AutoCAD® LT 2005 Tutorial

Text by
Randy H. Shih
Oregon Institute of Technology

MultiMedia CD by
Jack Zecher
Indiana University Purdue University Indianapolis

ISBN: 1-58503-202-6

SDC
PUBLICATIONS
Mission, Kansas

Schroff Development Corporation
P.O. Box 1334
Mission KS 66222
(913) 262-2664
www.**schroff**.com

Trademarks
The following are registered trademarks of Autodesk, Inc.: 3D Studio, ADI, Advanced Modeling Extension, AME, AutoCAD, AutoCAD Mechanical Desktop, AutoCAD Development System, AutoCAD LT, Autodesk, Autodesk Animator, AutoLISP, AutoShade, AutoVision, and Heidi.
The following are trademarks of Autodesk, Inc.: ACAD, Autodesk Device Interface, AutoCAD DesignCenter, AutoTrack, Heads-up Design, ObjectARX and Visual LISP.
Microsoft, Windows are either registered trademarks or trademarks of Microsoft Corporation.
All other trademarks are trademarks of their respective holders.

Shih, Randy H.
AutoCAD® LT 2005 Tutorial /
Randy H. Shih

ISBN 1-58503-202-6

The author and publisher of this book have used their best efforts in preparing this book. These efforts include the development, research and testing of the material presented. The author and publisher shall not be liable in any event for incidental or consequential damages with, or arising out of, the furnishing, performance, or use of the material.

Printed and bound in the United States of America.

Preface

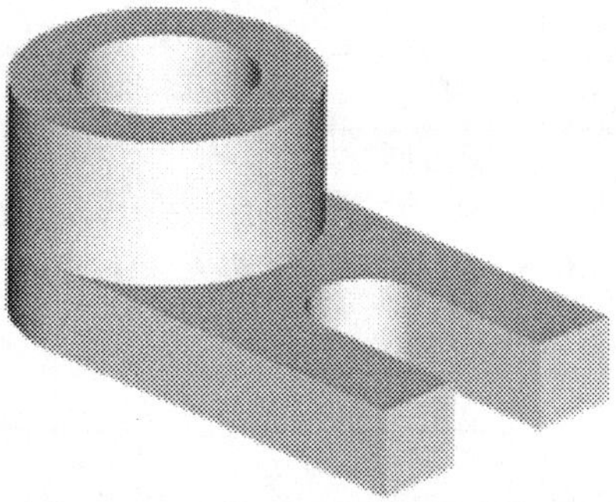

The primary goal of ***AutoCAD® LT 2005 Tutorial*** is to introduce the aspects of **Computer Aided Design and Drafting (CADD)**. This text is intended to be used as a training guide for students and professionals. This text covers *AutoCAD® LT 2005* and the lessons proceed in a pedagogical fashion to guide you from constructing basic shapes to making multiview drawings and building three-dimensional wireframe models. This text takes a hands-on, exercise-intensive approach to all the important CAD techniques and concepts. This textbook contains a series of ten tutorial style lessons designed to introduce beginning CAD users to **AutoCAD® LT 2005**. This text is also helpful to AutoCAD LT users upgrading from a previous release of the software. The new improvements and key enhancements of the software are incorporated into the lessons. You will learn to use the AutoCAD Heads-up Design™ interface, which enables you to focus on the design, not on the keyboard. The AutoCAD® AutoTrack™ feature, the WYSIWYG (What You See Is What You Get) plotting feature, the Named Plot Style feature, and Layout plotting are also introduced in the lessons. The CAD techniques and concepts discussed in this text are also designed to serve as the foundation to the more advanced feature-based parametric CAD packages such as AutoCAD® Mechanical Desktop and Autodesk Inventor. The basic premise of this book is that the more designs you create using AutoCAD® LT 2005, the better you learn the software. With this in mind, each lesson introduces a new set of commands and concepts, building on previous lessons. This book does not attempt to cover all of AutoCAD® LT 2005's features, only to provide an introduction to the software. It is intended to help you establish a good basis for exploring and growing in the exciting field of Computer Aided Engineering.

Acknowledgments

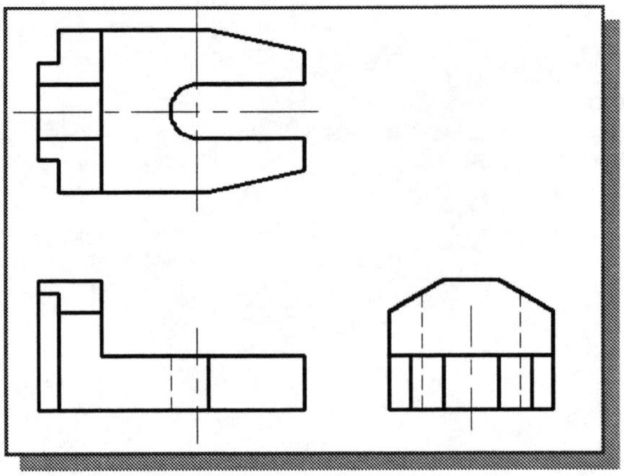

This book would not have been possible without a great deal of support. First, special thanks to two great teachers, Prof. George R. Schade of University of Nebraska-Lincoln and Mr. Denwu Lee, who taught me the fundamentals, the intrigue, and the sheer fun of Computer Aided Engineering.

My deep appreciation goes to Prof. Jack Zecher, Indiana University Purdue University Indianapolis, for the production of the multimedia CD, the audio-visual format of this text.

The effort and support of the editorial and production staff of Schroff Development Corporation is gratefully acknowledged. I would especially like to thank Stephen Schroff and Mary Schmidt for their support and helpful suggestions during this project.

I am grateful that the Mechanical Engineering Technology Department of Oregon Institute of Technology has provided me with an excellent environment in which to pursue my interests in teaching and research. Thanks to Prof. Brian Moravec, Emeritus Professor Charles Hermach and all of my colleagues at Oregon Institute of Technology for their support and contributions.

Finally, truly unbounded thanks are due to my wife Hsiu-Ling and our daughter Casandra for their understanding and encouragement throughout this project.

Randy H. Shih
Klamath Falls, Oregon
Fall, 2004

Table of Contents

Lesson 2
Construction and Editing Tools

Lesson 3
Object Properties and Organization

Lesson 7
Auxiliary Views and Editing with GRIPS

Lesson 8
Section Views

Lesson 9
Assembly Drawings and AutoCAD Blocks

Introduction

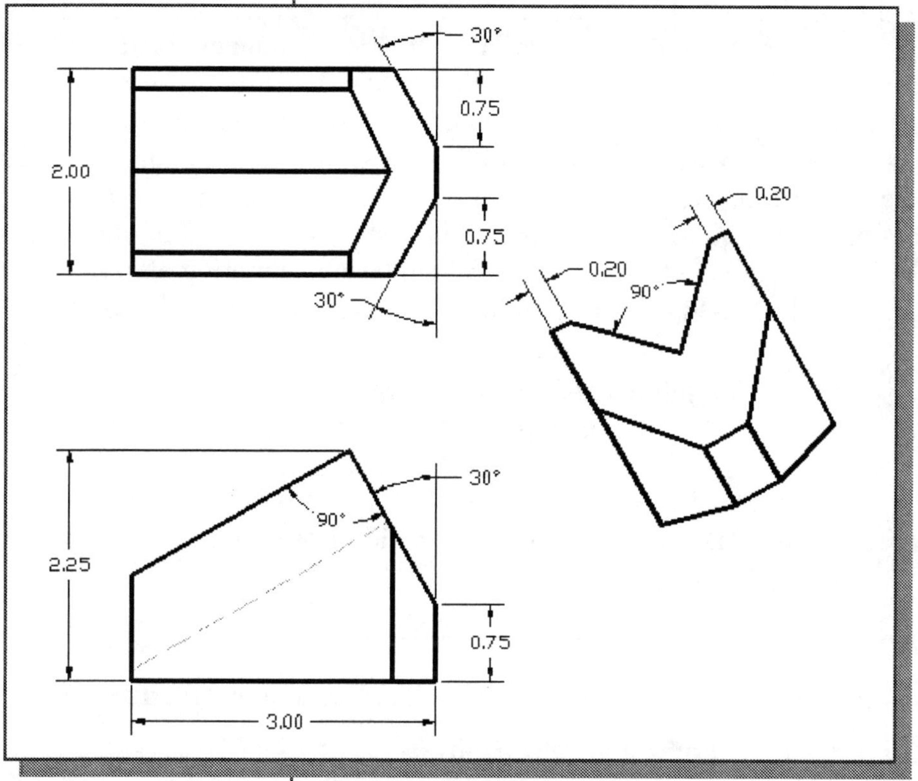

Learning Objectives

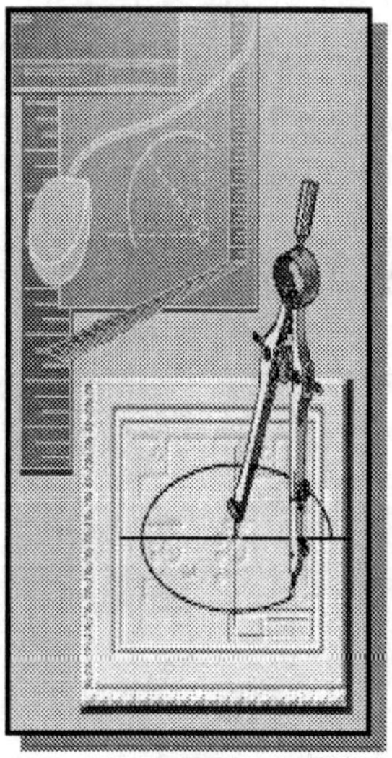

- ♦ **Development of Computer Aided Design**
- ♦ **Why use AutoCAD LT 2005**
- ♦ **Get started with AutoCAD LT 2005**
- ♦ **Access the AutoCAD LT Online Help**
- ♦ **AutoCAD LT 2005 Screen Layout**
- ♦ **Mouse Buttons**
- ♦ **Start and Exit AutoCAD LT**

Introduction

The rapid changes in the field of **Computer Aided Engineering** (CAE) have brought exciting advances in the engineering community. Recent advances have made the long-sought goal of **concurrent engineering** closer to a reality. CAE has become the core of concurrent engineering and is aimed at reducing design time, producing prototypes faster, and achieving higher product quality. **AutoCAD® LT 2005** is a computer aided design software package developed by *Autodesk Inc*. The **AutoCAD® LT 2005** software is a tool that can be used for design and drafting activities. The two-dimensional and three-dimensional models created in **AutoCAD® LT 2005** can be transferred to other computer programs for further analysis and testing. The computer models can also be used in manufacturing equipment such as machining centers, lathes, mills, or rapid prototyping machines to manufacture the product. In this text, we will be concentrating mainly with the drafting and part drawings used for part designs.

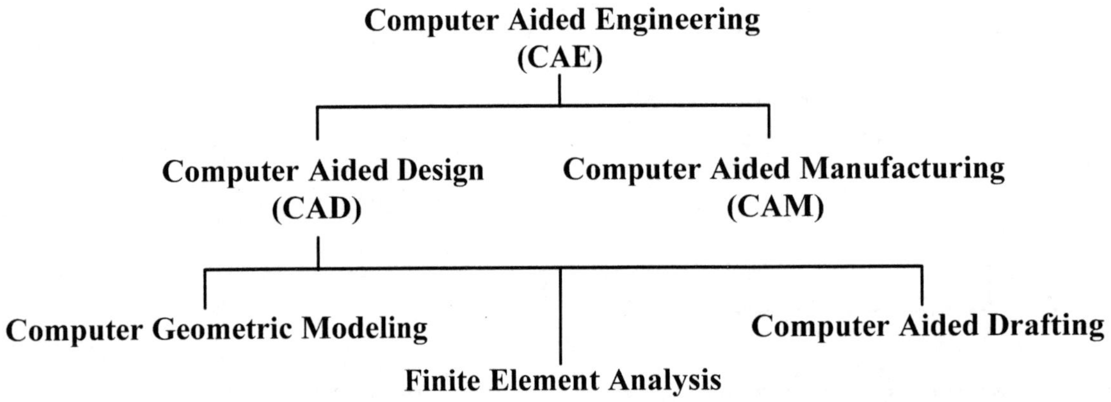

Development of Computer Geometric Modeling

Computer geometric modeling is a relatively new technology and its rapid expansion in the last fifty years is truly amazing. Computer-modeling technology has advanced along with the development of computer hardware. The first generation CAD programs, developed in the 1950s, were mostly non-interactive; CAD users were required to create program codes to generate the desired two-dimensional (2D) geometric shapes. Initially, the development of CAD technology occurred mostly in academic research facilities. The Massachusetts Institute of Technology, Carnegie-Mellon University, and Cambridge University were the leading pioneers at that time. The interest in CAD technology spread quickly and several major industry companies, such as General Motors, Lockheed, McDonnell, IBM, and Ford Motor Co., participated in the development of interactive CAD programs in the 1960s. Usage of CAD systems was primarily in the automotive industry, aerospace industry, and government agencies that developed their own programs for their specific needs. The 1960s also marked the beginning of the development of finite element analysis methods for computer stress analysis and computer aided manufacturing for generating machine toolpaths.

The 1970s are generally viewed as the years of the most significant progress in the development of computer hardware, namely the invention and development of **microprocessors**. With the improvement in computing power, new types of 3D CAD programs that were user-friendly and interactive became reality. CAD technology quickly expanded from very simple **computer aided drafting** to very complex **computer aided design**. The use of 2D and 3D wireframe modelers was accepted as the leading edge technology that could increase productivity in industry. The development of surface modeling and solid modeling technology was taking shape by the late 1970s, but the high cost of computer hardware and programming slowed the development of such technology. During this period, the available CAD systems all required extremely expensive room-sized mainframe computers.

In the 1980s, improvements in computer hardware brought the power of mainframes to the desktop at less cost and with more accessibility to the general public. By the mid-1980s, CAD technology had become the main focus of a variety of manufacturing industries and was very competitive with traditional design/drafting methods. It was during this time that 3D solid modeling technology experienced major advancements, which boosted the usage of CAE technology in industry.

The introduction of the *feature-based parametric solid modeling* approach, at the end of the 1980s, elevated CAD/CAM/CAE technology to a new level. In the 1990s, CAD programs evolved into powerful design/manufacturing/management tools. CAD technology has come a long way, and during these years of development, modeling schemes progressed from two-dimensional (2D) wireframe to three-dimensional (3D) wireframe, to surface modeling, to solid modeling and, finally, to feature-based parametric solid modeling.

The first generation CAD packages were simply 2D **computer aided drafting** programs, basically the electronic equivalents of the drafting board. For typical models, the use of this type of program would require that several to many views of the objects be created individually as they would be on the drafting board. The 3D designs remained in the designer's mind, not in the computer database. The mental translation of 3D objects to 2D views is required throughout the use of these packages. Although such systems have some advantages over traditional board drafting, they are still tedious and labor intensive. The need for the development of 3D modelers came quite naturally, given the limitations of 2D drafting packages.

The development of three-dimensional modeling schemes started with three-dimensional (3D) wireframes. Wireframe models are models consisting of points and edges, which are straight lines connecting between appropriate points. The edges of wireframe models are used, similar to lines in 2D drawings, to represent transitions of surfaces and features. The use of lines and points is also a very economical way to represent 3D designs.

The development of the 3D wireframe modeler was a major leap in the area of computer geometric modeling. The computer database in the 3D wireframe modeler contains the locations of all the points in space coordinates and it is typically sufficient to create just one model rather than multiple views of the same model. This single 3D model can then be viewed from any direction as needed. Most 3D wireframe modelers allow the user to create projected lines/edges of 3D wireframe models. In comparison to other types of 3D modelers, the 3D wireframe modelers require very little computing power and generally can be used to achieve reasonably good representations of 3D models. However, because surface definition is not part of a wireframe model, all wireframe images have the inherent problem of ambiguity.

Surface modeling is the logical development in computer geometry modeling to follow the 3D wireframe modeling scheme by organizing and grouping edges that define polygonal surfaces. Surface modeling describes the part's surfaces but not its interiors. Designers are still required to interactively examine surface models to insure that the various surfaces on a model are contiguous throughout. Many of the concepts used in 3D wireframe and surface modelers are incorporated in the solid modeling scheme, but it is solid modeling that offers the most advantages as a design tool.

In the solid modeling presentation scheme, the solid definitions include nodes, edges, and surfaces, and it is a complete and unambiguous mathematical representation of a precisely enclosed and filled volume. Unlike the surface modeling method, solid modelers start with a solid or use topology rules to guarantee that all of the surfaces are stitched together properly. Two predominant methods for representing solid models are **constructive solid geometry** (CSG) representation and **boundary representation** (B-rep).

By the 1980s, a new paradigm called *concurrent engineering* had emerged. With concurrent engineering, designers, design engineers, analysts, manufacturing engineers, and management engineers all work together closely right from the initial stages of the design. In this way, all aspects of the design can be evaluated and any potential problems can be identified right from the start and throughout the design process. Using the principles of concurrent engineering, a new type of computer modeling technique appeared.

In this text, we will follow the logical order, parallel to the development of computer geometric modeling, in learning the fundamental concepts and commands of **AutoCAD® LT 2005**. We will begin with basic geometric constructions, orthographic projections and then move toward the more advanced features of **AutoCAD® LT 2005**. We will also discuss and demonstrate the general procedure required in creating three-dimensional wireframe models. The techniques presented in this text will also serve as the foundation to enter the world of the advanced three-dimensional solid modeling using packages such as ***AutoDesk Mechanical Desktop*** and ***Autodesk Inventor***.

Why use *AutoCAD® LT 2005*

AutoCAD® was first introduced to the public in late 1982, and was one of the first CAD software products that were available for personal computers. Since 1984, **AutoCAD®** has established the reputation for being the most widely used PC-based CAD software around the world. By 2002, it is estimated that there are over 3.75 million **AutoCAD®** users in more than 150 countries worldwide. **AutoCAD® 2005** is the seventeenth release, with many added features and enhancements, of the original **AutoCAD®** software produced by *Autodesk Inc*. The first version of **AutoCAD LT** (the scaled-down version of **AutoCAD**) was first introduced in late 1993. It has become quite popular in several CAD market segments, including new CAD users, the 2D-only drafting population, and those who review and mark up AutoCAD drawings. Since then, new versions of this CAD drafting package appeared at yearly intervals, often incorporating many of the current AutoCAD's features but just as often introducing features and capabilities not in AutoCAD. **AutoCAD® LT 2005** software offers design capability to everyone by providing a basic CAD product for CAD users. **AutoCAD® LT 2005**'s features are designed to improve productivity, extend design capabilities through intuitive and well-designed features.

CAD provides us with a wide range of benefits; in most cases, the result of using CAD is increased accuracy and productivity. First of all, the computer offers much higher accuracy than the traditional method of drafting and design. Traditionally, drafting and detailing are the most expensive cost elements in a project and the biggest bottlenecks. With CAD systems, such as **AutoCAD® LT 2005,** the tedious drafting and detailing tasks are simplified through the use of many of the CAD geometric construction tools, such as *grids*, *snap*, *trim,* and *auto-dimensioning*. Dimensions and notes are always legible in CAD drawings and, in most cases, CAD systems can produce higher quality prints compared to traditional hand drawings.

CAD also offers much-needed flexibility in design and drafting. A CAD model generated on a computer consists of numeric data that describe the geometry of the object. This allows the designers and clients to see something tangible and to interpret the ramifications of the design. In many cases, it is also possible to simulate the operating conditions on the computer and observe the results. Any kind of geometric shape stored in the database can be easily duplicated. For large and complex designs and drawings, particularly those involving similar shapes and repetitive operations, CAD approaches are very efficient and effective. Because computer designs and models can be altered easily, a multitude of design options can be examined and presented to a client before any construction or manufacturing actually takes place. Making changes to a CAD database is generally much faster than making changes to a traditional hand drawing. Only the affected components of the design need to be modified and the drawings can be plotted again. In addition, the greatest benefit is that, once the CAD model is created, it can be used over and over again. The CAD models can also be transferred into manufacturing equipment such as machining centers, lathes, mills, or rapid prototyping machines to manufacture the product directly.

CAD, however, does not replace every design activity. CAD may help, but it does not replace the designer's experience with geometry, graphical conventions and standards for the specific field. CAD is a powerful tool, but the use of this tool does not guarantee correct results; the designer is still responsible for using good design practice and applying good judgement. CAD will supplement these skills to ensure that the best design is obtained.

CAD designs and drawings are stored in binary form, usually as CAD files, to magnetic devices such as diskettes and hard disks. The information stored in CAD files usually requires much less physical space in comparison to traditional hand drawings. However, the information stored inside the computer is not indestructible. On the contrary, the electronic format of information is very fragile and sensitive to the environment. Heat or cold can damage the information stored on magnetic storage devices. A power failure while you are creating a design could wipe out the many hours you spent working in front of your computer monitor. It is a good habit to save your work periodically, just in case something might go wrong while you are working on your design. In general, you should save your work onto the disk at an interval of every 15 to 20 minutes. You should also save your work before you make any major modifications to the design. It is also a good habit to periodically make backup copies of your work and put them in a safe place.

AutoCAD® LT 2005 offers significant ease of use and affordability, without all of AutoCAD 2005 software's advanced capabilities. The system requirements for **AutoCAD® LT 2005**, such as RAM memory and disk space are considerably lower than the system requirements for AutoCAD 2005. In most cases, **AutoCAD® LT 2005** loads and runs faster than AutoCAD 2005. **AutoCAD® LT 2005**, mostly used as a 2D drafting product, does not offer any of the 3D solid-modeling and visualization features found in the AutoCAD 2005 software. However, 3D wireframe features are available in the **AutoCAD® LT 2005** software; it also has limited customization capabilities. Many of the add-on applications that are designed for use with AutoCAD 2005 software cannot be used with AutoCAD L*T*, but a lot of them are being developed to be used with AutoCAD LT. **AutoCAD® LT 2005** software reads and displays AutoCAD 2005 files with 100 percent visual fidelity. And no data will be lost or changed when modifications are done on AutoCAD 2005 DWG files. With its unique ease of use and low cost for professionals, **AutoCAD® LT 2005** software provides an alternative to the complexity of AutoCAD 2005.

This textbook contains a series of ten tutorial style lessons designed to introduce students to **AutoCAD® LT 2005**. The improvements and key enhancements of the software are incorporated into the lessons. You will learn to use the **AutoCAD Heads-up Design™** interface, which enables you to focus on the design, not on the keyboard. The **AutoCAD AutoTrack™** feature, the onscreen lineweight feature, the WYSIWYG (What You See Is What You Get) plotting feature, the Named Plot Style feature and Layout plotting feature are also introduced in the lessons.

Getting Started with *AutoCAD® LT 2005*

Now that you have some grounding and are ready to move on, let us begin the learning experience with **AutoCAD® LT 2005,** which you will find interesting and fun. And welcome to the exciting world of **computer aided design**.

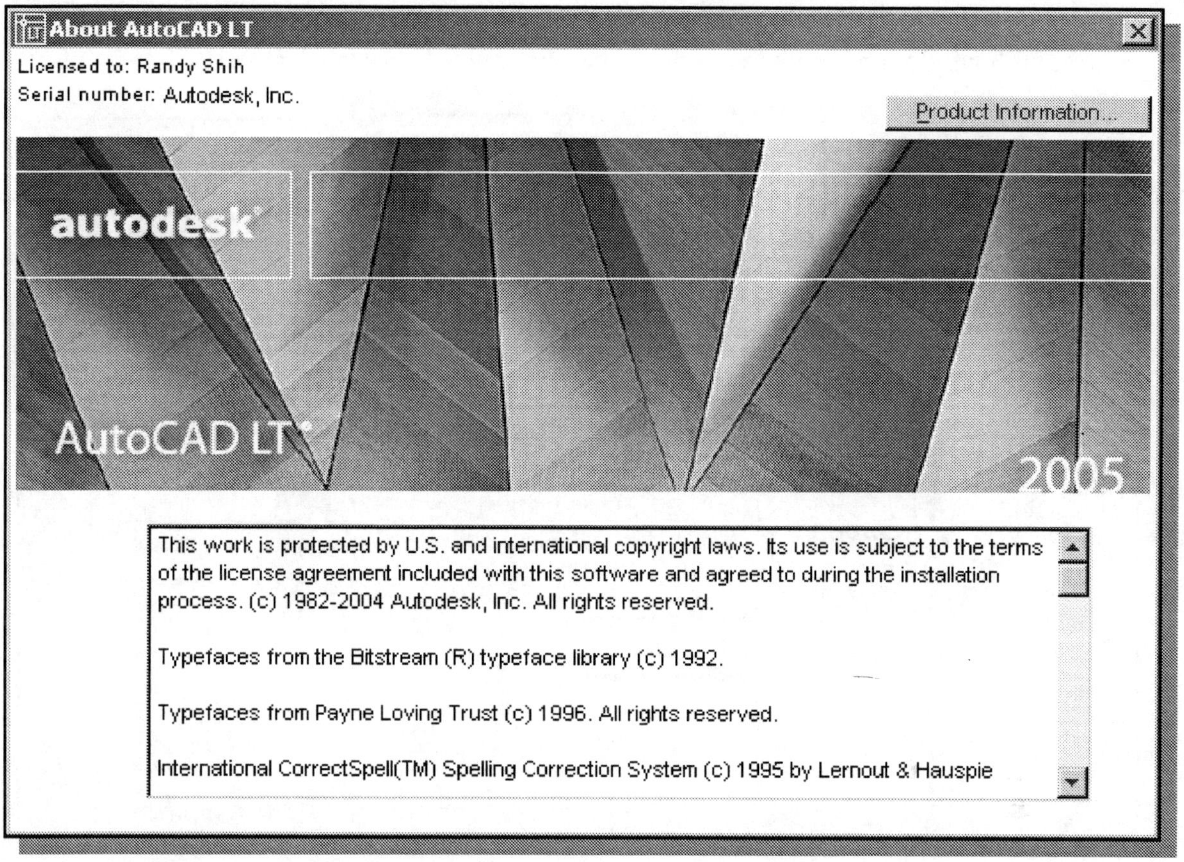

How to start **AutoCAD® LT 2005** depends on the type of workstation and the particular software configuration you are using. With most *Windows* systems, you may select the **AutoCAD LT 2005** option on the *Start* menu or select the **AutoCAD LT 2005** icon on the desktop. Consult your instructor or the technical support personnel if you have difficulty starting the software.

The program takes a while to load, so be patient. Eventually the **AutoCAD® LT 2005** *Drawing Screen* and the *AutoCAD LT Today* startup dialog box will appear on the screen.

The tutorials in this text are based on the assumption that you are using **AutoCAD® LT 2005**'s default settings. If your system has been customized for other uses, some of the settings may not work with the step-by-step instructions in the tutorials. Contact your instructor and/or the technical support personnel to restore the default software configuration.

AutoCAD® LT 2005 Screen Layout

The default **AutoCAD® LT 2005** *Drawing Screen* contains the *pull-down menus*, the *Standard* toolbar, the *Object Properties* toolbar, the *Draw* toolbar, the *Modify* toolbar, the *command prompt* area, and the *Status Bar*. A line of quick help text appears at the bottom of the window as you move the *mouse cursor* over different icons. You may resize the **AutoCAD® LT 2005** drawing window by click and drag at the edges of the window, or relocate the window by click and drag at the window title area.

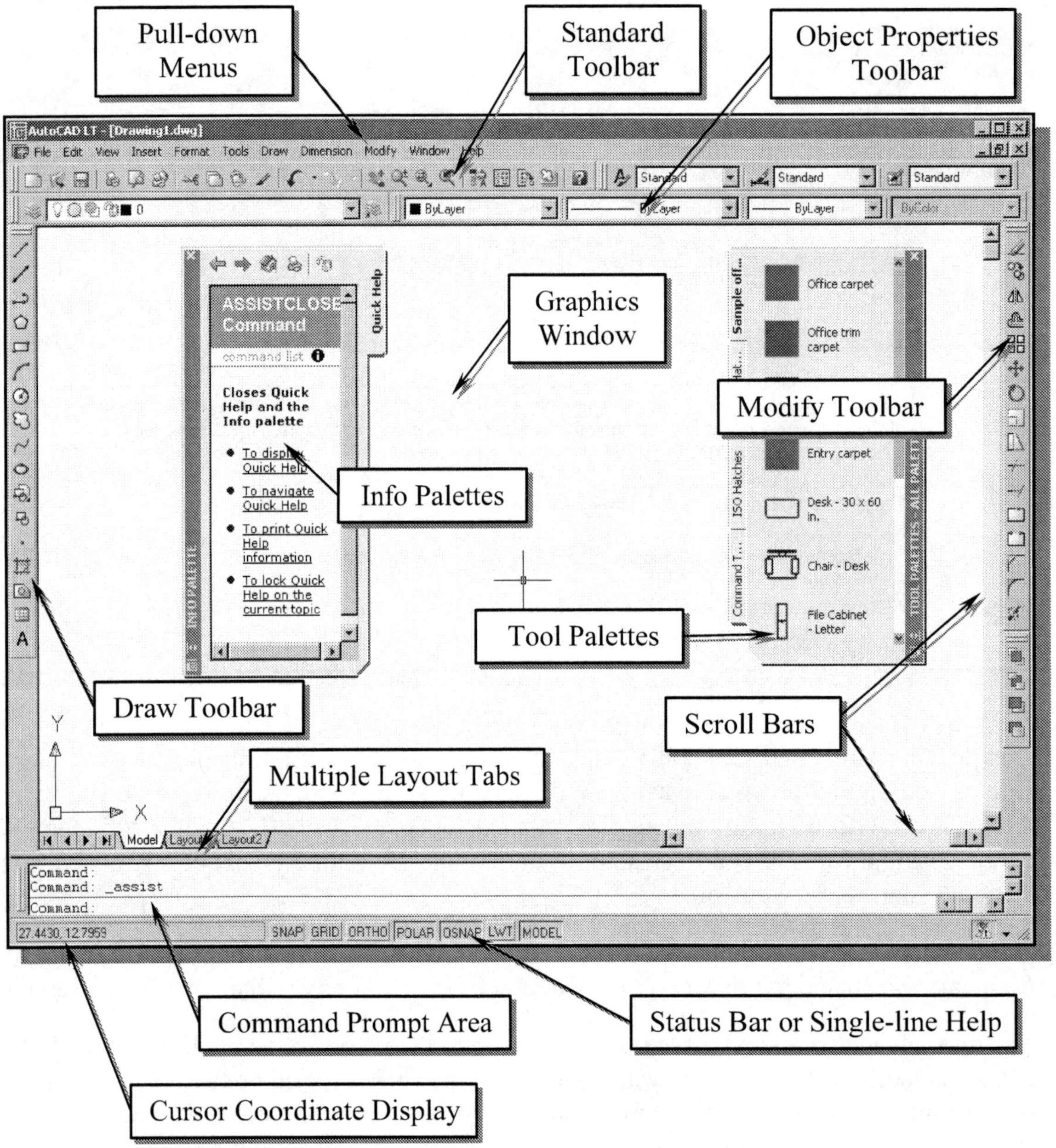

- **Pull-down Menus**

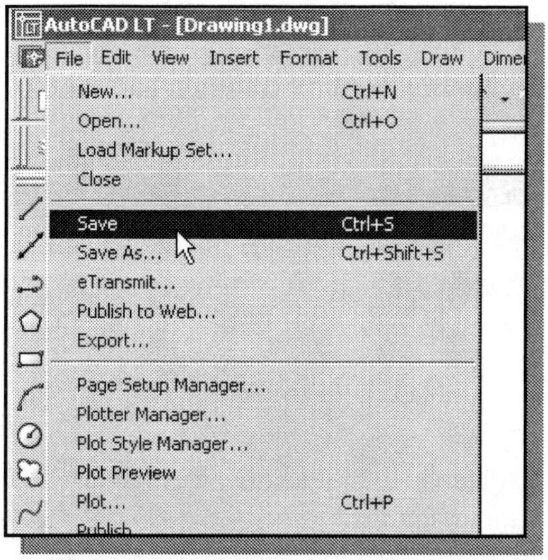

The *pull-down menus* at the top of the main window contain operations that you can use for all modes of the system.

- **Standard Toolbar**

The *Standard* toolbar at the top of the screen window allows us quick access to frequently used commands. We can customize the toolbar by adding and removing sets of options or individual commands.

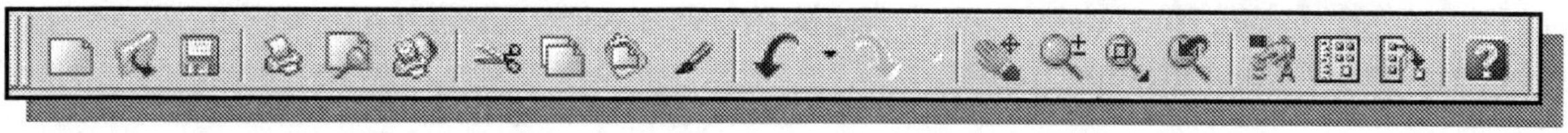

- **Object Properties Toolbar**

The *Object Properties* toolbar contains tools to help manipulate the graphical object properties, such as color, line type, and layer.

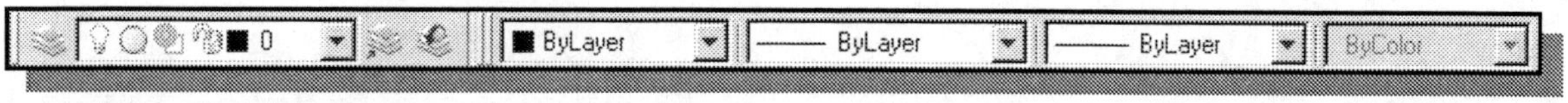

- **Graphics Window**

The *graphics window* is the area where models and drawings are displayed.

- **Graphics Cursor or Crosshairs**

The *graphics cursor*, or *crosshairs*, shows the location of the pointing device in the graphics window. The coordinates of the cursor are displayed at the bottom of the screen layout. The cursor's appearance depends on the selected command or option.

- **Command Prompt Area**

The bottom section of the *screen layout* provides status information for an operation and it is also the area for data input.

- **Draw Toolbar and Modify Toolbar**

Additional toolbars are available in **AutoCAD® LT 2005**, which contain groups of buttons that allow us to pick commands quickly, without searching through a menu structure. The *Draw* toolbar and *Modify* toolbar contain icons for basic draw and modify commands.

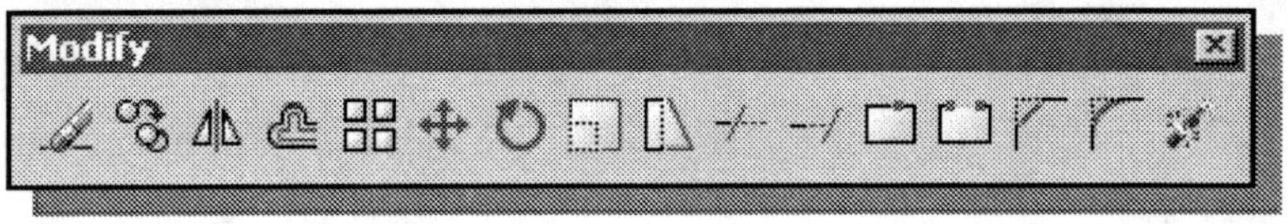

Mouse Buttons

AutoCAD® LT 2005 utilizes the mouse buttons extensively. In learning **AutoCAD® LT 2005**'s interactive environment, it is important to understand the basic functions of the mouse buttons. It is highly recommended that you use a mouse or a tablet with **AutoCAD® LT 2005** since the package uses the buttons for various functions.

- **Left mouse button**

The **left-mouse-button** is used for most operations, such as selecting menus and icons, or picking graphic entities. One click of the button is used to select icons, menus and form entries, and to pick graphic items.

- **Right mouse button**

The **right-mouse-button** is used to bring up additional available options. The software also utilizes the **right-mouse-button** as the same as the **ENTER** key, and is often used to accept the default setting to a prompt or to end a process.

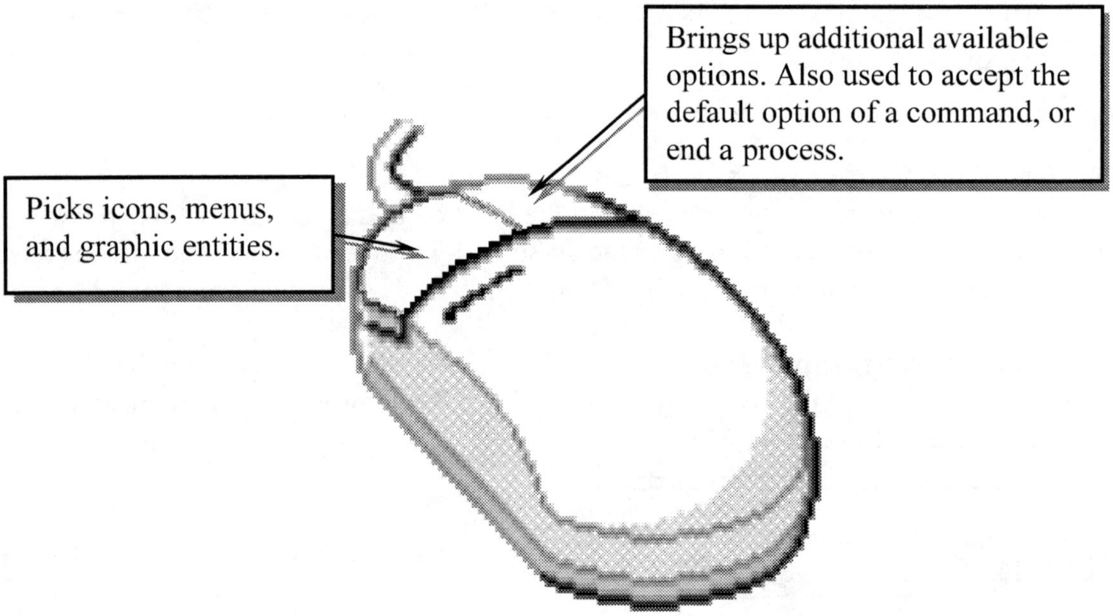

[Esc] - Canceling Commands

The [**Esc**] key is used to cancel a command in **AutoCAD® LT 2005**. The [**Esc**] key is located near the top left corner of the keyboard. Sometimes, it maybe necessary to press the [**Esc**] key twice to cancel a command; it depends on where we are in the command sequence. For some commands, the [**Esc**] key is used to exit the command.

On-Line Help

❖ Several types of on-line help are available at any time during an **AutoCAD LT 2005** session. The **AutoCAD LT® 2005** software provides many on-line help options:

- **Info Palette**:

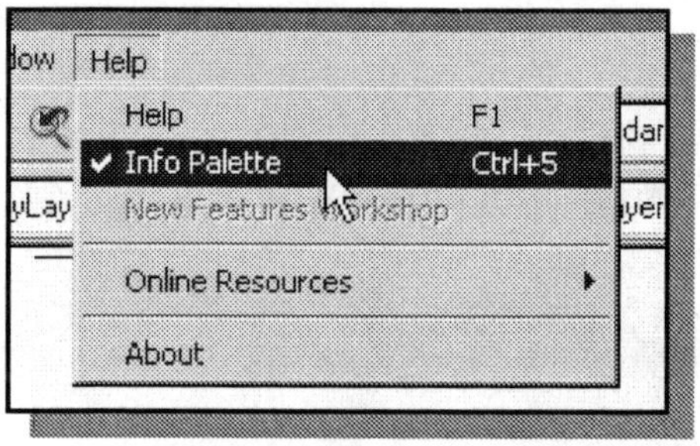

The **Info Palette** option provides an instant help that dynamically displays information on the activated command. The guidance from the **Info Palette** system enables users to quickly get started on performing desired tasks. In the **Info Palette** window, links to additional information are also available. Clicking a blue-text-link expands the current **Info Palette** topic.

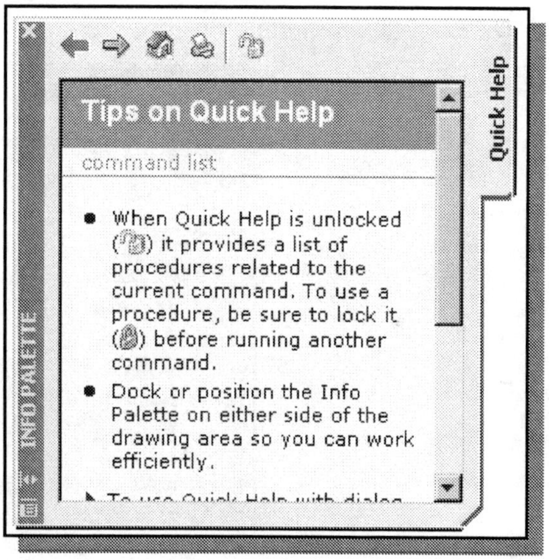

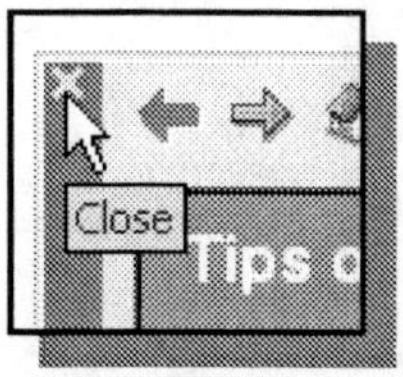

- To *close* the **Info Palette**, left-click the [**X**] icon located in the upper left corner of the ***Info Palette*** window as shown.

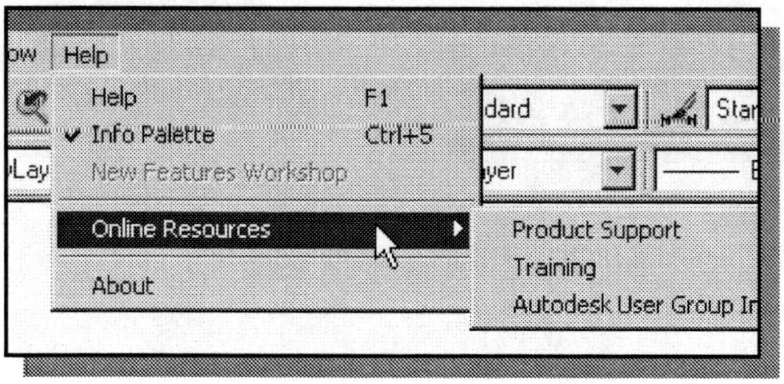

- **Online Resources**: Click on the **HELP** option in the pull-down menu to access the **AutoCAD® 2005 Help menu system**. Notice the different online resources available in the pull-down list.

- **Standard toolbar**: Click on the **[?]** icon in the *Standard* toolbar to access Autodesk On-line Help: User Documentation.

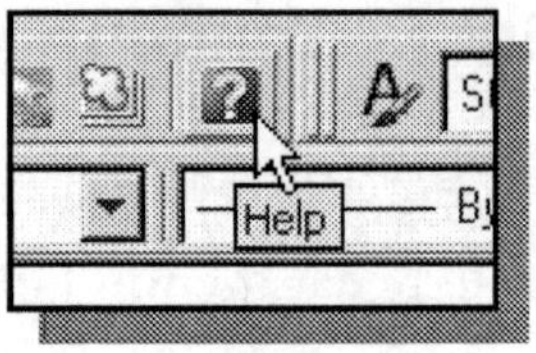

- **Command line and function key [F1]**: Press the [**F1**] key or enter a question mark [**?**] at the command prompt to access the **AutoCAD On-line Help system**.

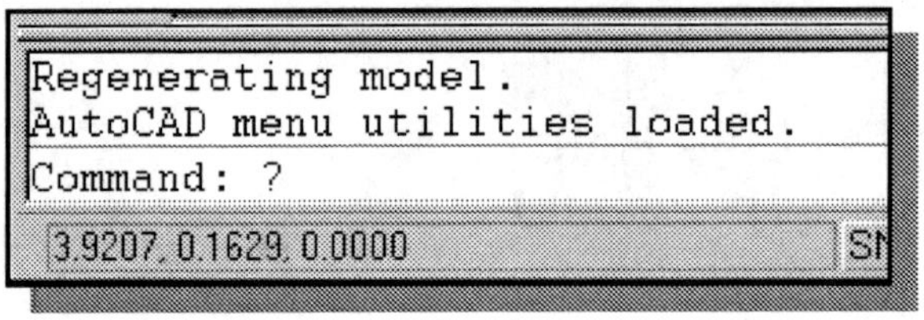

Leaving *AutoCAD® LT 2005*

To leave **AutoCAD® LT 2005**, use the left mouse button and click on **File** at the top of the *AutoCAD LT* screen window, then choose **Exit** from the pull-down menu or type ***QUIT*** at the command prompt area.

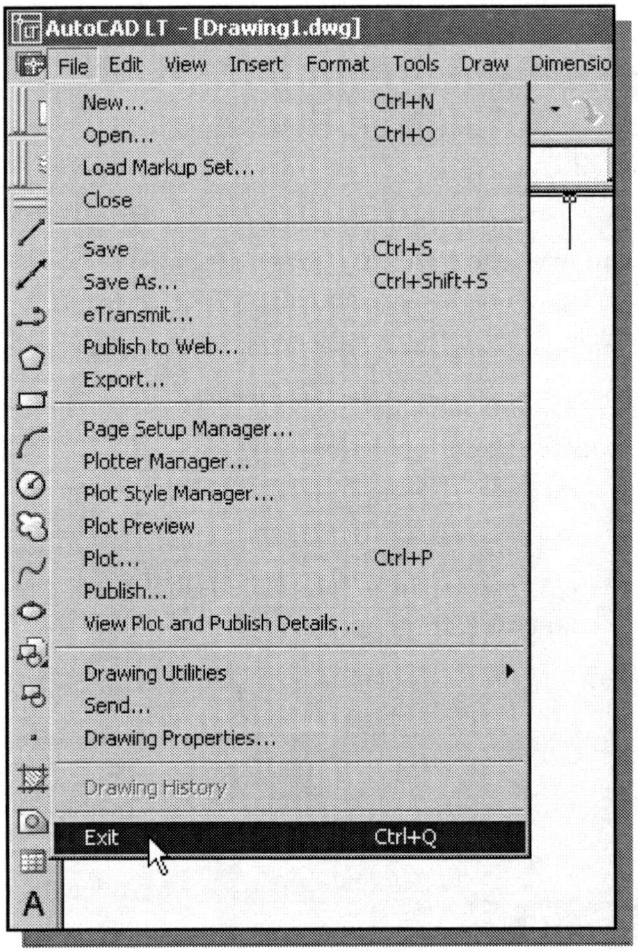

Creating a CAD Files Folder

It is a good practice to create a separate folder to store your CAD files. You should not save your CAD files in the same folder where the **AutoCAD® LT 2005** application is located. It is much easier to organize and backup your project files if they are in a separate folder. Making folders within this folder for different types of projects will help you organize your CAD files even further. When creating CAD files in **AutoCAD® LT 2005**, it is strongly recommended that you *save* your CAD files on the hard drive. However, if you do want to save your files on a floppy drive, be sure to exit the **AutoCAD® LT 2005** program before removing the diskette from the drive. The better alternative is to save the files on the hard drive and then copy the files onto a floppy diskette under the operating system.

➢ To create a new folder in the *Windows* environment:

1. In *My Computer*, or start *Windows Explorer* under the *Start* menu, open the folder in which you want to create a new folder.

2. On the **File** menu, point to **New**, and then click **Folder**. The new folder appears with a temporary name.

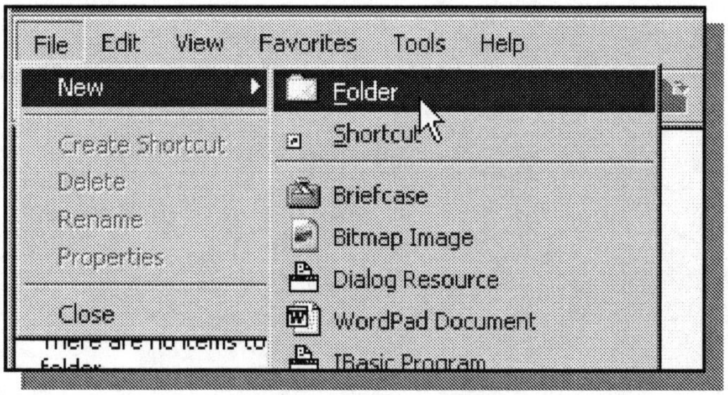

3. Type a name for the new folder, and then press **ENTER**.

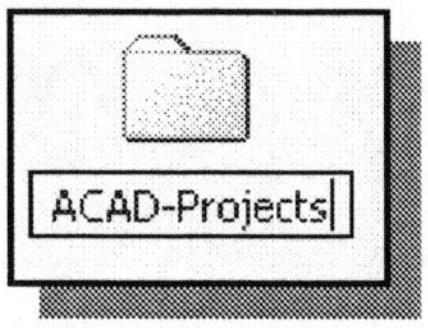

Notes:

Lesson 1
Geometric Construction Basics

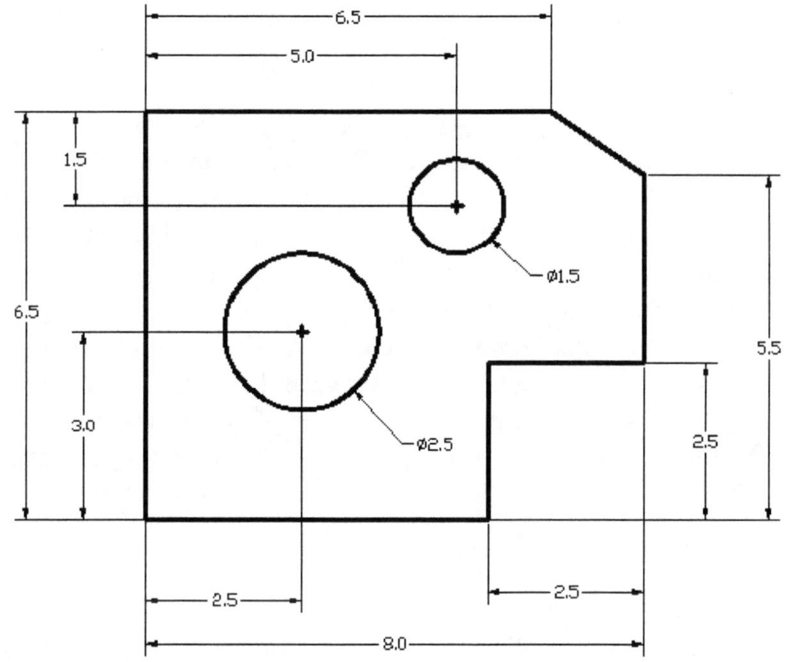

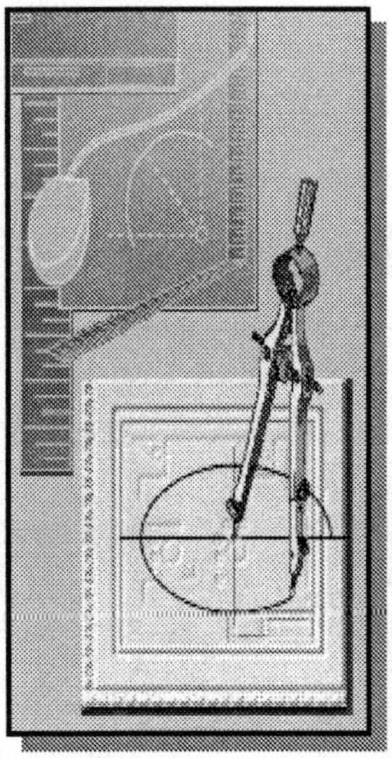

Learning Objectives

- Create and Save AutoCAD Drawing Files
- Use the AutoCAD LT Visual Reference Commands
- Draw, Using the LINE and CIRCLE Commands
- Use the ERASE Command
- Define Positions Using the Basic Entry Methods
- Use the Pan Realtime Option

Introduction

Learning to use a CAD system is similar to learning a new language. We need to begin with the basic alphabet and learn how to use the basic alphabet correctly and effectively through practice. This will require learning some new concepts and skills as well as learning a different vocabulary. All CAD systems create designs using basic geometric entities. Most of the constructions used in technical designs are based upon two-dimensional planar geometry. The method and number of operations that are required to accomplish the construction are different from one system to another.

In order to become effective in using a CAD system, we must learn to create geometric entities quickly and accurately. In learning to use a CAD system, **lines** and **circles** are the first two, and perhaps the most important two, geometric entities that we need to master the skills in creating and modifying. Straight lines and circles are used in almost all technical designs. In examining the different types of planar geometric entities, we can see that triangles and polygons are planar figures bounded by straight lines. Ellipses and splines can be constructed by connecting arcs with different radii. As we gain some experience in creating lines and circles, similar procedures can be applied to create other geometric entities. In this lesson, we will examine the different ways of creating lines and circles in **AutoCAD® LT 2005**.

Starting Up *AutoCAD LT 2005*

1. Select the **AutoCAD LT 2005** option on the *Program* menu or select the **AutoCAD LT 2005** icon on the *Desktop*. Once the program is loaded into memory, the *AutoCAD LT 2005* drawing screen will appear on the screen.

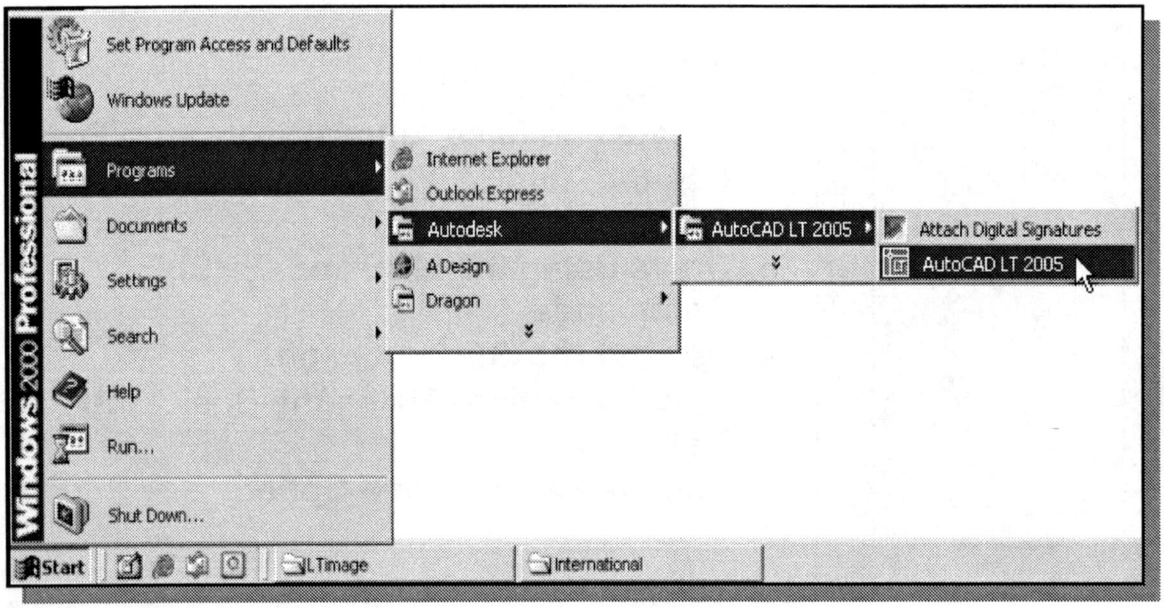

➢ Note that AutoCAD LT automatically assigns generic names, *Drawing X*, as new drawings are created. In our example, AutoCAD LT opened the graphics window using the default system units and assigned the drawing name *Drawing1*.

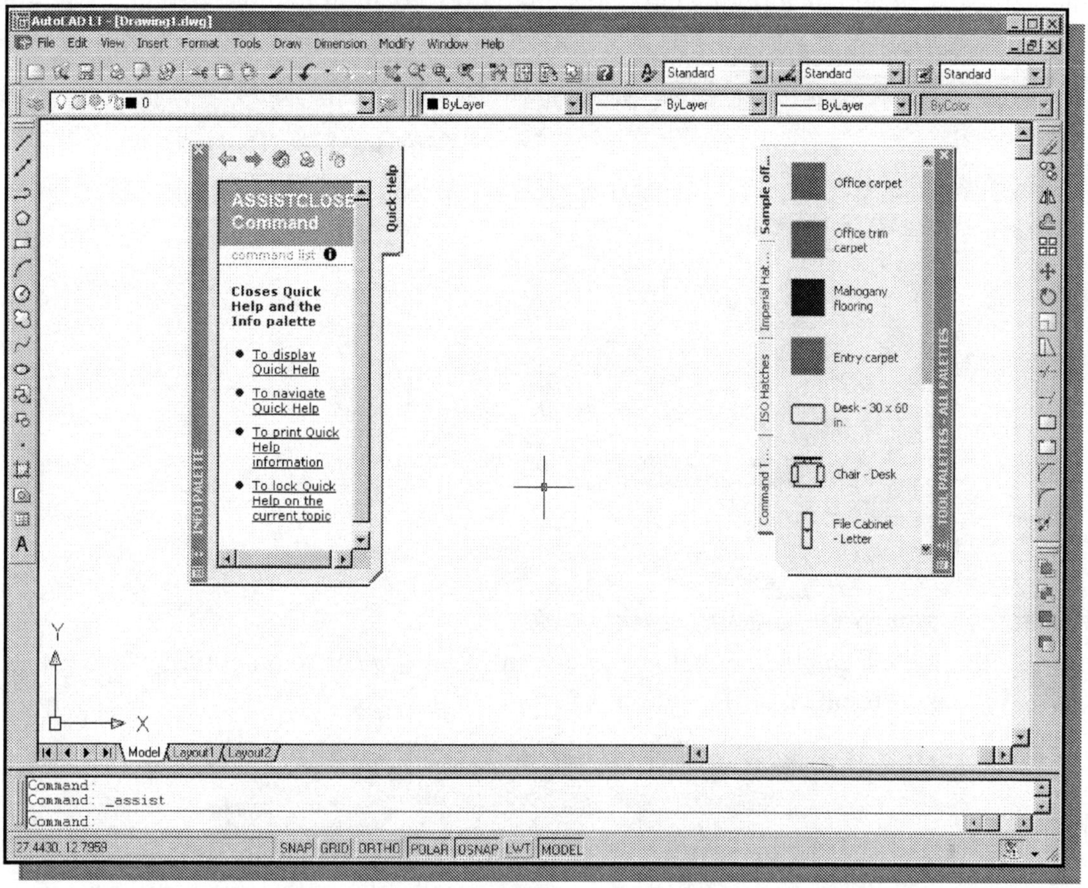

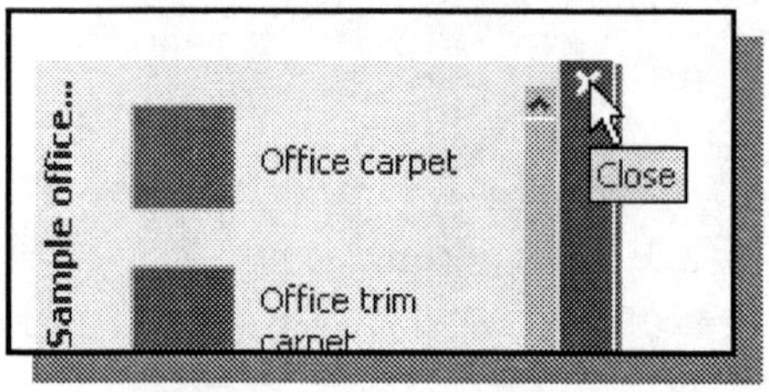

2. Close the *Tool Palettes* by clicking once on **Close** button located at the upper right corner of the window as shown.

3. Close the *Info Palettes* by clicking once on the **Close** button located at the upper left corner of the window as shown.

Drawing Units Setup

Every object we construct in a CAD system is measured in **units**. We should determine the value of the units within the CAD system before creating the first geometric entities.

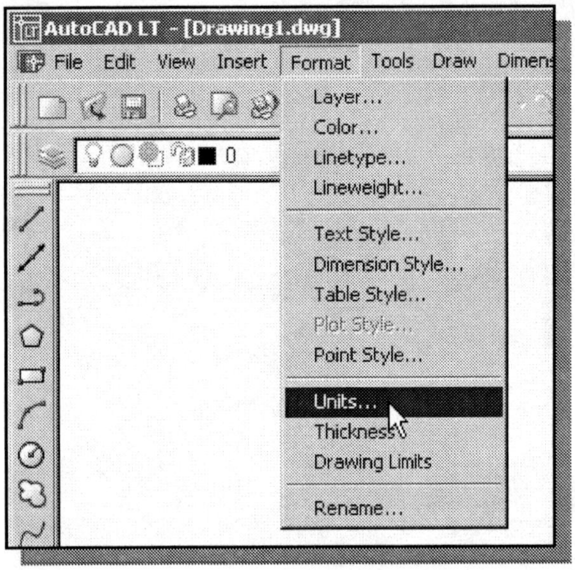

1. In the pull-down menus, select **[Format] → [Units]**

2. In the *Drawing Units* dialog box, set the *Length Type* to **Decimal**. This will set the measurement to the default English units, inches.

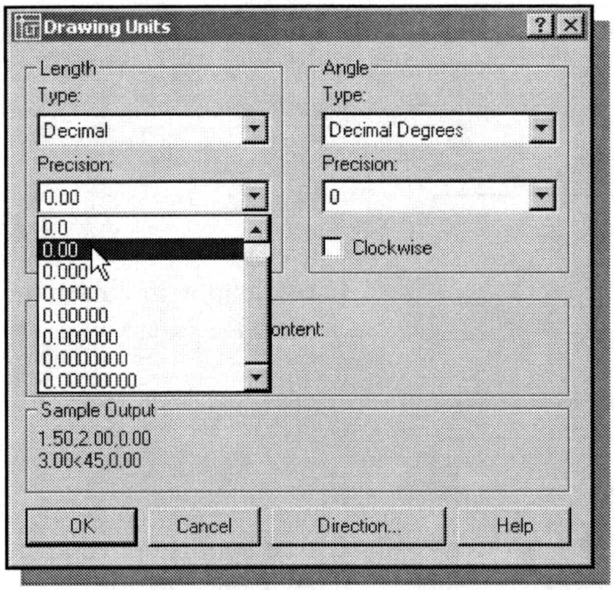

3. Set the *Precision* to **two digits** after the decimal point as shown in the above figure.

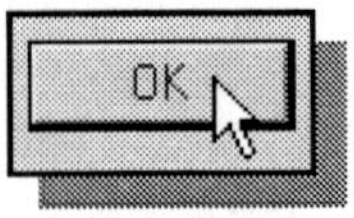

4. Pick **OK** to exit the *Drawing Units* dialog box.

Drawing Area Setup

Next, we will set up the **Drawing Limits**; setting the Drawing Limits controls the extents of the display of the *grid.* It also serves as a visual reference that marks the working area. It can also be used to prevent construction outside the grid limits and as a plot option that defines an area to be plotted/printed. Note that this setting does not limit the region for geometry construction.

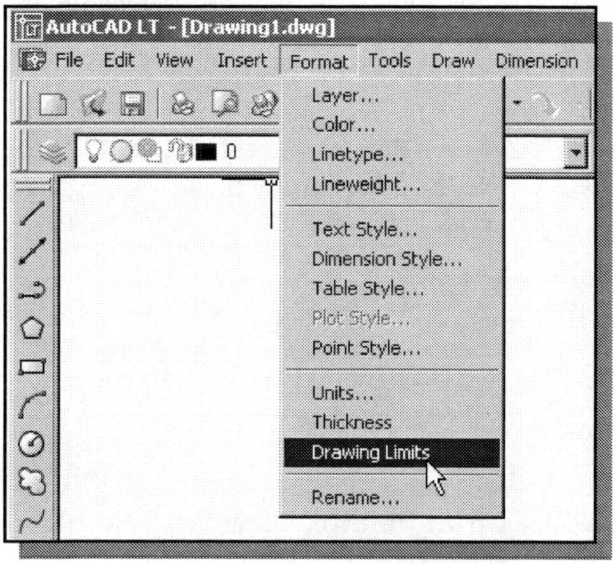

1. In the pull-down menus, select **[Format] → [Drawing Limits]**

2. In the command prompt area, near the bottom of the *AutoCAD LT* drawing screen, the message "*Reset Model Space Limits: Specify lower left corner or [On/Off] <0.00,0.00>:*" is displayed. Press the **Enter** key once to accept the default coordinates <**0.00,0.00**>.

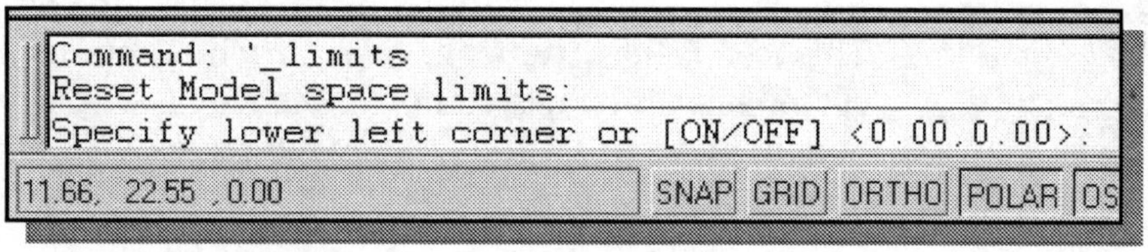

3. In the command prompt area, the message "*Specify upper right corner <0.00,0.00>:*" is displayed. Press the **ENTER** key once to accept the default coordinates <**12.00,9.00**>.

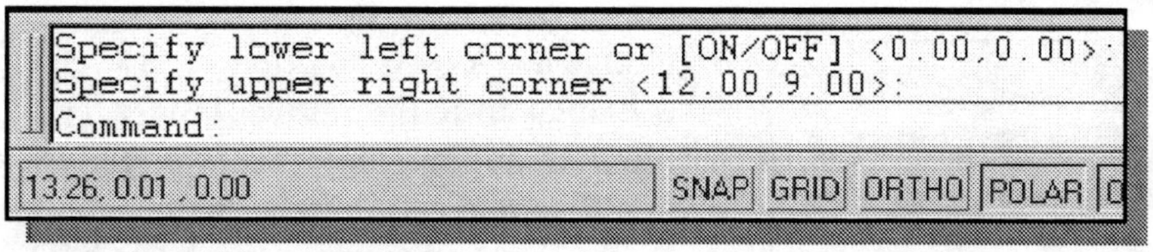

4. On your own, move the graphic cursor near the upper-right comer inside the drawing area and note that the drawing area is unchanged. (The Drawing Limits command is used to set the drawing area; but the display will not be adjusted until a display command is used.)

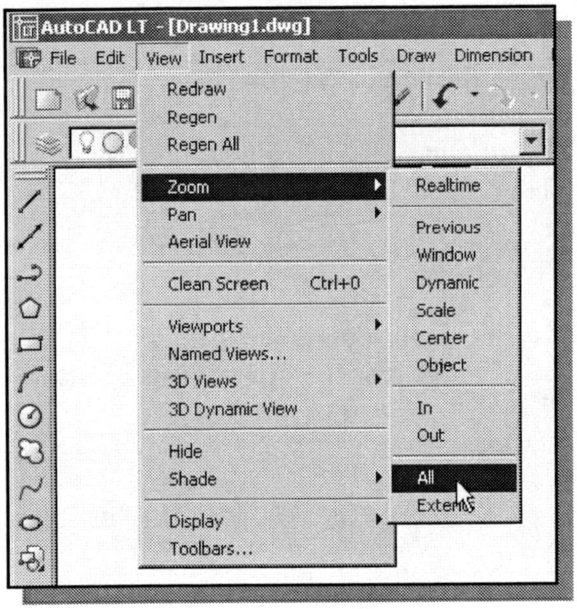

5. In the pull-down menus, select **[View] → [Zoom All]**

➢ The **Zoom All** command will adjust the display so that all objects in the drawing are displayed to be as large as possible. If no objects are constructed, the **Drawing Limits** are used to adjust the current viewport.

6. Move the graphic cursor near the upper right comer inside the drawing area and note that the display area is updated.

Using the *Line* Command

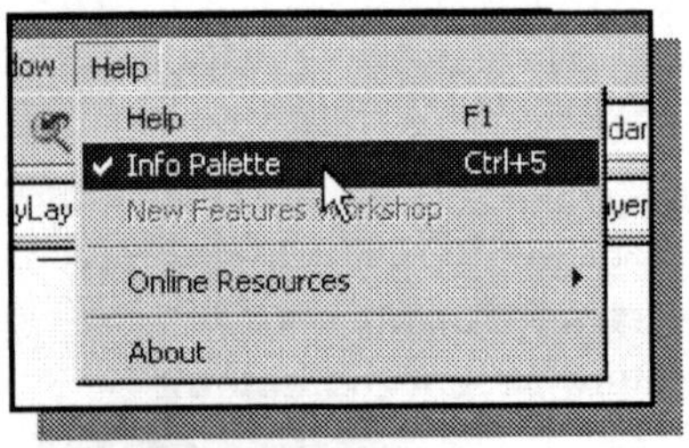

1. Switch ***ON*** the **Info Palette** option in the **Help** pull-down menu as shown.

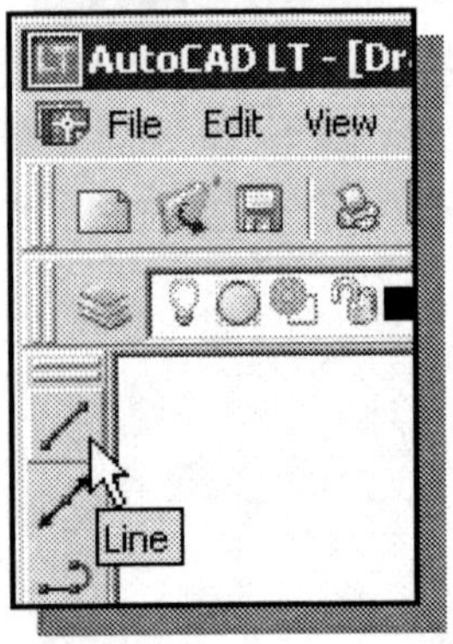

2. Move the graphics cursor to the first icon in the *Draw* toolbar. This icon is the **Line** icon. A *help-tip* box appears next to the cursor and a brief description of the icon is displayed at the bottom of the *AutoCAD LT* drawing screen: *"Creates Straight line segments: LINE."*

3. Select the icon by clicking once with the left-mouse-button; this will activate the **Line** command.

➢ Notice a brief explanation of the selected command is displayed in the *Active Assistance* window. It is highly recommended that you read the explanations to gain some insights on the basic assumptions and general procedure of using AutoCAD LT.

4. In the *Active Assistance* window, click **To draw lines** to open the *AutoCAD LT Help* window and get a more detailed explanation on the procedure.

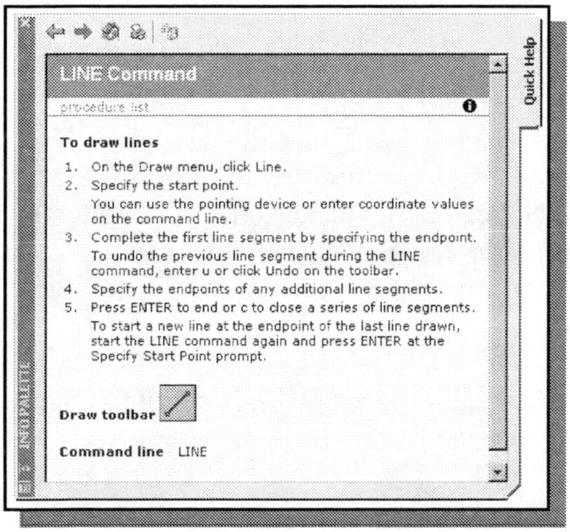

5. Click on **Close** button located at the upper left corner of the *AutoCAD LT Info Palette* window as shown.

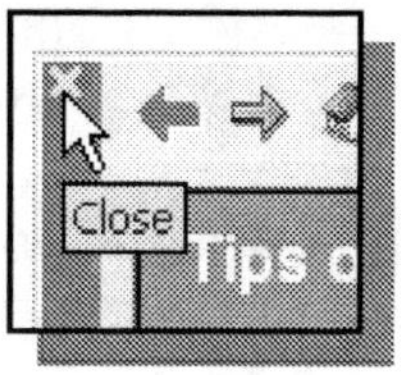

6. In the command prompt area, near the bottom of the *AutoCAD LT* drawing screen, the message *"_line Specify first point:"* is displayed. AutoCAD LT expects us to identify the starting location of a straight line. Move the graphics cursor inside the graphics window and watch the display of the coordinates of the graphics cursor at the bottom of the *AutoCAD LT* drawing screen. The two numbers represent the location of the cursor in the X, and Y directions. We can treat the graphics window as if it were a piece of paper and we are using the graphics cursor as if it were a pencil with which to draw.

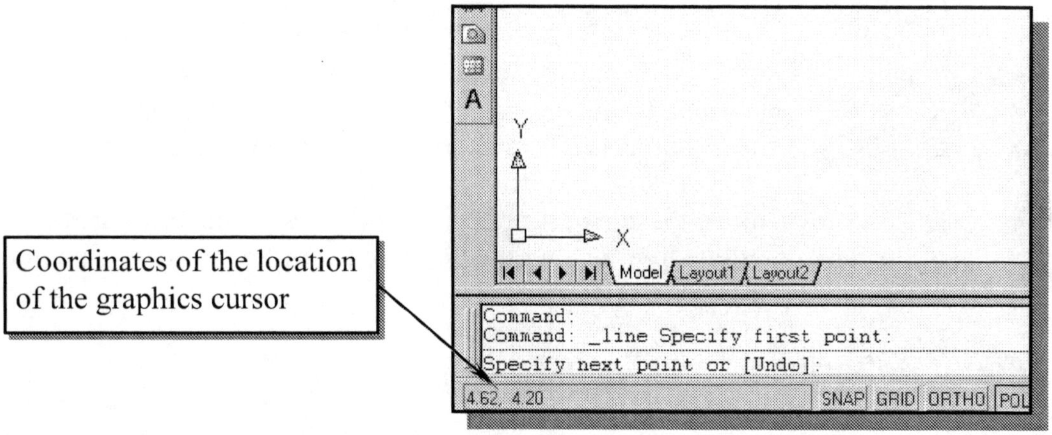

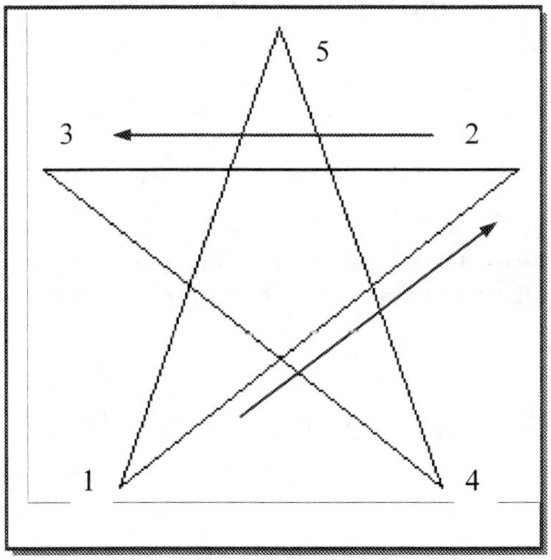

➢ We will create a freehand sketch of a five-point star using the Line command. Create the sketch by placing the first corner of the star near the lower left corner of the drawing window. Do not be overly concerned with the actual size or the accuracy of your freehand sketch. This exercise is to give you a feel for the **AutoCAD® LT 2005** user interface.

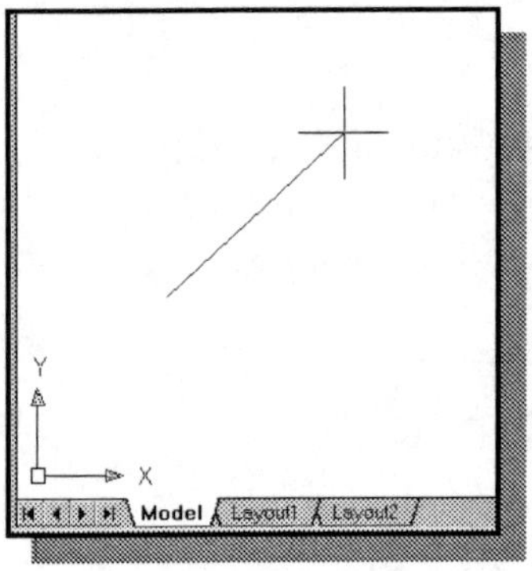

7. We will start at a location about one-third from the bottom of the graphics window. Left-click once to position the starting point of our first line. This will be *point 1* of our sketch. Next move the cursor upward and toward the right side of *point 1*. Notice the rubber-band line that follows the graphics cursor in the graphics window. Left-click again (*point 2*) and we have created the first line of our sketch.

8. Move the cursor to the left of *point 2* and create a horizontal line about the same length as the first line on the screen.

9. Repeat the above steps and complete the freehand sketch by adding three more lines (from *point 3* to *point 4*, *point 4* to *point 5*, and then connect to *point 5* back to *point 1*).

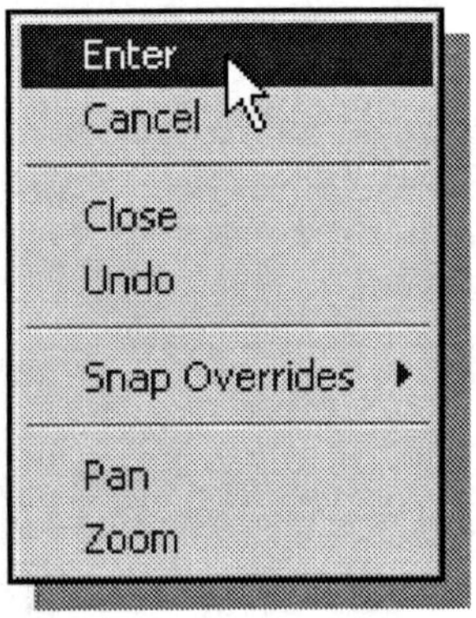

10. Notice that the Line command remains activated even after we connected the last segment of the line to the starting point *(point 1)* of our sketch. Inside the graphics window, **click once with the right-mouse-button** and a popup menu appears on the screen.

11. Select **Enter** with the left-mouse-button to end the Line command. (This is equivalent to hitting the **[ENTER]** key on the keyboard. The right-mouse-click brings up more options and we should get used to using the option menu.)

12. On your own, move the cursor near *point 2* and *point 3*, and estimate the length of the horizontal line by watching the displayed coordinates for each point at the bottom of the screen.

Visual Reference

The method we just used to create the freehand sketch is known as the **interactive method**, where we use the cursor to specify locations on the screen. This method is perhaps the fastest way to specify locations on the screen. However, it is rather difficult to try to create a line of a specific length by watching the displayed coordinates. It would be helpful to know what one-inch or one-meter looks like on the screen while we are creating entities. **AutoCAD® LT 2005** provides us with many tools to aid the construction of our designs. We will use the ***GRID*** and ***SNAP*** options to get a visual reference as to the size of objects and learn to restrict the movement of the cursor to a set increment on the screen.

The *Status Bar* area is located at the bottom of the *AutoCAD LT* drawing screen. The words *SNAP*, *GRID*, *ORTHO*, *POLAR*, *OSNAP*, *LWT* and *MODEL* appearing to the right of the coordinates are buttons that we can left-click to turn these special options *ON* and *OFF*. When the corresponding button is *highlighted*, the specific option is turned on. These buttons act as toggle switches; each click of the button will toggle the option on or off. Using the buttons is a quick and easy way to make changes to these *drawing aid* options. We can toggle the options ***ON*** and ***OFF*** in the middle of another command.

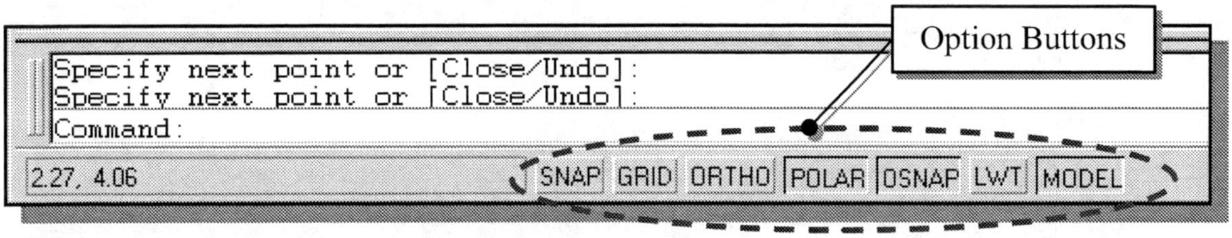

GRID ON

1. Left-click the ***GRID*** button in the *Status Bar* to turn ***ON*** the *GRID* option. (Notice in the command prompt area, the message *"<Grid on>"* is also displayed.)

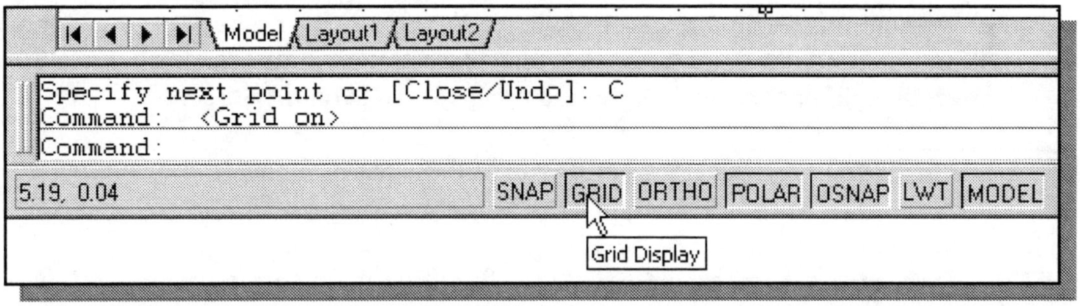

2. Move the cursor inside the graphics window, and estimate the distance between the grid points by watching the coordinates display at the bottom of the screen.

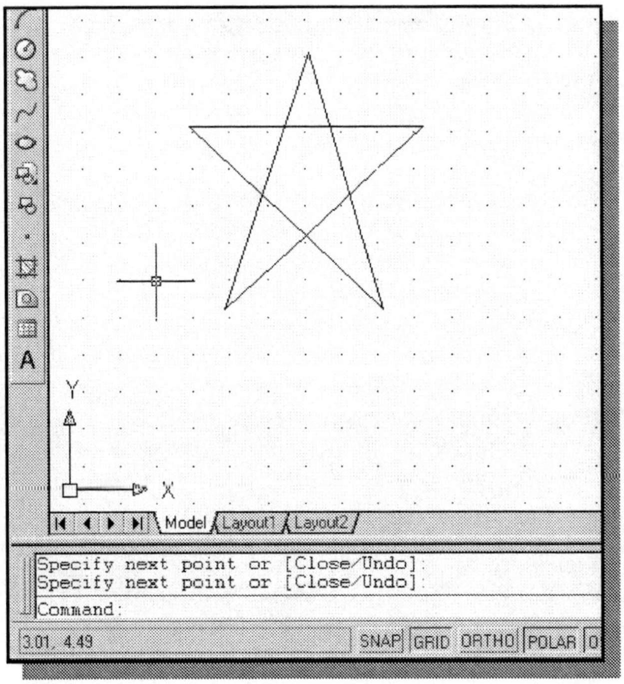

➢ The *GRID* option creates a pattern of dots that extends over an area on the screen. Using the grid is similar to placing a sheet of grid paper under a drawing. The grid helps you align objects and visualize the distance between them. The grid is not displayed in the plotted drawing. The default grid spacing, which means the distance in between two dots on the screen, is 0.5 inches. We can see that the sketched horizontal line in the above sketch is about 3.0 inches long.

SNAP ON

1. Left-click the ***SNAP*** button in the *Status Bar* to turn ***ON*** the *SNAP* option.

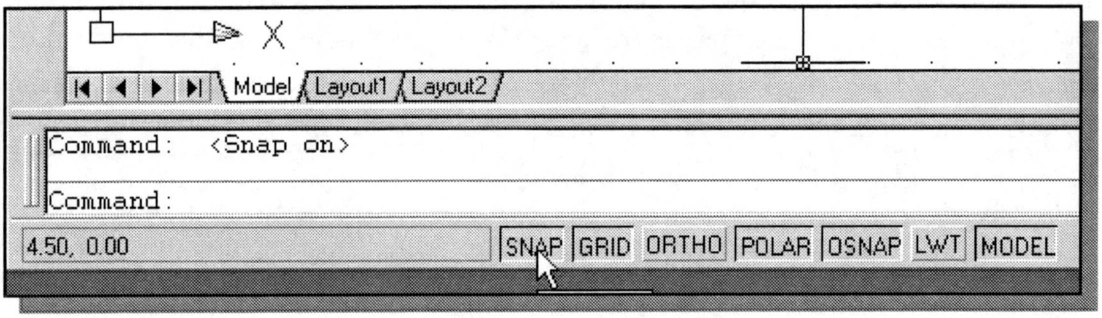

2. Move the cursor inside the graphics window, and move the cursor diagonally on the screen. Observe the movement of the cursor and watch the *coordinates display* at the bottom of the screen.

➢ The *SNAP* option controls an invisible rectangular grid that restricts cursor movement to specified intervals. When *SNAP* mode is on, the screen cursor and all input coordinates are snapped to the nearest point on the grid. The default snap interval is 0.5 inches, and aligned to the grid points on the screen.

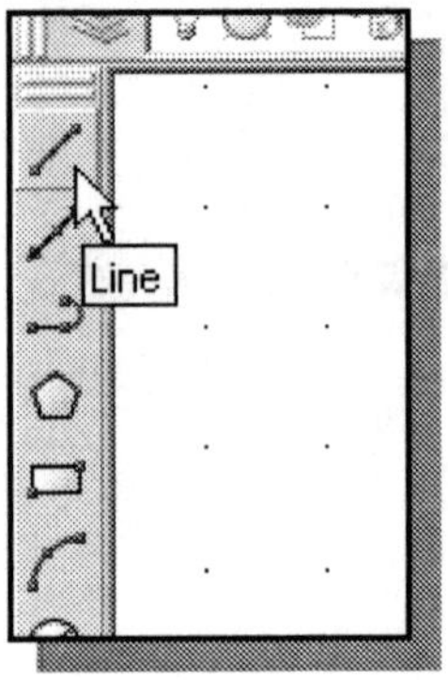

3. Click on the **Line** icon in the *Draw* toolbar. In the command prompt area, the message *"_line Specify first point:"* is displayed.

4. Create another sketch of the five-point star with the *GRID* and *SNAP* options switched *ON*.

5. Use the right-mouse-button and select **Enter** in the popup menu to end the Line command if you have not done so.

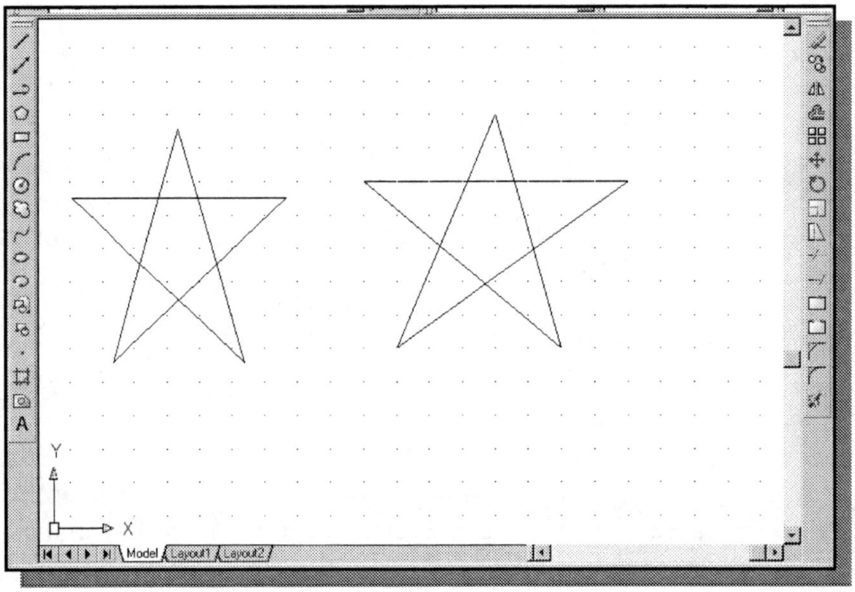

Using the *ERASER*

One of the advantages of using a CAD system is the ability to remove entities without leaving any marks. We will erase two of the lines using the **Erase** command.

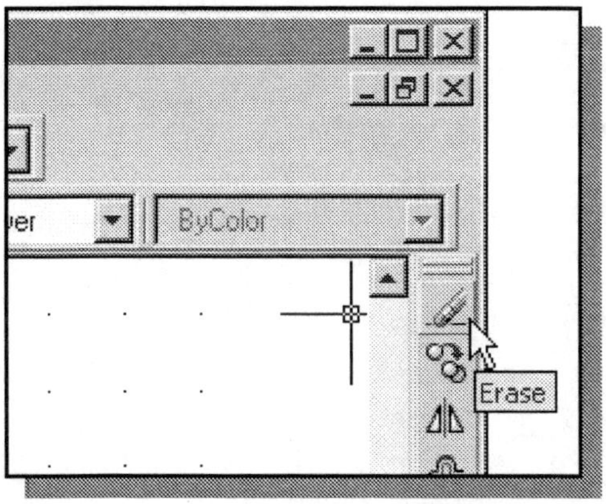

1. Pick **Erase** in the *Modify* toolbar. (The icon is the first icon in the *Modify* toolbar. The icon is a picture of an eraser at the end of a pencil.) The message *"Select objects"* is displayed in the command prompt area and AutoCAD LT waits for us to select the objects to erase.

2. Left-click the ***SNAP*** button on the *Status Bar* to turn ***OFF*** the *SNAP* option so that we can more easily move the cursor on top of objects. We can toggle the *Status Bar* options ***ON*** or ***OFF*** in the middle of another command.

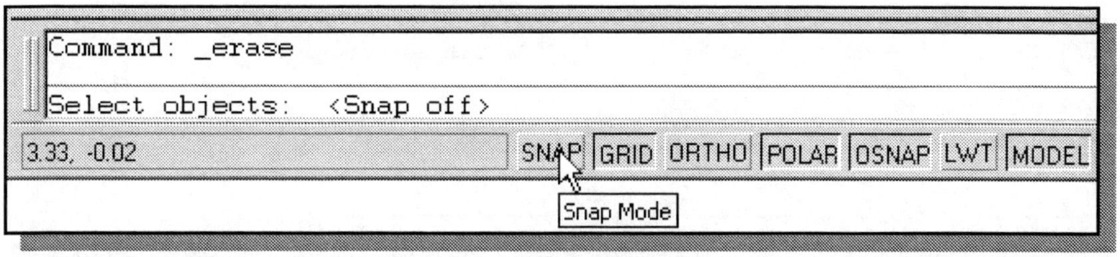

3. Select any two lines on the screen, and right-mouse-click once to accept the selections. The selected two lines are erased.

Repeat the Last Command

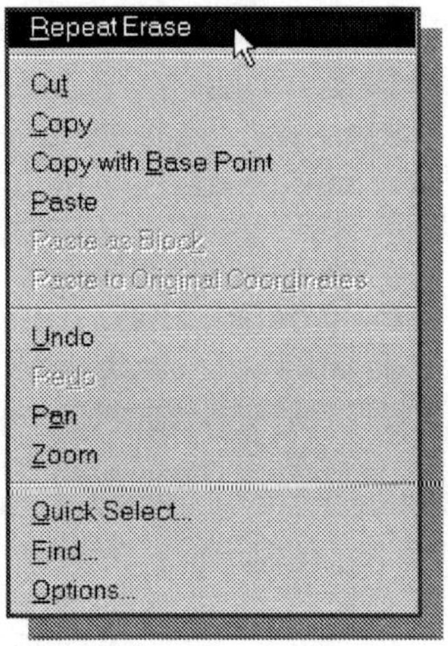

1. Inside the graphics window, click once with the right-mouse-button to bring up the popup option menu.

2. Pick **Repeat Erase**, with the left-mouse-button, in the popup menu to repeat the last command. Notice the other options available in the popup menu.

- **AutoCAD® LT 2005** offers many options to assist us in accomplishing this task. Throughout this text, we will emphasize the use of the **AutoCAD Heads-up Design™** interface, which means that we can focus on the screen, not on the keyboard.

3. Move the cursor to a location that is above and toward the left side of the entities on the screen. Left-mouse-click once to start a corner of a rubber-band window.

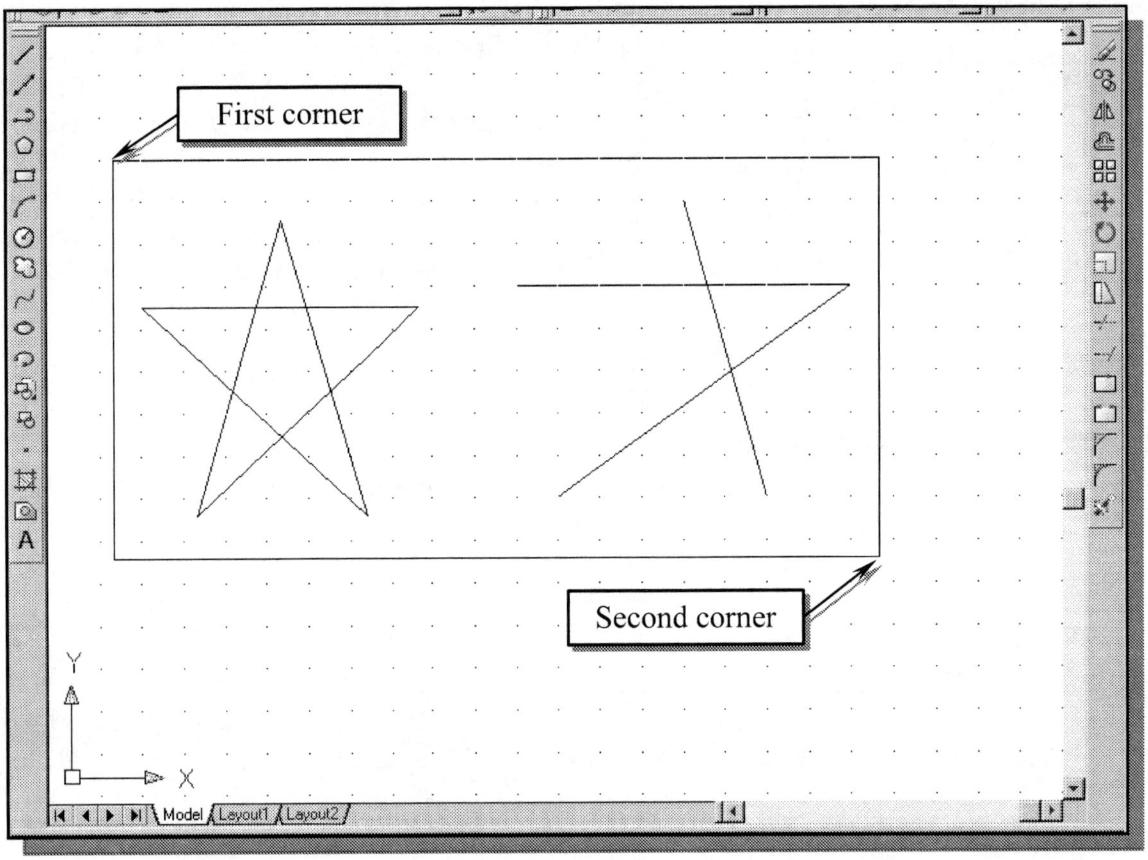

4. Move the cursor toward the right and below the entities, and then left-mouse-click to enclose all the entities inside the **selection window**. Notice all entities that are inside the window are selected.

5. Inside the graphics window, **right-mouse-click** to proceed with erasing the selected entities.

➢ On your own, create a sketch of your choice using the **Line** command. Experiment with using the different commands we have discussed so far, such as switching the *GRID* and *SNAP* options ***ON*** and ***OFF*** in the middle of a command.

❖ Do not be in a hurry to rush through the tutorials. Build up your CAD skills by familiarizing yourself with the commands and options demonstrated, along with the concepts discussed in the lessons. Feel free to repeat, at any time, any of the lessons.

➢ Use the Erase command and erase all entities on the screen before proceeding to the next section.

The CAD Database and the User Coordinate System

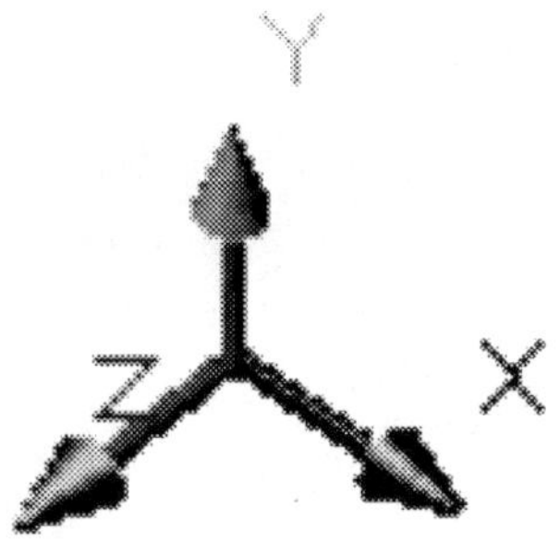

❖ Designs and drawings created in a CAD system are usually defined and stored using sets of points in what is called **world space**. In most CAD systems, the world space is defined using a three-dimensional *Cartesian coordinate system*. Three mutually perpendicular axes, usually referred to as the X, Y, and Z-axes, define this system. The intersection of the three coordinate axes forms a point called the **origin**. Any point in world space can then be defined as the distance from the origin in the X, Y and Z- directions. In most CAD systems, the directions of the arrows shown on the axes identify the positive sides of the coordinates.

A CAD file, which is the electronic version of the design, contains data that describe the entities created in the CAD system. Information such as the coordinate values in world space for all endpoints, center points, etc., along with the descriptions of the types of entities is all stored in the file. Knowing that AutoCAD LT stores designs by keeping coordinate data helps us understand the inputs required to create entities.

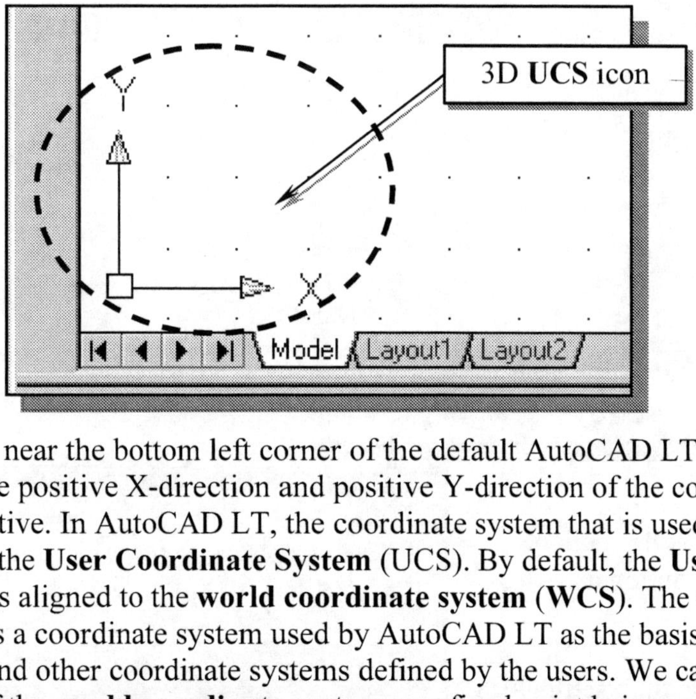

The icon near the bottom left corner of the default AutoCAD LT graphics window shows the positive X-direction and positive Y-direction of the coordinate system that is active. In AutoCAD LT, the coordinate system that is used to create entities is called the **User Coordinate System** (UCS). By default, the **User Coordinate System** is aligned to the **world coordinate system (WCS)**. The **world coordinate system** is a coordinate system used by AutoCAD LT as the basis for defining all objects and other coordinate systems defined by the users. We can think of the **origin** of the **world coordinate system** as a fixed point being used as a reference for all measurements. The default orientation of the Z-axis can be considered as positive values in front of the monitor and negative values inside the monitor.

Changing to the 2D UCS Icon Display

❖ In **AutoCAD® LT 2005**, the UCS icon is displayed in various ways to help us visualize the orientation of the drawing plane.

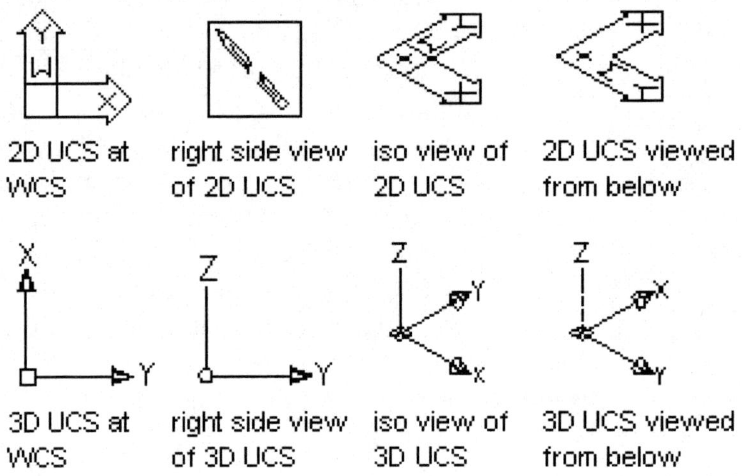

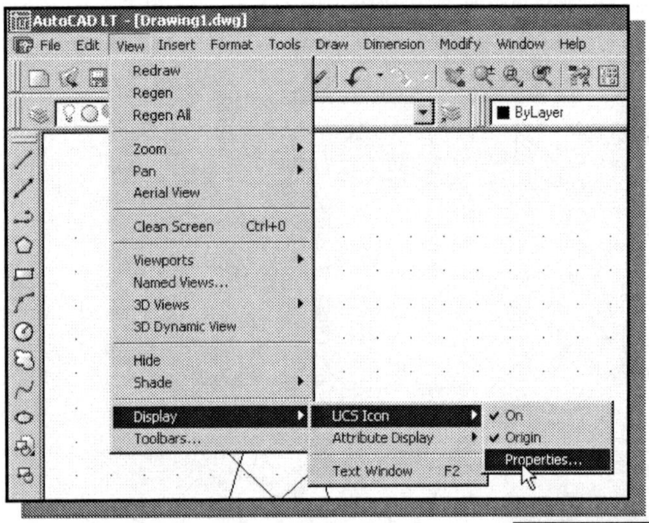

1. In the pull-down menus, select **[View] → [Display] → [UCSIcon] → [Properties]**

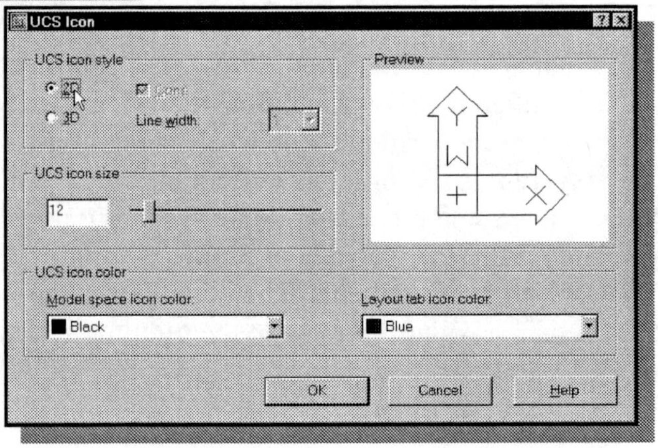

2. In the UCS icon style section, switch to the **2D** option as shown.

3. Click **OK** to accept the settings.

➢ Note the W symbol in the UCS icon indicates the UCS is aligned to the world coordinate system.

Cartesian and Polar Coordinate Systems

In two-dimensional space, a point can be represented using different coordinate systems. The point can be located, using *Cartesian coordinate system*, as X and Y units away from the origin. The same point can also be located using the *polar coordinate system*, as **r** and θ units away from the origin.

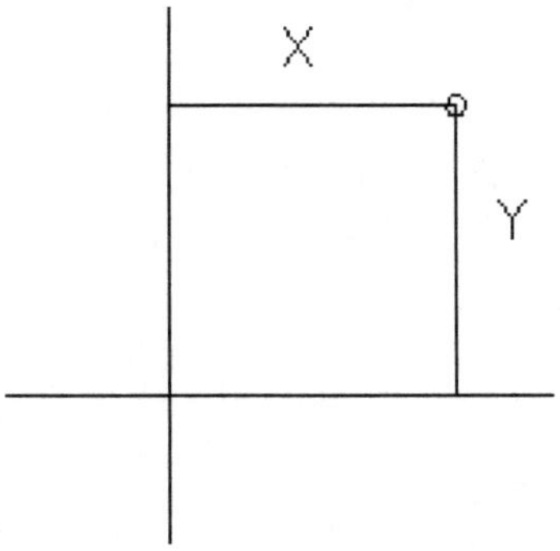

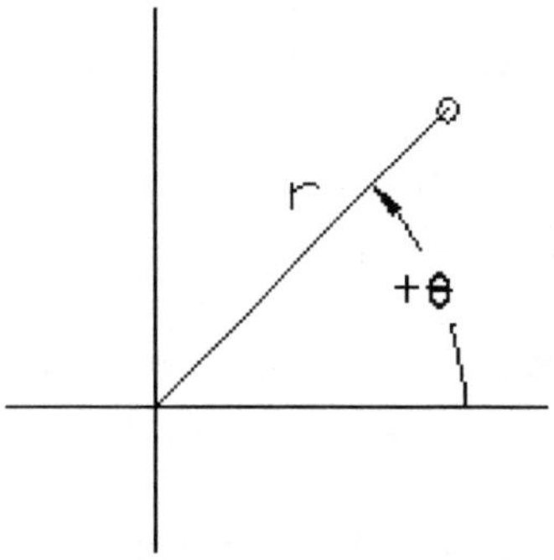

For planar geometry, the polar coordinate system is very useful for certain applications. In the polar coordinate system, points are defined in terms of a radial distance, r, from the origin and an angle, θ, between the direction of r and the positive X-axis. The default system for measuring angles in **AutoCAD® LT 2005** defines positive angular values as counter-clockwise from the positive X-axis.

Absolute and Relative Coordinates

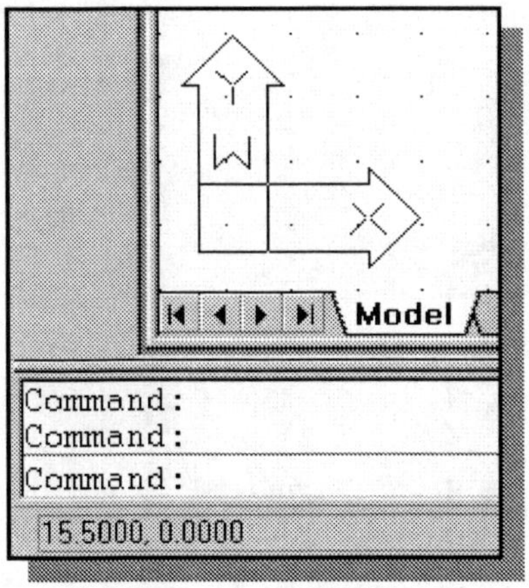

AutoCAD® LT 2005 also allows us to use *absolute* and *relative coordinates* to quickly construct objects. **Absolute coordinate values** are measured from the current coordinate system's origin point. **Relative coordinate values** are specified in relation to previous coordinates.

- The *coordinate display area* can also be used as a toggle switch; each left-mouse-click will toggle the coordinate display on or off.

In **AutoCAD® LT 2005**, the *absolute* coordinates and the *relative* coordinates can be used in conjunction with the *Cartesian* and *polar* coordinate systems. By default, AutoCAD LT expects us to enter values in *absolute Cartesian coordinates*, distances measured from the current coordinate system's origin point. We can switch to using the *relative* coordinates by using the **@** symbol. The @ symbol is used as the *relative coordinates specifier*, which means that we can specify the position of a point in relation to the previous point.

Defining Positions

In AutoCAD LT, there are five methods to specify the locations of points when we create planar geometric entities.

- **Interactive method:** Use the cursor to select on the screen.

- **Absolute coordinates (Format: X,Y):** Type the X and Y coordinates to locate the point on the current coordinate system relative to the origin.

- **Relative rectangular coordinates (Format: @X,Y):** Type the X and Y coordinates relative to the last point.

- **Relative polar coordinates (Format: @distance<angle):** Type a distance and angle relative to the last point.

- **Direct distance entry technique**: Specify a second point by first moving the cursor to indicate direction and then entering a distance.

The *Guide Plate*

We will next create a mechanical design using the different coordinate entry methods.

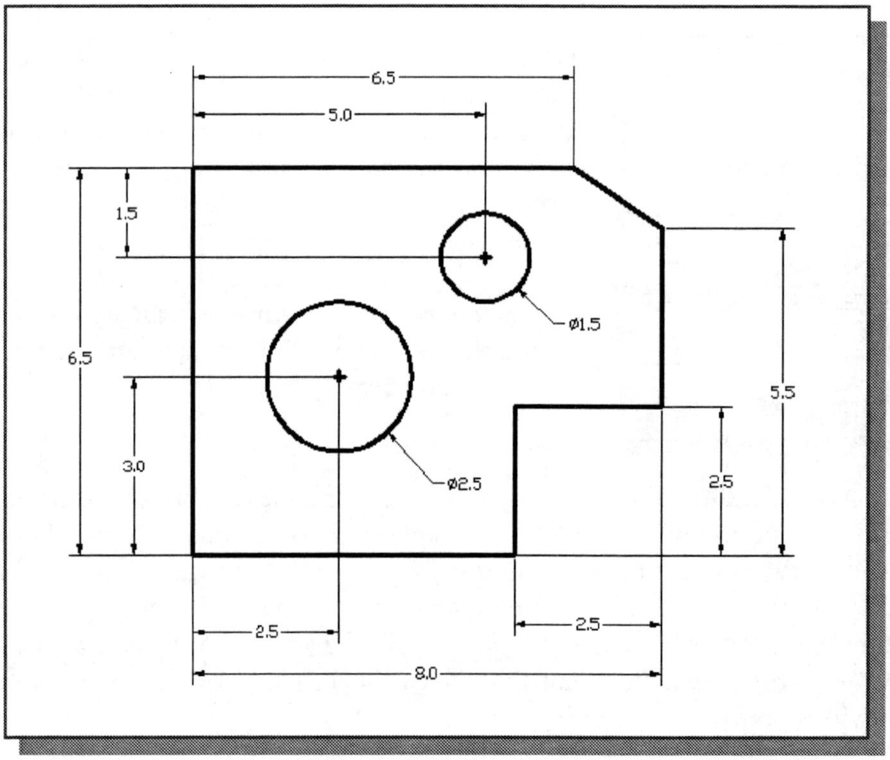

The rule for creating CAD designs and drawings is that they should be created **full size** using real-world units. The CAD database contains all the definitions of the geometric entities and the design is considered as a virtual, full-sized object. Only when a printer or plotter transfers the CAD design to paper is the design scaled to fit on a sheet. The tedious task of determining a scale factor so that the design will fit on a sheet of paper is taken care of by the CAD system. This allows the designers and CAD operators to concentrate their attention on the more important issues – the design.

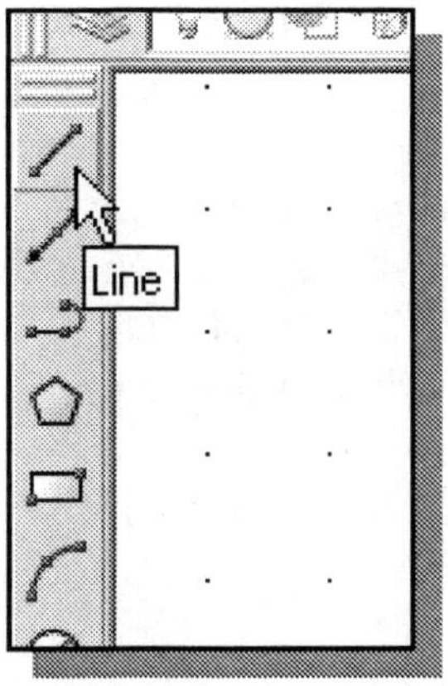

1. Select the **Line** command icon in the *Draw* toolbar. In the command prompt area, near the bottom of the *AutoCAD LT* graphics window, the message *"_line Specify first point:"* is displayed. AutoCAD LT expects us to identify the starting location of a straight line.

2. In the command prompt area, we will locate the starting point of our design at the origin of the *world coordinate system.*

   Command: _line Specify first point: **0,0 [ENTER]**
   (Type **0,0** in the command prompt area and press the **[ENTER]** key once.)

3. We will create a horizontal line by entering the absolute coordinates of the second point.

   Specify next point or [Undo]: **5.5,0 [ENTER]**

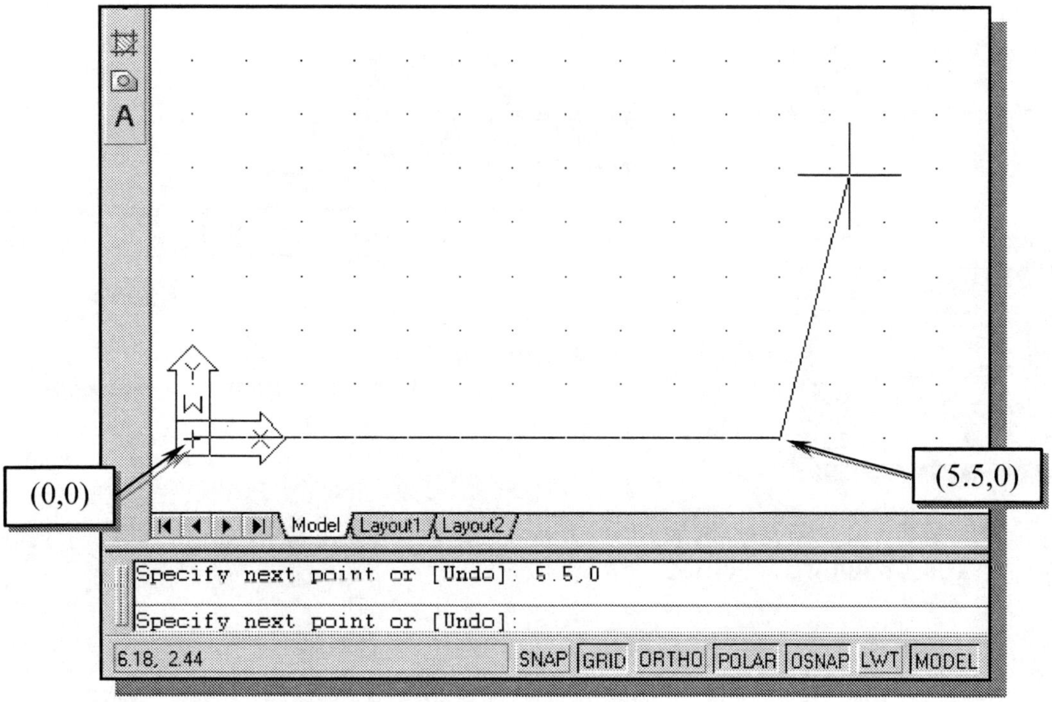

➢ The line we created is aligned to the bottom edge of the drawing window. Let us adjust the viewing of the line by using the Pan Realtime command.

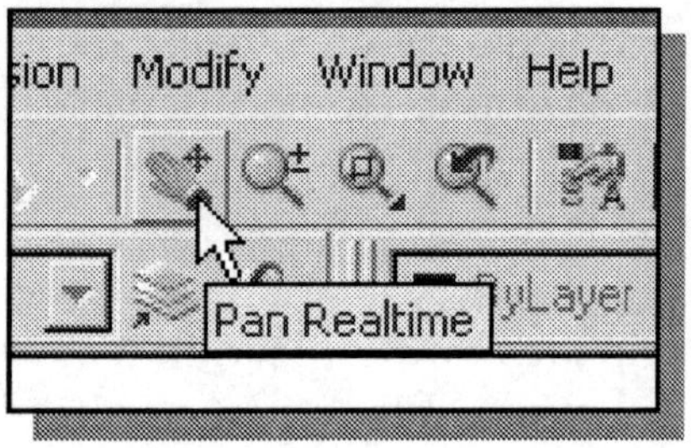

4. Click on the **Pan Realtime** icon in the *Standard* toolbar area. The icon is the picture of a hand with four arrows.

➢ The Pan command enables us to move the view to a different position. This function acts as if you are using a video camera.

5. Move the cursor, which appears as a hand inside the graphics window, near the center of the drawing window, then push down the left-mouse-button and drag the display toward the right and top side until we can see the sketched line. (Notice the scroll bars can also be used to adjust viewing of the display.)

6. Press the [**Esc**] key to exit the Pan command. Notice that AutoCAD LT goes back to the Line command.

7. We will create a vertical line by using the *relative rectangular coordinates entry method*, relative to the last point we specified

   Specify next point or [Close/Undo]: **@0,2.5** **[ENTER]**

8. We can mix any of the entry methods in positioning the location of an endpoint. Move the cursor to the *Status Bar* area, and turn ***ON*** the *GRID* and *SNAP* options.

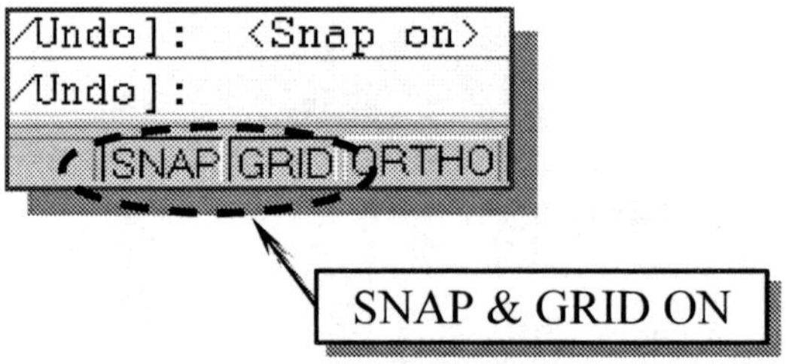

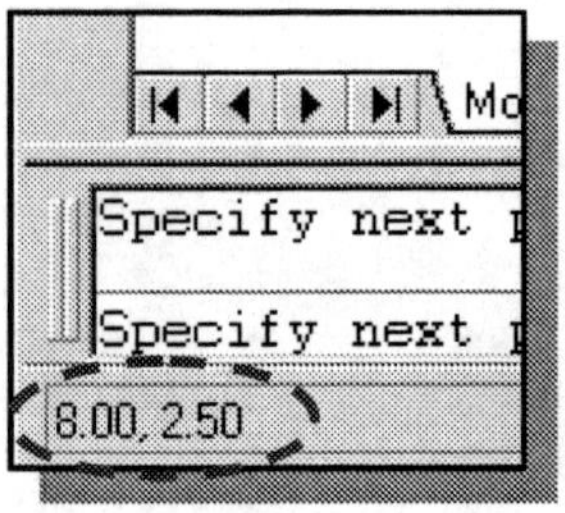

9. Create the next line by picking the location, *world coordinates* ***(8,2.5)***, on the screen.

10. We will next use the *relative polar coordinates entry method*, relative to the last point we specified

   Specify next point or [Close/Undo]: **@3<90** **[ENTER]**
   (Distance is **3** inches and an angle of **90** degrees)

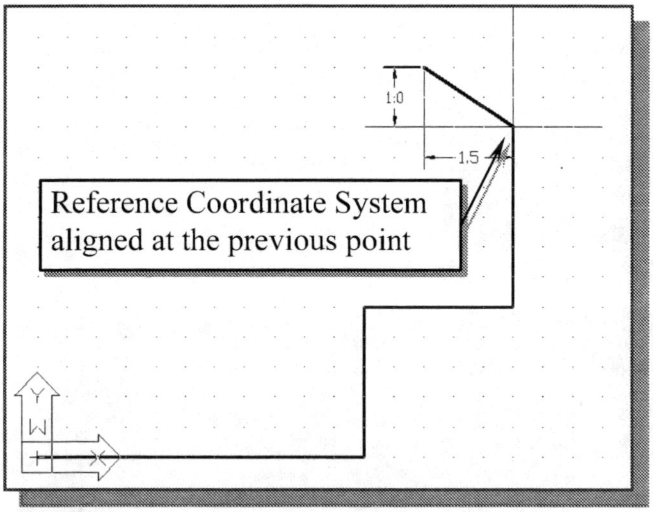

11. Using the *relative rectangular coordinates entry method* to create the next line, we can imagine a *reference coordinate system* aligned at the previous point. Coordinates are measured along the two reference axes.

Specify next point or [Close/Undo]: @**-1.5,1** **[ENTER]**

(**-1.5** and **1** inches are measured relative to the reference point.)

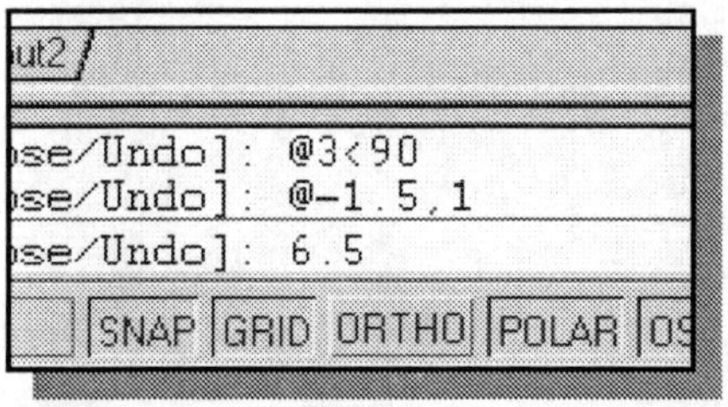

12. Move the cursor directly to the left of the last point and use the *direct distance entry technique* by entering **6.5 [ENTER]**.

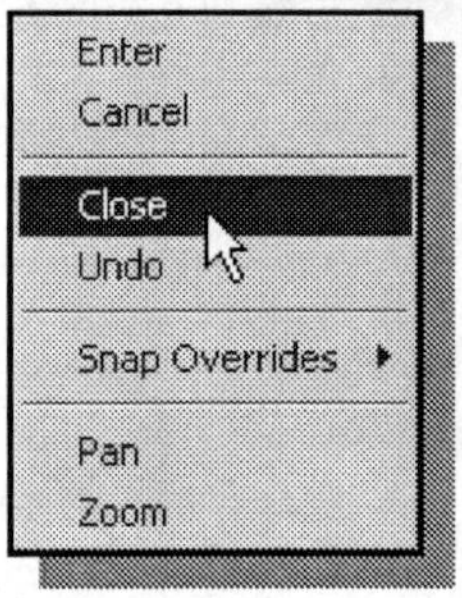

13. For the last segment of the sketch, we can use the Close option to connect back to the starting point. Inside the graphics window, **right-mouse-click** and a popup menu appears on the screen.

14. Select **Close** with the left-mouse-button to connect back to the starting point and end the Line command.

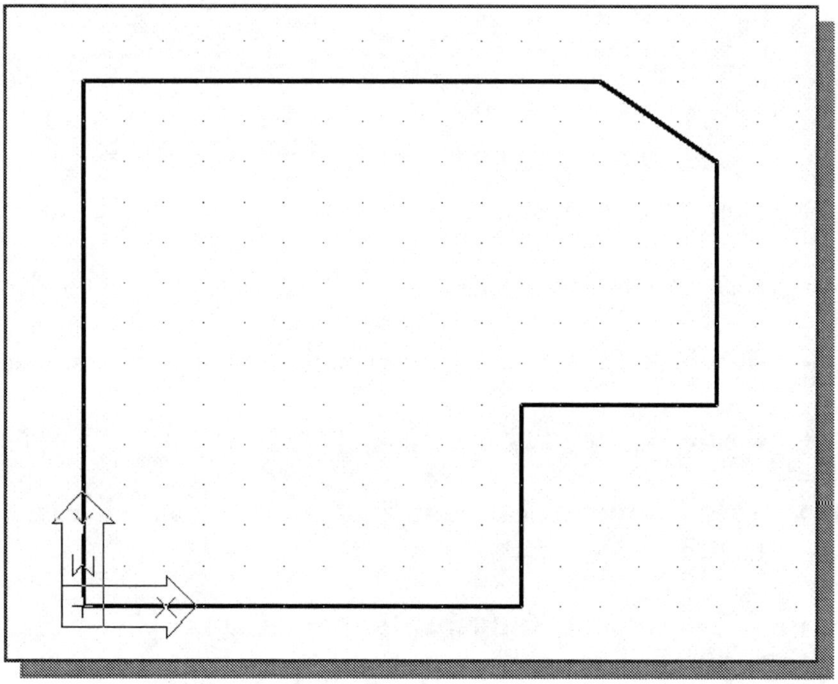

Creating *Circles*

The menus and toolbars in **AutoCAD® LT 2005** are designed to allow the CAD operators to quickly activate the desired commands. Besides using the *Draw* toolbar, we can also select the different *Draw* commands through the *pull-down menus*.

1. In the pull-down menus, select
   [Draw] → [Circle] → [Center, Diameter]

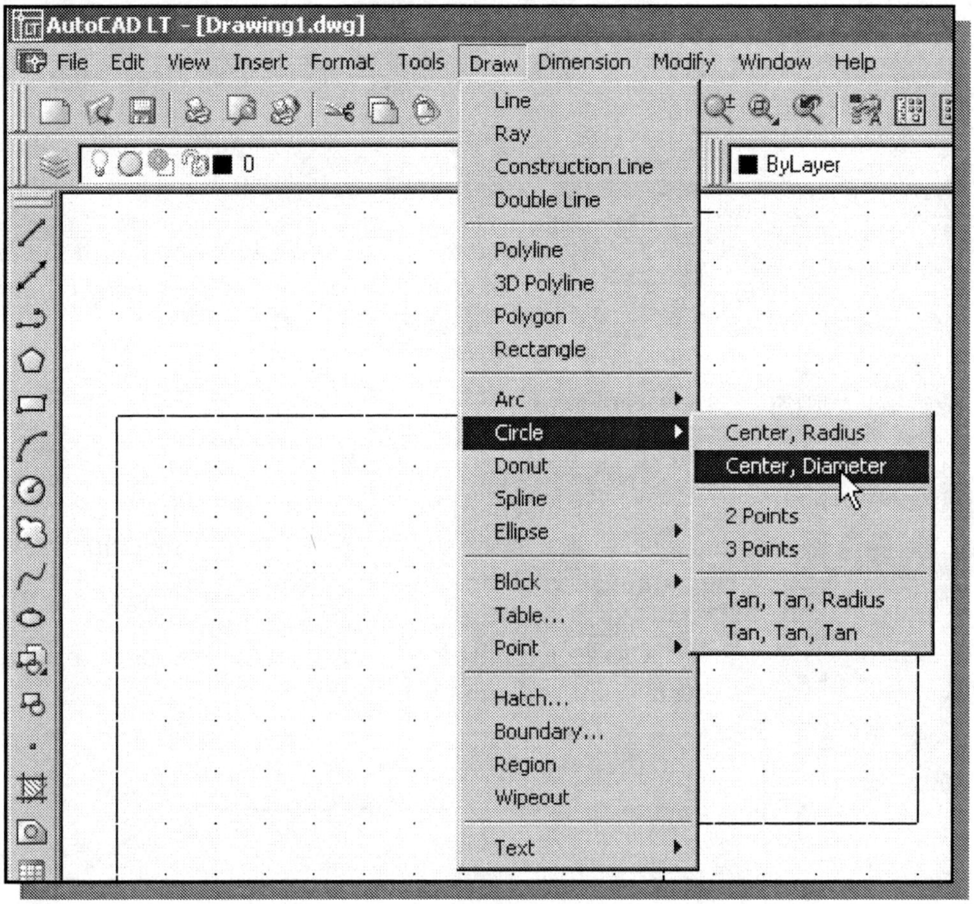

➢ Notice the different options available under the circle submenu:

- **Center Point**: Draws a circle based on a center point and a diameter or a radius.
- **3 Points**: Draws a circle based on three points on the circumference.
- **2 Points**: Draws a circle based on two endpoints of the diameter.
- **TTR – Tangent, Tangent, Radius**: Draws a circle with a specified radius tangent to two objects.
- **TTT– Tangent, Tangent, Tangent**: Draws a circle tangent to three objects.

2. In the command prompt area, the message *"Specify center point for circle or [3P/2P/Ttr (tan tan radius)]:"* is displayed. AutoCAD LT expects us to identify the location of a point or enter an option. We can use any of the four coordinate entry methods to identify the desired location. We will enter the world coordinates **(2.5,3)** as the center point for the first circle.

   Specify center point for circle or [3P/2P/Ttr (tan tan radius)]: **2.5,3 [ENTER]**

3. In the command prompt area, the message *"Specify diameter of circle:"* is displayed.

   Specify diameter of circle: **2.5 [ENTER]**

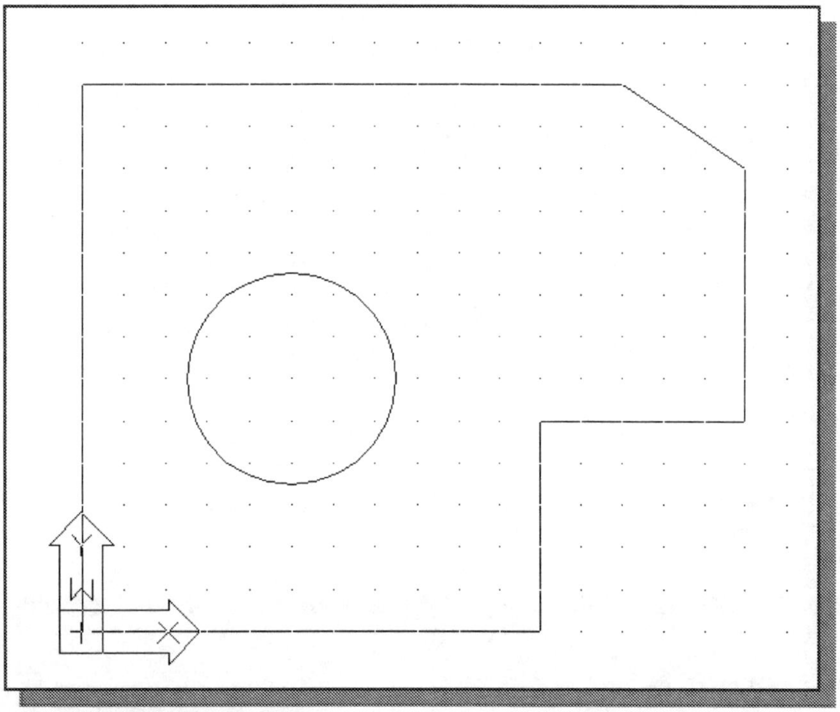

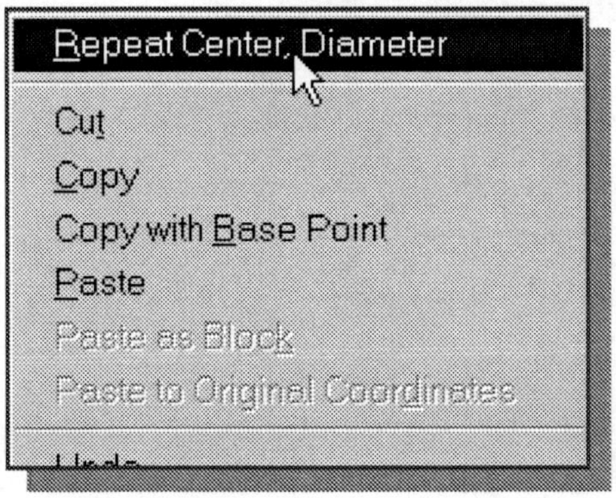

4. Inside the graphics window, **right-mouse-click** to bring up the popup option menu.

5. Pick **Repeat Center, Diameter** with the left-mouse-button in the popup menu to repeat the last command.

6. Using the *relative rectangular coordinates entry method*, relative to the center-point coordinates of the first circle, we specify the location as **(2.5,2)**.

Specify center point for circle or [3P/2P/Ttr (tan tan radius)]: **@2.5,2 [ENTER]**

7. In the command prompt area, the message *"Specify Diameter of circle: <2.50>"* is displayed. The default option for the **Circle** command in AutoCAD LT is to specify the *radius*, and the last radius used is also displayed in brackets.

   Specify Diameter of circle<2.50>: **1.5 [ENTER]**

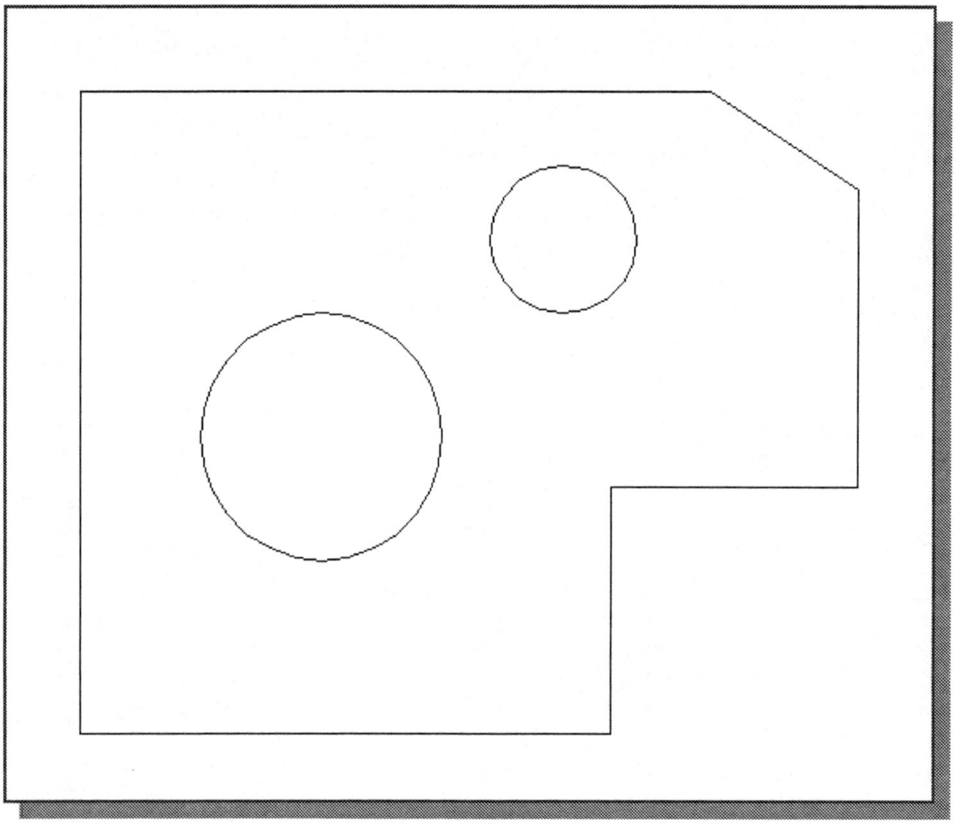

Saving the CAD File

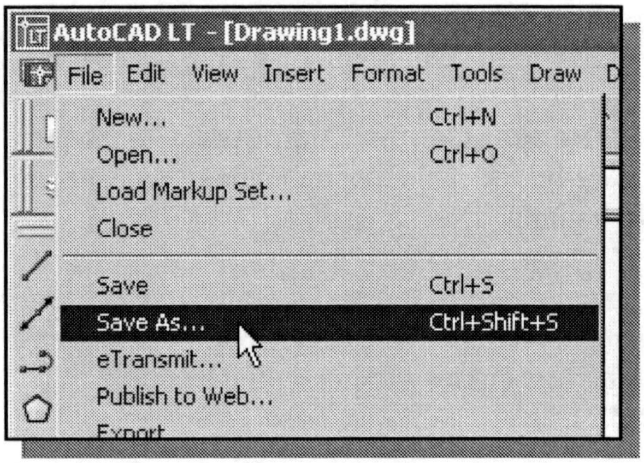

1. In the pull-down menus, select **[File] → [Save As]**

2. In the *Save Drawing As* dialog box, select the folder in which you want to store the CAD file and enter ***GuidePlate*** in the *File name* box.

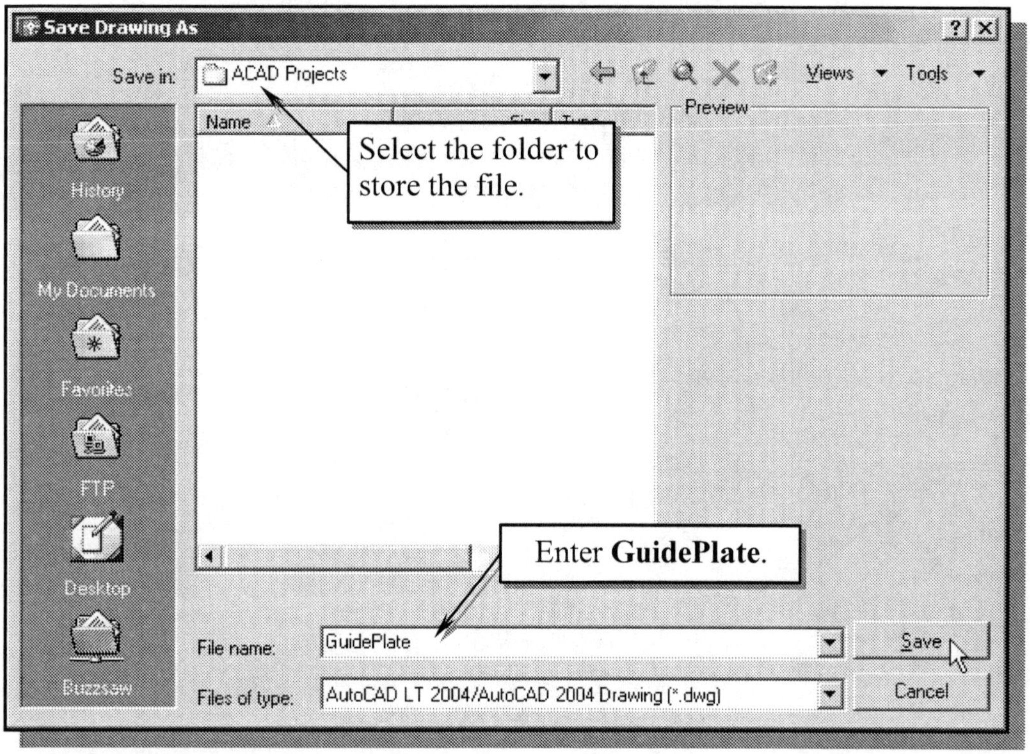

3. Pick **Save** in the *Save Drawing As* dialog box to accept the selections and save the file.

Exit *AutoCAD LT 2005*

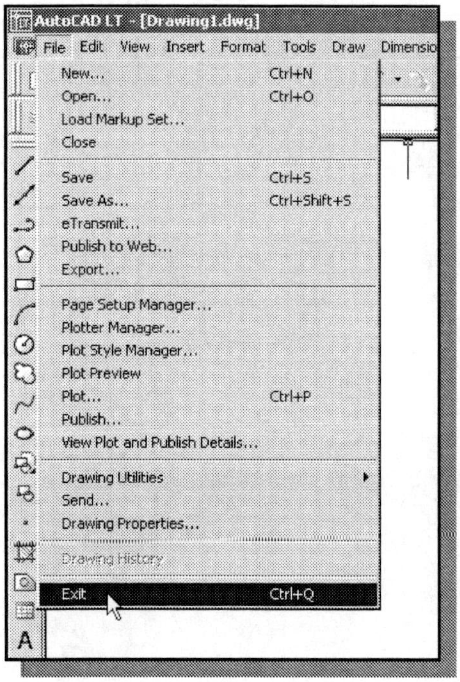

To exit **AutoCAD® LT 2005**, select **File** then choose **Exit** from the pull-down menu or type ***QUIT*** at the command prompt.

Questions:

1. What are the advantages and disadvantages of using CAD systems to create engineering drawings?

2. How do the *GRID* and *SNAP* options assist us in sketching?

3. List and describe the different **coordinate entry methods** available in AutoCAD LT?

4. List and describe two types of coordinate systems commonly used for planar geometry.

5. Identify the following commands:

(a)

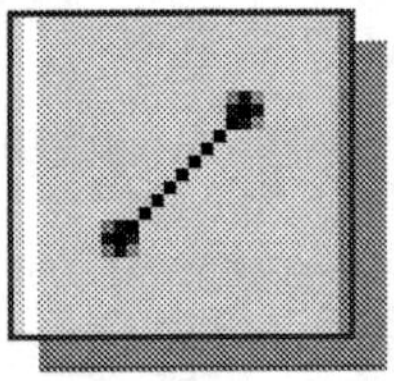

(b)

(c)

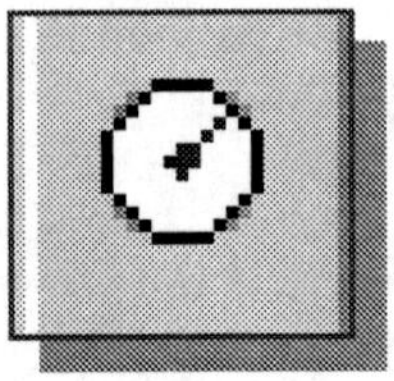

(d)

Tan, Tan, Radius

Exercises: (All dimensions are in inches.)

1.

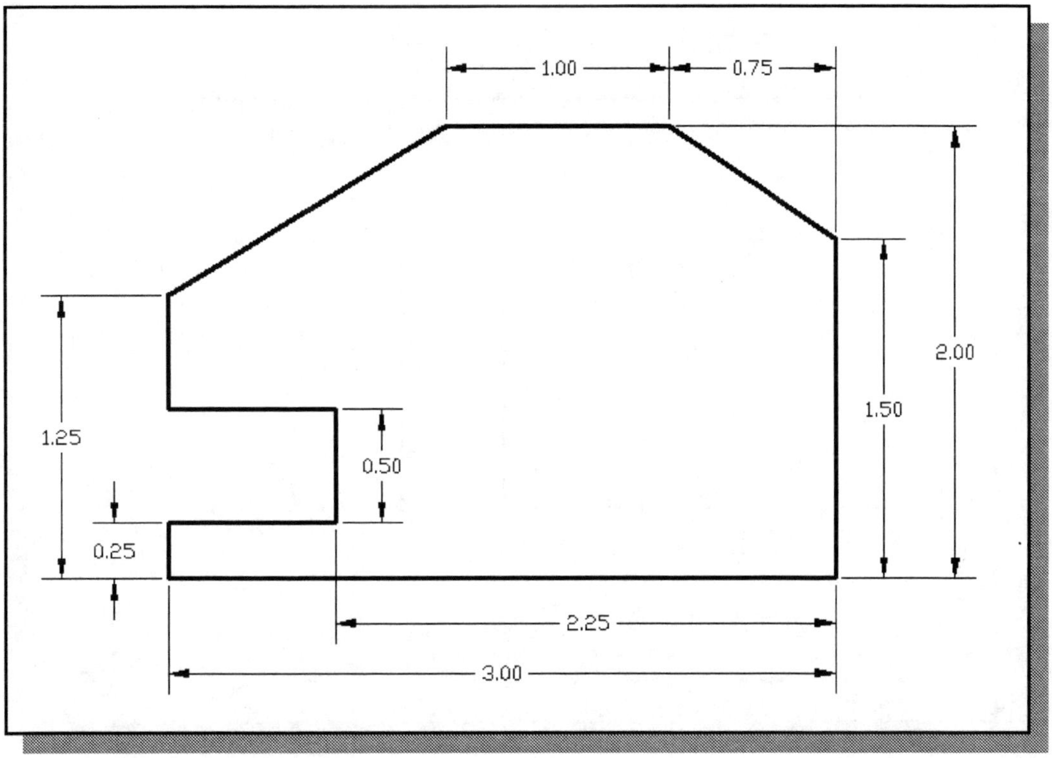

2.

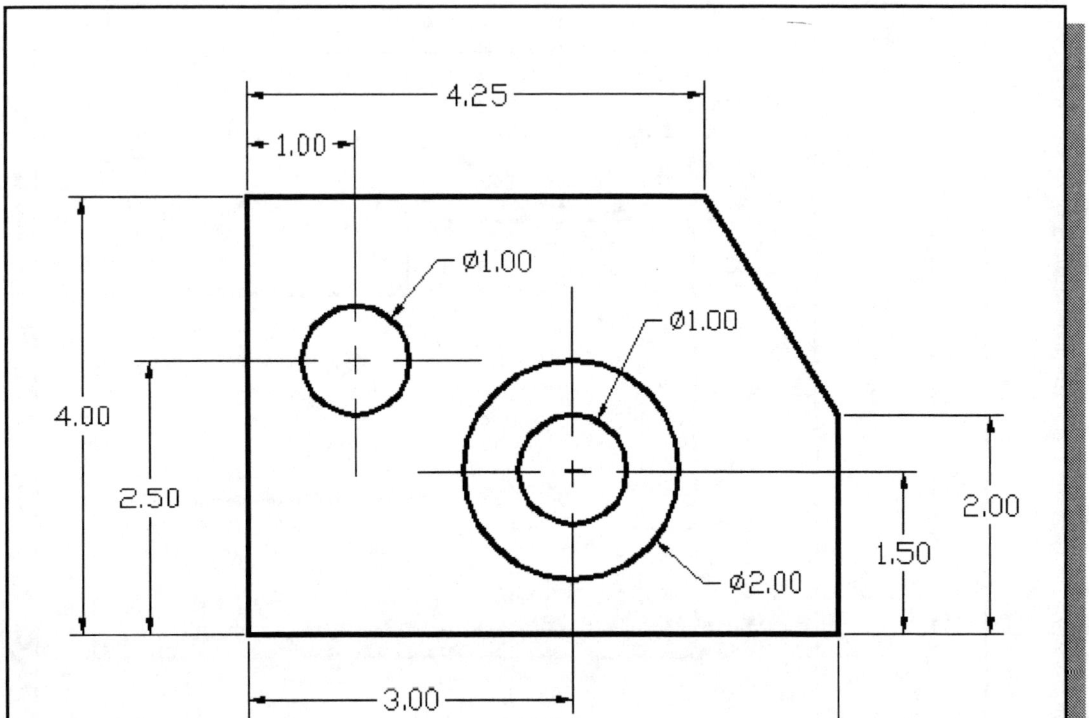

3.

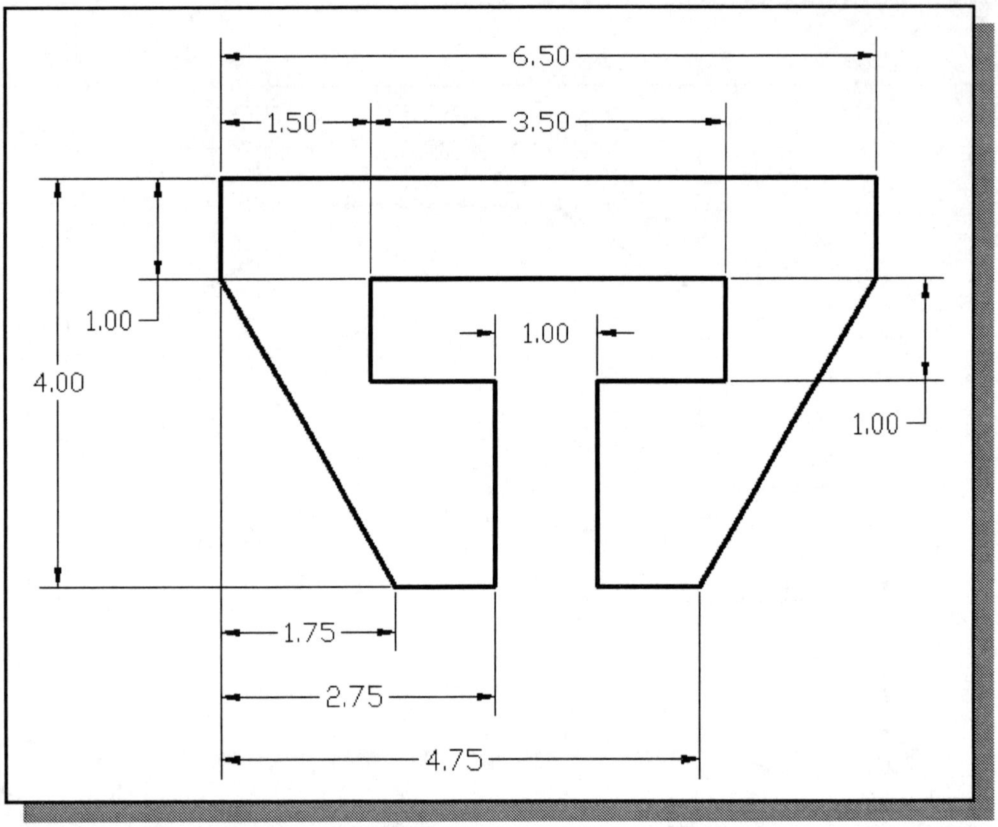
6.50
1.50
3.50
1.00
4.00
1.00
1.00
1.75
2.75
4.75

4.

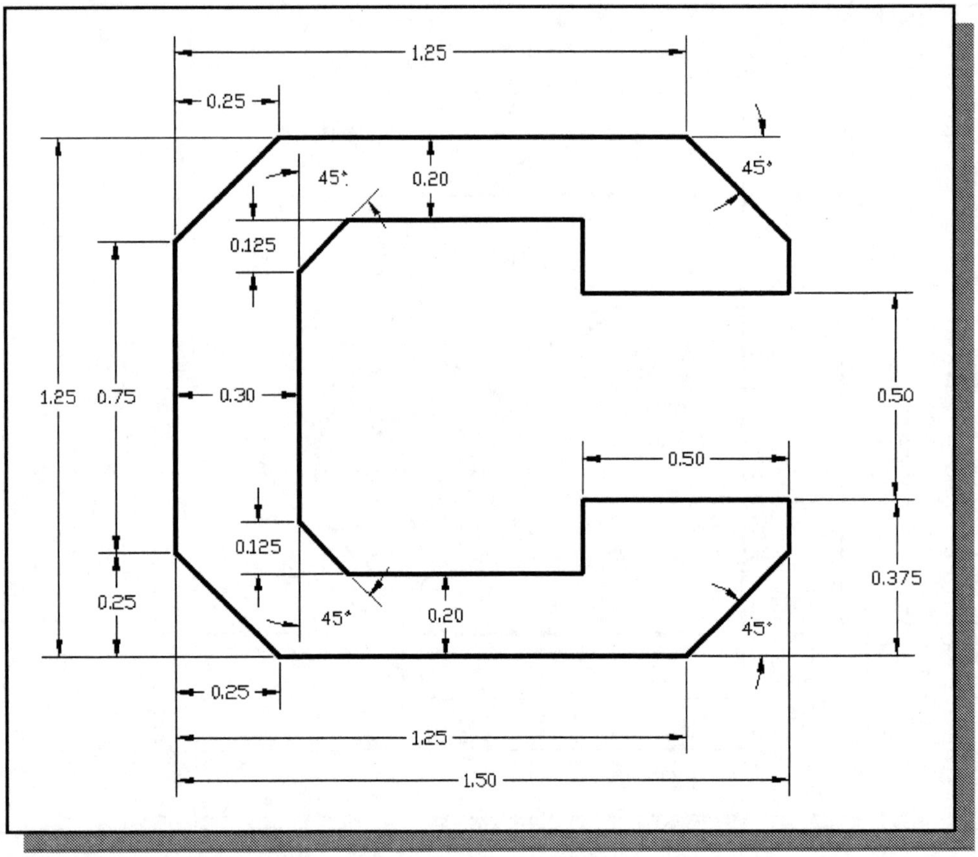
1.25
0.25
45°
0.20
45°
0.125
1.25
0.75
0.30
0.50
0.50
0.125
0.25
45°
0.20
45°
0.375
0.25
1.25
1.50

Lesson 2
Construction and Editing Tools

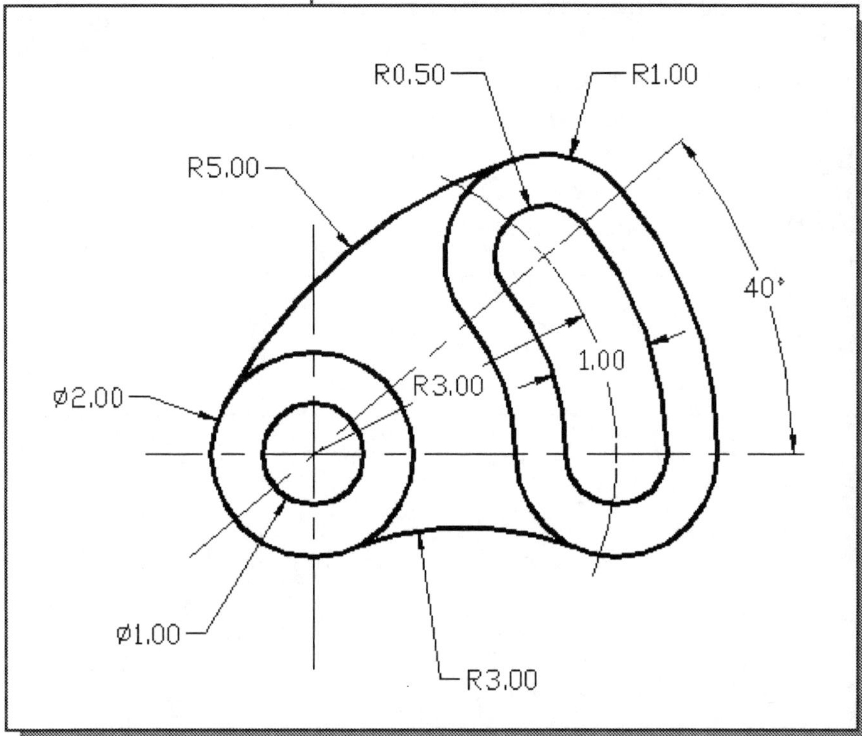

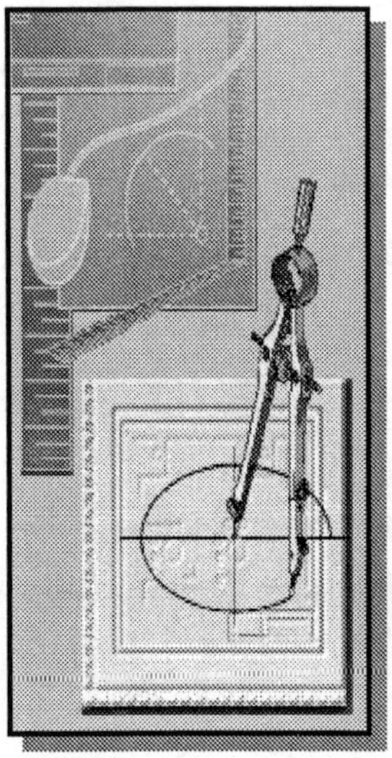

Learning Objectives

- Set Up Drawing Units
- Set Up GRID & SNAP Intervals
- Display AutoCAD's Toolbars
- Set Up and Use OBJECT SNAPS
- Edit, Using EXTEND and TRIM
- Use the FILLET Command
- Create Parallel Geometric Entities
- Use the EXPLODE Command

Introduction

The main characteristic of any CAD system is its ability to create and modify geometric entities quickly and accurately. Most CAD systems provide a variety of construction and editing tools to relieve the designer of the tedious drudgery of this task, so that the designer can concentrate more on the design content.

In this lesson, we will examine the basic construction and editing tools provided by **AutoCAD® LT 2005**. We will first look at tools such as *UNITS, GRID, SNAP* intervals setup and *OSNAP* option, followed by editing tools such as Trim, Extend, Fillet, Pedit and Offset. **AutoCAD® LT 2005** offers many different input options and we will take a different approach in constructing the design in this example.

The *Gasket* Design:

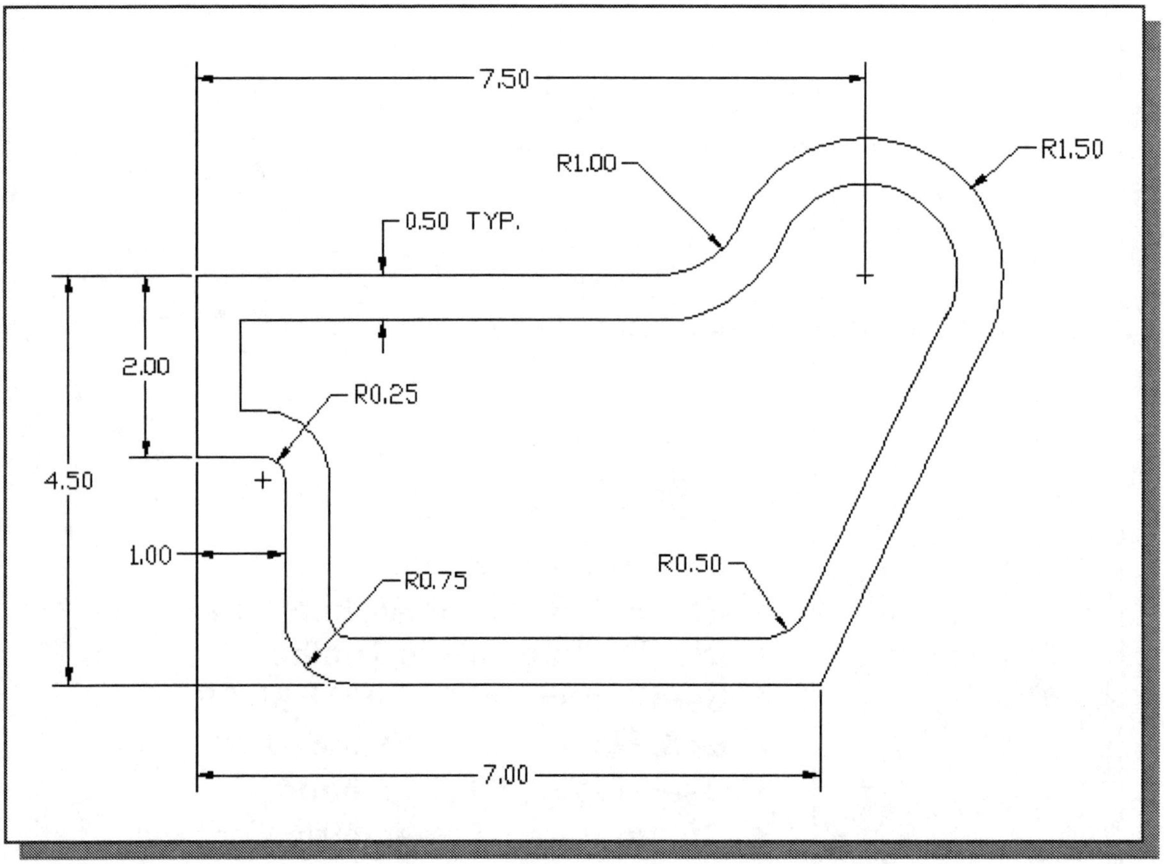

➤ Before continuing to the next page, on your own make a rough sketch showing the steps that can be used to create the design. Be aware that there are many different approaches to accomplishing the same task.

Starting Up *AutoCAD LT 2005*

1. Select the **AutoCAD LT 2005** option on the *Program* menu or select the **AutoCAD LT 2005** icon on the *Desktop*. Once the program is loaded into the memory, the *AutoCAD LT 2005* drawing screen will appear on the screen.

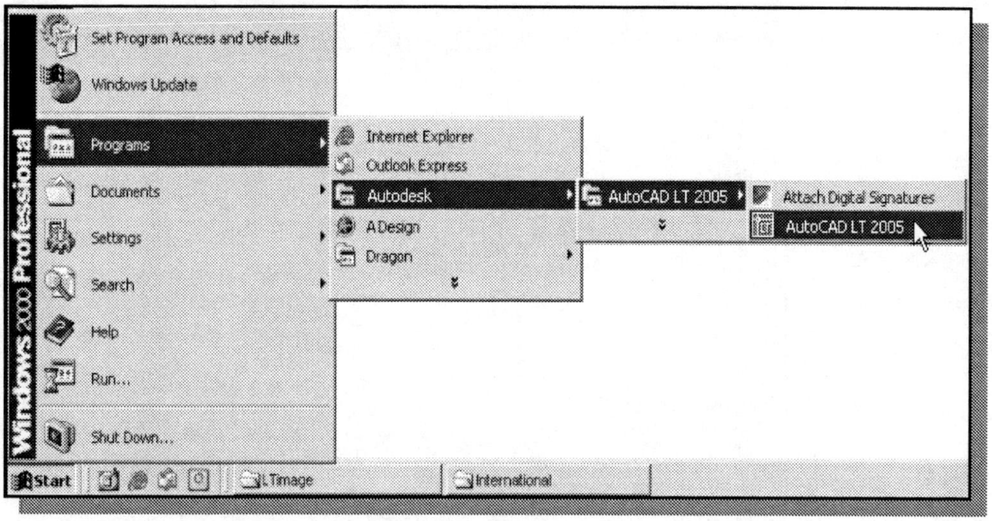

➢ Note that AutoCAD LT automatically assigns generic names, *Drawing X*, as new drawings are created. In our example, AutoCAD LT opened the graphics window using the default system units and assigned the drawing name *Drawing1*. **AutoCAD® LT 2005** provides several options to control the units settings.

Drawing Units Setup

Every object we construct in a CAD system is measured in units. We should determine the value of the units within the CAD system before creating the first geometric entities. For example, in one drawing, a unit might equal one millimeter of the real-world object. In another drawing, a unit might equal an inch. In AutoCAD LT, *drawing unit settings* control how AutoCAD LT interprets the coordinate and angle entries and how it displays coordinates and units in the *Status Bar* and in dialog boxes.

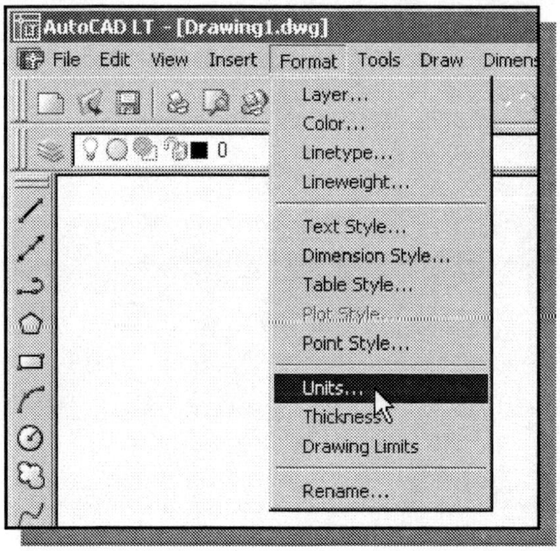

1. In the pull-down menus, select **[Format] → [Units]**

2. In the *Drawing Units* dialog box, set the *Length Type* to **Decimal**. This will set the measurement to the default English units, inches.

3. Set the *Precision* to **two digits** after the decimal point.

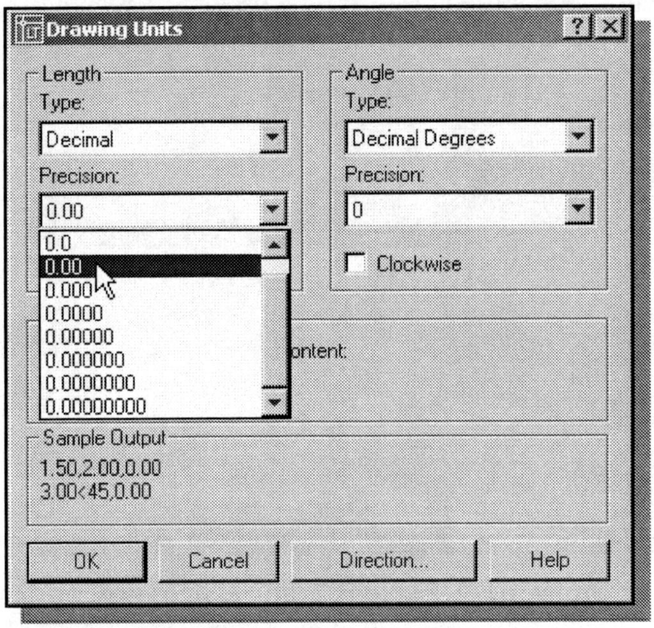

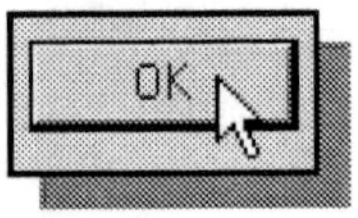

4. Pick **OK** to exit the *Drawing Units* dialog box.

GRID and *SNAP* Intervals Setup

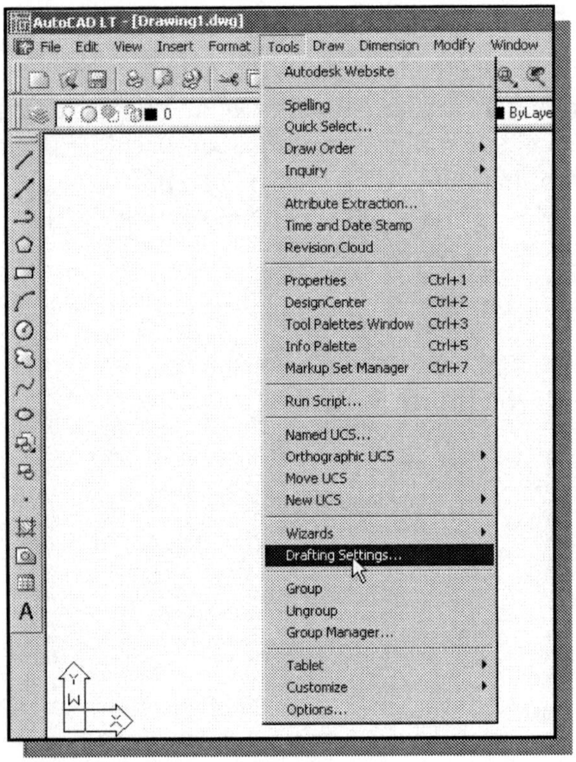

1. In the pull-down menus, select **[Tools] → [Drafting Settings]**

2. In the *Drafting Settings* dialog box, select the **SNAP and GRID** tab if it is not the page on top.

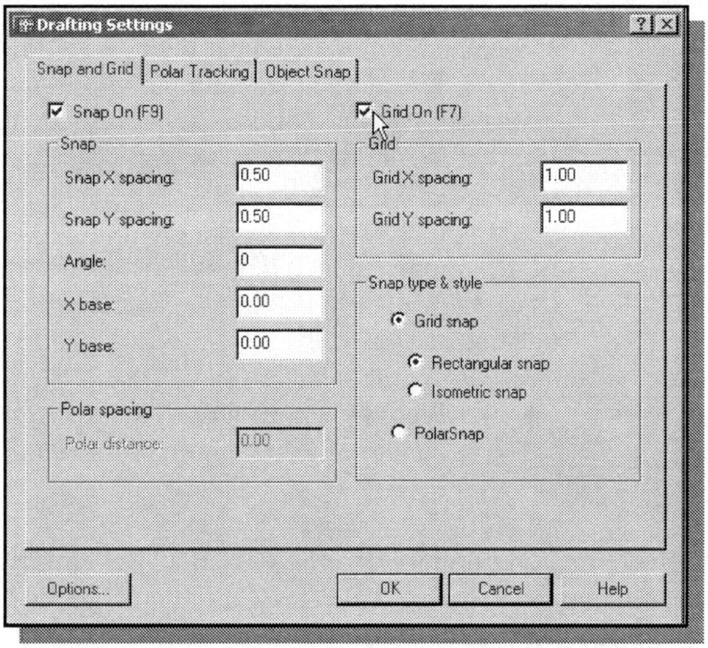

3. Change *Grid Spacing* to **1.00** for both X and Y directions.

4. Pick **OK** to exit the *Drawing Units* dialog box.

5. In the *Standard* toolbar, select **Zoom All** with the left-mouse-button on the **Zoom** icon stack.

➢ Notice in the *Status Bar* area, the *GRID* and *SNAP* options are pressed down indicating they are switched *ON*. The grid spacing is set to **1** inch and the snap interval is set to **0.5** inch.

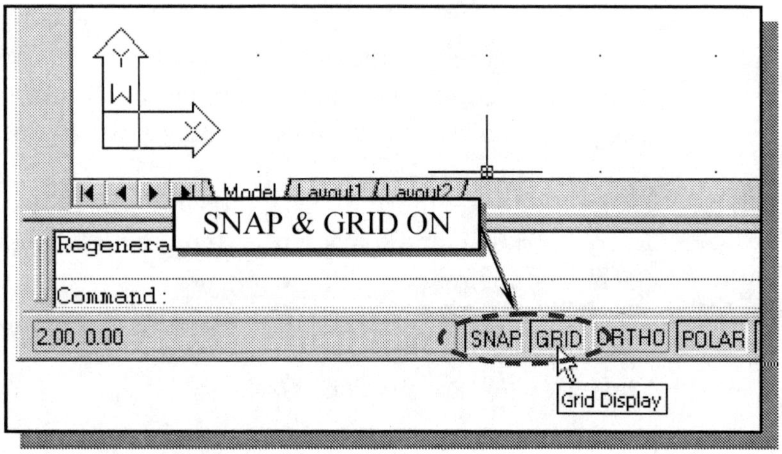

Using the *Line* Command

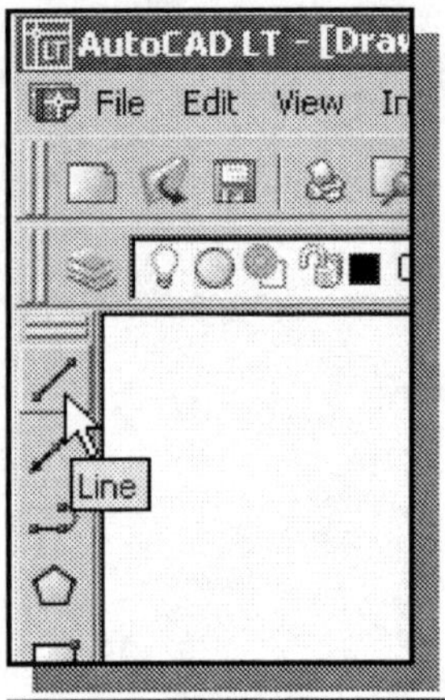

1. Select the **Line** command icon in the *Draw* toolbar. In the command prompt area, near the bottom of the AutoCAD LT drawing screen, the message *"_line Specify first point:"* is displayed. AutoCAD LT expects us to identify the starting location of a straight line.

2. In the graphics window, move the cursor to *world coordinates* **(2,6)**. **Left-click** to position the starting point of the line at that location.

3. We will next turn ***ON*** the *ORTHO* option by toggling on the ***ORTHO*** button in the *Status Bar* area.

❖ The *ORTHO* option constrains cursor movement to the horizontal or vertical directions, relative to the current coordinate system. With the **Line** command, we are now restricted to creating only horizontal or vertical lines with the *ORTHO* option.

4. Move the graphics cursor below the last point we selected on the screen and create a vertical line that is two units long (*Y coordinate: 4.00*).

5. Move the graphics cursor to the right of the last point and create a horizontal line that is one unit long (*X coordinate: 3.00*).

6. Move the graphics cursor below the last point and create a vertical line that is 2.5 units long (*Y coordinate: 1.50*).

7. Turn ***OFF*** the *SNAP* option in the *Status Bar* area.

8. Move the graphics cursor to the right of the last point and create a horizontal line that is about seven units long (near *X coordinate: 10.00*). As is quite common during the initial design stage, we do not know all of the dimensions.

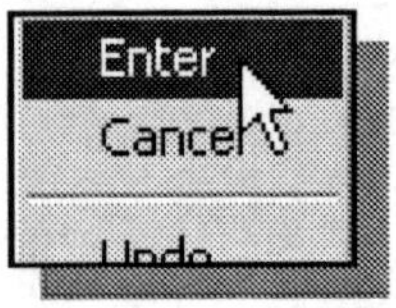

9. Inside the graphics window, **right-mouse-click** to activate the option menu and select **Enter** with the left-mouse-button to end the **Line** command.

10. In the *Status Bar* area, reset the option buttons so that only *GRID*, *ORTHO* and *MODEL* are switched ***ON***.

Toolbar List

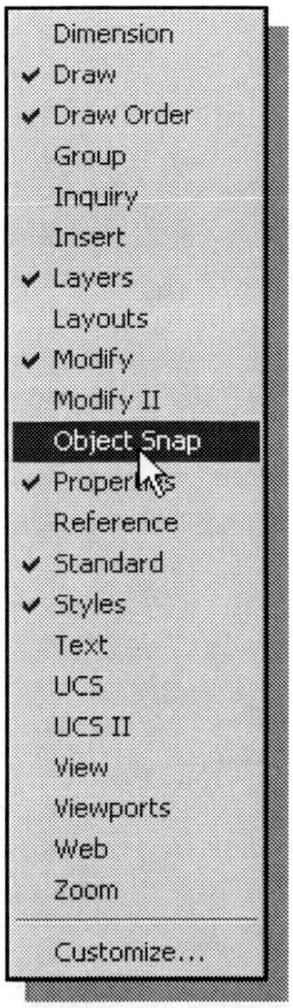

1. Move the cursor to the *Standard* toolbar area and **right-mouse-click** once on any icon in the toolbar area to display a list of toolbar menu groups.

❖ AutoCAD LT provides 22 pre-defined toolbars for access to frequently used commands, settings, and modes. The *Standard*, *Object Properties*, *Draw*, and *Modify* toolbars are displayed by default. The *check marks* in the list identify the toolbars that are currently displayed on the screen.

2. Select **Object Snap**, with the left-mouse-button, to display the *Object Snap* toolbar on the screen.

❖ ***Object Snap*** is an extremely powerful construction tool available on most CAD systems. During an entity's creation operations, we can snap the cursor to points on objects such as endpoints, midpoints, centers, and intersections. For example, we can turn on ***Object Snap*** and quickly draw a line to the center of a circle, the midpoint of a line segment, or the intersection of two lines.

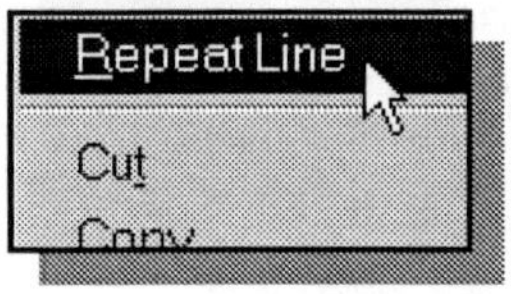

3. Activate the **Line** command by picking the icon in the *Draw* toolbar or **right-mouse-click** to activate the option menu and select **Repeat Line**.

4. Move the cursor over the icons in the *Object Snap* toolbar and read the description of each icon in the *Status Bar* area.

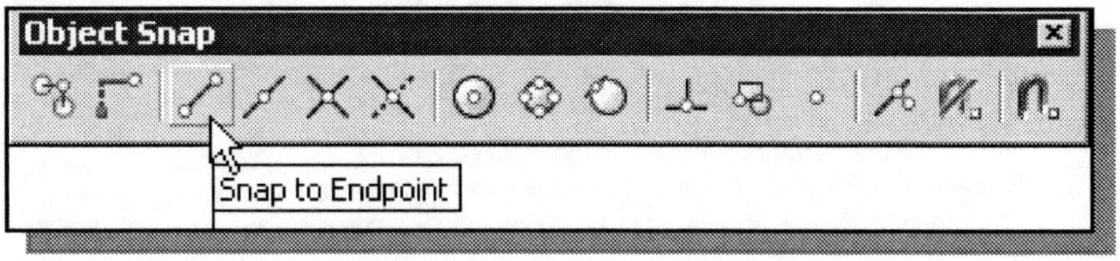

5. In the *Object Snap* toolbar, pick **Snap to Endpoint**. In the command prompt area, the message *"_endp of"* is displayed. *AutoCAD LT* now expects us to select a geometric entity on the screen.

➢ The **Snap to Endpoint** option allows us to snap to the closest endpoint of objects such as lines or arcs. AutoCAD LT uses the midpoint of the entity to determine which end to snap to.

6. Pick the **top-left vertical line** by selecting a location above the midpoint of the line. Notice AutoCAD LT automatically snaps to the top endpoint of the line.

7. Move the graphics cursor to the right of the last point and create a horizontal line that is about three units long (near *X coordinate: 5.00*).

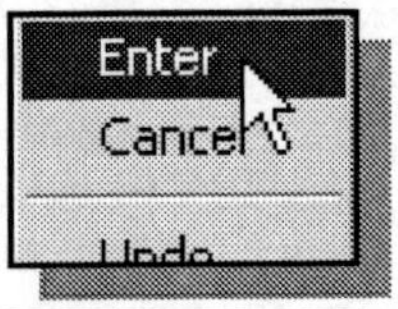

8. Inside the graphics window, right-mouse-click to activate the option menu and select **Enter** with the left-mouse-button to end the **Line** command.

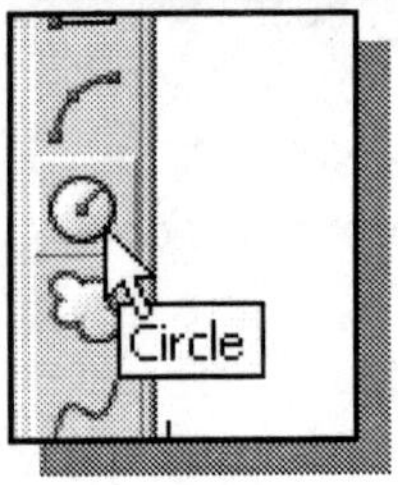

9. Select the **Circle** command icon in the *Draw* toolbar. In the command prompt area, the message *"Specify center point for circle or [3P/2P/Ttr (tan tan radius)]:"* is displayed.

10. In the *Status Bar* area, switch ***ON*** the ***SNAP*** option.

11. In the graphics window, move the cursor to *world coordinates* ***(9.5,6).*** **Left-click** to position the center point of the circle at this location.

12. Move the graphics cursor to *world coordinates* ***(11,6).*** **Left-click** at this location to create a circle (radius **1.5 inches**).

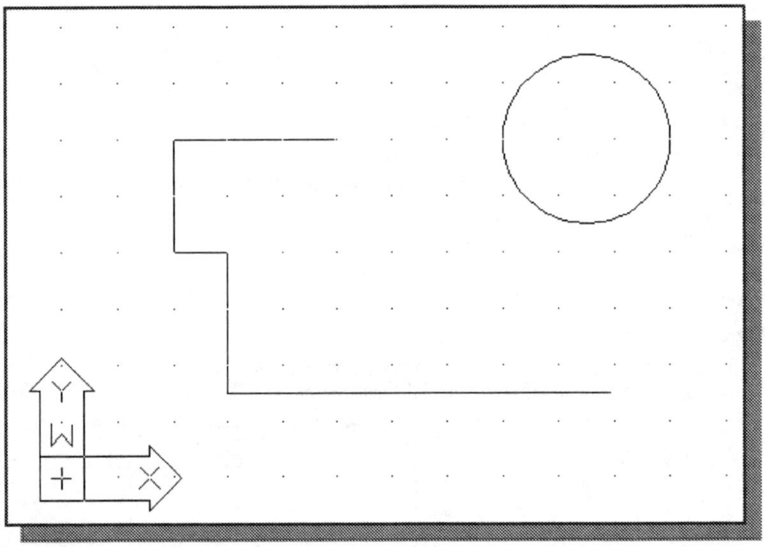

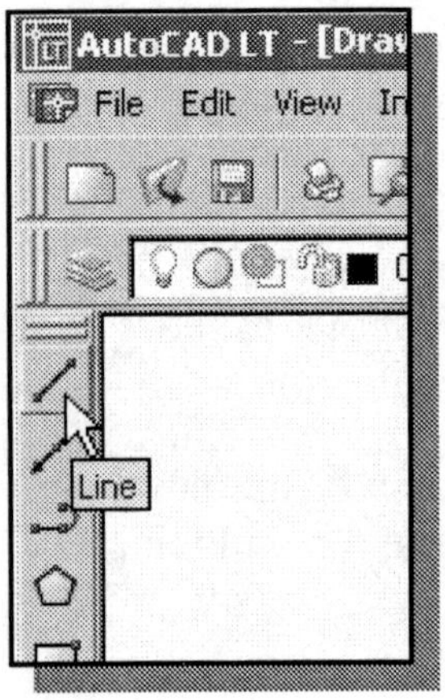

13. Select the **Line** command icon in the *Draw* toolbar. In the command prompt area, the message *"_line Specify first point:"* is displayed.

14. In the graphics window, move the cursor to *world coordinates* ***(9,1.5).*** **Left-click** to position the first point of a line at this location.

15. Pick **Snap to Tangent** in the *Object Snap* toolbar. In the command prompt area, the message *"_tan to"* is displayed. AutoCAD LT now expects us to select a circle or an arc on the screen.

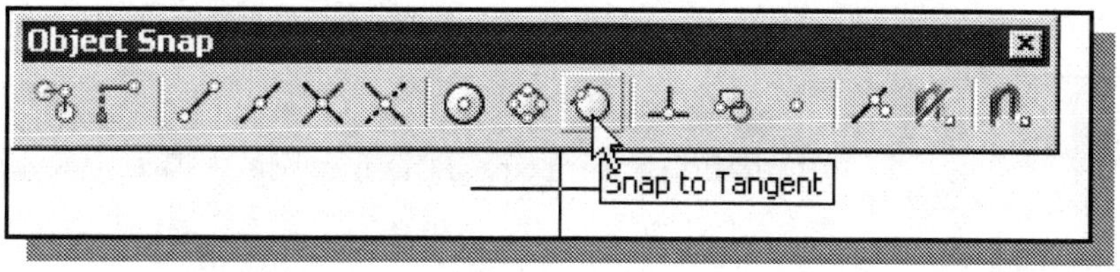

➢ The **Snap to Tangent** option allows us to snap to the point on a circle or arc that, when connected to the last point, forms a line tangent to that object.

16. Pick a location on the right side of the circle and create the line tangent to the circle.

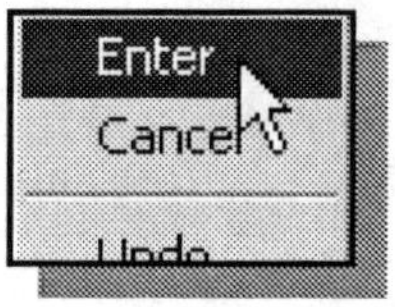

17. Inside the graphics window, **right-mouse-click** to activate the option menu and select **Enter** with the left-mouse-button to end the Line command.

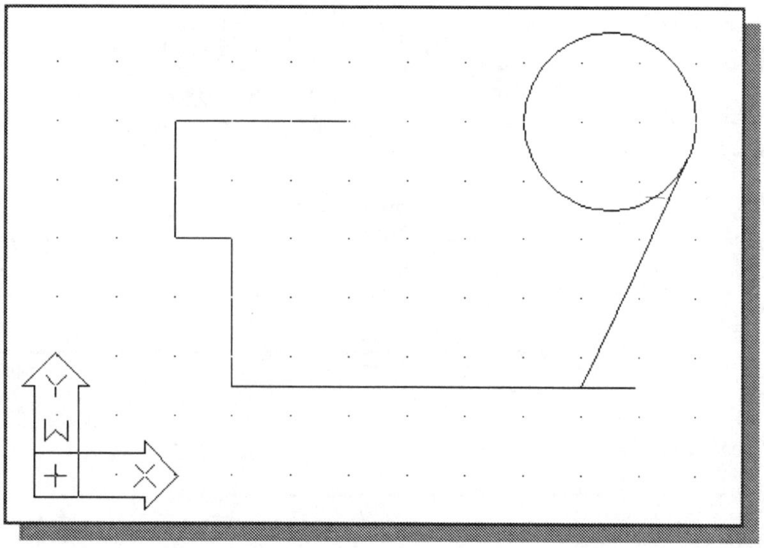

18. In the *Status Bar* area, reset the option buttons so that only the *MODEL* button is switched ***ON***.

19. Close the *Object Snap* toolbar by **left-clicking** the upper right corner **X** icon.

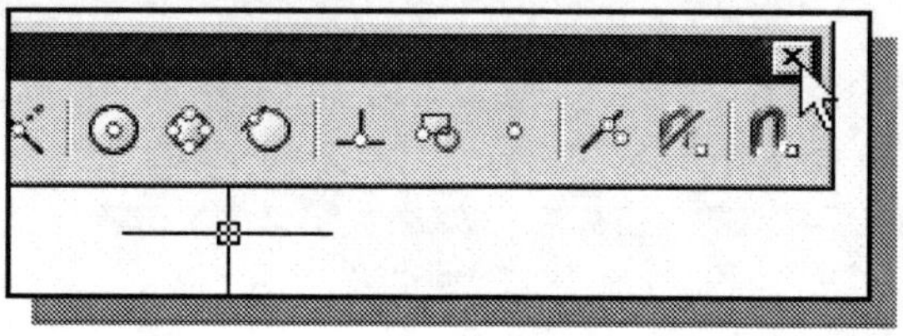

Using the *Extend* Command

The Extend command lengthens an object so that it ends precisely at a selected boundary.

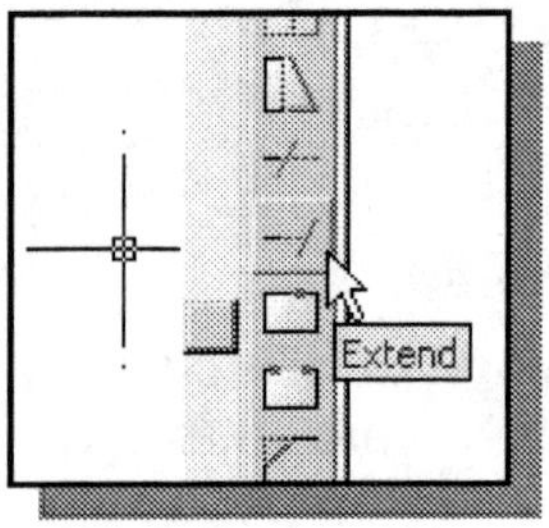

1. Select the **Extend** command icon in the *Modify* toolbar. In the command prompt area, the message *"Select boundary edges... Select objects:"* is displayed.

➢ First, we will select the objects that define the boundary edges to which we want to extend the object.

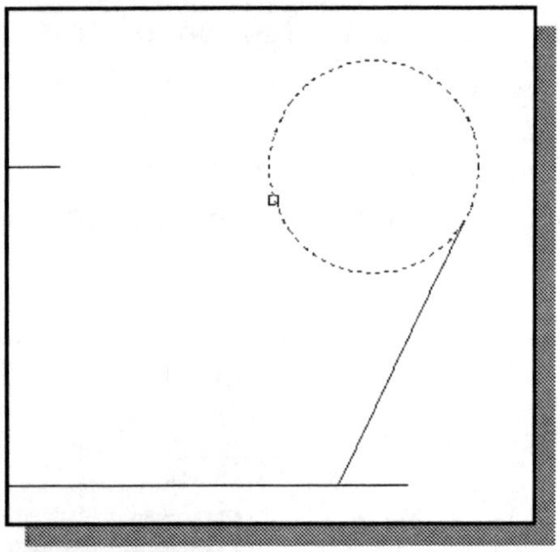

2. Pick the **circle** as the *boundary edge.*

3. Inside the graphics window, **right-mouse-click** to proceed with the Extend command. The message *"Select object to extend or [Project/Edge/Undo]:"* is displayed in the command prompt area.

4. Pick the **top horizontal line** that is to the left side of the circle.

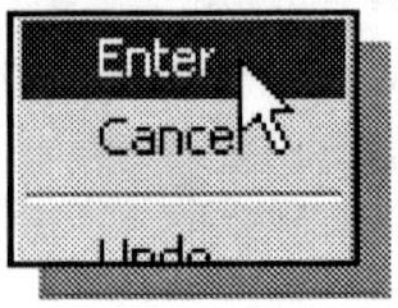

5. Inside the graphics window, **right-mouse-click** to activate the option menu and select **Enter** with the left-mouse-button to end the Extend command.

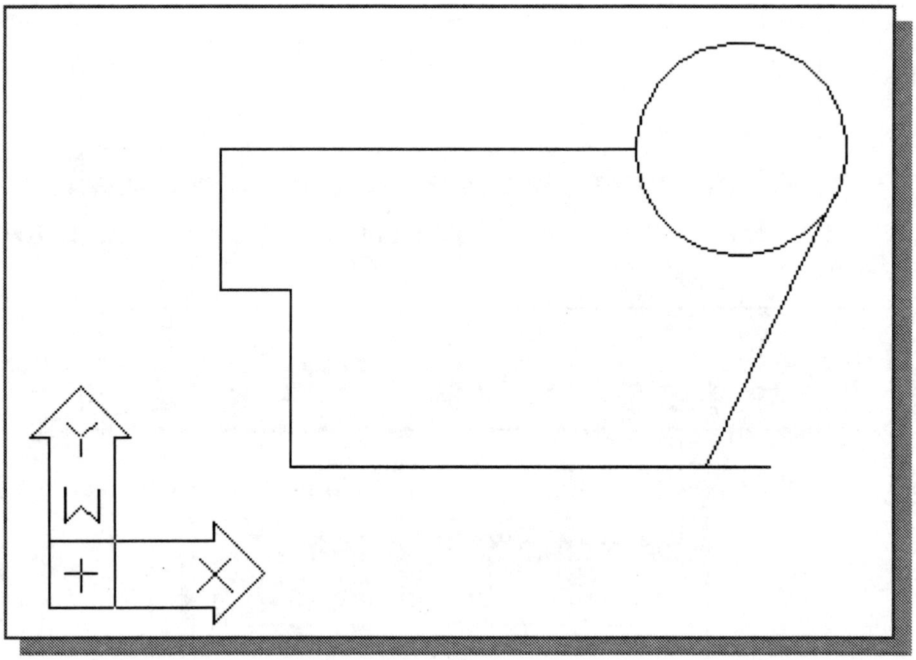

Using the *Trim* Command

The Trim command shortens an object so that it ends precisely at a selected boundary.

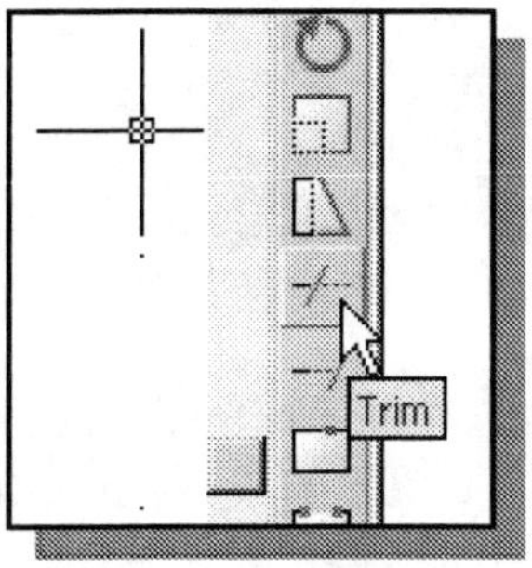

1. Select the **Trim** command icon in the *Modify* toolbar. In the command prompt area, the message *"Select boundary edges... Select objects:"* is displayed.

➤ First we will select the objects that define the boundary edges to which we want to trim the object.

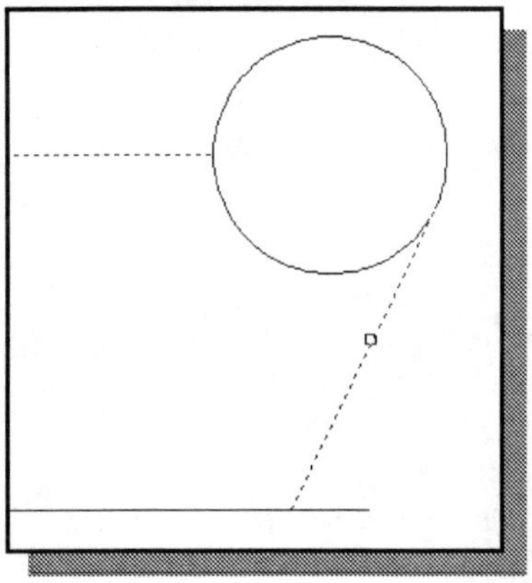

2. Pick the *inclined line* and the *top horizontal line* as the *boundary edges*.

3. Inside the graphics window, **right-mouse-click** to proceed with the Trim command. The message *"Select object to trim or [Project/Edge/Undo]:"* is displayed in the command prompt area.

4. Pick the right endpoint of the bottom horizontal line.

5. Pick the bottom of the circle by click on the lower portion of the circle

6. Inside the graphics window, **right-mouse-click** to activate the option menu and select **Enter** with the left-mouse-button to end the Trim command.

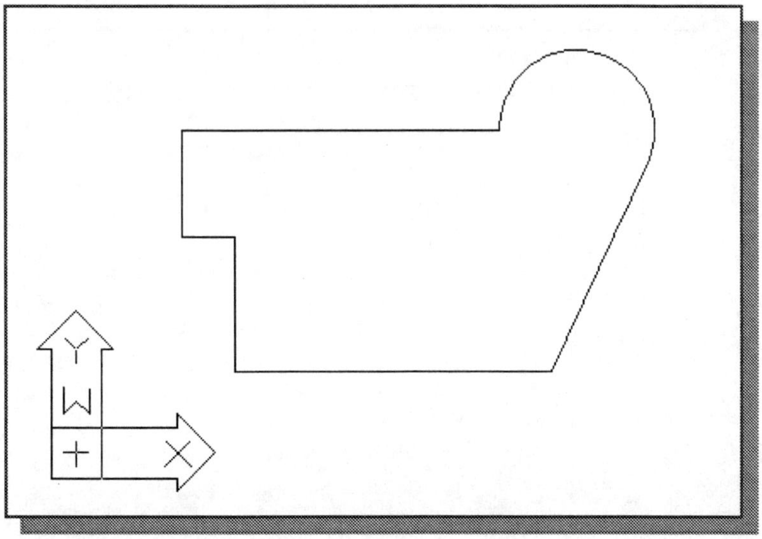

➤ Note that in **AutoCAD® LT 2005**, we can perform either trimming or extending an object using the Extend command or the Trim command. For example, when using the **Extend** command, we can select an object to *extend* or hold down **SHIFT** and select an object to *trim*.

Creating a *TTR circle*

1. Select the **Circle** command icon in the *Draw* toolbar. In the command prompt area, the message *"Specify center point for circle or [3P/2P/Ttr (tan tan radius)]:"* is displayed.

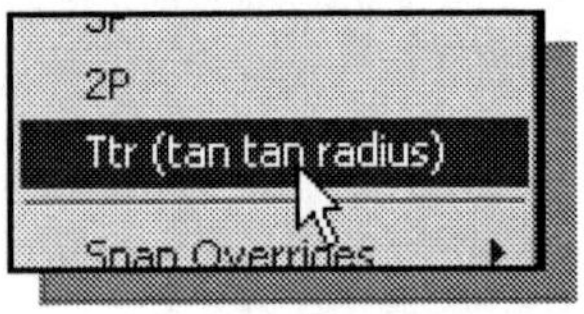

2. Inside the graphics window, right-mouse-click to activate the option menu and select the **Ttr (tan tan radius)** option with the left-mouse-button to create a circle that is tangent to two objects.

3. Pick the top horizontal line that is to the left side of the arc. We will create a circle that is tangent to this line and the circle.

4. Pick the circle by selecting a location that is above the right endpoint of the horizontal line. AutoCAD LT interprets the location we selected as being near the tangency.

5. In the command prompt area, the message *"Specify radius of circle <1.50>"* is displayed.

   Specify radius of circle <1.50>: **1.0 [ENTER]**

➢ On your own, trim the circle, the horizontal line and the arc as shown.

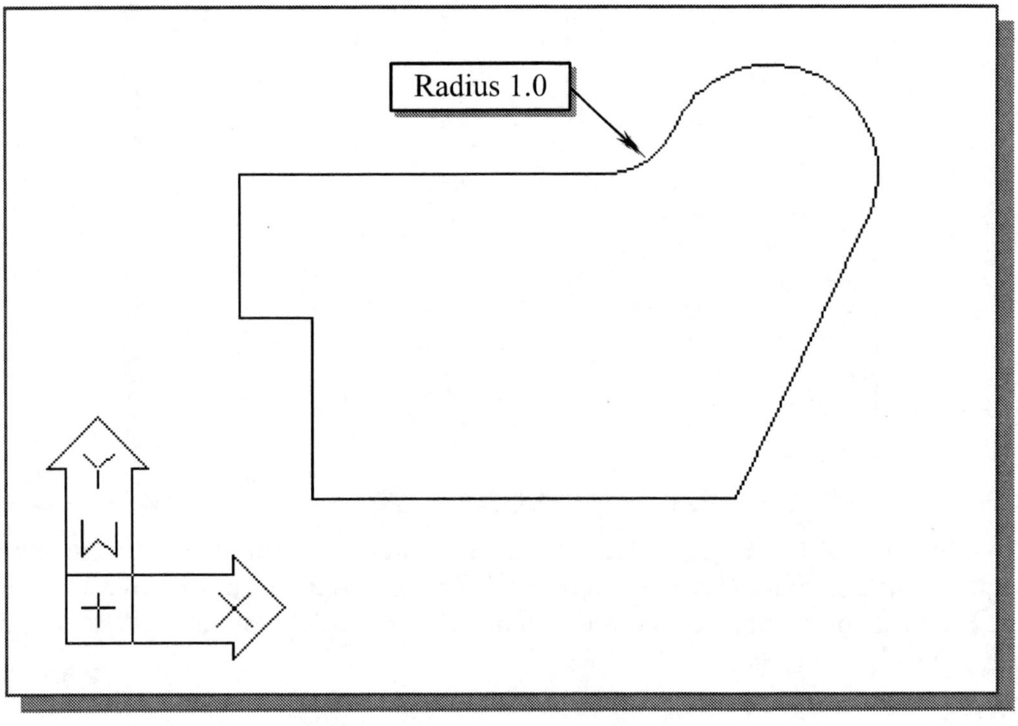

Using the *Fillet* Command

Fillet rounds, or fillets, the edges of two arcs, circles, elliptical arcs, or lines with an arc of a specified radius.

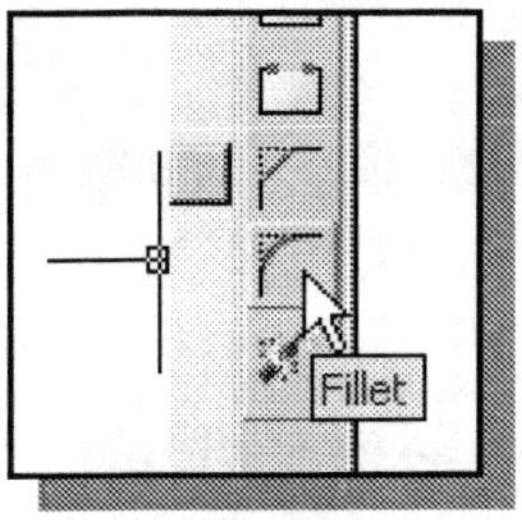

1. Select the **Fillet** command icon in the *Modify* toolbar. In the command prompt area, the message *"Select first object or [Polyline/Radius/Trim]:"* is displayed.

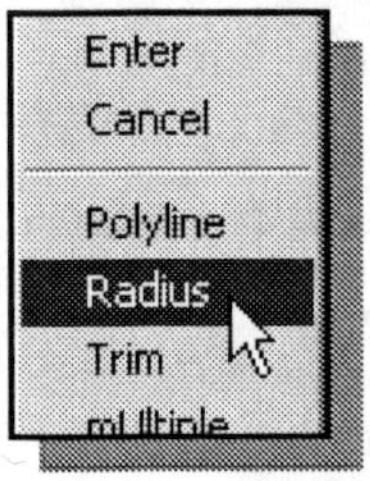

2. Inside the graphics window, **right-mouse-click** once to activate the option menu and select the **Radius** option with the left-mouse-button to specify the radius of the fillet.

3. In the command prompt area, the message *"Specify fillet radius:"* is displayed.

   Specify fillet radius: **0.75 [ENTER]**

4. Pick the **bottom horizontal line** and the **adjacent vertical line** to create a rounded corner as shown.

➢ On your own, use the Fillet command and create a 0.25 fillet at the corner as shown.

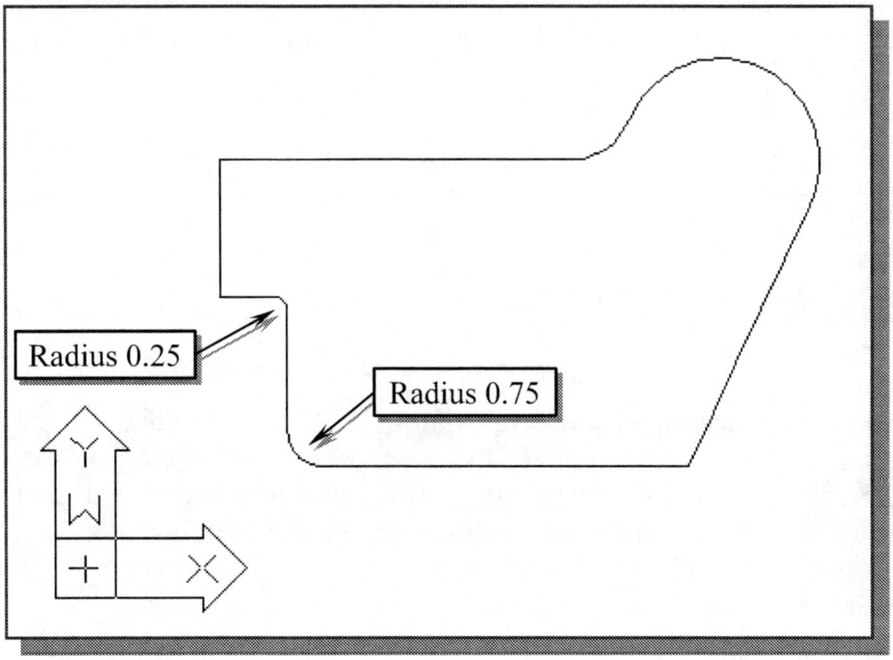

Converting Objects into a *Polyline*

The next task in our project is to create a copy, with an offset of 0.5, of all the objects we have constructed so far. Prior to using the **Offset** command, we will simplify the procedure by converting all objects into a **compound object** – a **polyline**.

❖ A *polyline* in AutoCAD LT is a 2D line of adjustable width composed of line and arc segments. A **polyline** is treated as a single object with definable options.

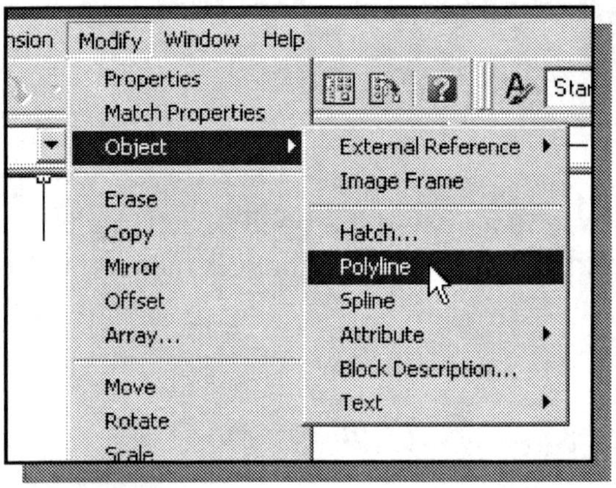

1. In the pull-down menus, select **[Modify] → [Object] →[Polyline]**

2. The message *"Select polyline:"* is displayed in the command prompt area. Select any of the objects on the screen.

3. The message *"Object selected is not a polyline, Do you want to turn it into one? <Y>"* is displayed in the command prompt area. **Right-mouse-click** to accept the *Yes* default.

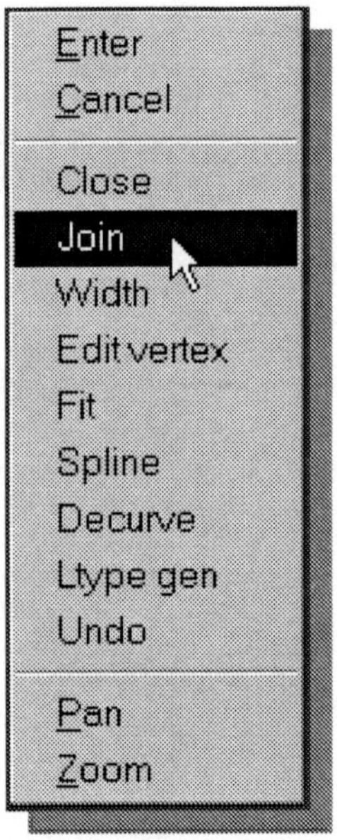

4. Inside the graphics window, right-mouse-click to activate the option menu and select the **Join** option with the left-mouse-button to add objects to the polyline.

5. **Pick all objects** by enclosing them inside a *selection window.*

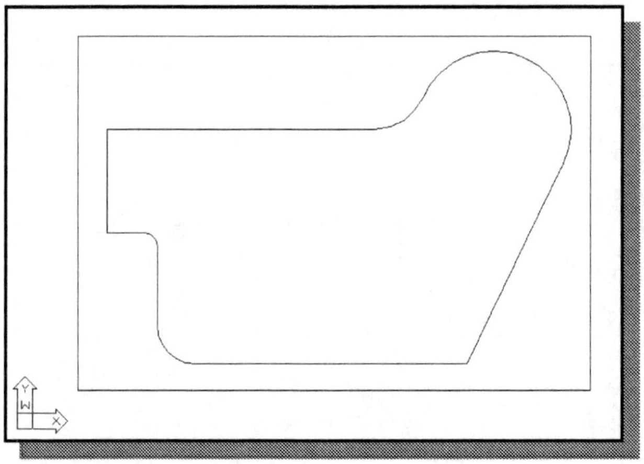

6. Inside the graphics window, **right-mouse-click** to accept the selected objects.

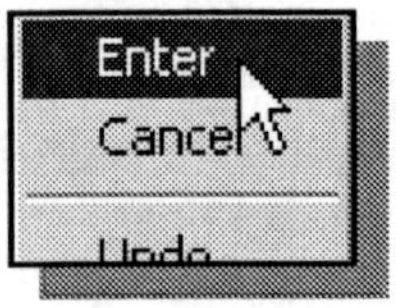

7. Inside the graphics window, **right-mouse-click** to activate the option menu and select **Enter** to end the PEdit command.

Using the *Offset* Command

The Offset command creates a new object at a specified distance from an existing object or through a specified point.

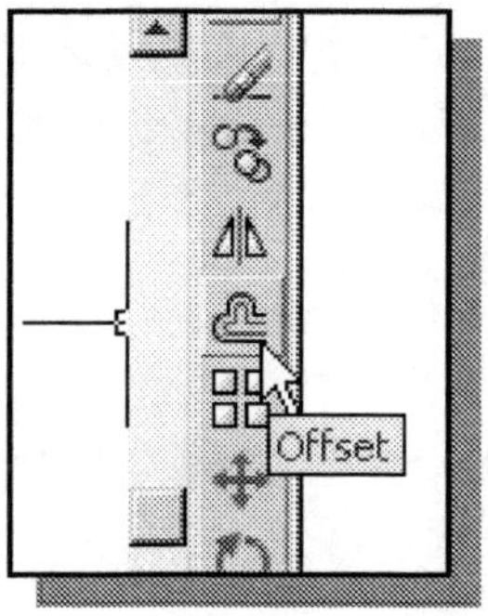

1. Select the **Offset** command icon in the *Modify* toolbar. In the command prompt area, the message *"Specify offset distance or [Through]:"* is displayed.

   Specify offset distance or [Through]: **0.5 [ENTER]**

2. In the command prompt area, the message *"Select object to offset or <exit>:"* is displayed. Pick any object on the screen.

3. Since all the lines and arcs have been converted into a single object, all segments are selected.

4. AutoCAD LT next asks us to identify the direction of the offset. Pick a location that is *inside* the polyline.

5. Inside the graphics window, right-mouse-click to end the Offset command.

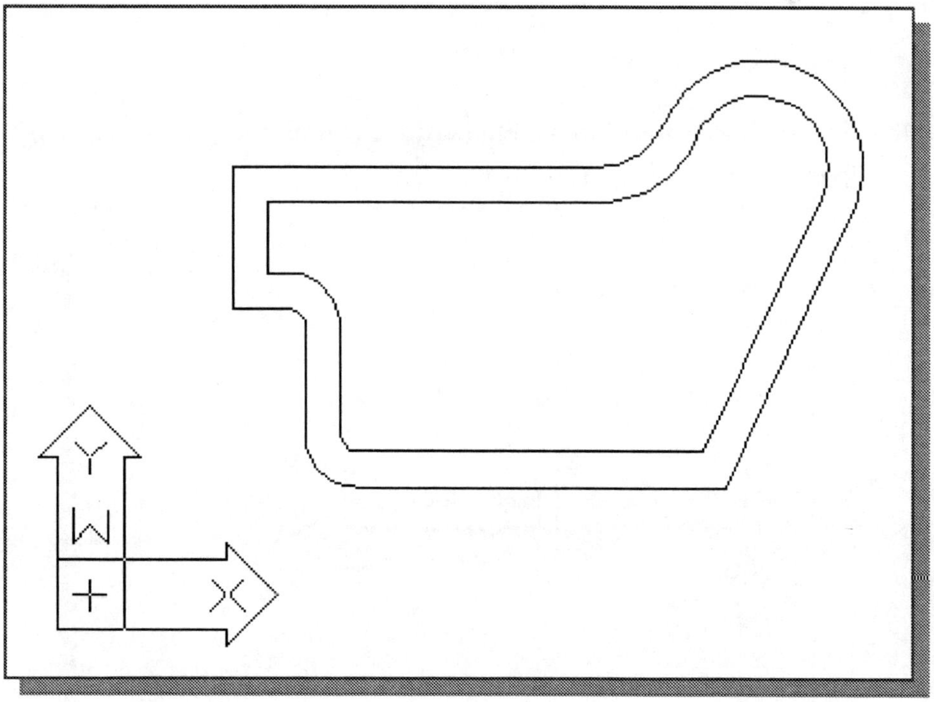

Using the *Explode* Command

The Explode command breaks a compound object into its component objects.

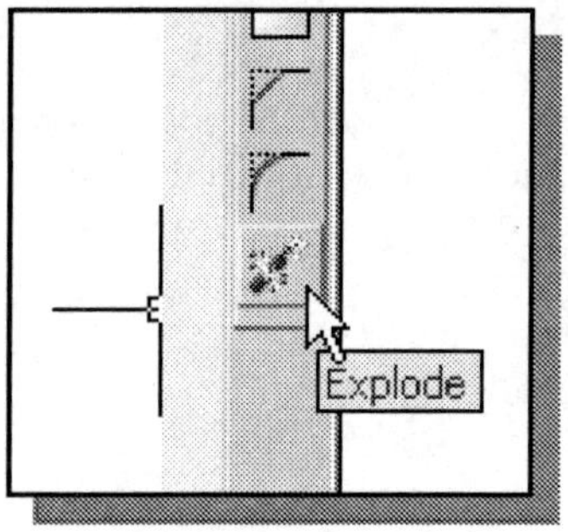

1. Select the **Explode** command icon in the *Modify* toolbar. In the command prompt area, the message *"Select objects:"* is displayed.

2. Pick the polyline that we created using the Offset command.

3. Inside the graphics window, right-mouse-click to end the Explode command.

Create Another *Fillet*

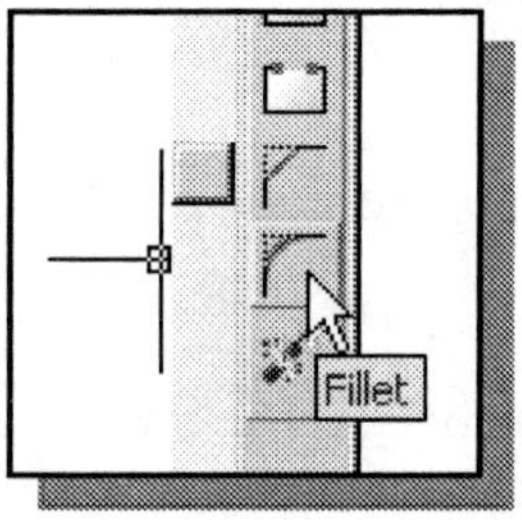

1. Select the **Fillet** command icon in the *Modify* toolbar. In the command prompt area, the message *"Select first object or [Polyline/Radius/Trim]:"* is displayed.

2. Inside the graphics window, right-mouse-click to activate the option menu and select the **Radius** option with the left-mouse-button to specify the radius of the fillet.

3. In the command prompt area, the message *"Specify fillet radius:"* is displayed.

   Specify fillet radius: **0.5 [ENTER]**

4. Pick the **horizontal line** and the **adjacent inclined line** to create a rounded corner as shown.

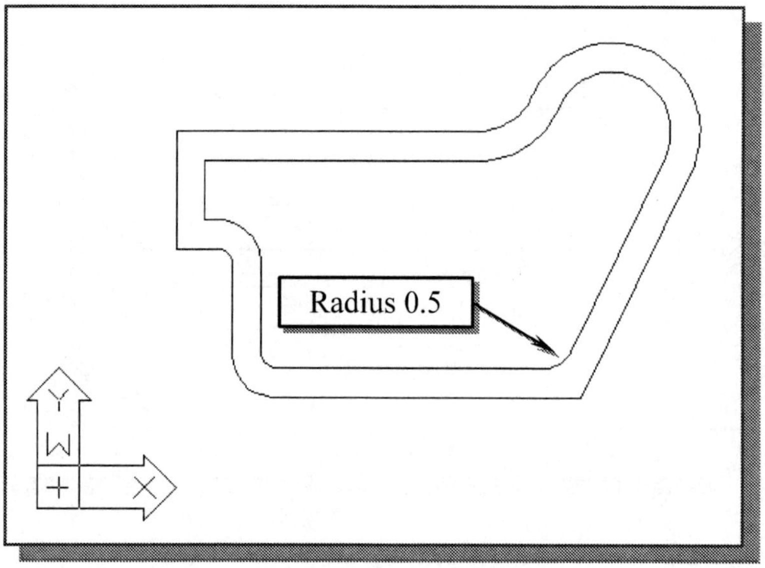

Saving the CAD File

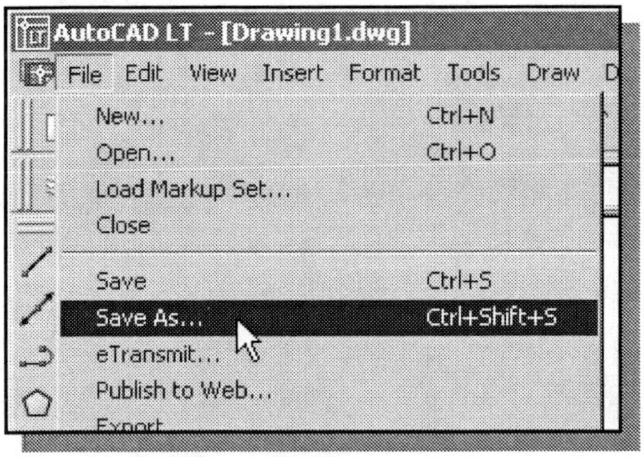

1. In the pull-down menus, select **[File] → [Save As]**

2. In the *Save Drawing As* dialog box, select the folder in which you want to store the CAD file and enter ***Gasket*** in the *File name* box.

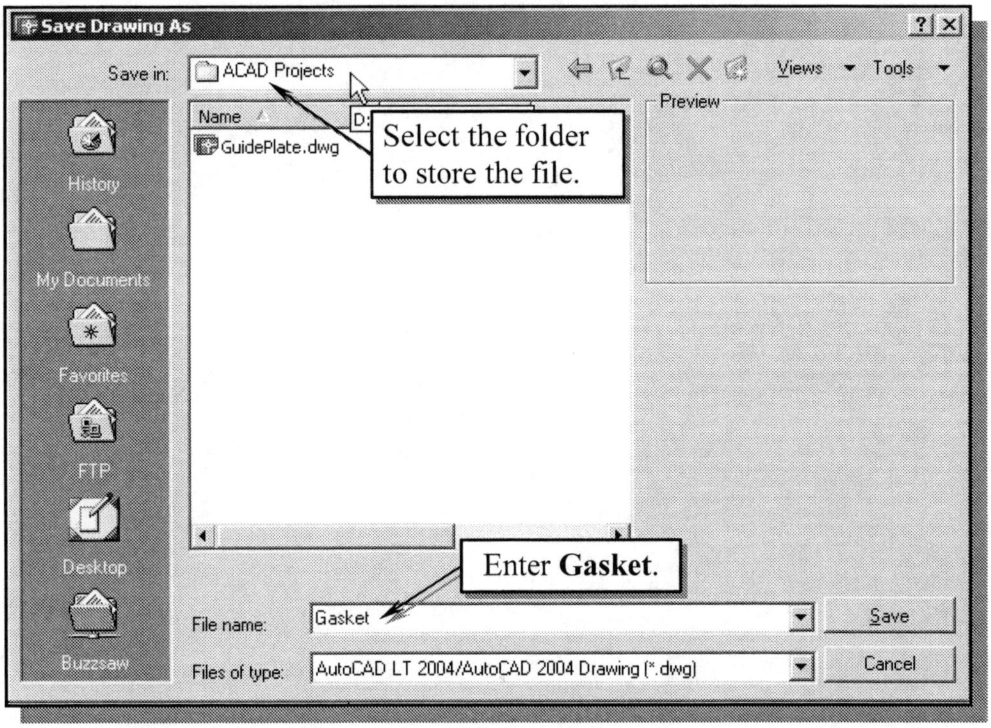

3. Pick **Save** in the *Save Drawing As* dialog box to accept the selections and save the file.

Exit AutoCAD

To exit **AutoCAD® LT 2005**, select **File** then choose **Exit** from the pull-down menu or type ***QUIT*** at the command prompt.

Questions:

1. Describe the AutoCAD LT ***ORTHO*** option.

2. List and describe three AutoCAD LT ***Object Snap*** options.

3. Which AutoCAD LT command can we use to create rounded corners?

4. Describe the AutoCAD LT **Offset** command.

5. Identify the following commands:

(a)

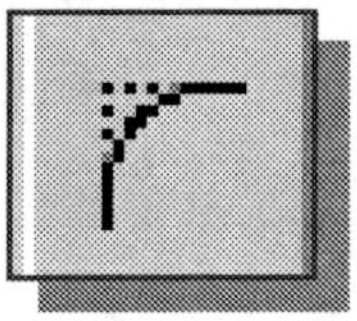

(b)

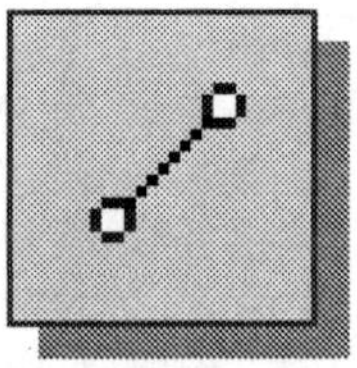

(c)

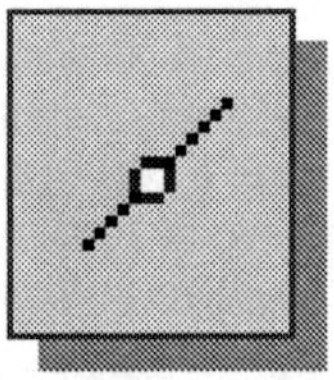

(d)

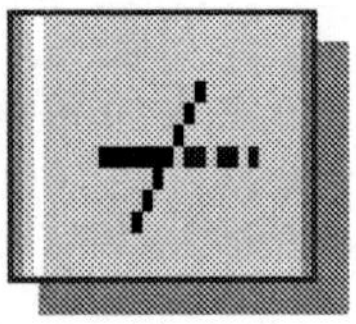

Exercises: Unless otherwise specified, dimensions are in inches.

1.

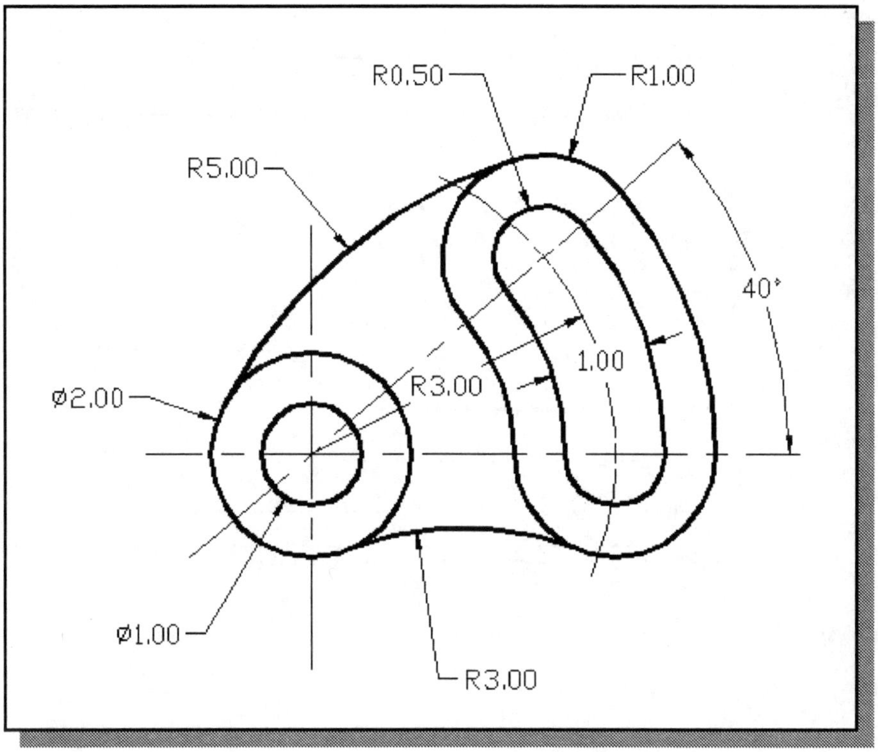

2. (Note: This design has two sets of parallel lines with implied tangency.)

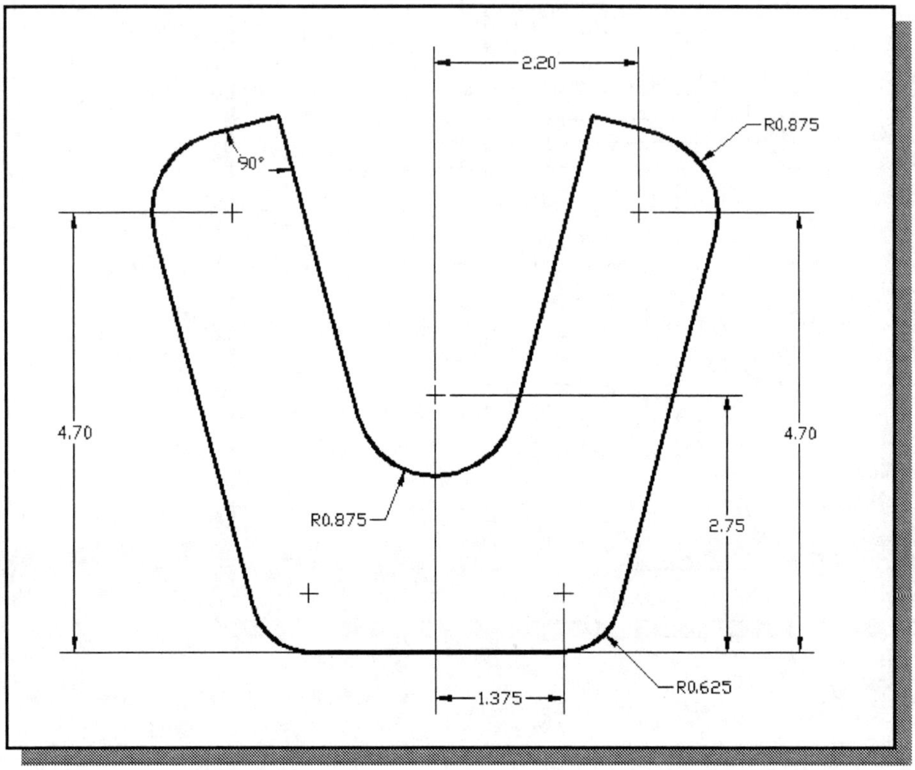

3. Dimensions are in millimeters.

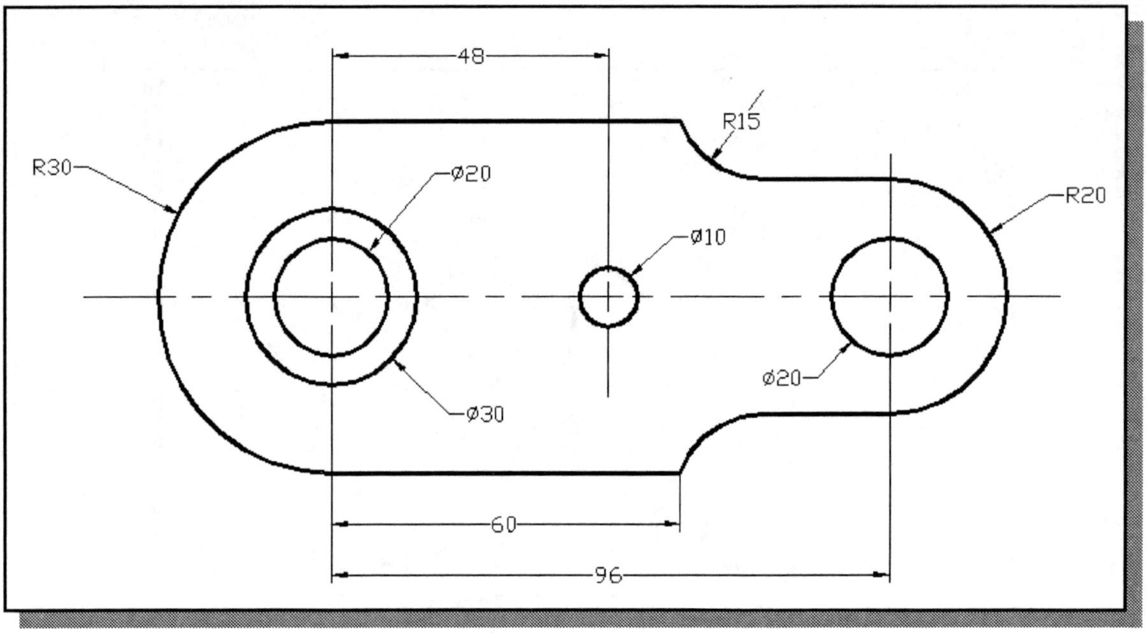

4.

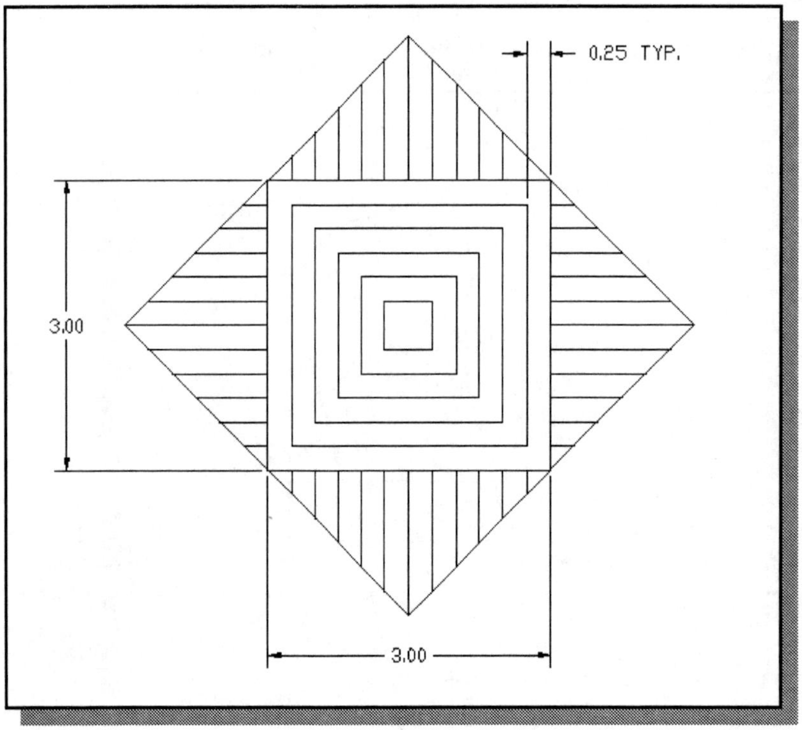

5.

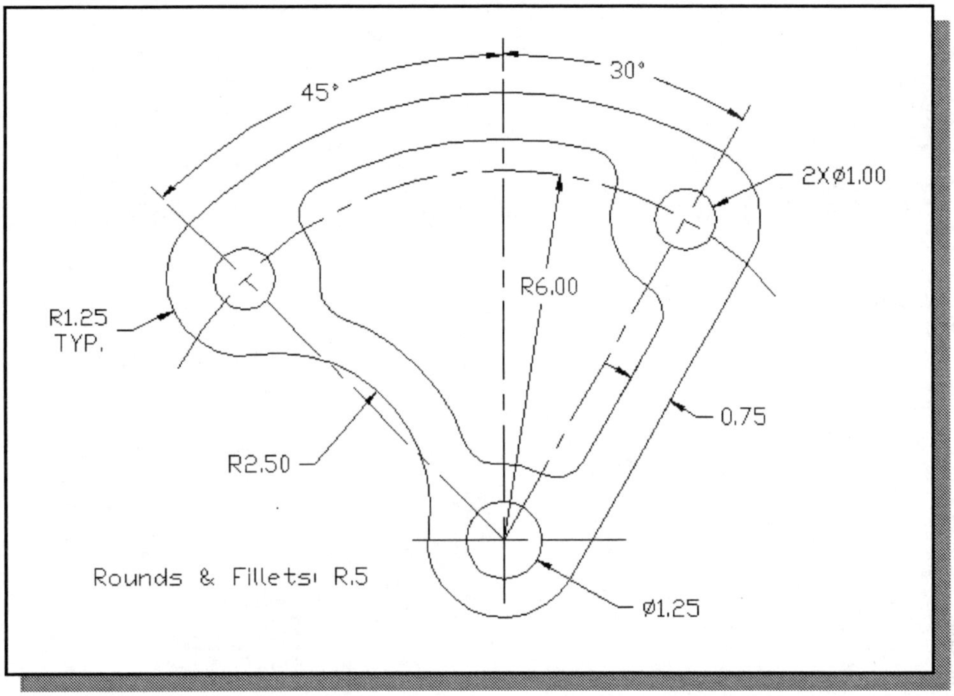
45°
30°
2X⌀1.00
R6.00
R1.25
TYP.
0.75
R2.50
Rounds & Fillets: R.5
⌀1.25

6.

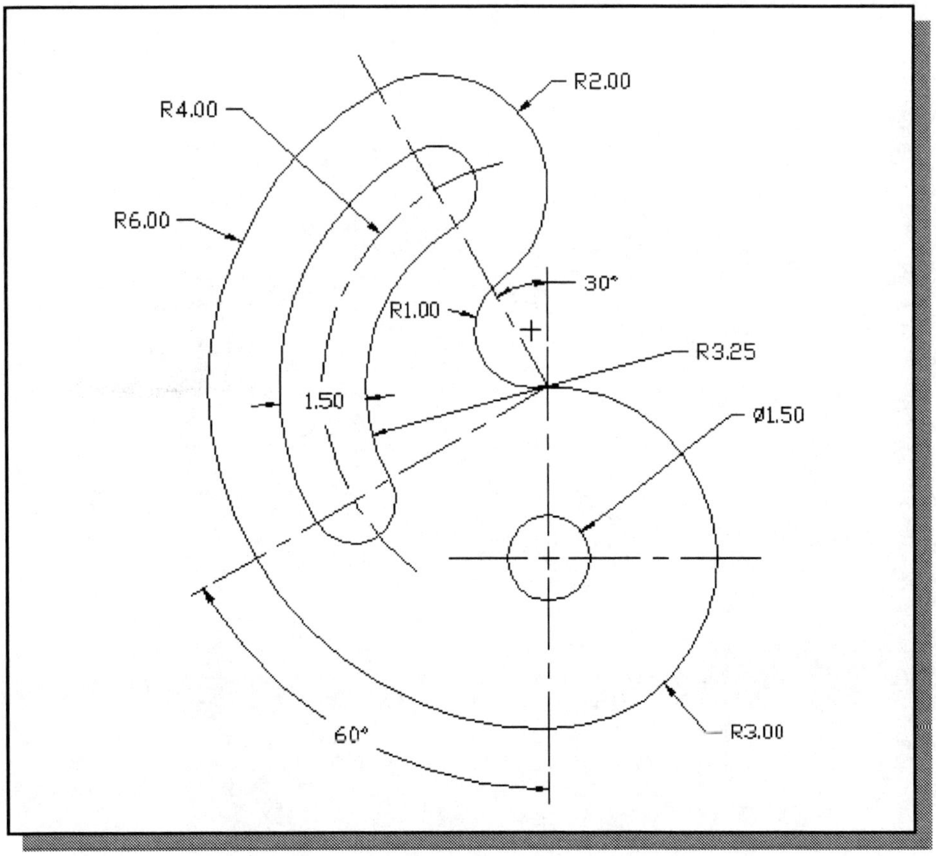
R2.00
R4.00
R6.00
30°
R1.00
R3.25
1.50
⌀1.50
60°
R3.00

Notes:

Lesson 3
Object Properties and Organization

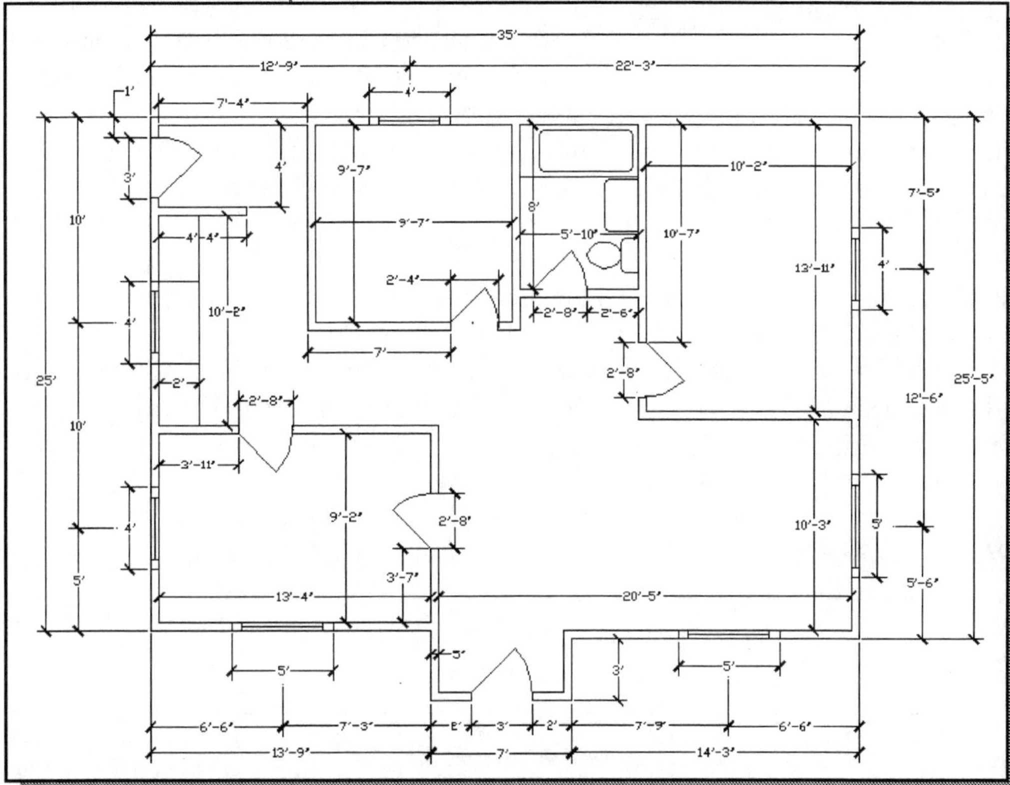

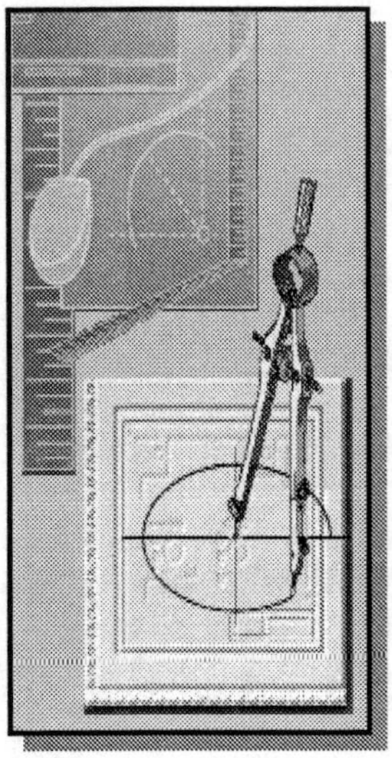

Learning Objectives

- Use the AutoCAD Quick Setup Wizard
- Draw, Using the Double Line Command
- Use the ZOOM ALL Command
- Create New Layers
- Pre-selection of Objects
- Controll Layer Visibility
- Move Objects to a Different Layer

Introduction

The CAD database of a design may contain information regarding the hundreds of CAD entities that are used to create the CAD model. One of the advantages of using a CAD system is its ability to organize and manage the database so that the designer can access the information quickly and easily. Typically, CAD entities that are created to describe one feature, function, or process of a design are perceived as related information and therefore are organized into the same group. In AutoCAD, the **Layer** command is used extensively for this purpose. For example, an architectural drawing typically will show walls, doors, windows and dimensions. Using layers, we can choose to display or hide sub-systems for clarity; we can also change object properties, such as colors and linetypes, quickly and easily.

In this lesson, we will continue to explore the different construction and editing tools that are available in **AutoCAD® LT 2005**. We will demonstrate the use of the Limits, Double Line, and Layer commands. As you become proficient with the CAD tools and understand the underlying CAD modeling concepts, you are encouraged to experiment with new ideas in using the CAD tools and develop your own style of using the system.

Floor Plan Design

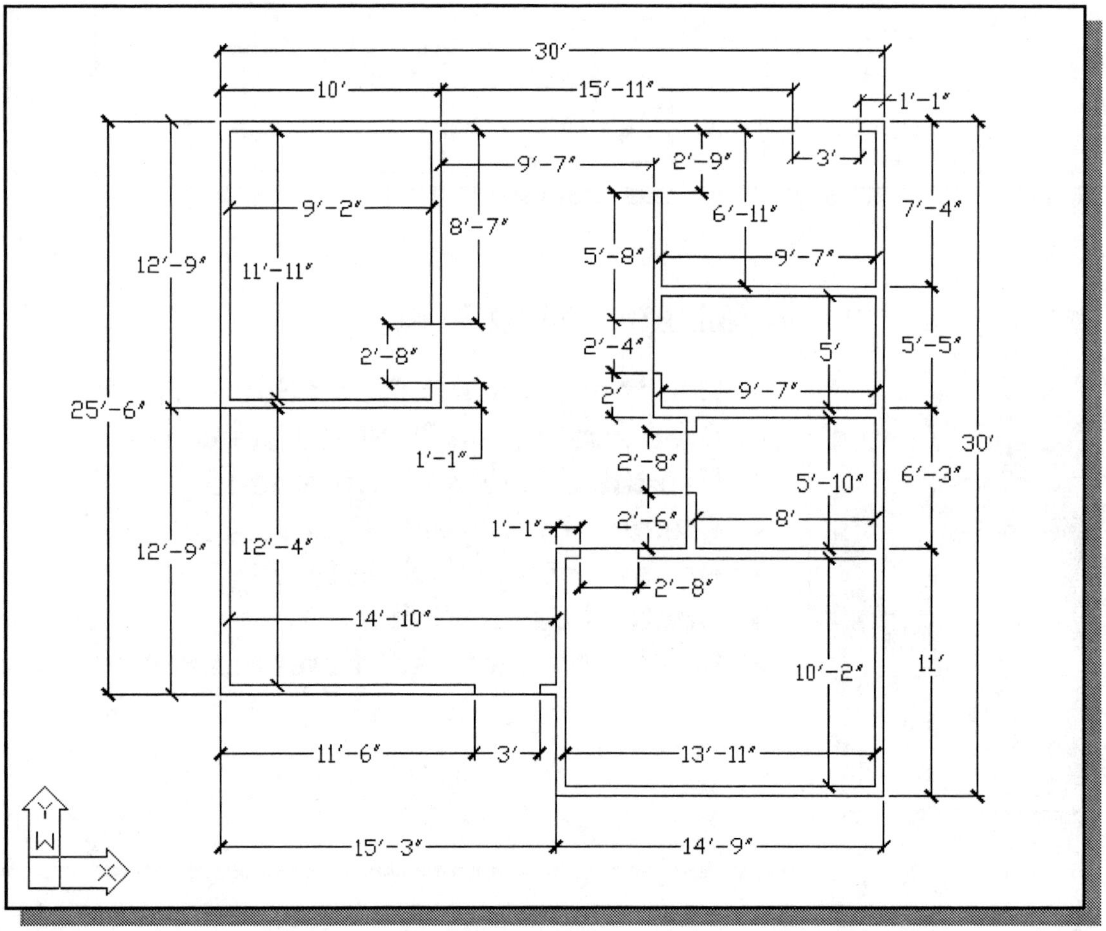

Starting Up *AutoCAD LT 2005*

1. Select the **AutoCAD LT 2005** option on the *Program* menu or select the **AutoCAD LT 2005** icon on the *Desktop*. Once the program is loaded into the memory, the *AutoCAD LT 2005* drawing screen will appear on the screen.

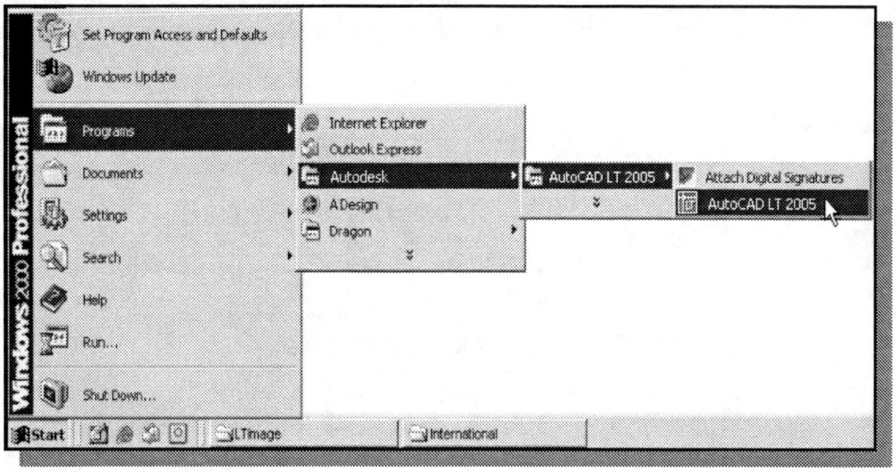

➢ Note that AutoCAD automatically assigns generic names, *Drawing X*, as new drawings are created. In our example, AutoCAD opened the graphics window using the default system units and assigned the drawing name *Drawing1.*

Using the Setup Wizard

In **AutoCAD® LT 2005**, we can use the *setup wizards* to establish, step by step, several of the drawing settings. This option can be activated through the **Options** command.

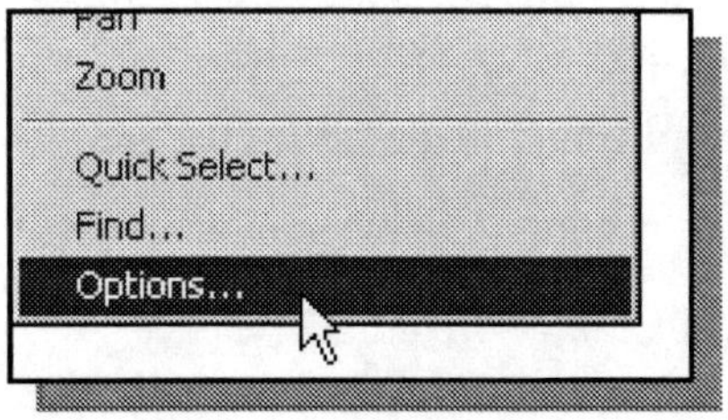

1. Inside the *graphics area*, **right-mouse-click** once to display the option list.

2. Select **Options**, with the left-mouse-button, to display the *Options* dialog box.

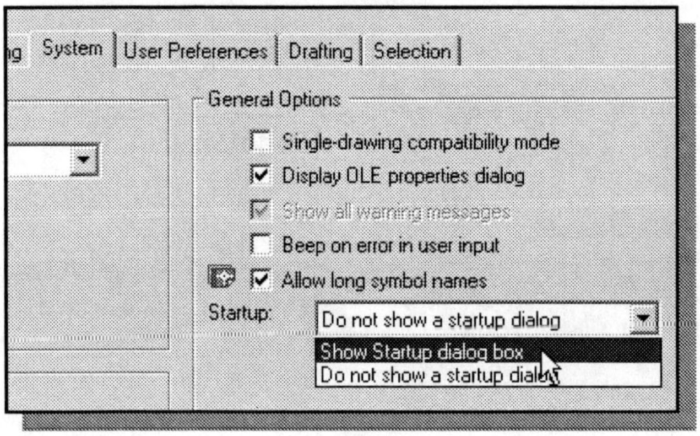

3. Switch to the **System** tab as shown.

4. In the *General Options* list, set the ***Startup*** option to **Show Startup dialog box** as shown.

5. Pick **OK** to exit the *Options* dialog box.

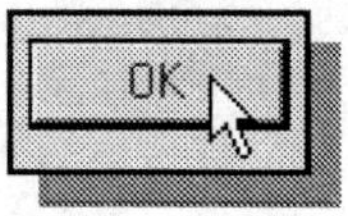

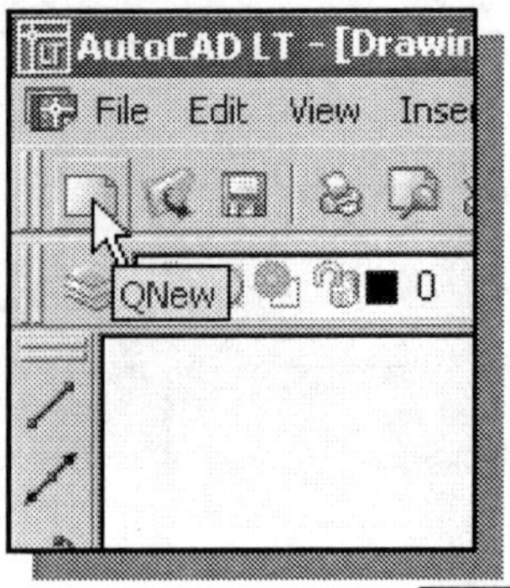

6. In the *Standard* toolbar, click **QNew** to start a new drawing.

➢ Note that the currently opened drawing is *Drawing1*.

7. In the *Create New Drawing* dialog box, select the ***Use a Wizard*** option as shown in the figure below.

8. In the *Select a Wizard* section, pick **Quick Setup**.

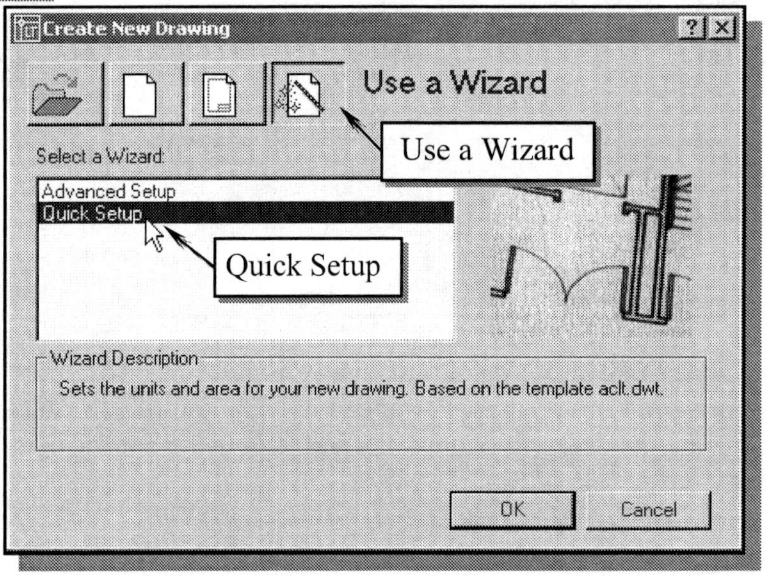

❖ AutoCAD LT setup wizards allow us to customize several of the AutoCAD LT settings depending on the wizard we choose. The *Quick Setup* wizard sets the units and grid display area. Choices for units include *Decimal, Engineering, Architectural, Fractional,* and *Scientific*. We can also specify the width and length of a two-dimensional area to establish the extents of the *grid* displayed, also known as the *limits* of the working area.

Drawing Units Setup

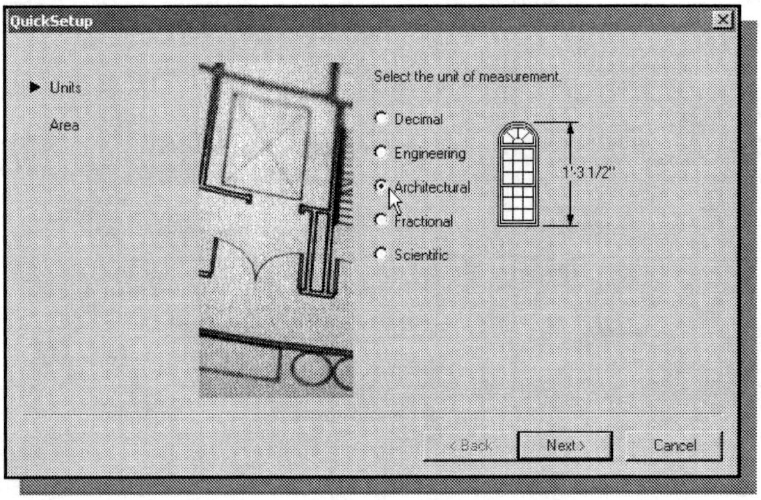

1. In the *Quick Setup Units* option, select **Architectural**.

2. Pick **Next** to continue with the *Quick Setup* settings.

Reference Area Setup

1. In the *Quick Setup Area* option, enter **60′** and **40′** for the width and length.

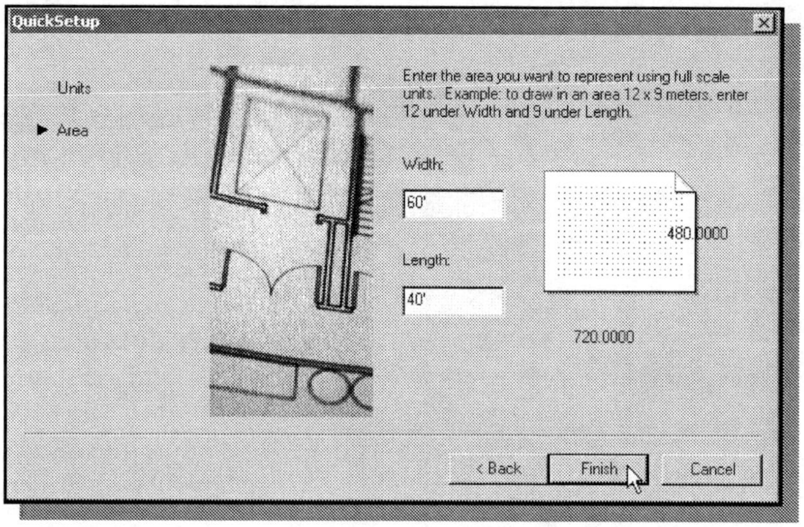

➢ The two-dimensional area we set up in the *Quick Setup* is the *drawing limits* in AutoCAD LT.

2. Pick **Finish** to accept the settings and end the *Quick Setup* wizard.

➢ We have two drawing windows opened in the AutoCAD LT screen window. Note that the units setting of *Drawing1* is set to the default system units. The *Drawing2* window is set up through the AutoCAD LT *Quick Setup* wizard, which sets the units to the architectural style. To avoid any confusion in following through the tutorial, let's close the *Drawing1* window.

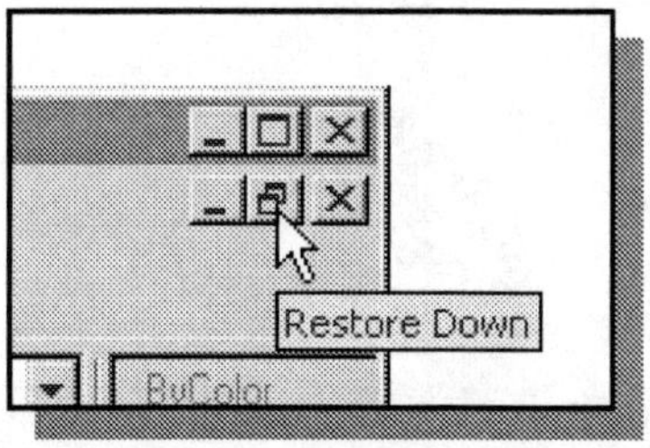

3. Click on the **Restore Down** button located at the upper right corner of the AutoCAD LT main window.

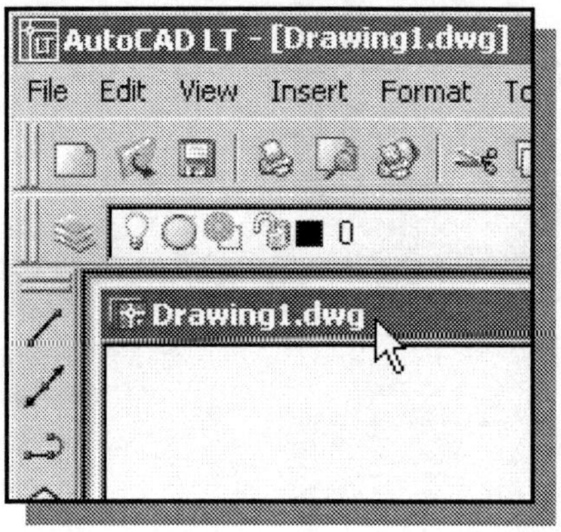

4. Switch to the *Drawing1* window by left-clicking once in the title area of the window.

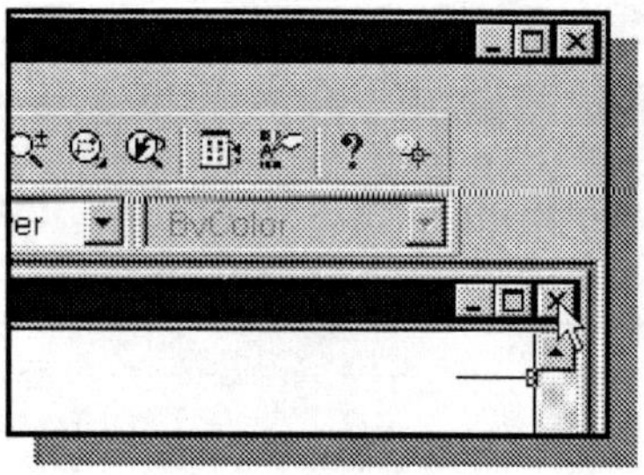

5. Close the window by clicking the **Close** icon located at the upper right corner of the *Drawing1* window.

GRID and *SNAP* Intervals Setup

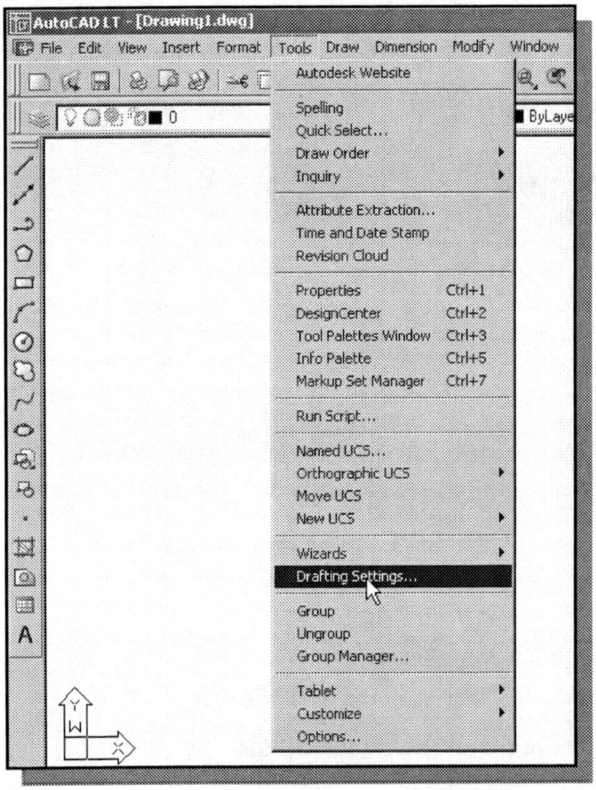

1. In the pull-down menus, select **[Tools] → [Drafting Settings]**

2. In the *Drafting Settings* dialog box, select the **SNAP and GRID** tab if it is not the page on top.

3. Change *Grid Spacing* to **6″** for both X and Y directions.

4. Also adjust the *Snap Spacing* to **6″** for both X and Y directions.

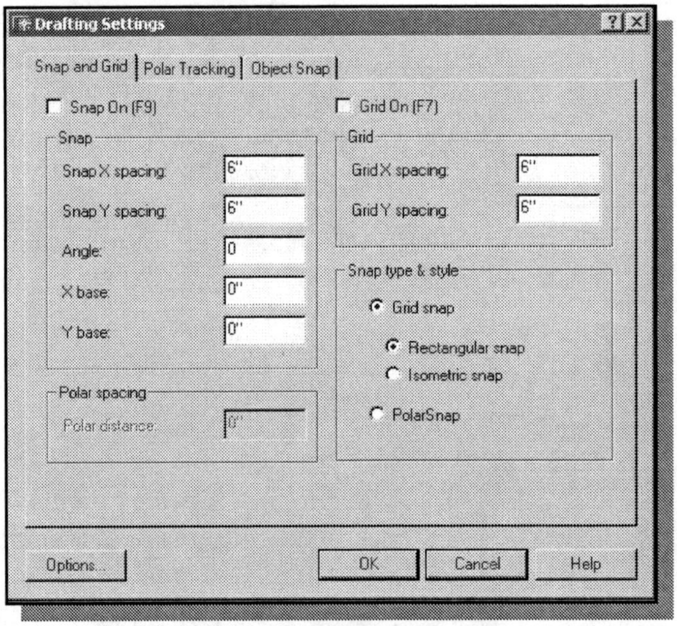

5. Pick **OK** to exit the *Drafting Settings* dialog box.

6. In the *Status Bar* area, reset the option buttons so that only *SNAP, GRID*, and *MODEL* are switched ***ON***.

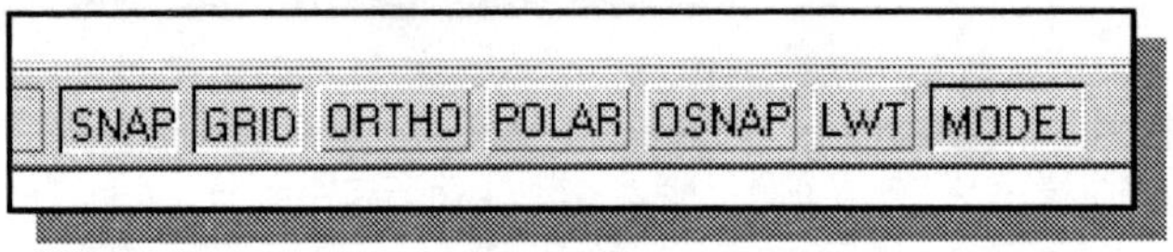

Using the *ZOOM ALL* Command

1. Move the cursor inside the graphics window and notice that, although we have set the *limits* to 40′ by 60′, the default display is still 9″ by 12″. In the graphics window, only a few grid points are displayed.

2. In the *Standard* toolbar area, click and hold down the Zoom Window button, and the list of available Zoom options appears. Move the cursor over the different icons and read the brief description of each icon to get a feel for what each option is.

3. Move the cursor over the **Zoom All** icon, the second icon from the bottom of the list, and release the left-mouse-button to select the command.

➢ The Zoom All command displays all objects in the current design. In a two-dimensional view, AutoCAD LT zooms to the drawing limits or the area that shows all objects, whichever is greater.

The AutoCAD LT *Double Line* Command

The Double Line (DLine) command can be used to create parallel lines segments and arcs. This command is very useful for creating designs that contain parallel lines, such as walls for architectural designs and for highway designs in civil engineering. We can draw double lines as straight segments or as arcs. Each double line segment and its **endcap**, a line that connects the double line endpoints, is actually a separate line object that can be individually edited. For our floor plan design, we will use the DLine command to create parallel lines representing a five-inch wall.

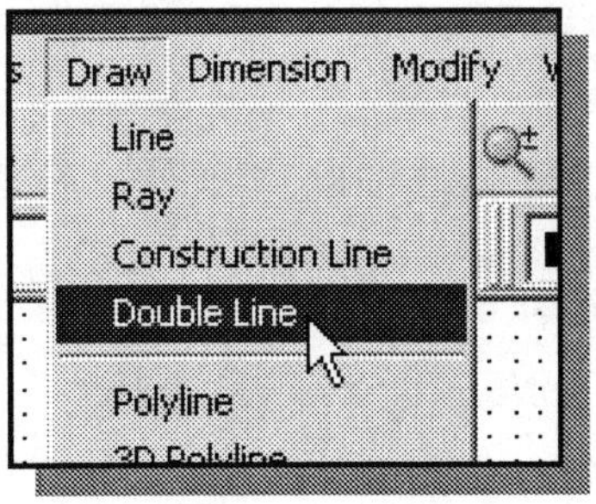

1. Select the **Double Line** command in the *Draw* pull-down menu as shown.

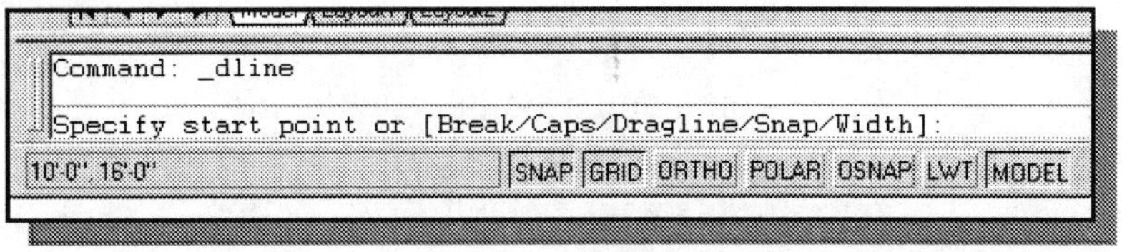

2. In the command prompt area, the message *"Specify start point or [Break/ Caps/ Dragline/ Offset/ Snap/ Undo/ Width]:"* is displayed. The items listed in the brackets are different settings available to control the creation of double lines. At this point, AutoCAD LT expects us to identify the starting location or adjust any of the settings. We will first setup the different DLine settings.

Setting the Offset Distance of Double Lines

The offset distance of double lines can be adjusted using the **Width** option. Once the offset distance is set, AutoCAD LT maintains the value until a different value is set.

1. Inside the command prompt window, enter *W* to select the **Width** option. The Width option is used to set the double line offset distance.

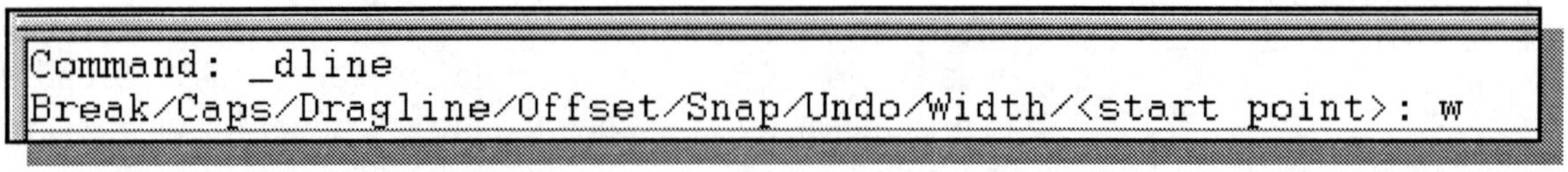

2. In the command prompt area, the message *"Specify Width of Dline <0.05>:"* is displayed. Enter **5"** as the new DLine offset distance.

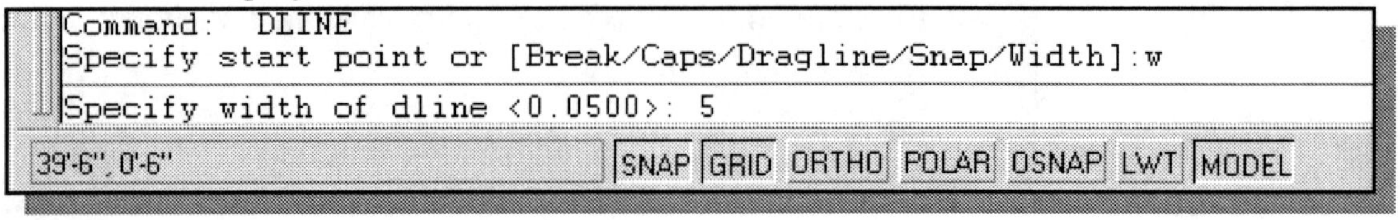

Setting the Appearance of Endpoints

The ends of double lines can be open, closed, or different on each end. When endcaps are turned on, AutoCAD LT automatically connects the specified ends. The **Auto** option automatically caps only the ends that are not snapped to an object.

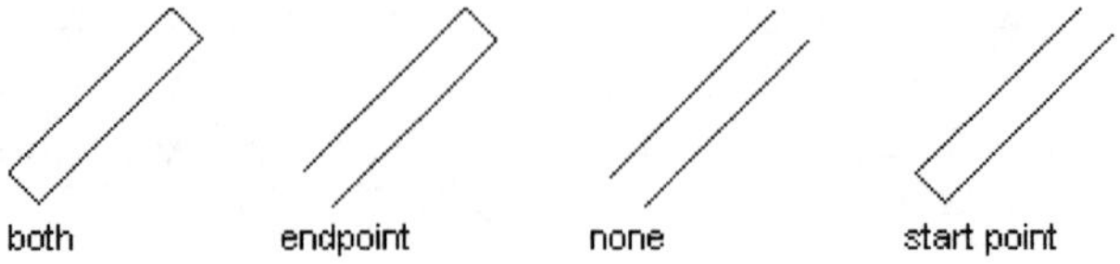

1. Inside the command prompt window, enter *C* to select the **Caps** option. The Caps option is used to set the endcaps option.

2. In the command prompt area, the message *"Enter option for drawing endcaps [Both/End/None/Start/Auto] <Auto>:"* is displayed. Press the **ENTER** key once to select the default **Auto** option.

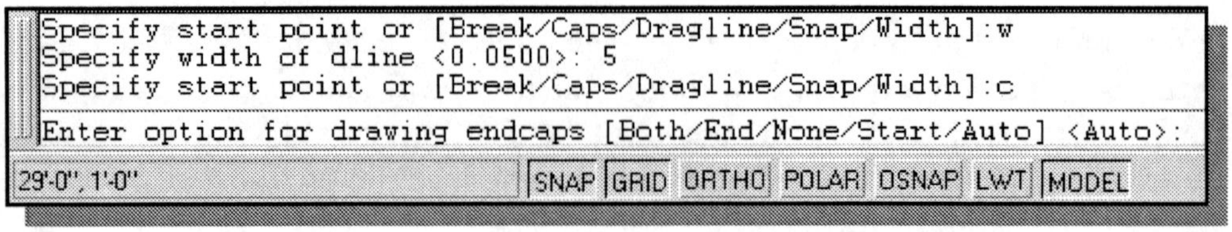

Controlling Placement of Double Lines

We can control the placement of double lines by using the Dragline option. The ***dragline*** is a rubber-band line that determines the placement of a double line. We can control whether the double line is centered on or offset to the right or left of the dragline.

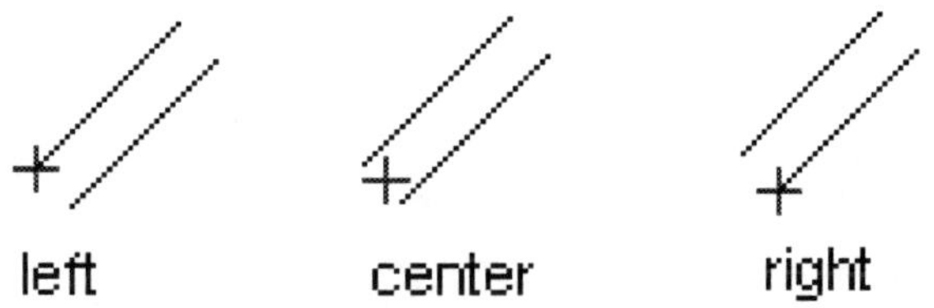

- Note that we can also enter an offset value to adjust the placement position to a specific location between the double lines. A negative offset value positions the offset side of the double line to the left of the dragline; a positive value positions the offset side to the right.

1. Inside the command prompt window, enter ***D*** to select the **Dragline** option. The Dragline option is used to set the placement of the double line.

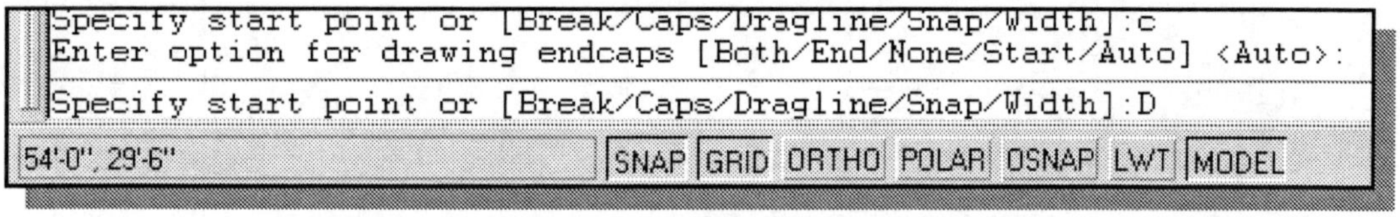

2. In the command prompt area, the message *"Enter offset from center or dragline position option [Left/Center/Right]:"* is displayed. Inside the command prompt window, enter ***L*** to set the placement option to the **Left** option.

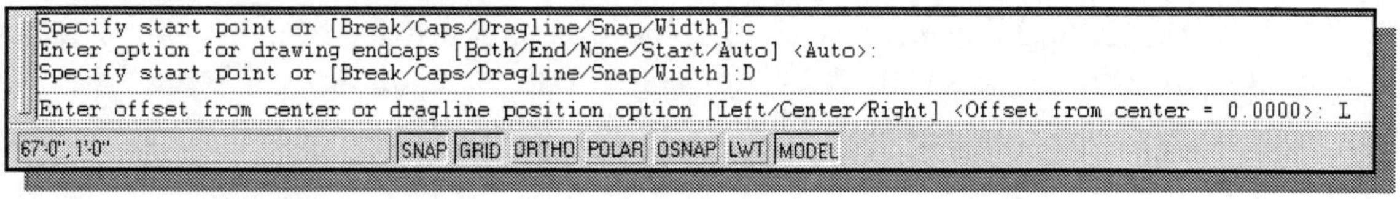

The DLINE Break Option

We can also create a break where double lines intersect by turning ***ON*** the Break option. The use of the option is illustrated in the following sections.

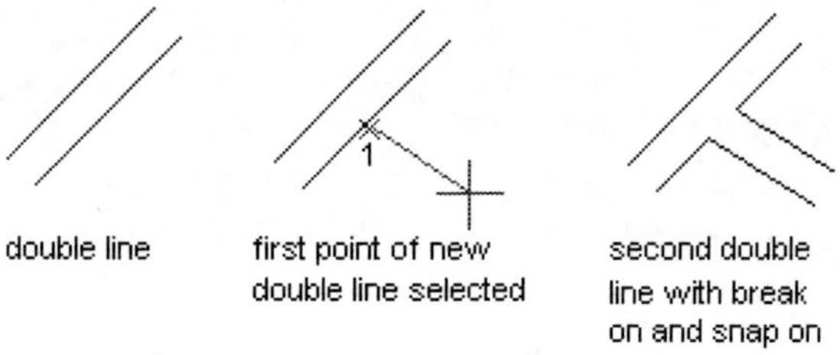

Drawing Double Lines

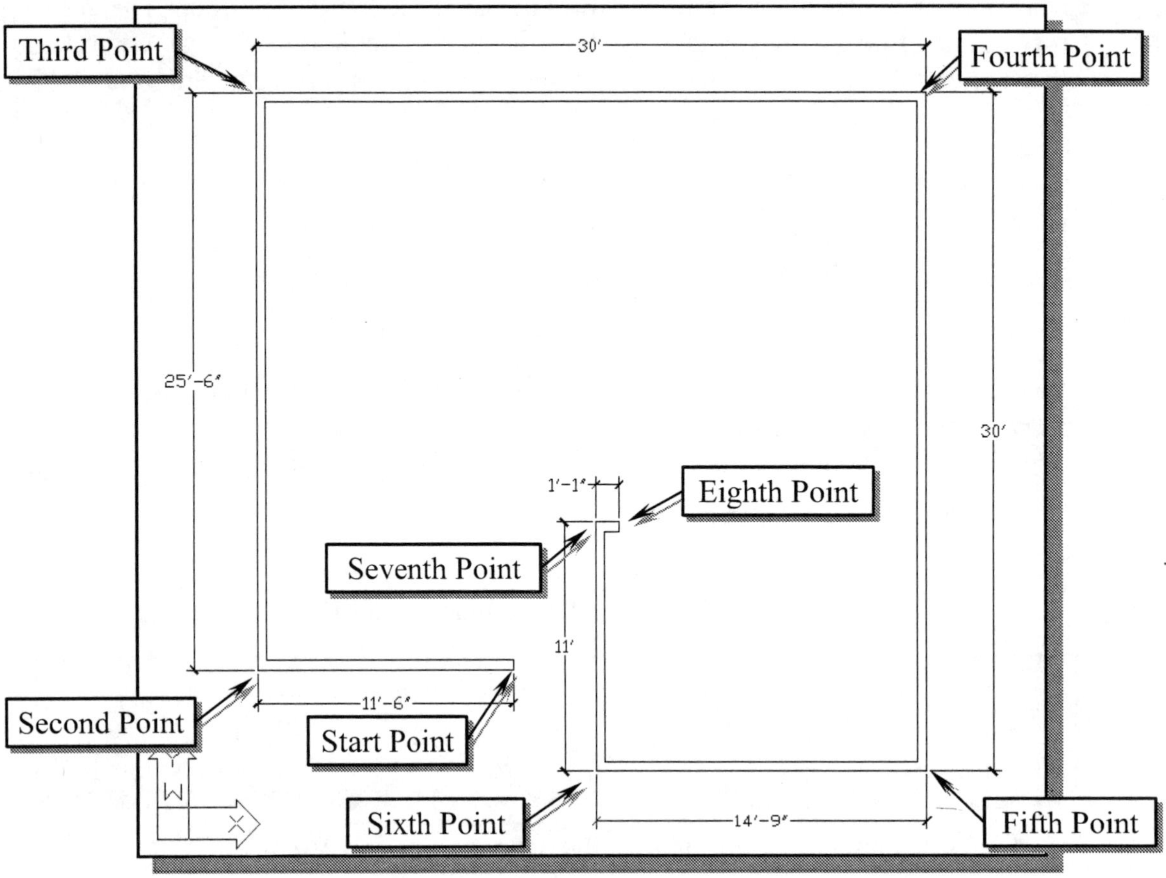

1. In the command prompt area, the message *"Specify start point or [Break/ Caps/ Dragline/ Offset/ Snap/ Undo/ Width]: "* is displayed. AutoCAD LT expects us to identify the starting location or adjust any of the settings. Select the coordinate location (22′,10′) as the **start point** of the double line by left-clicking the mouse at that location.

2. In the command prompt area, create a vertical line by using the *relative rectangular coordinates entry method*, relative to the last point we specified

   Specify next point: **@-11′6″,0 [Enter]**

3. Complete the double line by specifying the points, **point three** through **point eight**, as shown in the above figure.

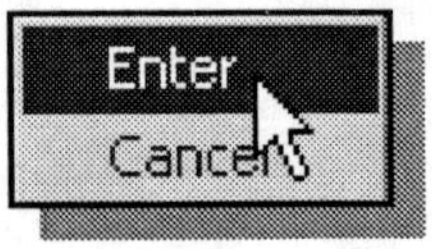

3. Inside the graphics window, right-mouse-click and select **Enter** to end the **Dline** command.

Display the Object Snap Toolbar

1. Move the cursor on any icon in the *Standard* toolbar area and right-mouse-click once to display a list of toolbar menu groups.

2. Select **Object Snap**, with the left-mouse-button, to display the *Object Snap* toolbar on the screen to assist the construction of the floor plan.

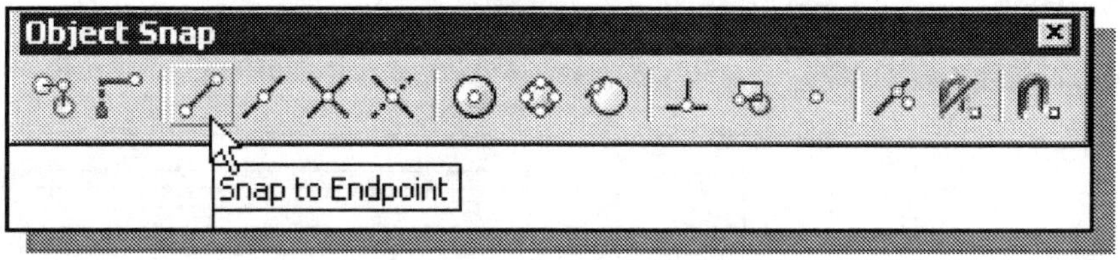

Controlling the Appearance of Intersections

We can also control the appearance of intersections between double lines. The Break option allows us to specify whether DLine creates a break in a double line, line, or arc when we snap a double line to it.

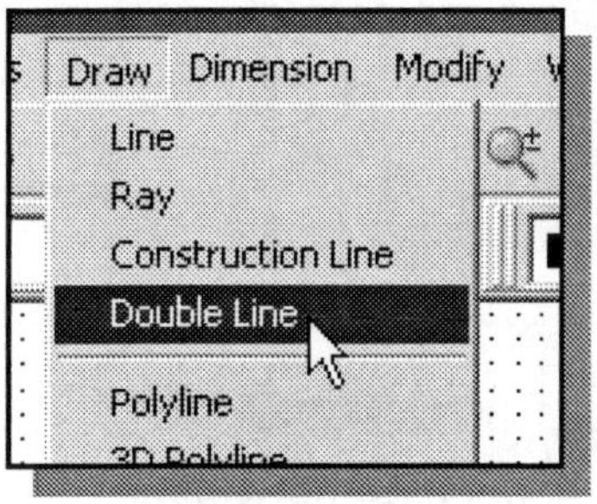

1. Select the **Double Line** command in the *Draw* pull-down menu as shown.

2. In the command prompt area, the message *"Specify start point or [Break/ Caps/ Dragline/ Offset/ Snap/ Undo/ Width]:"* is displayed. Inside the prompt window, enter ***B*** to select the **Break** option.

```
Command:
Command: _dline
Specify start point or [Break/Caps/Dragline/Snap/Width]:B
```

3. In the command prompt area, the message *"Break dlines at start and end points [OFf/ON]:"* is displayed. Inside the prompt window, enter ***ON*** to turn on the Break option.

```
Command: _dline
Specify start point or [Break/Caps/Dragline/Snap/Width]:B
Break Dlines at start and end points? [OFF/ON] <ON>: ON
```

4. *On your own,* set the **Dragline** option to **Right** as shown.

```
Specify start point or [Break/Caps/Dragline/Snap/Width]:D
Enter offset from center or dragline position option [Left/Center/Right] <Offset from center = -2.5000>: R
```

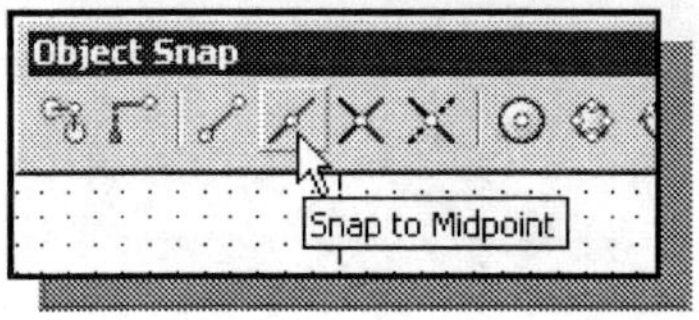

5. In the *Object Snap* toolbar, pick **Snap to Midpoint**. In the command prompt area, the message *"_midp of"* is displayed. AutoCAD LT now expects us to select a geometric entity on the screen.

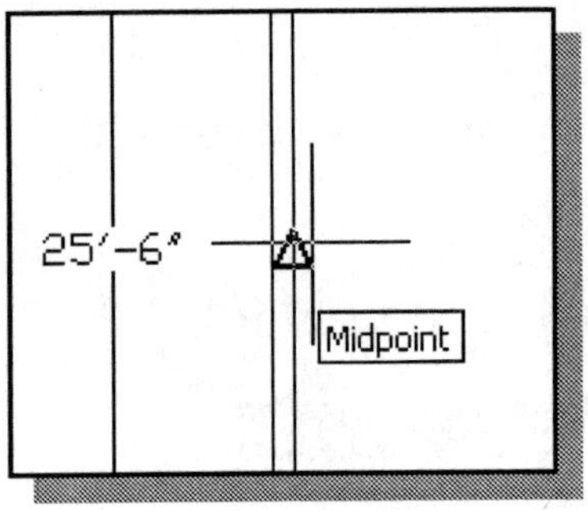

6. Select the inside vertical line on the left as shown.

7. At the command prompt, enter **@10′,0** **[ENTER]**.

8. Now enter **@0,1′1″**, to define the vertical stub wall.

9. Inside the graphics window, right-mouse-click and select **Enter** to end the Dline command.

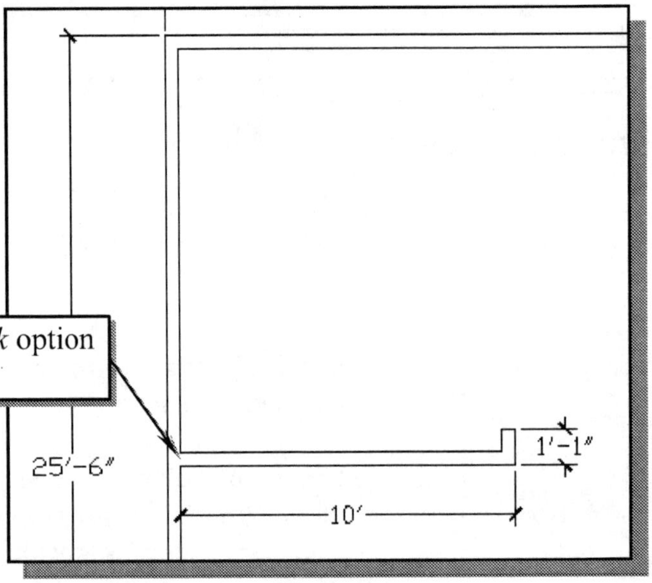

➢ The appearance of the intersection of the two double lines is adjusted automatically when the Break option is turned *ON*.

Creating Interior Walls

Next, we will create a line representing the location of a 2′-8″ door.

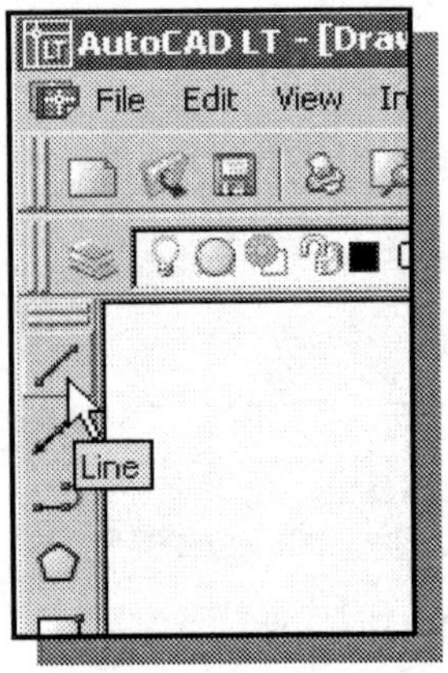

1. Select the **Line** command icon in the *Draw* toolbar. In the command prompt area, the message *"_line Specify first point:"* is displayed.

2. In the *Object Snap* toolbar, pick **Snap to Endpoint**. In the command prompt area, the message *"_endp of"* is displayed. AutoCAD LT now expects us to select a geometric entity on the screen.

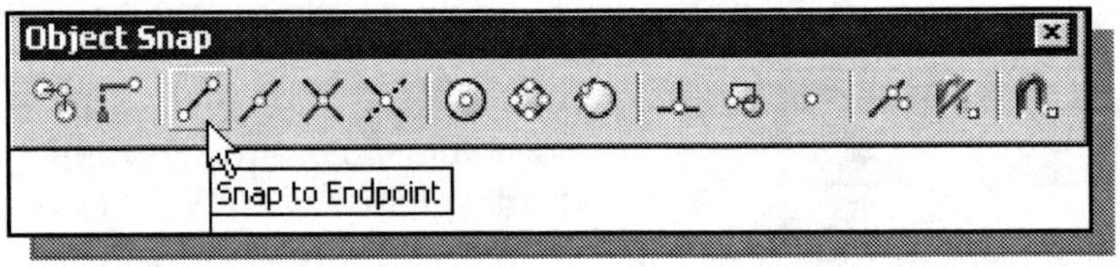

3. Pick the **top right corner** of the multiline we just created.

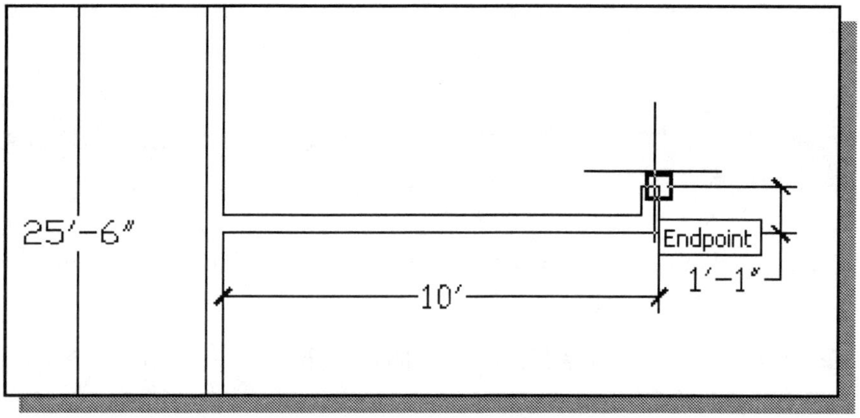

4. At the command prompt, enter **@0,2′8″ [ENTER]**

5. Inside the graphics window, right-mouse-click and select **Enter** to end the Line command.

6. Select the **Double Line** command icon in the *Draw* toolbar. In the command prompt area, the message *"Specify start point or [Break/ Caps/ Dragline/ Offset/ Snap/ Undo/ Width]:"* is displayed.

7. In the *Object Snap* toolbar, pick **Snap to Endpoint**. In the command prompt area, the message *"_endp of"* is displayed.

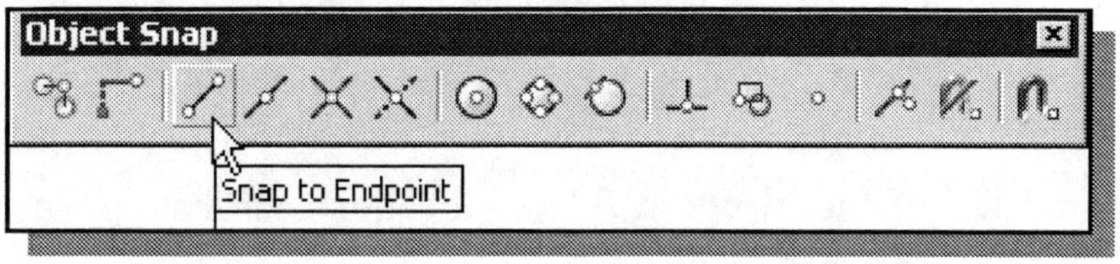

8. Pick the **top endpoint** of the reference line we just created.

9. In the *Status Bar* area, turn *ON* the *ORTHO* option by toggling the button with the left-mouse-button as shown.

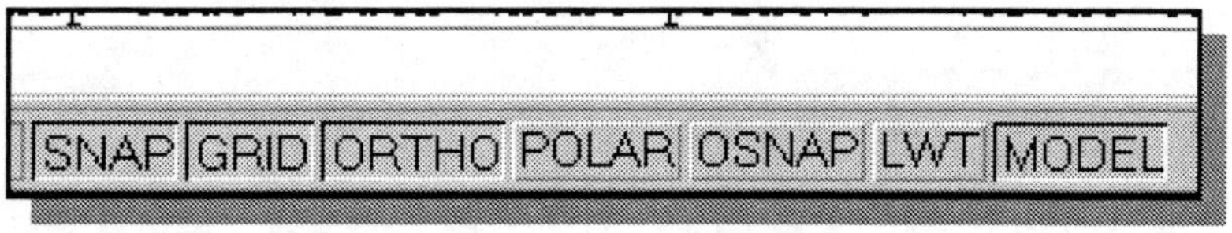

10. We will create another inside wall using the DLINE SNAP option. Inside the prompt window, enter *S* to select the Snap option

```
Command: _dline
Break/Caps/Dragline/Offset/Snap/Undo/Width/<start point>: _endp of
Arc/Break/CAps/CLose/Dragline/Snap/Undo/Width/<next point>: S
```

11. In the command prompt area, enter ***ON*** to turn on the SNAP option.

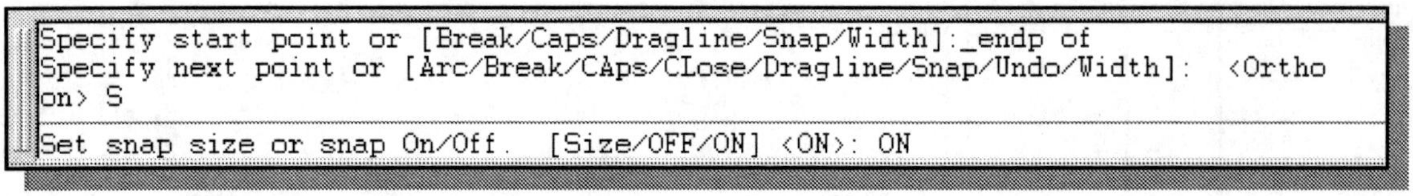

➢ The SNAP option sets the double line to start or end by snapping to an existing object. When the SNAP option is turned ***ON***, the Break option determines automatically whether to break the object at the intersection of the double line or not.

12. We will also set the CAPS option to **START**. Note that the **Auto** option automatically caps only the ends that are not snapped to an object. Inside the graphics window, **right-mouse-click** to bring up the option list.

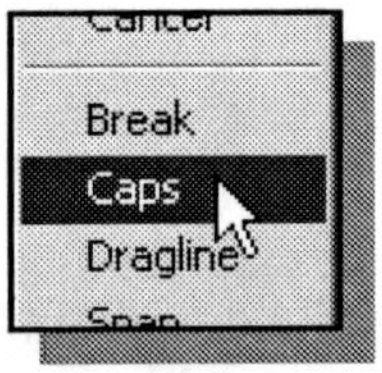

13. Select **Caps** in the option list to set the CAPS option.

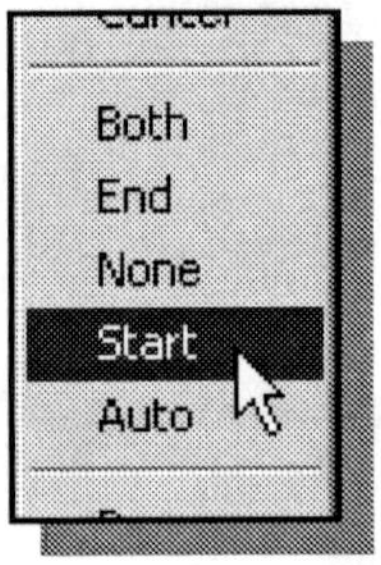

14. Inside the graphics window, **right-mouse-click** to bring up the option list.

15. Select **Start** in the option list. This will CAP only the first point of the DLINE segment we create next.

16. Inside the graphics window, select a location near the top outside wall and create the wall as shown.

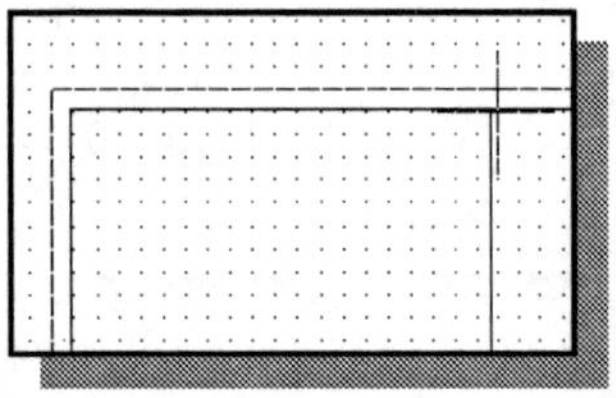

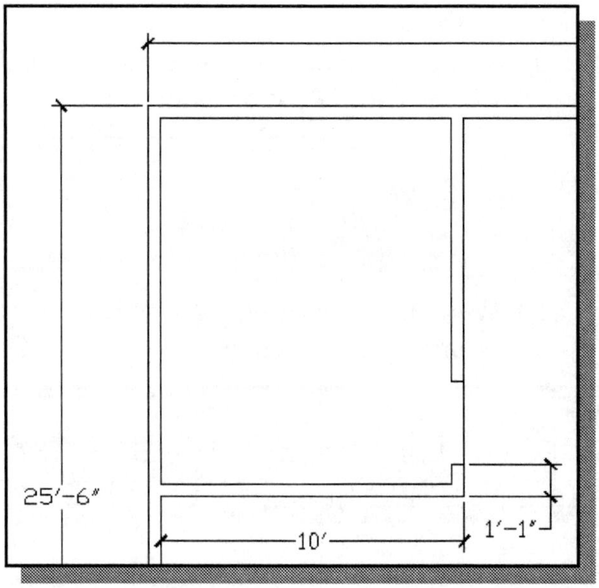

17. On your own, use the **DLine, Snap, Extend, Trim** commands and create the additional walls and doorways as shown below.

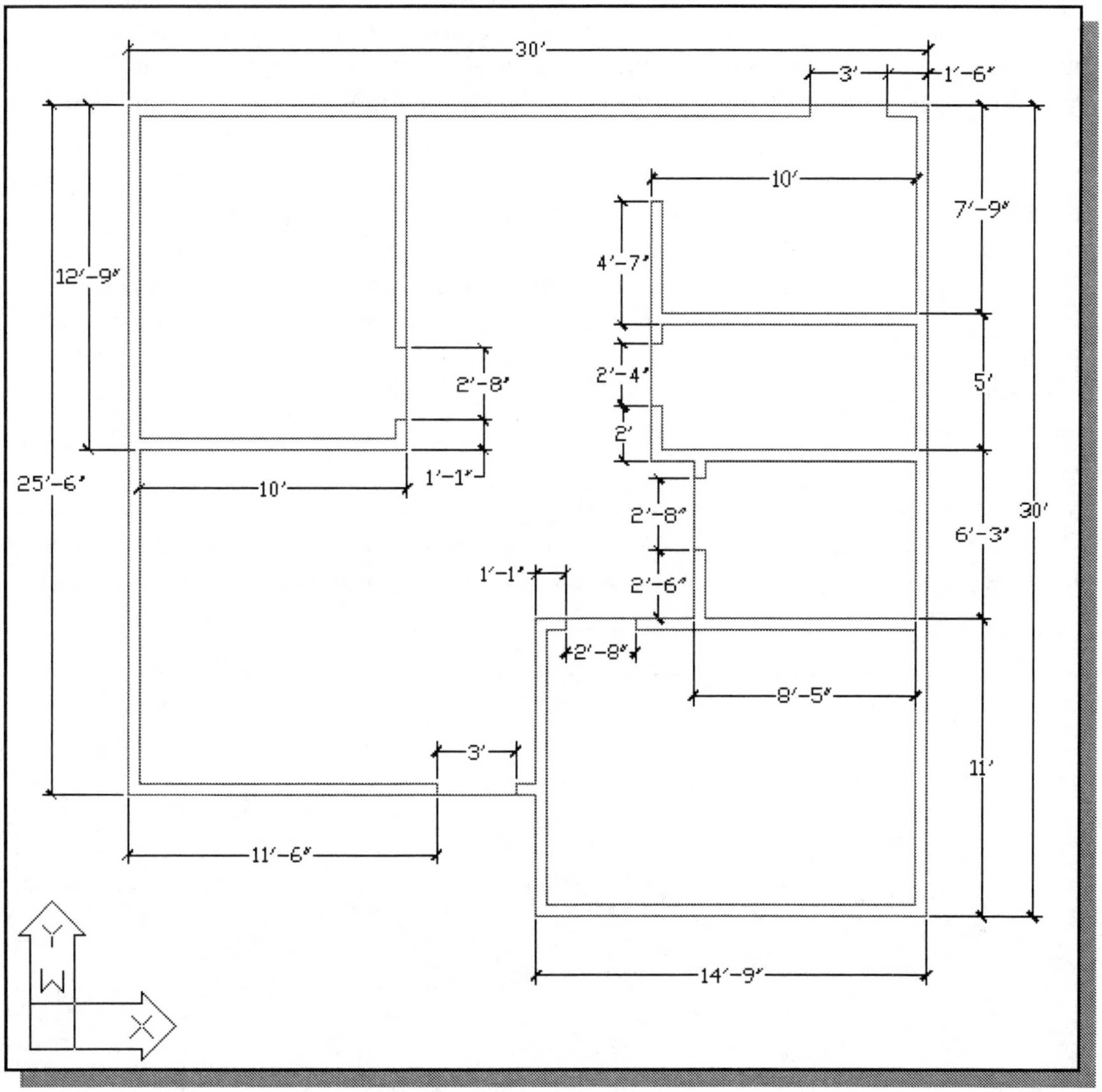

➢ Use the **Undo** and **Erase** commands to assist the construction of the floor plan.

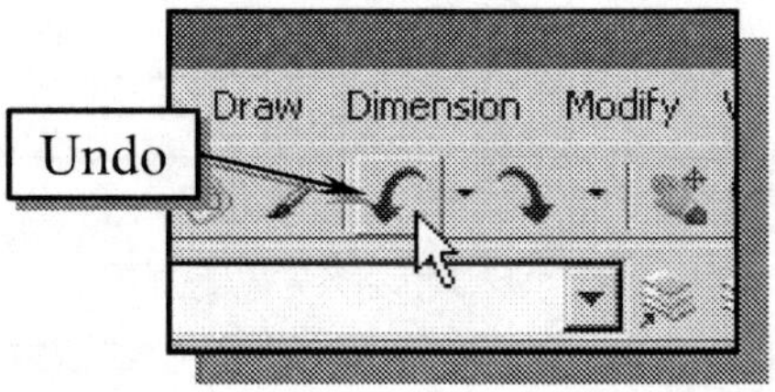

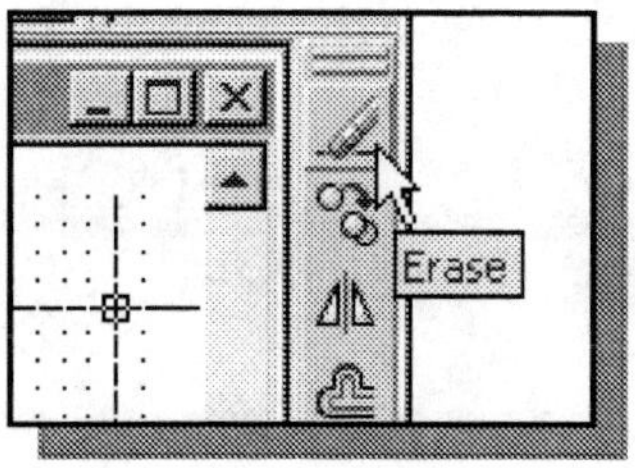

Using *Layers* and *Object Properties*

In AutoCAD LT, **layers** can be thought of as transparent overlays on which we organize different kinds of design information. Typically, CAD entities that are created to describe one feature or function of a design are considered as related information and therefore can be organized into the same group. The objects we organized into the same group will usually have common properties such as colors, linetypes, and lineweights. Color helps us visually distinguish similar elements in our designs. Linetype helps us identify easily the different drafting elements, such as centerlines or hidden lines. Lineweight increases the legibility of an object through width. Consider the floor plan we are currently working on. The floor plan can be placed on one layer, electrical layout on another and plumbing on a third layer. Organizing layers and the objects on layers makes it easier to manage the information in our designs. Layers can be used as a method to control the visibility of objects. We can temporarily switch *ON* or *OFF* any layers to help construction and editing of our designs.

AutoCAD LT allows us to create an infinite number of layers. In general, twenty to thirty layers are sufficient for most designs. Most companies also require designers and CAD operators to follow the company standards in organizing objects in layers.

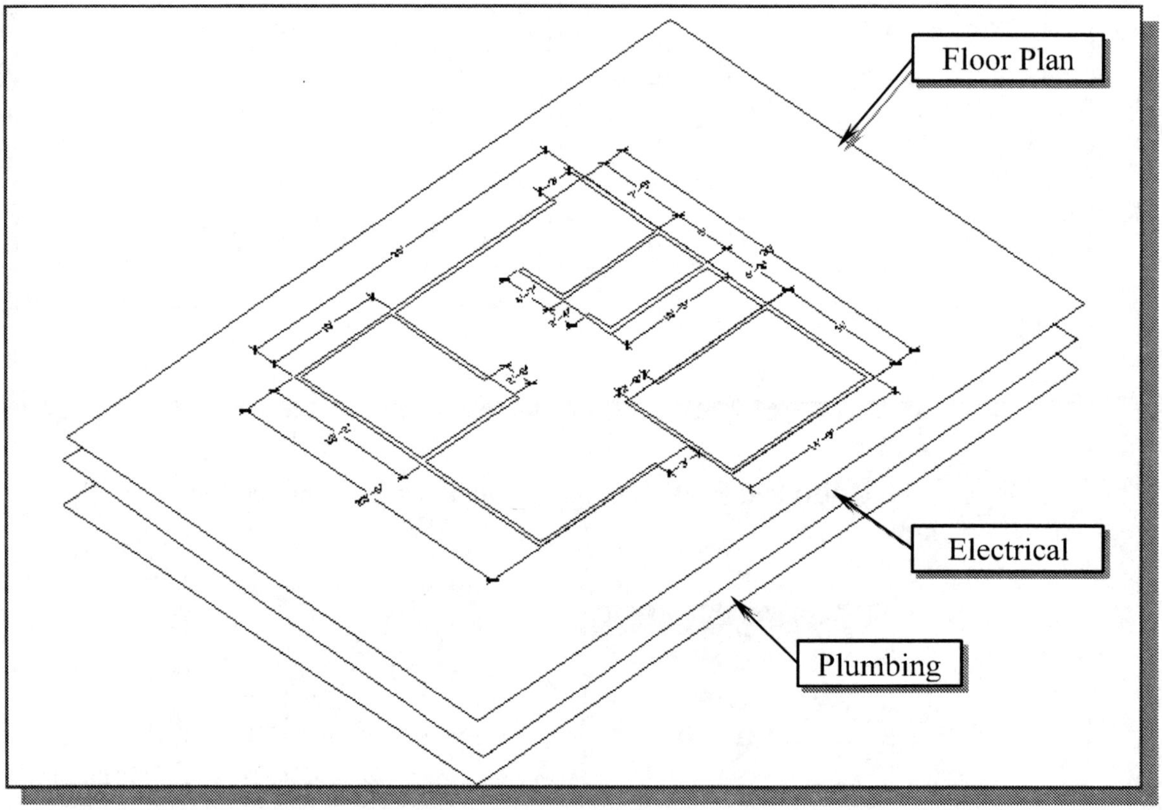

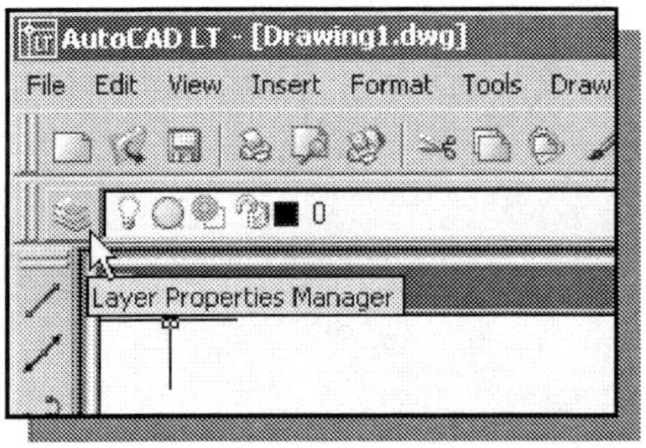

1. Pick **Layers Properties Manager** in the *Object Properties* toolbar.

➢ The *Layer Properties Manager* dialog box appears. AutoCAD LT creates a default layer, *layer 0*, which we cannot rename or delete. *Layer 0* has special properties used by the system.

❖ In AutoCAD LT, we always construct entities on a layer. It may be the default layer or a layer that we create. Each layer has associated properties such as the visibility setting, color, linetype, lineweight, and plot style.

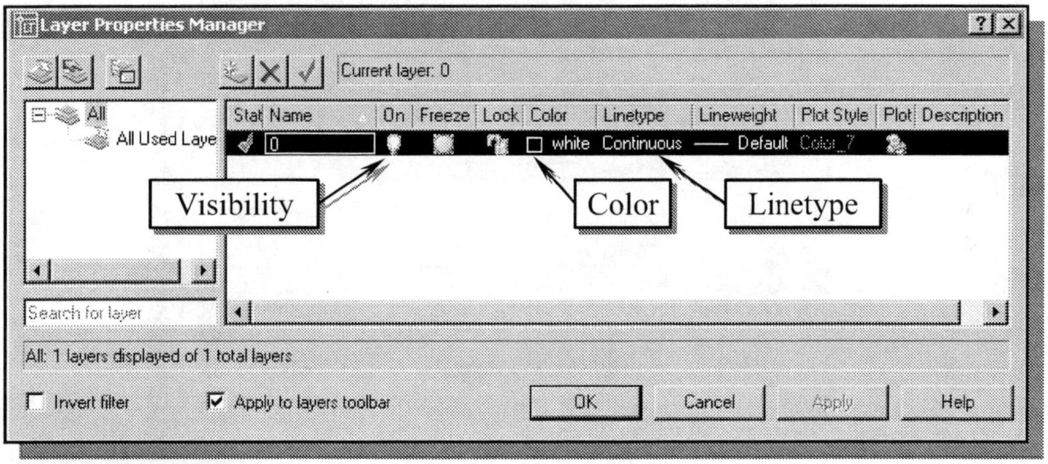

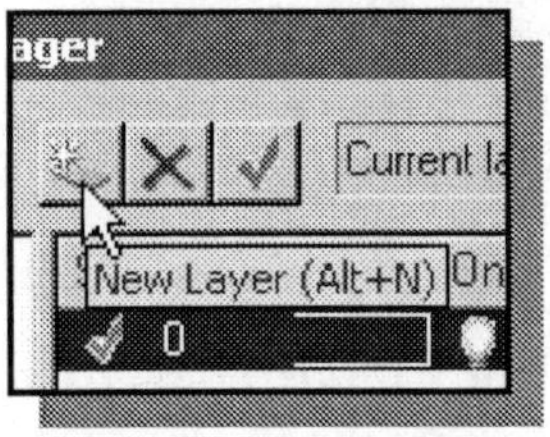

2. Click on the **New** button. Notice a layer is automatically added to the list of layers.

3. AutoCAD LT will assign a generic name to the new layer (*Layer1*). Enter ***BathRoom*** as the name of the new layer.

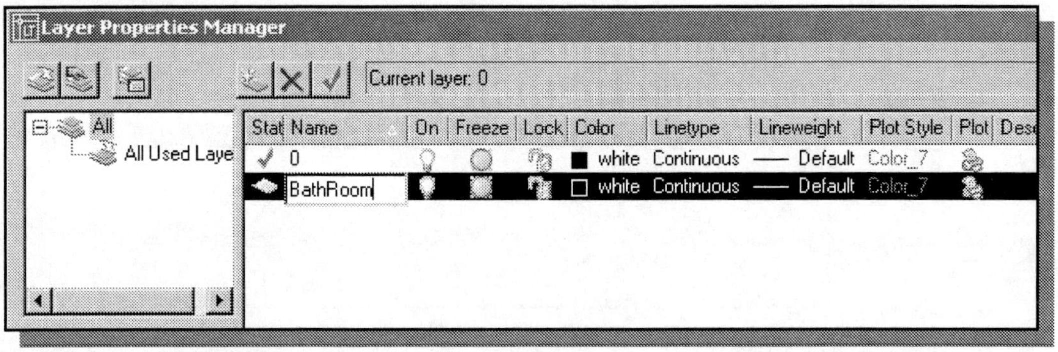

➢ Layer properties can be adjusted by clicking on the icon or name of a property; for example, clicking on the *light-bulb* icon will toggle the visibility of the layer *ON* or *OFF*.

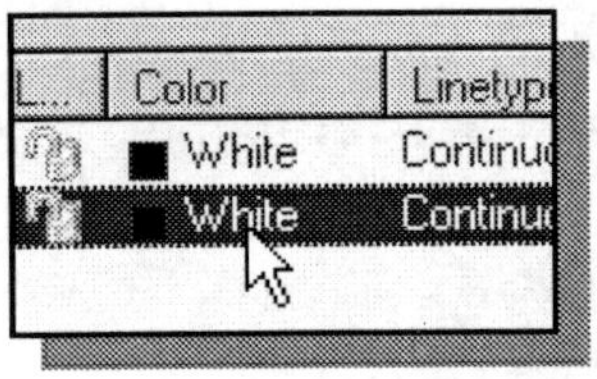

4. Pick the color swatch or the color name (**White**) of the *BathRoom* layer. The *Select Color* dialog box appears.

5. Pick **Cyan** in the *Standard Colors* section. Notice the current color setting is displayed at the bottom of the dialog box.

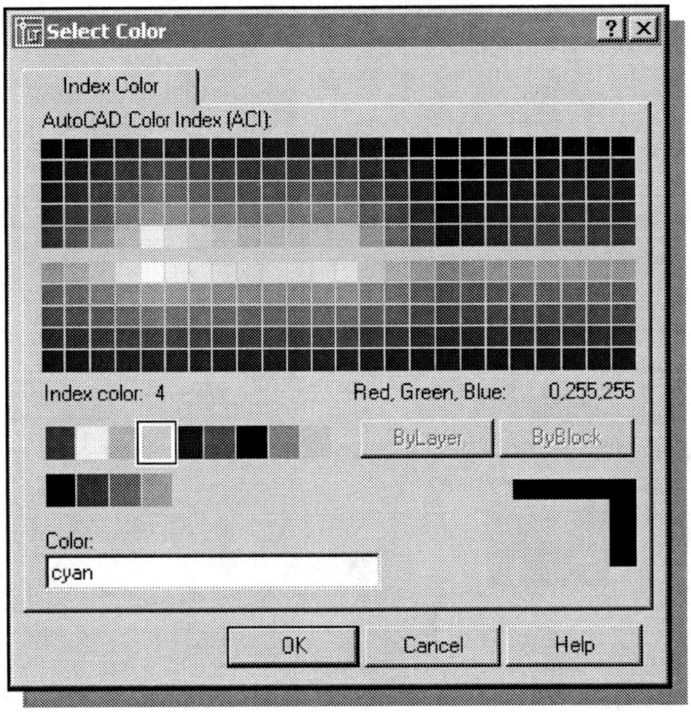

6. Click on the **OK** button to accept the color assignment.

7. Click on the **Current** button to make *BathRoom* the *Current Layer*. There can only be one *Current Layer*, and new entities are automatically placed on the layer that is set to be the *Current Layer*.

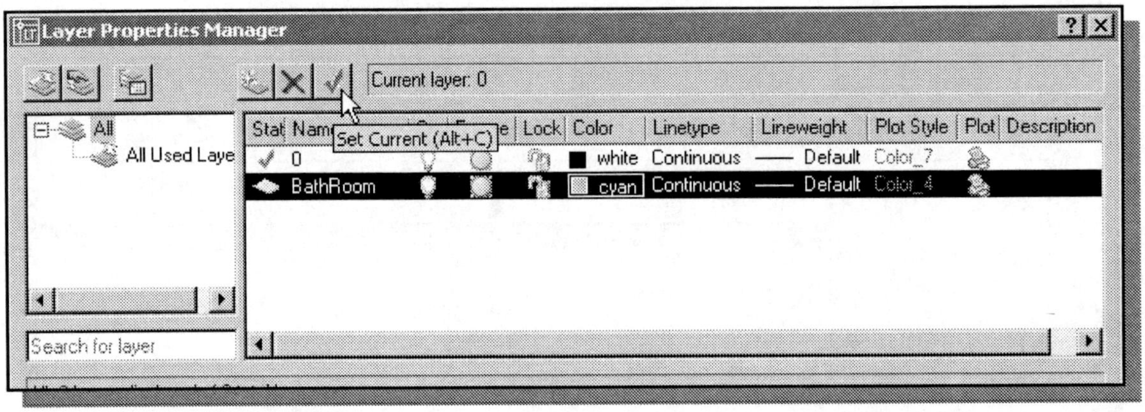

8. Click on the **OK** button to accept the settings and exit the *Layer Properties Manager* dialog box.

➢ The *Object Properties* toolbar near the top of the *AutoCAD LT* screen shows the status of object properties. There are two strategies for assigning colors, linetypes, and lineweights in *AutoCAD LT*: assign to individual objects, or assign *ByLayer* properties. Using the ***ByLayer*** method is the preferred method, since it allows us to modify all related objects quickly and easily.

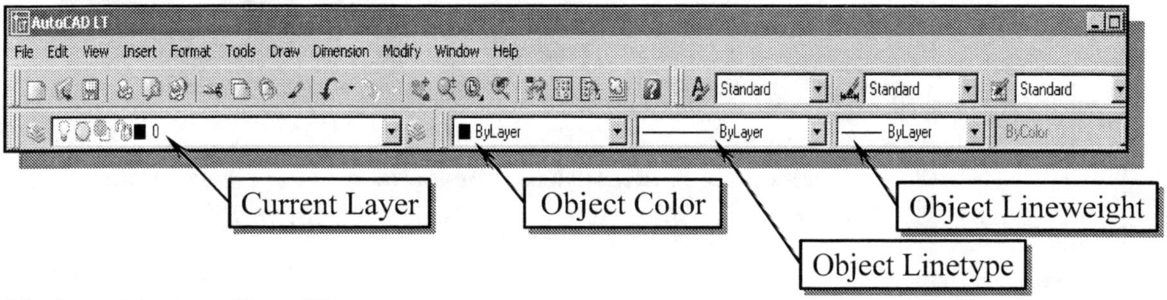

Using *Zoom Realtime*

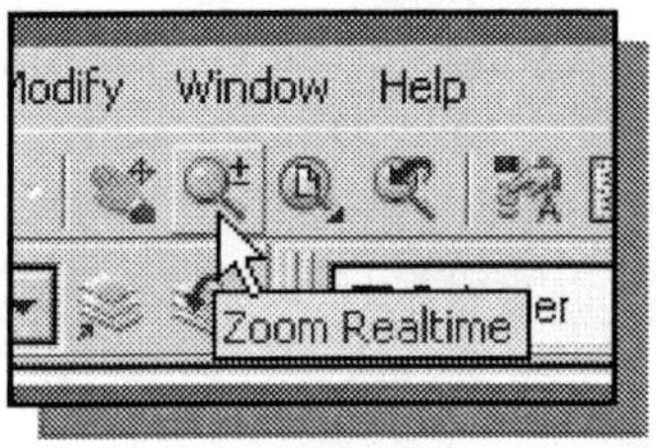

1. Click on the **Zoom Realtime** icon in the *Standard* toolbar area.

2. Move the cursor near the center of the graphics window.

3. Inside the graphics window, **push and hold down the left-mouse-button,** then move upward to enlarge the current display scale factor. (Press the [**Esc**] key to exit the Zoom command.)

4. Use the **Pan Realtime** option to reposition the display so that we can work on the bathroom of the floor plan.

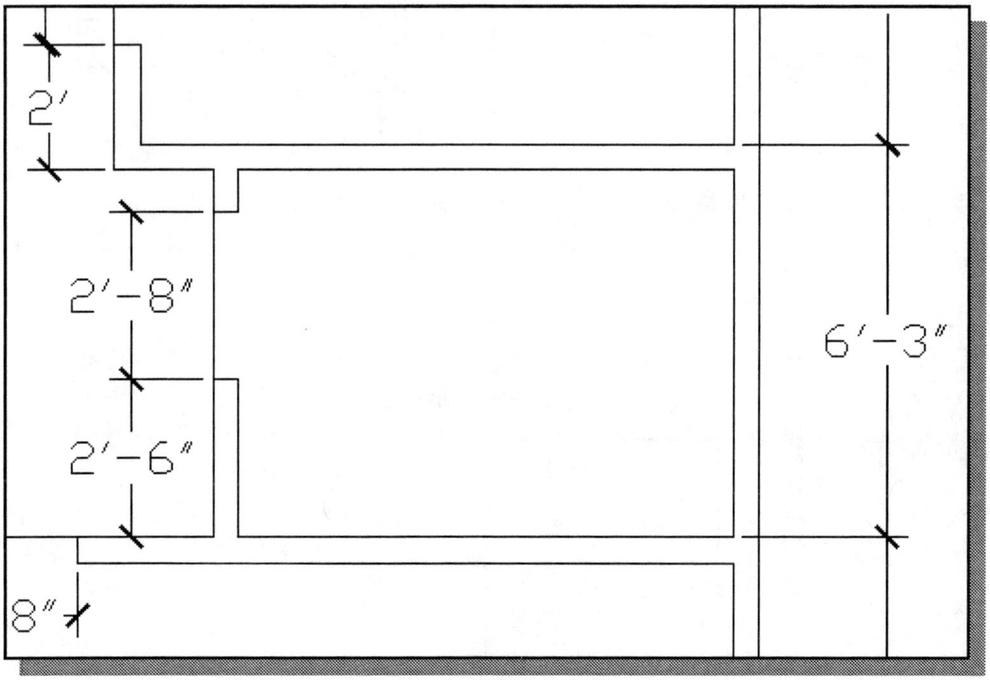

Modeling the *BathRoom*

1. In the *Status Bar* area, reset the option buttons so that only the *MODEL* button is switched ***ON***.

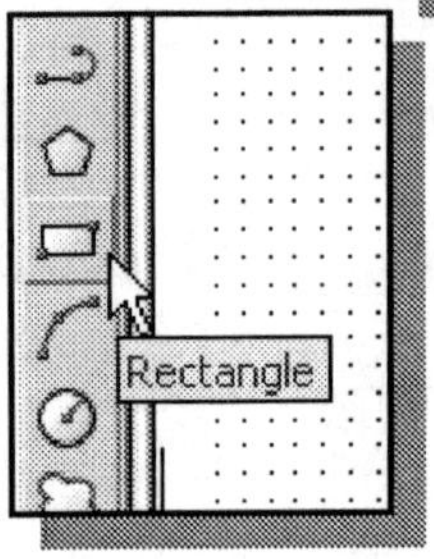

2. Click on the **Rectangle** command icon in the *Draw* toolbar. In the command prompt area, the message *"Specify first corner point:"* is displayed.

3. In the *Object Snap* toolbar, pick **Snap to Endpoint**. In the command prompt area, the message *"_endp of"* is displayed. AutoCAD LT now expects us to select a geometric entity on the screen.

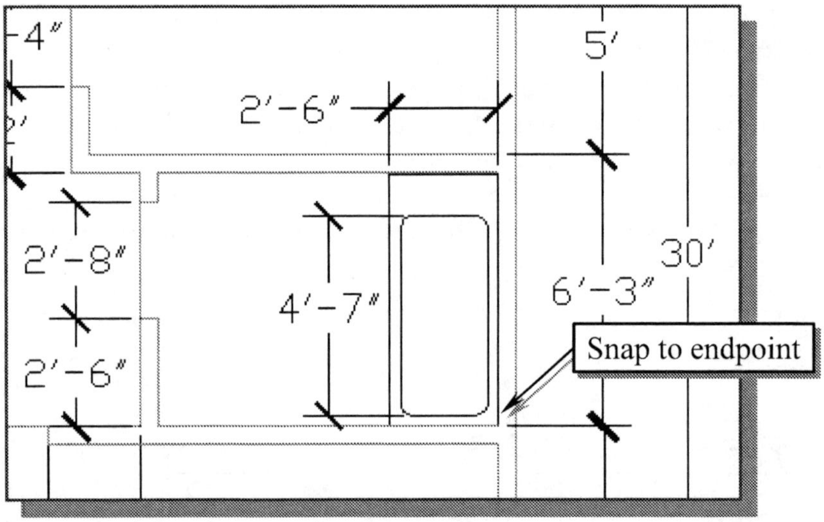

4. Use the *relative coordinate entry method* and create the outer rectangle of the tub.

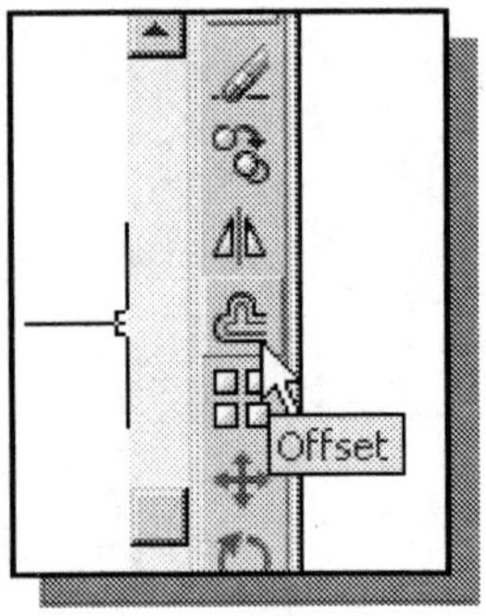

5. Complete the inner shape by creating an offset distance of **3"** and rounded corners of **3"** radius.

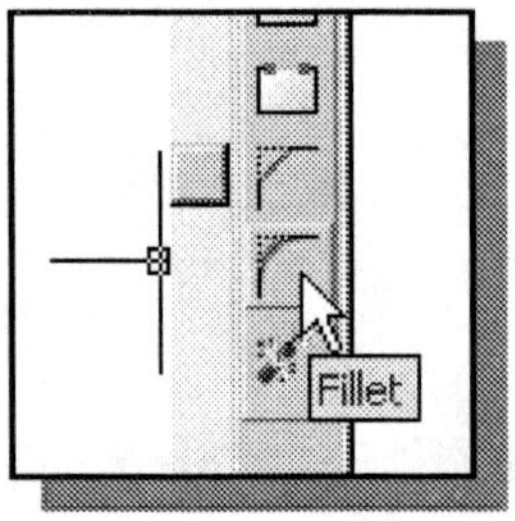

6. Create two rectangles (**10″** × **20″** and **20″** × **30″**) with rounded corners (Radius 3″) and position them as shown. Use the **Explode** command to change the rectangle into lines prior to creating the fillets.

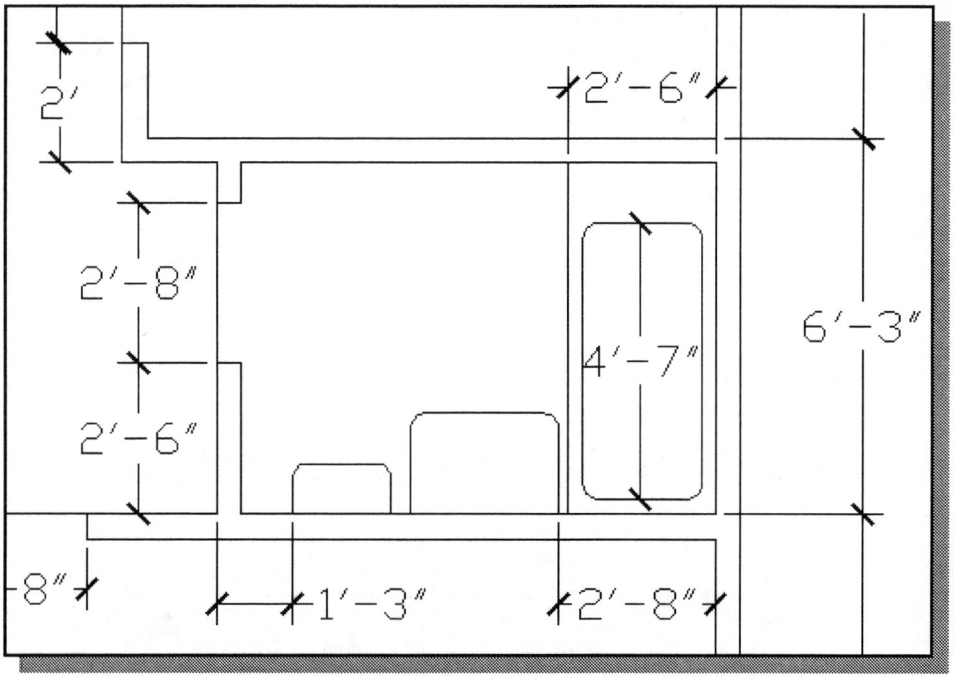

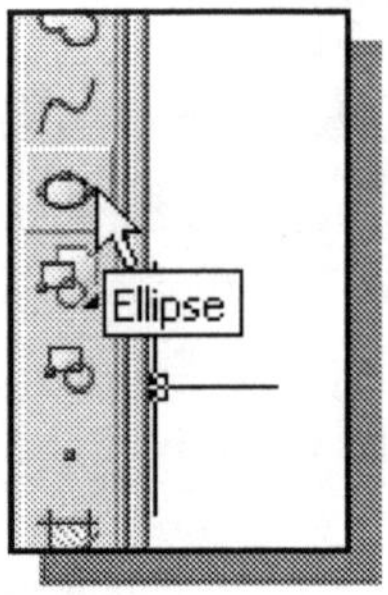

7. Select the **Ellipse** command icon in the *Draw* toolbar. In the command prompt area, the message *"Specify axis endpoint of ellipse or [Arc/Center]:"* is displayed.

8. In the *Object Snap* toolbar, pick **Snap to Midpoint**. In the command prompt area, the message *"_mid of"* is displayed.

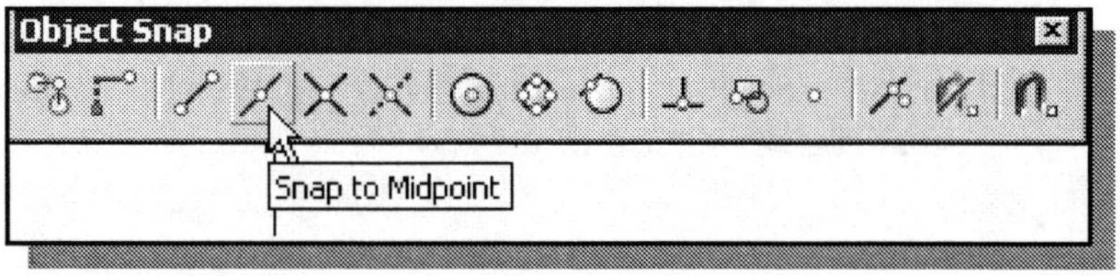

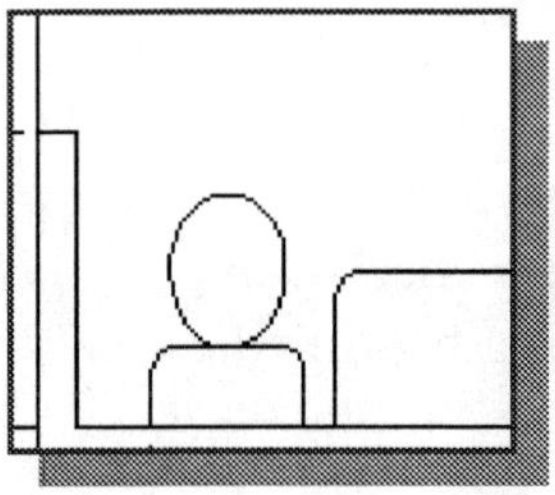

9. Pick the top horizontal line of the small rectangle we just created.

10. For the second point location, enter **@0,20 [ENTER]**

11. For the third point, enter **@7.5,0 [ENTER]**

➢ An ellipse has a major axis, the longest distance between two points on the ellipse, and a minor axis, the shorter distance across the ellipse. The three points we specified identify the two axes.

Controlling *Layer Visibility*

AutoCAD LT does not display or plot the objects that are on invisible layers. To make layers invisible, we can *freeze* or *turn off* those layers. Turning off layers only temporary removes the objects from the screen; the objects remain active in the CAD database. Freezing layers will make the objects invisible and also disable the objects in the CAD database. Freezing layers will improve object selection performance and reduce regeneration time for complex designs. When we ***thaw*** a frozen layer, AutoCAD LT updates the CAD database with the screen coordinates for all objects in the design.

1. On the *Object Properties* toolbar, choose the ***Layer Control*** box with the left-mouse-button.

2. Move the cursor over the **light-bulb** icon for *layer 0*. The *tool tip "Turn a layer On or Off"* appears.

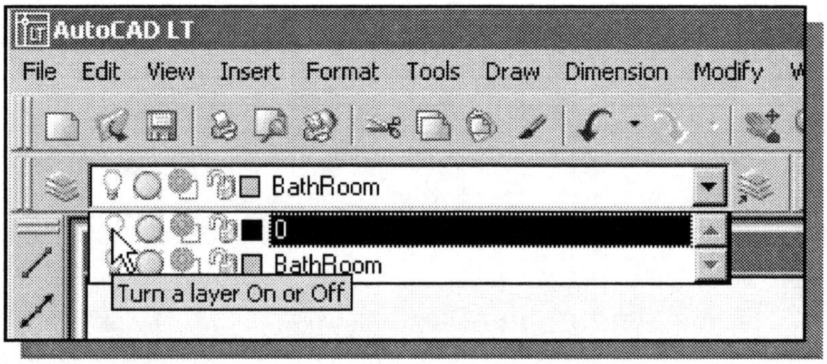

3. **Left-mouse-click once** and notice the icon color is changed to a dark color, representing the layer (*layer 0*) is turned *OFF*.

4. Move the cursor into the graphics window and **left-mouse-click once** to accept the layer control settings.

➢ On your own, practice turning on *layer 0* and freezing/thawing *layer 0*. What would happen if we turn off all layers?

Adding a New Layer

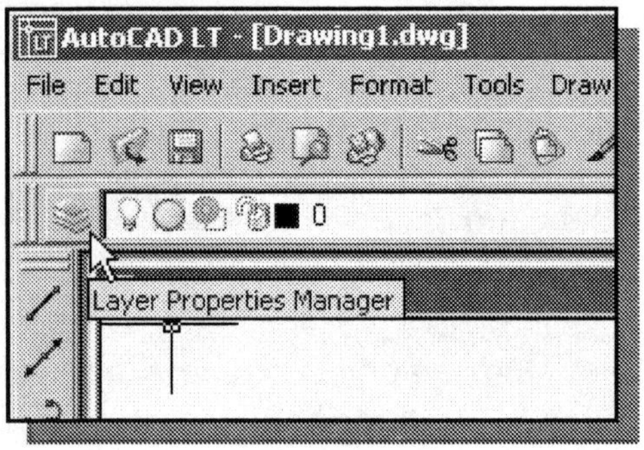

1. Pick **Layers Properties Manager** in the *Object Properties* toolbar. The *Layer Properties Manager* dialog box appears.

2. On your own, create a new layer (layer name: ***Walls***) and change the layer color to **Green**.

3. Set the ***Walls*** layer as the *Current Layer* and turn ***OFF*** the *BathRoom* layer.

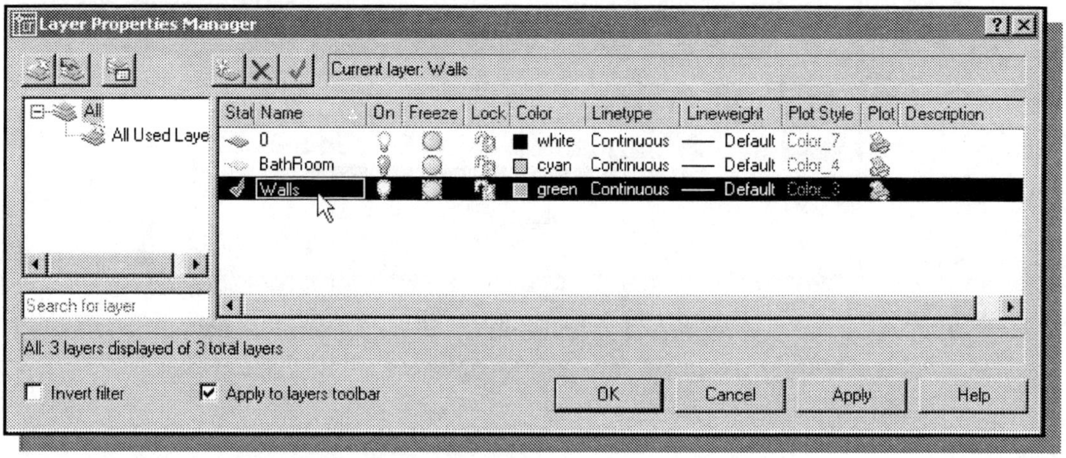

4. Click on the **OK** button to accept the settings.

Moving Objects to a Different Layer

AutoCAD LT 2005 provides a flexible graphical user interface that allows users to select graphical entities BEFORE the command is selected (*pre-selection*), or AFTER the command is selected (*post-selection*). The procedure we have used so far is the *post-selection* option. We can pre-select one or more objects by clicking on the objects at the command prompt (***Command:***). To deselect the selected items, press the [**Esc**] key twice.

1. Inside the graphics window, pre-select all objects by enclosing all objects inside a **selection window** as shown.

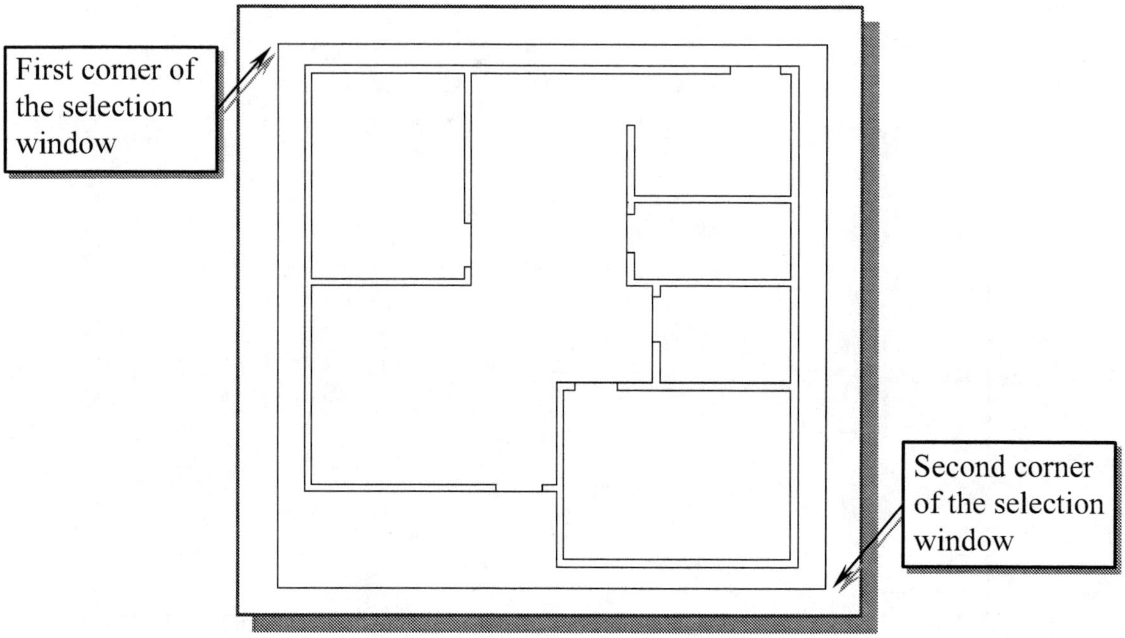

2. On the *Object Properties* toolbar, choose the ***Layer Control*** box with the left-mouse-button.

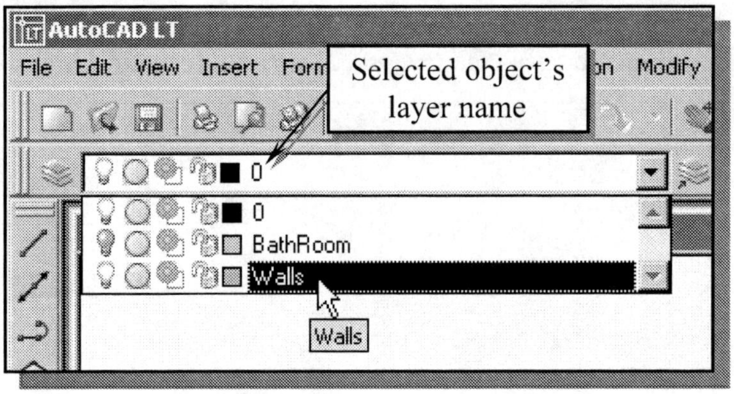

❖ Notice the layer name displayed in the *Layer Control* box is the selected object's assigned layer and layer properties.

3. In the *Layer Control* box, click on the **Walls** layer name

4. On your own, make the *Walls* invisible by turning the *Walls layer* **OFF**.

➢ On your own, experiment with turning layers *ON* or *OFF* and moving objects from one layer to another.

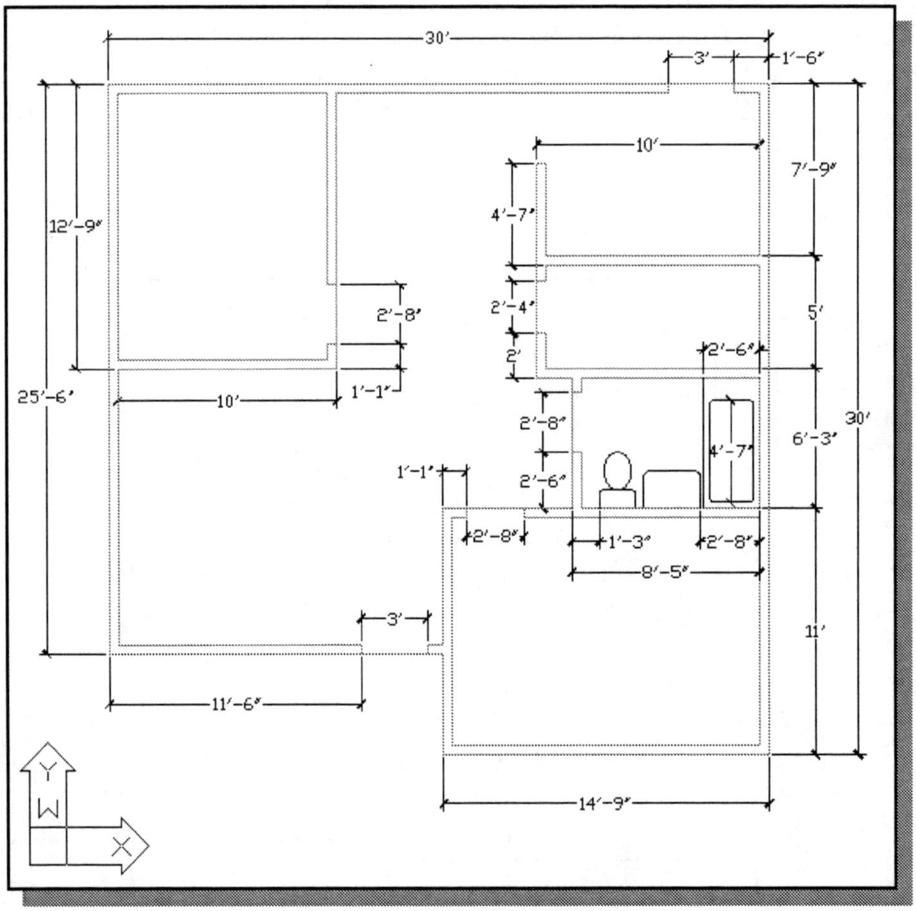

Questions:

1. Describe some of the advantages of using *layers*.

2. List two methods to control the layer *visibility* in **AutoCAD® LT 2005**.

3. What is the difference between *freezing a layer* and *turning off a layer*?

4. When and why would you use the Double Line command?

5. Identify the following commands:

(a)

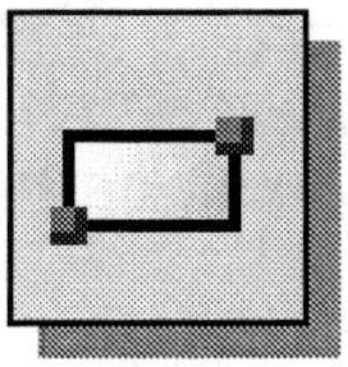

(b)

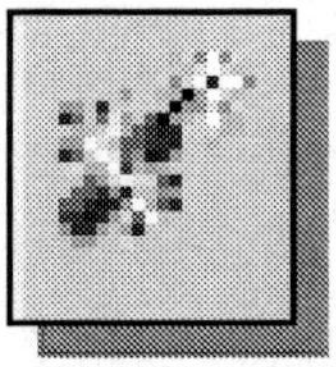

(c)

(d)

Exercises:

1. Wall thickness: 5 inches

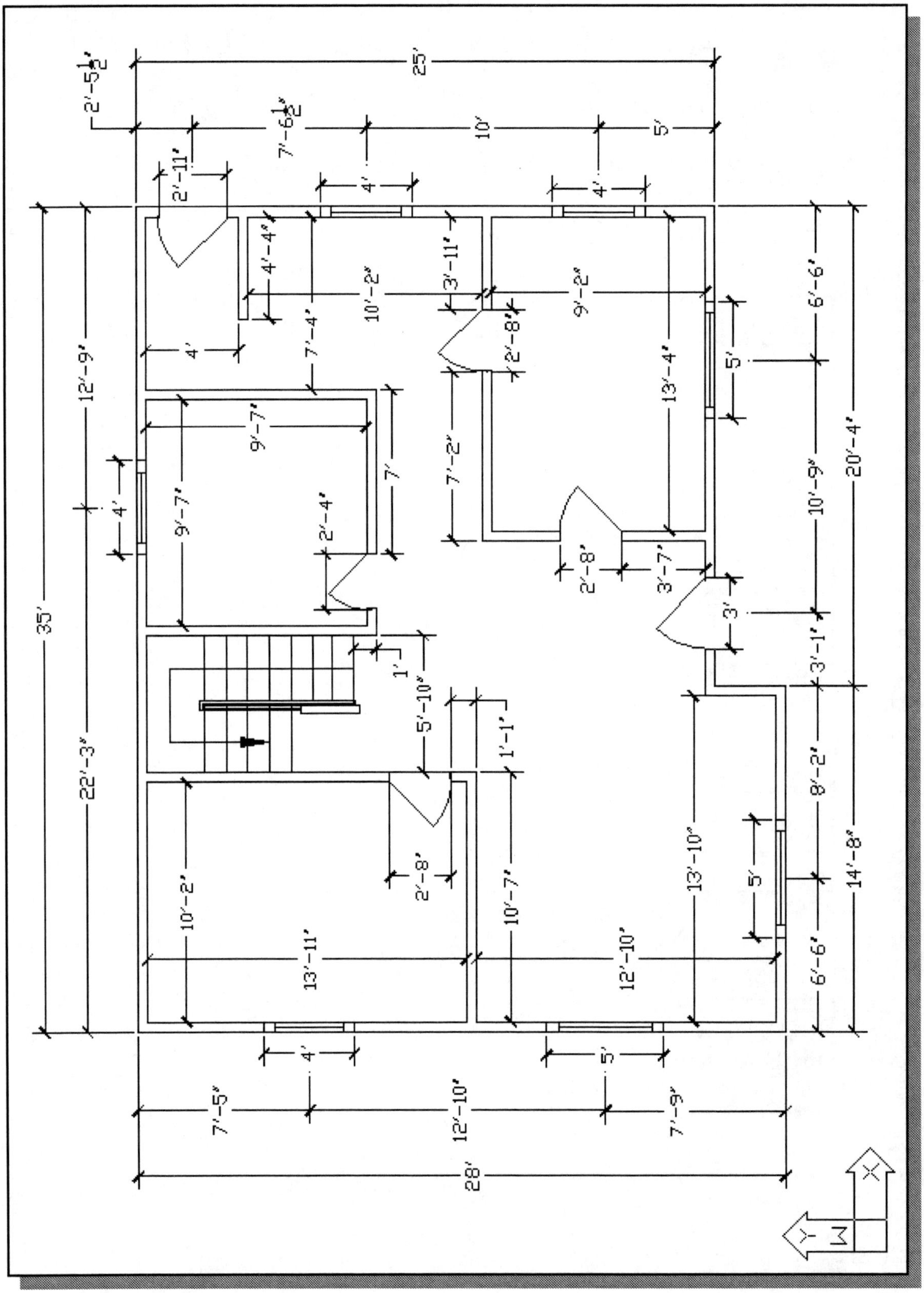

2. Wall thickness: 5 inches

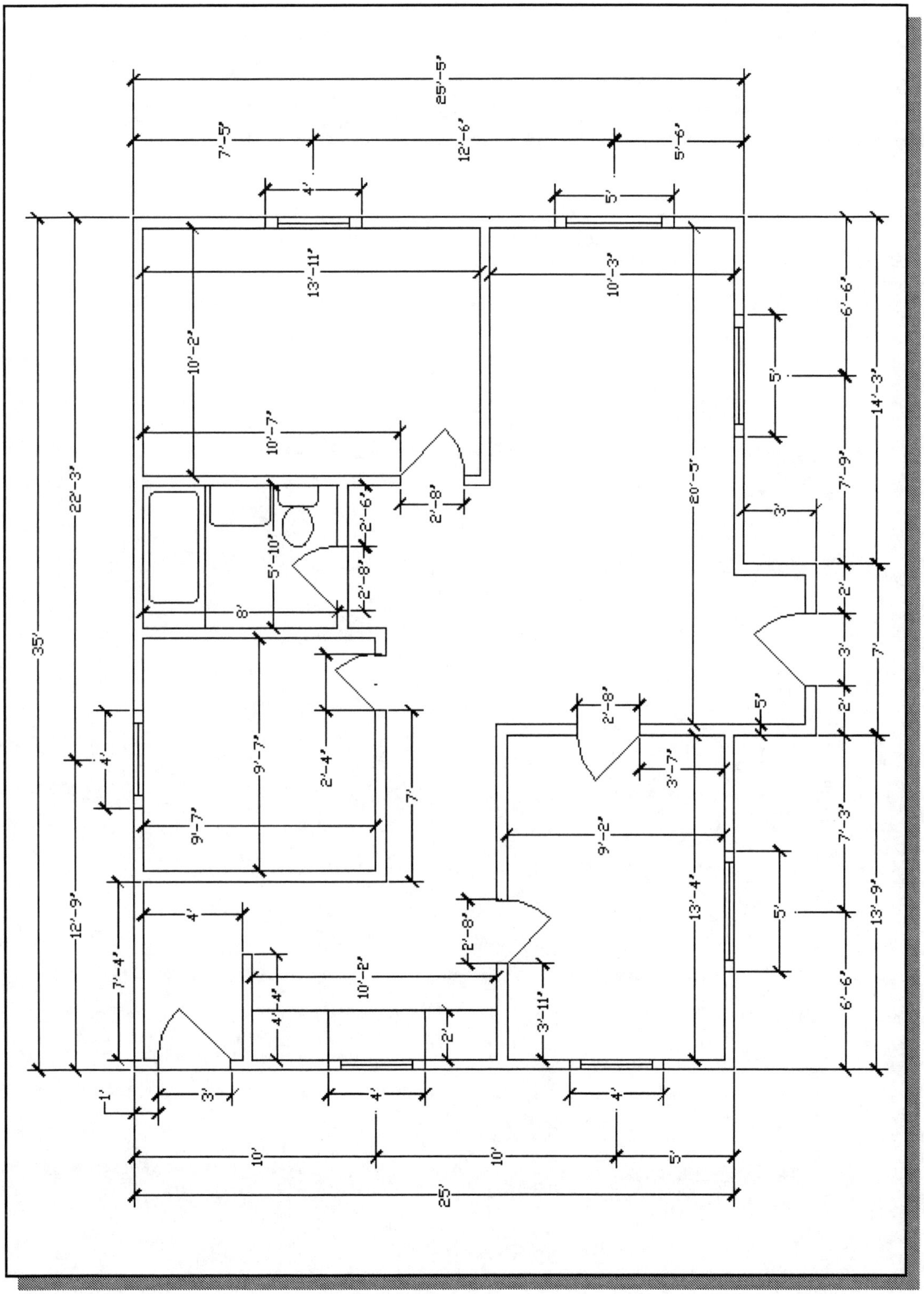

Notes:

Lesson 4
Orthographic Views in Multiview Drawings

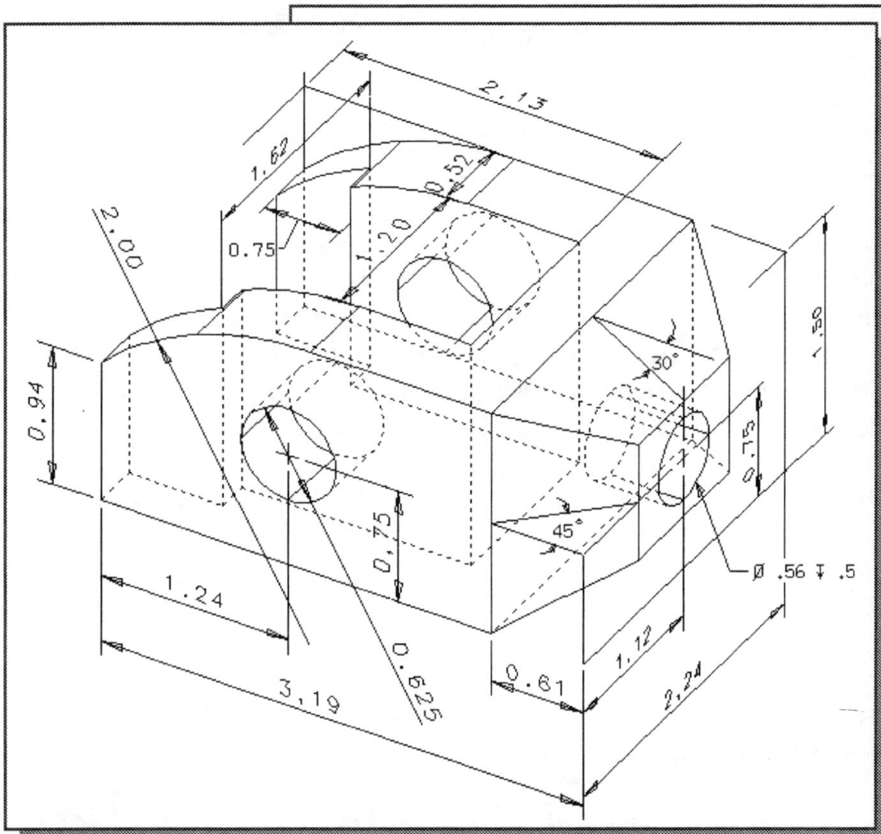

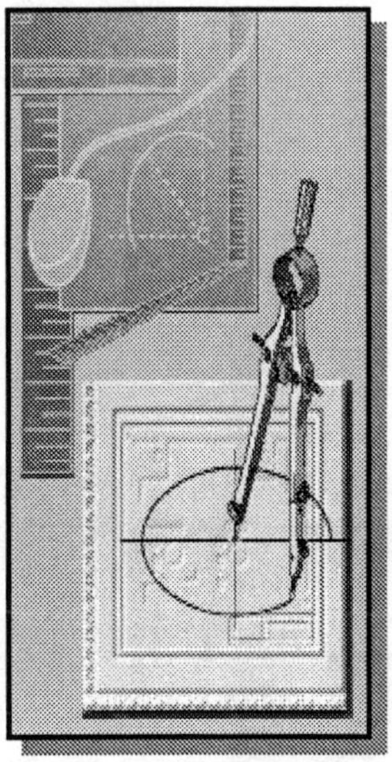

Learning Objectives

- **Create 2D Orthographic Views Using AutoCAD LT**
- **Use the CONSTRUCTION LINE Command to Draw**
- **UseRunning Object Snaps**
- **Use AutoCAD LT's *AutoSnap* and *AutoTrack* Features**
- **Create a Miter Line to Transfer Dimensions**
- **Use Projection Lines Between Orthographic Views**
- **Use the POLAR Tracking Option**

Introduction

Most drawings produced and used in industry are ***multiview drawings***. Multiview drawings are used to provide accurate three-dimensional object information on two-dimensional media, a means of communicating all of the information necessary to transform an idea or concept to reality. The standards and conventions of multiview drawings have been developed over many years, which equips us with a universally understood method of communication. The age of computers has greatly altered the design process, and several CAD methods are now available to help generate multiview drawings using CAD systems.

Multiview drawings usually require several orthographic views to define the shape of a three-dimensional object. Each orthographic view is a two-dimensional drawing showing only two of the three dimensions of the three-dimensional object. Consequently, no individual view contains sufficient information to completely define the shape of the three-dimensional object. We must look at all orthographic views together to comprehend the shape of the three-dimensional object. The arrangement and relationship between the views are therefore very important in multiview drawings. In this lesson, we will look at the more common methods of creating two-dimensional orthographic views with AutoCAD LT.

The *Locator* Design

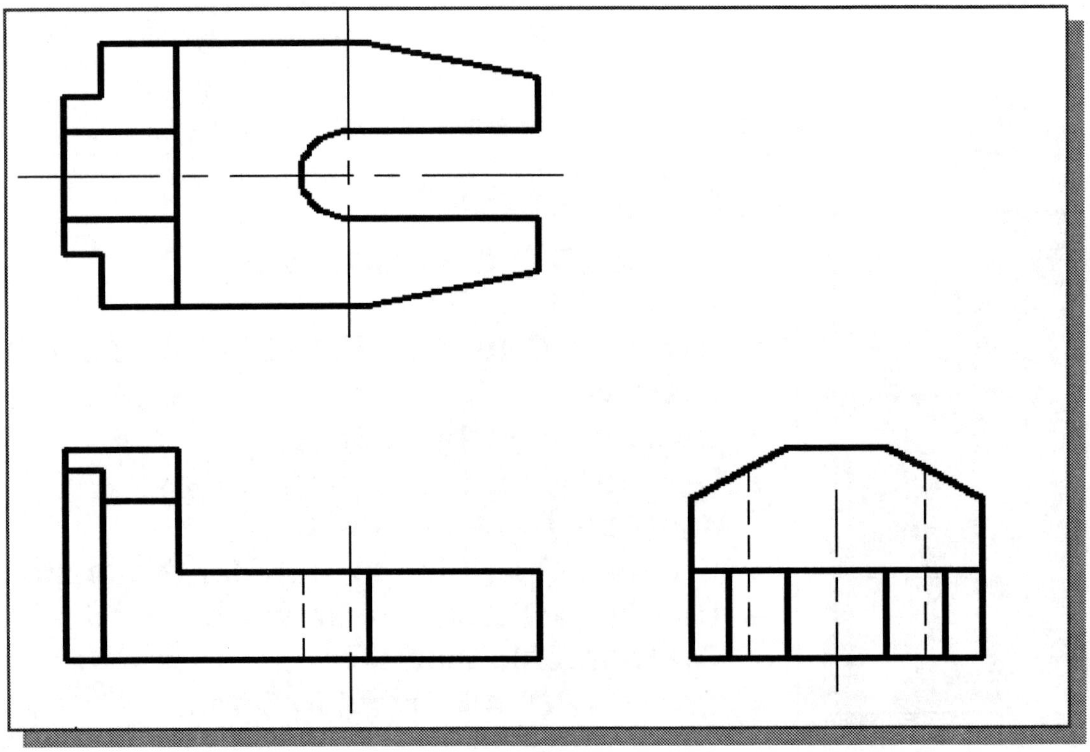

The *Locator* Part

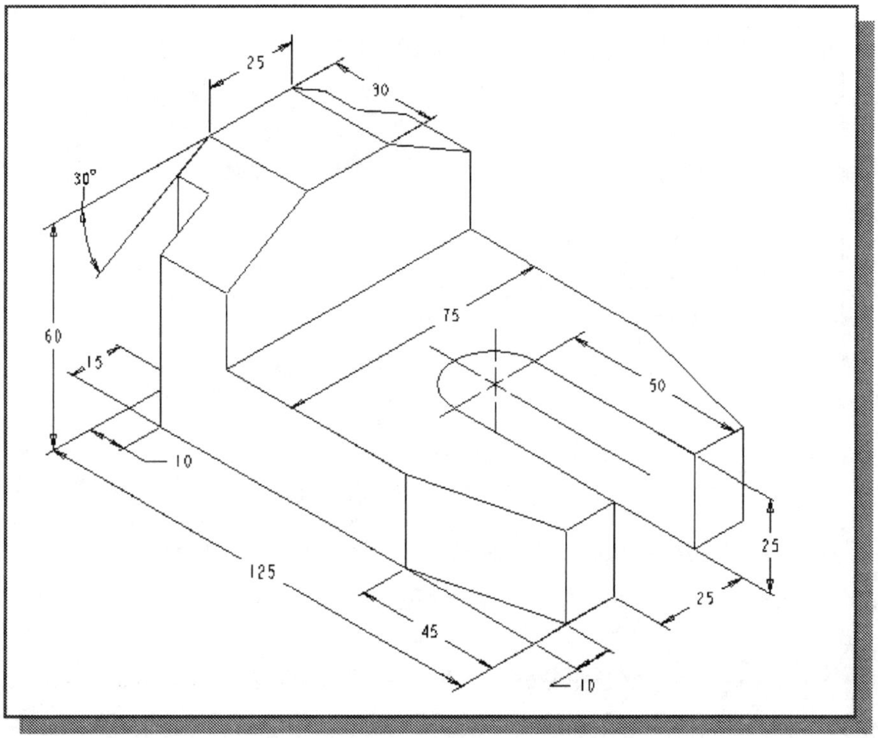

➢ Before going through the tutorial, make a rough sketch of a multiview drawing of the part. How many 2D views will be necessary to fully describe the part? Based on your knowledge of **AutoCAD® LT 2005** so far, how would you arrange and construct these 2D views? Take a few minutes to consider these questions and do the preliminary planning by sketching on a piece of paper. You are also encouraged to construct the orthographic views on your own prior to following through the tutorial.

Starting Up *AutoCAD LT 2005*

1. Select the **AutoCAD LT 2005** option on the *Program* menu or select the **AutoCAD LT 2005** icon on the *Desktop*. Once the program is loaded into the memory, the *AutoCAD LT 2005* drawing screen will appear on the screen.

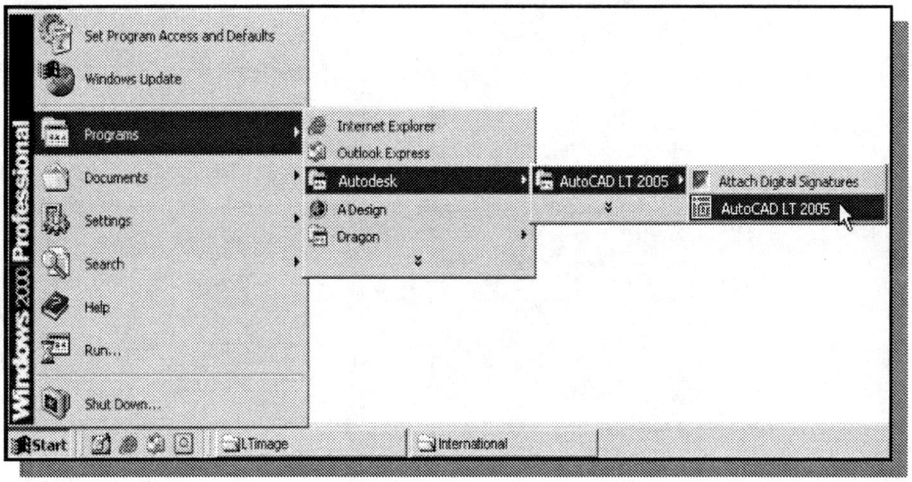

2. In the *Startup* dialog box, select the ***Start from Scratch*** option with a single click of the left-mouse-button.

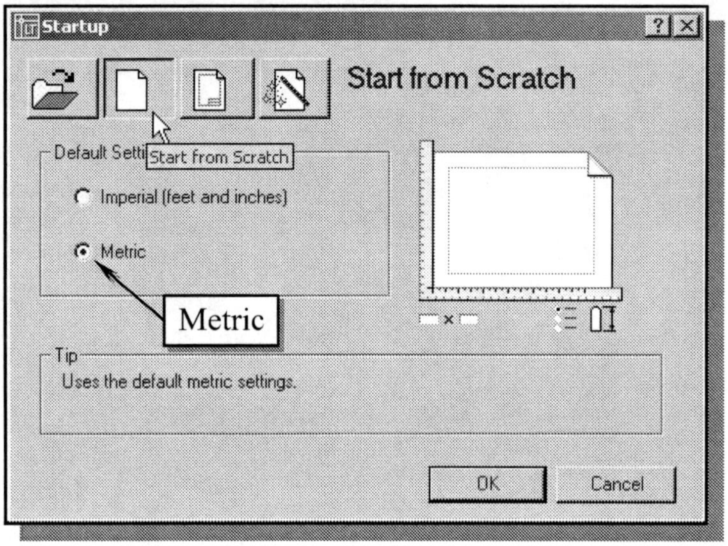

3. In the *Default Settings* section, pick **Metric** as the drawing units.

4. Click **OK** to accept the settings and exit the *Startup* window.

GRID and *SNAP* Intervals Setup

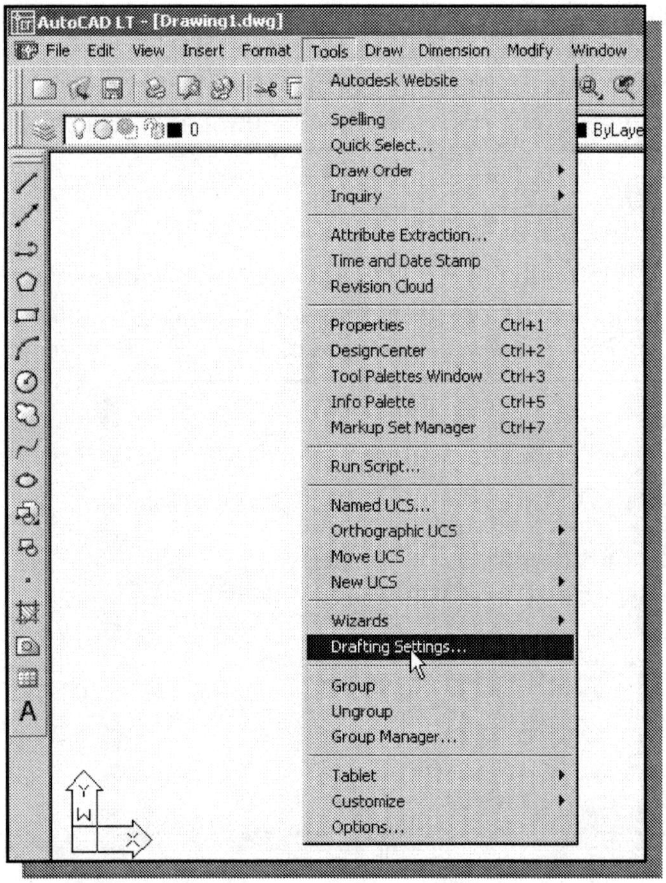

1. In the pull-down menus, select **[Tools] → [Drafting Settings]**

2. In the *Drafting Settings* dialog box, select the **SNAP and GRID** tab if it is not the page on top.

3. Change *Grid Spacing* to **10** for both X and Y directions.

4. Also adjust the *Snap Spacing* to **10** for both X and Y directions.

5. Pick **OK** to exit the *Drafting Settings* dialog box.

Layers Setup

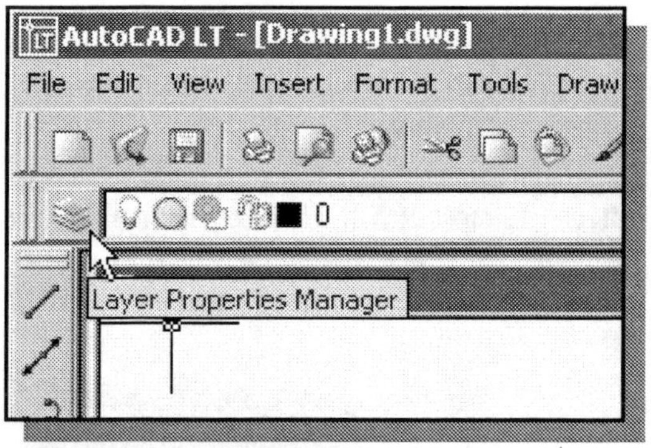

1. Pick **Layers Properties Manager** in the *Object Properties* toolbar.

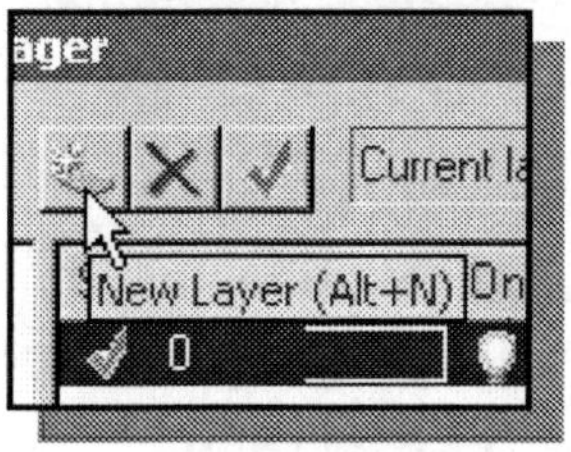

2. Click on the **New** button to create new layers.

3. Create **two new layers** with the following settings:

Layer	***Color***	***LineType***
Construction	**White**	**Continuous**
Object	**Cyan**	**Continuous**

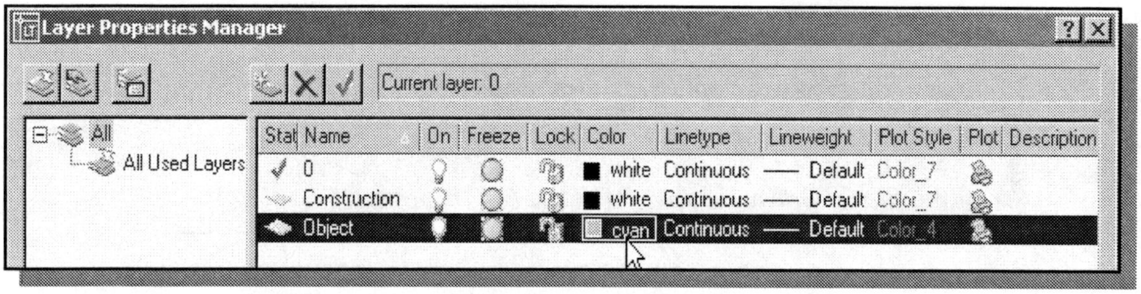

4. Select the layer ***Construction*** in the list of layers.

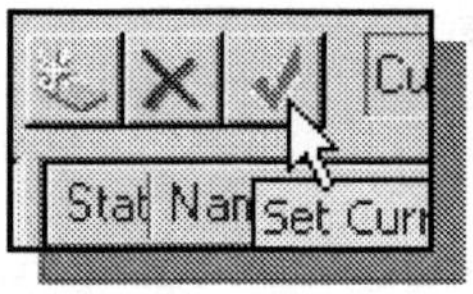

5. Click on the **Current** button to set layer ***Construction*** as the *Current Layer*.

6. Click on the **OK** button to accept the settings and exit the *Layer Properties Manager* dialog box.

7. In the *Status Bar* area, reset the option buttons so that only *SNAP, GRID*, and *MODEL* are switched ***ON***.

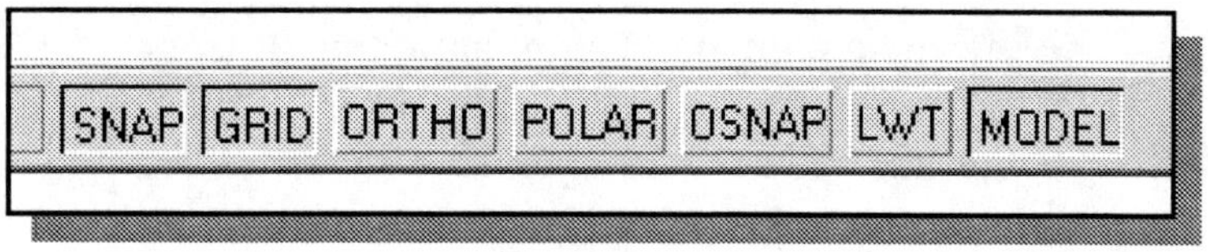

Drawing *Construction Lines*

Construction lines are lines that extend to infinity. Construction lines are usually used as references for creating other objects. We will also place the construction lines on the *Construction* layer so that the layer can later be frozen or turned off.

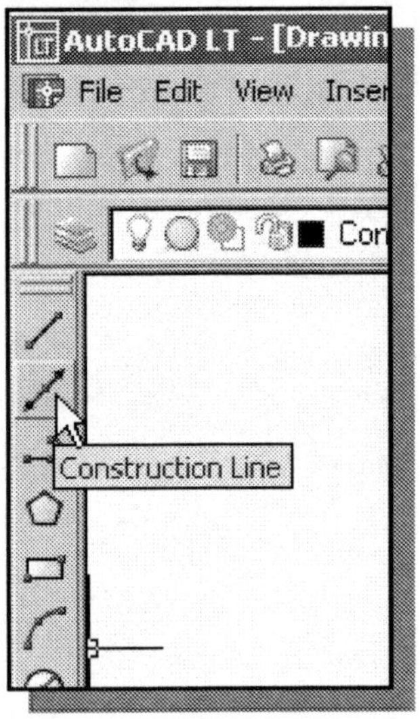

1. Select the **Construction Line** icon in the *Draw* toolbar. In the command prompt area, the message *"_xline Specify a point or [Hor/Ver/Ang/Bisect/Offset]:"* is displayed.

➢ To orient construction lines, we generally specify two points, though other orientation options are also available.

2. Select a location near the lower left corner of the graphics window. It is not necessary to align objects to the world coordinate origin. CAD systems provide us with many powerful tools to manipulate geometry. Our main goal is to use CAD systems as flexible and powerful tools, and to be very efficient and effective with the systems.

3. Pick a location above the last point to create a **vertical line**.

4. Move the cursor toward the right of the first point and pick a location to create a **horizontal line**.

5. Inside the graphics window, **right-mouse-click** to end the Construction Line command.

6. In the *Status Bar* area, turn ***OFF*** the *SNAP* option.

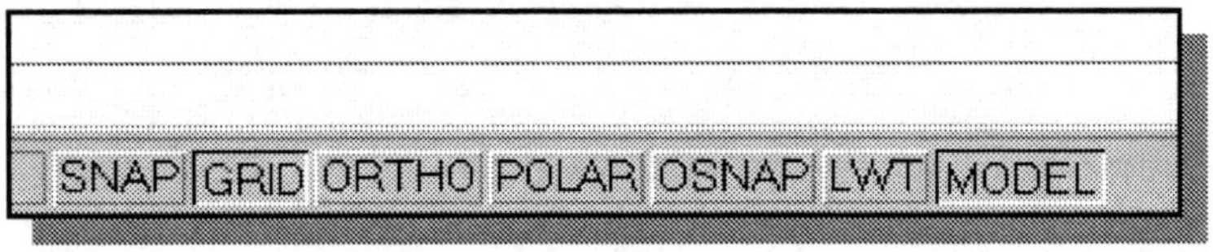

Using the *Offset* Command

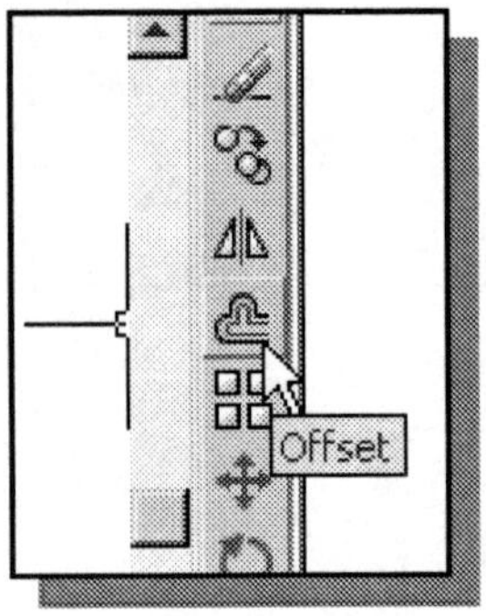

1. Select the **Offset** icon in the *Modify* toolbar. In the command prompt area, the message *"Specify offset distance or [Through]:"* is displayed.

2. In the command prompt area, enter **125 [ENTER]**

3. In the command prompt area, the message *"Select object to offset or <exit>:"* is displayed. Pick the **vertical line** on the screen.

4. AutoCAD LT next asks us to identify the direction of the offset. Pick a location that is to the **right** of the vertical line.

5. Inside the graphics window, **right-mouse-click** to end the Offset command.

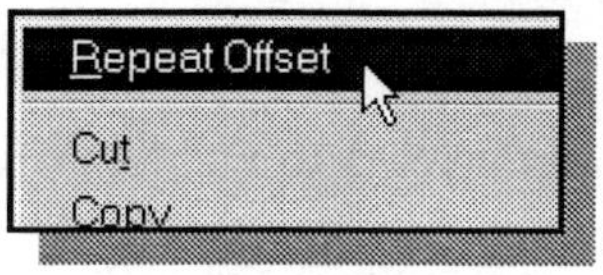

6. Hit the **[SPACE BAR]**, or **right-mouse-click** inside the graphics window and select **Repeat Offset** in the popup list, to repeat the Offset command.

7. In the command prompt area, enter **60 [ENTER]**

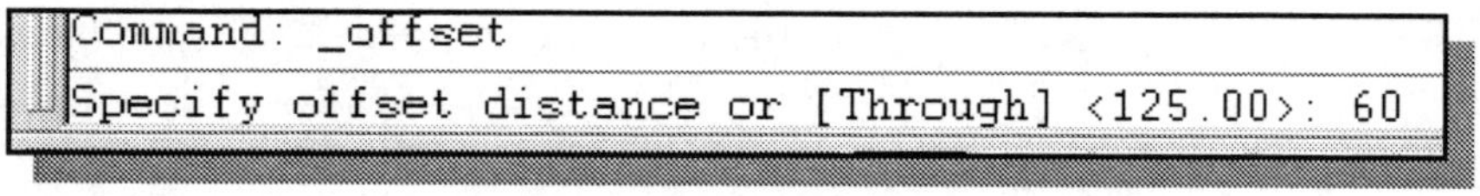

8. In the command prompt area, the message *"Select object to offset or <exit>:"* is displayed. Pick the **horizontal line** on the screen.

9. AutoCAD LT next asks us to identify the direction of the offset. Pick a location that is **above** the horizontal line.

10. Inside the graphics window, right-mouse-click to end the Offset command.

11. Repeat the **Offset** command and create the lines as shown.

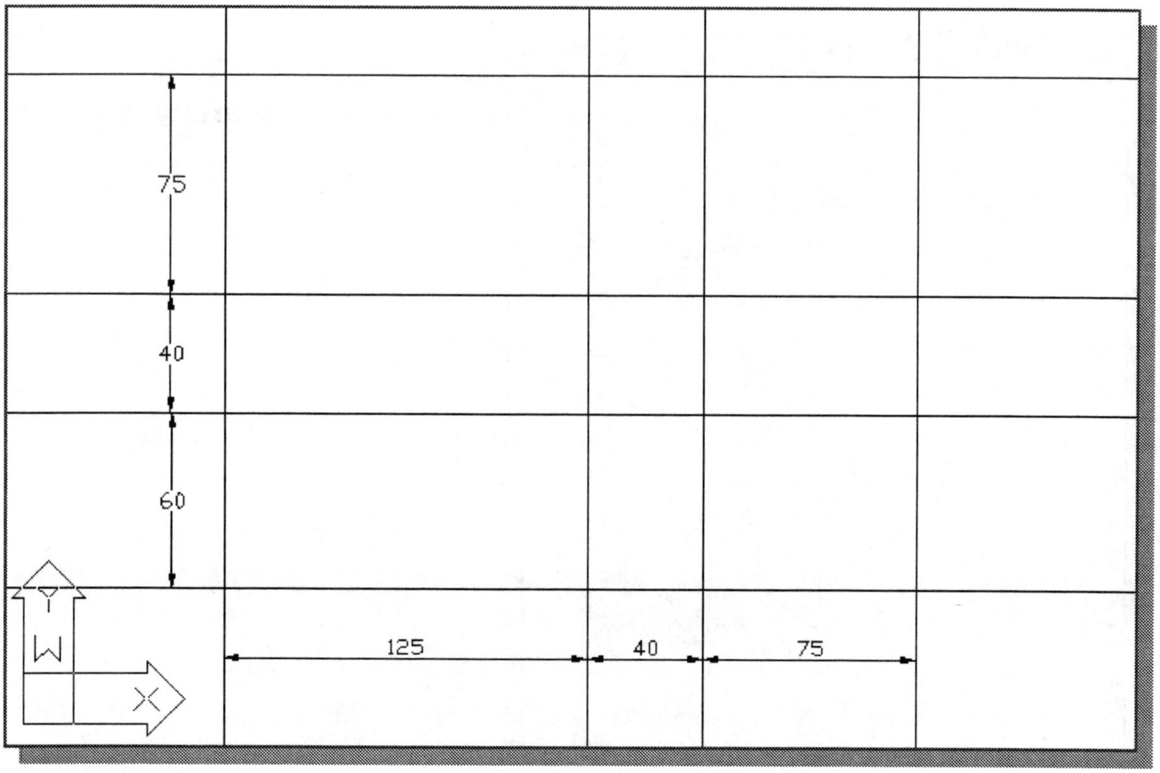

Set Layer *Object* as the Current Layer

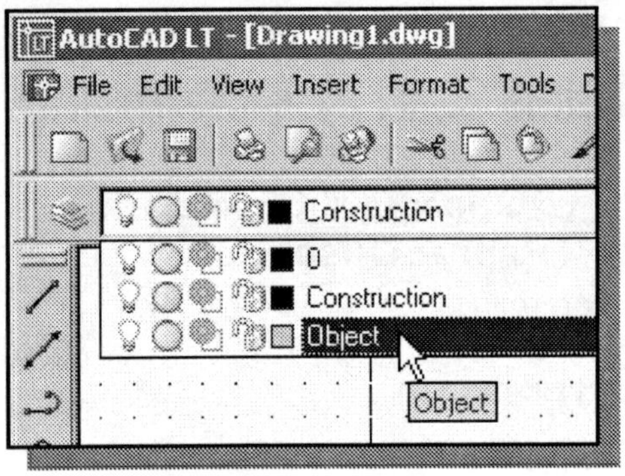

1. On the *Object Properties* toolbar, choose the **Layer Control** box with the left-mouse-button.

2. Move the cursor over the name of the layer ***Object***. The tool tip *"Object"* appears.

3. **Left-mouse-click once** on the *Object* layer name to set the layer as the *Current Layer*.

Using the *Running Object Snaps*

In **AutoCAD® LT 2005**, while using geometry construction commands, we can snap the cursor to points on objects such as endpoints, midpoints, centers, and intersections. In AutoCAD LT, this tool is called the ***Object Snap***.

We can turn on *object snaps* in one of two ways:

- **Single Point (or override) Object Snaps**: Sets an object snap for one use.
- **Running Object Snaps**: Sets Object Snaps *active* until we turn them off.

The procedure we have used so far is the *Single Point Object Snaps* option, where we select the specific object snap, from the *Object Snap* toolbar, for one use only. We will next demonstrate using the *Running Object Snaps* to assist our construction.

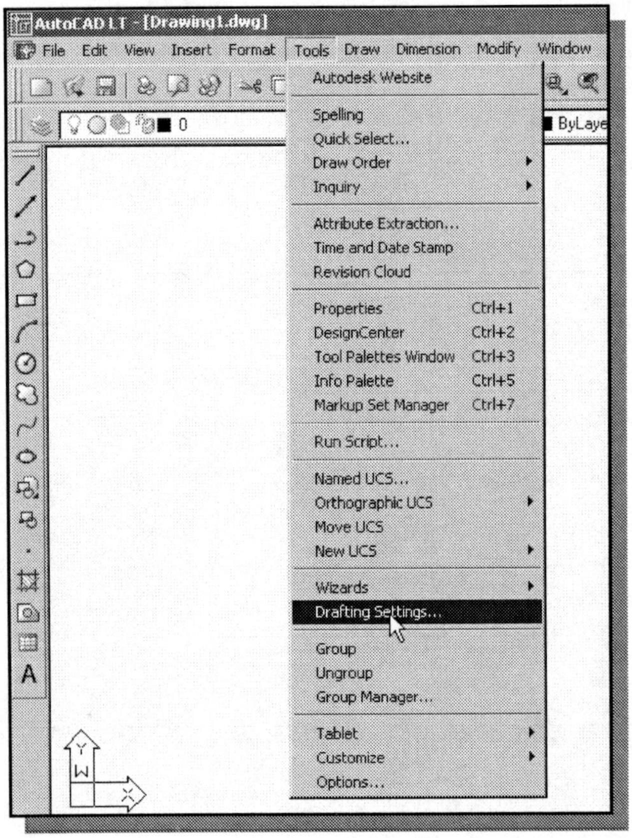

1. In the pull-down menus, select **[Tools] → [Drafting Settings]**

2. In the *Drafting Settings* dialog box, select the **Object Snap** tab.

➢ The *Running Object Snap* options can be turned on or off by clicking the different options listed. Notice the different symbols for the different *Object Snap* options, especially the *Intersection* option.

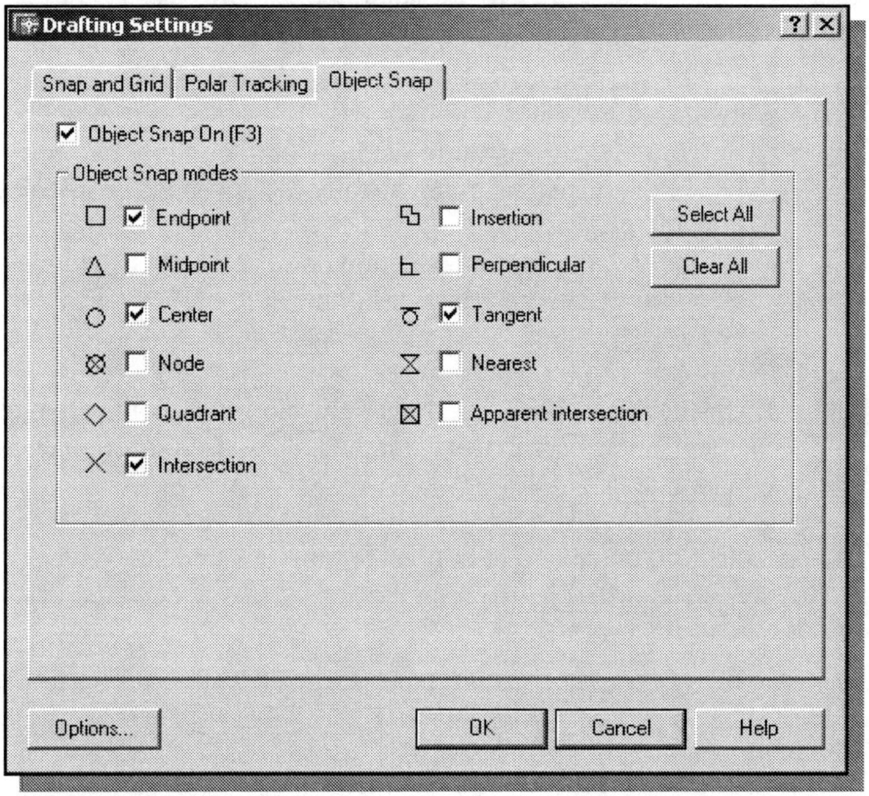

3. Turn ***ON*** the *Running Object Snap* by clicking the ***Object Snap On*** box, or hit the **[F3]** key once.

4. Turn ***ON*** the ***Intersection, Endpoint, Center*** and ***Tangent*** options and click on the **OK** button to accept the settings and exit from the *Drafting Settings* dialog box.

➢ Notice in the *Status Bar* area, the ***OSNAP*** button is switched ***ON***. We can toggle the *Running Object Snap* option on or off by clicking the *OSNAP* button.

5. Press the **[F3]** key once and notice the *OSNAP* button is switched ***OFF*** in the *Status Bar* area.

6. Press the **[F3]** key again and notice the *OSNAP* button is now switched ***ON*** in the *Status Bar* area.

❖ **AutoCAD® LT 2005** provides many input methods and shortcuts; examine the different options and choose the option that best fit your own style.

Creating *Object Lines*

We will define the areas for the front view, top view and side view by adding object lines using the *Running Object Snap* option.

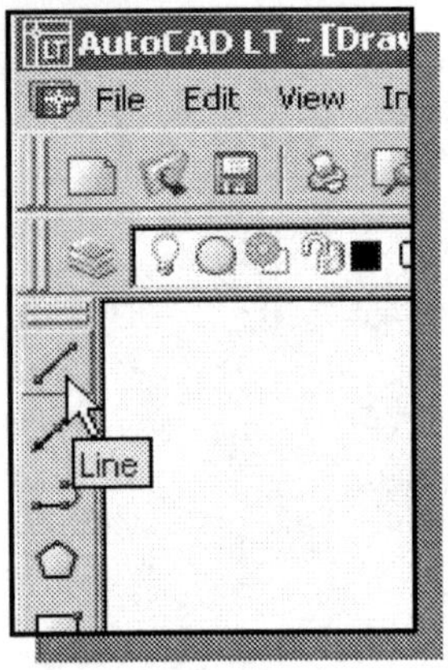

1. Select the **Line** command icon in the *Draw* toolbar. In the command prompt area, the message *"_line Specify first point:"* is displayed.

2. Move the cursor to the intersection of any two lines and notice the visual aid automatically displayed at the intersection.

3. Pick the four intersection points closest to the lower left corner to create the four sides of the area of the front view.

4. Inside the graphics window, right-mouse-click to activate the option menu and select **Enter** with the left-mouse-button to end the Line command.

5. Repeat the Line command to define the top-view and side-view as shown.

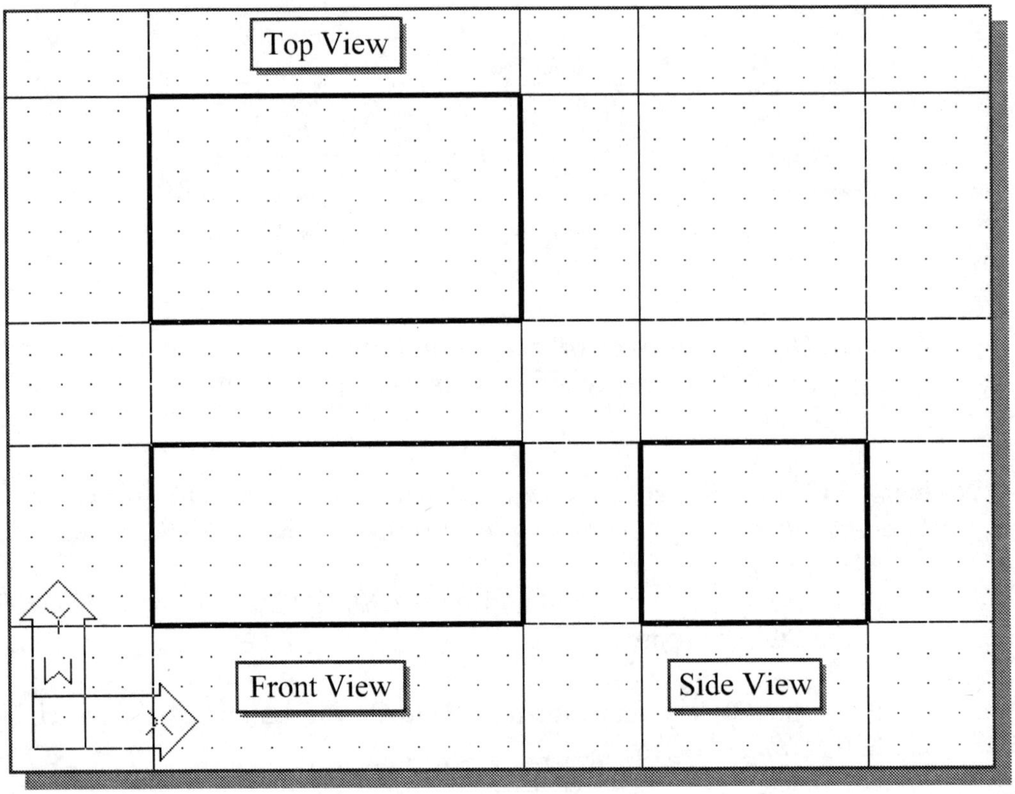

Turn *OFF* the Construction Lines

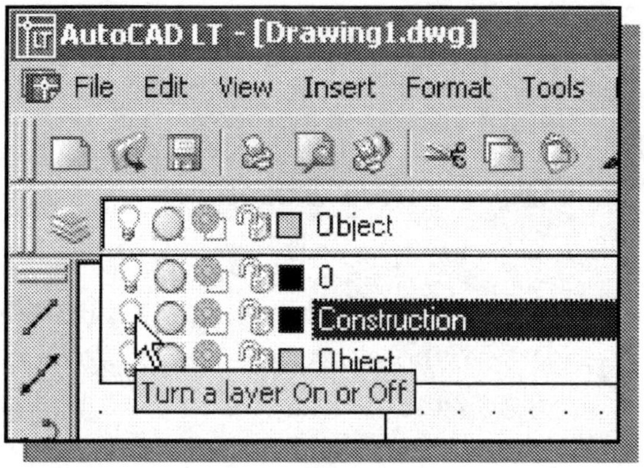

1. On the *Object Properties* toolbar, choose the ***Layer Control*** box with the left-mouse-button.

2. Move the cursor over the light-bulb icon for layer *Construction*. The tool tip *"Turn a layer On or Off"* appears.

3. **Left-mouse-click once** and notice the icon color is changed to gray color, representing the layer is turned *OFF*.

Adding More Objects in the Front View

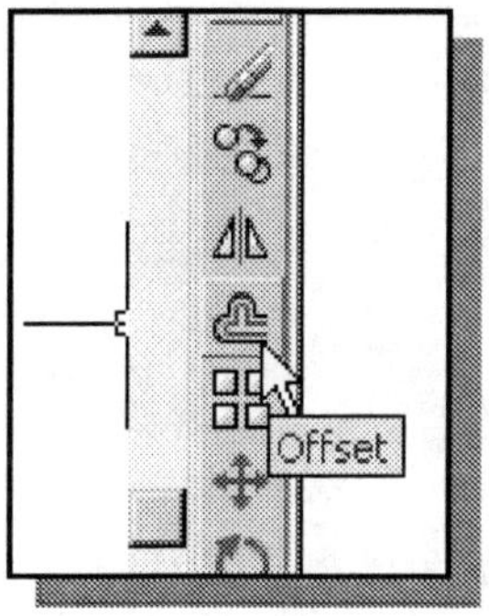

1. Use the **Offset** command and create the two parallel lines in the front view as shown.

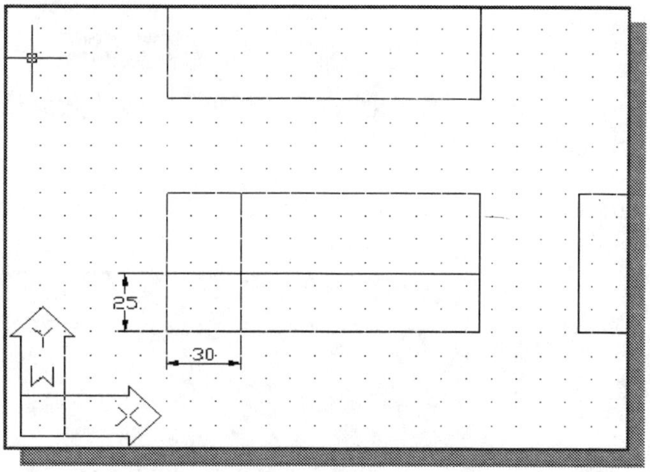

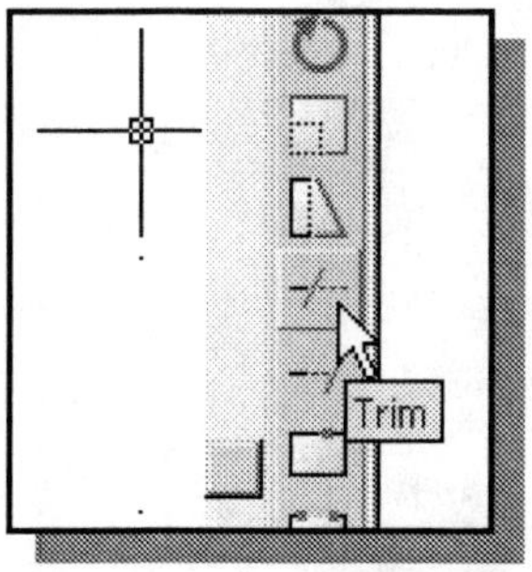

2. Use the **Trim** command and modify the front view as shown.

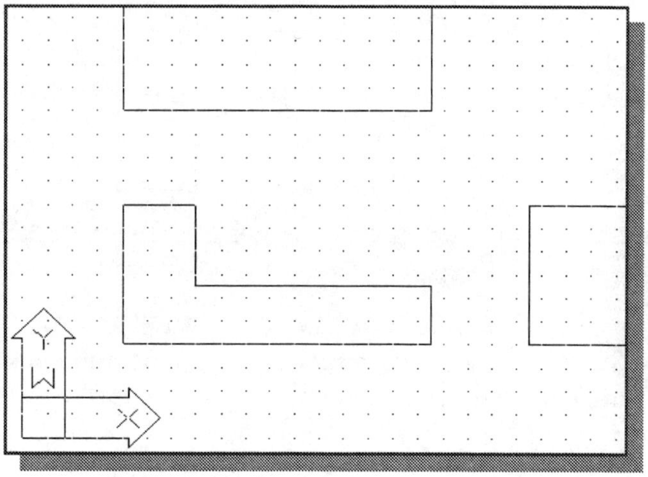

The *AutoSnap*™ and *AutoTrack*™ Features

AutoCAD's AutoSnap and *AutoTrack* provide visual aids when we are using *Object Snap*. The main advantages of *AutoSnap* and *AutoTrack* are as follows:

- **Symbols**: Automatically displays the *Object Snap* type at the object snap location.
- **Tooltips**: Automatically displays the *Object Snap* type below the cursor.
- **Magnet**: Locks the cursor onto a snap point when the cursor is near the point.

The **Polar** option button, displayed at the bottom of the screen, can be used to control the **polar tracking** and **polar snap** options that are part of the *AutoSnap* and *AutoTrack* features. With **polar tracking** and **polar snap,** the cursor can track along alignment paths based on the polar angle settings relative to the selected point in a command.

1. In the *Status Bar* area, turn ***ON*** the ***POLAR*** option.

2. In the *Status Bar* area, move the cursor on top of ***POLAR*** option and right mouse-click to bring up the option menu.

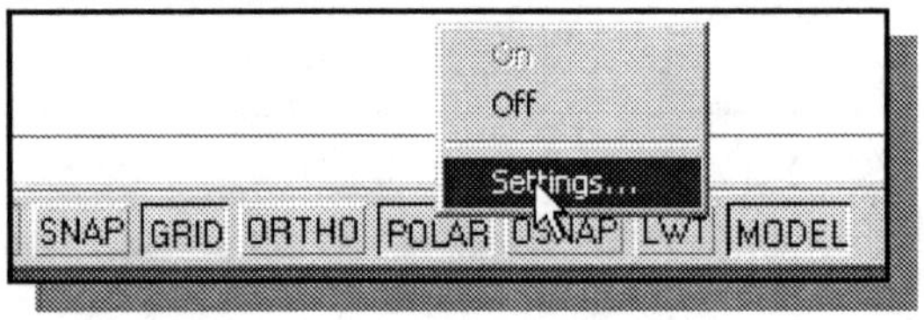

3. Select **Settings** in the popup menu.

4. In the *Drafting Settings – Polar Tracking* dialog box, select **30** as the increment angle as shown.

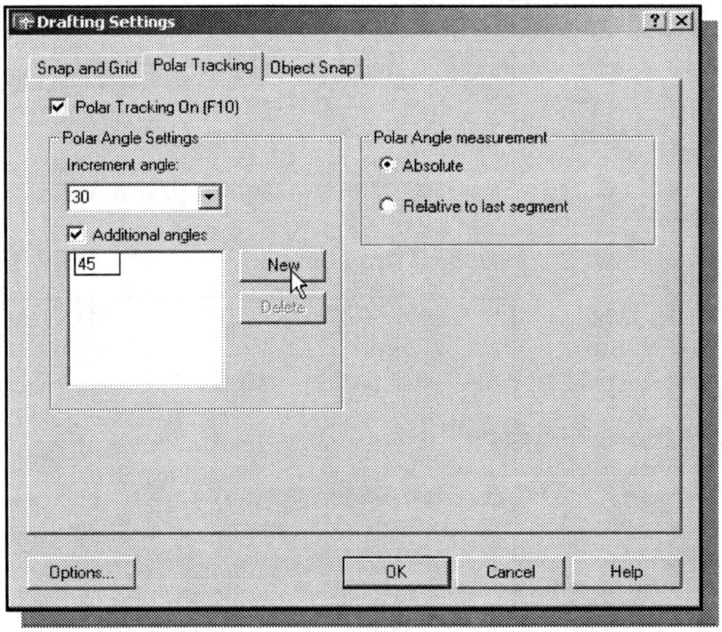

5. Switch on the ***Additional Angles*** option and click on the **New** button to also track **45** degrees as shown.

6. Click on the **OK** button to accept the settings.

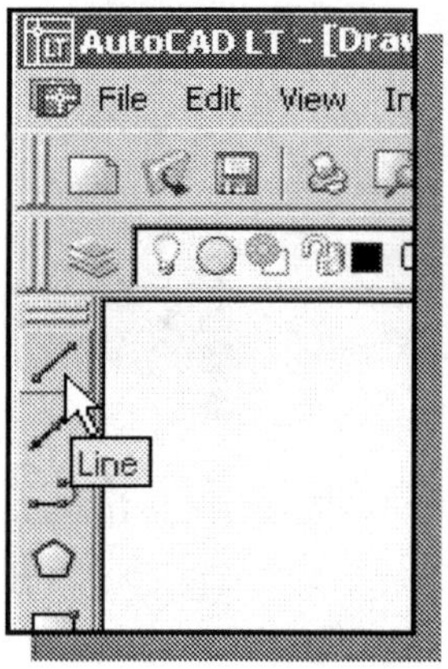

7. Select the **Line** command icon in the *Draw* toolbar. In the command prompt area, the message *"_line Specify first point:"* is displayed.

8. Move the cursor near the top right corner of the vertical protrusion in the front view. Notice that *AutoSnap* automatically locks the cursor to the corner and displays the **Endpoint** symbol. Left click once to select the corner as the starting point of a line.

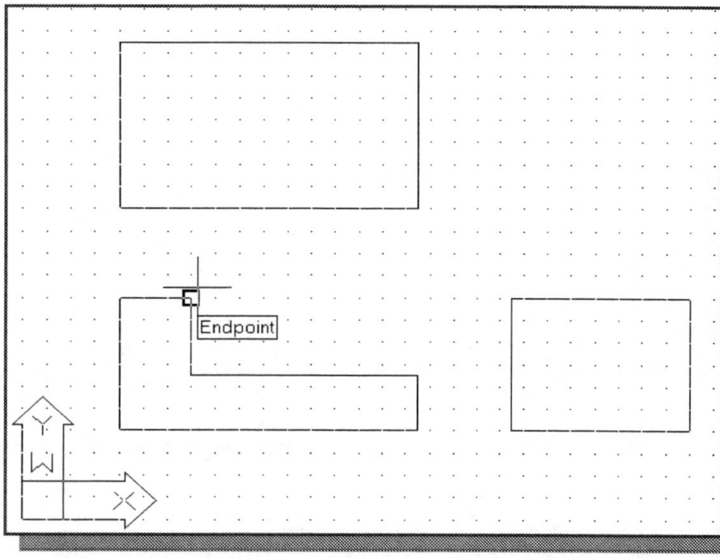

9. Move the cursor upward and notice the *polar tracking* displays a dashed line, showing the alignment to the top right corner of the vertical protrusion in the front view. Move the cursor near the top horizontal line of the top view and notice that *PolarSnap* displays the intersection point. Left-mouse-click once to create a line to the intersection point.

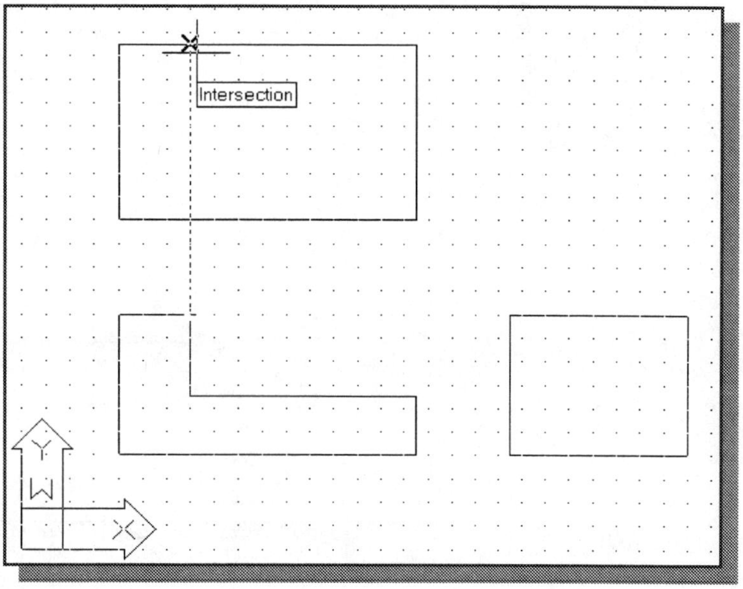

10. Inside the graphics window, right-mouse-click to activate the option menu and select **Enter** with the left-mouse-button to end the **Line** command.

11. On your own, use the **Trim** command and modify the line as shown below.

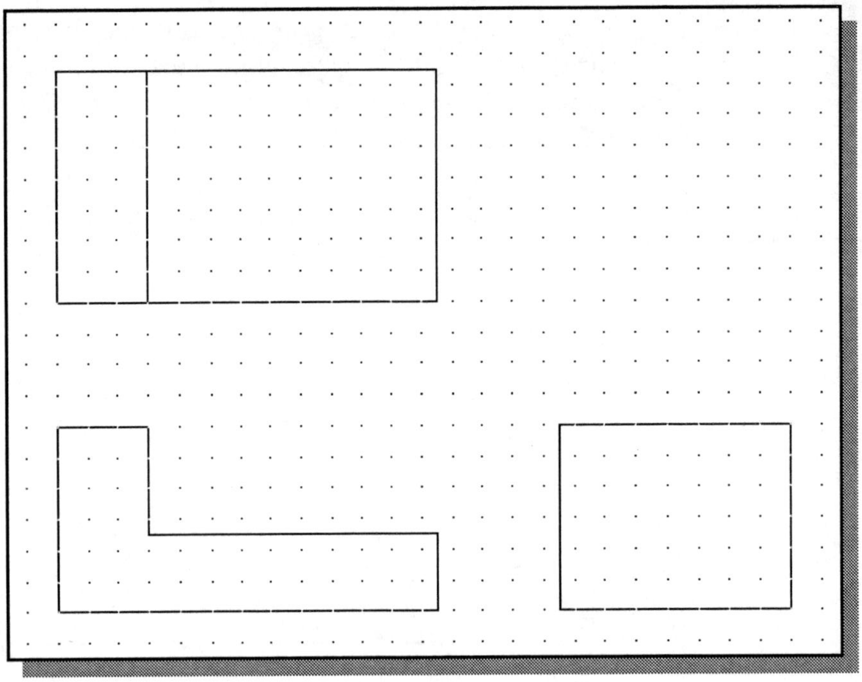

Adding More Objects in the Top View

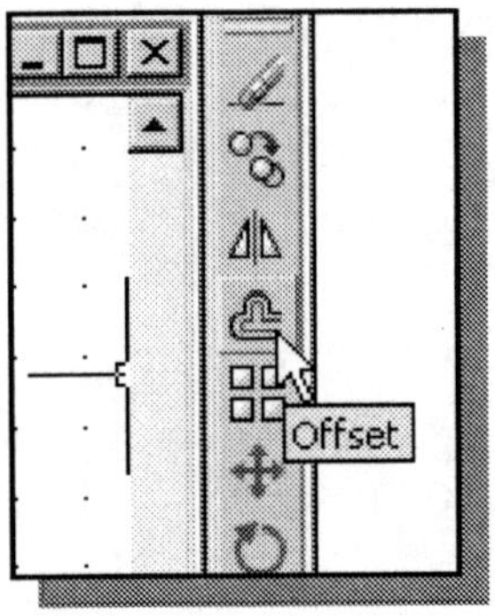

1. Use the **Offset** command and create the two parallel lines in the top view as shown.

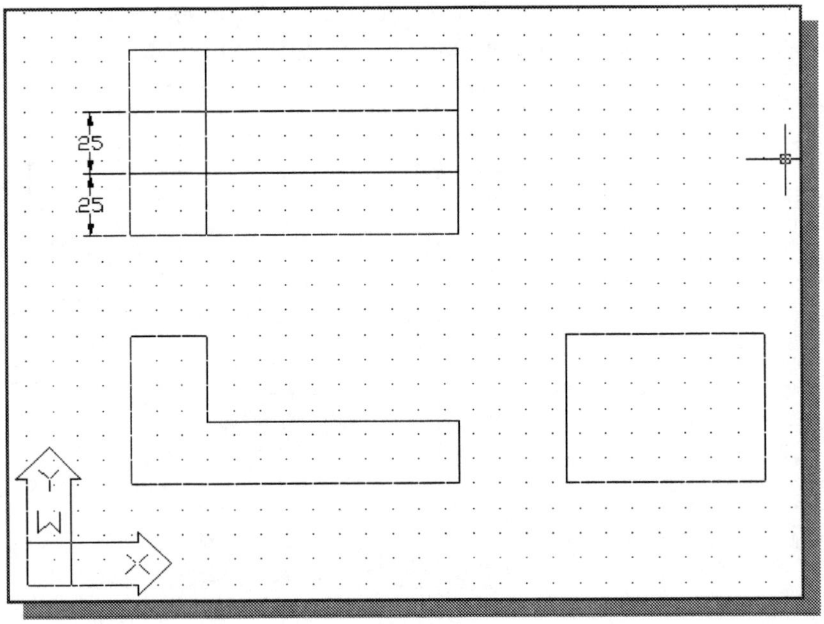

2. Move the cursor to the *Standard* toolbar area and **right-mouse-click** on any icon to display a list of toolbar menu groups.

3. Select **Object Snap**, with the left-mouse-button, to display the *Object Snap* toolbar on the screen.

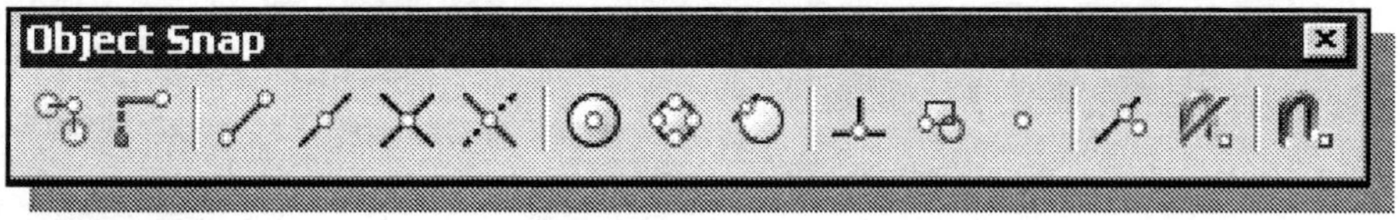

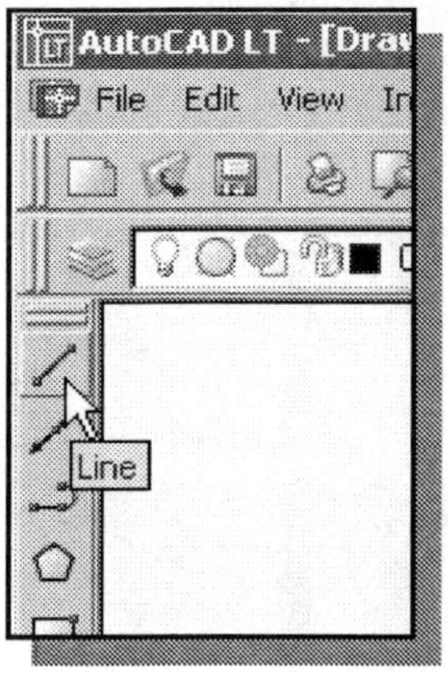

4. Select the **Line** command icon in the *Draw* toolbar. In the command prompt area, the message *"_line Specify first point:"* is displayed.

5. In the *Object Snap* toolbar, pick **Snap From**. In the command prompt area, the message *"_from Base point"* is displayed. AutoCAD LT now expects us to select a geometric entity on the screen.

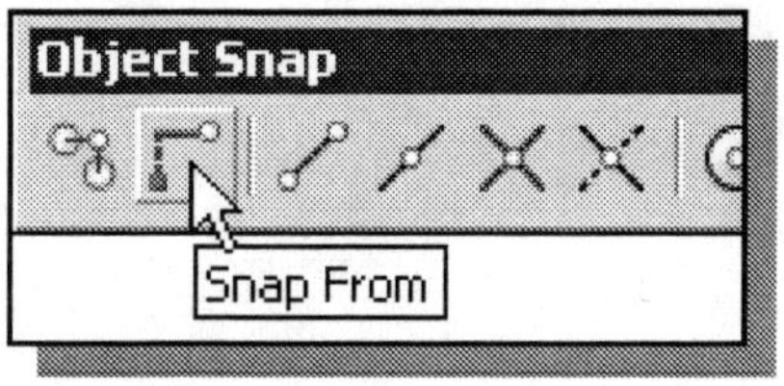

➢ The ***Single Point* (or override) *Object Snap*** overrides the ***Running Object Snap*** option**.**

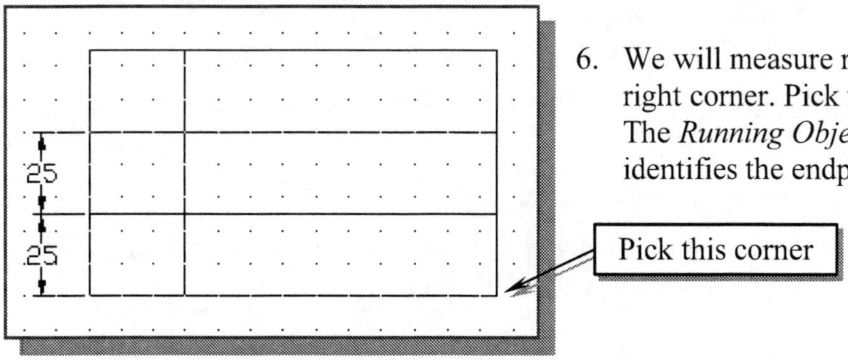

6. We will measure relative to the lower right corner. Pick the corner as shown. The *Running Object Snap* automatically identifies the endpoint as specified.

7. In the command prompt area, enter **@0,10 [ENTER]**

8. In the *Object Snap* toolbar, pick **Snap From.** Pick the lower right corner of the top view again.

9. In the command prompt area, enter **@-45,0 [ENTER]**

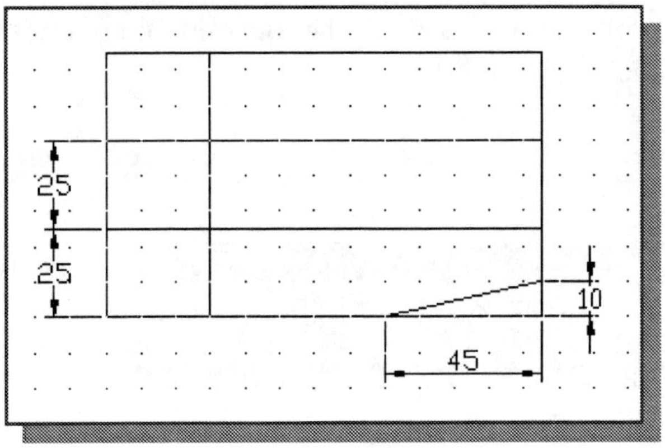

10. Inside the graphics window, right-mouse-click to activate the option menu and select **Enter** with the left-mouse-button to end the **Line** command.

11. Repeat the procedure and create another inclined line and a circle (diameter **25mm**) as shown.

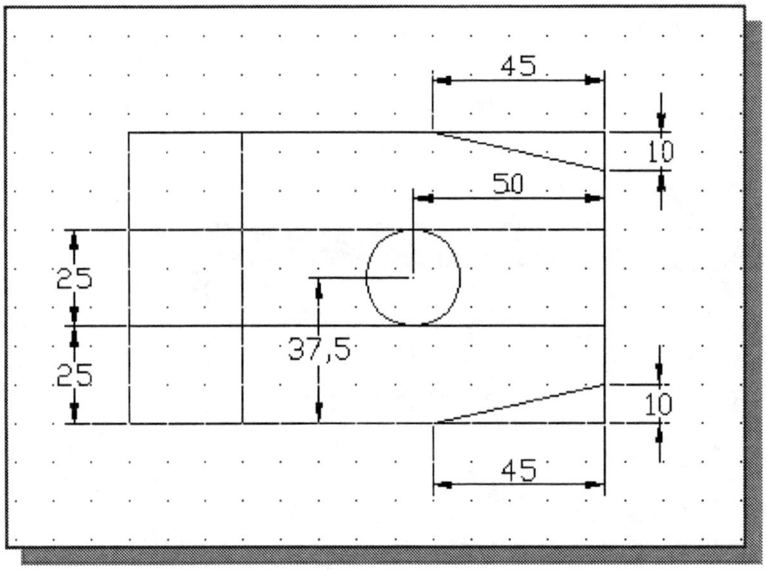

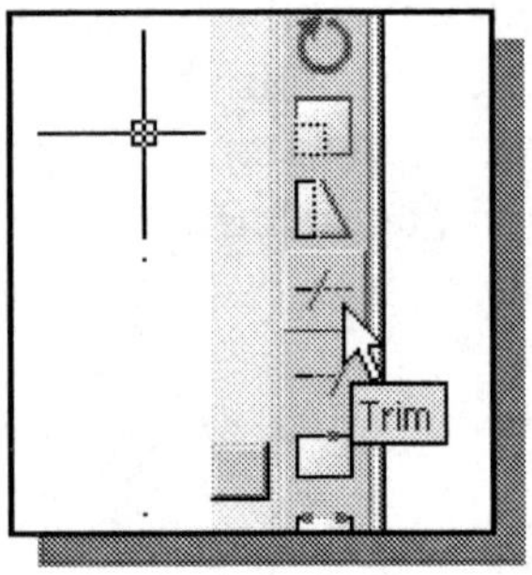

12. Select the **Trim** icon in the *Modify* toolbar. In the command prompt area, the message *"Select boundary edges... Select objects:"* is displayed.

13. Pick the following objects as boundary edges: the circle, and the lines that are near the circle.

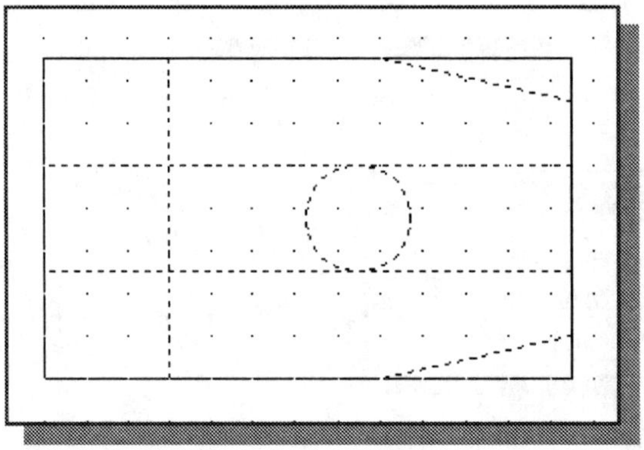

14. Inside the graphics window, **right-mouse-click** to accept the selected objects.

15. Select the unwanted portions and modified the objects as shown.

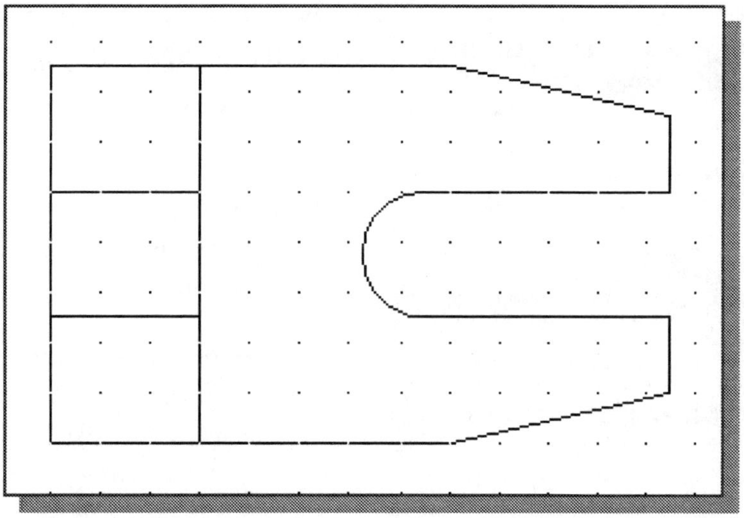

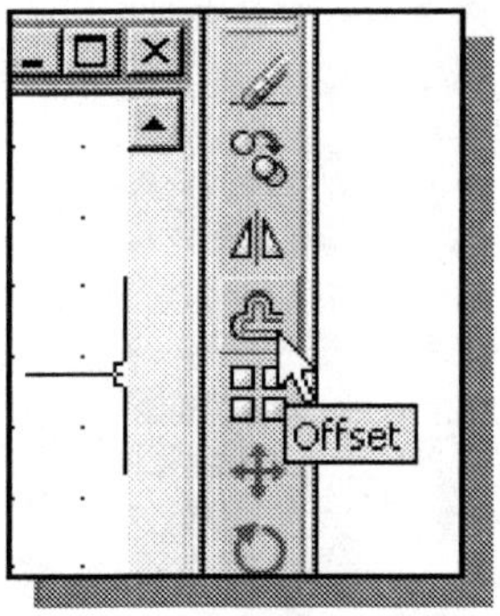

16. On your own, use the **Offset** and **Trim** commands and modify the top view as shown.

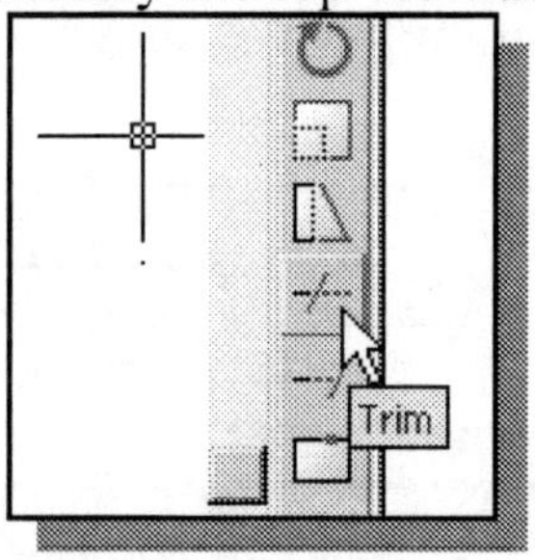

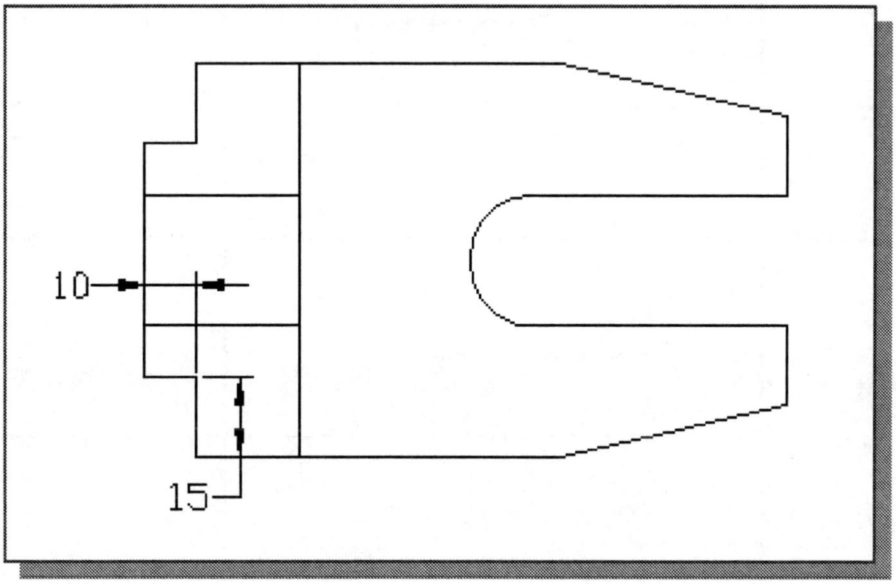

Drawing a *Miter Line*

The *45° miter line* method is a simple and straightforward procedure to transfer measurements in between the top view and the side view.

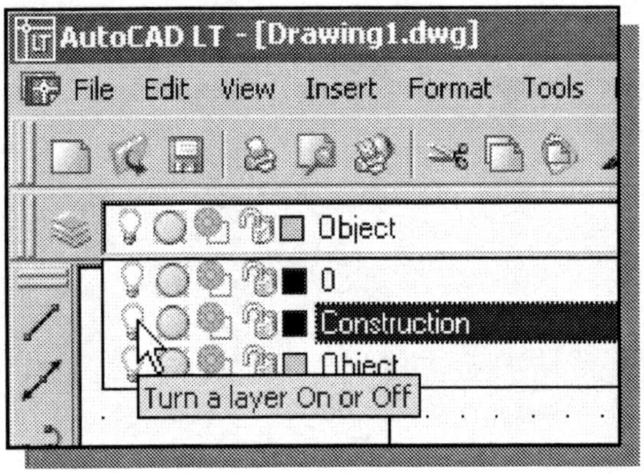

1. On the *Object Properties* toolbar, choose the ***Layer Control*** box with the left-mouse-button.

2. Move the cursor over the light-bulb icon for layer *Construction*. The tool tip *"Turn a layer On or Off"* appears.

3. **Left-mouse-click once** and notice the icon color is changed to a light color, representing the layer is turned *ON*.

4. **Left-mouse-click once** over the name of the layer ***Construction*** to set it as the *Current Layer*.

5. Use the **Line** command and create the *miter line* by connecting the two intersections of the construction lines as shown.

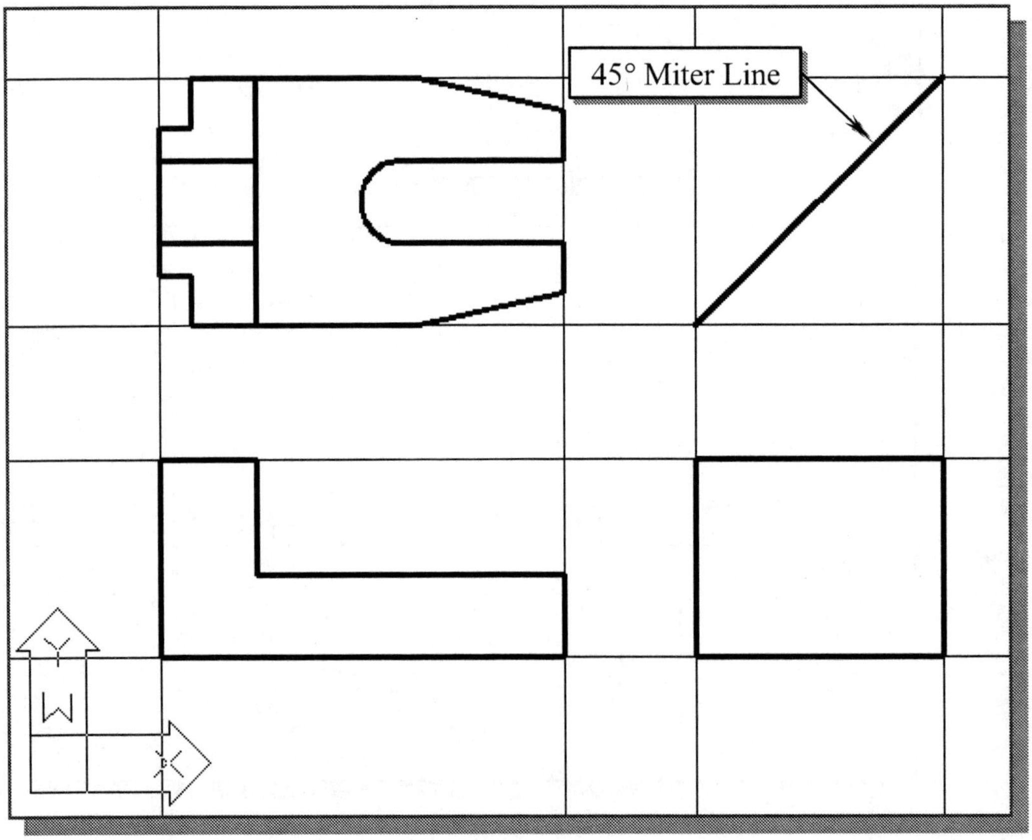

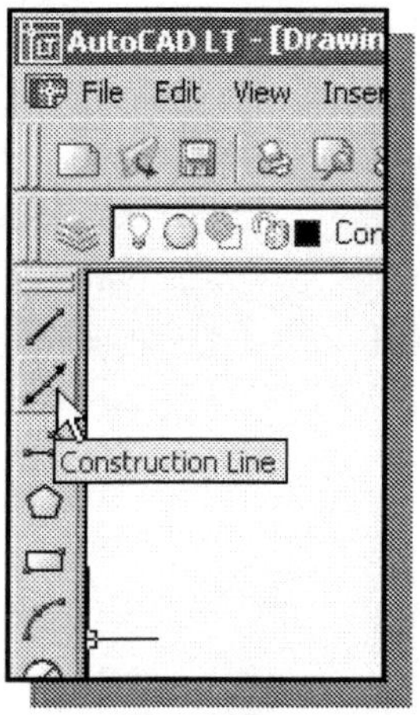

6. Use the **Construction Line** command and create horizontal projection lines (**right-mouse-click** and select the **Horizontal** option) through all the corners in the top view as shown.

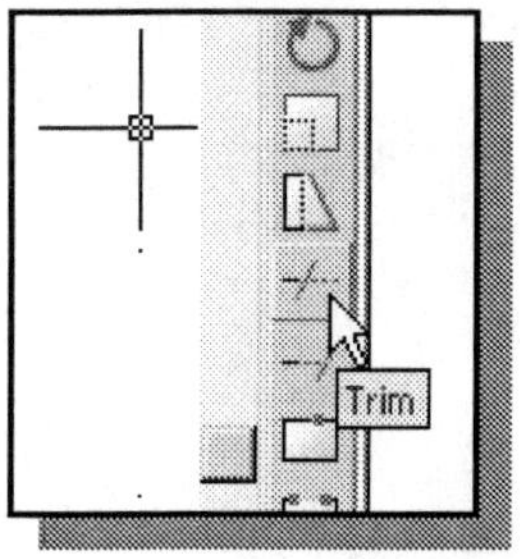

7. Use the **Trim** command and trim the projection lines as shown.

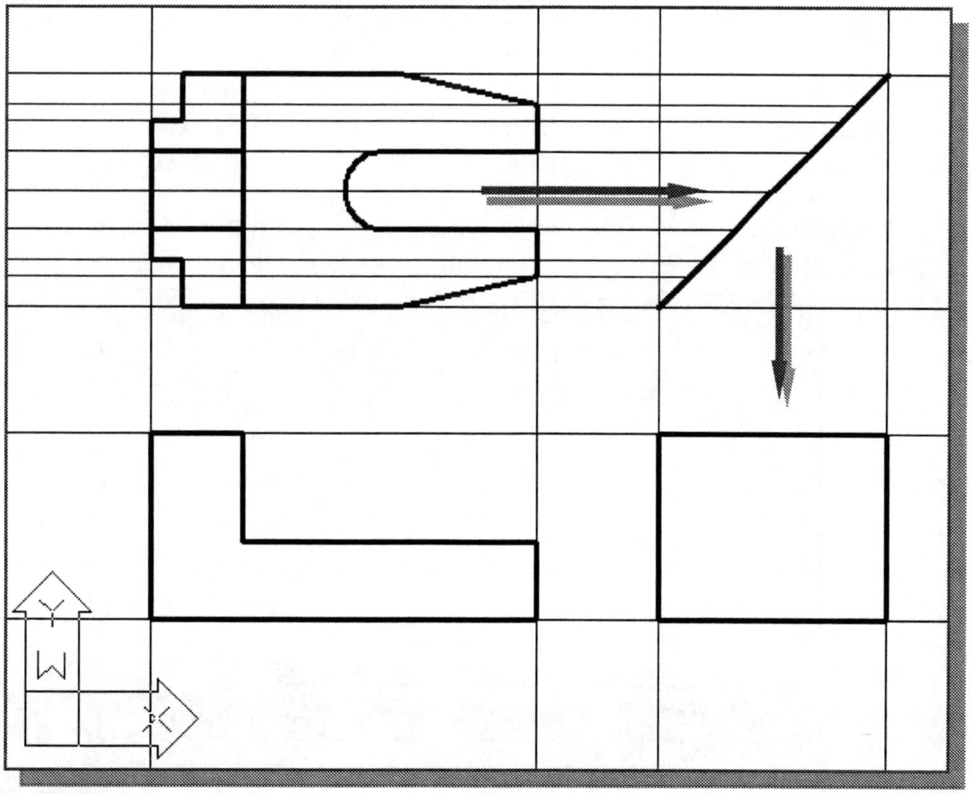

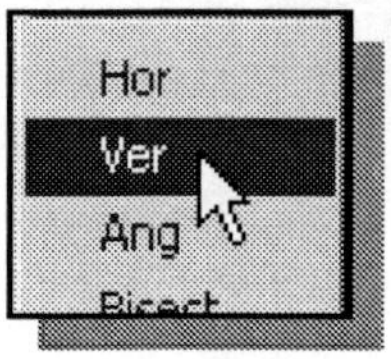

8. On your own, add Vertical Construction Lines (using the *vertical* option) through all the intersection points that are on the miter line.

More Layers Setup

1. Pick **Layers Properties Manager** in the *Object Properties* toolbar.

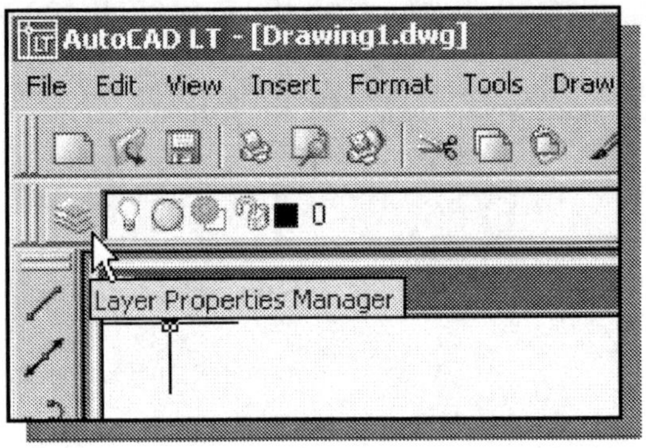

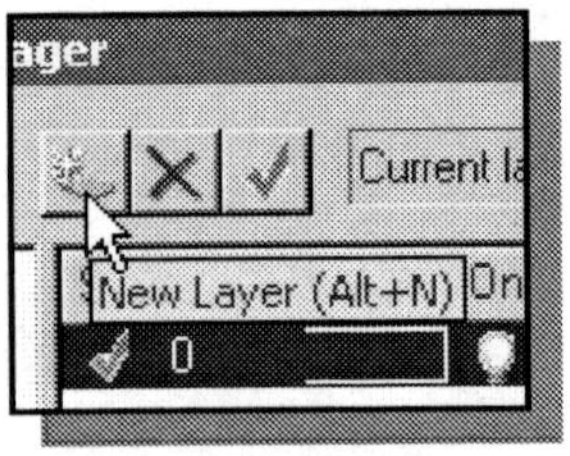

2. Click on the **New** button to create new layers.

3. Create two **new layers** with the following settings:

Layer	***Color***	***LineType***
Hidden	**Blue**	**HIDDEN**
Center	**Red**	**CENTER**

➢ The default linetype is *Continuous.* To use other **linetypes**, click on the **Load** button in the *Select Linetype* dialog box and select the desired linetypes.

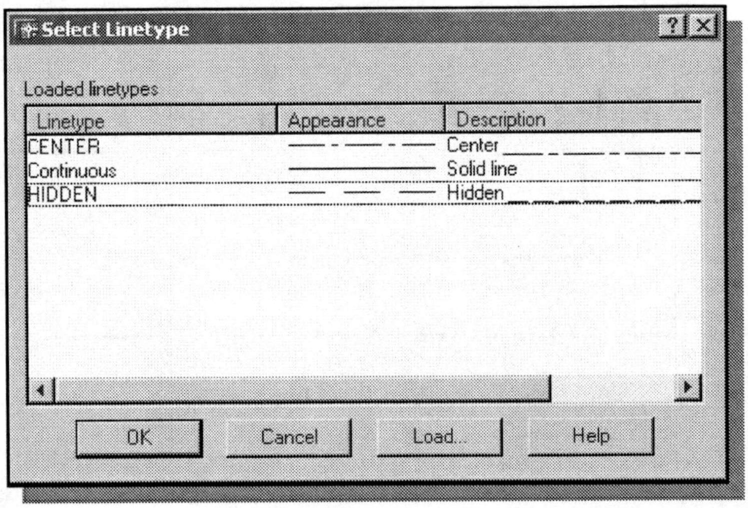

4. On your own, set the layer ***Object*** as the *Current Layer.*

Top View to Side View Projection

1. Using the *Running Object Snaps*, create the necessary **object lines** in the side view.

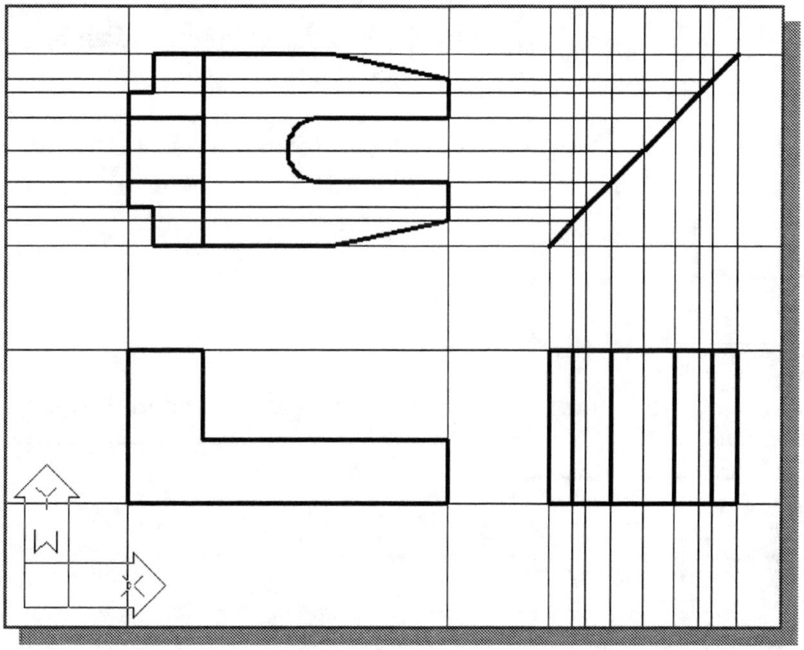

2. Set layer ***Hidden*** as the *Current Layer* and create the two necessary hidden lines in the side view.

3. Set layer ***Center*** as the *Current Layer* and create the necessary centerlines in the side view.

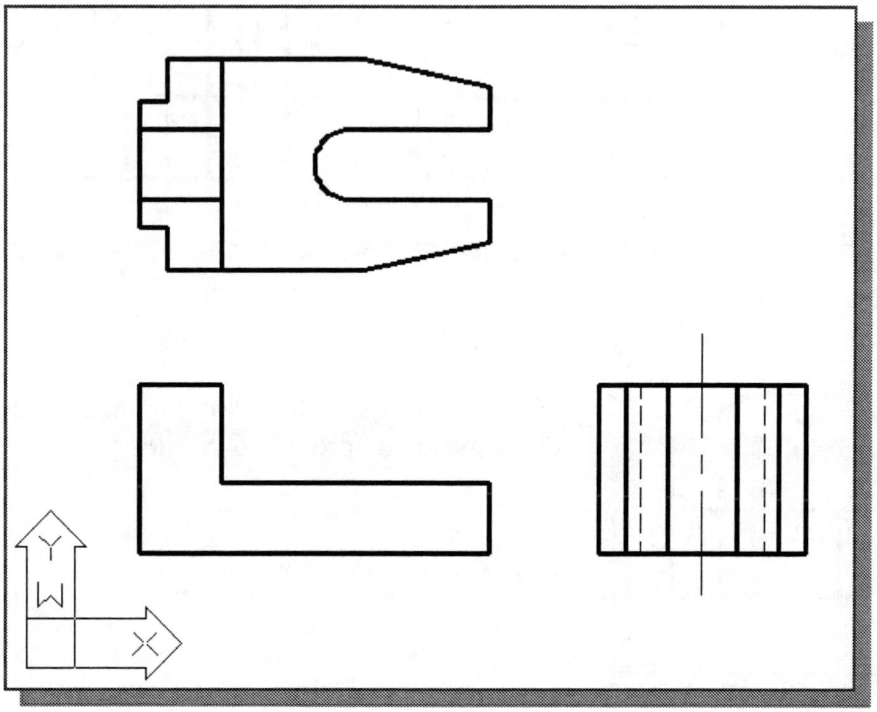

4. In the *Layer Control* box, turn ***OFF*** the construction lines.

5. Set layer ***Object*** as the *Current Layer*.

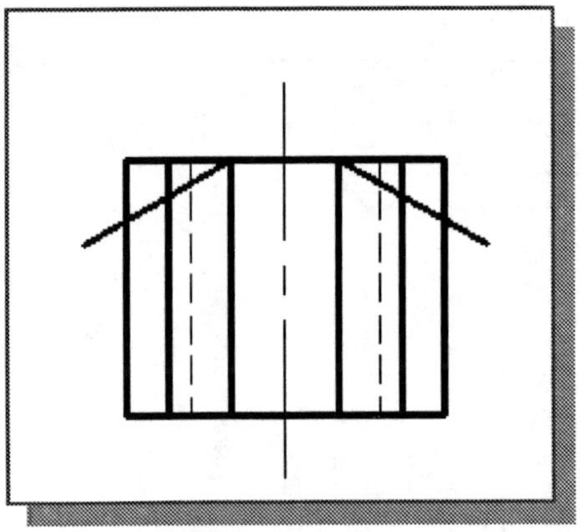

6. Use the **Line** command and create the two 30° inclined lines as shown.

➤ Note that with the *Polar Tracking* option, the inclined lines are constructed very easily and quickly.

7. Use the Line command and create a horizontal line in the side view as shown.

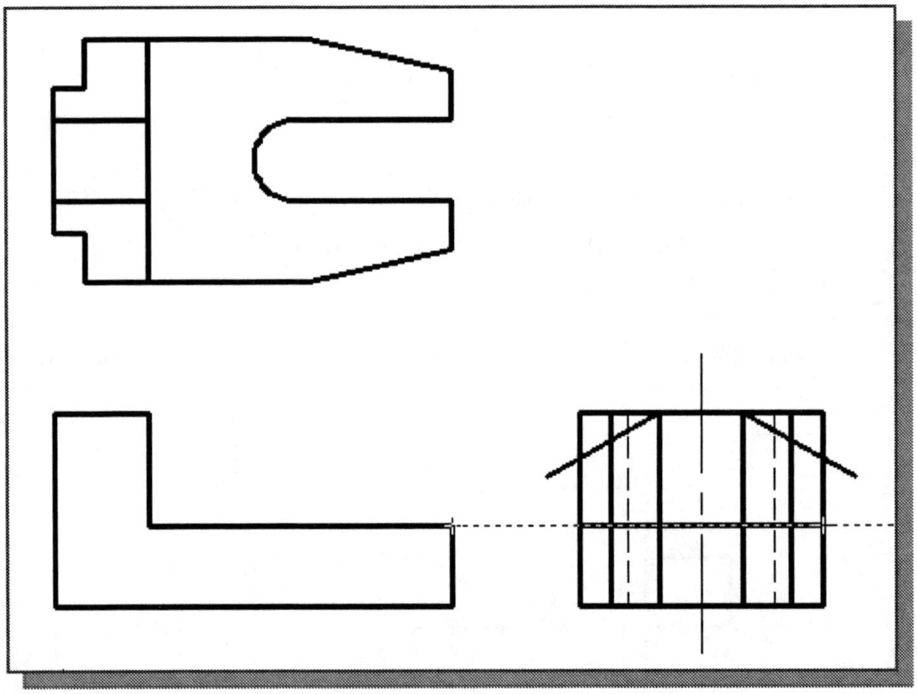

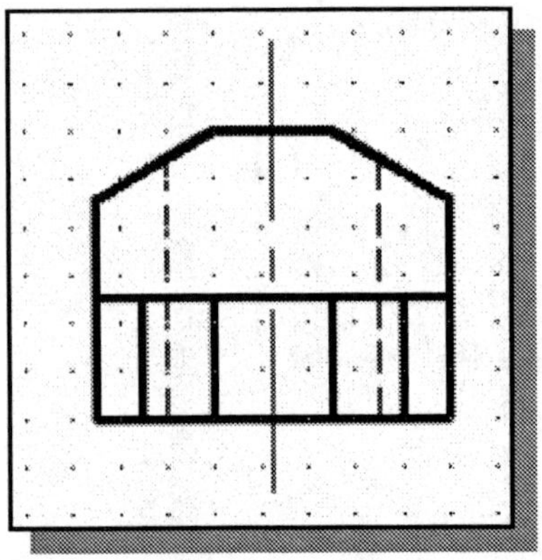

8. On your own, use the **Trim** command and remove the unwanted portions in the side view.

Completing the Front View

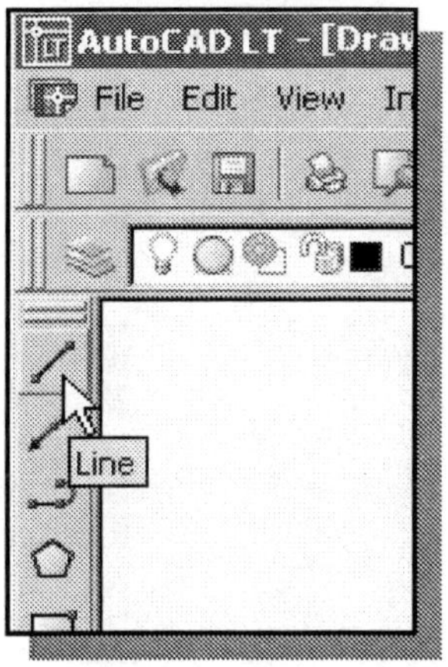

1. Select the **Line** command icon in the *Draw* toolbar. In the command prompt area, the message *"_line Specify first point:"* is displayed.

2. Create a horizontal line by connecting from the top left corner in the side view to the left edge of the front view using the *Polar Tracking/Snap* options.

3. Create a vertical line connecting from the lower left corner of the top view to the bottom edge of the front view as shown.

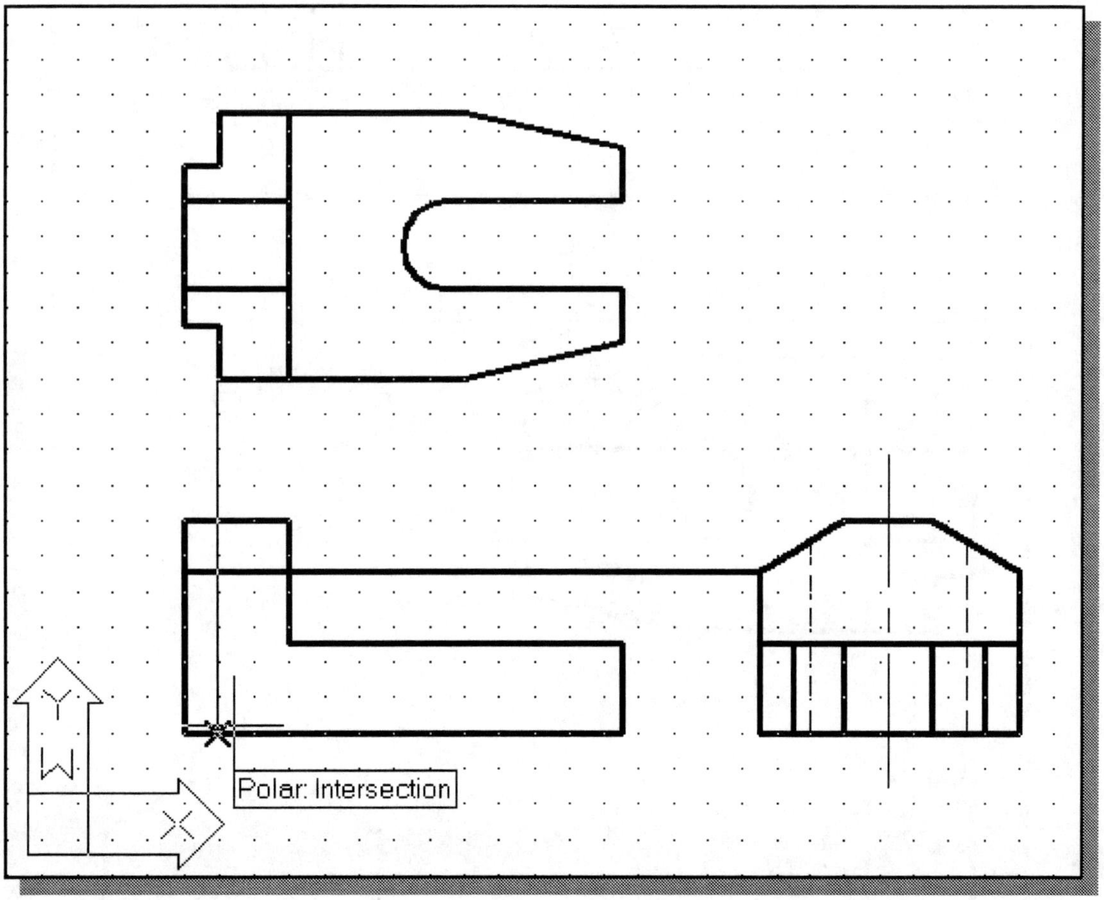

4. Create the **horizontal line** as shown.

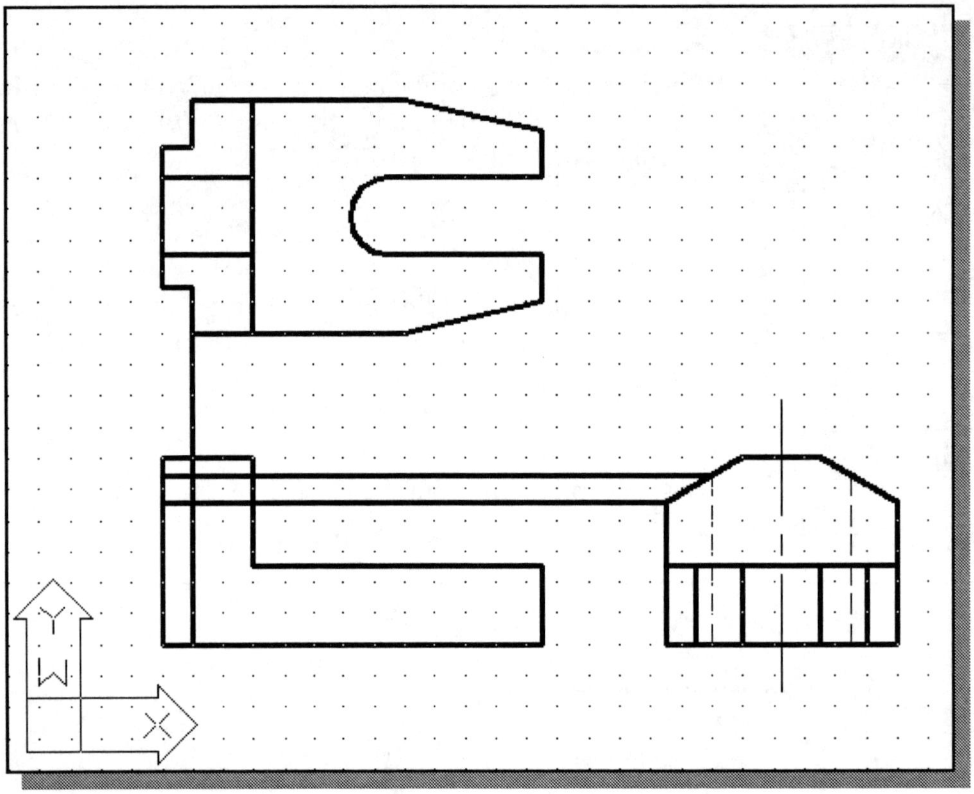

5. Use the **Trim** command and modify the lines in the front view as shown.

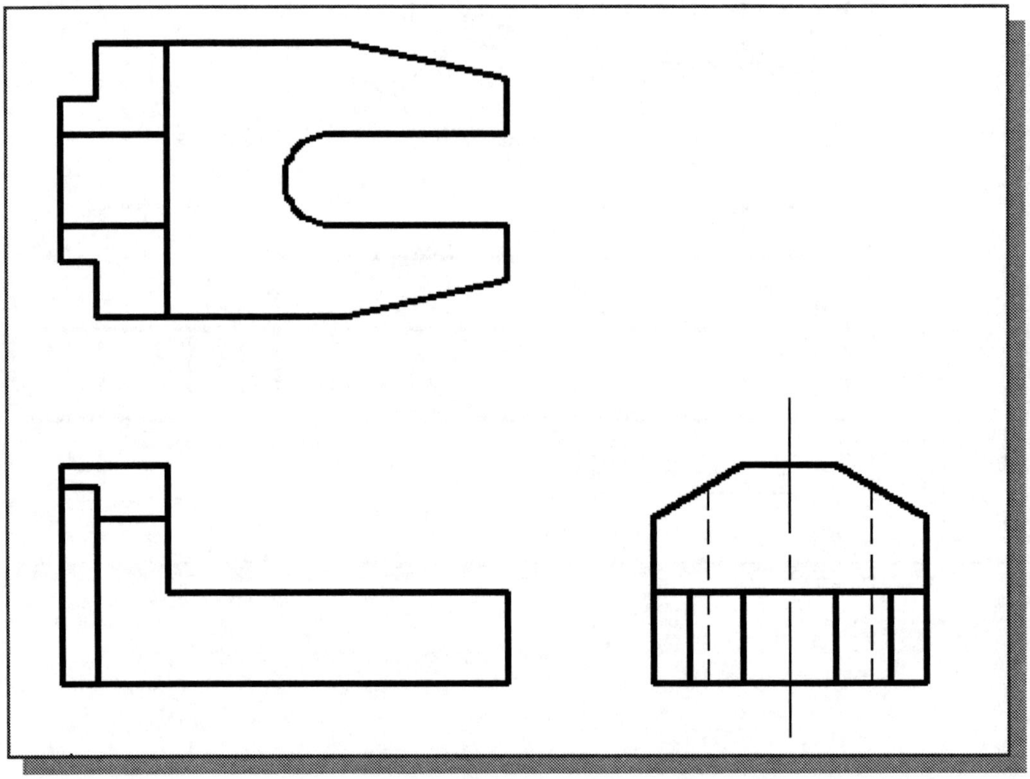

6. On your own, add additional object lines as shown in the figure below.

7. Set layer ***Hidden*** as the *Current Layer* and create the necessary hidden lines in the front view.

8. Set layer ***Center*** as the *Current Layer* and create the necessary centerlines in the top view and front view.

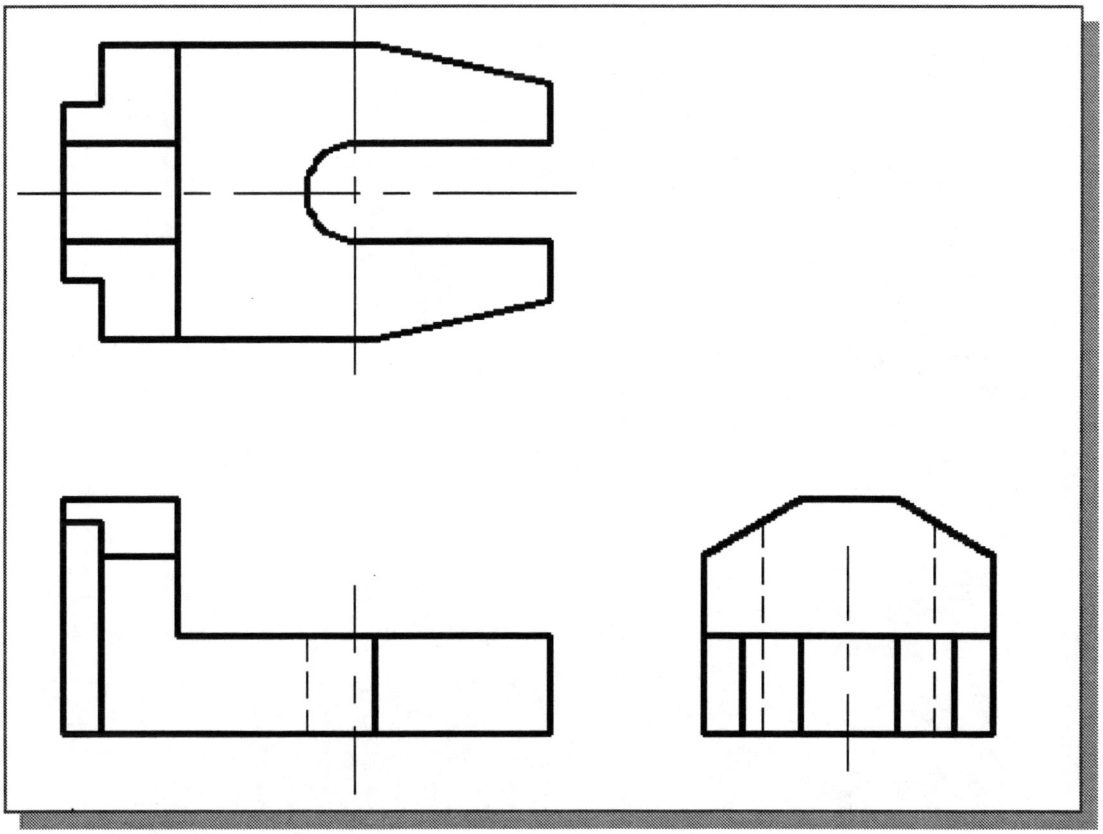

Saving the CAD File

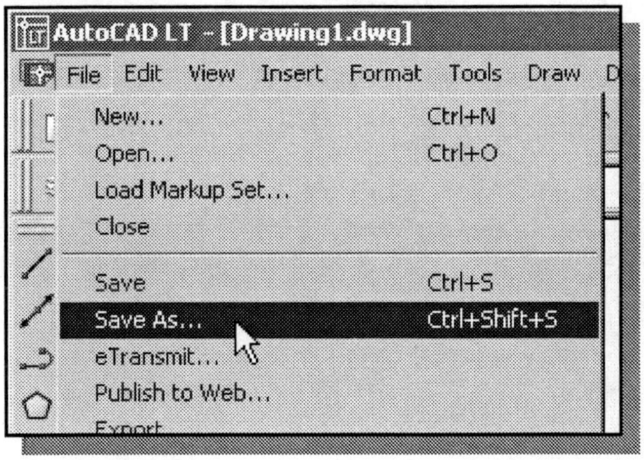

1. In the pull-down menus, select **[File] → [Save As]**

2. In the *Save Drawing As* dialog box, select the folder you want to store the CAD file and enter ***Locator*** in the *File name* box.

3. Pick **Save** in the *Save Drawing As* dialog box to accept the selections and save the file.

Questions:

1. Explain what an *orthographic view* is and why it is important to engineering graphics.

2. What does the *Running Object Snaps* option allow us to do?

3. Explain how a *miter line* can assist us in creating orthographic views.

4. Describe the *AutoCAD LT AutoSnap* and *PolarTrack* options.

5. Identify the following commands:

(a)

(b)

(c)

(d)

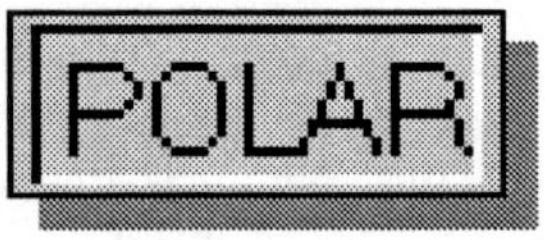

Exercises: (Unless otherwise specified, dimensions are in inches.)

1.

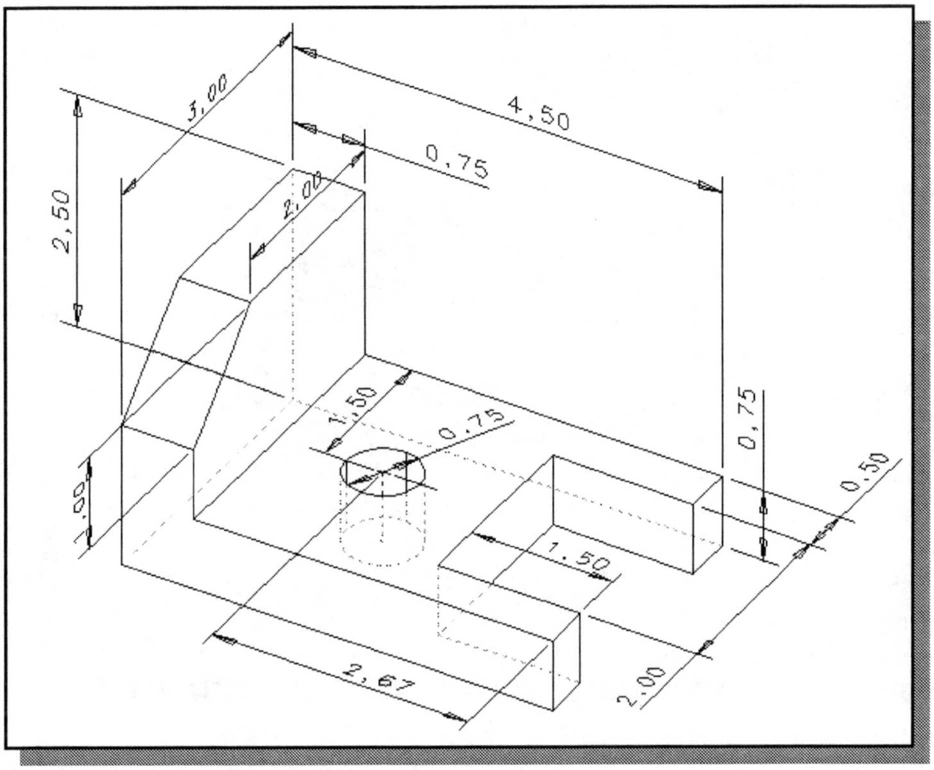

2.

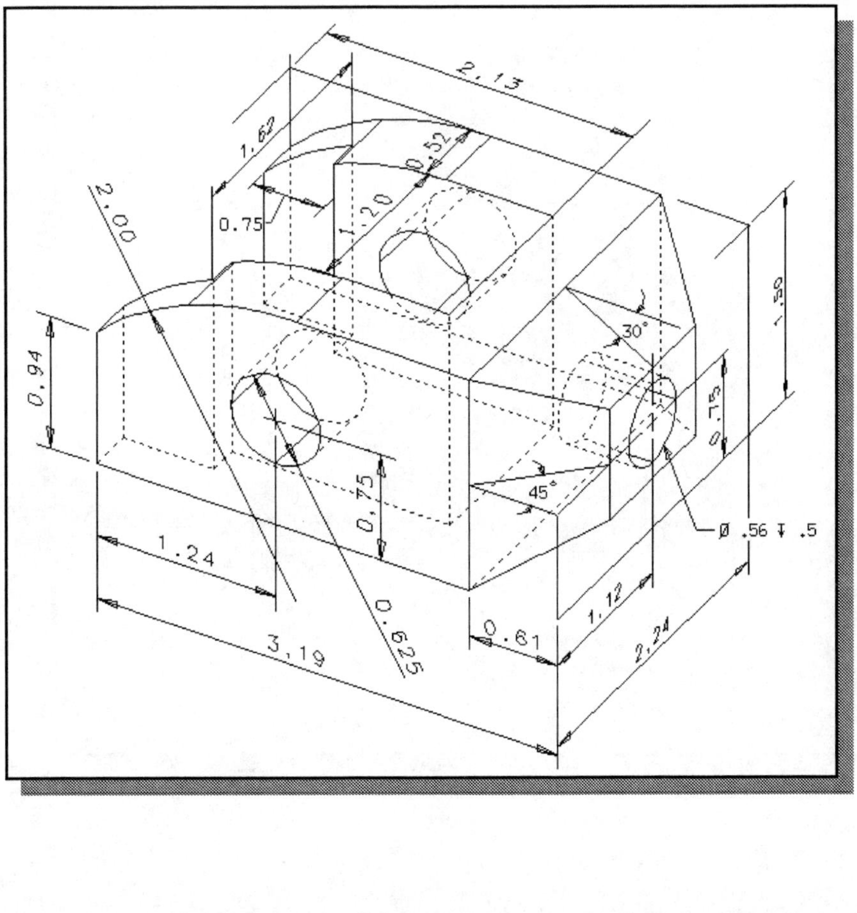

3.

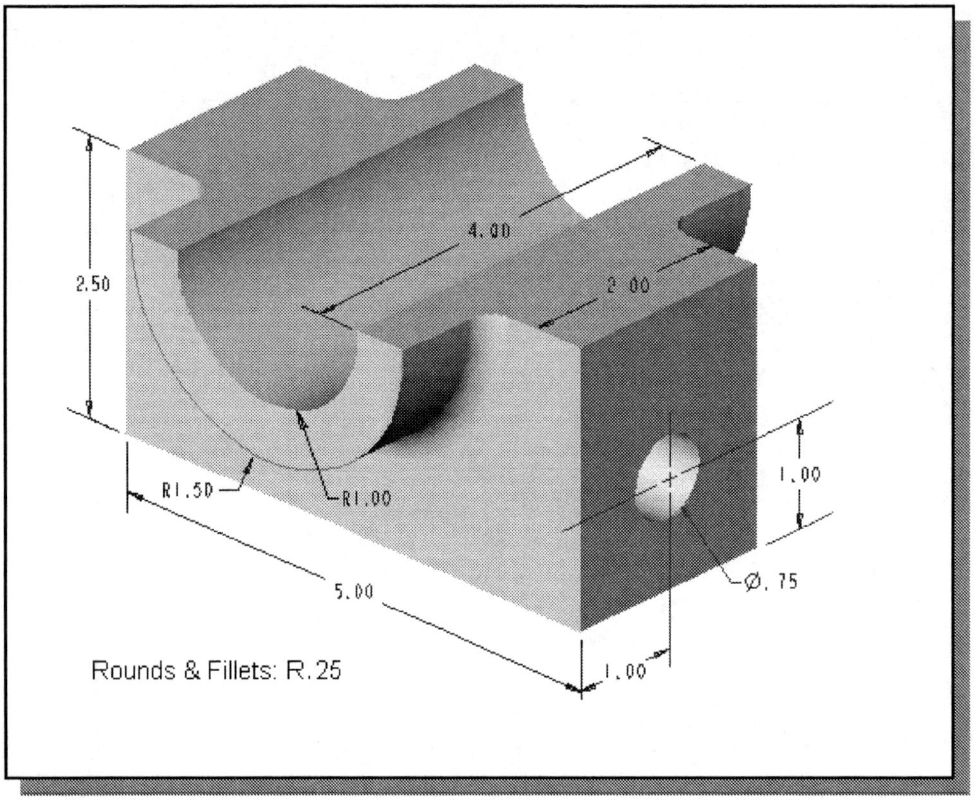

4. Dimensions are in millimeters.

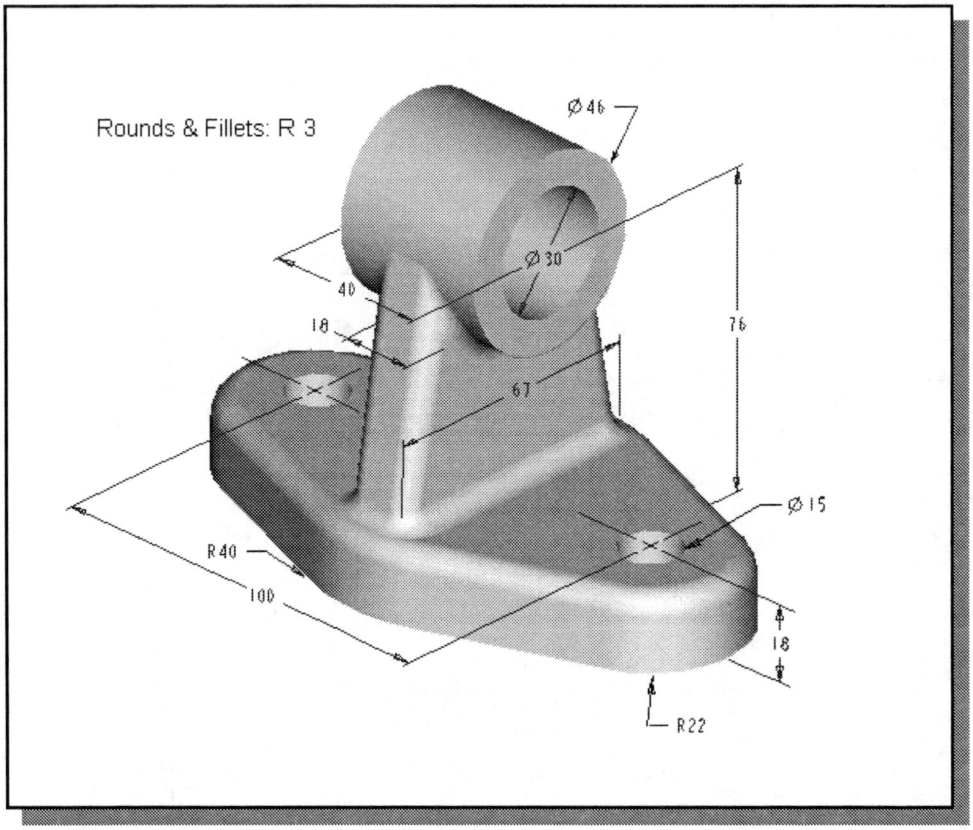

5.

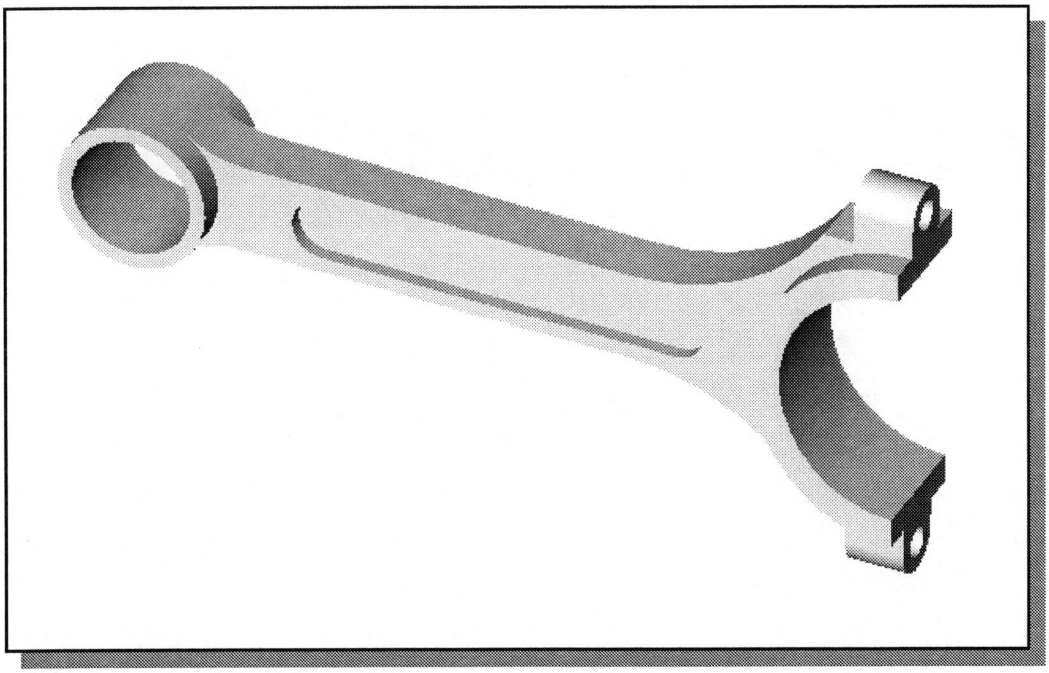

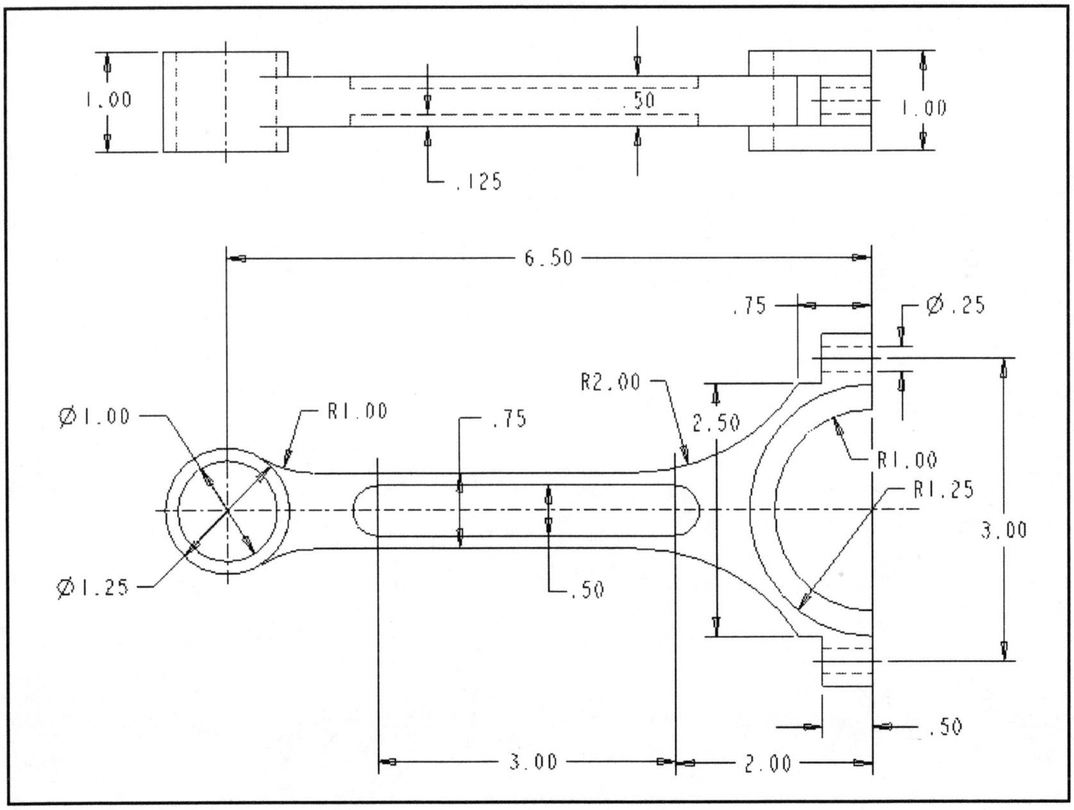
1.00
.50
1.00
.125
6.50
.75
Ø.25
R2.00
2.50
Ø1.00
R1.00
.75
R1.00
R1.25
3.00
Ø1.25
.50
.50
3.00
2.00

Notes:

Lesson 5
Basic Dimensioning and Notes

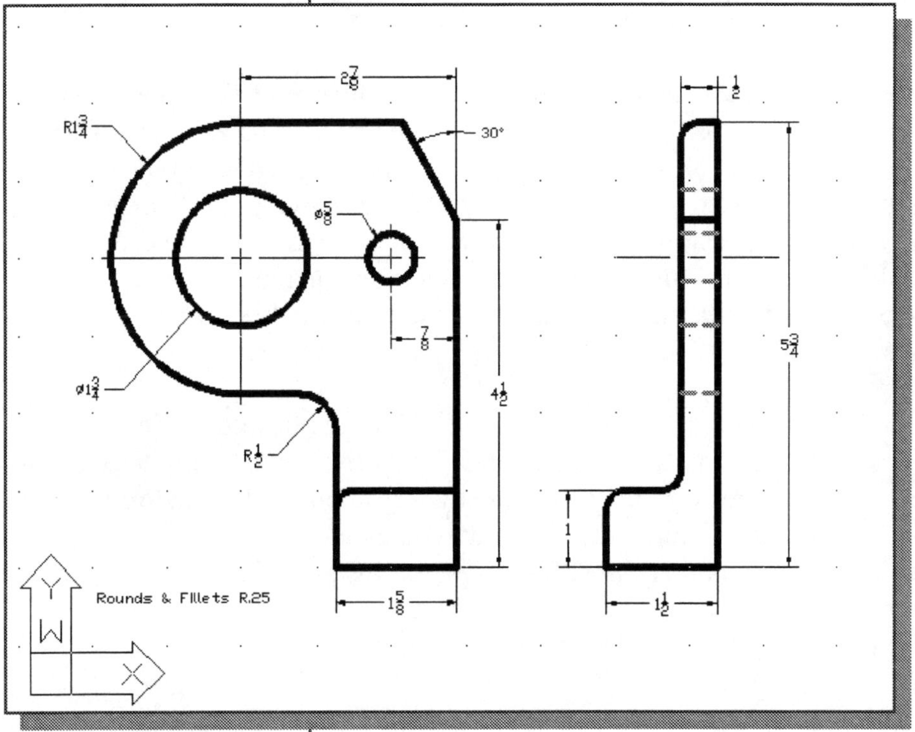

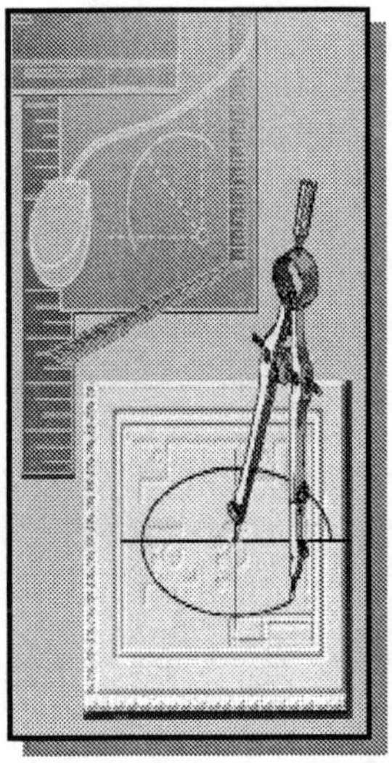

Learning Objectives

- **Understand Dimensioning Nomenclature and Basics**
- **Display and Use the Dimension Toolbar**
- **Use the AutoCAD LT Dimension Style Manager**
- **Create Center Marks**
- **Add Linear and Angular Dimensions**
- **Use the SINGLE LINE TEXT Command**
- **Create Special Characters in Notes**

Introduction

In order to manufacture the design, the complete ***shape*** and ***size*** description must be shown on the drawings of the design. Thus far, we have illustrated how to use **AutoCAD® LT 2005** to define the ***shape*** of designs. In this lesson, we will discuss the procedures to define the ***size*** of designs using **AutoCAD® LT 2005**. The *tools of size description* are known as *dimensions* and *notes*.

Considerable experience and judgment is required for accurate size description. Detail drawings should contain only those dimensions that are necessary to make the design. Dimensions for the same feature of the design should be given only once in the same drawing. Nothing should be left to chance or guesswork on a drawing. Drawings should be dimensioned to avoid any possibility of questions. Dimensions should be carefully positioned; preferably near the profile of the feature being dimensioned. The designer and CAD operator should be as familiar as possible with materials, method of manufacturing, and shop processes.

Traditionally, detailing a drawing is the biggest bottleneck of the design process; and when doing board drafting, dimensioning is one of the most time consuming and tedious tasks. Today, most CAD systems provide what is known as an **auto-dimensioning feature**, where the CAD systems automatically create the extension lines, dimensional lines, arrowheads, and dimension text. Most CAD systems also provide an **associative-dimensioning feature** so that the system automatically updates the dimensions when the drawing is modified.

The *Bracket* Design

Starting Up *AutoCAD LT 2005*

1. Select the **AutoCAD LT 2005** option on the *Program* menu or select the **AutoCAD LT 2005** icon on the *Desktop*.

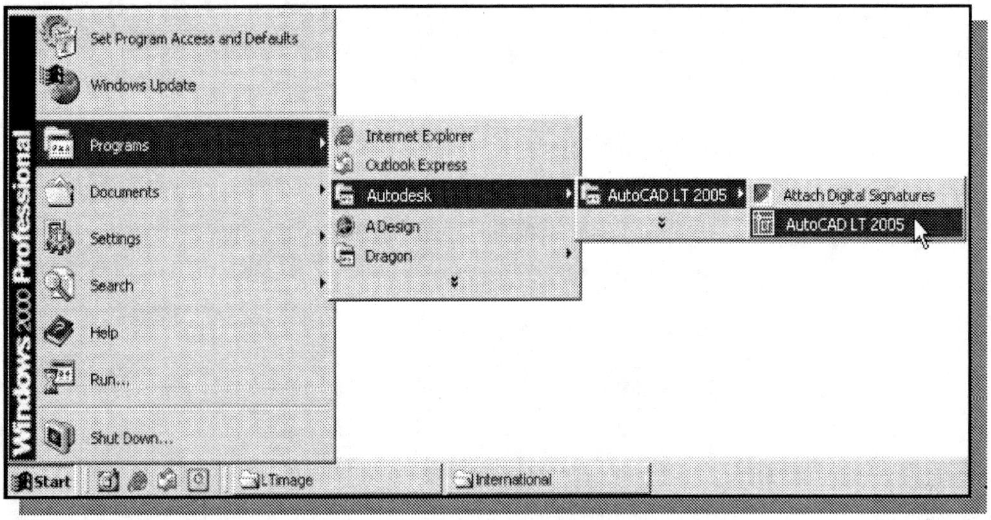

2. Choose ***Start from Scratch*** as the startup option, as shown in the figure below.

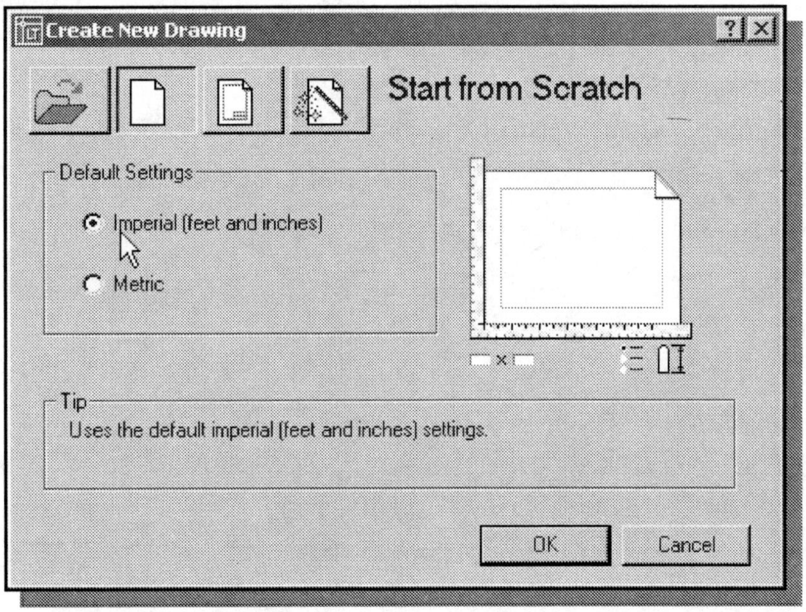

3. In the *Default Settings* section, pick **Imperial (feet and inches)** as the drawing units.

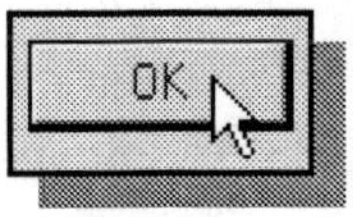

4. Pick **OK** in the *Startup* dialog box to accept the selected settings.

GRID and *SNAP* Intervals Setup

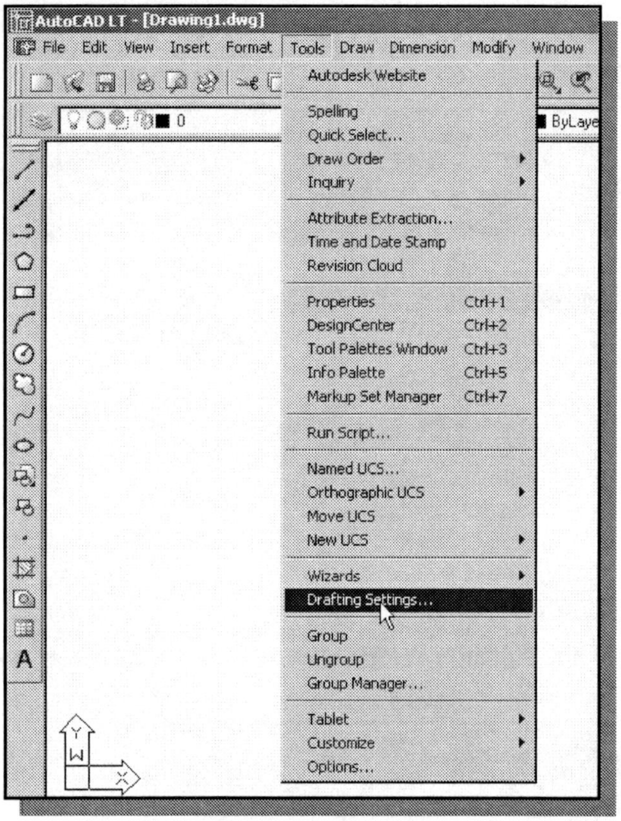

1. In the pull-down menus, select **[Tools] → [Drafting Settings]**

2. In the *Drafting Settings* dialog box, select the **SNAP and GRID** tab if it is not the page on top.

3. Change *Grid Spacing* to **1.0** for both X and Y directions.

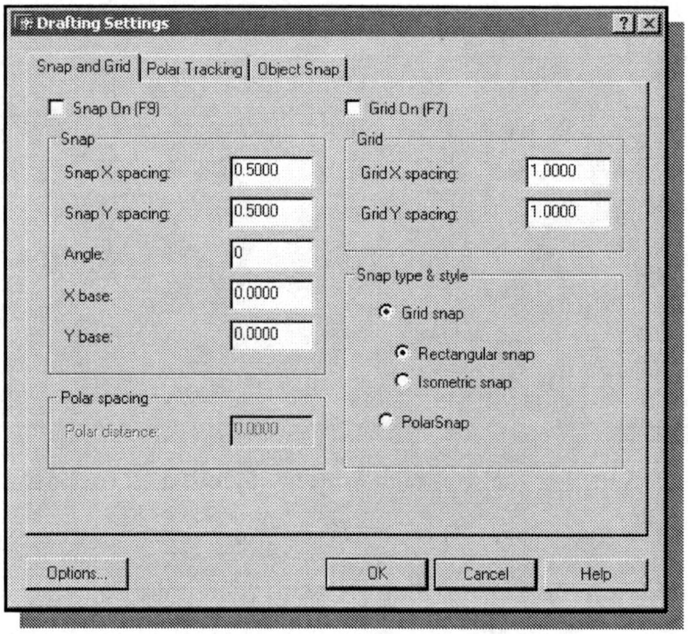

4. Also adjust the *Snap Spacing* to **0.5** for both X and Y directions.

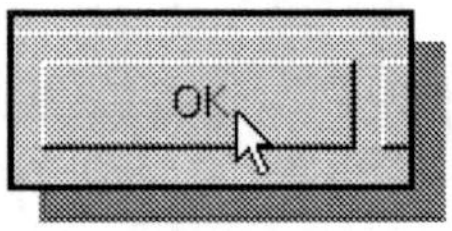

5. Pick **OK** to exit the *Drafting Settings* dialog box.

Layers Setup

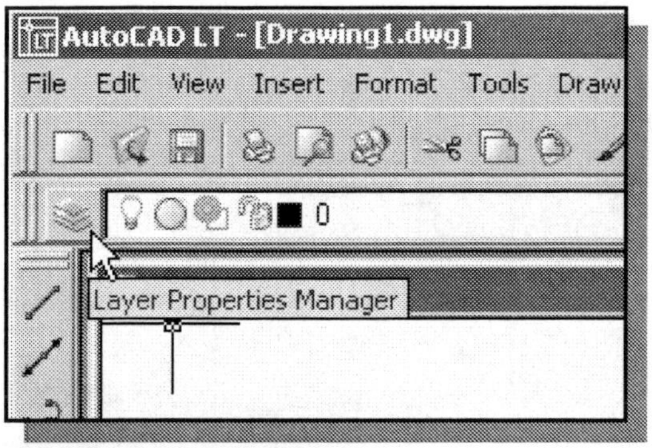

1. Pick **Layers Properties Manager** in the *Object Properties* toolbar.

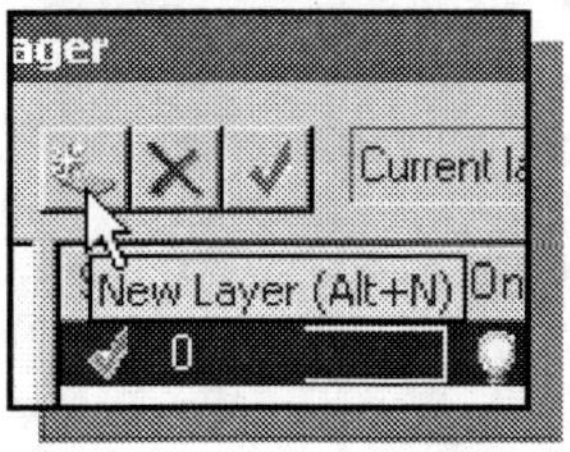

2. In the *Layer Properties Manager* dialog box, click on the **New** button to create new layers.

3. Create **layers** with the following settings:

Layer	***Color***	***LineType***	***Lineweight***
Construction	**Gray**	**Continuous**	**Default**
Object_Lines	**Blue**	**Continuous**	**0.6mm**
Hidden_Lines	**Cyan**	**Hidden**	**0.3mm**
Center_Lines	**Red**	**Center**	**Default**
Dimensions	**Magenta**	**Continuous**	**Default**
Section_Lines	**Black/White**	**Continuous**	**Default**
CuttingPlane_Lines	**Dark Gray**	**Phantom**	**0.6mm**
Title_Block	**Green**	**Continuous**	**1.2mm**
Viewport	**Black/White**	**Continuous**	**Default**

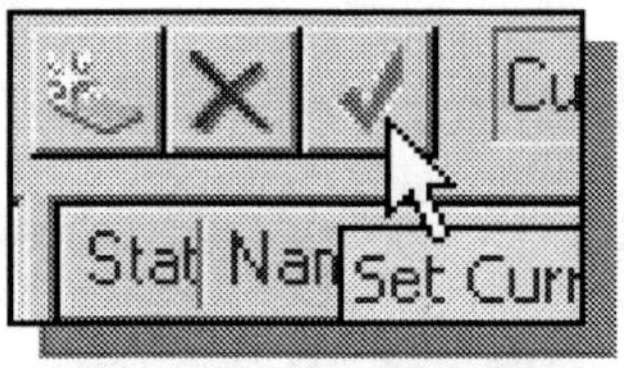

4. Highlight the layer ***Construction*** in the list of layers.

5. Click on the **Current** button to set layer ***Construction*** as the *Current Layer*.

6. Click on the **OK** button to accept the settings and exit the *Layer Properties Manager* dialog box.

7. In the *Status Bar* area, reset the option buttons so that only *SNAP, GRID* and *MODEL* are switched ***ON***.

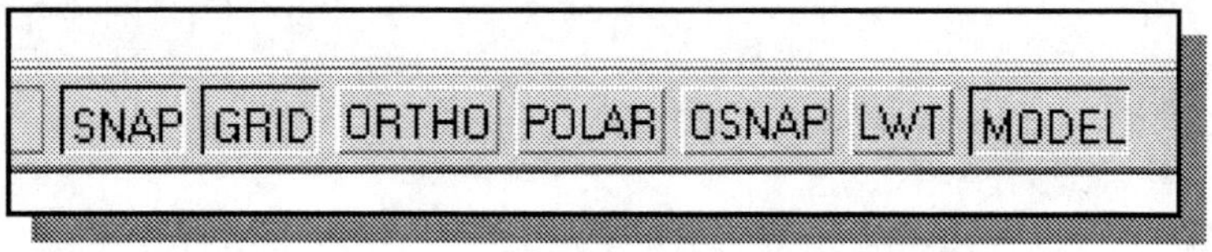

The *Bracket* Design

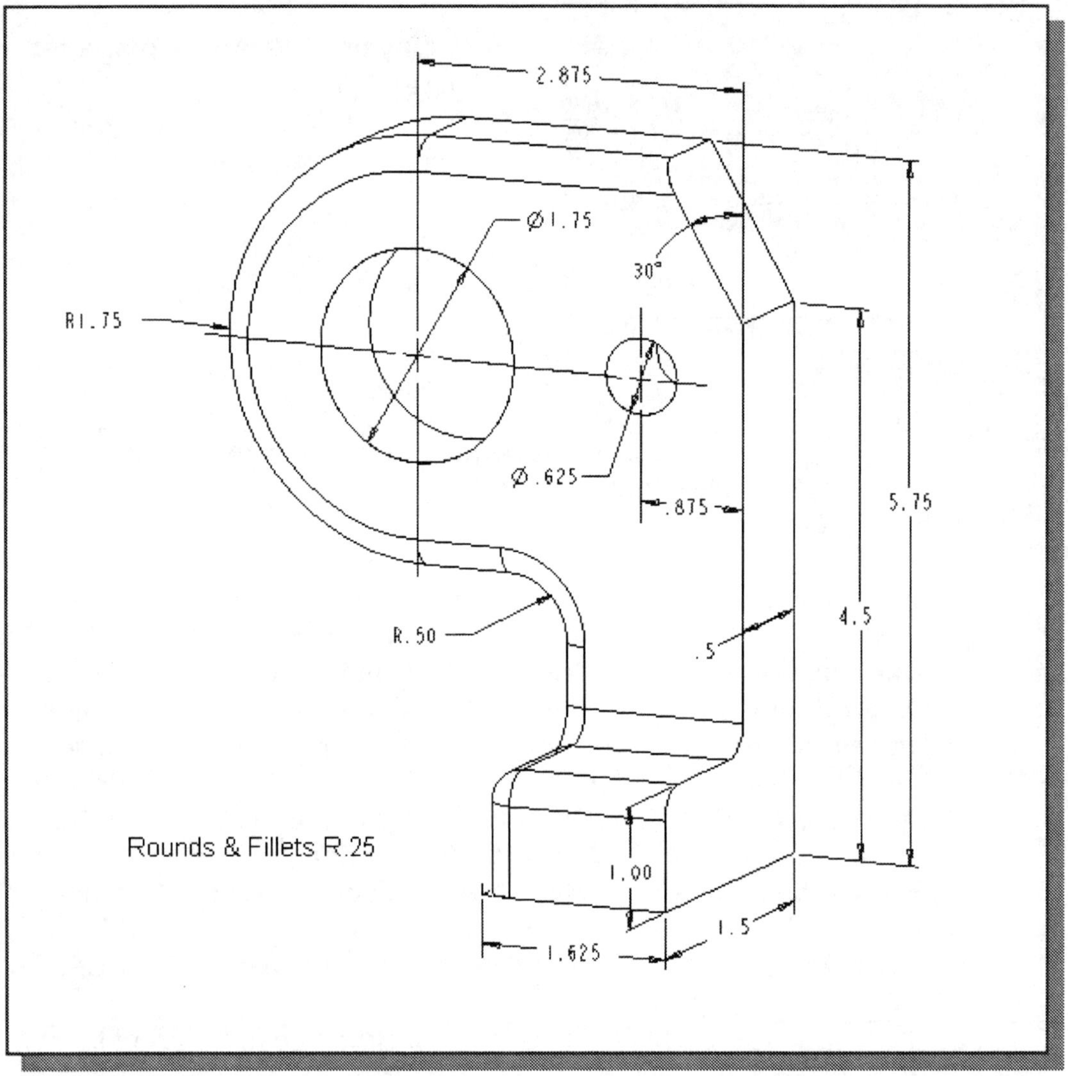

➢ Before going through the tutorial, make a rough sketch of a multiview drawing of the part. How many 2D views will be necessary to fully describe the part? Based on your knowledge of **AutoCAD® LT 2005** so far, how would you arrange and construct these 2D views? Take a few minutes to consider these questions and do preliminary planning by sketching on a piece of paper. You are also encouraged to construct the orthographic views on your own before continuing.

Drawing Construction Lines

We will place the construction lines on the *Construction* layer so that the layer can later be frozen or turned off.

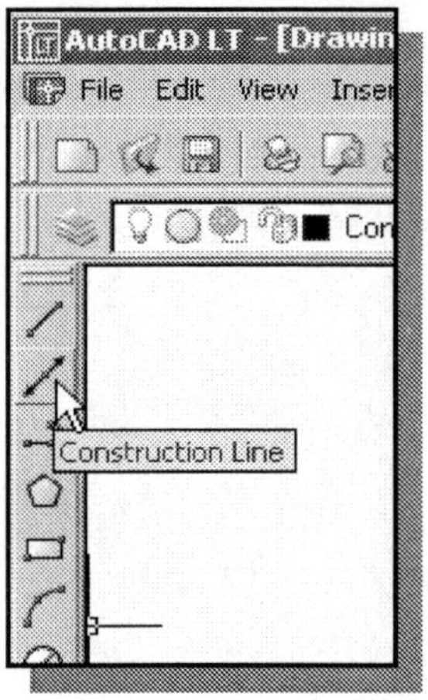

1. Select the **Construction Line** icon in the *Draw* toolbar. In the command prompt area, the message *"_xline Specify a point or [Hor/Ver/Ang/Bisect/Offset]:"* is displayed.

➢ To orient construction lines, we generally specify two points, though other orientation options are also available.

2. Place the first point at world coordinate (**3,2**) on the screen.

3. Pick a location above the last point to create a **vertical line**.

4. Move the cursor toward the right of the first point; pick a location to create a **horizontal line**.

5. Inside the graphics window, **right-mouse-click** to end the command.

6. In the *Status Bar* area, turn ***OFF*** the *SNAP* option.

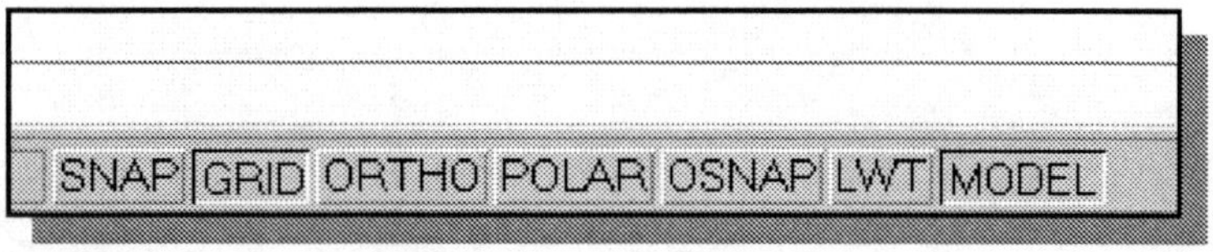

Using the *Offset* Command

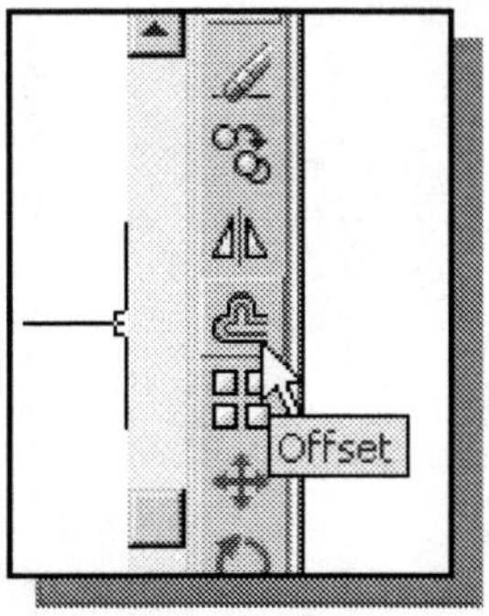

1. Select the **Offset** icon in the *Modify* toolbar. In the command prompt area, the message *"Specify offset distance or [Through]:"* is displayed.

2. In the command prompt area, enter **2.875 [ENTER]**

3. In the command prompt area, the message *"Select object to offset or <exit>:"* is displayed. Pick the **vertical line** on the screen.

4. AutoCAD LT next asks us to identify the direction of the offset. Pick a location that is to the **right** of the vertical line.

5. Inside the graphics window, right-mouse-click to end the Offset command.

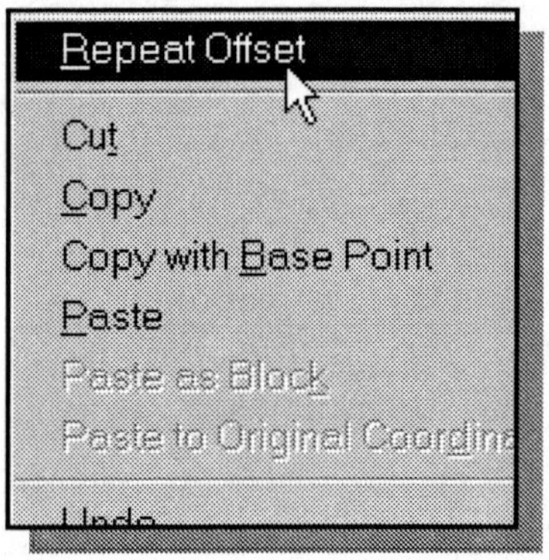

6. Hit the [**SPACE BAR**], or **right-mouse-click** inside the graphics window and select **Repeat Offset** in the popup list, to repeat the Offset command.

7. In the command prompt area, enter **5.75 [ENTER]**

8. In the command prompt area, the message *"Select object to offset or <exit>:"* is displayed. Pick the **horizontal line** on the screen.

9. AutoCAD LT next asks us to identify the direction of the offset. Pick a location that is **above** the horizontal line.

10. Inside the graphics window, right-mouse-click to end the Offset command.

11. Repeat the **Offset** command and create the lines as shown.

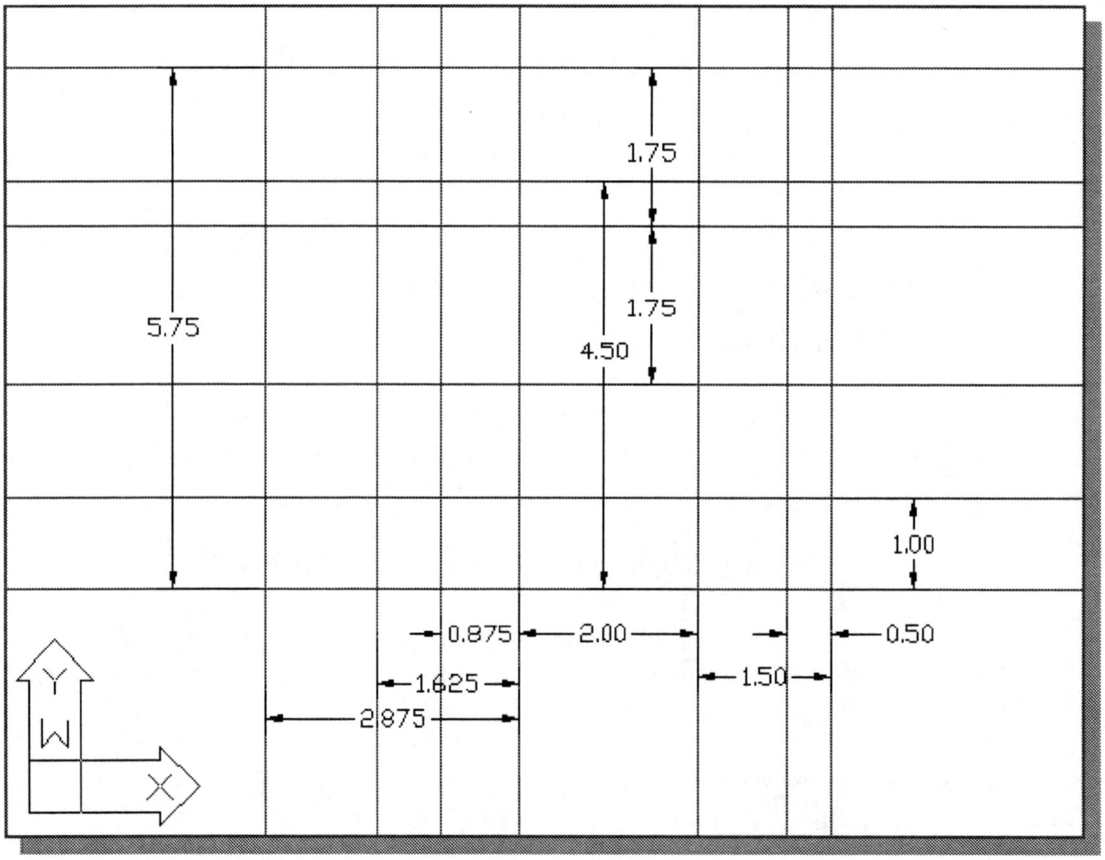

Set layer *Object_Lines* as the Current Layer

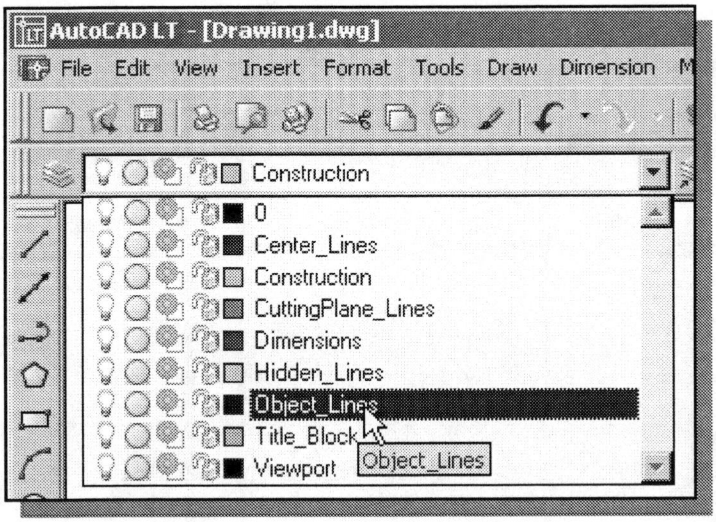

1. On the *Object Properties* toolbar, choose the ***Layer Control*** box with the left-mouse-button.

2. Move the cursor over the name of layer ***Object_Lines***, the tool tip *"Object_Lines"* appears.

3. **Left-mouse-click once** and layer *Object_Lines* is set as the *Current Layer*.

4. In the *Status Bar* area, turn ***ON*** the *OSNAP, POLAR* and *LWT* options.

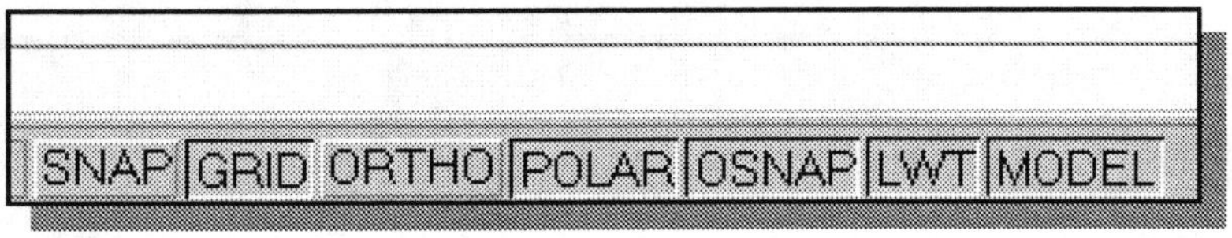

Creating Object Lines

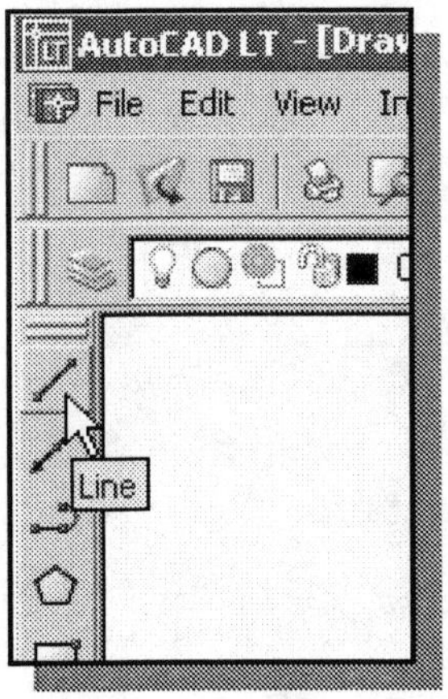

1. Select the **Line** command icon in the *Draw* toolbar. In the command prompt area, the message *"_line Specify first point:"* is displayed.

2. Move the cursor to the intersection of any two lines and notice the visual aid automatically displayed at the intersection.

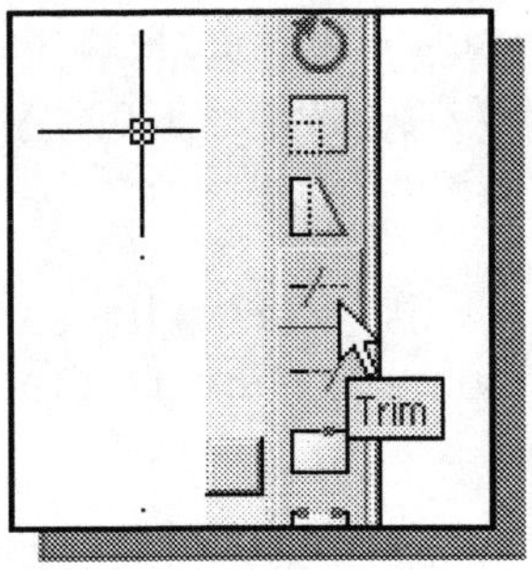

3. Create the object lines as shown on the next page. (Hint: Use the *Polar Tracking* option and the Trim command to construct the 30° line.)

4. Use the Arc and Circle commands to complete the object lines as shown.

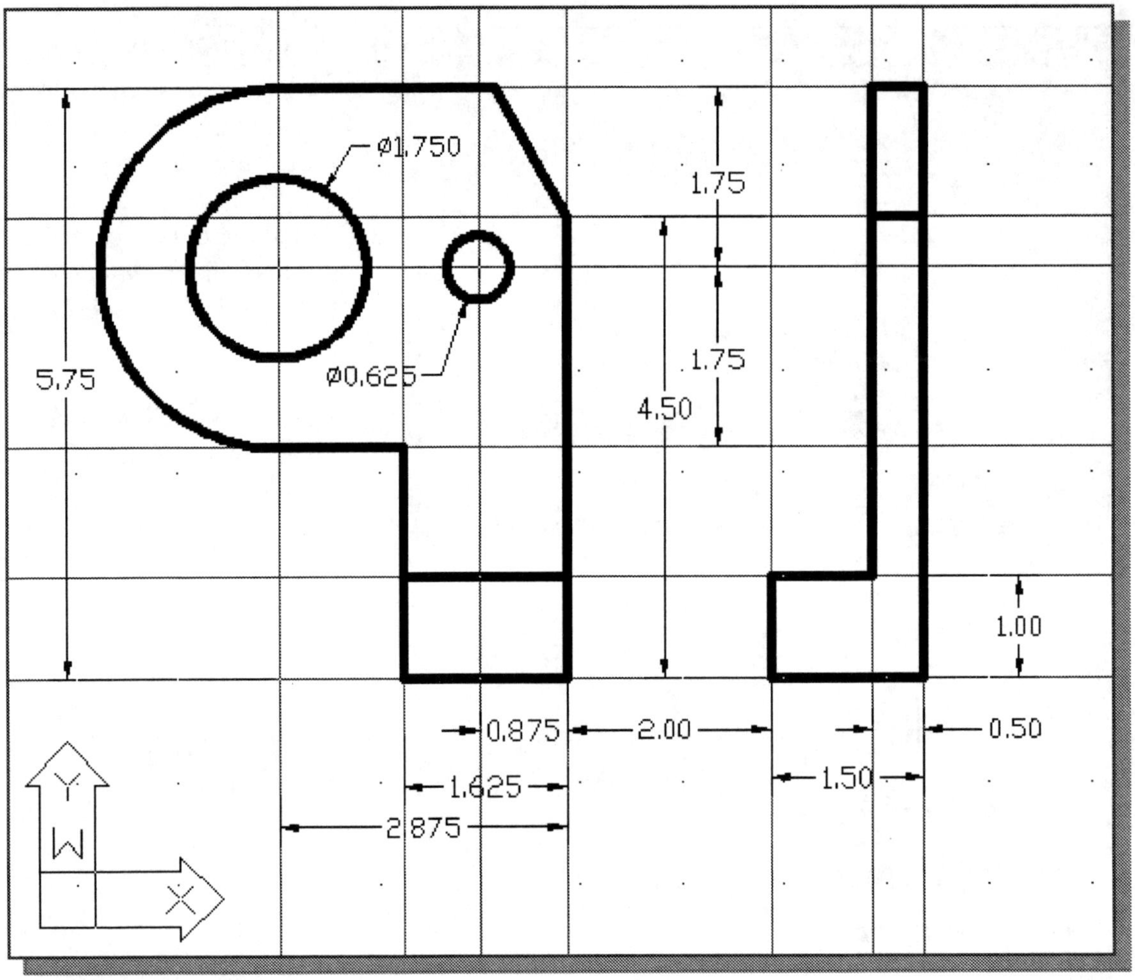

Creating Hidden Lines

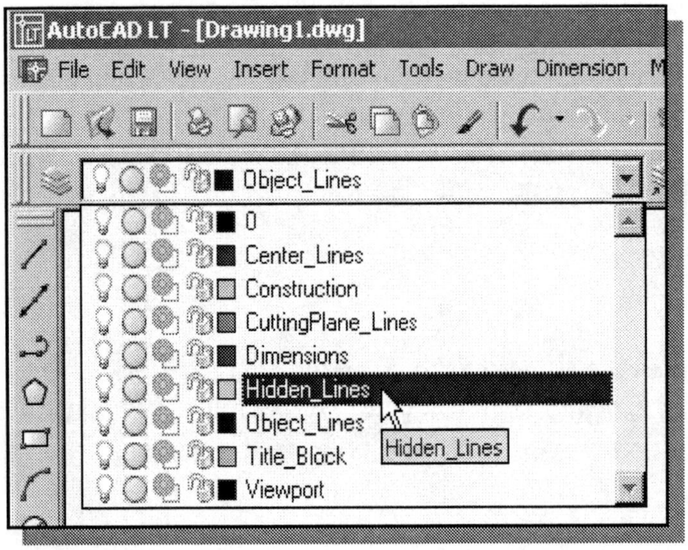

1. On the *Object Properties* toolbar, choose the ***Layer Control*** box with the left-mouse-button.

2. Move the cursor over the name of layer ***Hidden_Lines***, left-mouse-click once and set layer *Hidden_Lines* as the *Current Layer.*

3. Create the five hidden lines in the side view as shown on the next page.

Creating Center Lines

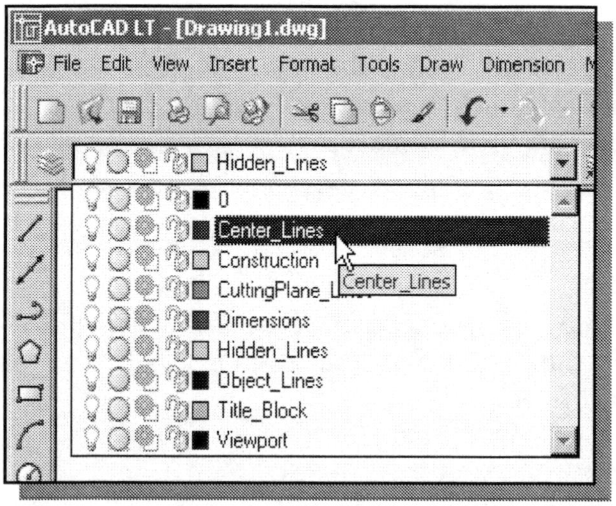

1. On the *Object Properties* toolbar, choose the ***Layer Control*** box with the left-mouse-button.

2. Move the cursor over the name of layer ***Center_Lines***, left-mouse-click once and set layer *Center_Lines* as the *Current Layer.*

3. Create the center line in the side view as shown. (We will add the center lines in the front view using the *Center Mark* option.)

Turn *OFF* the Construction Lines

1. On the *Object Properties* toolbar, choose the ***Layer Control*** box with the left-mouse-button.

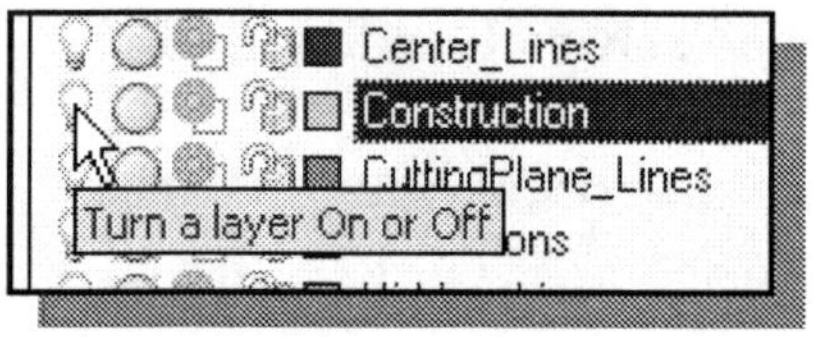

2. Move the cursor over the light-bulb icon for layer *Construction_Lines*, **left-mouse-click once** and notice the icon color is changed to a gray tone color, representing the layer is turned *OFF.*

3. Move the cursor over the name of layer ***Object_Lines***, left-mouse-click once and set layer *Object_Lines* as the *Current Layer.*

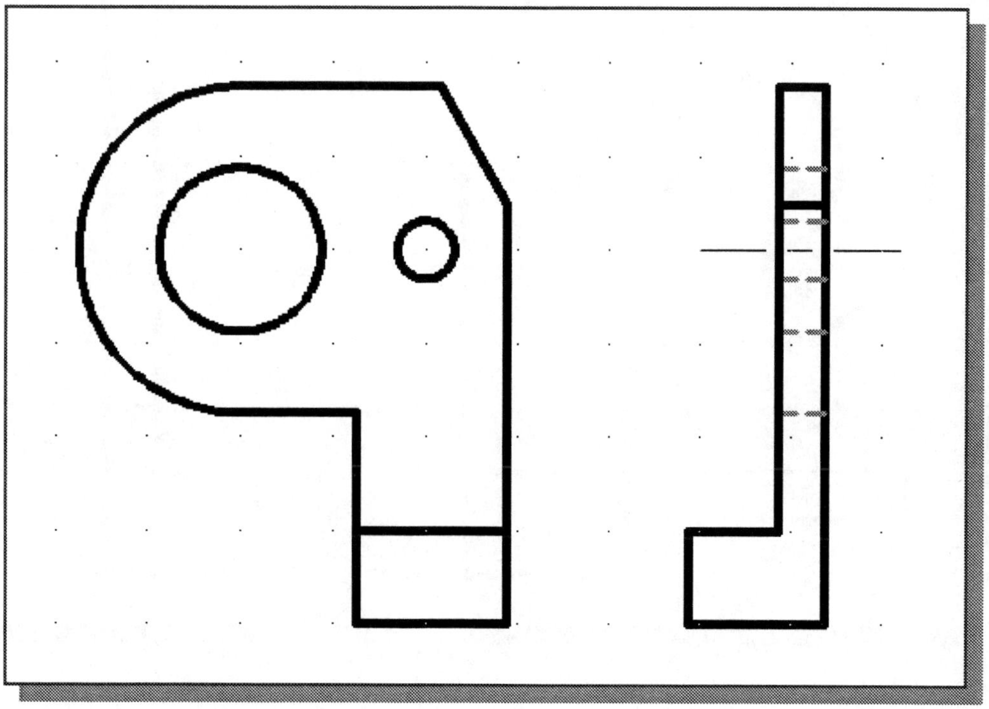

Using the *Fillet* Command

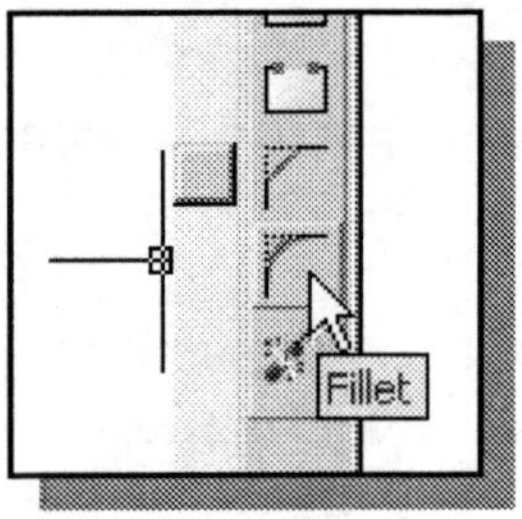

1. Select the **Fillet** command icon in the *Modify* toolbar. In the command prompt area, the message *"Select first object or [Polyline/Radius/Trim]:"* is displayed.

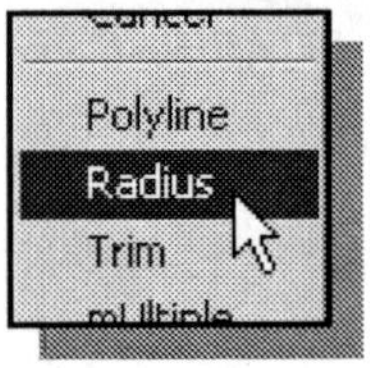

2. Inside the graphics window, right-mouse-click to activate the option menu and select the **Radius** option with the left-mouse-button to specify the radius of the fillet.

3. In the command prompt area, the message *"Specify fillet radius:"* is displayed.

   Specify fillet radius: **0.5 [ENTER]**

4. Activate the **Fillet** command by picking the icon in the *Modify* toolbar or right-mouse-click to activate the option menu and select **Repeat Fillet**.

5. Pick the **bottom horizontal line** and the **adjacent vertical line** connected to the arc to create a rounded corner as shown.

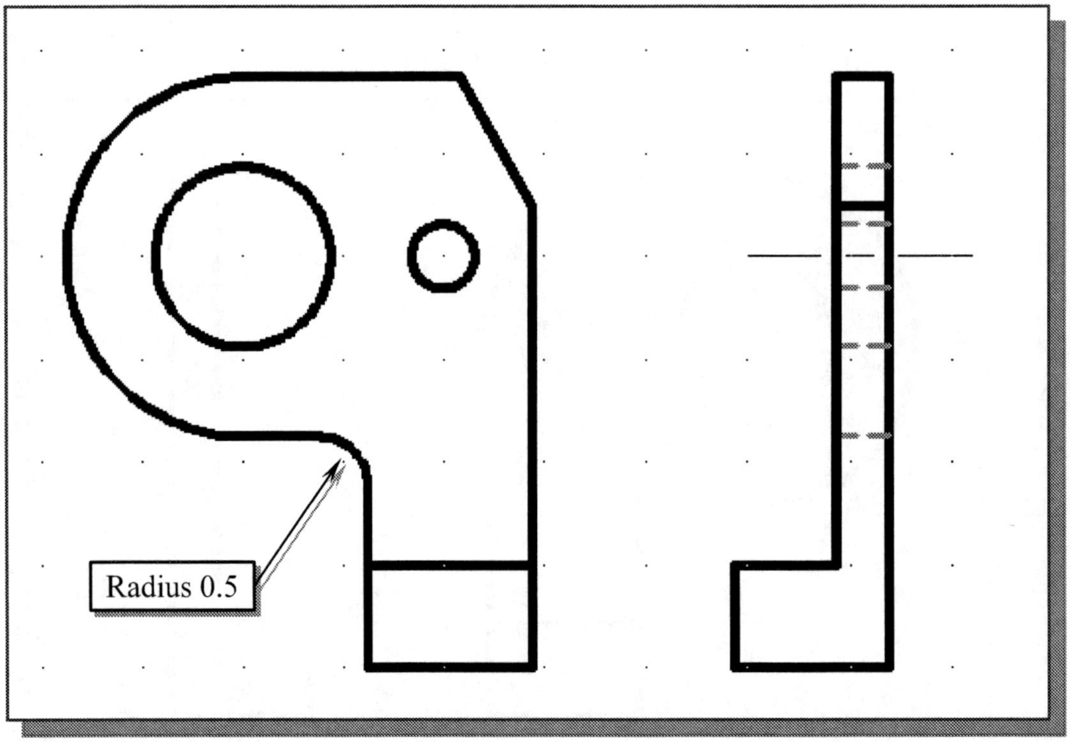

6. Repeat the **Fillet** command and create the four rounded corners (Radius **0.25**) as shown.

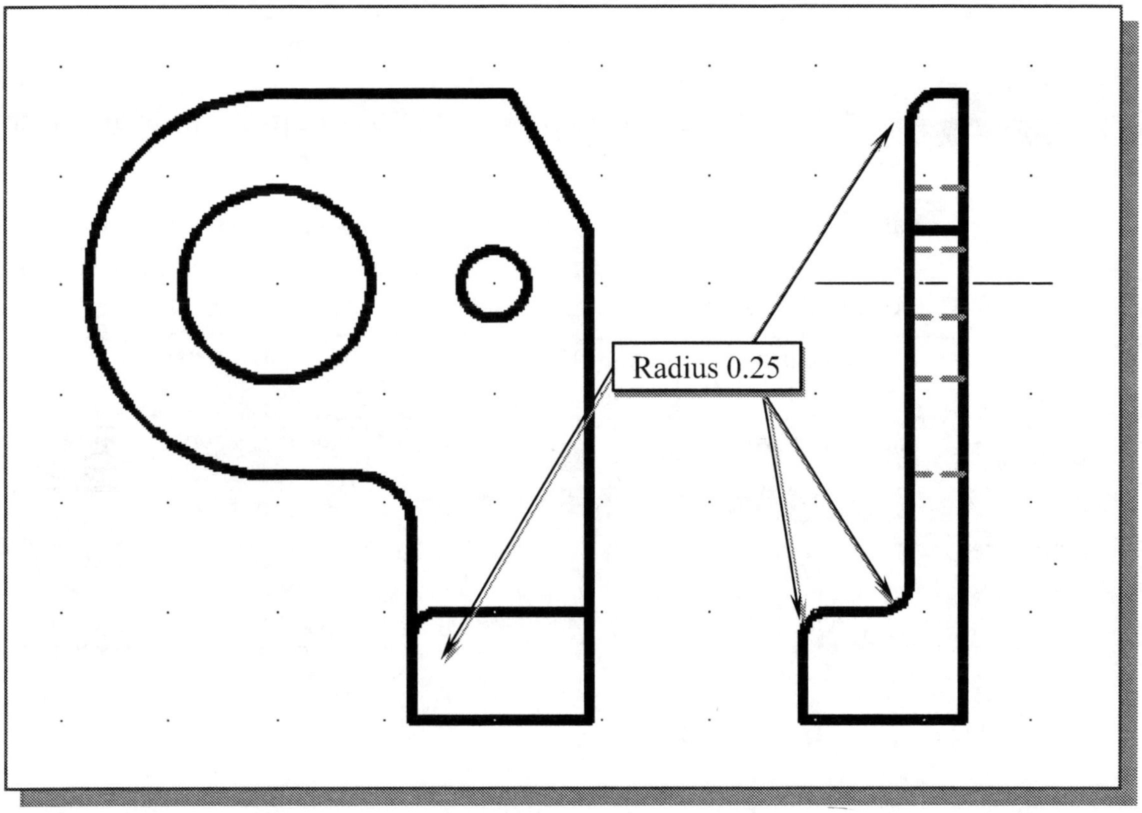

Saving the CAD File

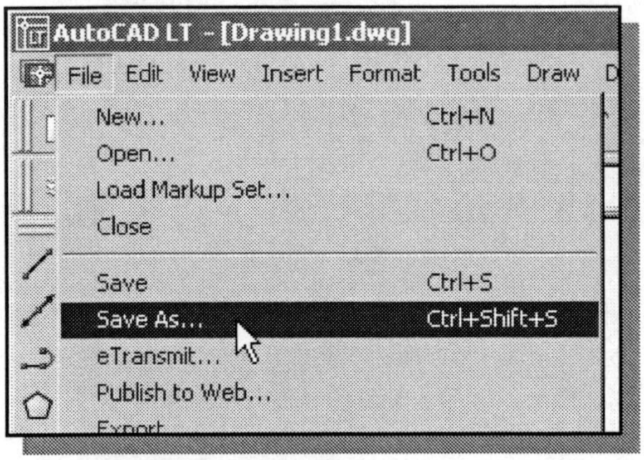

1. In the pull-down menus, select **[File] → [Save As]**

2. In the *Save Drawing As* dialog box, select the folder in which you want to store the CAD file and enter ***Bracket*** in the *File name* box.

3. Pick **Save** in the *Save Drawing As* dialog box to accept the selections and save the file.

The *Dimension* Toolbar

1. Move the cursor to the *Standard* toolbar area and **right-mouse-click** on any icon in the *Standard* toolbar to display a list of toolbar menu groups.

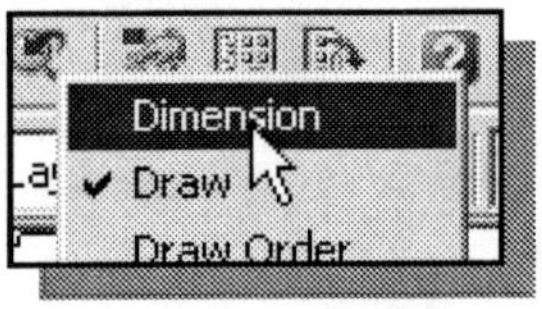

2. Select **Dimension**, with the left-mouse-button, to display the *Dimension* toolbar on the screen.

3. Move the cursor over the icons in the *Dimension* toolbar and read the description of each icon in the *Status Bar* area.

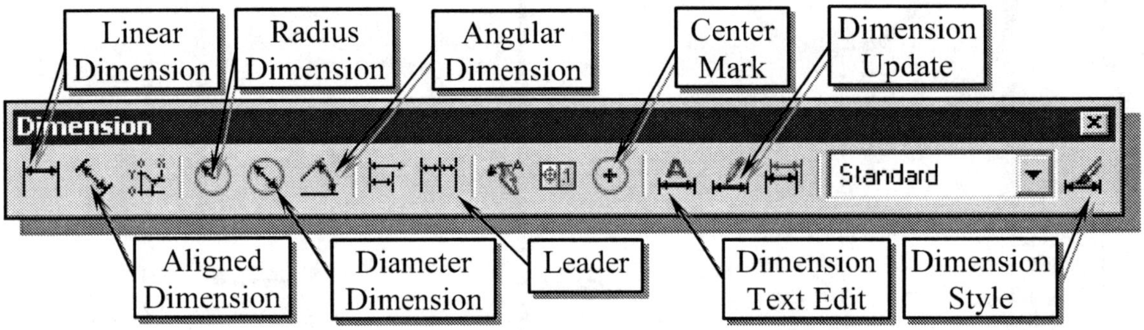

Using *Dimension Style Manager*

The appearances of the dimensions are controlled by *dimension variables*, which we can set using the *Dimension Style Manager* dialog box.

1. In the *Dimension* toolbar, pick **Dimension Style**. The *Dimension Style Manager* dialog box appears on the screen.

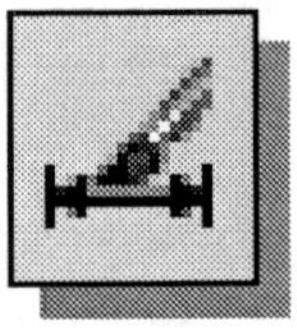

Dimensions Nomenclature and Basics

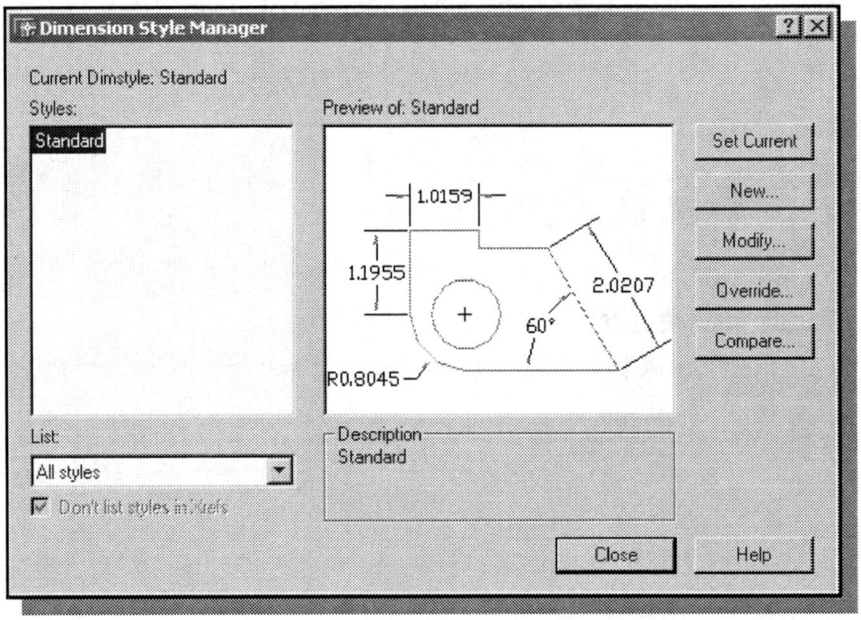

As was stated in *Lesson 1*, the rule for creating CAD designs and drawings is that they should be created **full size** using real-world units. The importance of this practice is evident when we begin applying dimensions to the geometry. The features that we specify for dimensioning are measured and displayed automatically.

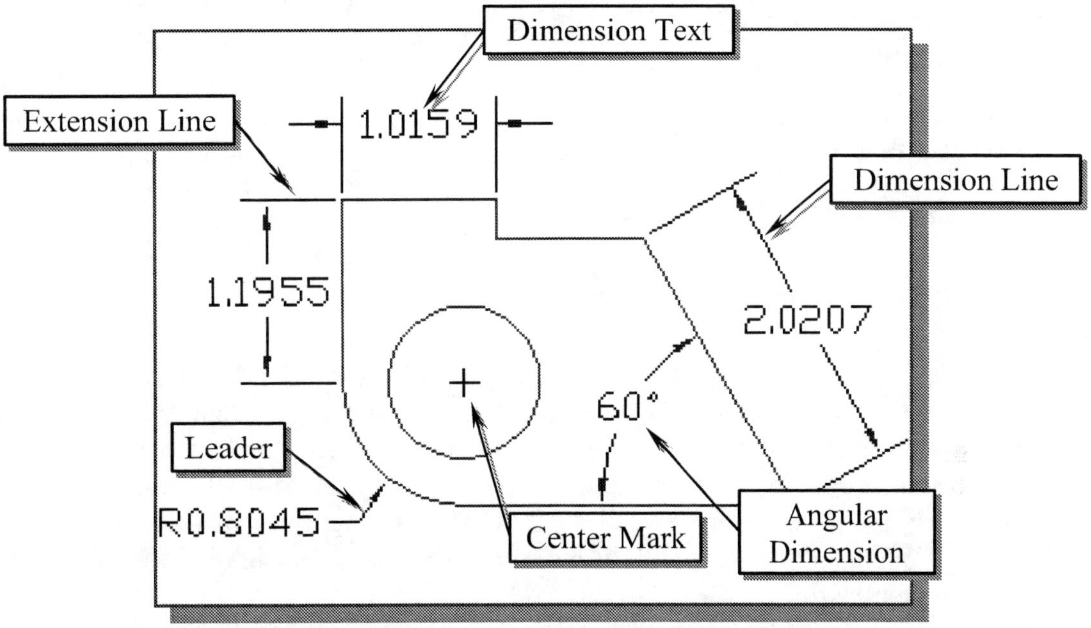

When selecting and placing dimensions, think about (1) the function of the part and (2) manufacturing operations. Detail drawings should contain only those dimensions that are necessary to make the design. Dimensions for the same feature of the design should be given only once in the same drawing. Nothing should be left to chance or guesswork on a drawing. Drawings should be dimensioned to avoid any possibility of questions. Dimensions should be carefully positioned; preferably near the profile of the feature being dimensioned.

Notice in the *Dimension Style Manager* dialog box, the AutoCAD LT default style name is *Standard.* We can create our own dimension style to fit the specific type of design we are working on, such as mechanical or architectual.

1. Click on the **New** button to create a new dimension style.

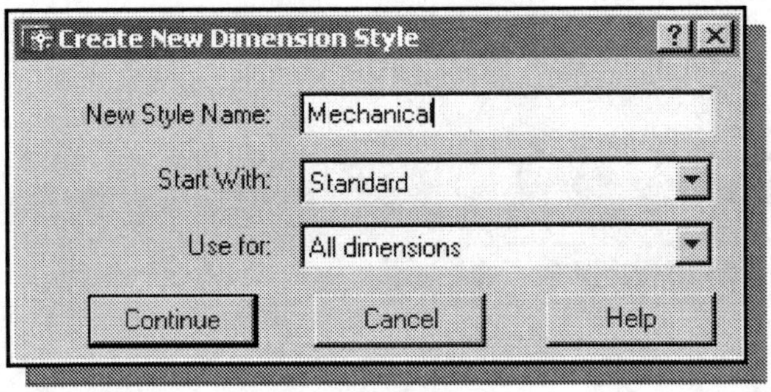

2. In the *Create New Dimension Style* dialog box, enter ***Mechanical*** as the dimension style name.

3. Click on the **Continue** button to proceed.

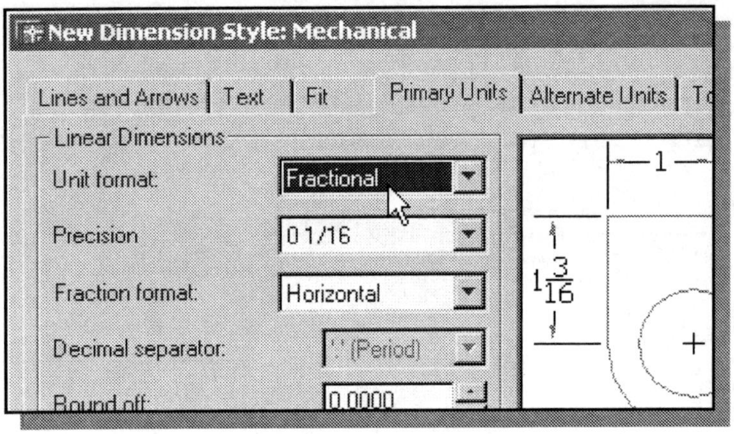

4. Click on the **Primary Units** tab.

5. Select ***Fractional*** as the *Unit format*.

➢ On your own, examine the different options available; most of the settings are self-explanatory.

6. Select the **Fit** tab and notice the two options under *Scale for Dimension Features*.

❖ We can manually adjust the dimension scale factor or let AutoCAD LT automatically adjust the scale factor. For example, our current drawing will fit on A-size paper, and therefore we will use the scale factor of 1. If we decided to plot the same drawing on B-size paper, then we will need to set the dimension scale factor to 2.0. It is possible to let AutoCAD LT determine the scale factor based on the *layout settings*; we will discuss more about the AutoCAD drawing layout in the next lesson.

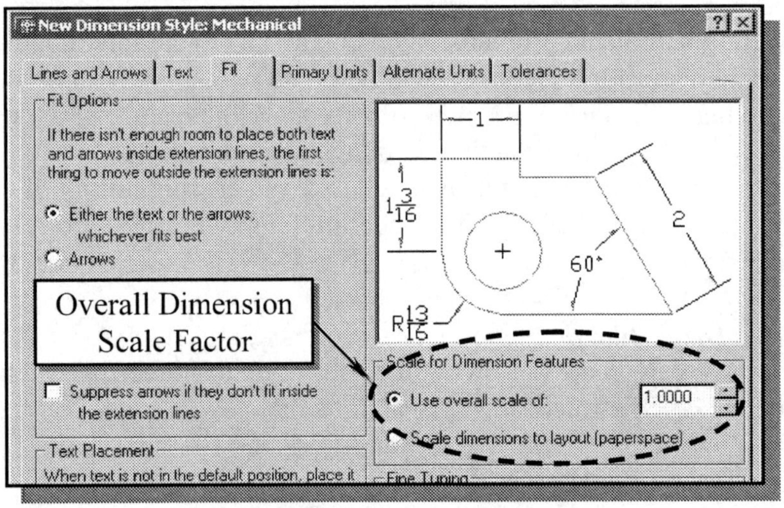

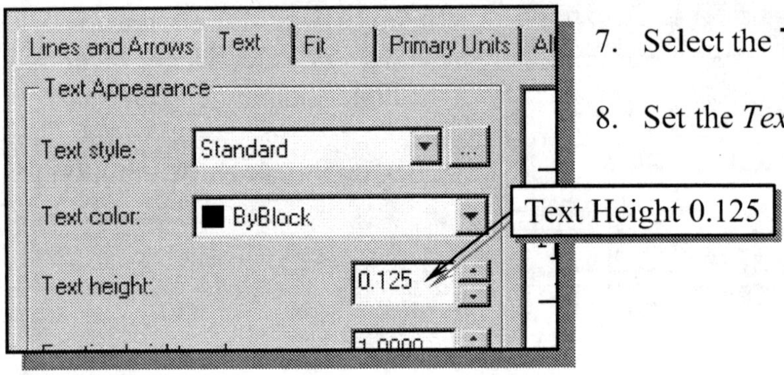

7. Select the **Text** tab.

8. Set the *Text Height* to **0.125**.

9. Select the **Line and Arrows** tab and set the *Arrow size* and *Extend beyond dim lines* to **0.125**. Also set the *Center Mark Type* to ***Line***.

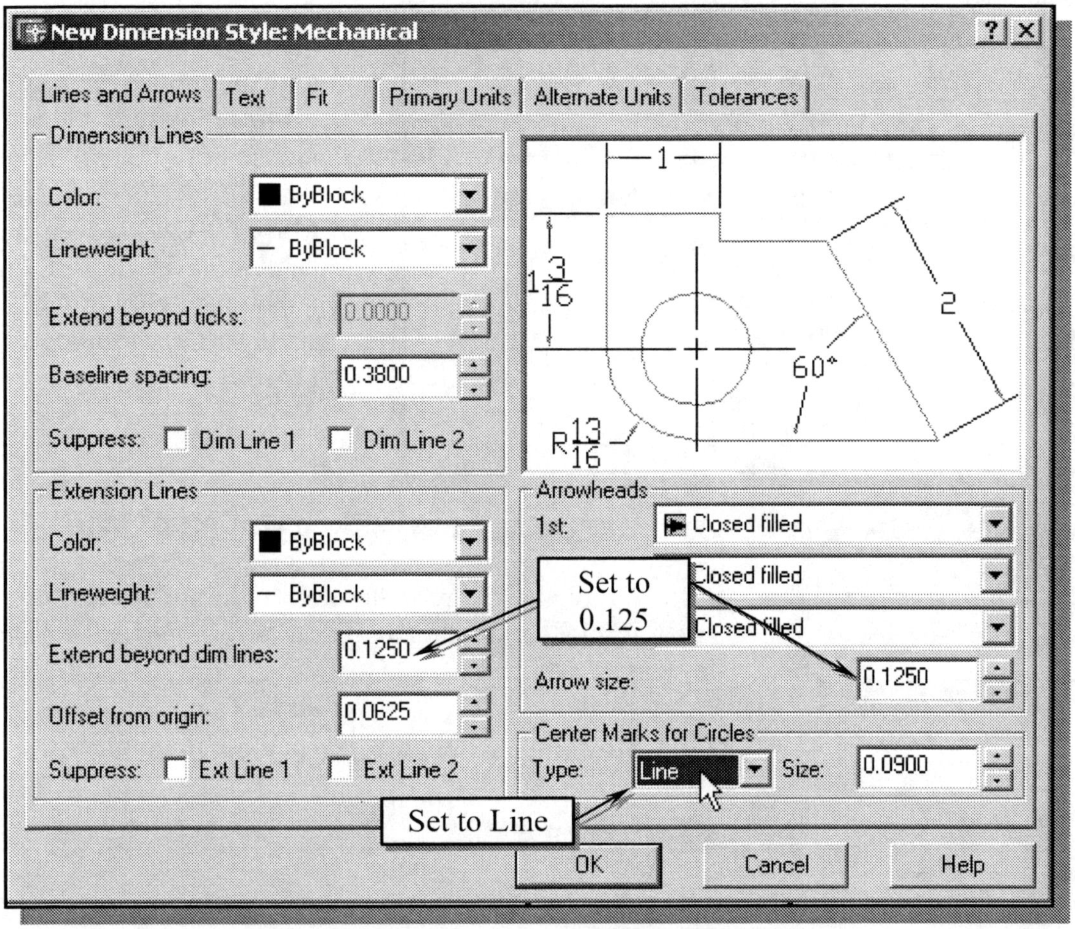

- Notice the different options available on this page, options that let us turn off one or both of the extension lines, dimension lines, and arrowheads. The *Dimension Style Manager* allows us to easily control the appearance of the dimensions in the drawing.

10. Click on the **OK** button to accept the settings and close the dialog box.

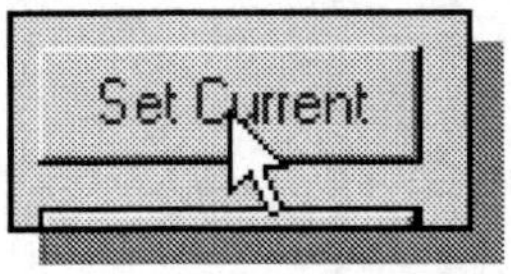

11. Pick the **Set Current** button to make the *Mechanical* dimension style the current dimension style.

12. Click on the **OK** button to accept the settings and close the dialog box.

13. Click on the **Close** button to accept the settings and close the *Dimension Style Manager* dialog box.

❖ The ***Center Mark*** option is used to control the appearance of center marks and centerlines for diameter and radial dimensions.

Using the *Center Mark* Command

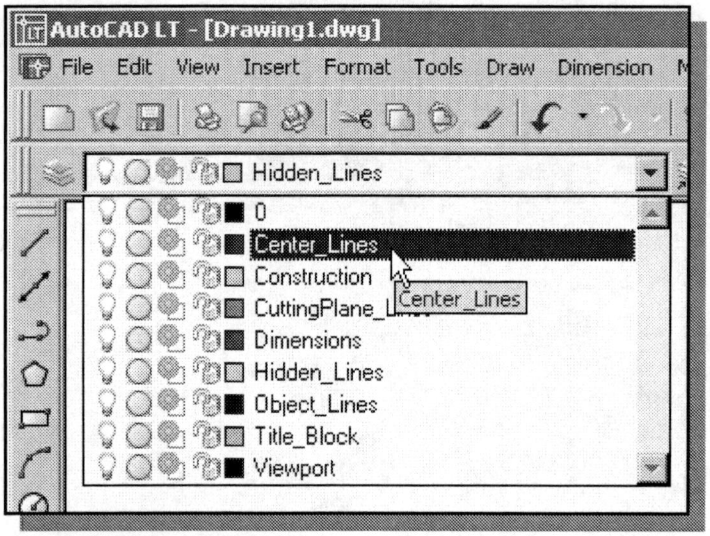

1. On the *Object Properties* toolbar, choose the ***Layer Control*** box with the left-mouse-button.

2. Move the cursor over the name of layer ***Center_Lines***, **left-mouse-click once**, and set layer *Center_lines* as the *Current Layer.*

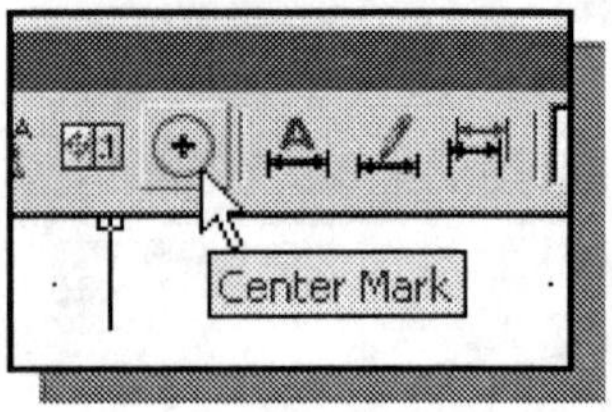

3. In the *Dimension* toolbar, click on the **Center Mark** icon.

4. Pick the radius 1.75 arc in the front view and notice AutoCAD LT automatically places two centerlines through the center of the arc.

5. Repeat the **Center Mark** command and pick the small circle to place the centerlines as shown.

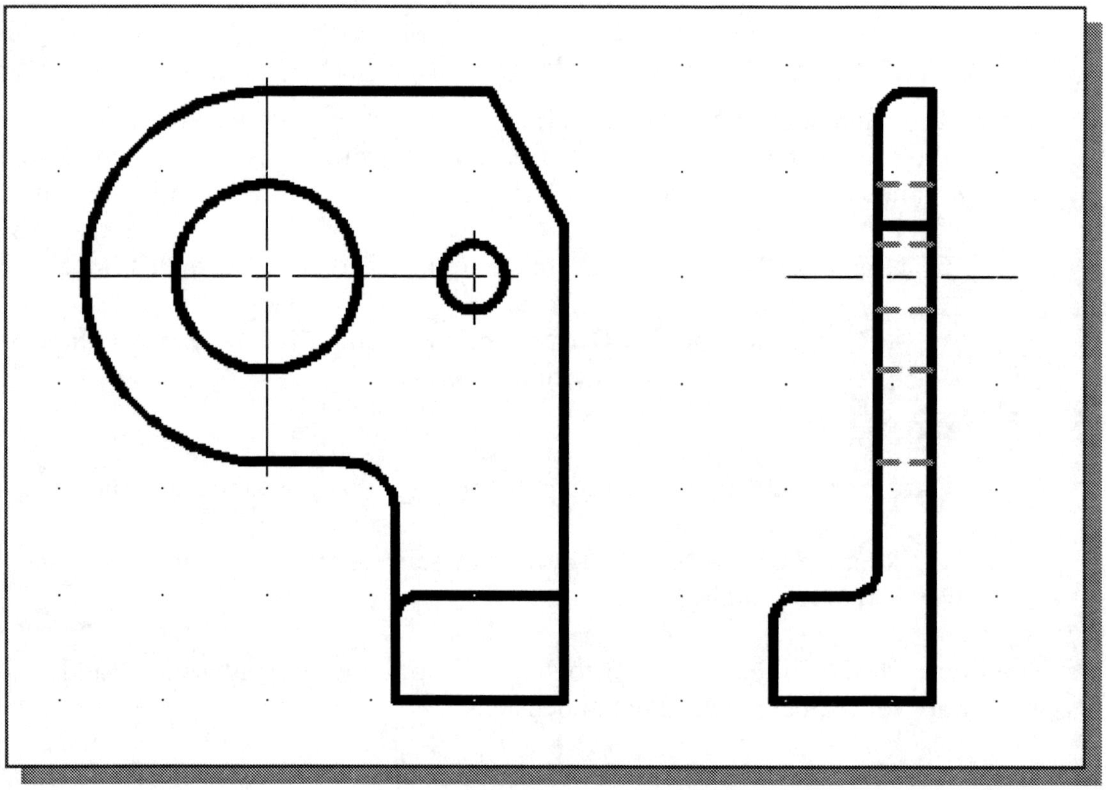

Adding *Linear* Dimensions

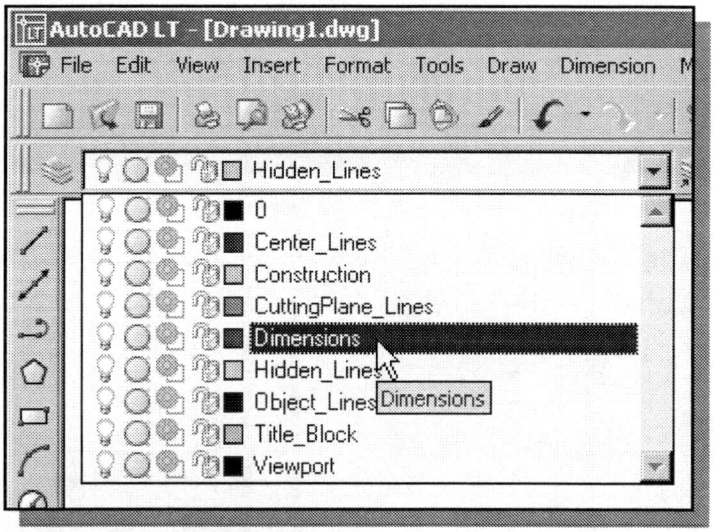

1. On the *Object Properties* toolbar, choose the ***Layer Control*** box with the left-mouse-button.

2. Move the cursor over the name of layer ***Dimensions***, left-mouse-click once, and set layer *Dimensions* as the *Current Layer.*

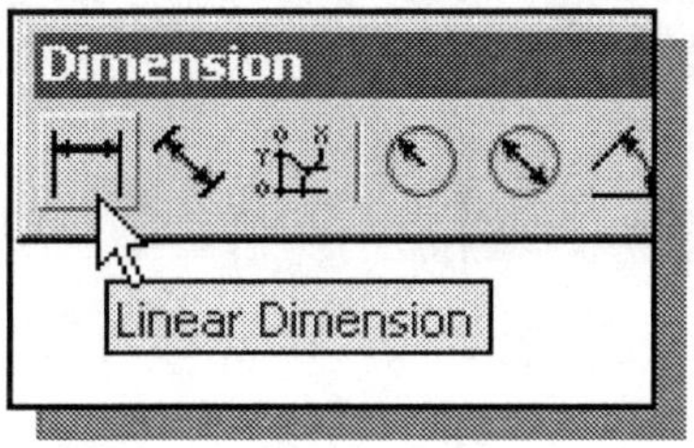

3. In the *Dimension* toolbar, click on the **Linear Dimension** icon.

➢ The Linear Dimension command measures and annotates a feature with a horizontal or vertical dimension.

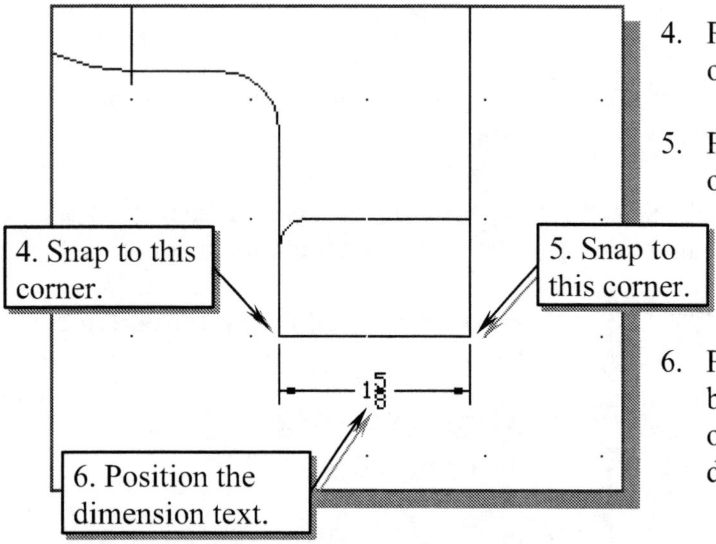

4. Pick the **lower left corner** of the front view of the part.

5. Pick the **lower right corner** of the front view of the part.

6. Pick a point that is about 0.5 inch below the bottom horizontal line of the front view to place the dimension text.

❖ Adding dimensions is this easy with AutoCAD LT's auto-dimensioning and associative-dimensioning features.

7. Repeat the **Linear Dimension** command and add the necessary linear dimensions as shown.

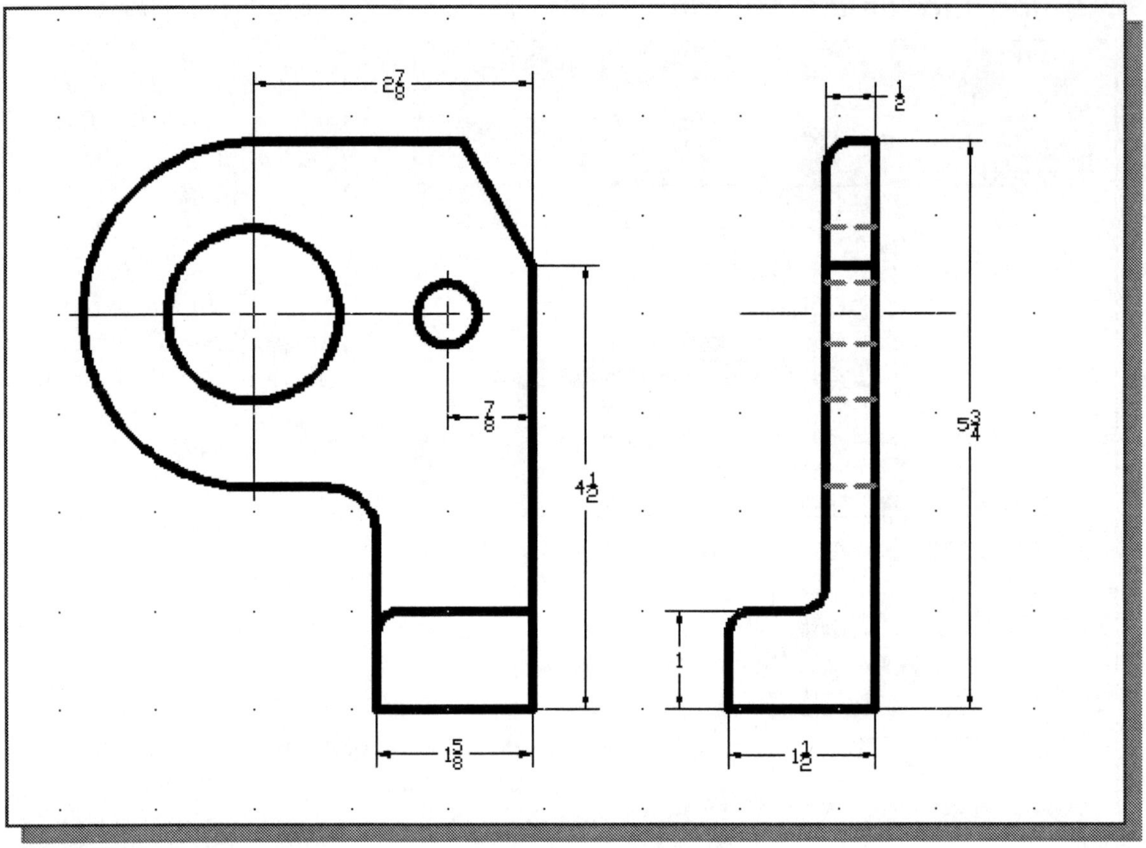

Adding an *Angular* Dimension

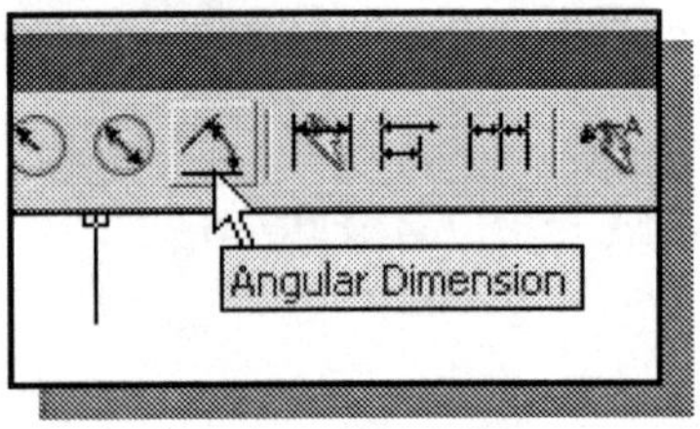

1. In the *Dimension* toolbar, click on the **Angular Dimension** icon.

➢ The Angular Dimension command measures and annotates a feature with an angle dimension.

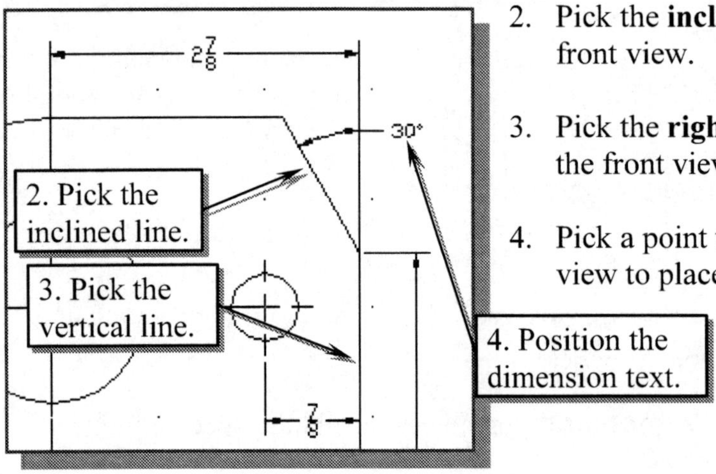

2. Pick the **inclined line** of the part in the front view.

3. Pick the **right vertical line** of the part in the front view.

4. Pick a point toward the right of the front view to place the dimension text.

Adding *Radius* and *Diameter* dimensions

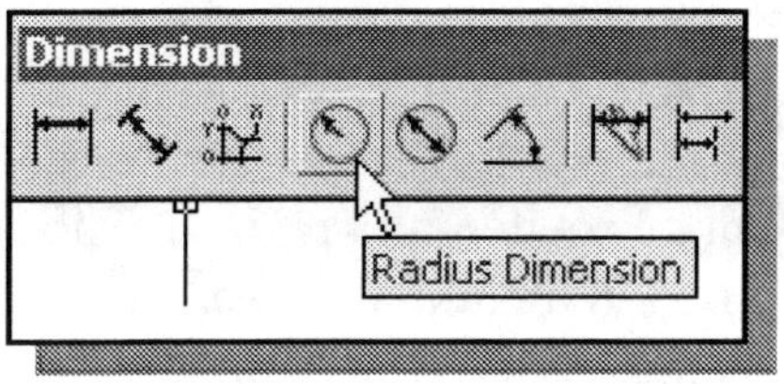

1. In the *Dimension* toolbar, click on the **Radius Dimension** icon.

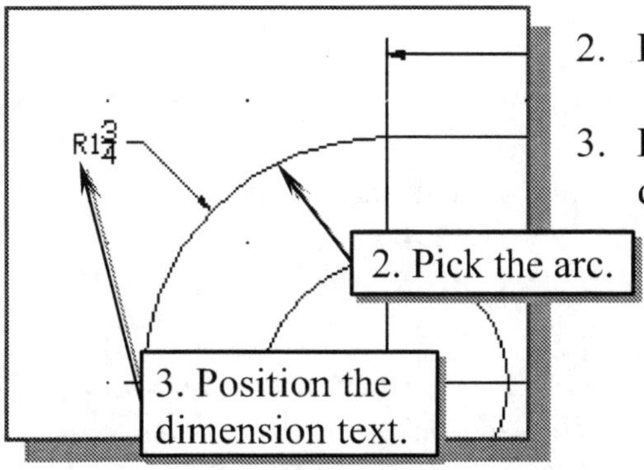

2. Pick the **large arc** in the front view.
3. Pick a point toward the left of the arc to place the dimension text.
4. Use the Radius Dimension and Diameter Dimension commands to add the necessary dimensions as shown.

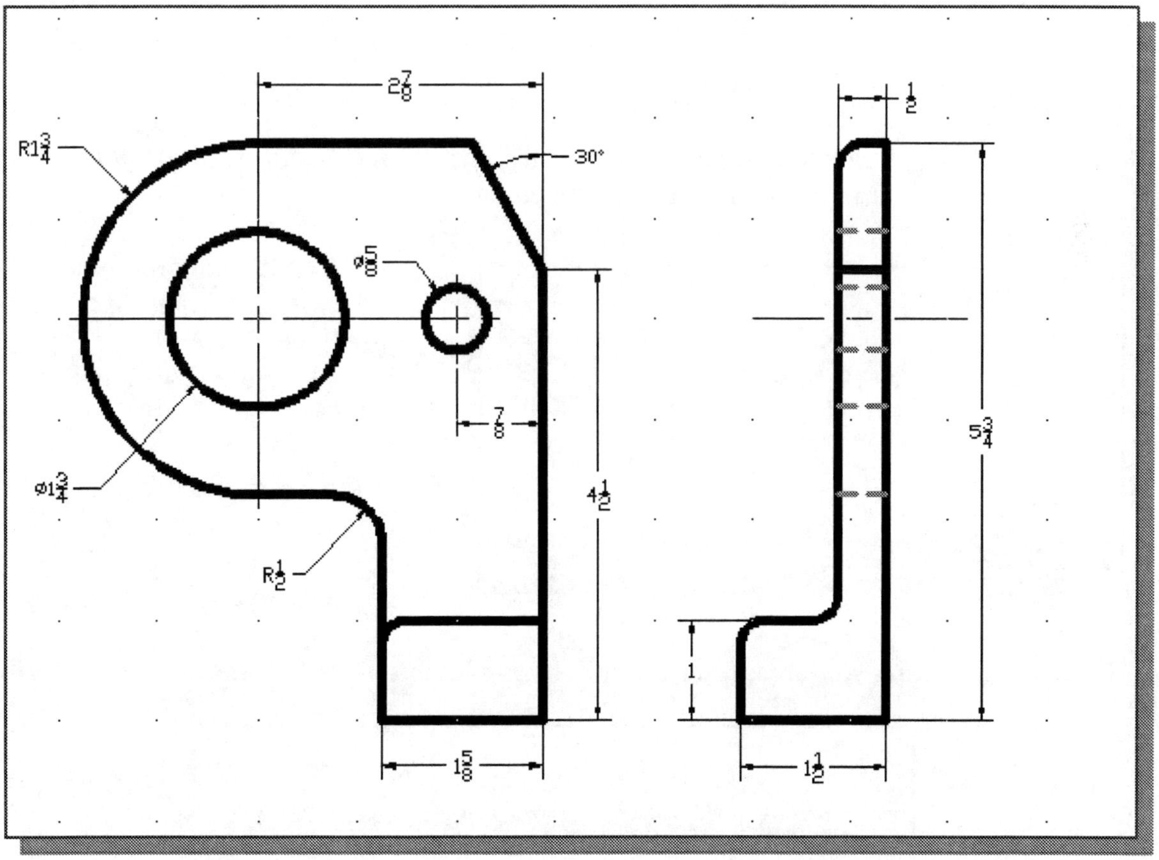

Using the *Single Line Text* Command

AutoCAD LT provides two options to create notes. For simple entries, we can use the **Single Line Text** command. For longer entries with internal formatting, we can use the **Multiline Text** command. The **Single Line Text** command, also known as the **Text** command, can be used to enter several lines of text that can be rotated and resized. The text we are typing is displayed on the screen. Each line of text is treated as a separate object in AutoCAD. To end a line and begin another, press the [**ENTER**] key after entering characters. To end the Text command, press the [**ENTER**] key without entering any characters.

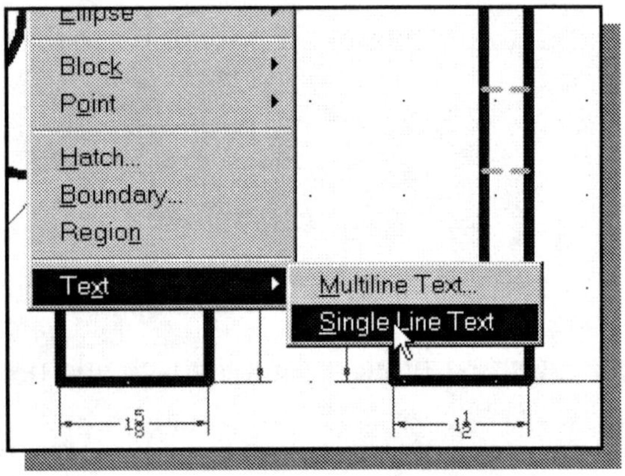

1. In the pull-down menus, select
   [Draw] → [Text] → [Single Line Text]

2. In the command prompt area, the message *"Specify start point of text or [Justify/Style]:"* is displayed. Pick a location near the world coordinate **(1,1.5)**.

3. In the command prompt area, the message *"Specify Height:"* is displayed. Enter **0.125** as the text height.

4. In the command prompt area, the message *"Specify rotation angle of text <0>:"* is displayed. Enter **0** at the command prompt.

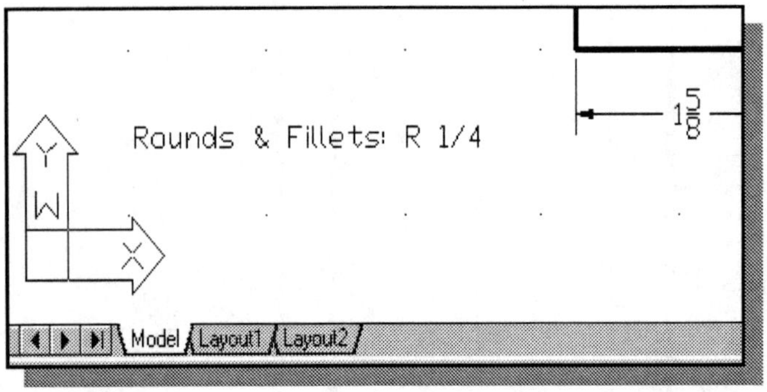

5. In the command prompt area, the message *"Enter Text:"* is displayed.
   Enter **Rounds & Fillets R.25 [ENTER]**

6. In the command prompt area, the message *"Enter Text:"* is displayed. Press the [**ENTER**] key once to end the command.

7. In the *Status Bar* area, reset the options as shown.

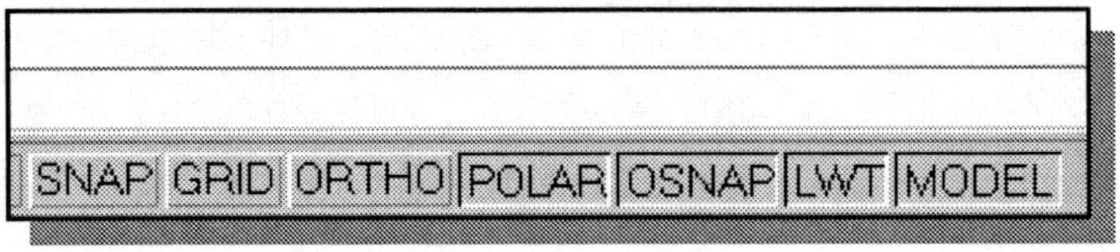

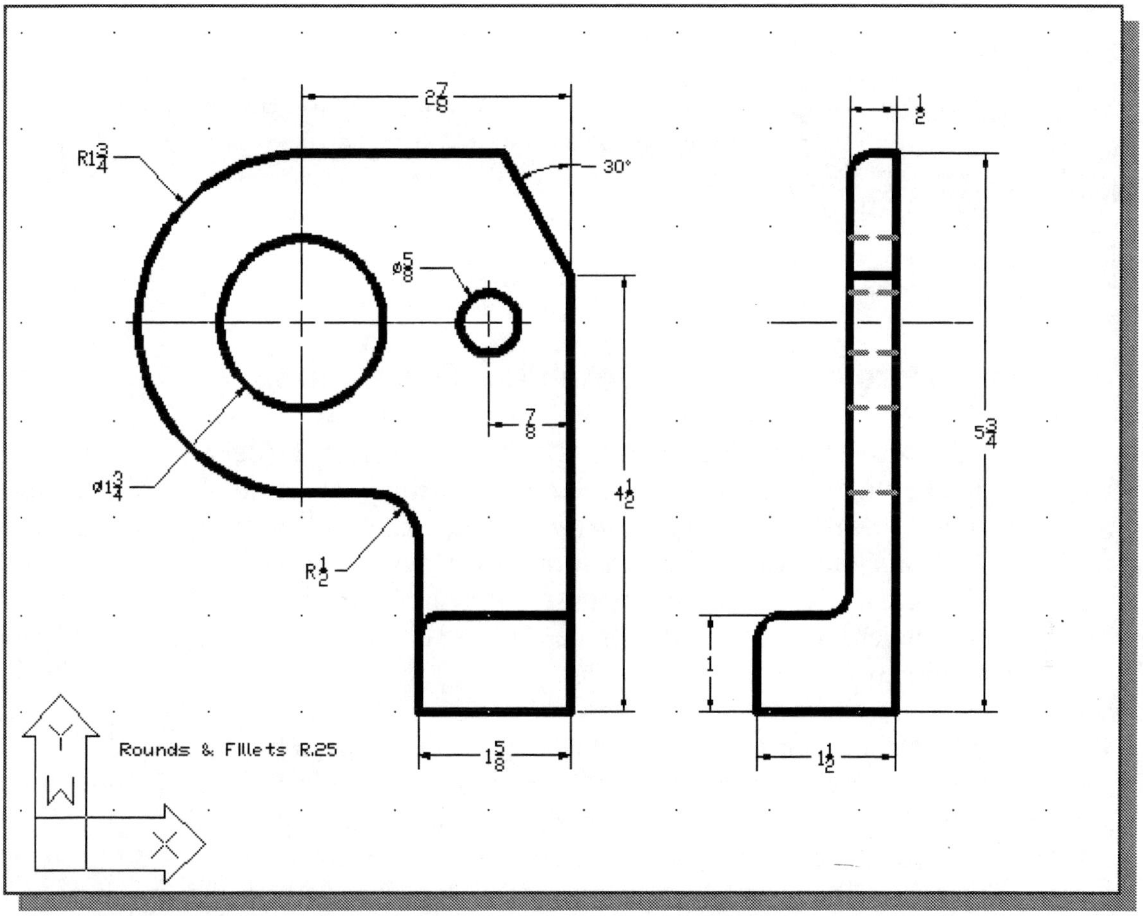

Adding Special Characters

We can add special text characters to the dimensioning text and notes. We can type in special characters during any text command and when entering the dimension text. The most common special characters have been given letters to make them easy to remember.

Code	*Character*	*Symbol*
%%C	Diameter symbol	∅
%%D	Degree symbol	°
%%P	Plus/Minus sign	±

- On your own, create notes containing the special characters.
- On your own, switch on and off different layers to examine the information stored on each layer.

Saving the CAD File

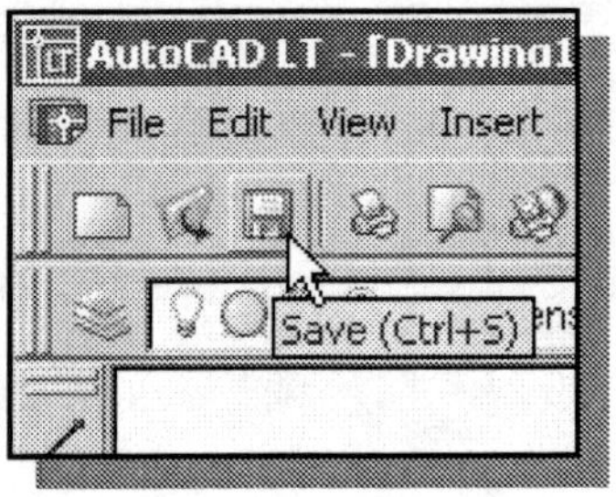

In the *Standard Toolbar* area, click on **Save** icon to save the CAD design.

A Special Note on Layers Containing Dimensions

AutoCAD LT creates several hidden **BLOCKS** when we create associative dimensions and we will take a more in depth look at **blocks** in *Lesson 9*. AutoCAD LT treats blocks as a special type of object called a ***named object***. Each kind of *named object* has a ***symbol table*** or a ***dictionary***, and each table or dictionary can store multiple *named objects*. For example, if we create five dimension styles, our drawing's dimension style symbol table will have five dimension style records. In general, we do not work with symbol tables or dictionaries directly.

When we create dimensions in AutoCAD LT, most of the hidden blocks are placed in the same layer where the dimension was first defined. Some of the definitions are placed in the *DEFPOINTS* layer. When moving dimensions from one layer to another, AutoCAD LT does not move these definitions. When deleting layers, we cannot delete the current layer, layer *0*, xref-dependent layers, or a layer that contains visible and/or invisible objects. Layers referenced by block definitions, along with the *DEFPOINTS* layer, cannot be deleted even if they do not contain visible objects.

To delete layers with hidden blocks, first use the **Purge** command **[File → Drawing Utilities → Purge → Block]** to remove the invisible blocks. (We will have to remove all visible objects prior to using this command.) The empty layer can now be *deleted* or *purged*.

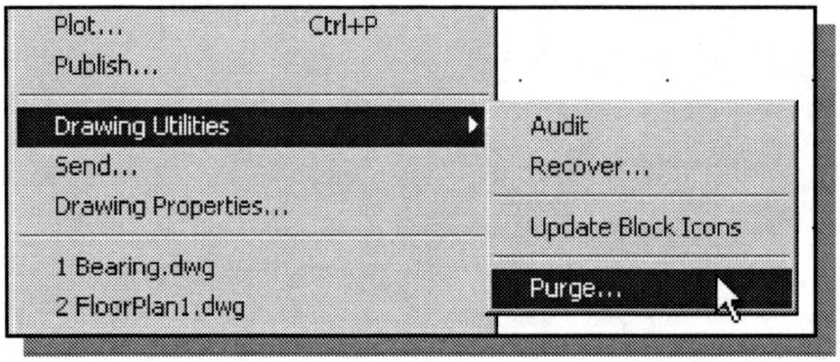

Questions:

1. Why are dimensions and notes important to a technical drawing?

2. List and describe some of the general-dimensioning practices.

3. Describe the procedure in setting up a new *dimension style.*

4. What is the special way to create a diameter symbol when entering a dimension text?

5. Identify the following commands:

(a)

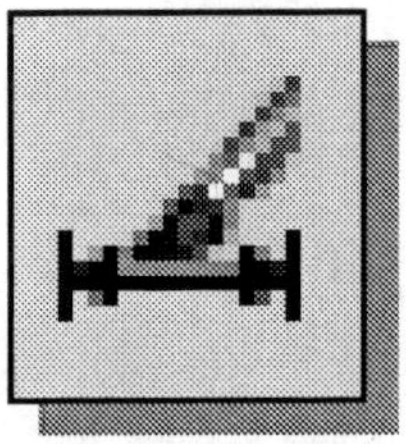

(b)

(c)

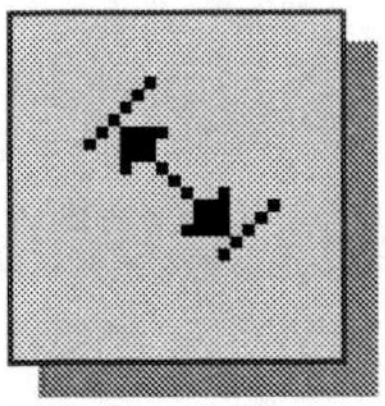

(d)

Exercises:

1. Dimensions are in inches.

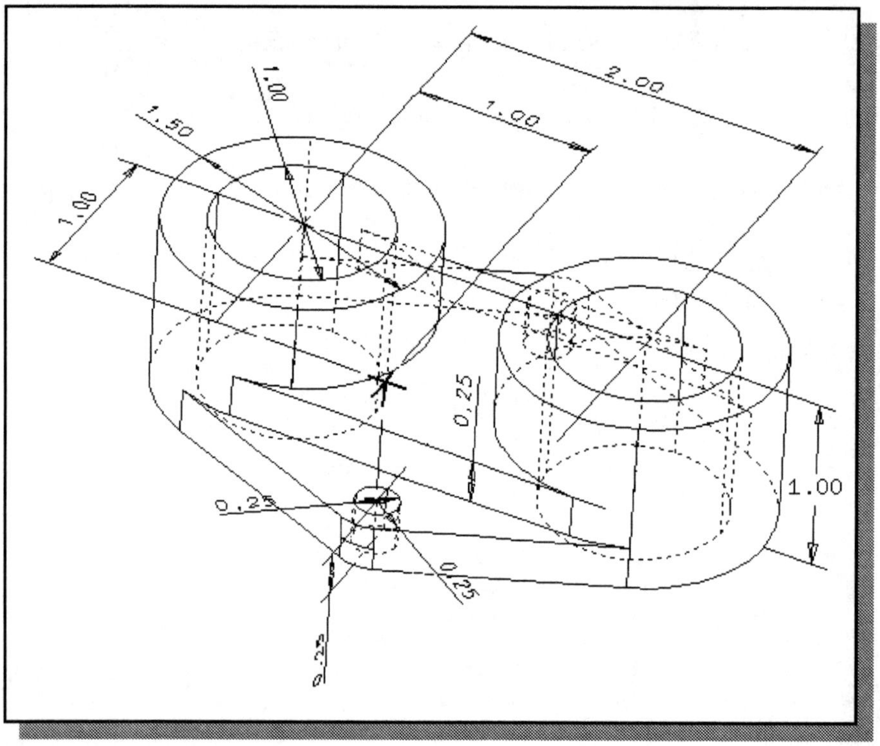

2. Dimensions are in inches.

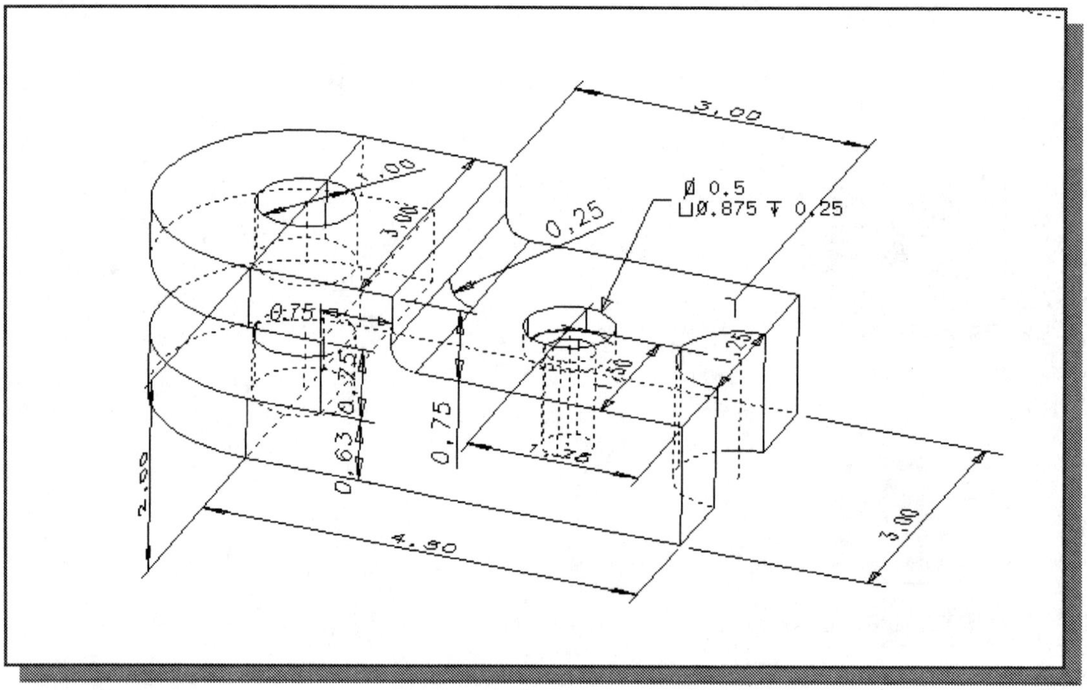

3. Dimensions are in millimeters.

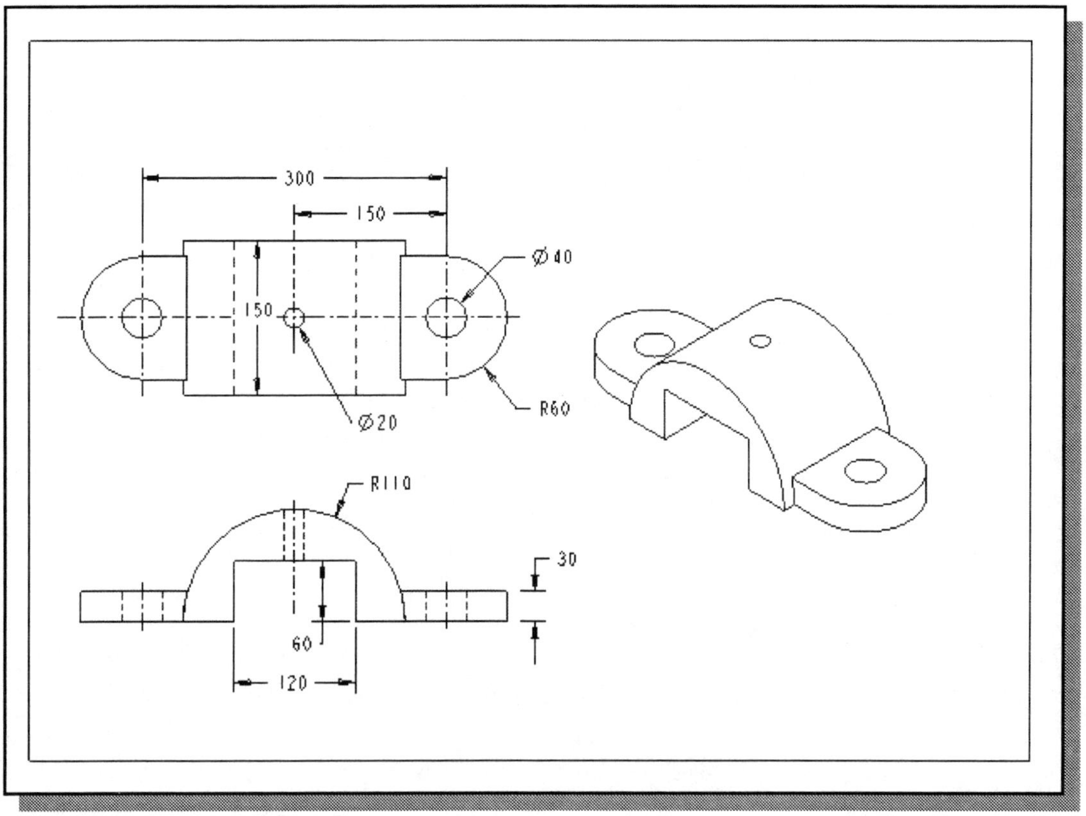

4. Dimensions are in inches.

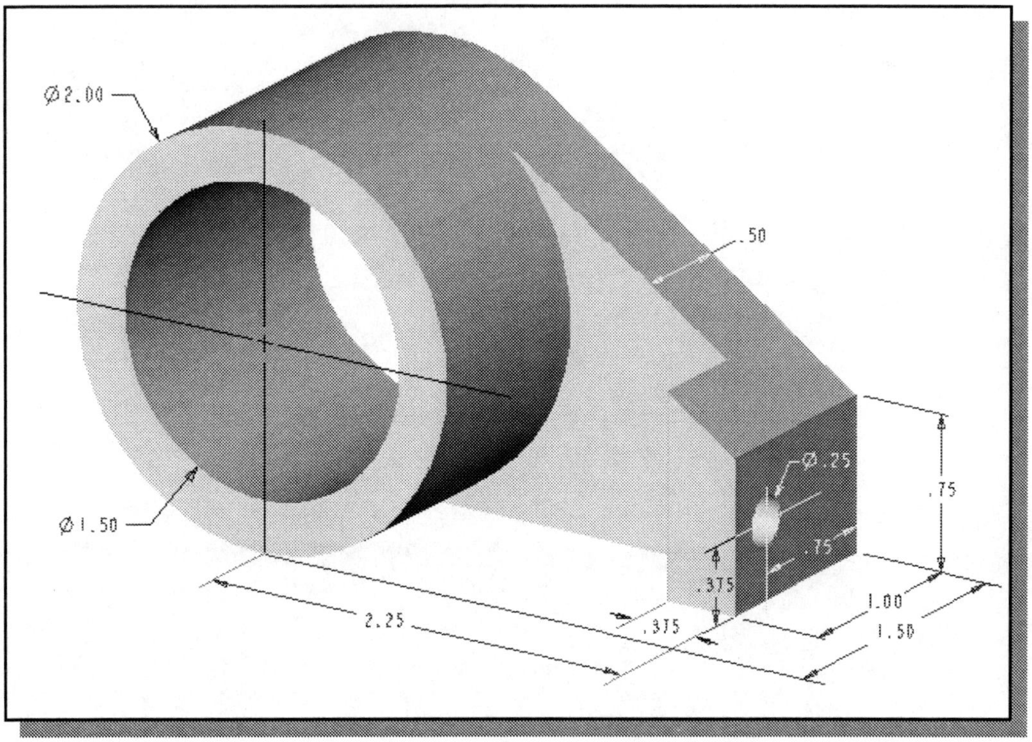

Notes:

Lesson 6
Templates and Plotting

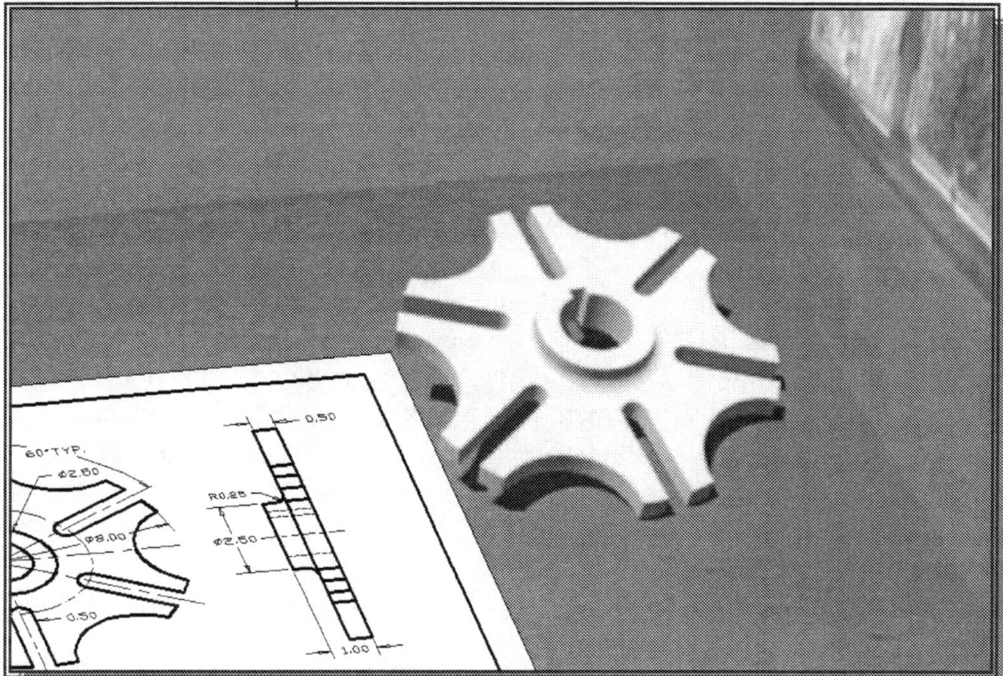

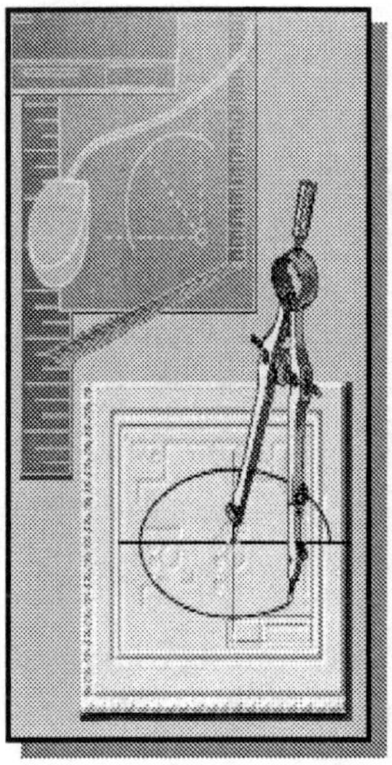

Learning Objectives

- Set up the AutoCAD LT Plot Style Option
- Create and Use a Template File
- Use the MIRROR Command
- Create Multiple Copies of Objects
- Set Up Layouts in Paper Space
- Create Viewports in Paper Space
- Use the PROPERTIES Command
- Adjust the Text Scale for Plotting

Introduction

One of the main advantages of using CAD systems is that we can easily reuse information that is already in the system. For example, many of the system settings, such as setting up layers, colors, linetypes and grids, are typically performed in all AutoCAD LT files. In **AutoCAD® LT 2005**, we can set up **template files** to eliminate these repetitive steps and make our work much more efficient. Using template files also helps us maintain a consistent design and drafting standard. We can also reuse any of the geometry information that is already in the system. For example, we can easily create multiple identical copies of geometry with the **Array** command, or create mirror images of objects using the **Mirror** command. In this lesson, we will examine the use of these more advanced construction features and techniques in **AutoCAD® LT 2005**.

In this lesson, we will also demonstrate the printing/plotting procedure to create a hardcopy of our design. **AutoCAD® LT 2005** provides plotting features that are very easy to use. The new **AutoCAD® LT 2005** plotting features include: WYSIWYG (What You See Is What You Get) layouts; onscreen lineweights; plot style tables; device-accurate paper sizes; and creating custom paper sizes.

The *Geneva Cam* Design

Starting Up *AutoCAD LT 2005*

1. Select the **AutoCAD LT 2005** option on the *Program* menu or select the **AutoCAD LT 2005** icon on the *Desktop*.

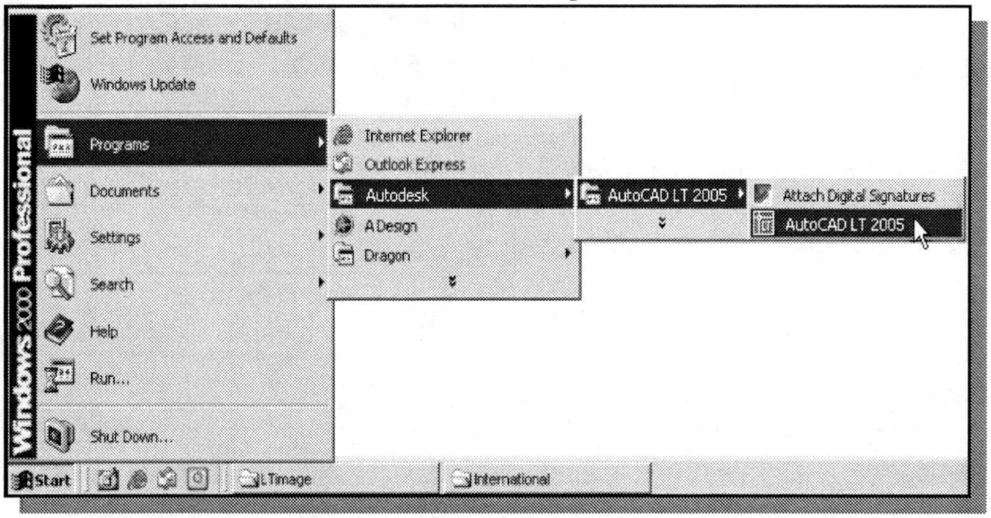

2. Choose ***Start from Scratch*** as the startup option, as shown in the figure below.

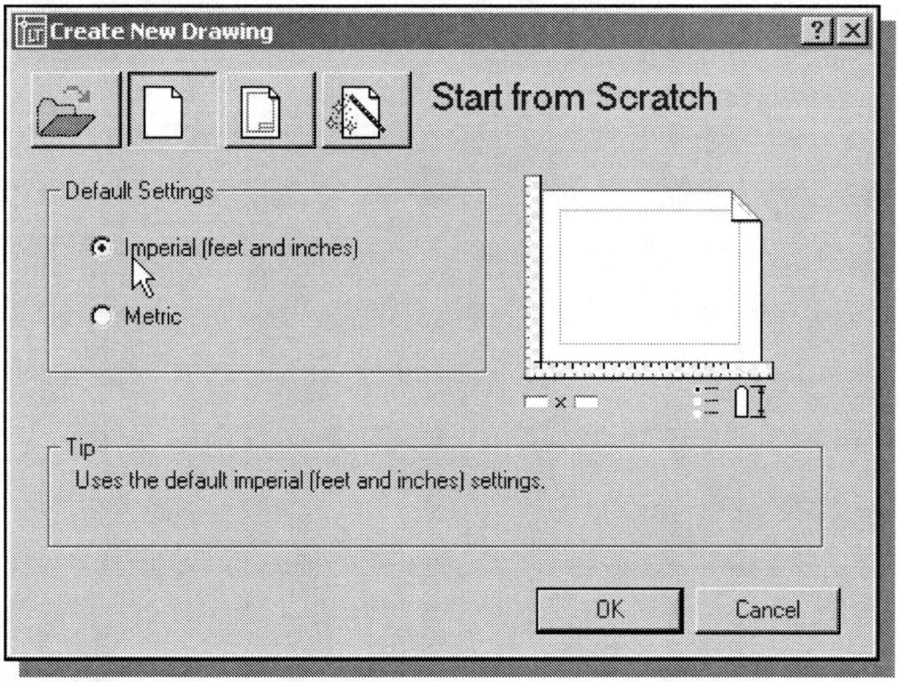

3. In the *Default Settings* section, pick **Imperial (feet and inches)** as the drawing units.

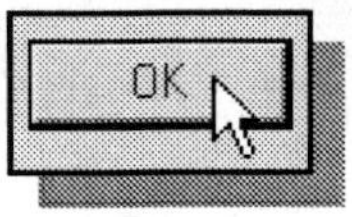

4. Pick **OK** in the *Startup* dialog box to accept the selected settings.

Setting Up the *Plot Style Mode*

Using **AutoCAD® LT 2005** ***plot styles*** and ***plot style tables*** allows us to control the way drawings look at plot time. We can reassign object properties, such as color, linetype, and lineweight, and plot the same drawing differently. The default **AutoCAD® LT 2005** ***plot style mode*** is set to use the ***Color-Dependent*** plot style, which controls the plotting of objects based on the object colors and is the traditional method of adjusting the plotted hardcopy in AutoCAD LT. Another method, first introduced in *AutoCAD 2000*, is to use the ***Named*** plot style table that works independently of color. In this lesson, we will learn to plot with the new AutoCAD LT ***Named*** plot style, which provides a very flexible and fast way to control the plotting of our designs.

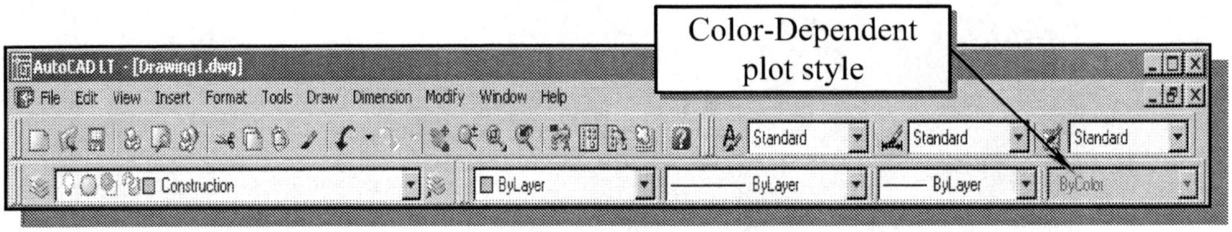

- Notice the ***Plot Style*** box, in the *Object Properties* toolbar, displays the default setting of *ByColor* and is grayed out. This indicates the plot style is set to the *Color-Dependent* plot style, and therefore the object color is used to control plotting.

1. In the pull-down menus, select
   [Tools] → [Options]

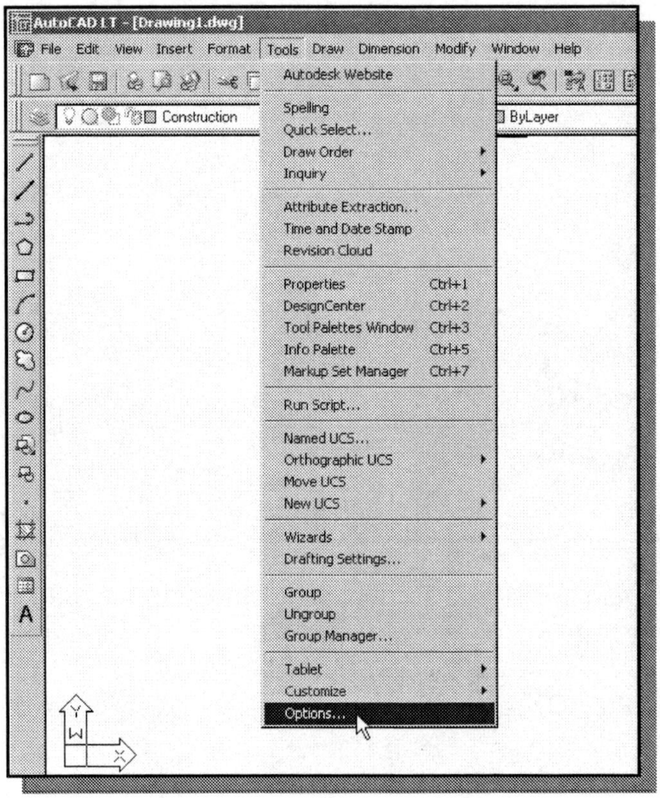

2. In the *Options* dialog box, select the **Plot and Publish** tab if it is not the page on top.

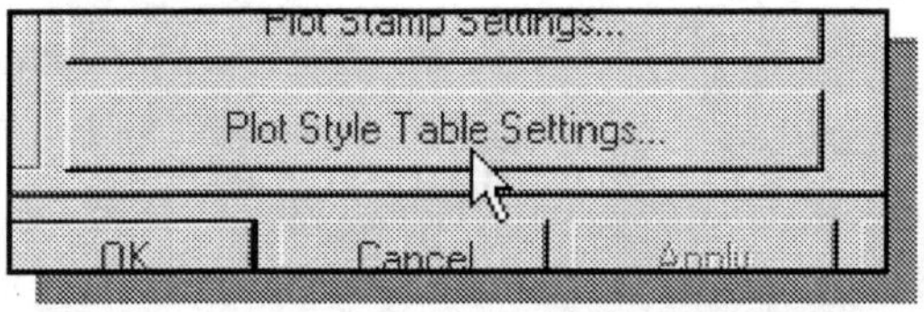

3. Click on the **Plot Style Table Settings** button as shown.

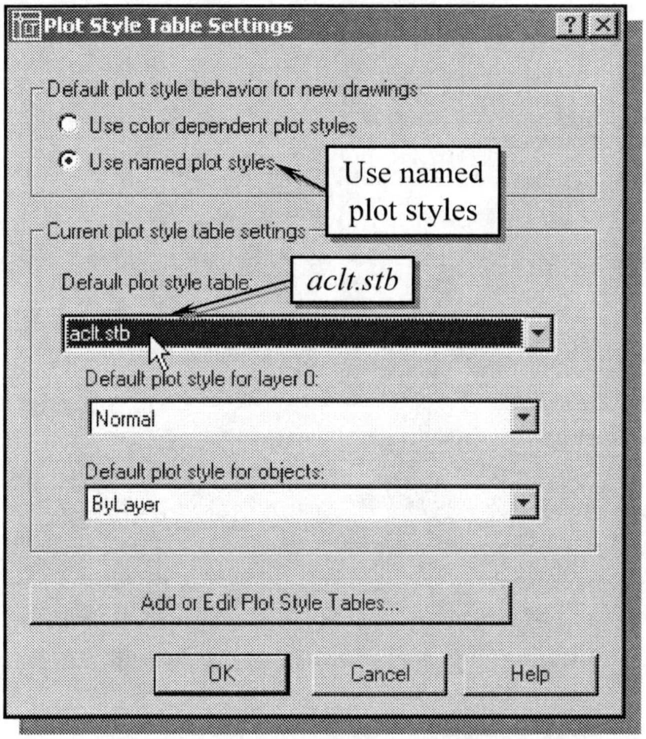

4. Switch *ON* the **Use named plot styles** as shown.

5. In the *Default plot style table*, select ***aclt.stb*** from the list of plot style tables.

6. Click on the **OK** button to accept the modified plot style table settings.

7. Pick **OK** to accept the selected settings and close the ***Options*** dialog box.

➢ Notice the *Plot Style* box in the *Object Properties* toolbar still displays the setting of *ByColor* and is still grayed out. This is because the plotting settings are stored in each file. We will close this file and start a new file to have the new settings take effect.

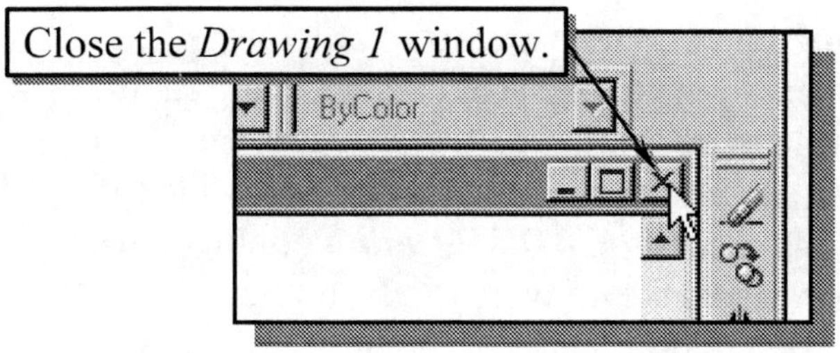

8. Click on the **[X]** button, located near the top right corner of the *Drawing 1* window, to close the file.

9. In the AutoCAD *Warning* dialog box, select **NO** to close the file without saving.

Starting a New File

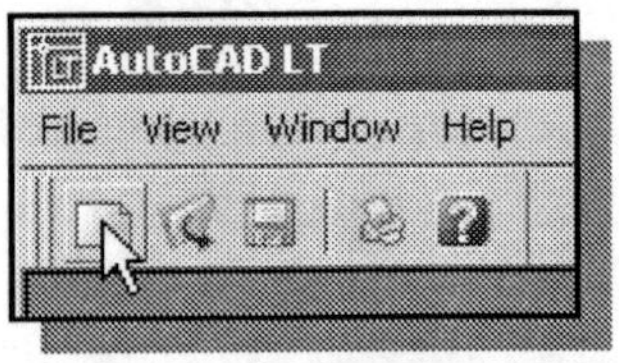

1. Select the **New** icon in the *Standard* toolbar area.

2. In the *AutoCAD LT* startup dialog box, select the **Create Drawings** icon.

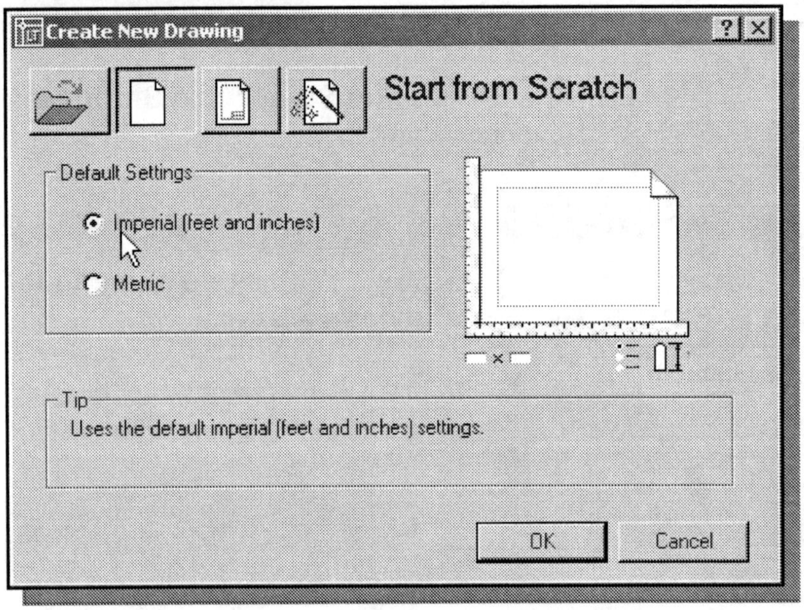

3. Select the ***Start from Scratch*** option as shown.

4. Pick **Imperial (feet and inches)** as the drawing units.

5. On your own, click OK to **close** the *AutoCAD LT* Startup dialog box.

➤ Notice the ***Plot Style*** box in the *Object Properties* toolbar now displays the setting of ***ByLayer*** and is no longer grayed out. This indicates we are now using a *named* plot style, and different options are available to control plotting of the design.

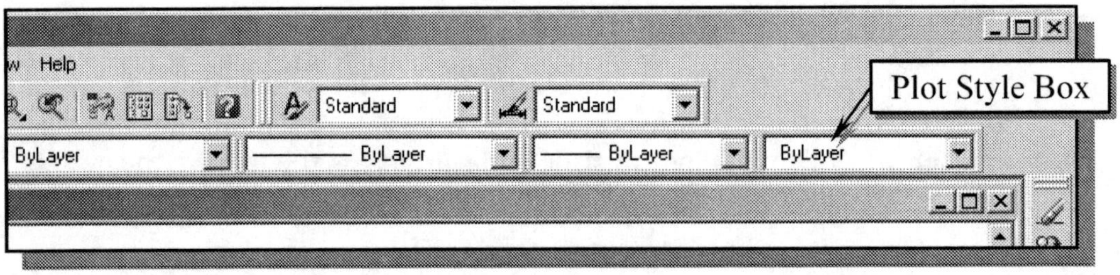

➤ We will demonstrate the use of the **named** plot style to create a hardcopy of the *Geneva Cam* design. The steps described in the above sections are required to set up the settings for the named plot style to be used in new drawings, and it should be done prior to creating the design. We can also convert an existing drawing to use named plot styles; it will require installing the ***AutoCAD Migration*** application and use the **Convertpstyles** command to perform the conversion. Note that after the conversion, any color-dependent plot style tables attached to layouts in the drawing are removed.

GRID and *SNAP* Intervals Setup

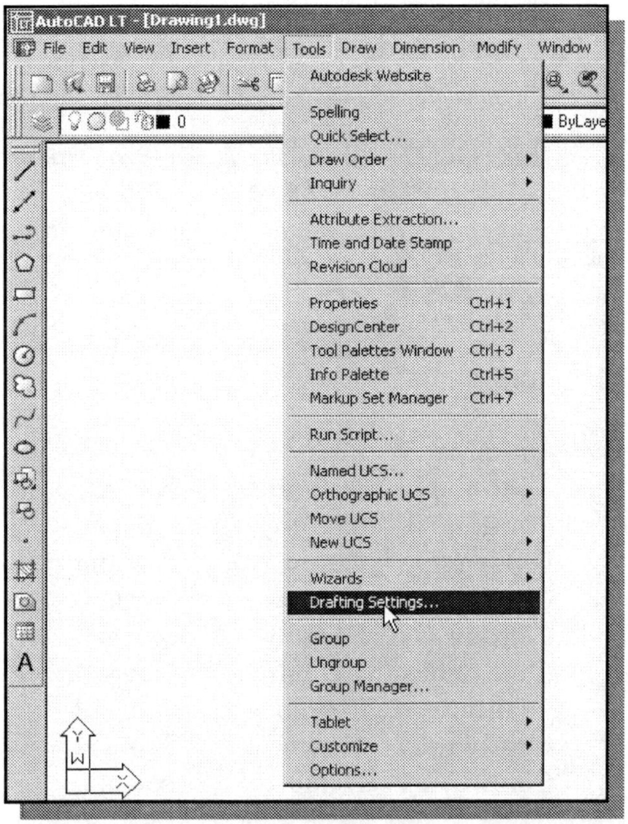

1. In the pull-down menus, select **[Tools] → [Drafting Settings]**

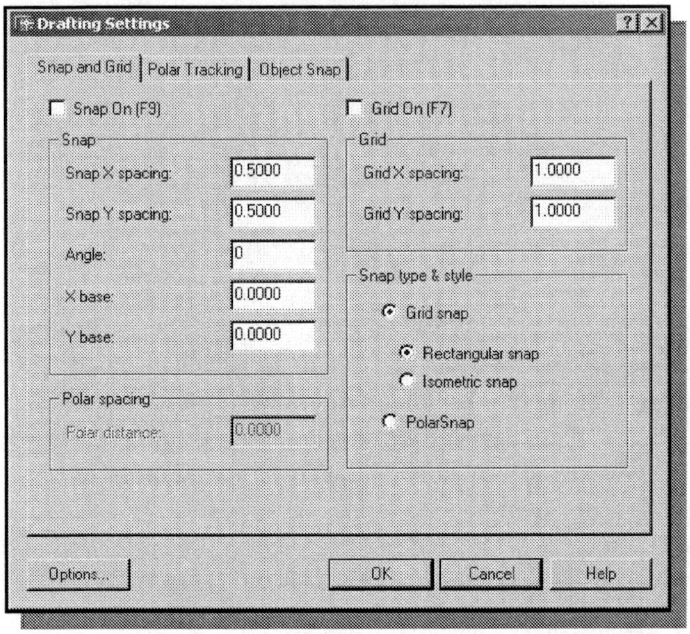

2. In the *Drafting Settings* dialog box, select the **SNAP and GRID** tab if it is not the page on top.

3. Change *Grid Spacing* to **1.0** for both X and Y directions.

4. Also adjust the *Snap Spacing* to **0.5** for both X and Y directions.

5. Pick **OK** to exit the *Drawing Units* dialog box.

6. In the *Status Bar* area, reset the option buttons so that only *SNAP, GRID*, and *MODEL* are switched ***ON***.

Layers Setup

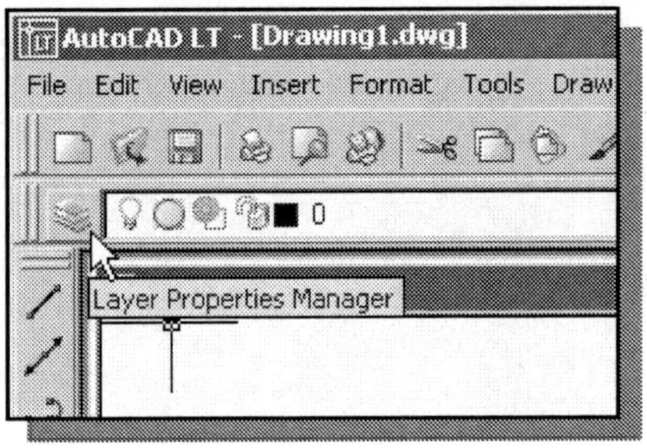

1. Pick **Layer properties manager** in the *Object Properties* toolbar.

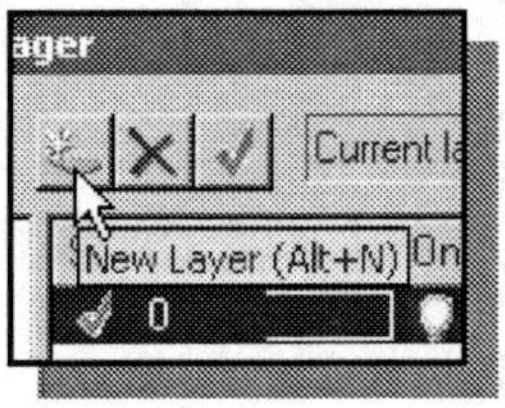

2. In the *Layer Properties Manager* dialog box, click on the **New** button to create new layers.

3. Create **layers** with the following settings:

Layer	*Color*	*LineType*	*Lineweight*	*PlotStyle*
Construction	**Gray**	**Continuous**	**Default**	**Normal**
Object_Lines	**Blue**	**Continuous**	**0.6mm**	**Normal**
Hidden_Lines	**Cyan**	**Hidden**	**0.3mm**	**Normal**
Center_Lines	**Red**	**Center**	**Default**	**Normal**
Dimensions	**Magenta**	**Continuous**	**Default**	**Normal**
Section_Lines	**White**	**Continuous**	**Default**	**Normal**
CuttingPlane_Lines	**Yellow**	**Phantom**	**0.6mm**	**Normal**
Title_Block	**Green**	**Continuous**	**1.2mm**	**Normal**
Viewport	**White**	**Continuous**	**Default**	**Normal**

➢ Using the ***Normal*** plot style enables plotting of *lineweights* defined in the specific layer.

4. Click on the **OK** button to accept the settings and exit the *Layer Properties Manager* dialog box.

Adding Borders and Title Block in the Layout

AutoCAD® LT 2005 allows us to create plots to any exact scale on the paper. Until now, we have been working in ***model space*** to create our design in ***full size***. When we are ready to plot, we can arrange our design on a two-dimensional sheet of paper so that the plotted hardcopy is exactly how we want. This two-dimensional sheet of paper is known as the ***paper space*** in AutoCAD LT. We can place borders and title blocks on *paper space*, the objects that are less critical to our design.

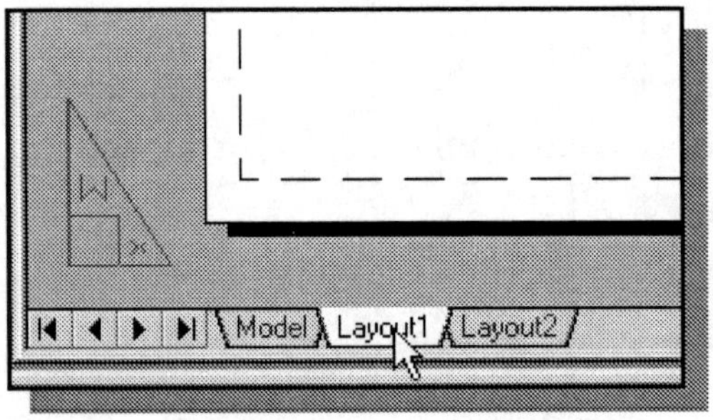

1. Pick the **Layout1** tab to switch to a two-dimensional paper space.

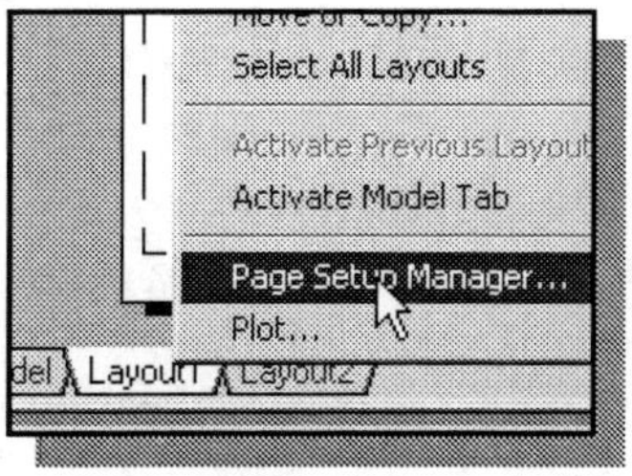

1. To adjust any *Page Setup* options, right-mouse-click once on the tab and select **Page Setup Manager**.

2. Choose the default layout in the *Page Setup Manager*.

3. In the *Page Setup* dialog box, select a plotter/printer that is available to plot/print your design. Consult with your instructor or technical support personnel if you have difficulty identifying the hardware.

❖ In this lesson, we will demonstrate the plotting procedure for an A-size plot on a LaserJet printer. The procedure described here is also applicable to other types of printers and plotters.

➢ Notice the *Printable area* listed in the *Paper size and paper units* section is typically smaller than the actual paper size, which is due to the limitations of the hardware.

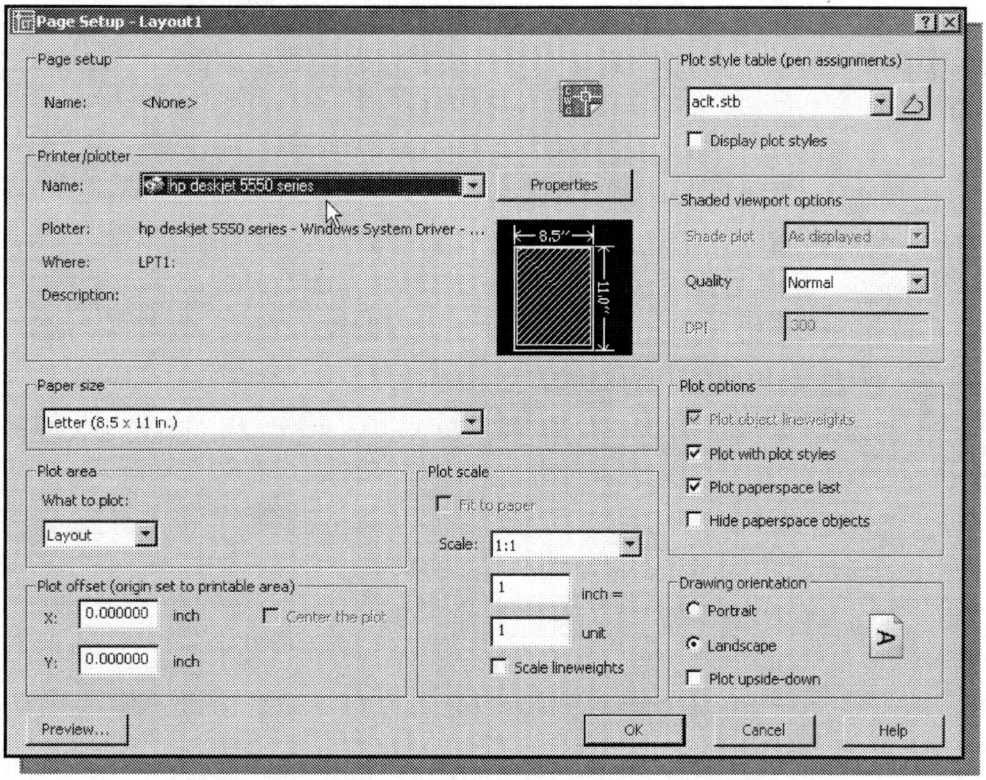

2. Confirm the *Paper size* is set to ***Letter*** or equivalent (8.5″ by 11″) and the *Drawing orientation* is set to ***Landscape***.

3. Click on the **OK** button to accept the settings and exit the *Page Setup* dialog box.

➢ In the graphics window, a rectangular outline on a gray background indicates the paper size. The dashed lines displayed within the paper indicate the *printable area*.

Change the Background Color of the Layout Graphics Window

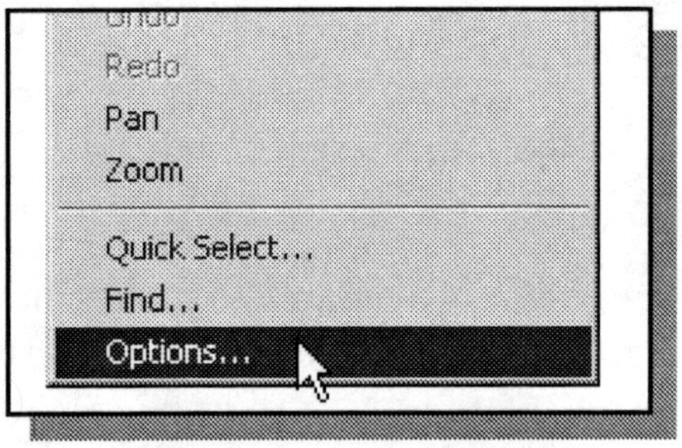

1. Move the cursor inside the graphics window, right-mouse-click to bring the option menu and select **Options** with the left-mouse-button.

➢ Note that many of the AutoCAD LT interface and drawing environment settings can be changed through the *Options* dialog box.

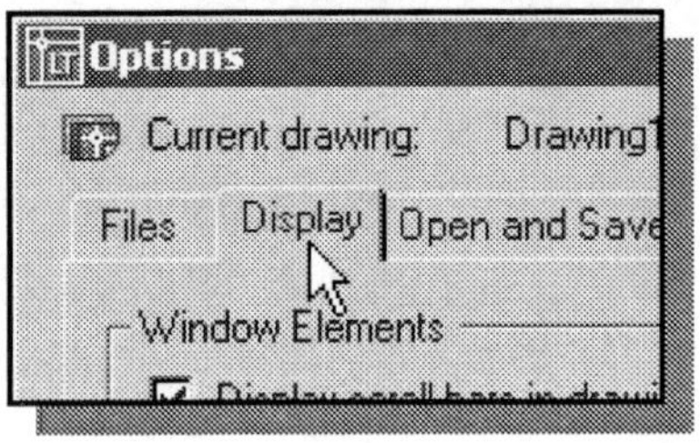

2. In the *Options* dialog box, select the **Display** tab if it is not the page on top.

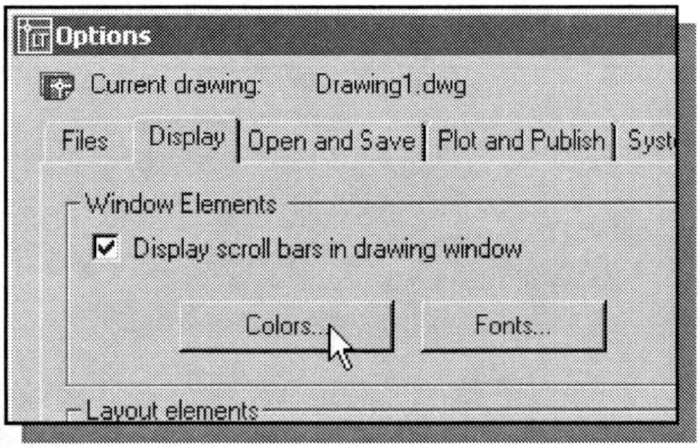

3. In the *Window Elements* section, click the **Colors** button as shown in the figure.

4. In the *Color Options* dialog box, select ***Layout tabs background*** as shown in the figure below.

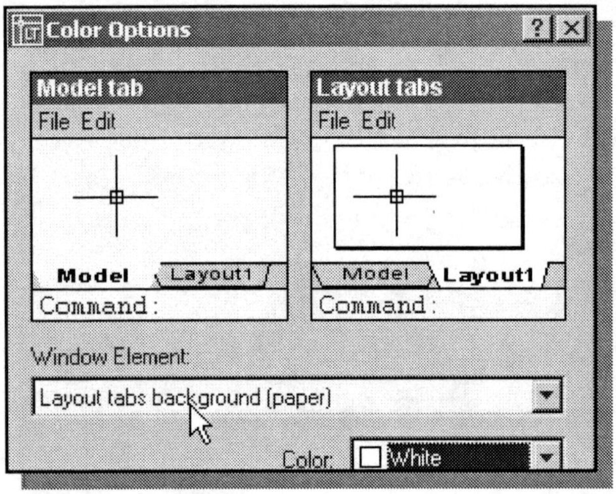

5. In the *Color* option, select ***White*** as shown.

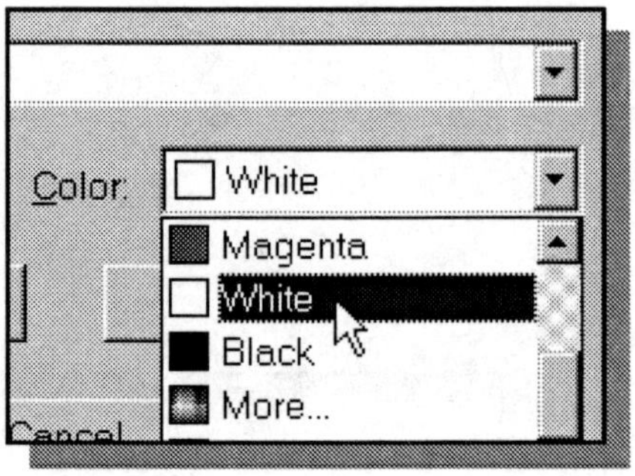

6. Click the **Apply & Close** button to accept the settings.

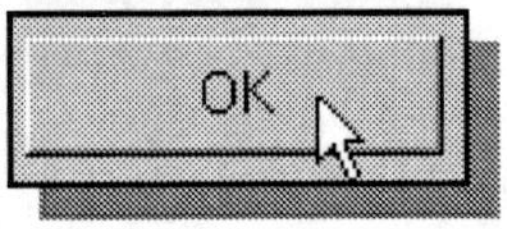

7. Click the **OK** button to exit the *Options* dialog box.

Create a Customized Title Block

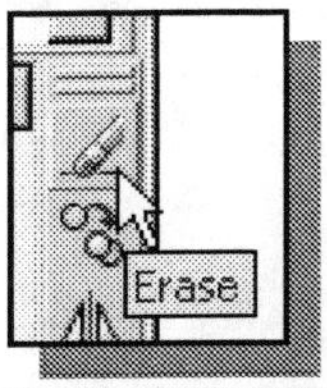

1. On your own, use the **Erase** command and delete the default *viewport*, the solid rectangle, inside the dashed lines.

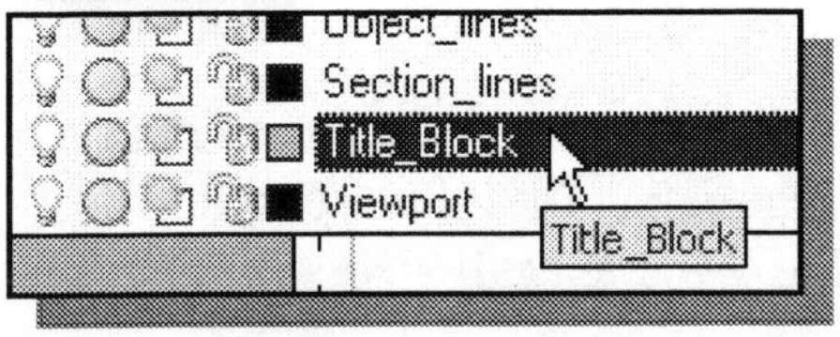

2. In the *Object Properties* toolbar area, select the ***Layer Control*** box and set layer *Title_Block* as the *Current Layer*.

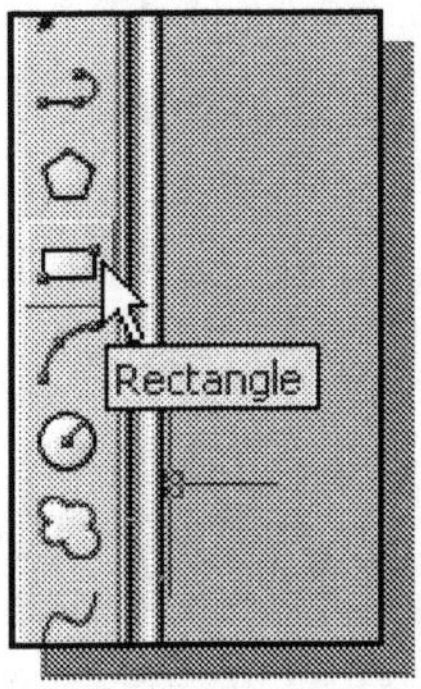

3. Select the **Rectangle** icon in the *Draw* toolbar. In the command prompt area, the message *"Specify first corner point or [Chamfer/Elevation/Fillet/Thickness/Width]:"* is displayed.

4. Pick a location that is on the inside and near the lower left corner of the dashed rectangle.

5. In the command prompt area, use the *relative coordinate entry method* and create a 10.25″ × 7.75″ rectangle.

6. Complete the title block as shown. (Place the text in the *Dimensions* layer.)

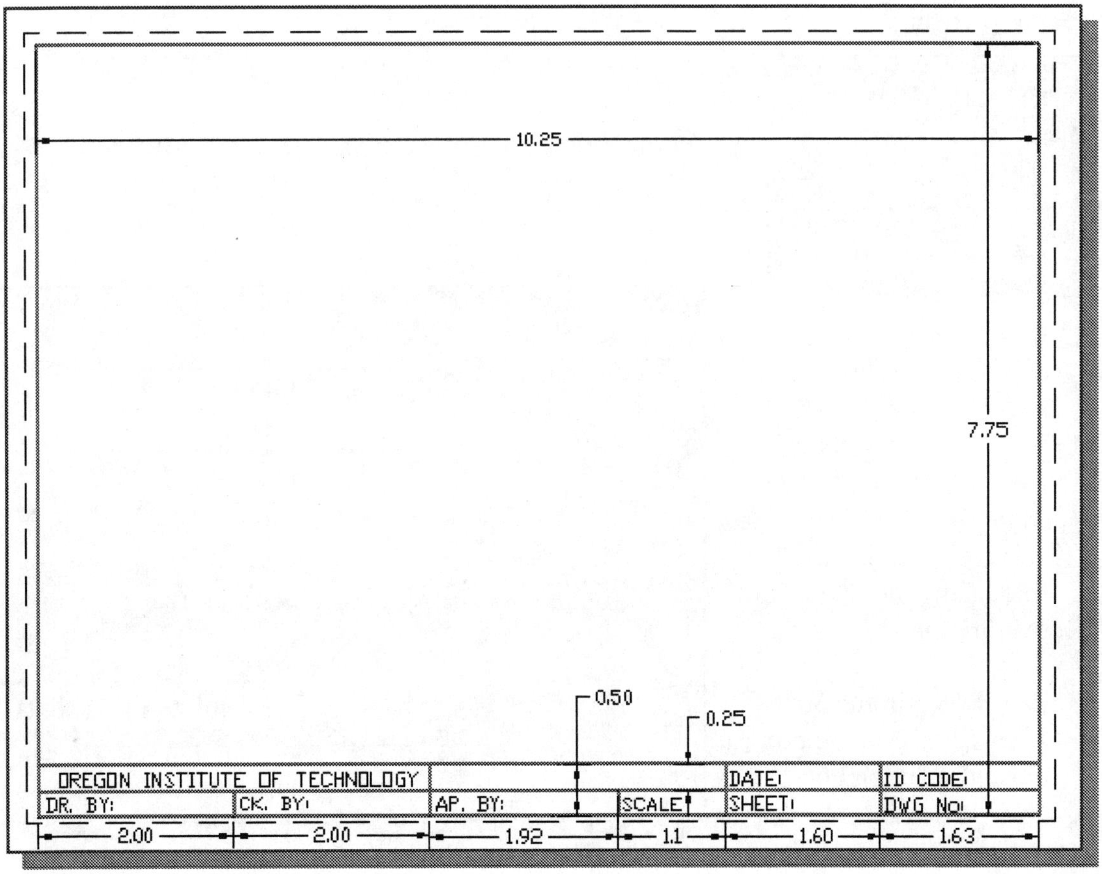

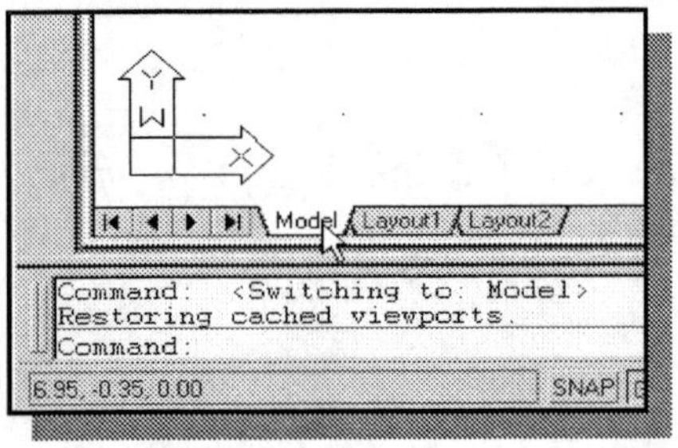

7. Pick the **Model** tab to switch back to *model space*.

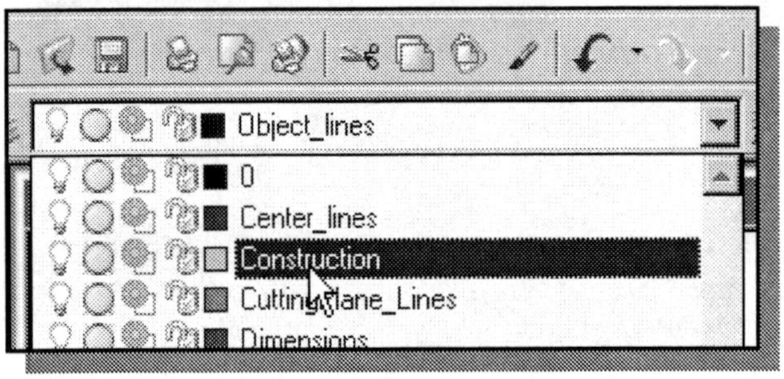

8. In the *Object Properties* toolbar area, select the ***Layer Control*** box and set layer ***Construction*** as the *Current Layer*.

➢ Notice the title block we created is shown only in *paper space*.

Create a Template File

The heart of any CAD system is the ability to reuse information that is already in the system. In the preceding sections, we spent a lot of time setting up system variables, such as layers, colors, linetypes, and plotting settings. We will make a **template file** containing all of the settings and the title block we have created so far.

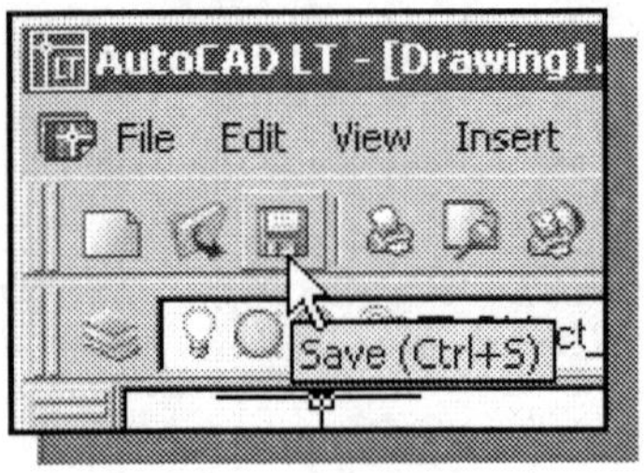

1. In the *Standard* toolbar area, select the **Save** icon.

2. In the *Save Drawing As* dialog box, select *AutoCAD LT Drawing Template (.dwt)* as the file type, enter ***Acad_A_Title*** in the *File name* box, and select the folder in which you want to store the file.

3. Pick **Save** in the *Save Drawing As* dialog box to close the dialog box.

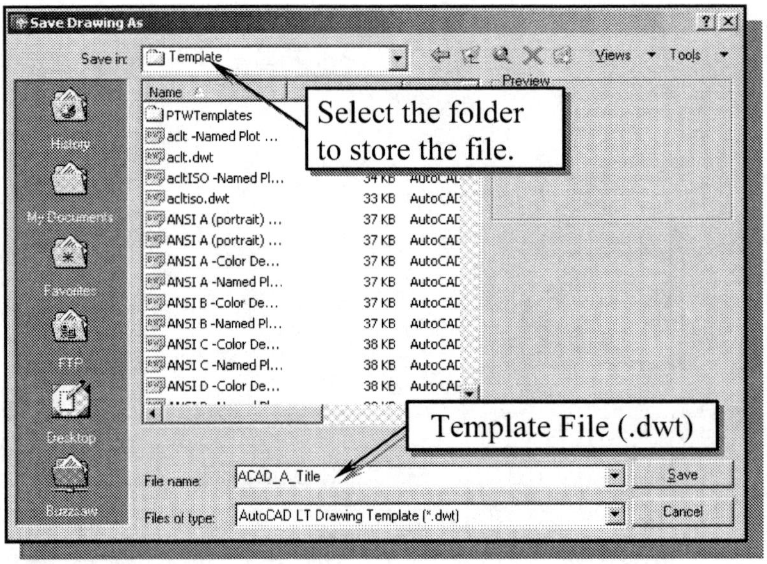

4. In the *Template Description* dialog box, enter ***A-size layout with title block*** in the *Description* box.

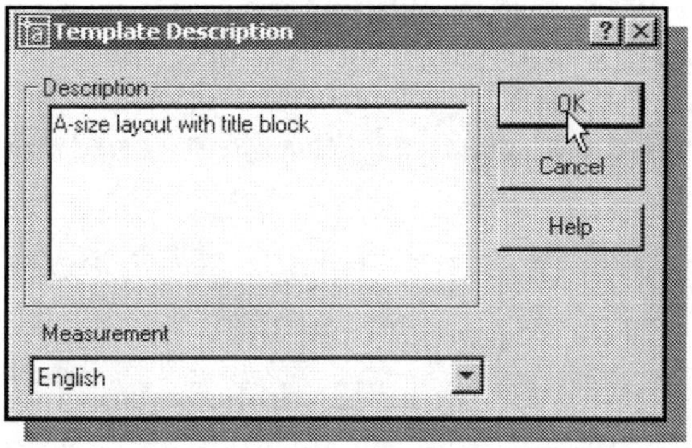

5. Pick **OK** to close the dialog box and save the template file.

➤ The only difference between an AutoCAD LT template file and a regular AutoCAD LT drawing file is the filename extension, (.dwt) versus (.dwg). We can convert any AutoCAD LT drawing into an AutoCAD LT template file by changing the filename extension to (.dwt). It is recommended that you keep a second copy of any template files on a separate floppy disk as a backup.

Exit *AutoCAD LT 2005*

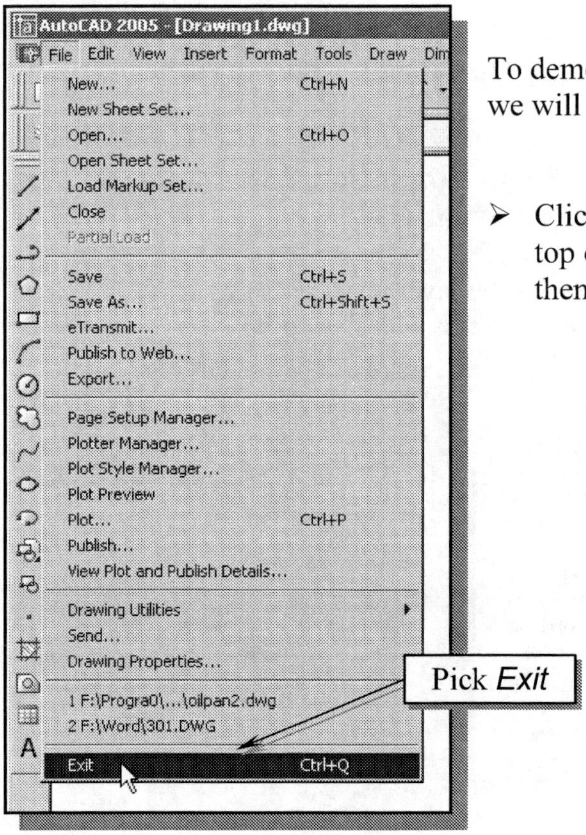

To demonstrate the effects of using a template file, we will exit and restart **AutoCAD® LT 2005**.

➤ Click on **File** at the pull-down menu near the top of the *AutoCAD LT* screen window, and then choose **Exit** from the pull-down menu.

Starting Up *AutoCAD LT 2005*

1. Select the **AutoCAD LT 2005** option on the program menu or select the **AutoCAD LT 2005** icon on the desktop.

2. In the *Startup* dialog box, select the ***Use a Template*** option with a single click of the left-mouse-button.

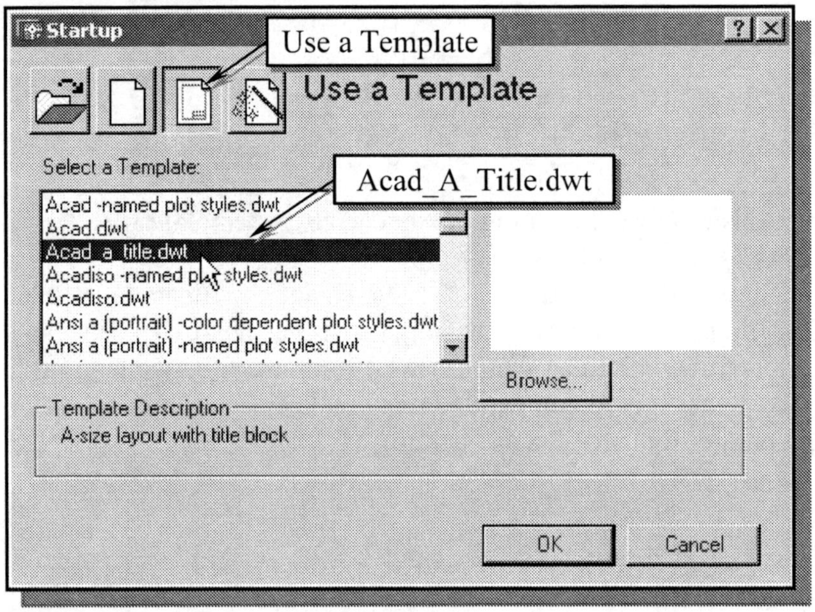

3. Select the ***Acad_A_Title*** template file from the list of template files. If the file is saved in a separate folder, click on the **Browse** button to locate the file.

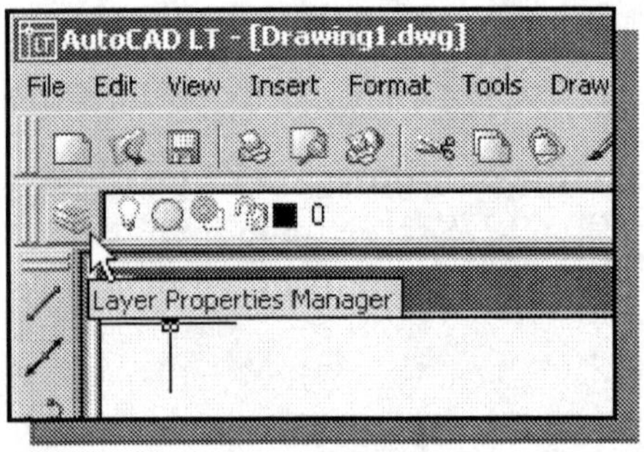

4. Pick **Layer Properties Manager** in the *Object Properties* toolbar.

5. Examine the layer property settings in the *Layer Properties Manager* dialog box.

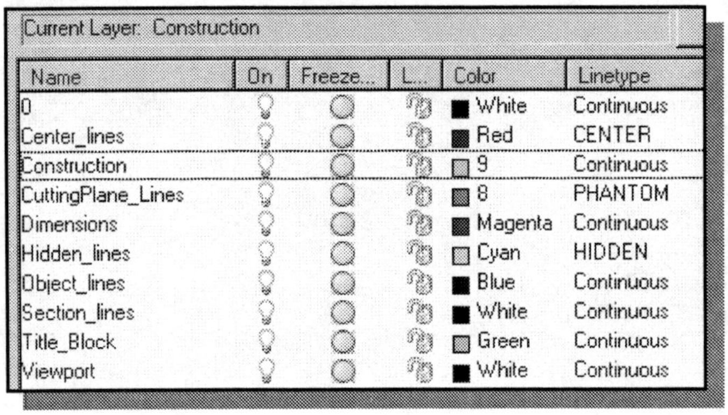

6. On your own, confirm that the layer ***Construction*** is set as the *Current Layer*.

7. Click on the **OK** button to exit the *Layer Properties Manager* dialog box.

The *Geneva Cam* Drawing

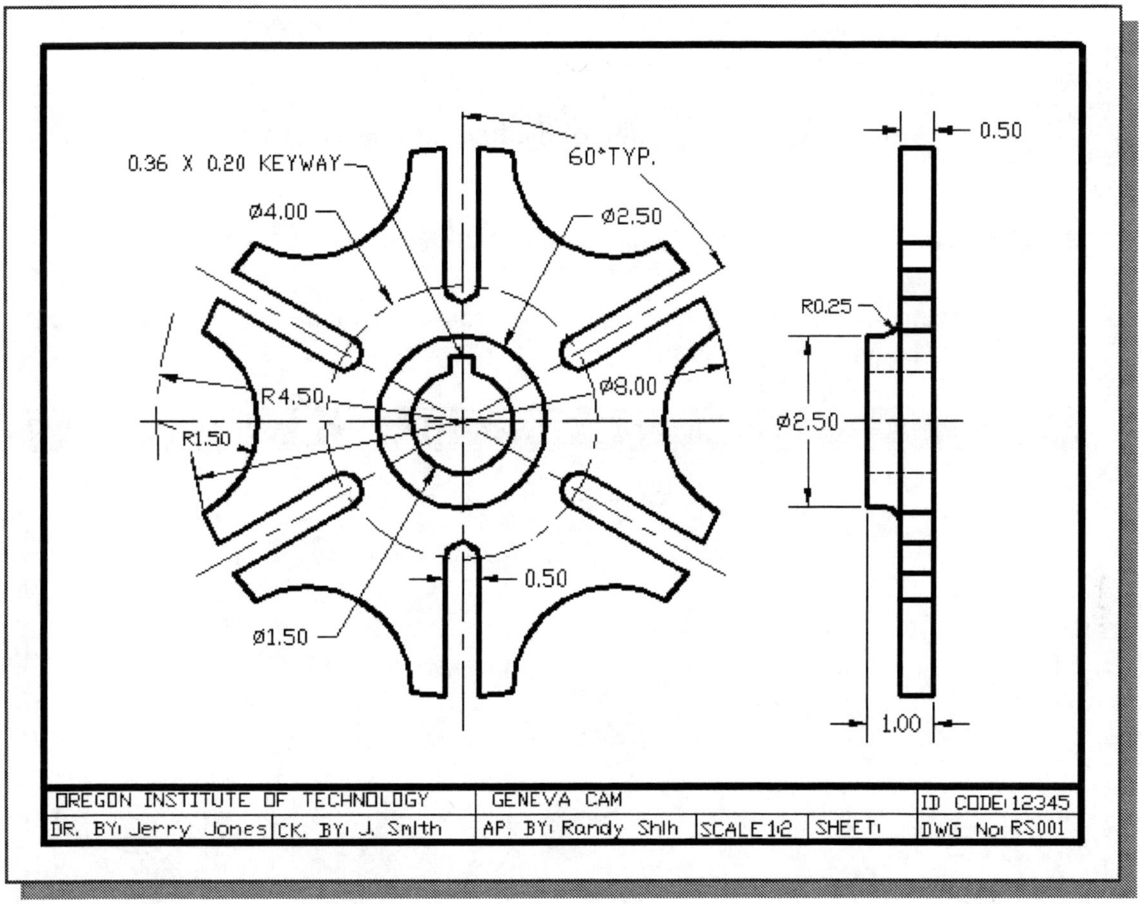

Drawing Construction Lines

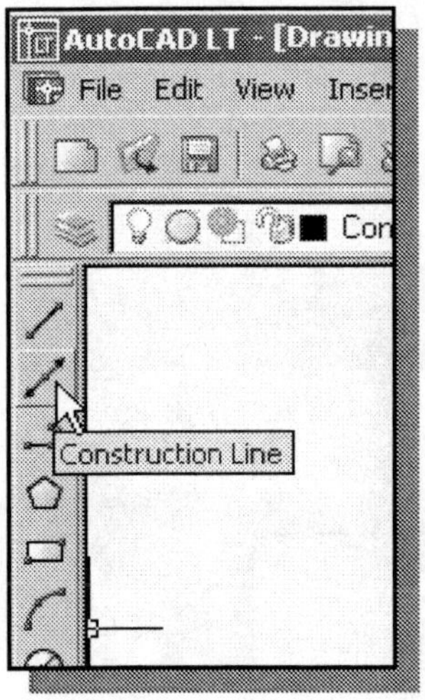

1. Select the **Construction Line** icon in the *Draw* toolbar. In the command prompt area, the message *"_xline Specify a point or [Hor/Ver/Ang/Bisect/Offset]:"* is displayed.

2. Place the first point at world coordinate **(5,4.5)** on the screen.

3. Pick a location above the last point to create a **vertical line**.

4. Move the cursor toward the right of the first point, then pick a location to create a **horizontal line**.

5. Next create a construction line that is rotated 30 degrees from horizontal, enter **@2<30 [ENTER]**.

6. Inside the graphics window, **right-mouse-click** to end the Construction Line command.

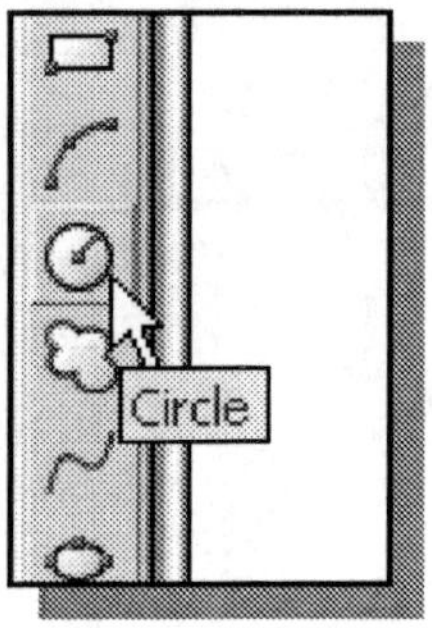

7. Select the **Circle** icon in the *Draw* toolbar. In the command prompt area, the message *"CIRCLE Specify center point for circle or [3P/2P/Ttr]:"* is displayed.

8. Pick the intersection of the lines as the center point of the circle.

9. In the command prompt area, the message *"Specify radius of circle or [Diameter]:"* is displayed. Enter **0.75 [ENTER]**

10. Repeat the Circle command and create four additional circles of radii **1.25**, **2.0**, **4.0** and **4.5** as shown.

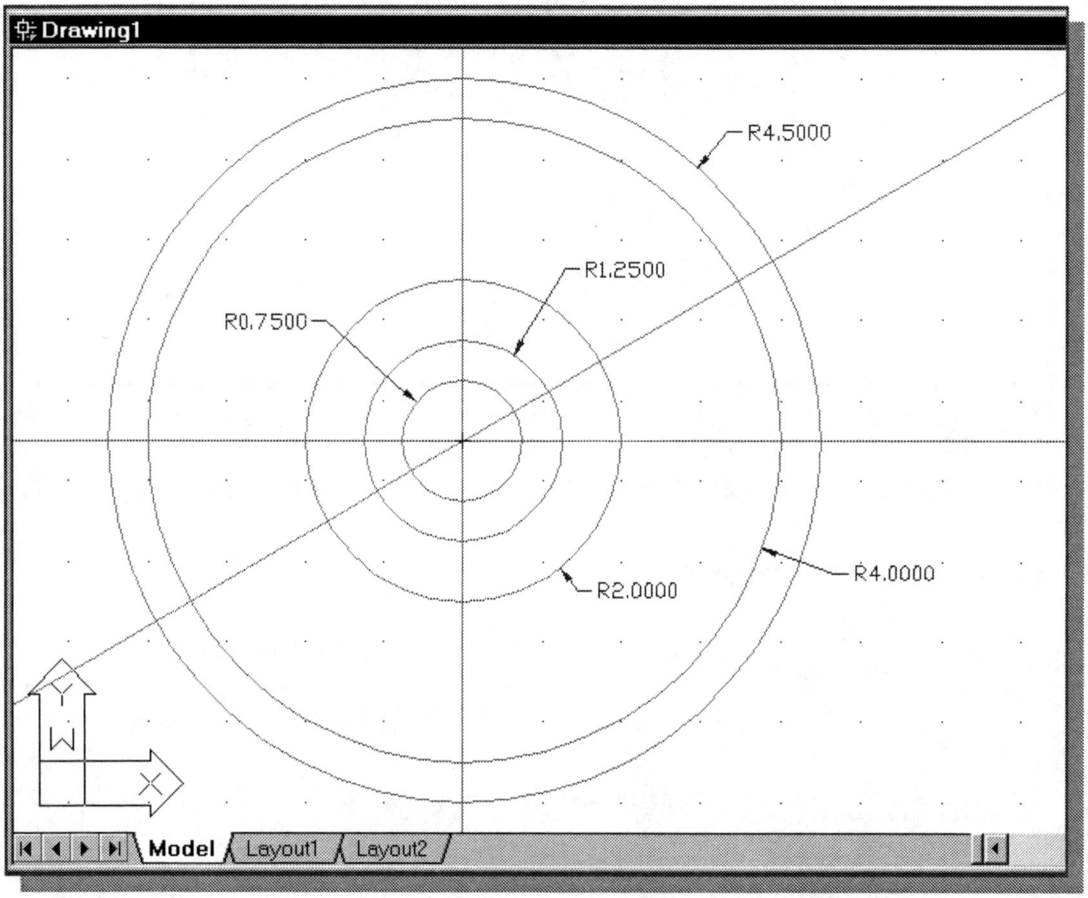

11. In the *Status Bar* area, reset the options and turn ***ON*** the *GRID*, *POLAR*, *OSNAP* and *LWT* options.

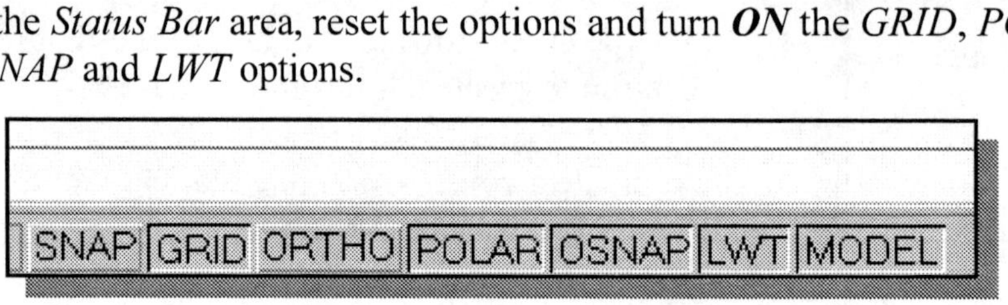

Creating Object Lines

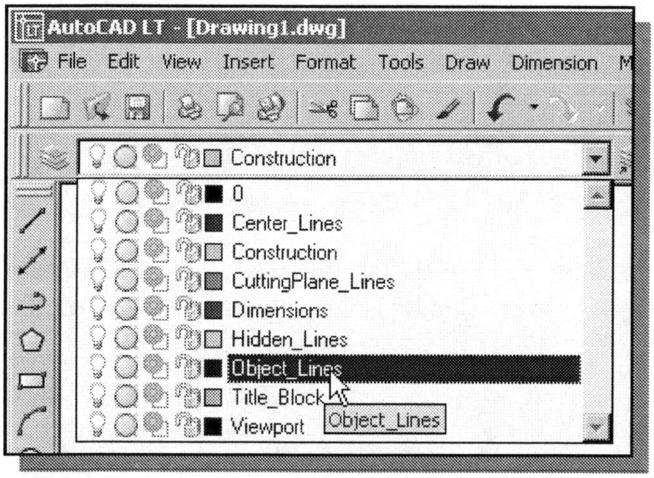

1. On the *Object Properties* toolbar, choose the ***Layer Control*** box with the left-mouse-button.

2. Move the cursor over the name of layer ***Object_Lines***, the tool tip *"Object_Lines"* appears.

3. Left-mouse-click once and layer *Object_Lines* is set as the *Current Layer.*

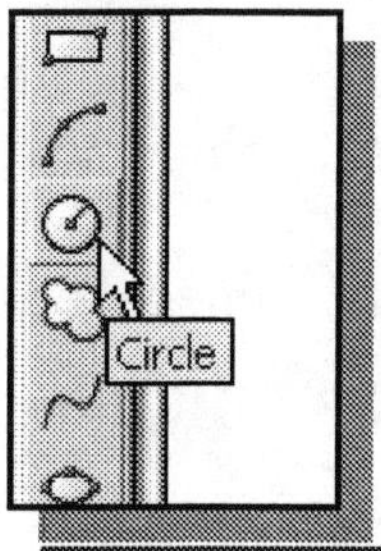

4. Select the **Circle** icon in the *Draw* toolbar. In the command prompt area, the message *"CIRCLE Specify center point for circle or [3P/2P/Ttr]:"* is displayed.

5. Move the cursor to the center of the circles, then left-click once to select the intersection as the center of the new circle.

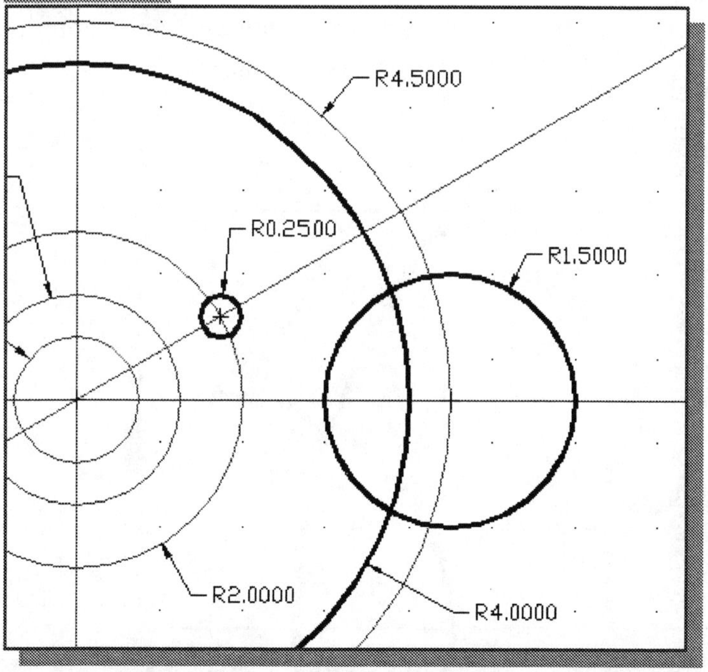

6. In the command prompt area, the message *"Specify radius of circle or [Diameter]:"* is displayed. Pick the **right intersection** of the horizontal line and the radius 4.0 circle as the center point of the circle. We are creating a circle that is also **radius 4.0** on the *Object_Lines* layer.

7. Repeat the **Circle** command and pick the **right intersection** of the horizontal line and the **radius 4.5 circle** as the center point of the circle.

8. In the command prompt area, the message *"Specify radius of circle or [Diameter]:"* is displayed. Enter **1.5 [ENTER]**

9. Repeat the **Circle** command and create a circle of radius **0.25** centered at the intersection of the inclined line and the radius 2.0 circle as shown.

Using the *Offset* Command

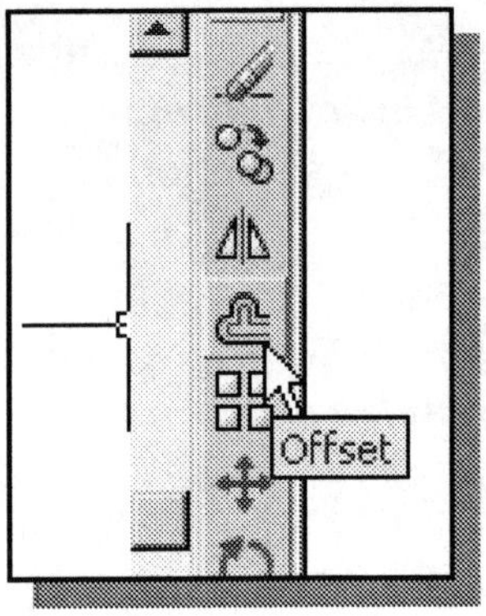

1. Select the **Offset** icon in the *Modify* toolbar. In the command prompt area, the message *"Specify offset distance or [Through]:"* is displayed.

2. In the command prompt area, enter **0.25 [ENTER]**

3. In the command prompt area, the message *"Select object to offset or <exit>:"* is displayed. Pick the **inclined line** on the screen.

4. AutoCAD LT next asks us to identify the direction of the offset. Pick a location that is **below** the inclined line.

5. Inside the graphics window, **right-mouse-click** to end the Offset command.

➢ Notice that the new line created by the Offset command is placed on the same layer as the line we selected to offset. Which layer is current does not matter; the offset object will always be on the same layer as the original object.

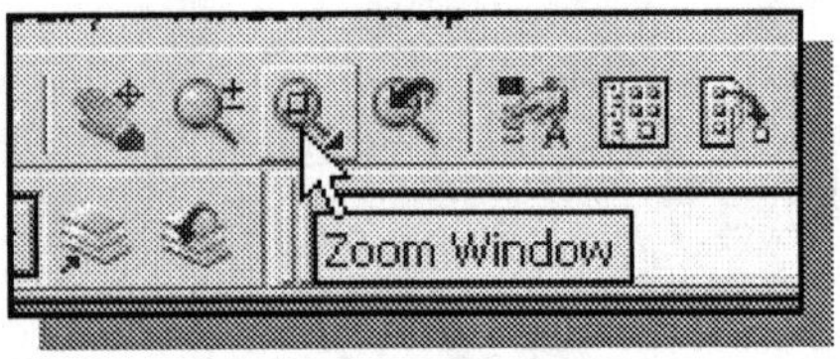

6. Use the **Zoom Window** command and zoom in on the 30 degrees region as shown.

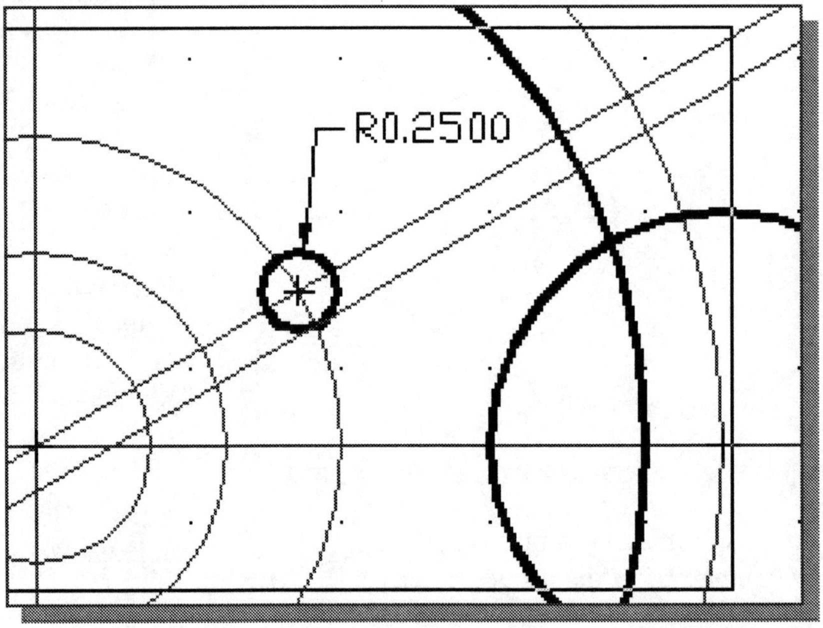

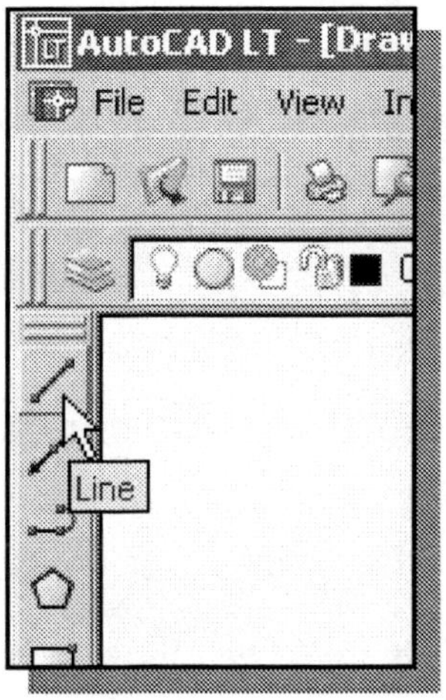

7. Select the **Line** command icon in the *Draw* toolbar. In the command prompt area, the message *"_line Specify first point:"* is displayed.

8. Move the cursor to the intersection of the small circle and the lower inclined line and notice the visual aid that automatically displays at the intersection. Left-click once to select the point.

9. Pick the next intersection point, toward the right side, along the inclined line.

➢ On your own, use the **Trim** and **Erase** commands to remove the unwanted portions of the objects until your drawing contains only the objects shown below.

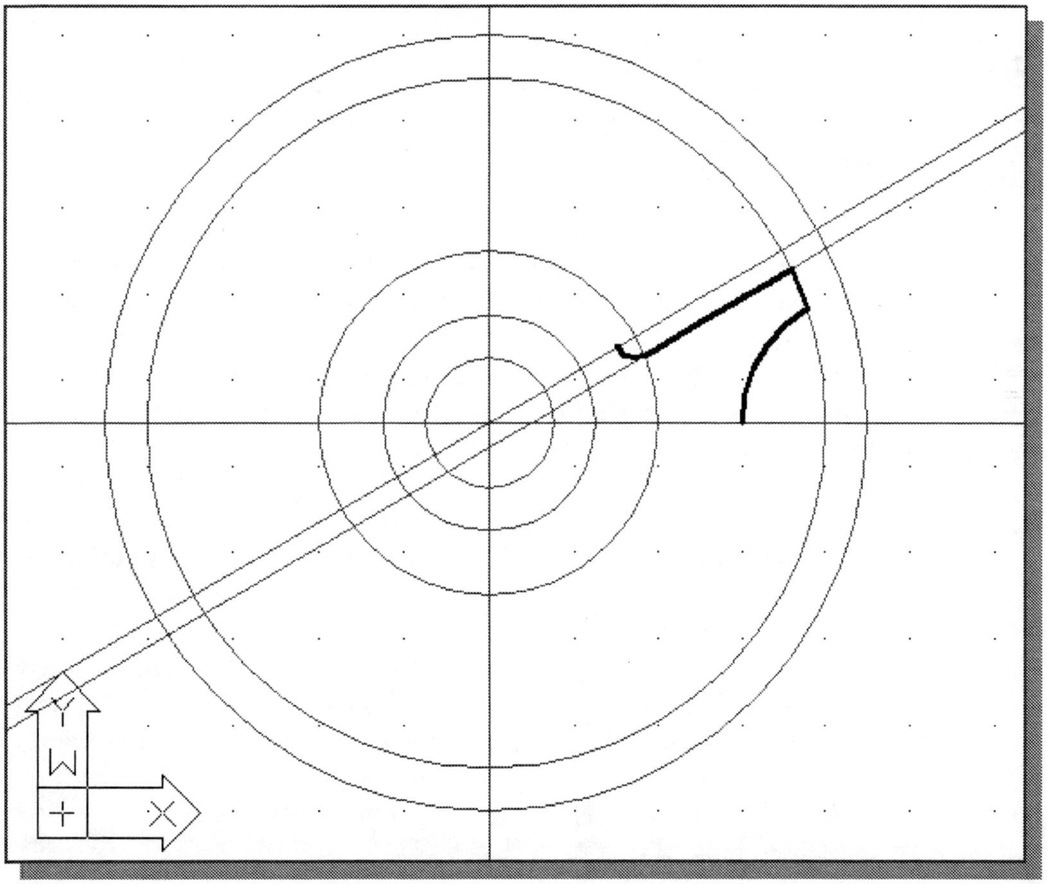

Using the *Mirror* Command

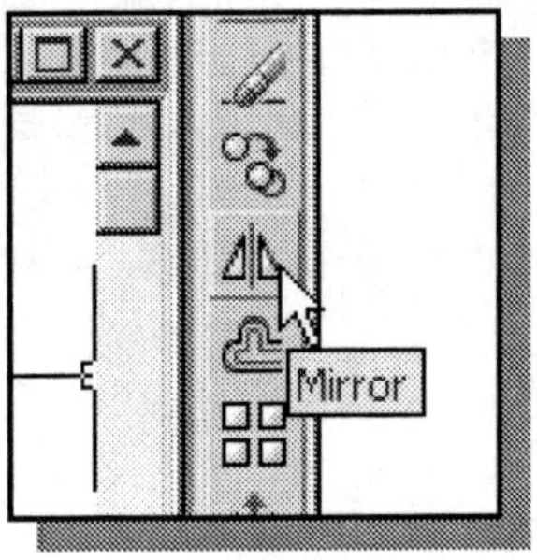

1. Select the **Mirror** command icon in the *Modify* toolbar. In the command prompt area, the message *" Select objects: "* is displayed.

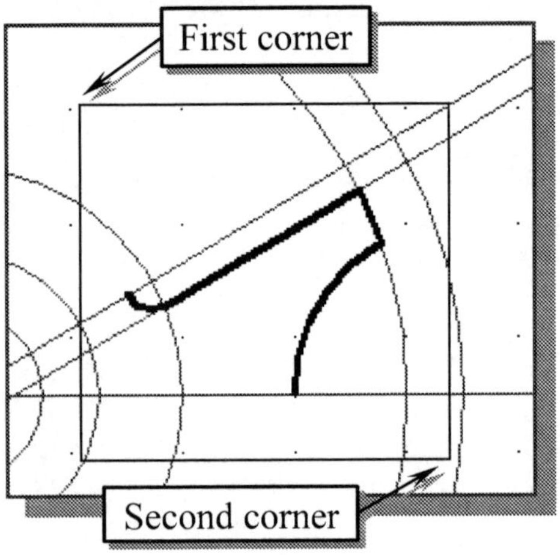

2. Create a **selection window** by selecting the two corners as shown.

➢ Note that in **AutoCAD® LT 2005**, creating the selection window from left to right will select only objects entirely within the selection area. Going from right to left (crossing selection) selects objects within and objects crossing the selection area. Objects must be at least partially visible to be selected.

3. Inside the graphics window, **right-mouse-click** to accept the selection and continue with the Mirror command.

4. In the command prompt area, the message *"Specify the first point of the mirror line:"* is displayed. Pick any intersection point along the horizontal line on the screen.

5. In the command prompt area, the message *"Specify the second point:"* is displayed. Pick any other intersection point along the horizontal line on the screen.

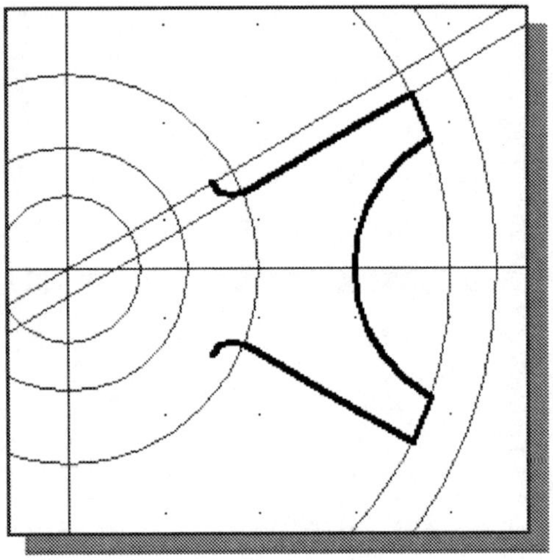

6. In the command prompt area, the message *"Delete source objects? [Yes/No] <N>:"* is displayed. Inside the graphics window, **right-mouse-click** and select **Enter** to retain the original objects.

Using the *Array* Command

We can make multiple copies of objects in polar or rectangular arrays (patterns). For polar arrays, we control the number of copies of the object and whether the copies are rotated. For rectangular arrays, we control the number of rows and columns and the distance between them.

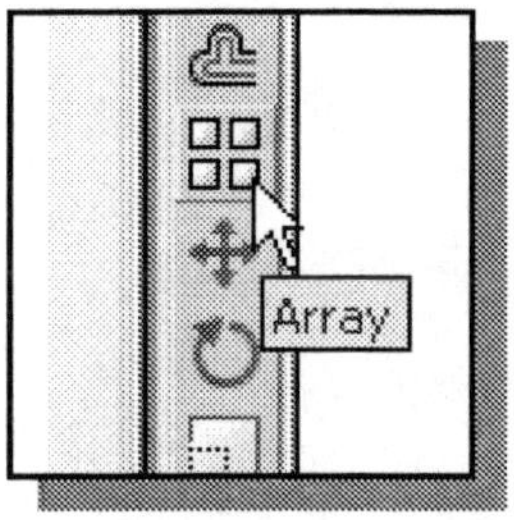

1. Select the **Array** command icon in the *Modify* toolbar. In the command prompt area, the message *"Select objects:"* is displayed.

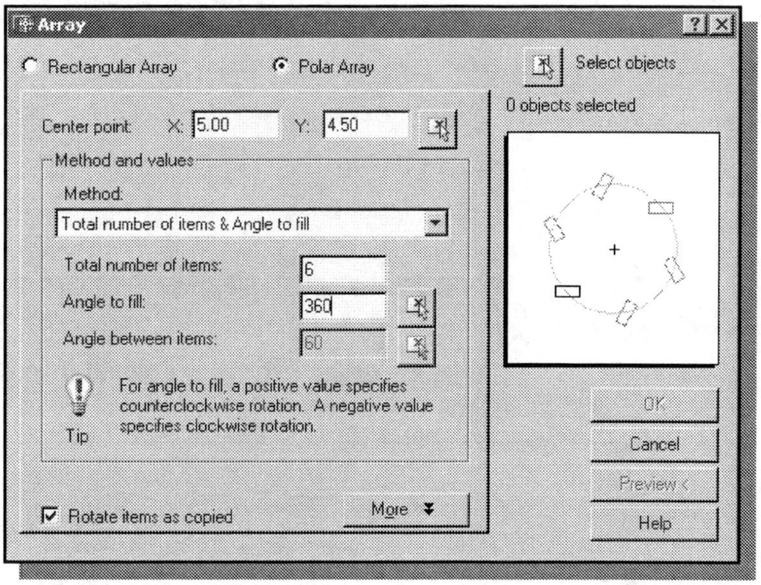

2. In the *Array* dialog box, select the ***Polar Array*** option.

3. Enter **5.0** and **4.5** as the X and Y coordinates of the *Center point* of the array.

4. Enter **6** as the number of items in the array.

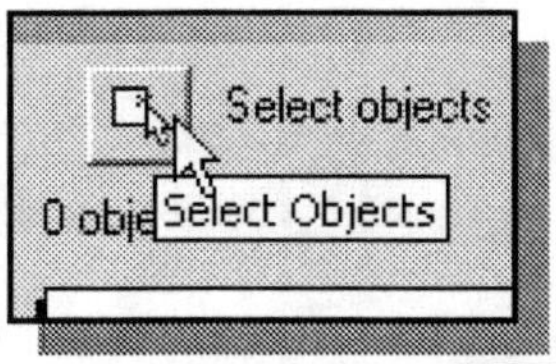

5. Click the **Select Objects** icon, as shown in the figure, to select objects to create the array.

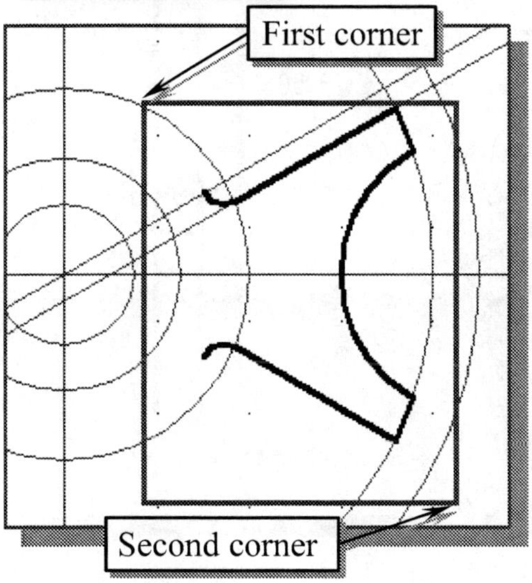

6. Using a *selection* window, enclose the objects we mirrored and the mirrored copies as shown.

7. In the command prompt area, the message "*Select Objects:*" is displayed. Inside the graphics window, **right-mouse-click** to end the selection.

8. In the *Array* dialog box, click the **OK** button to create the array.

9. Next construct the **0.36 × 0.20** keyway by first creating parallel lines at 0.95 and 0.18 distances from the horizontal and vertical construction lines.

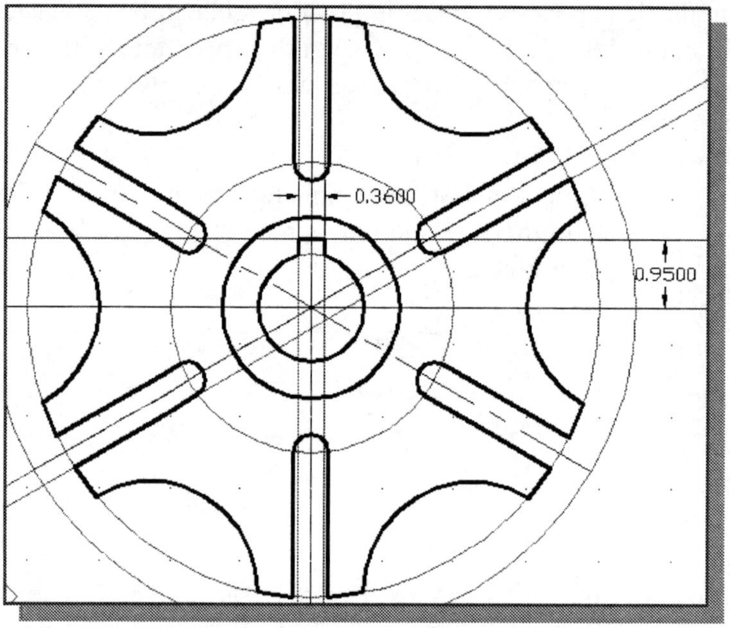

➢ On your own, complete the two views with dimensions. (In the *Dimension Style Manager*, set options under the **Fit** tab to control the appearance of radius and diameter dimensions.)

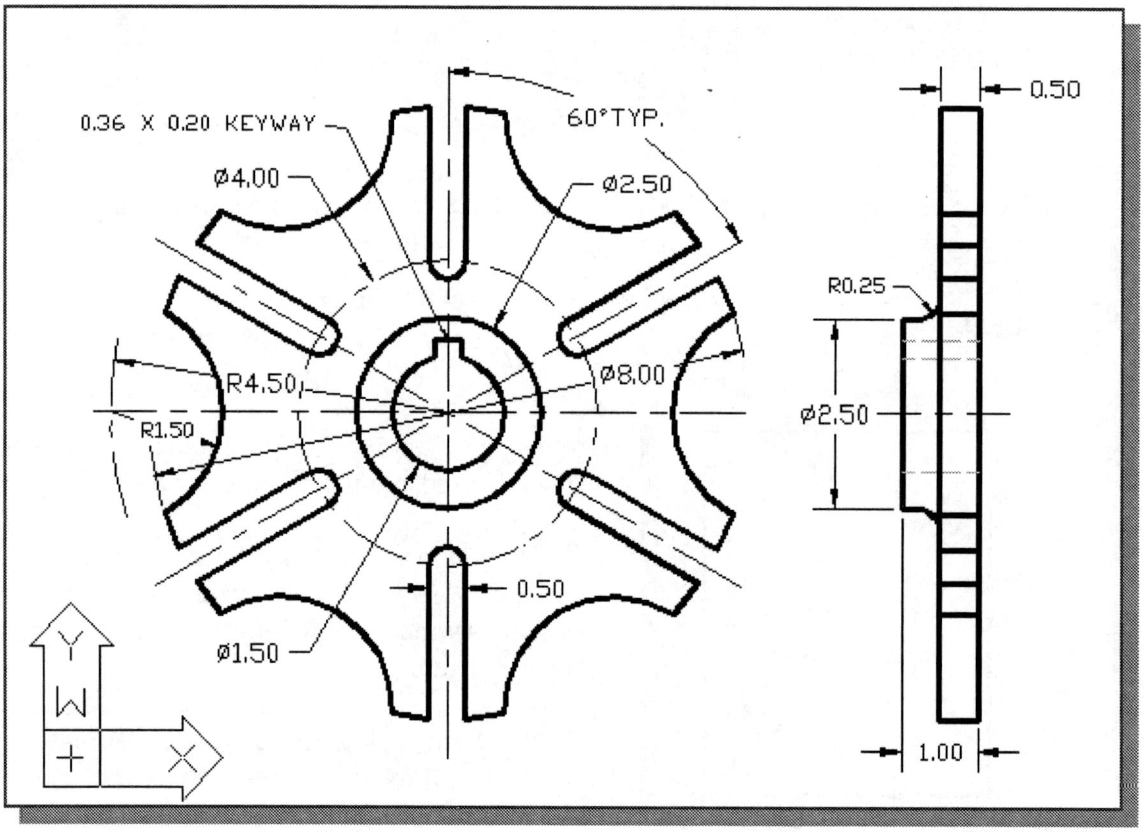

Creating a *Viewport* Inside the Title Block

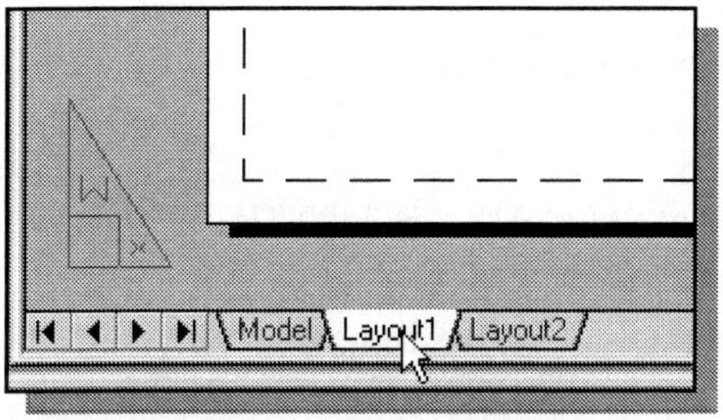

1. Pick the **Layout1** tab to switch to the two-dimensional paper space containing the title block.

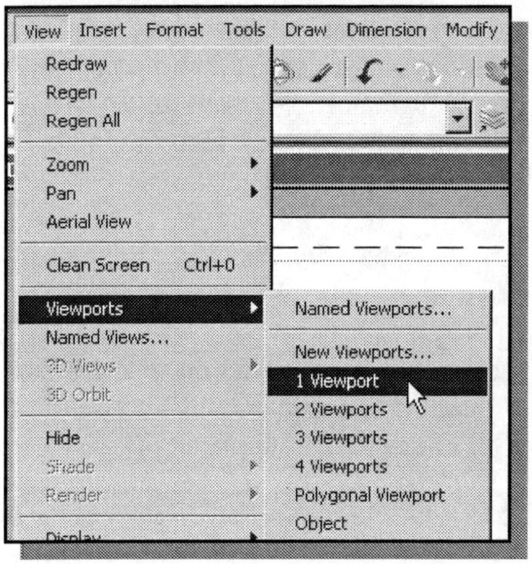

2. In the pull-down menus, select **[View] → [Viewports] →[1 Viewport]**

3. In the *Status Bar* area, turn ***OFF*** the *OSNAP* option.

4. Create a *viewport* inside the title block area as shown.

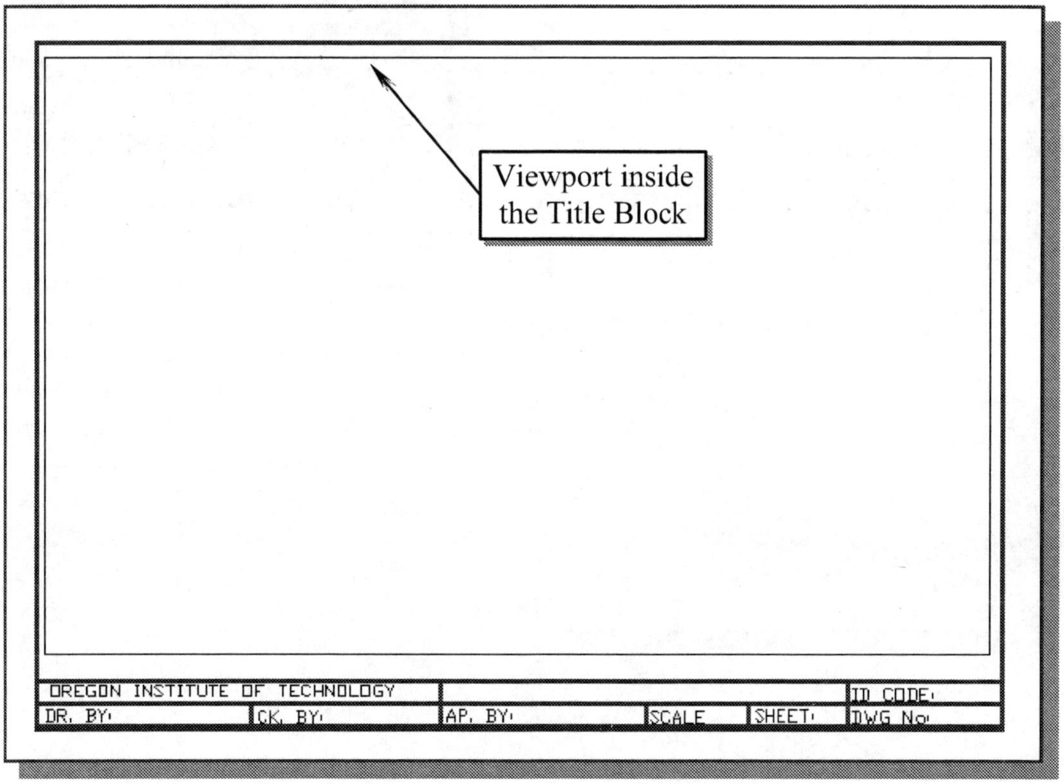

Viewport Properties

1. Pre-select the viewport by left-clicking once on any edge of the viewport.

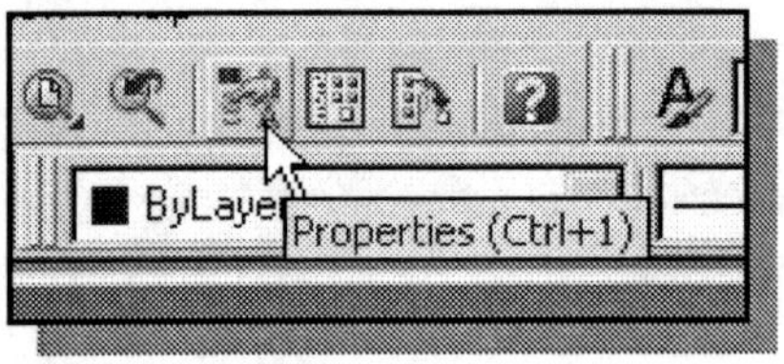

2. In the *Standard* toolbar, select the **Properties** icon.

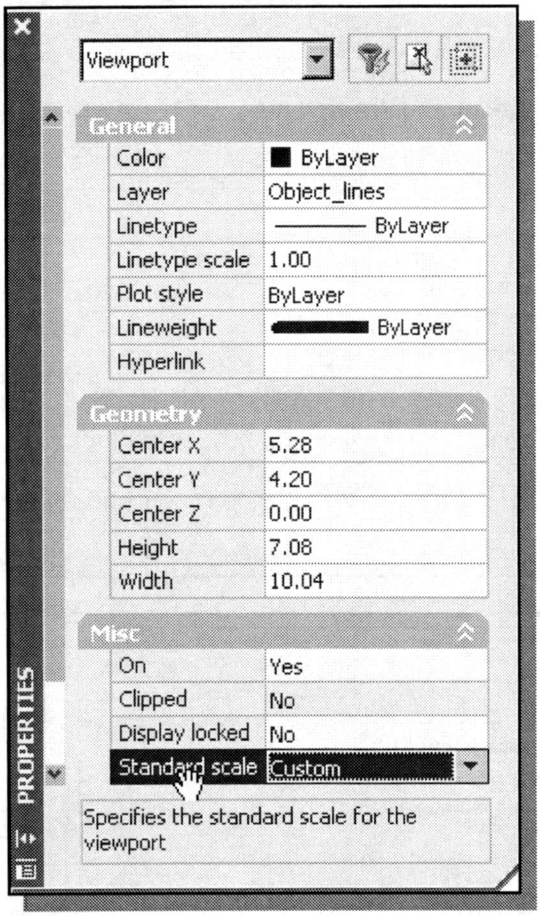

3. In the *Properties* dialog box, scroll down to the bottom of the list. Notice the current scale is set to ***Custom***, 0.5602. (The number on your screen might be different.)

4. **Left-click** the *Standard scale* box and notice an arrowhead appears.

5. Click on the arrowhead button and a list of standard scales is displayed. Use the scroll bar to look at the list.

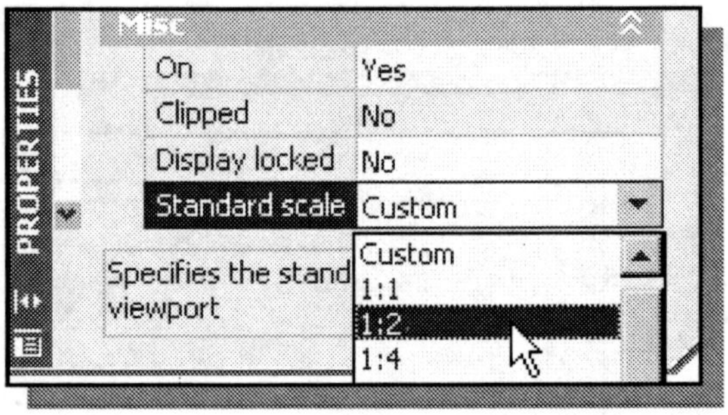

6. Select **1:2** in the *Standard scale* list. This will set the plotting scale factor to half scale.

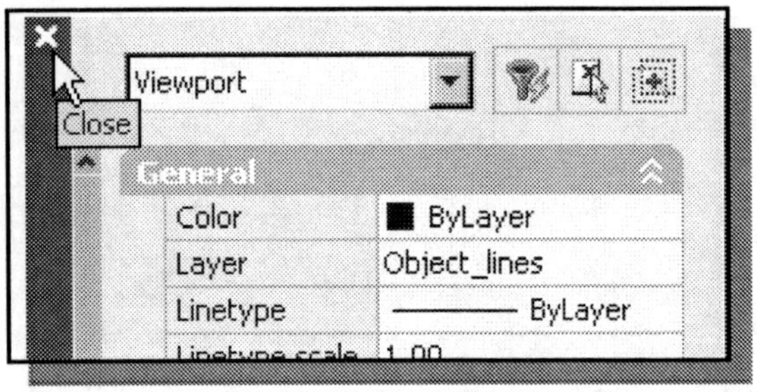

7. Click on the [**X**] button to exit the *Properties* dialog box.

Hide the *Viewport Borders*

We will **turn off** the *viewport borders*, so that the lines will not be plotted.

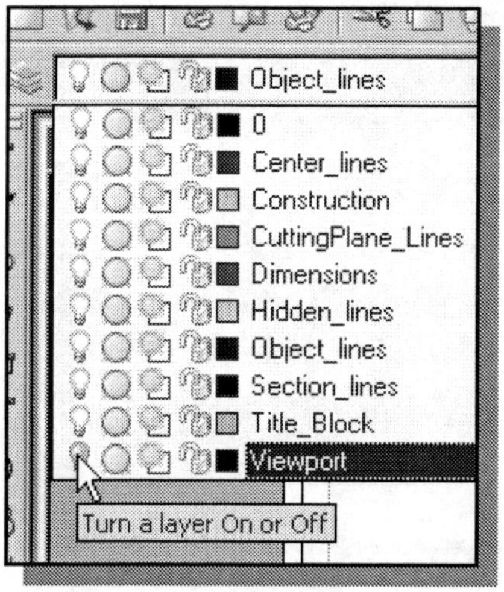

1. With the *viewport* pre-selected, choose the ***Layer Control*** box with the left-mouse-button.

2. Move the cursor over the name of layer ***Viewport***, **left-mouse-click once**, and move the viewport to layer *Viewport.*

3. Turn ***OFF*** layer *Viewport* in the *Layer Control* box.

Adjusting the Dimension Scale

1. Move the cursor to the *Standard* toolbar area and **right-click** the empty area (in between two icons) of the *Standard* toolbar to display a list of toolbar menu groups.

2. Select **Dimension**, with the left-mouse-button, to display the *Dimension* toolbar on the screen.

3. Click on the **Dimension Style** icon.

4. In the *Dimension Style Manager* dialog box, select **Modify**.

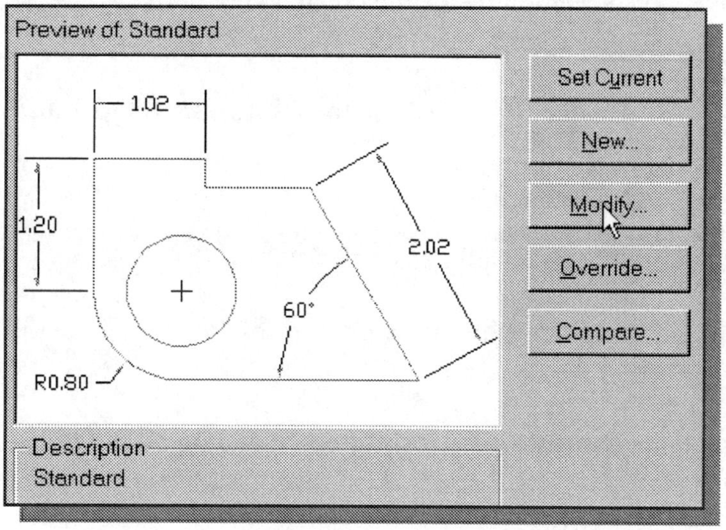

5. Use the ***Scale dimensions to layout (paperspace)*** option in the *Scale for Dimension Features* section under the **Fit** tab.

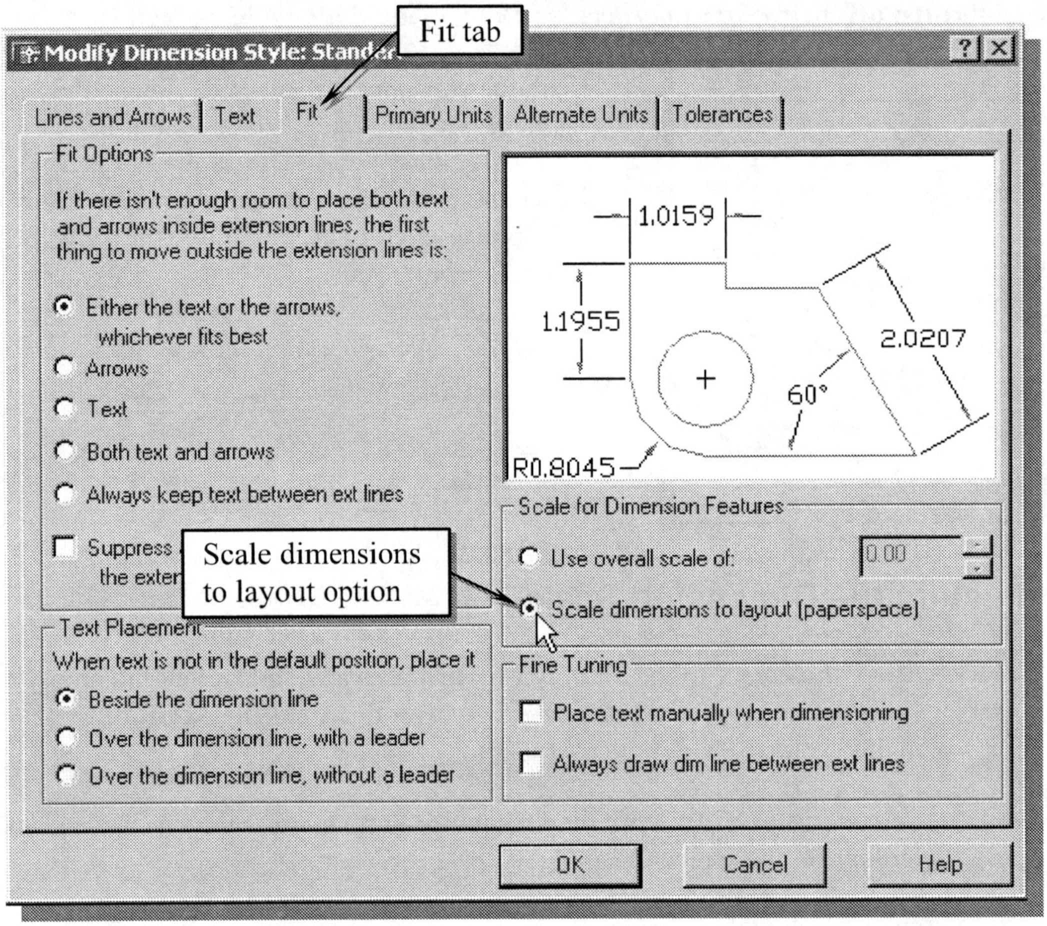

6. Click on the **OK** button to close the *Modify Dimension Style* dialog box.

7. Click on the **Close** button to close the *Dimension Style Manager* dialog box.

8. Double-click, with the left-mouse-button, near the center of the front view to activate the selection inside the created viewport.

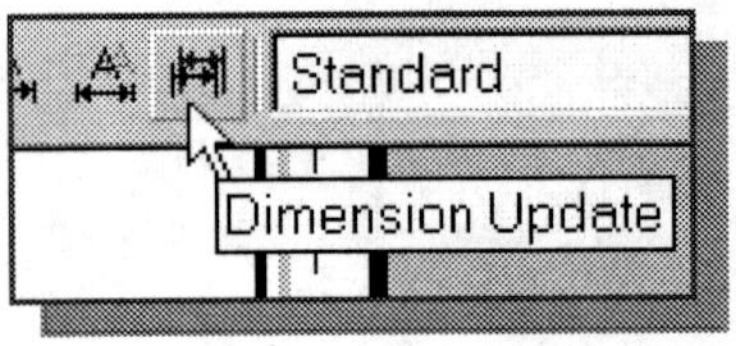

9. Click on the **Dimension Update** icon.

10. Pick one of the radius dimensions.

11. Inside the graphics window, right-mouse-click to update the selected dimension.

12. Repeat the **Dimension Update** command on all the dimensions.

Plot/Print the Drawing

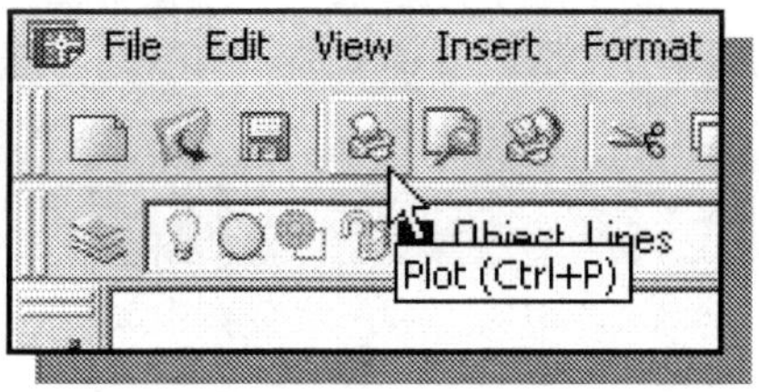

1. In the *Standard* toolbar, select the **Plot** icon.

2. Confirm the proper **plot device** is selected.

3. In the *Plot area* section, confirm it is set to ***Layout***.

4. In the *Plot scale* section, confirm it is set to ***1:1***. Our *paper space* is set to the correct paper size.

5. In the *Plot options* section, confirm the ***Plot with plot styles*** and ***Plot paper space last*** options are selected. (Click on the lower-right-button to expand the option list.)

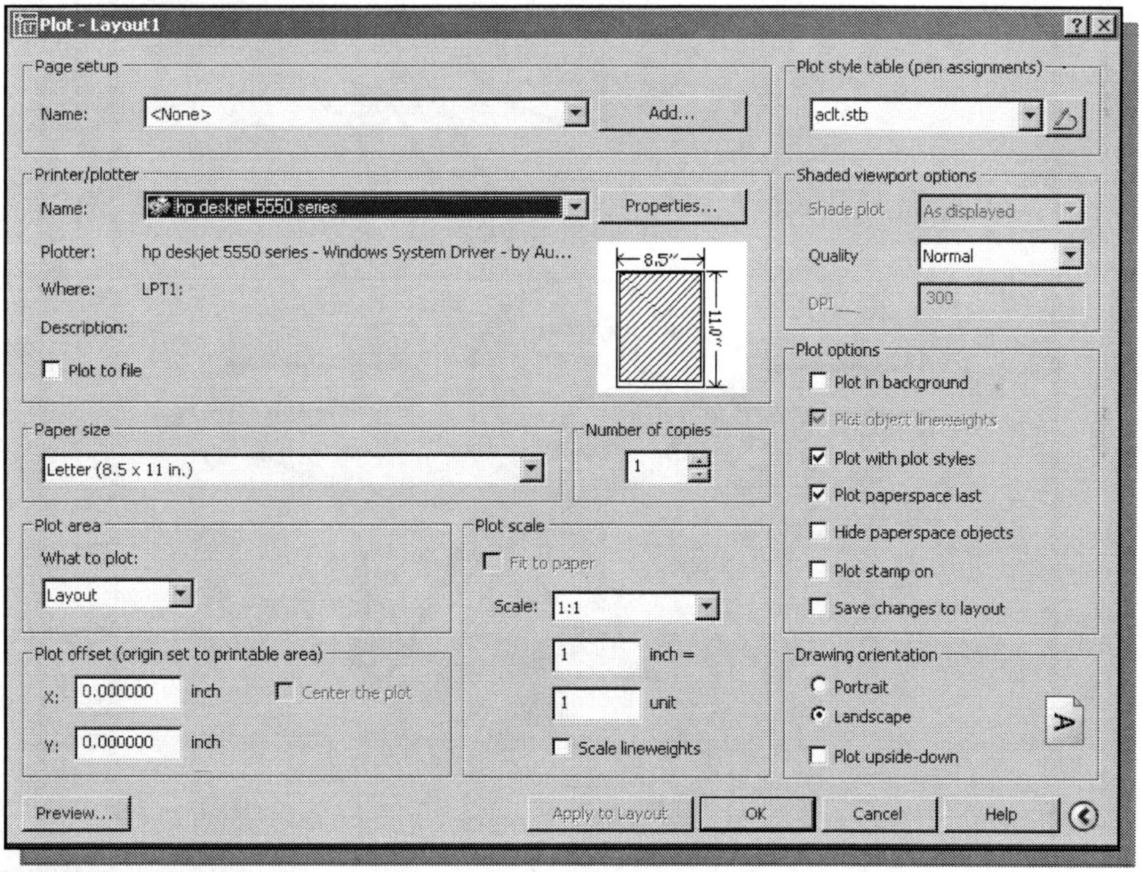

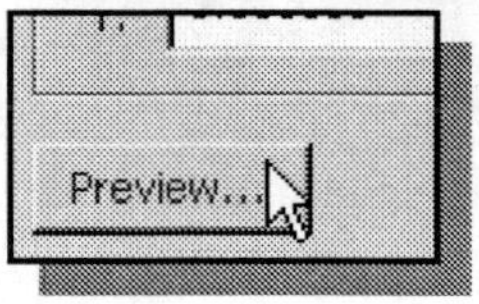

➢ Note the *Preview* option is also available.

6. Click on the **OK** button to proceed with plotting the drawing.

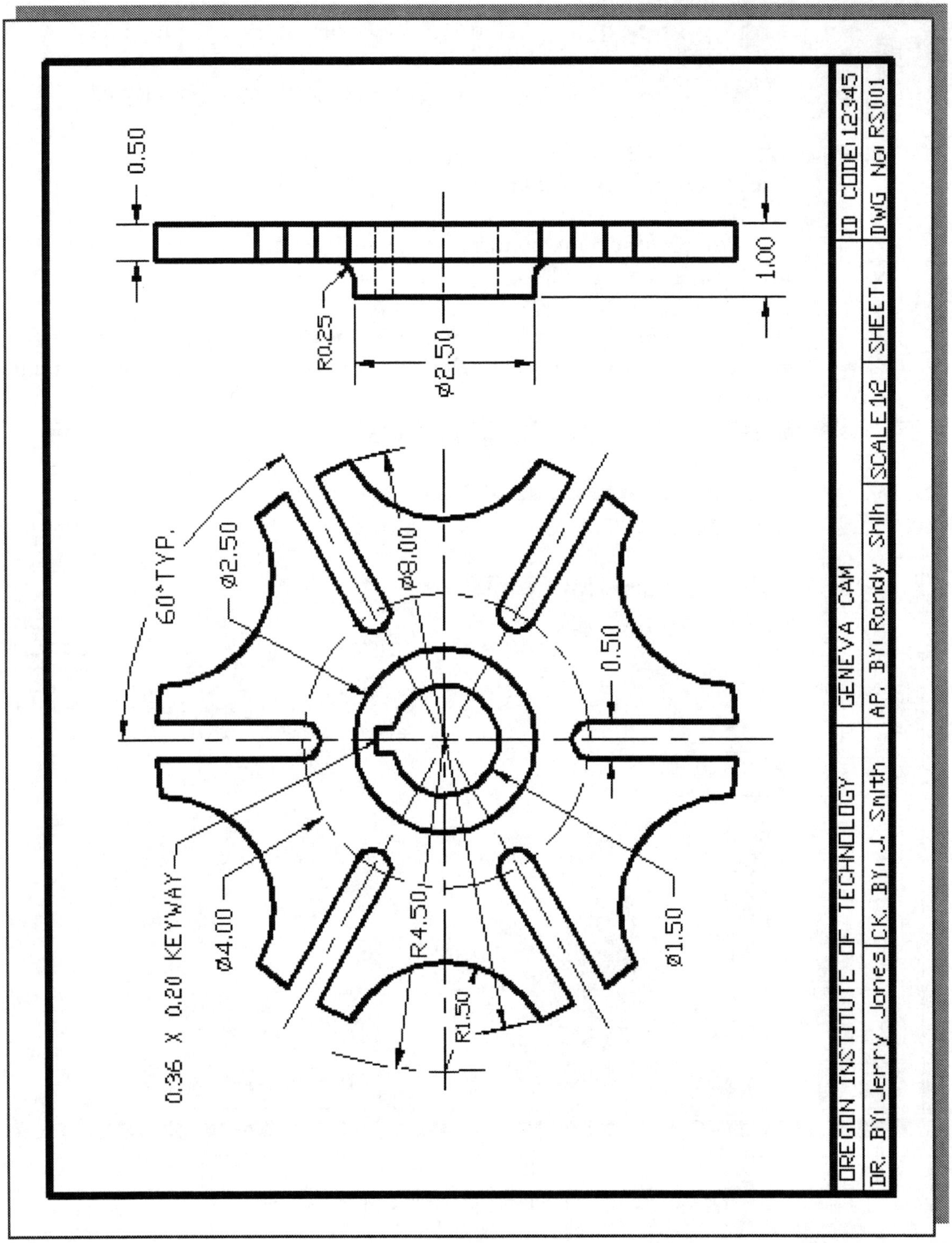
0.50
1.00
R0.25
Ø2.50
60°TYP.
Ø2.50
Ø8.00
0.50
0.36 X 0.20 KEYWAY
Ø4.00
R4.50
R1.50
Ø1.50
OREGON INSTITUTE OF TECHNOLOGY
GENEVA CAM
ID CODE: 12345
DR. BY: Jerry Jones
CK. BY: J. Smith
AP. BY: Randy Shih
SCALE 1:2
SHEET:
DWG No: RS001

Questions:

1. List and describe three advantages of using *template files*.

2. Describe the items that were included in the *Acad_A_Title* template file.

3. List and describe two methods of creating multiple copies of objects in **AutoCAD®** **LT 2005**.

4. Describe the procedure in determining the scale factor for plotting an **AutoCAD® LT 2005** layout.

5. Identify the following commands:

(a)

(b)

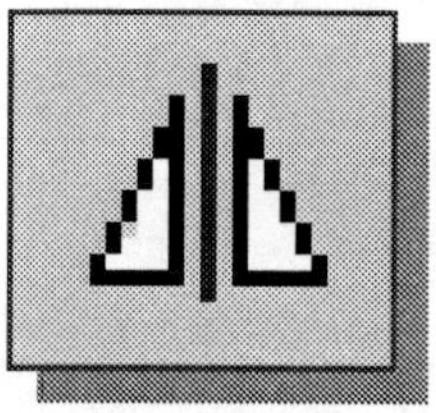

(c)

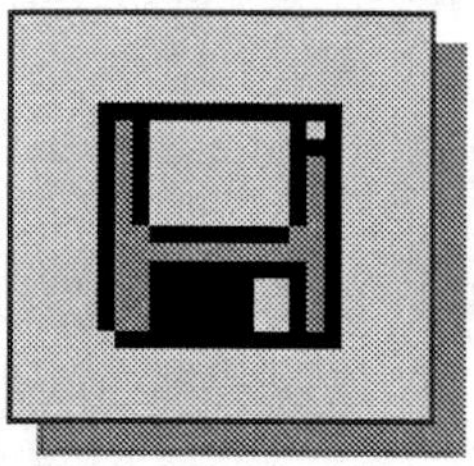

(d)

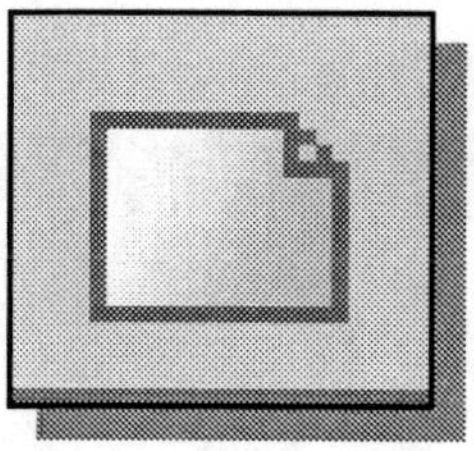

Exercises: (Unless otherwise specified, all dimensions are in inches.)

1. Plate thickness: 0.125 inch

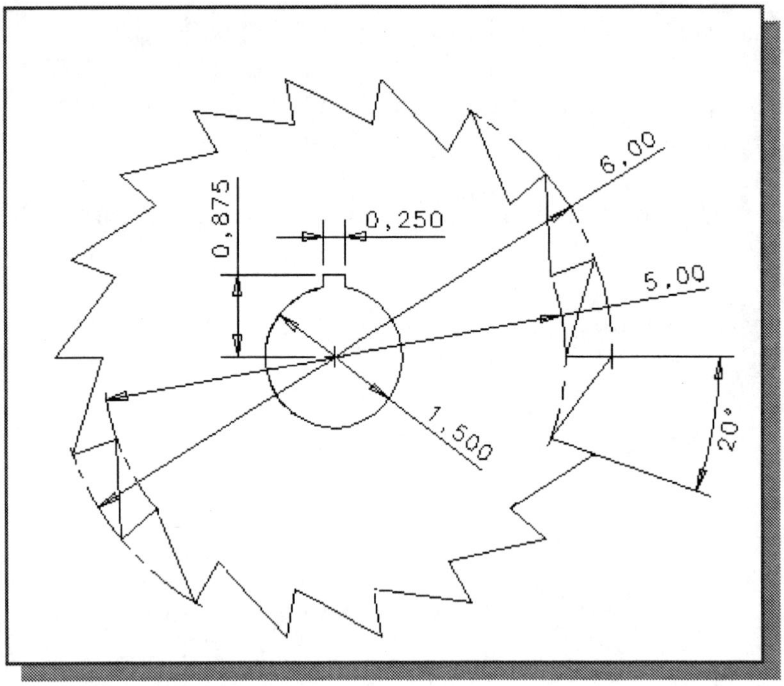

2.

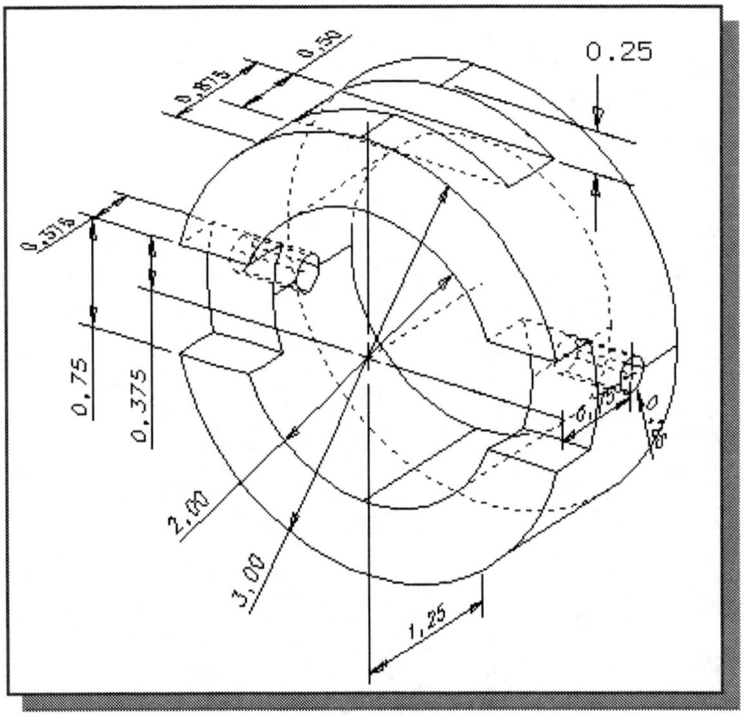

3.

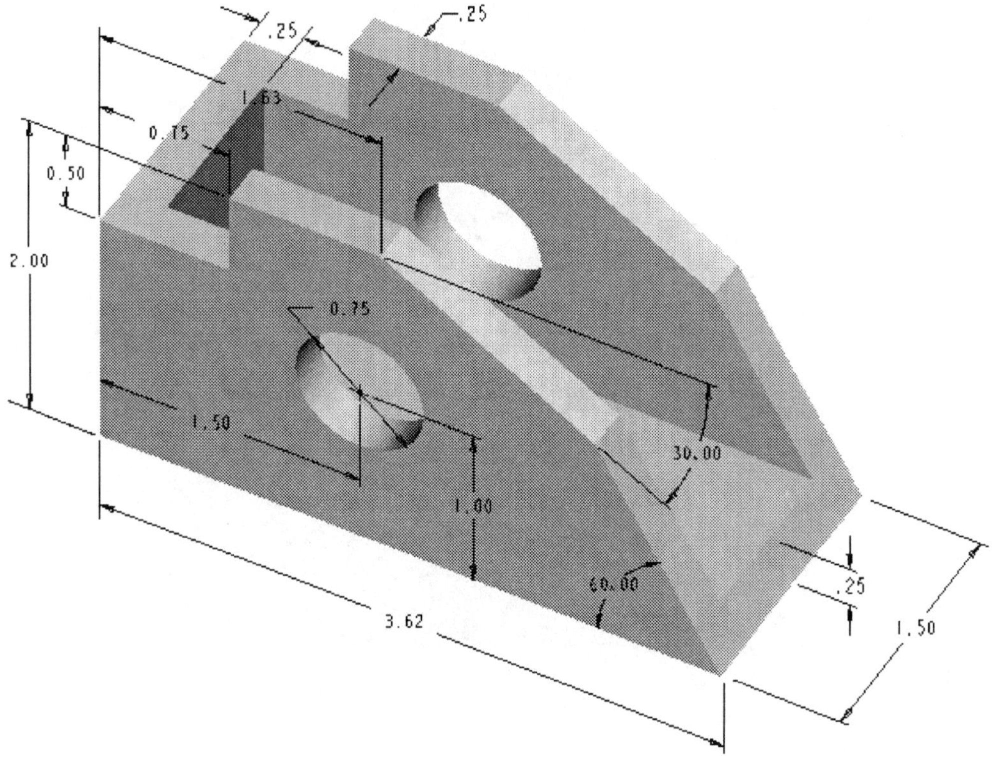
.25
.25
1.63
0.75
0.50
2.00
0.75
1.50
1.00
30.00
60.00
.25
3.62
1.50

4.

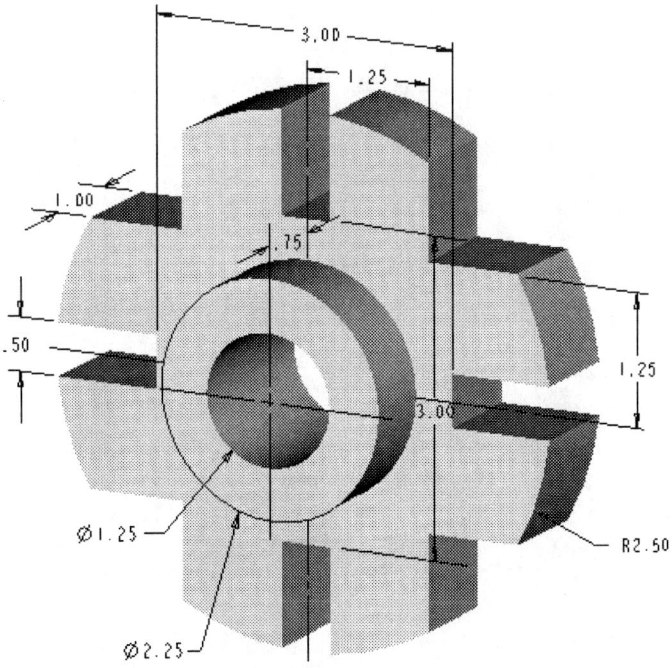
3.00
1.25
1.00
.75
.50
1.25
3.00
Ø1.25
R2.50
Ø2.25

5. Dimensions are in millimeters. (Thickness: 25 mm)

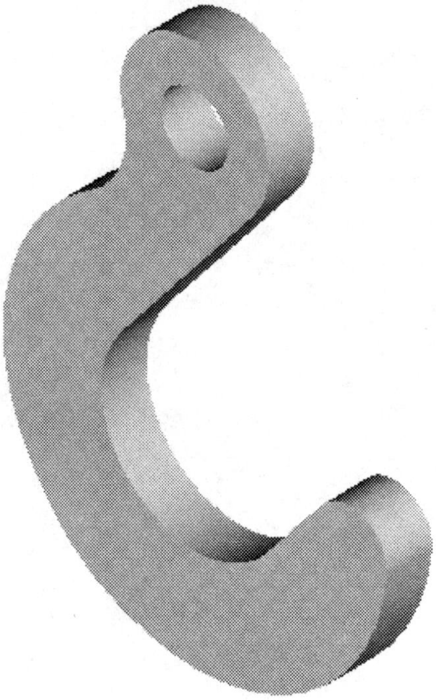

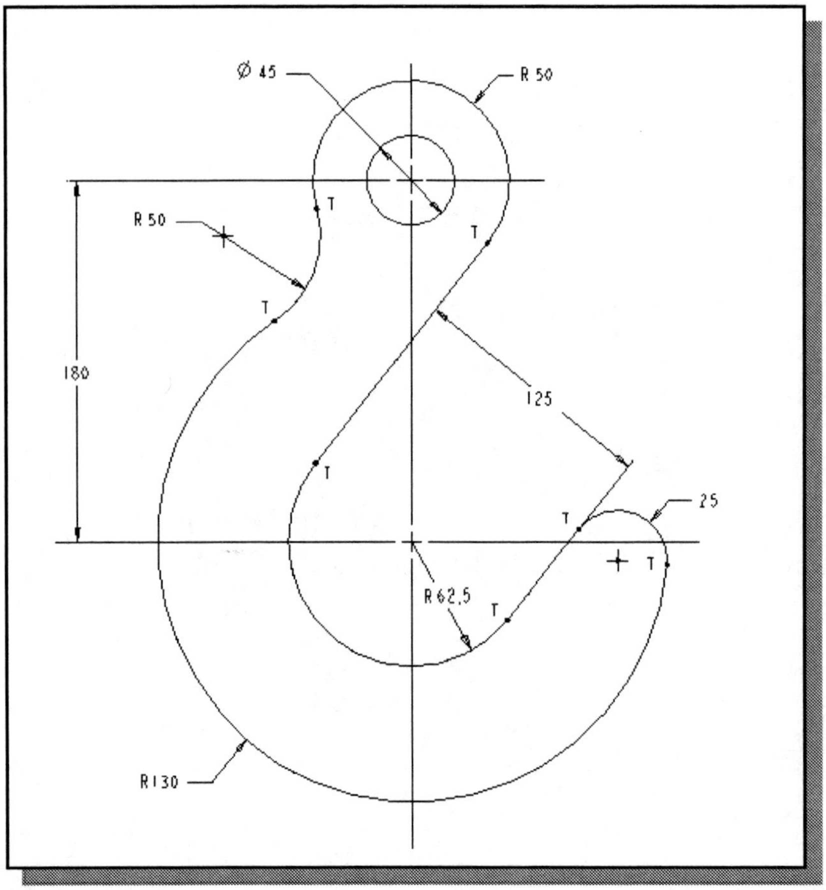

Lesson 7
Auxiliary Views and Grips Editing

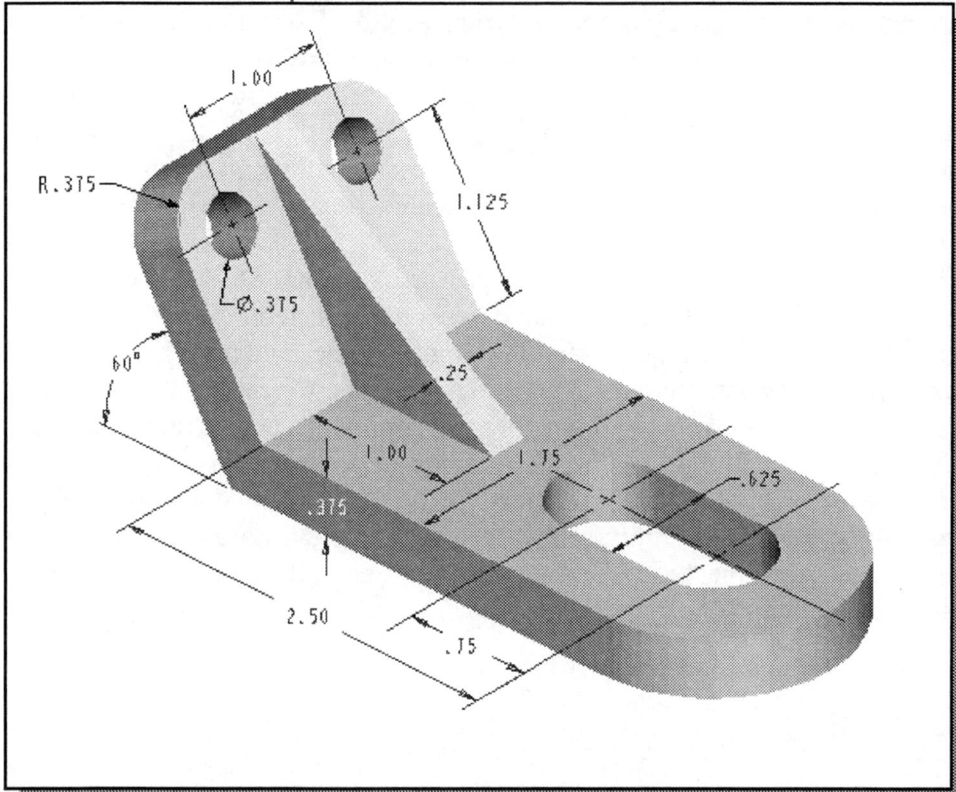

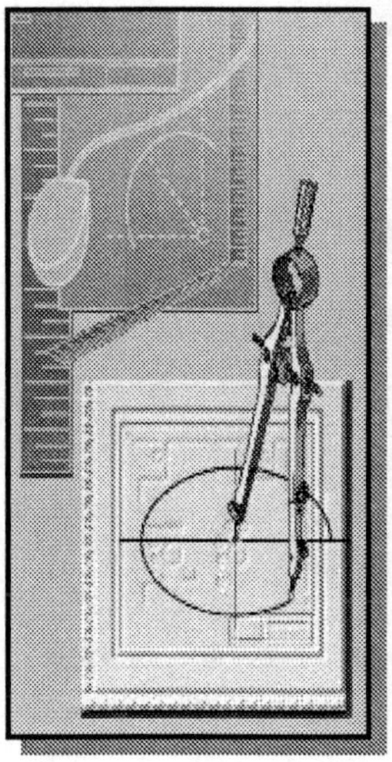

Learning Objectives

- Use 2D Projection Method to Draw Auxiliary Views
- Create Rectangles
- Use the Basic GRIPS Editing Commands
- Create and Edit the Plot Style Table
- Setup and Use the Polar Tracking Option
- Create Multiple Viewports in Paper Space

Introduction

An important rule concerning multiview drawings is to draw enough views to accurately describe the design. This usually requires two or three of the regular views, such as a front view, a top view and/or a side view. Many designs have features located on inclined surfaces that are not parallel to the regular planes of projection. To truly describe the feature, the true shape of the feature must be shown using an **auxiliary view**. An *auxiliary view* has a line of sight that is perpendicular to the inclined surface, as viewed looking directly at the inclined surface. An *auxiliary view* is a supplementary view that can be constructed from any of the regular views. This lesson will demonstrate the construction of an auxiliary view using various CAD techniques.

In this lesson, we will examine the use of the very powerful AutoCAD LT ***Grips*** feature. In AutoCAD LT, a ***Grip*** is a small square displayed on a pre-selected object. Grips are key control locations such as the endpoints and midpoints of lines and arcs. Different types of objects display different numbers of grips. Using grips, we can *stretch*, *move*, *mirror*, *scale*, *rotate*, and *copy* objects without entering commands or clicking toolbars. Grips reduce the keystrokes and object selection required in performing common editing commands. To edit with grips, we select the objects before issuing any commands. To remove a specific object from a selection set that displays grips, we hold down the **[SHIFT]** key as we select the object. To exit the grip modes and return to the command prompt, press the **[ESC]** key.

The *V-Block* Design

Starting Up *AutoCAD LT 2005*

1. Select the **AutoCAD LT 2005** option on the program menu or select the **AutoCAD LT 2005** icon on the desktop.

2. In the *Startup* dialog box, select the ***Use a Template*** option with a single click of the left-mouse-button.

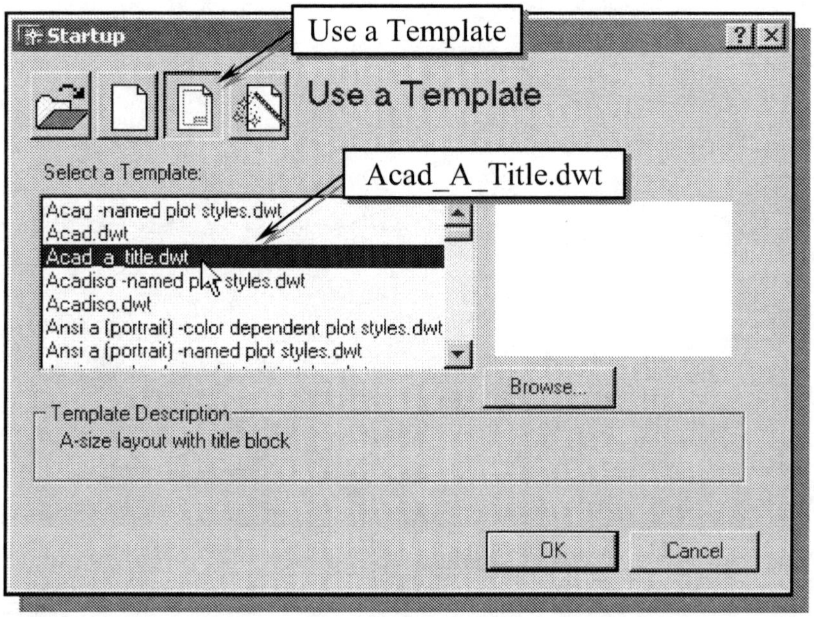

3. Select the ***Acad_A_Title*** template file from the list of template files. If the file is saved in a separate folder, click on the **Browse** button to locate the file.

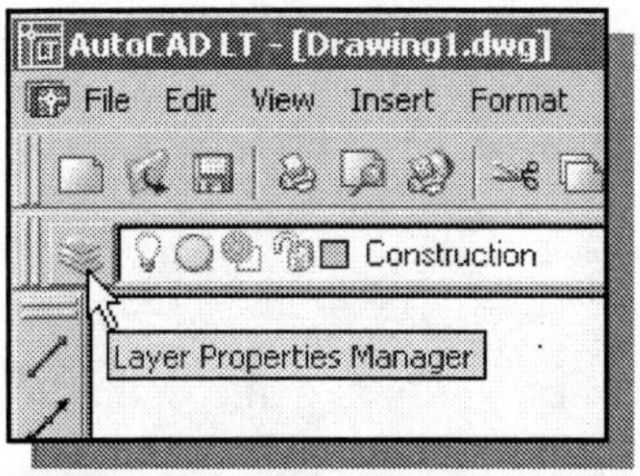

4. Pick **Layer Properties Manager** in the *Object Properties* toolbar.

5. Examine the layer property settings in the *Layer Properties Manager* dialog box.

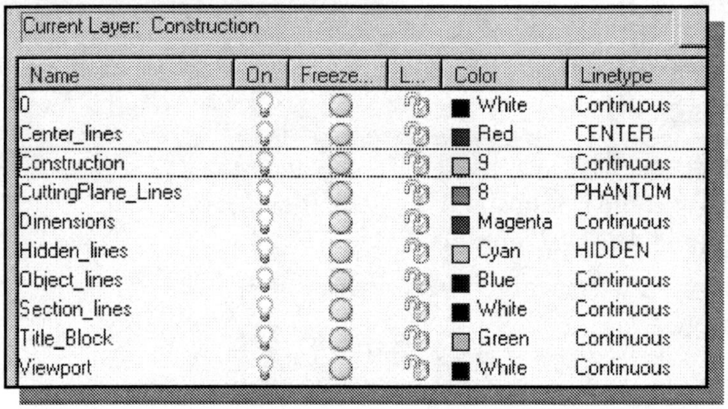

6. Click on the **OK** button to exit the *Layer Properties Manager* dialog box.

The *V-Block* Example

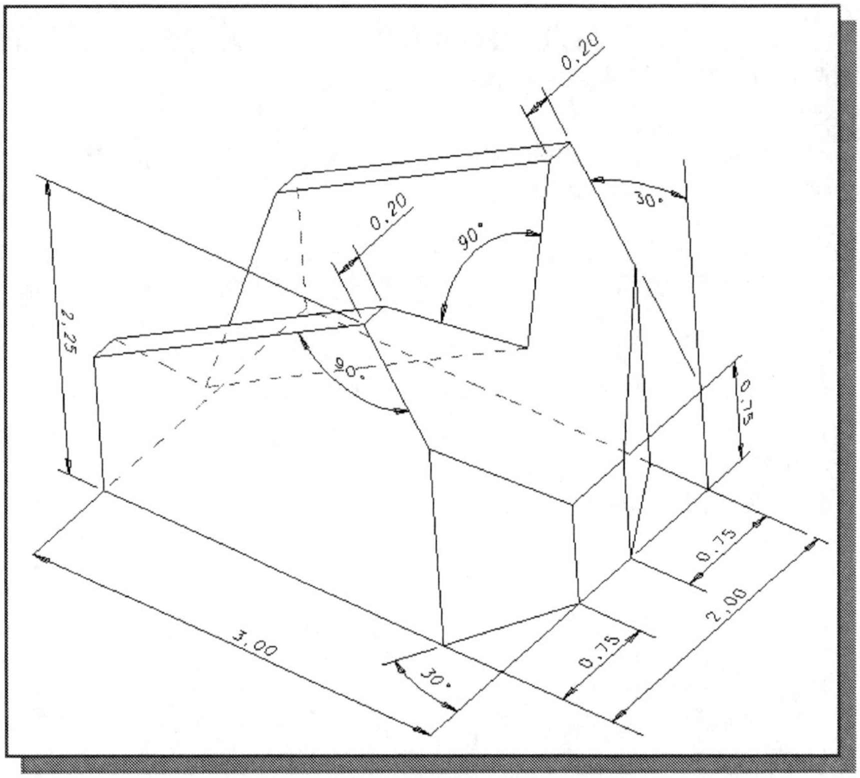

➤ Before going through the tutorial, make a rough sketch of a multiview drawing of the part. How many 2D views will be necessary to fully describe the part? Based on your knowledge of **AutoCAD® LT 2005** so far, how would you arrange and construct these 2D views? Take a few minutes to consider these questions and do preliminary planning by sketching on a piece of paper. You are also encouraged to construct the orthographic views on your own prior to going through the tutorial.

Setting Up the Principal Views

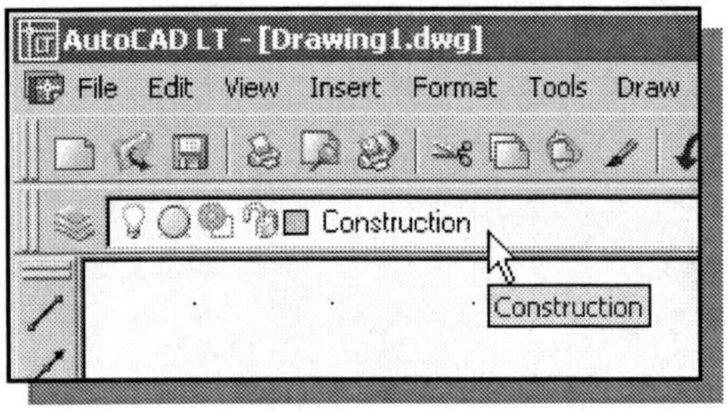

1. In the ***Layer Control*** box, confirm that layer *Construction* is set as the *Current Layer*.

2. In the *Status Bar* area, reset the options and turn ***ON*** the *SNAP, GRID, POLAR, OSNAP, LWT* and *MODEL* options.

➢ We will first create construction geometry for the front view.

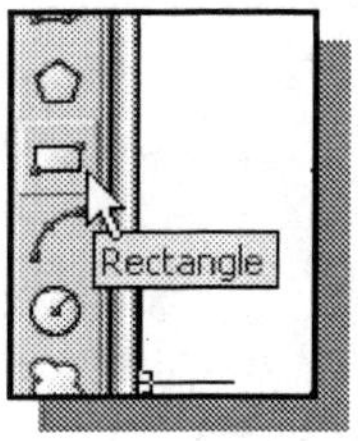

3. Select the **Rectangle** icon in the *Draw* toolbar. In the command prompt area, the message *"Specify first corner point or [Chamfer/Elevation/Fillet/Thickness/Width]:"* is displayed.

4. Place the first corner point of the rectangle near the lower left corner of the screen. Do not be overly concerned about the actual coordinates of the location; the drawing space is as big as you can imagine.

5. Next, create a 3″ × 2.25″ rectangle by entering **@3,2.25 [ENTER]**

❖ The **Rectangle** command creates rectangles as *polyline* features, which means all segments of a rectangle are created as a single object.

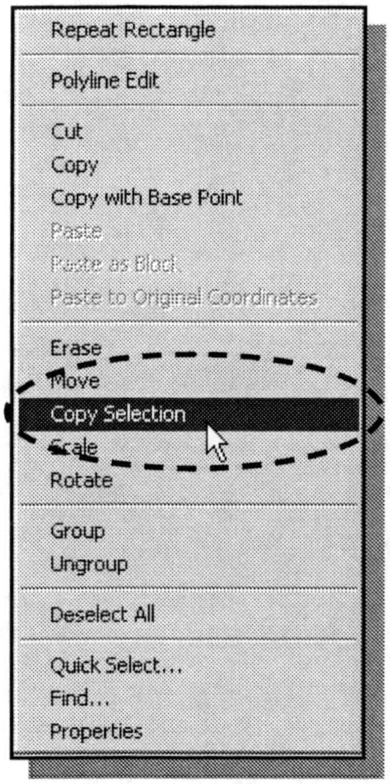

6. Next, use the *GRIPS* editing tools to make a copy of the rectangle. Pick any edge of the rectangle we just created. Notice that small squares appear at different locations on the rectangle.

7. Inside the graphics window, **right-mouse-click** to bring up the popup option menu.

➢ In the center section of the popup menu, the set of ***Grips*** editing commands includes Erase, Move, Copy Selection, Scale, and Rotate.

8. In the popup menu, select the **Copy Selection** option.

9. In the command prompt area, the message "*Specify base point or displacement, or [Multiple]:*" is displayed. Pick the **lower right corner** as the base point. A copy of the rectangle is attached to the cursor at the base point.

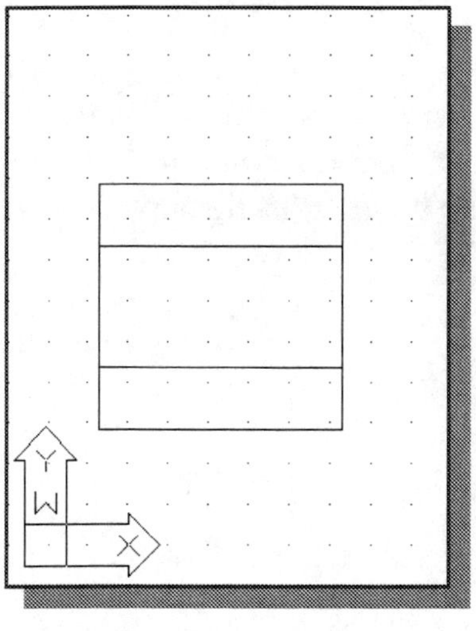

10. In the command prompt area, the message "*Specify second point of displacement, or <use first point as displacement>:*" is displayed. Enter **@0,0.75 [ENTER]**.

➢ This will position the second rectangle at the location for the 30-degree angle.

11. Pre-select the copy by picking the top horizontal line on the screen. The second rectangle, the copy we just created, is selected.

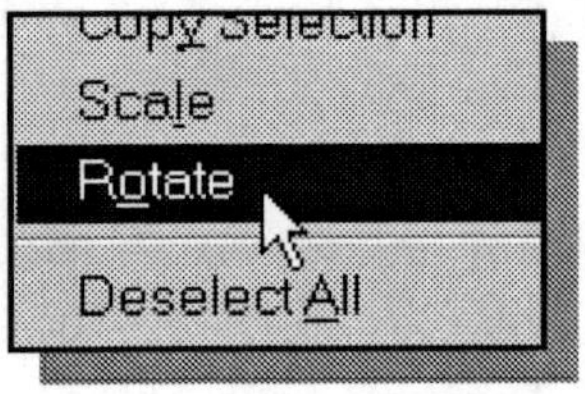

12. Inside the graphics window, **right-mouse-click** to bring up the popup option menu and select the **Rotate** option.

13. In the command prompt area, the message "*Specify base point:*" is displayed. Pick the **lower right corner** of the selected rectangle as the base point.

14. In the command prompt area, the message "*Specify the rotation angle or [Reference]:*" is displayed. Enter **30 [ENTER]**.

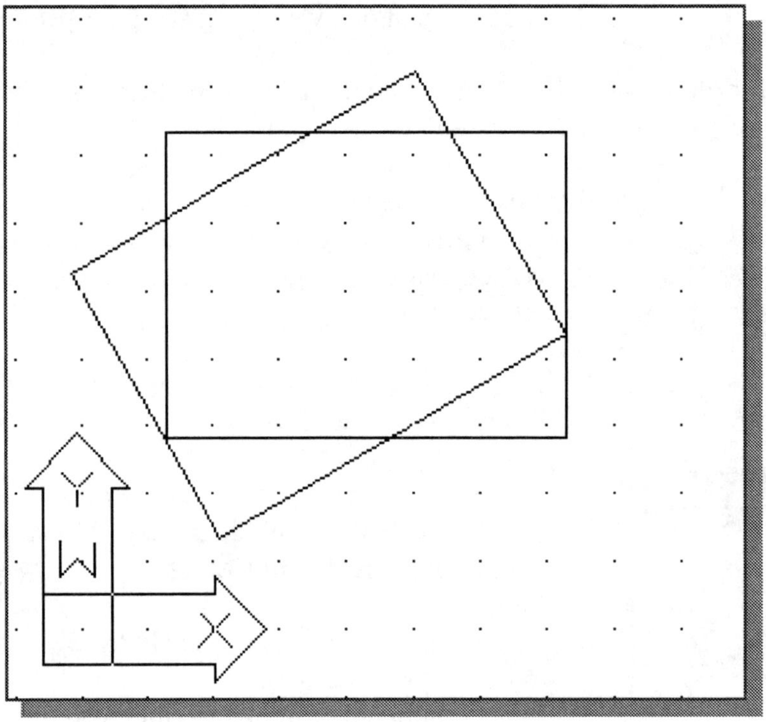

Setting Up the Outer Edges of the Top View

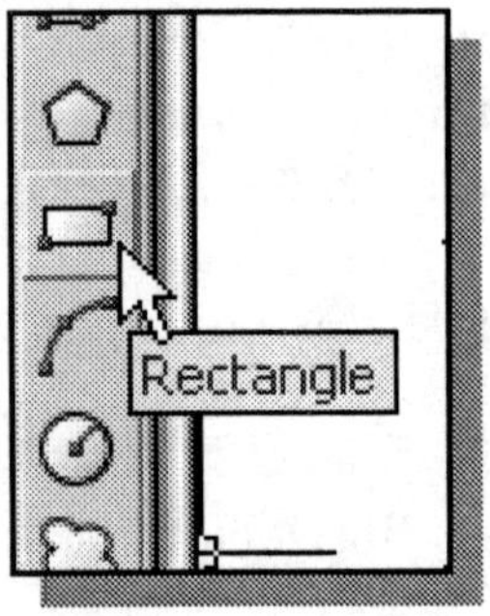

1. Select the **Rectangle** icon in the *Draw* toolbar. In the command prompt area, the message *"Specify first corner point or [Chamfer/Elevation/Fillet/Thickness/Width]:"* is displayed.

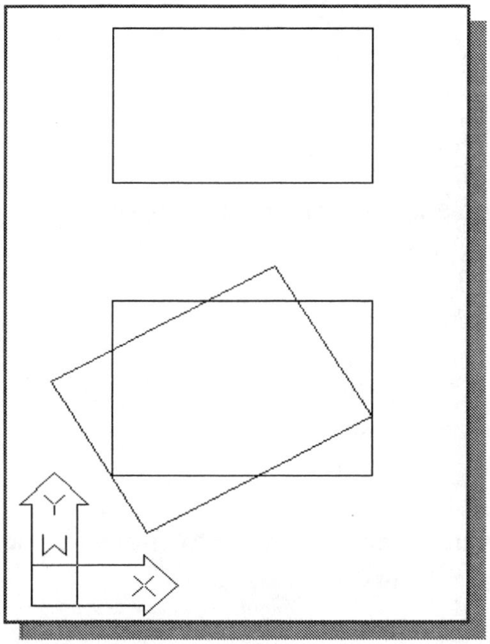

2. On your own, create a 3″ × 2″ rectangle that is about 2″ above the front view as shown.

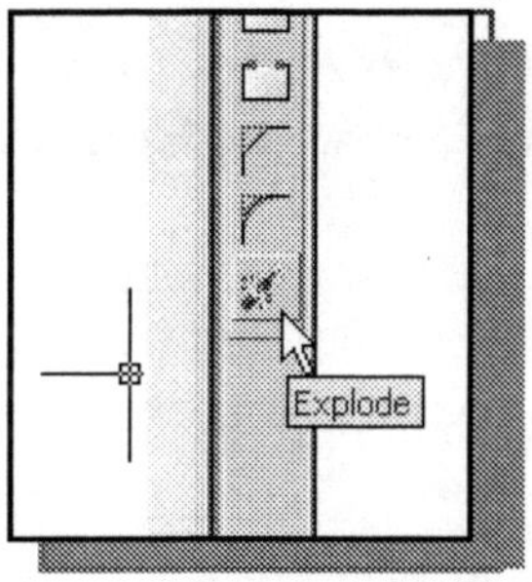

3. Pre-select the rectangle we just created by left-clicking any edge of the rectangle.

4. Select the **Explode** icon in the *Modify* toolbar.

➢ The top rectangle is no longer a single object; it now consists of four separate line segments.

5. In the *Status Bar* area, turn ***OFF*** the *SNAP* option.

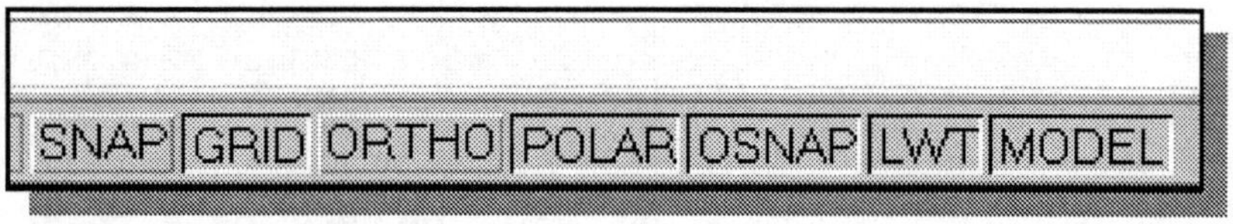

Using the *Offset* Command

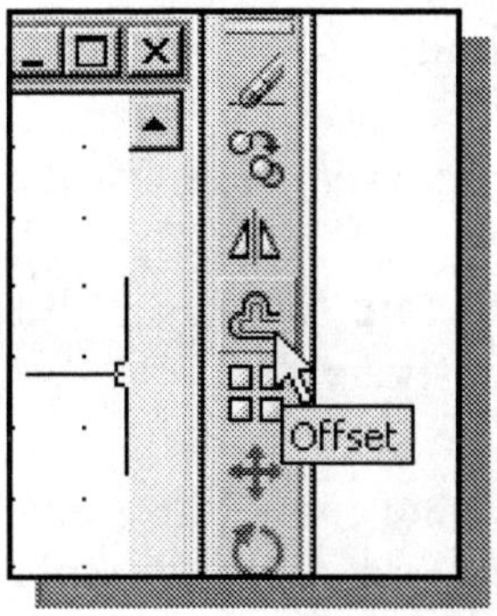

1. Select the **Offset** icon in the *Modify* toolbar. In the command prompt area, the message *"Specify offset distance or [Through]:"* is displayed.

2. In the command prompt area, enter **0.2** [**ENTER**]

3. In the command prompt area, the message *"Select object to offset or <exit>:"* is displayed. Pick the **top horizontal line** of the top view on the screen.

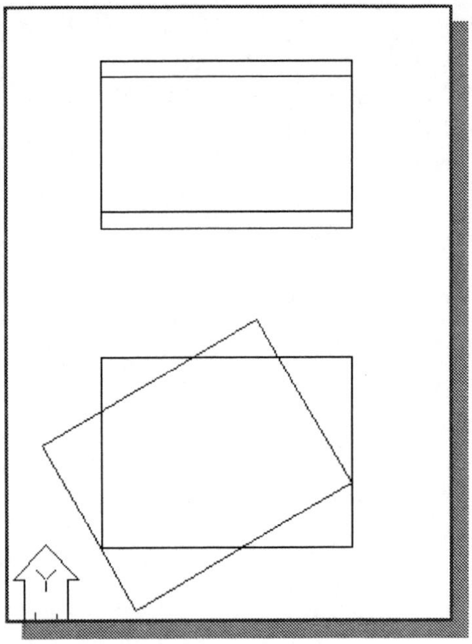

4. AutoCAD LT next asks us to identify the direction of the offset. Pick a location that is **below** the selected line.

5. In the command prompt area, the message *"Select object to offset or <exit>:"* is displayed. Pick the **bottom horizontal line** of the top view on the screen.

6. AutoCAD LT next asks us to identify the direction of the offset. Pick a location that is above the selected line.

7. Inside the graphics window, **right-mouse-click** to end the **Offset** command.

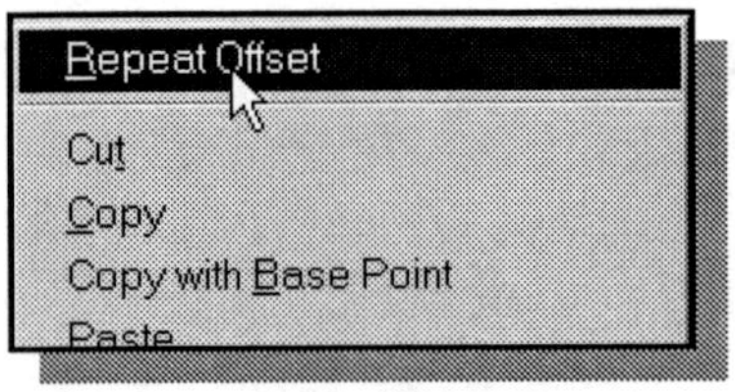

8. Inside the graphics window, **right-mouse-click** to bring up the popup option menu and select the **Repeat Offset** option.

9. In the command prompt area, the message *"Specify offset distance or [Through]:"* is displayed.

10. In the command prompt area, enter **0.75** [**ENTER**]

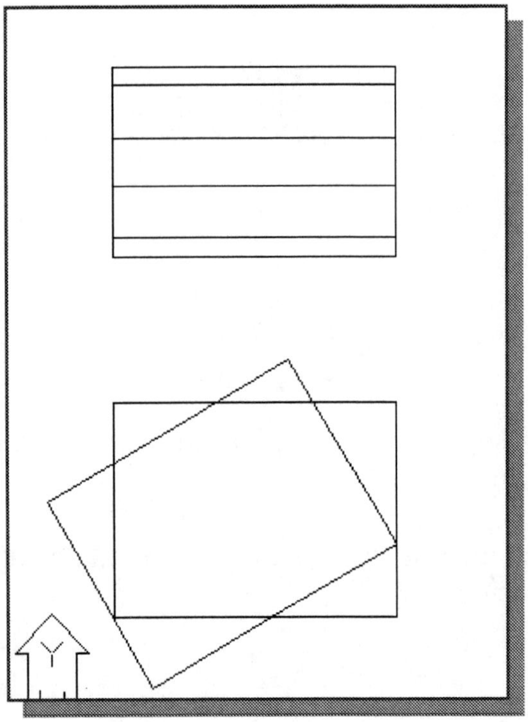

11. In the command prompt area, the message *"Select object to offset or <exit>:"* is displayed. Pick the **top horizontal line** of the top view on the screen.

12. AutoCAD LT next asks us to identify the direction of the offset. Pick a location that is **below** the selected line.

13. In the command prompt area, the message *"Select object to offset or <exit>:"* is displayed. Pick the **bottom horizontal line** of the top view on the screen.

14. AutoCAD LT next asks us to identify the direction of the offset. Pick a location that is above the selected line.

15. Inside the graphics window, **right-mouse-click** to end the **Offset** command.

➢ The four parallel lines we just created will help us locate the top V-cut feature and the two 0.75″ × 30° cut features at the base of the *V-Block*.

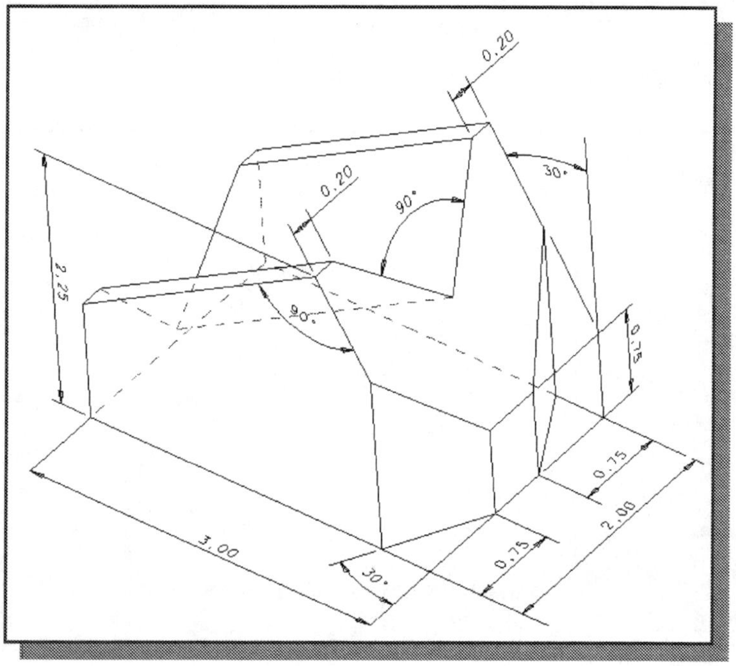

Creating Object Lines in the Front View

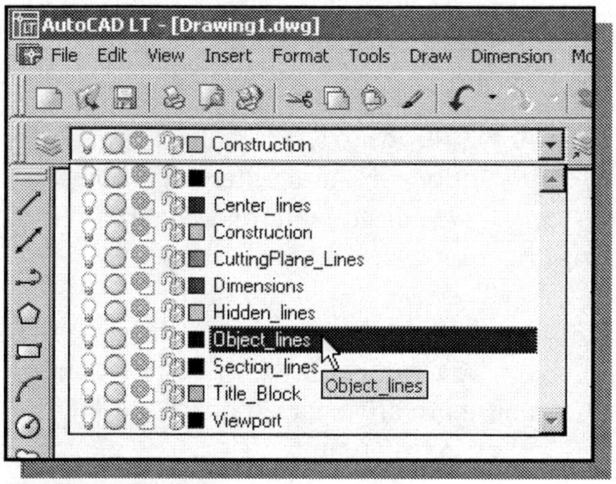

1. On the *Object Properties* toolbar, choose the ***Layer Control*** box with the left-mouse-button.

2. Move the cursor over the name of layer ***Object_Lines***; the tool tip *"Object_Lines"* appears.

3. **Left-mouse-click once** to set layer *Object_Lines* as the *Current Layer*.

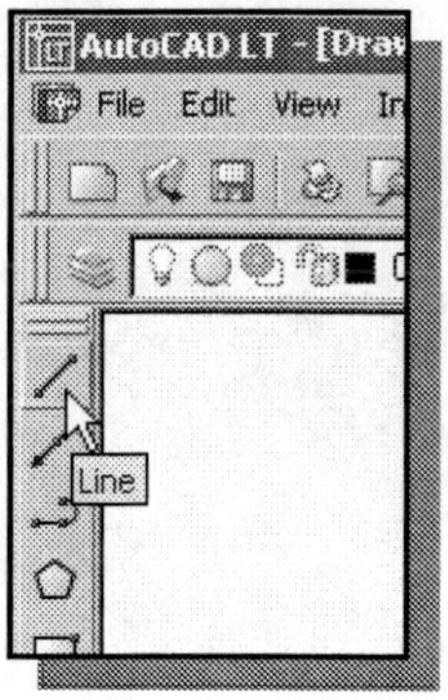

4. Select the **Line** command icon in the *Draw* toolbar. In the command prompt area, the message *"_line Specify first point:"* is displayed.

5. Pick the lower left corner of the bottom horizontal line in the front view as the starting point of the line segments.

6. Pick the lower right corner of the bottom horizontal line in the front view as the second point.

7. Select the **third** and **fourth** points as shown.

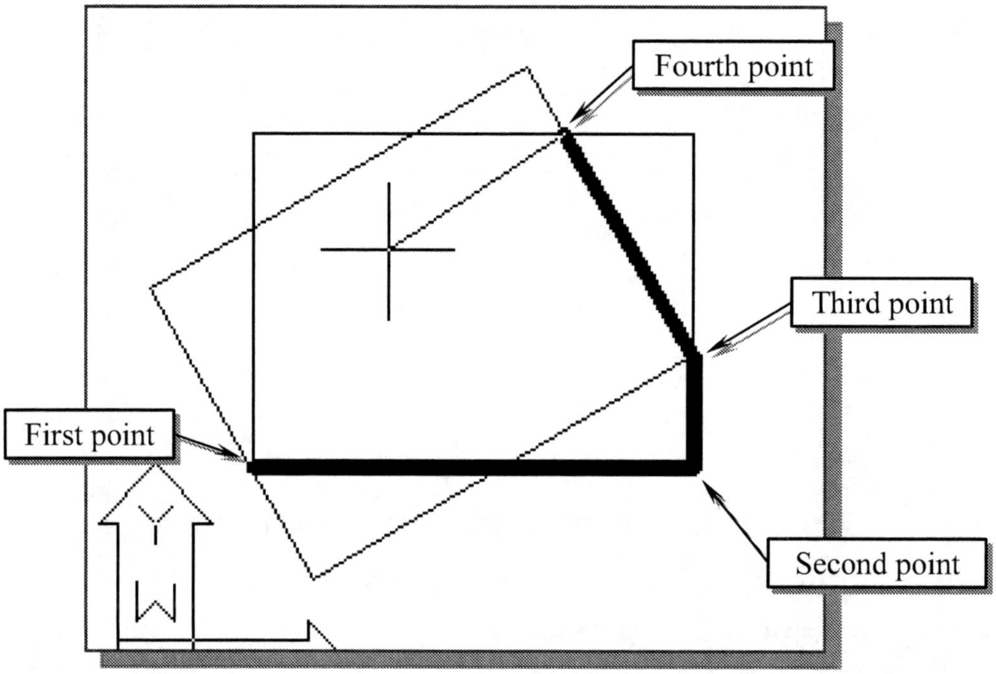

❖ The *POLAR* option is one of the **AutoCAD® LT 2005** AutoTrack/AutoSnap features. The *AutoTrack*™ feature includes two tracking options: polar tracking and object snap tracking. When the *POLAR* option is turned *ON*, alignment markers are displayed to help us create objects at precise positions and angles.

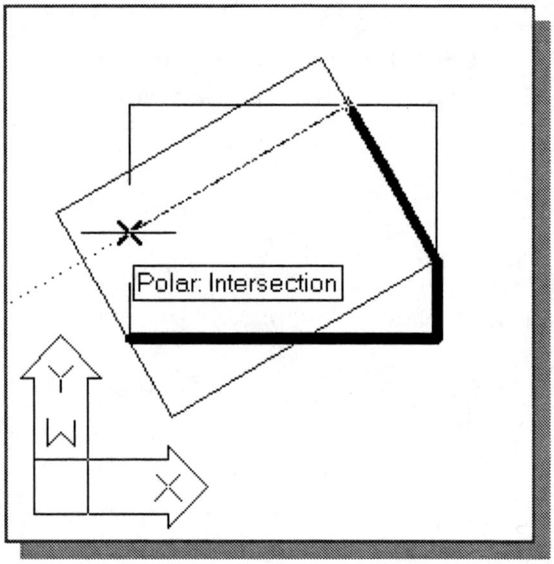

8. Move the cursor near the left vertical line and notice the *AutoTrack* feature automatically snaps the cursor to the intersection point.

9. Left-click at the intersection point as shown.

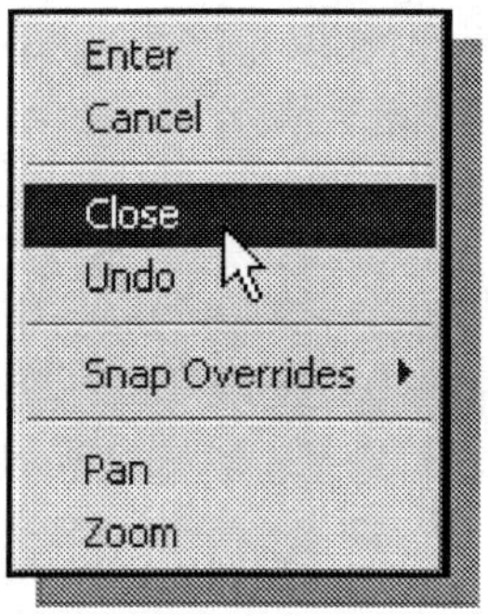

10. Inside the graphics window, right-mouse-click once to bring up the popup menu.

11. Pick the **Close** option in the popup menu. AutoCAD LT will create a line connecting the last point to the first point of the line sequence.

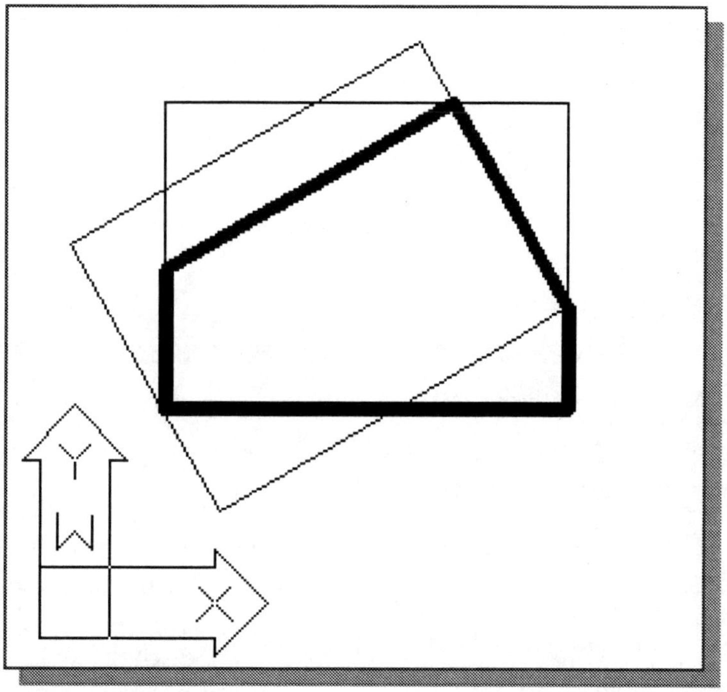

Stretch and Copy with Grips

We can stretch an object by moving selected ***Grips*** to new locations. Moving grips that are on text, block references, midpoints of lines, centers of circles, and point objects will move the object rather than stretching it. This is an excellent method for quickly adjusting existing objects on the screen.

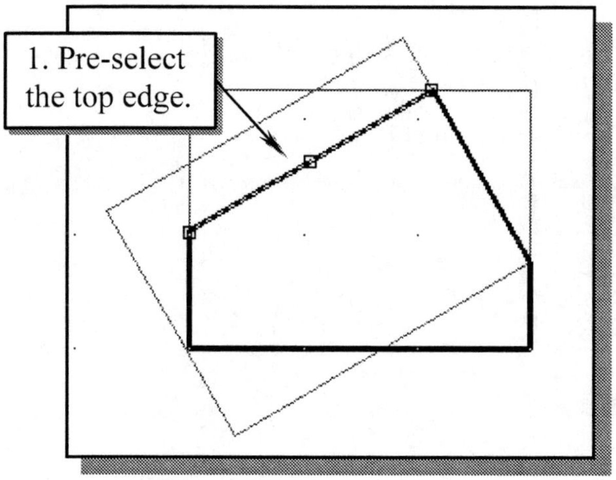

1. **Pre-select** the top edge of the *V-Block* in the front view as shown.

2. Left-click once on the right grip point on the selected line.

➢ Selecting the grip points located at the end of the line or arc allows us to STRETCH the selected line.

3. Move the cursor toward the left side and pick a location that is about 2″ away from the top corner of the *V-Block* in the front view as shown below.

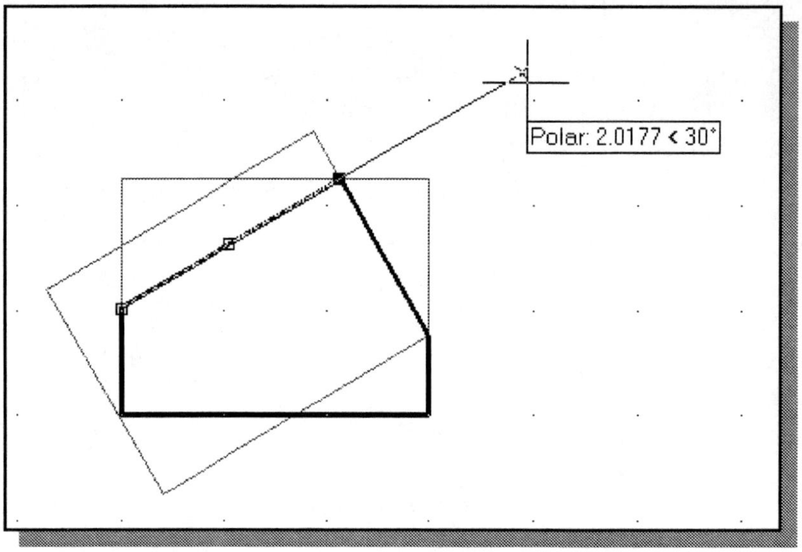

➤ Note that with the ***POLAR*** option, the alignment of objects can be accomplished quite easily.

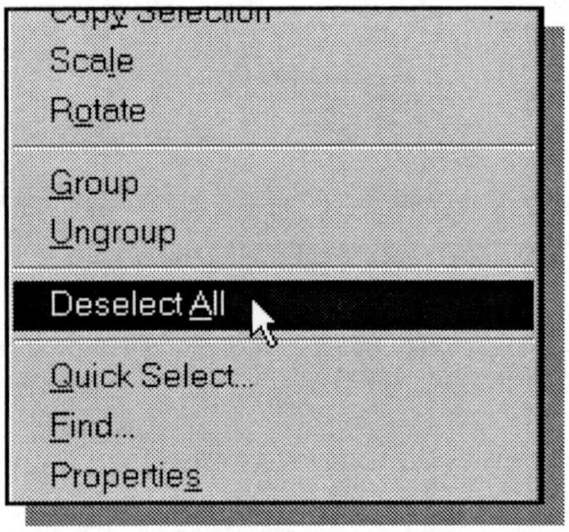

4. Inside the graphics window, right-mouse-click once to bring up the popup menu.

5. Pick **Deselect All** in the popup menu to release all of the pre-selected objects.

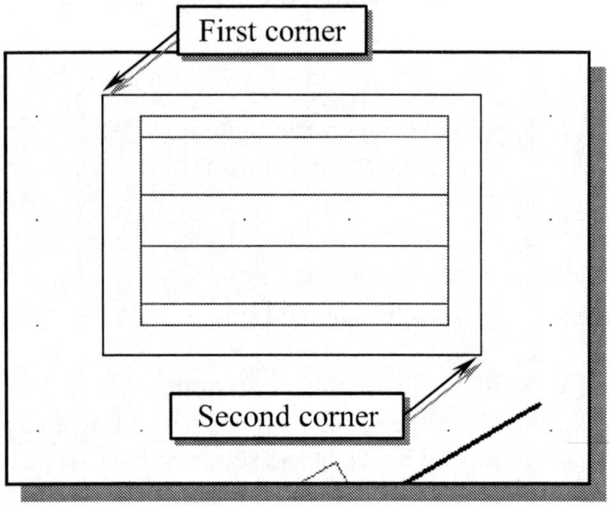

6. **Pre-select** all objects in the top-view by enclosing the objects inside a selection window.

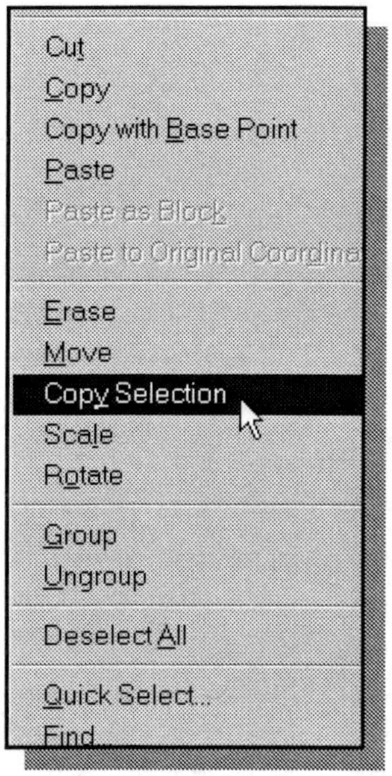

7. Inside the graphics window, **right-mouse-click** to bring up the popup option menu and select the **Copy Selection** option.

➢ In the center section of the popup menu, the set of *Grips* editing commands includes Erase, Move, Copy Selection, Scale, and Rotate.

8. In the command prompt area, the message *"Specify base point or displacement, or [Multiple]:"* is displayed. Pick the **lower left corner** of the top view as the base point.

9. Using the ***OSNAP*** feature, place the copy of the top view by aligning it to the *endpoint* of the inclined object line we just stretched. Left-click once to position the copy at the endpoint of the stretched line.

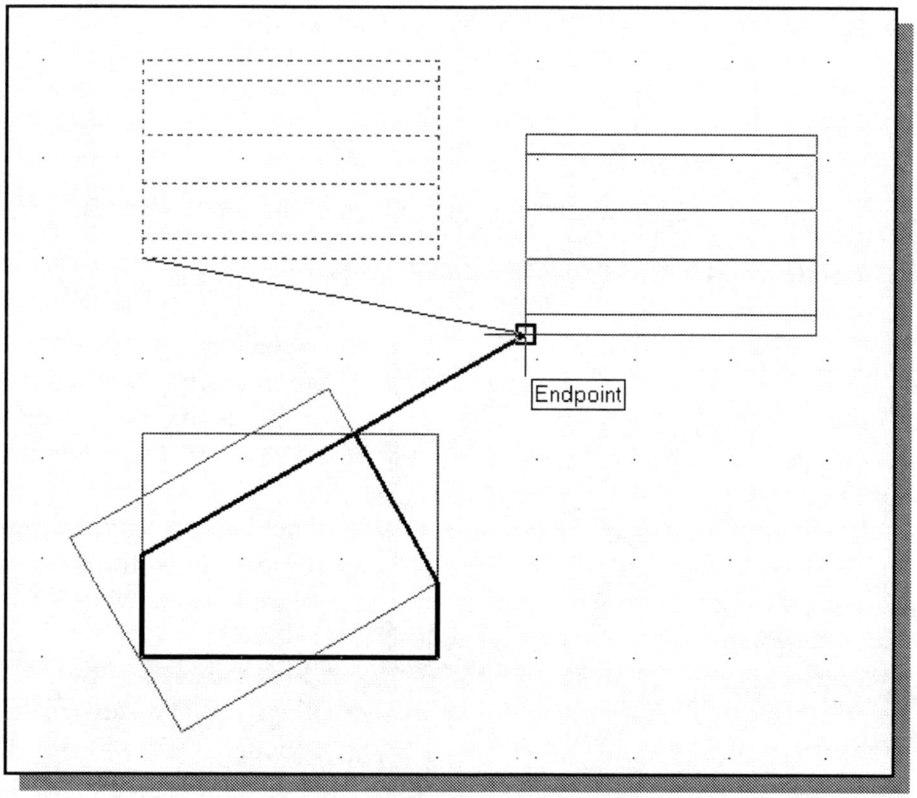

10. On your own, use the ***Grips*** **Stretch** option and readjust the top edge of the *V-Block* in the front view to its correct length.

Aligning the Auxiliary View to the Front View

1. **Pre-select** all objects in the auxiliary view by enclosing the objects inside a selection window.

2. Inside the graphics window, **right-mouse-click** to bring up the popup option menu and select the **Rotate** option.

3. In the command prompt area, the message *"Specify base point:"* is displayed. Pick the **left corner** of the auxiliary view as the base point.

4. In the command prompt area, the message *"Specify the rotation angle or [Reference]:"* is displayed. Enter: **-60 [ENTER]**

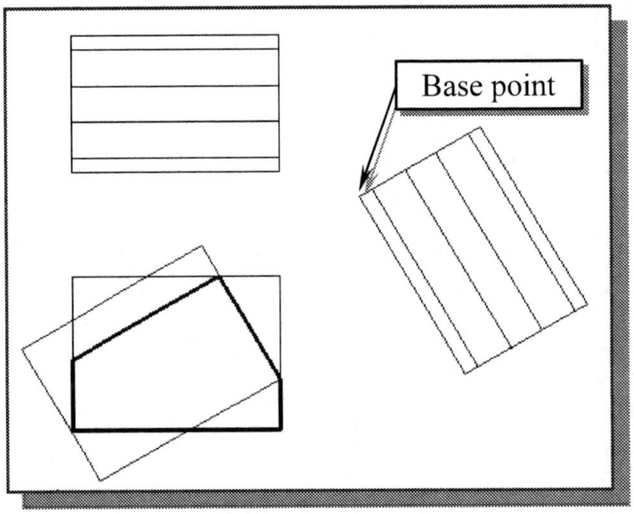

Creating the V-Cut in the Auxiliary View

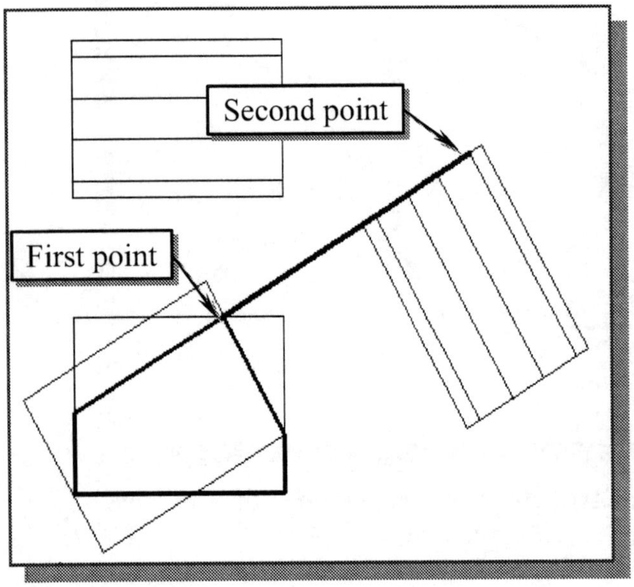

1. Select the **Line** icon in the *Draw* toolbar. In the command prompt area, the message *"_line Specify first point:"* is displayed.

2. Pick the **top corner** of the inclined object line in the front view as the starting point of the line segments.

3. Pick the **second top end point** in the auxiliary view as the second point.

4. Inside the graphics window, **right-mouse-click** and select **Enter** to end the **Line** command.

5. Pre-select the line we just created.

6. Inside the graphics window, **right-mouse-click** to bring up the popup option menu and select the **Rotate** option.

7. In the command prompt area, the message *"Specify base point:"* is displayed. Pick the top-right endpoint of the line as the base point.

8. In the command prompt area, the message *"Specify the rotation angle or [Reference]:"* is displayed. Enter **45 [ENTER]**

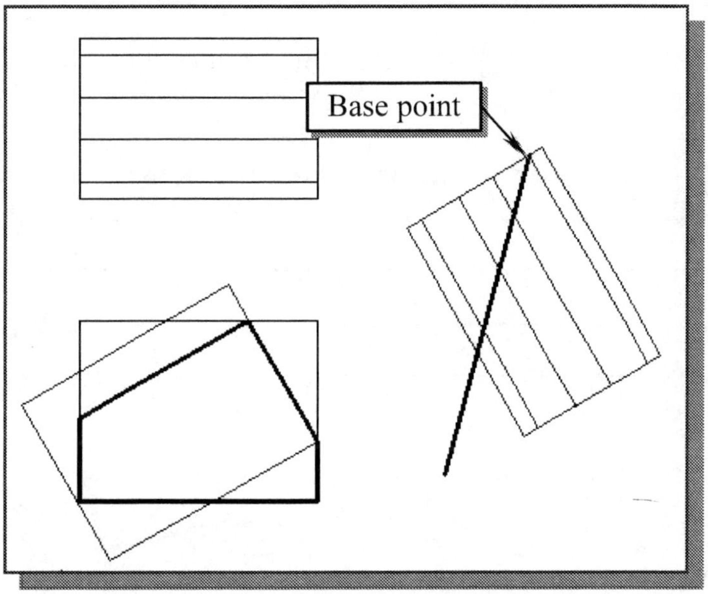

9. On your own, repeat the steps and create the other line as shown.

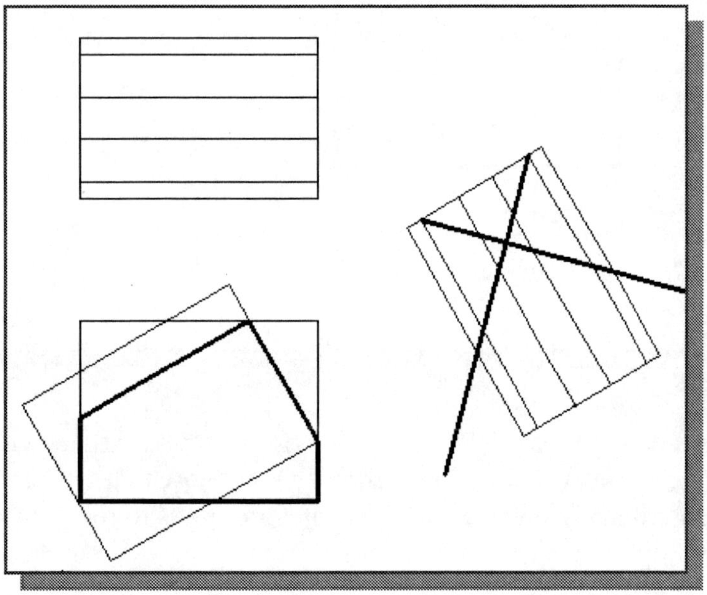

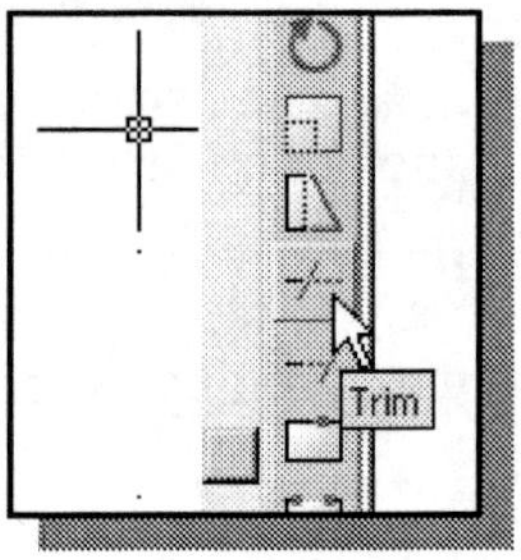

10. Select the **Trim** command icon in the *Modify* toolbar. In the command prompt area, the message *"Select boundary edges... Select objects:"* is displayed.

11. Pick the two inclined lines we just created in the auxiliary view as the *boundary edges*.

12. Inside the graphics window, **right-mouse-click** to proceed with the Trim command. The message *"Select object to trim or [Project/Edge/Undo]:"* is displayed in the command prompt area.

13. Pick the two lower endpoints of the two inclined lines to remove the unwanted portions.

14. Inside the graphics window, **right-mouse-click** to activate the option menu and select **Enter** with the left-mouse-button to end the **Trim** command.

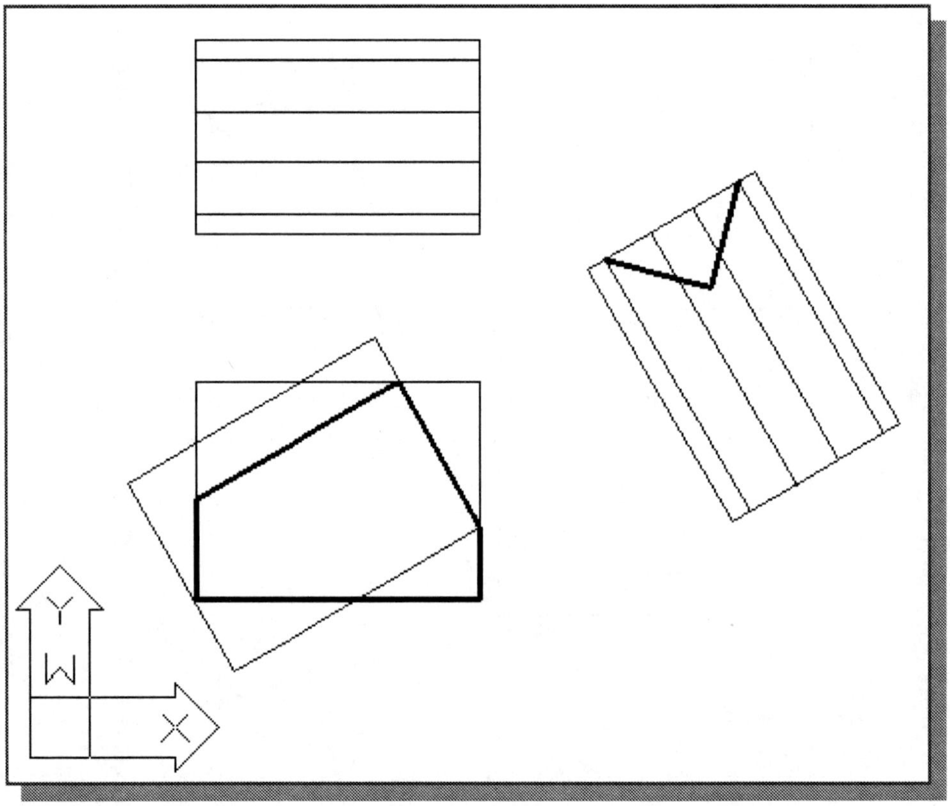

- The V-cut is shown at its true size and shape only in the auxiliary view. It is therefore necessary to create the V-cut in the auxiliary view. Now that we have constructed the feature in the auxiliary view, we can use projection lines to transfer the feature to the front view and top view.

Creating the V-cut in the Front-View and Top-View

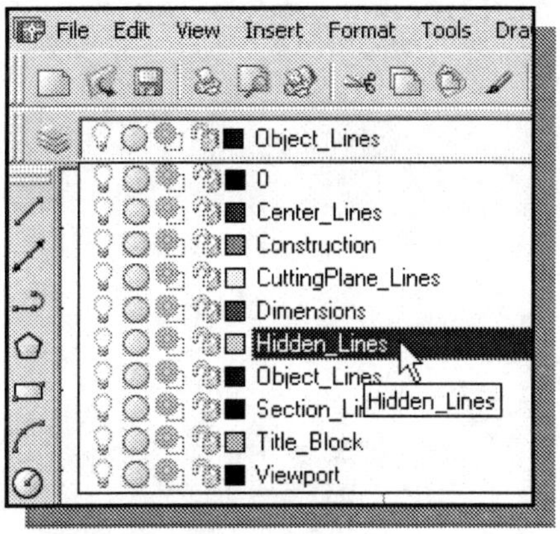

1. On the *Object Properties* toolbar, choose the ***Layer Control*** box with the left-mouse-button.

2. Move the cursor over the name of layer ***Hidden_Lines***; the tool tip *"Hidden_Lines"* appears.

3. **Left-mouse-click once** and layer *Hidden_Lines* is set as the *Current Layer.*

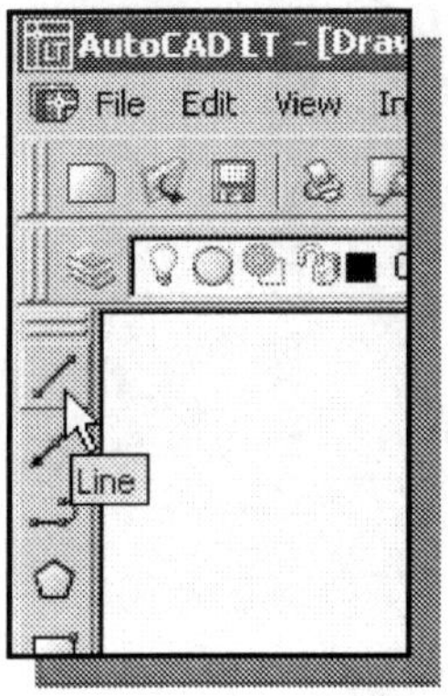

4. Select the **Line** command icon in the *Draw* toolbar. In the command prompt area, the message *"_line Specify first point:"* is displayed.

5. Pick the vertex of the V-cut in the side view as the first point of the line.

6. Inside the graphics window, hold down the **[SHIFT]** key and **right-mouse-click** once to bring up the *Object Snap* shortcut menu.

7. Select the **Perpendicular** option in popup window. Move the cursor to the front view and notice the perpendicular symbol appears at different locations. The *Single Object Snap* option overrides the *Running Object Snap* option.

8. Left-click at the location shown.

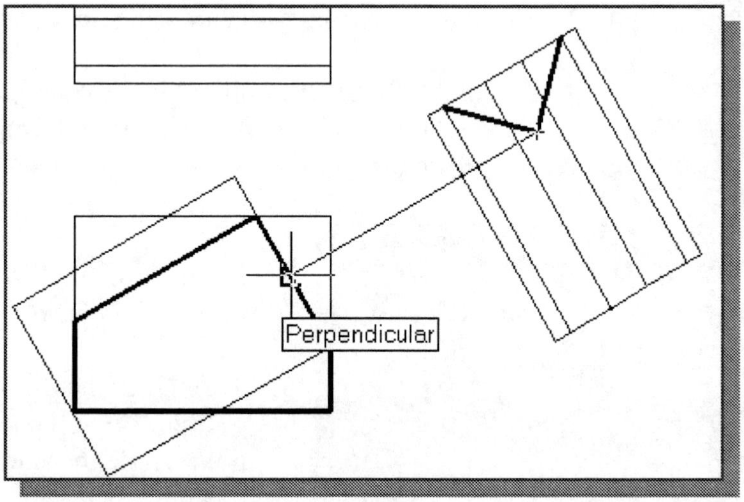

9. Inside the graphics window, right-mouse-click to activate the option menu and select **Enter** with the left-mouse-button to end the Line command.

10. Use the ***Grips editing options*** to adjust the hidden line in the front view.

➢ On your own, first create the two construction lines and then construct the V-cut feature in the top-view. Use the *Grips* editing options, **Trim** and **Extend** commands to assist the construction.

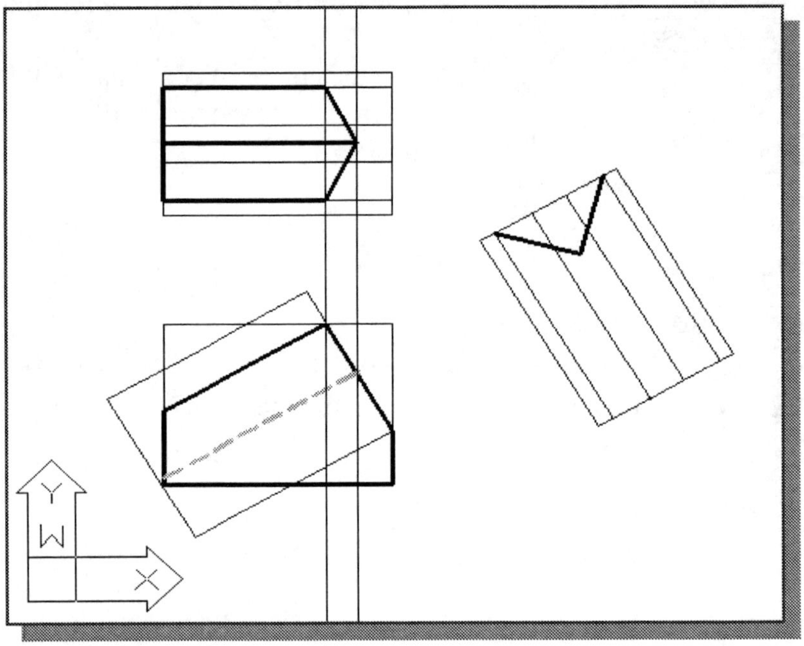

Setting the *Polar Tracking* Option

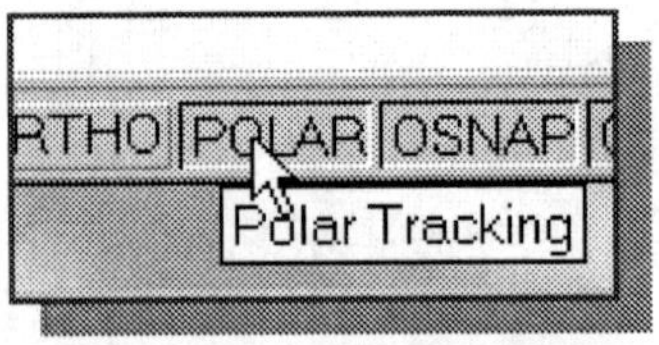

1. Move the cursor to the *Status Bar* area, over the *POLAR* option button.

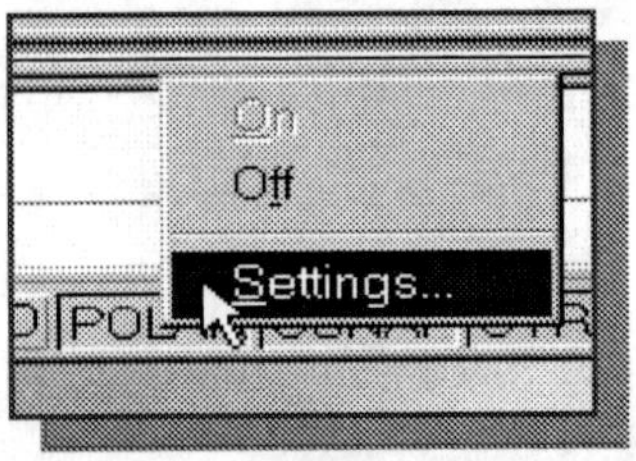

2. **Right-mouse-click once** to bring up a popup option menu.
3. Select the **Settings** option by clicking once with the left-mouse-button. This is the shortcut to bring up the *Drafting Settings* dialog box.

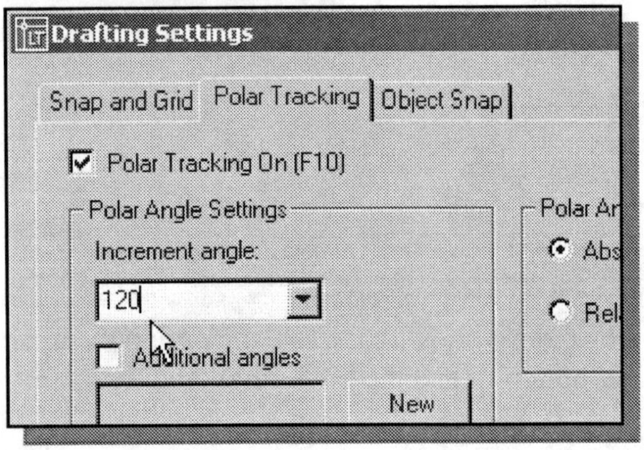

4. In the *Drafting Settings* dialog box, set the *Increment angle* to **120**.
5. Turn ***OFF*** the *Additional angles* option. We will use the absolute polar angle measurement for this example.
6. Click on the **OK** button to accept the settings.

Completing the Top-View

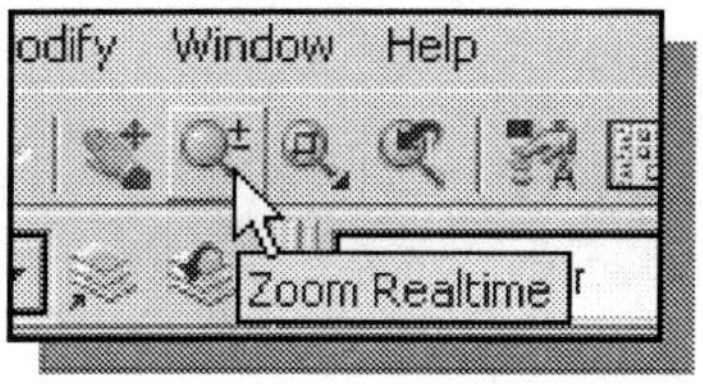

1. Click on the **Zoom Realtime** icon in the *Standard* toolbar area.

2. Move the cursor near the center of the graphics window.

3. **Push and hold down the left-mouse-button**, then move upward to enlarge the current display scale factor. (Press the [**Esc**] key to exit the command.)

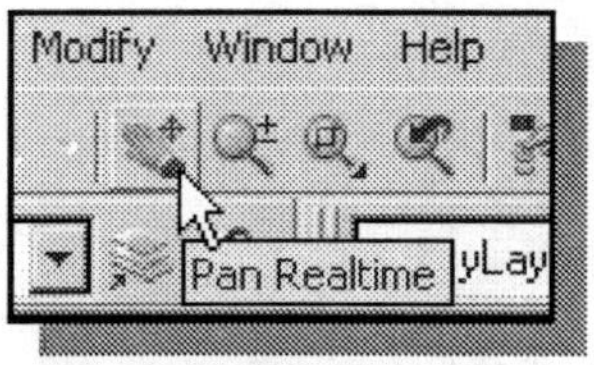

4. On your own, use the **Pan Realtime** option to reposition the display so that we can work on the top view of the *V-Block*.

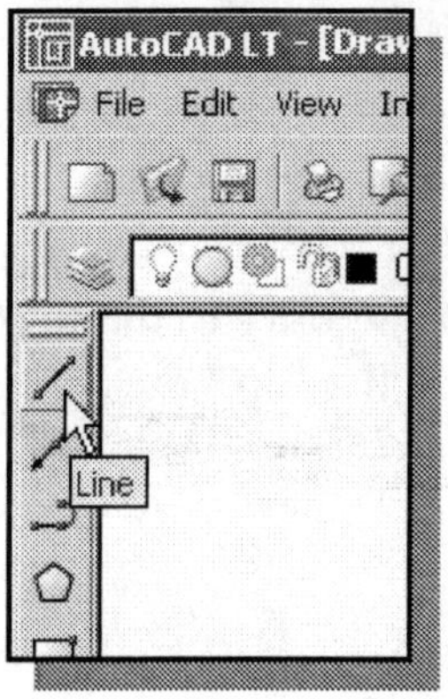

5. Select the **Line** icon in the *Draw* toolbar. In the command prompt area, the message *"_line Specify first point:"* is displayed.

6. Pick the **right endpoint** of the third horizontal line in the top view as the starting point of the line segments.

7. Move the cursor toward the top horizontal line and observe the *AutoTracking markers* over different locations.

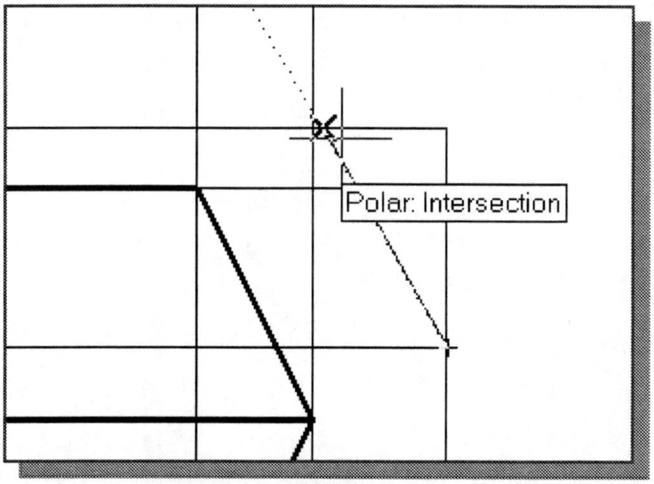

8. **Left-click** at the intersection of the polar tracking and the top horizontal line as shown. Do not select the intersection between the top horizontal line and the vertical line. (Use the **Zoom Realtime** command to zoom in further if necessary.)

9. Inside the graphics window, right-mouse-click and select **Enter** to end the **Line** command.

10. Repeat the above steps and create the other inclined line in the top view.

- On your own, complete the top view by adding all the necessary object lines. Use the *Grips* editing options to assist the construction.

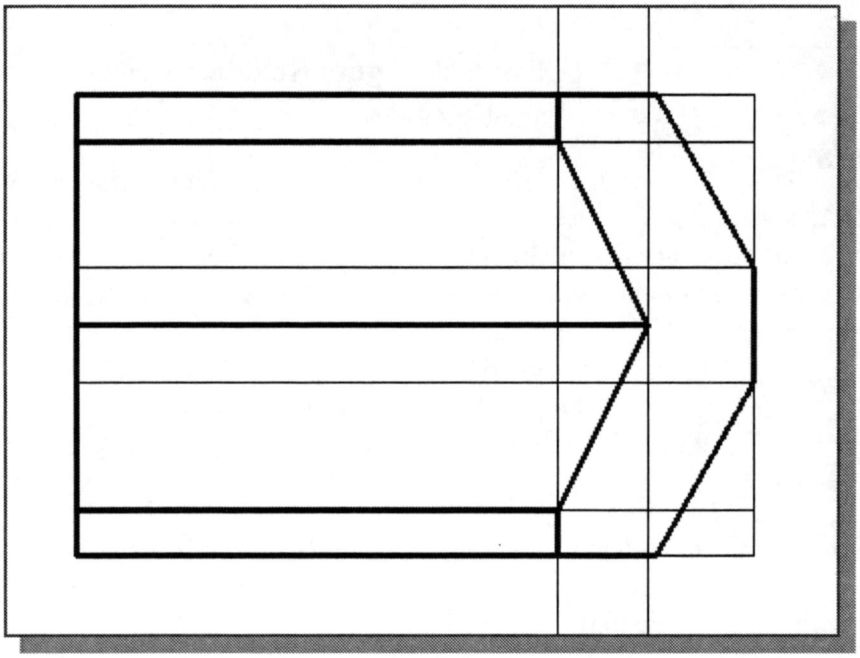

❖ Notice that the two 30° cut features are shown as **true size and shape** only in the top view, and therefore it is necessary for us to construct the features in the top view.

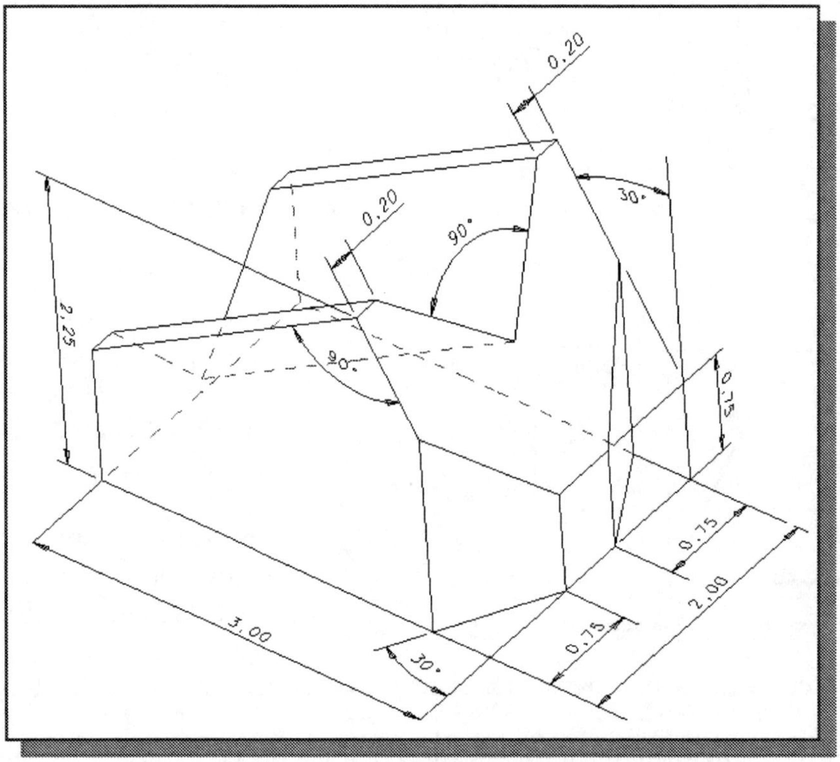

➤ On your own, create the **vertical construction line** through the corner of the 30° cut as shown.

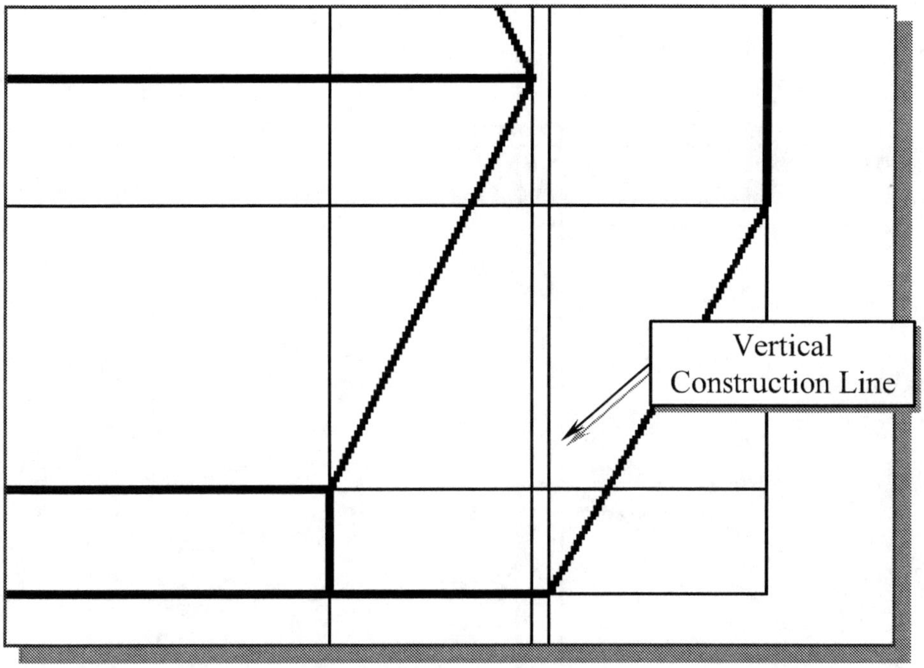

11. Complete the front view by adding the object line along the construction line as shown.

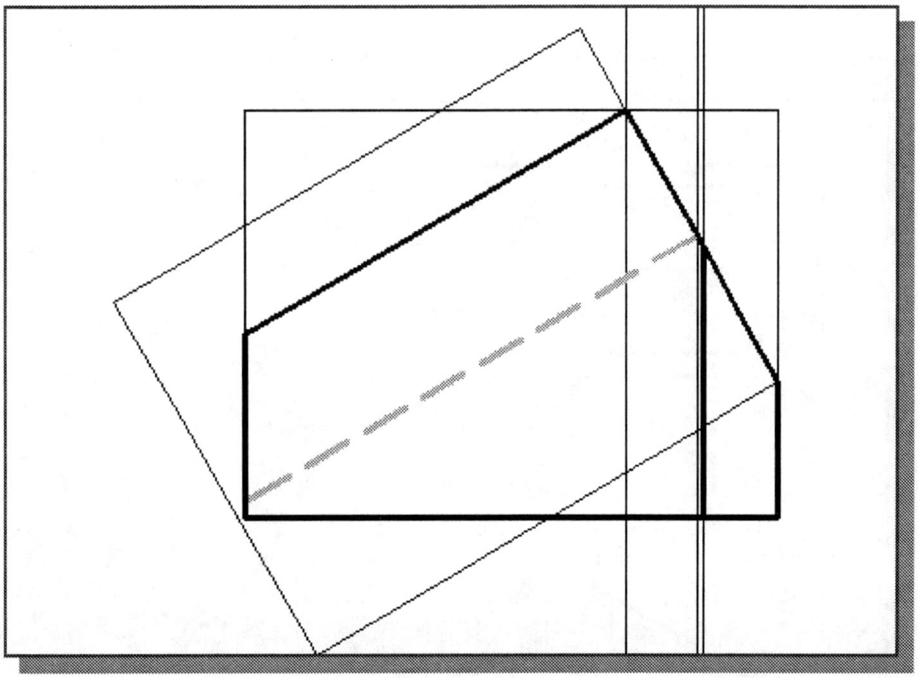

➢ On your own, complete the views by adding all the necessary object lines in the views.

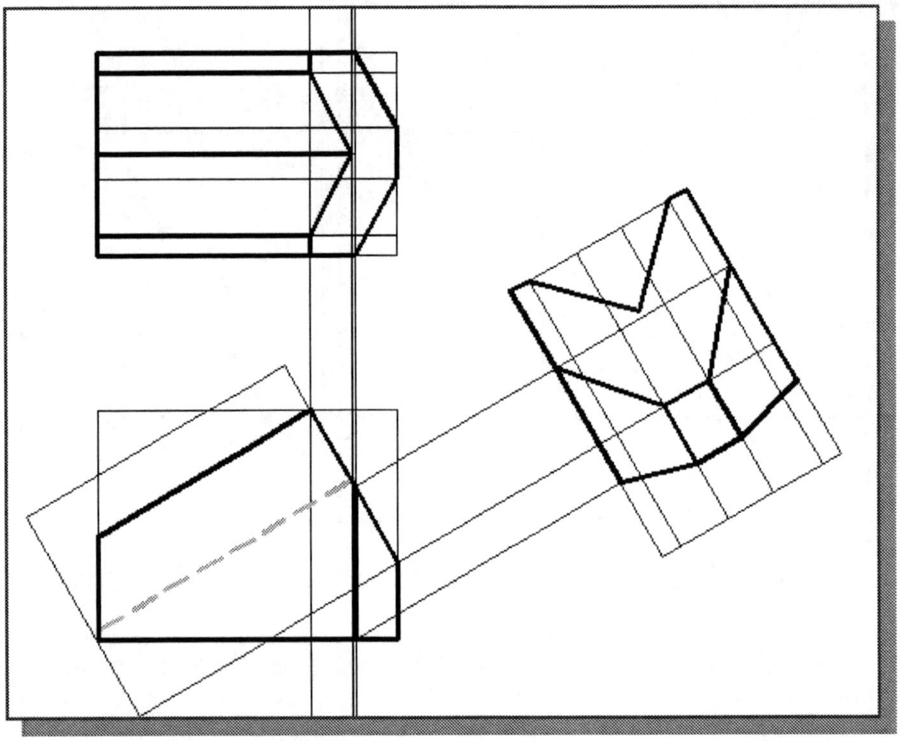

➢ Complete the drawing by adding the proper dimensions.

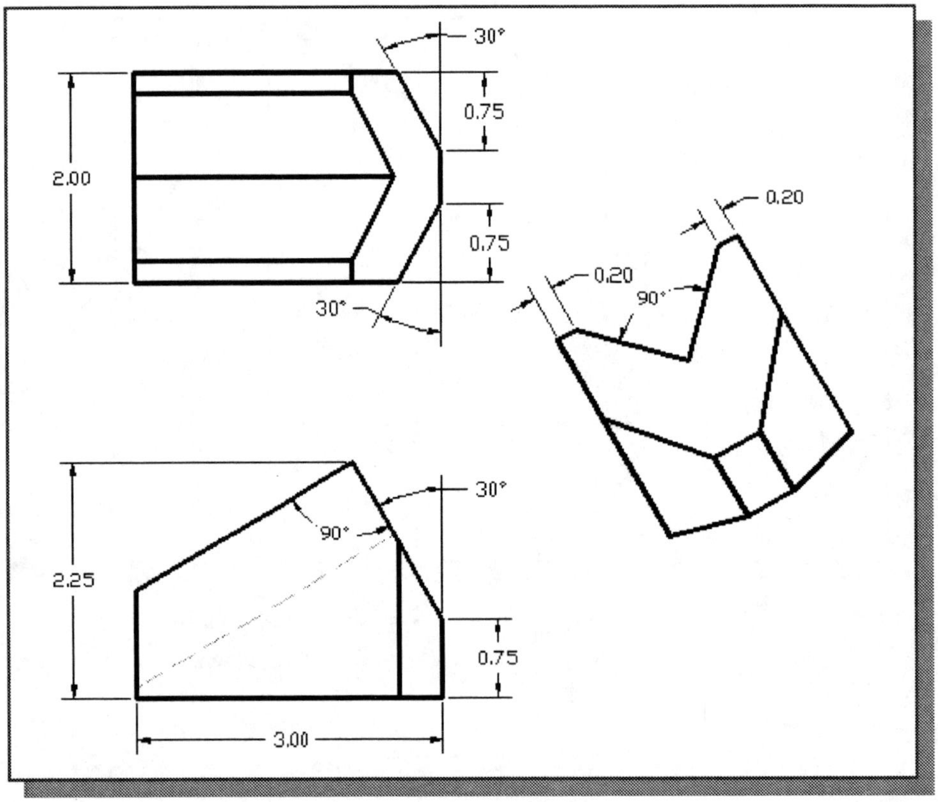

Edit the Plot Style Table

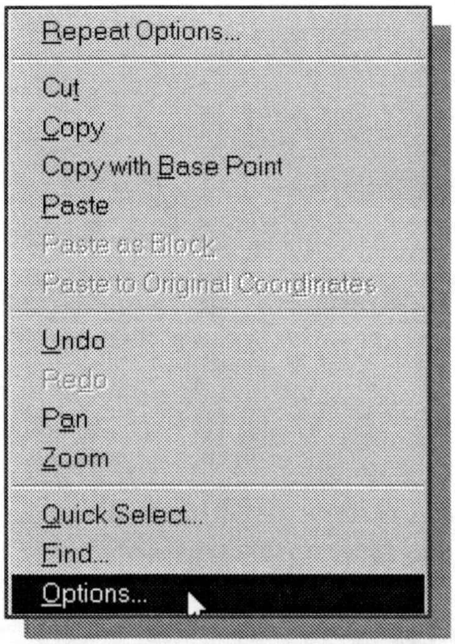

1. Inside the graphics window, right-mouse-click and select **Options** in the popup menu.

2. In the *Options* dialog box, select the **Plotting** tab.

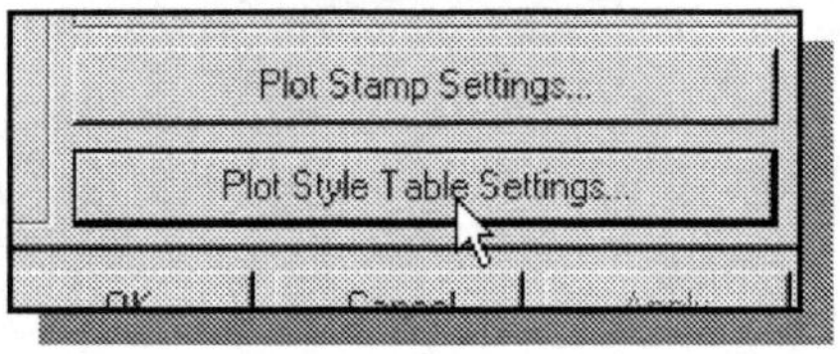

3. Click on the **Plot Style Table Settings** button as shown.

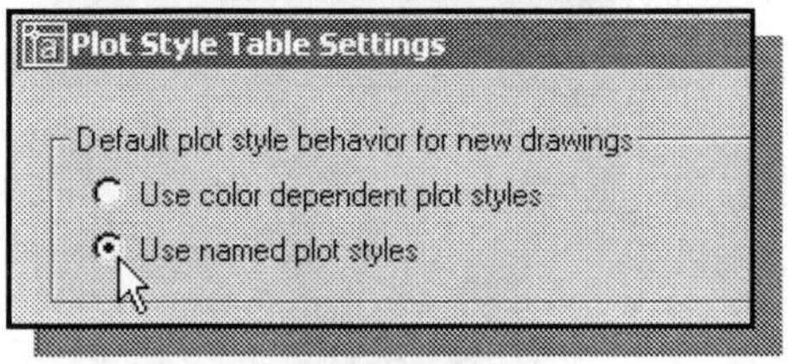

4. In the *Plot Style Table Settings* dialogue box, switch ***ON*** the ***Use named plot styles*** option as shown.

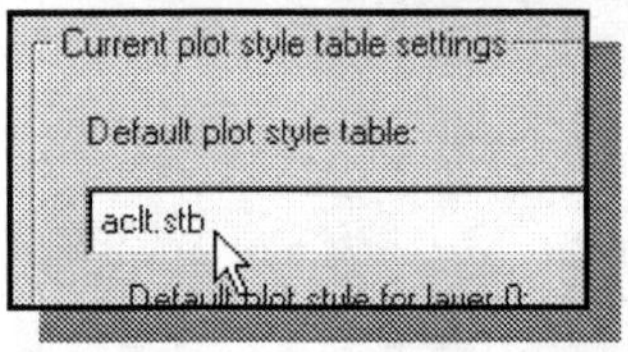

5. Choose the *aclt.stb* as the default plot style table as shown.

6. In the *Options* dialog box, click on the **Add or Edit Plot Style Tables** button.

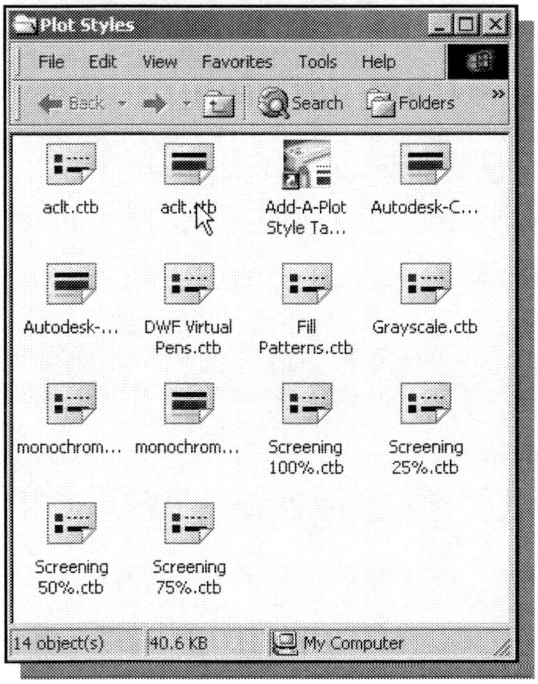

7. The *Plot Styles* folder appears on the screen.

8. Double-click the **aclt.stb** icon with the left-mouse-button to open the plot style file.

9. In the *Plot Style Table Editor*, select the **Table View** tab.

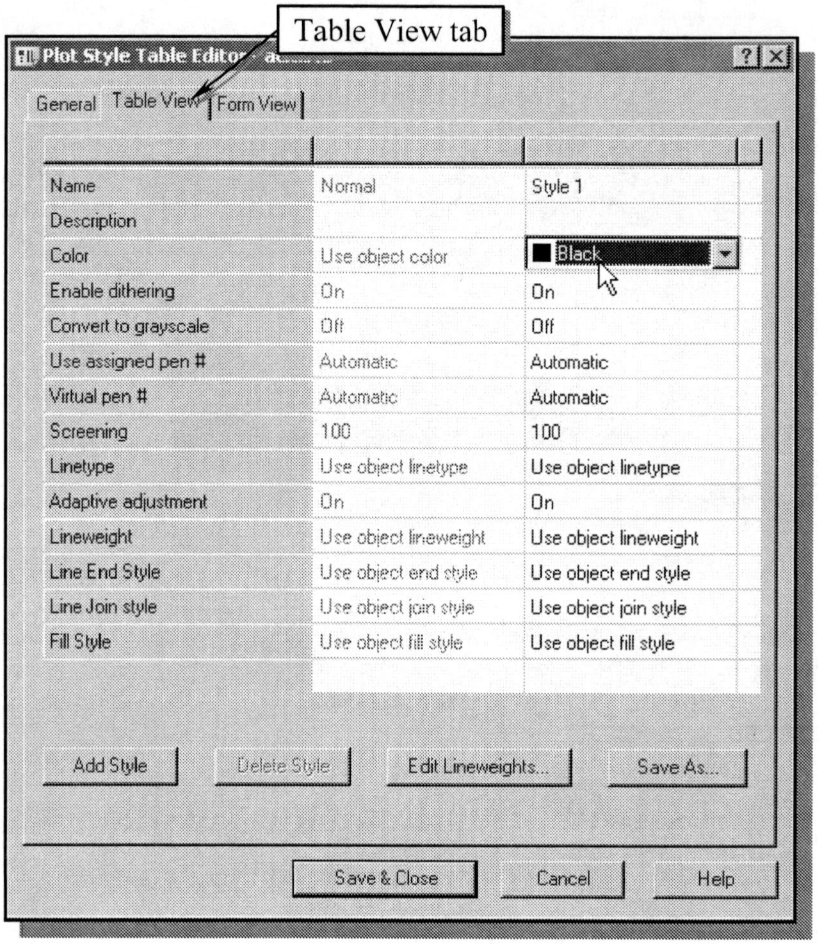

❖ The *Plot Style Table Editor* displays the plot styles that are in the current plot style table. The **Table View** and **Form View** tabs provide two methods to modify the existing plot style settings. Both tabs list all of the plot styles in the plot style table and their settings. In general, the **Table View** tab is more convenient if there are only a small number of plot styles. We can modify plot style color, screening, linetype, lineweight, and other settings. The first plot style in a named plot style table is *Normal* and represents an object's default properties (no plot style applied). We cannot modify or delete the *Normal* style.

10. Change the *Color* setting for *Style 1* to ***Black***, so that all layers using this plot style will print using black.

11. Pick the **Save & Close** button to accept the settings and exit the *Plot Style Table Editor*.

➢ On your own, print out a copy of the *V-Block* drawing using the modified plot style table.

Questions:

1. What is an *auxiliary view* and why would it be important?
2. When is a line viewed as a point? How can a line be shown in true length?
3. What is a *GRIP*? What are the advantages of using the *GRIPS*?
4. List three *GRIPS editing commands* you have used in the tutorial.
5. Identify the following commands:

(a)

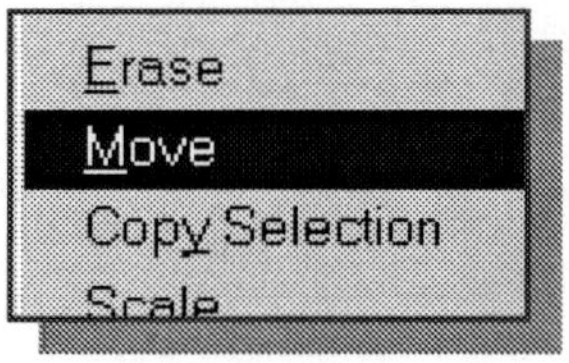

(b)

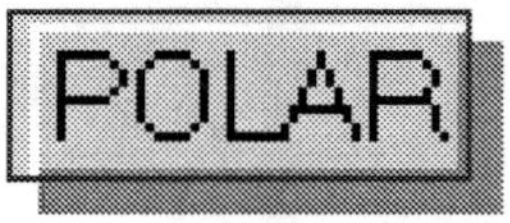

(c)

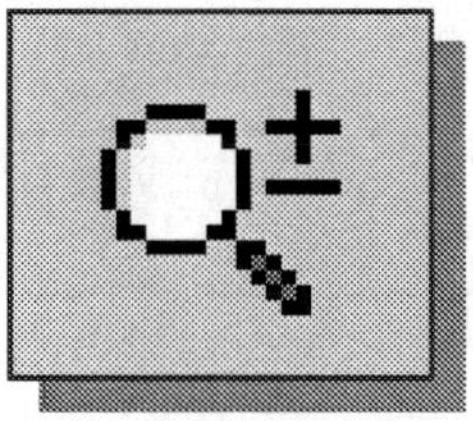

(d)

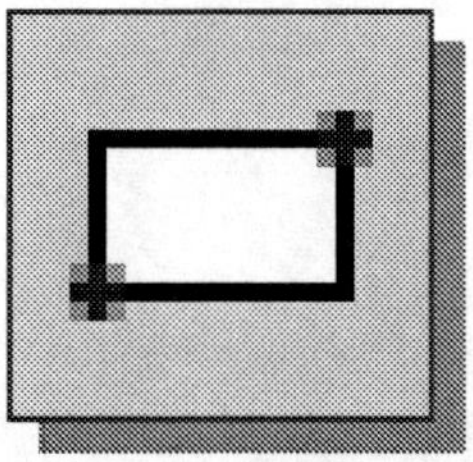

Exercises: (Unless otherwise specified, all dimensions are in inches.)

1.

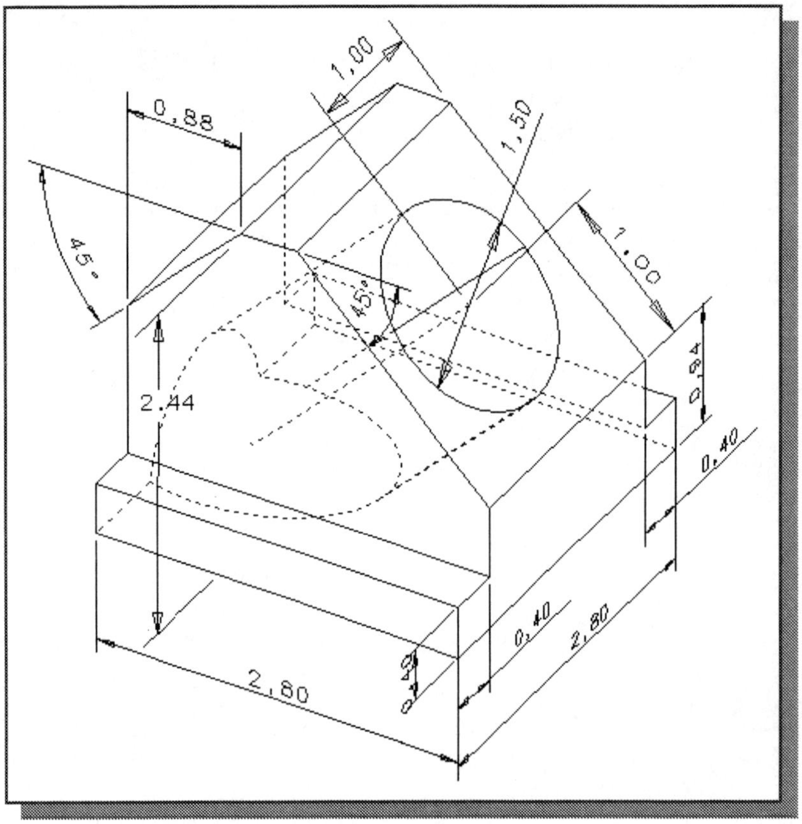

2.

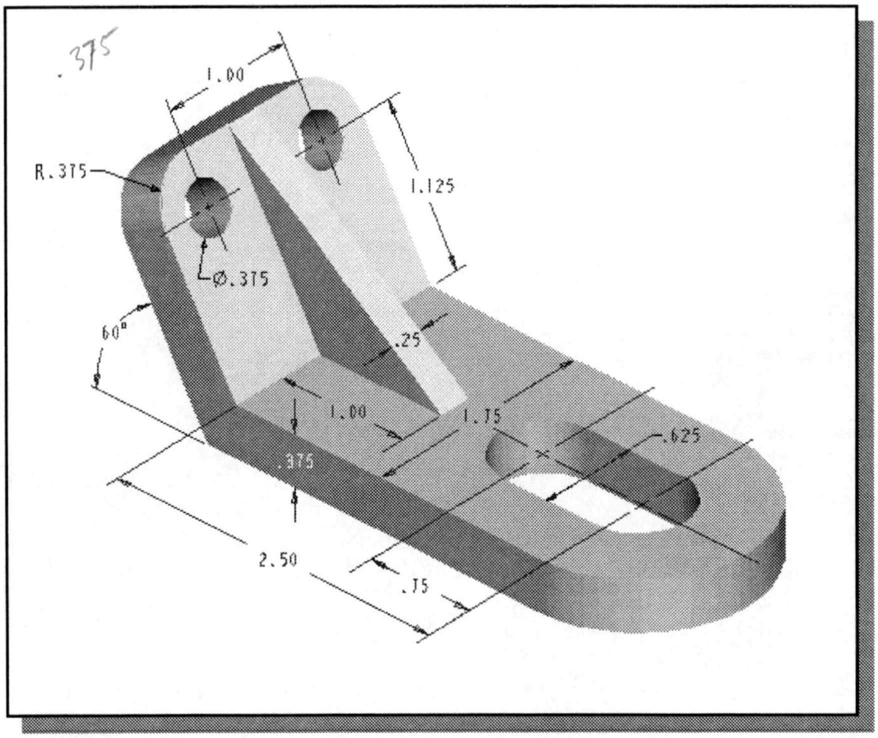

3.

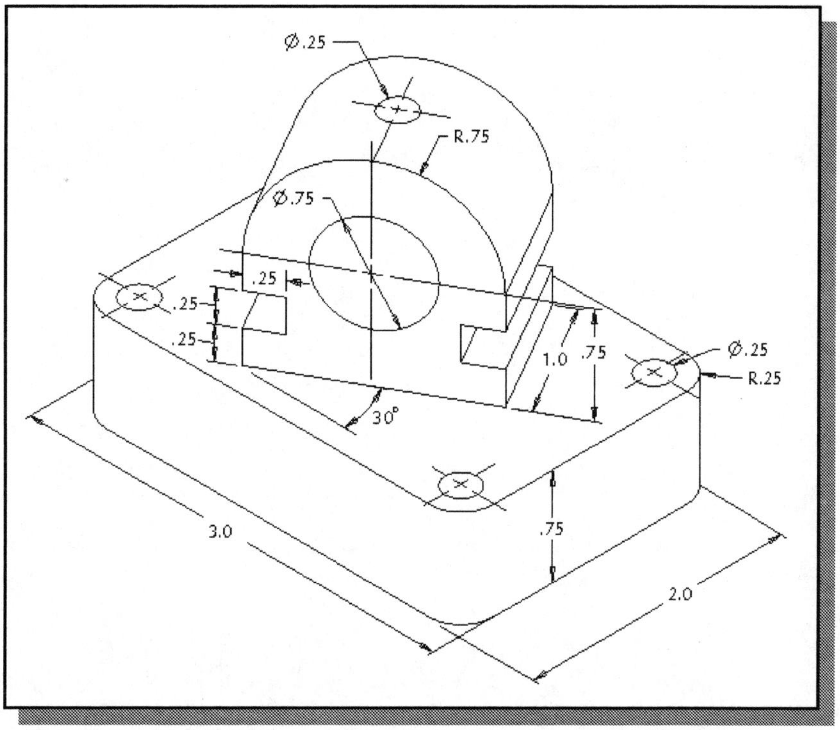

Notes:

Lesson 8
Section Views

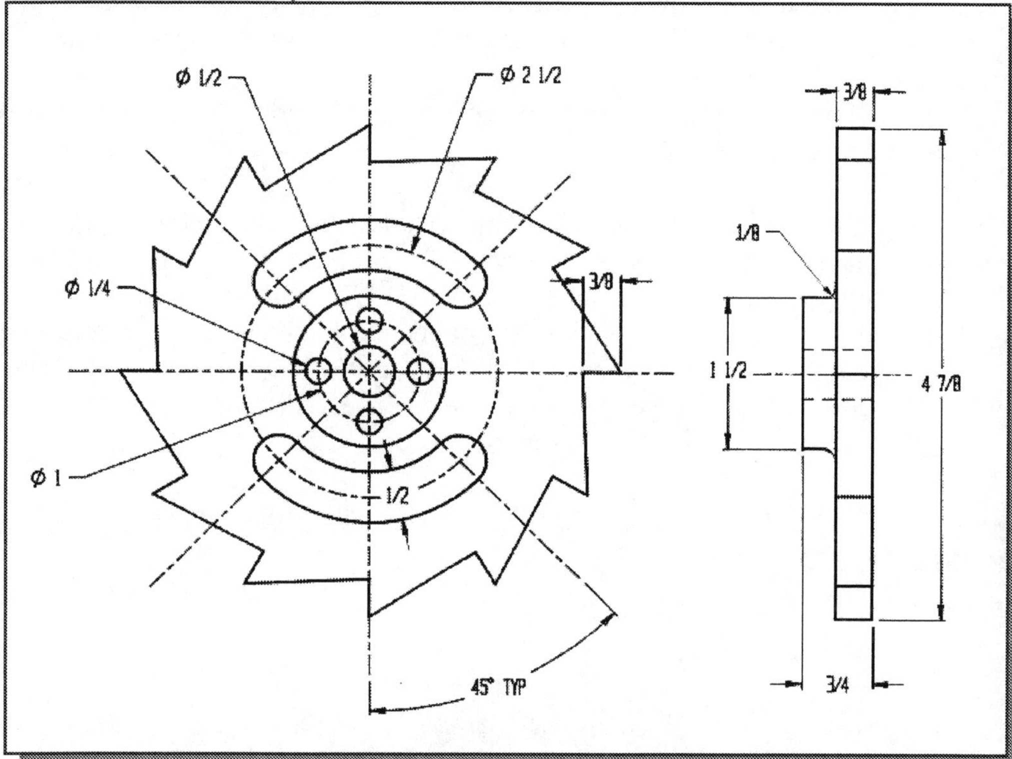

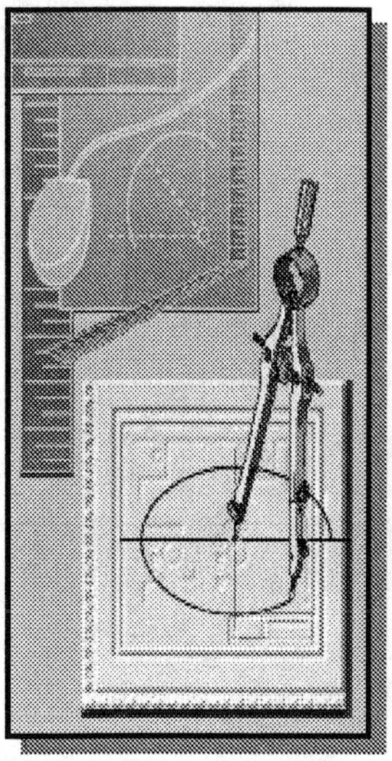

Learning Objectives

- Use CAD Methods to Create Section Views
- Use the Object Snap Shortcut Options
- Change the Linetype Scale Property
- Stretch and Move Objects with GRIPS
- Create Cutting Plane Lines
- Use the HATCH Command

Introduction

In the previous lessons, we have explored the basic CAD methods of creating orthographic views. By carefully selecting a limited number of views, the external features of most complicated designs can be fully described. However, we are frequently confronted with the necessity of showing the interiors of parts that cannot be shown clearly by means of hidden lines. We accomplish this by passing an imaginary cutting plane through the part and creating a cutaway view of the part. This type of view is known as a **section view**. In this lesson, we will demonstrate the procedure to construct a section view using **AutoCAD® LT 2005**.

In a section view, section lines, or cross-hatch lines, are added to indicate the surfaces that are cut by the imaginary cutting plane. The type of section line used to represent a surface varies according to the type of material. AutoCAD LT's **Hatch** command can be used to fill a pattern inside an area. We define a boundary that consists of an object or objects that completely enclose the area. **AutoCAD® LT 2005** comes with a solid fill and more than 50 industry-standard hatch patterns that we can use to differentiate the components of objects or represent object materials.

The *Bearing* Design

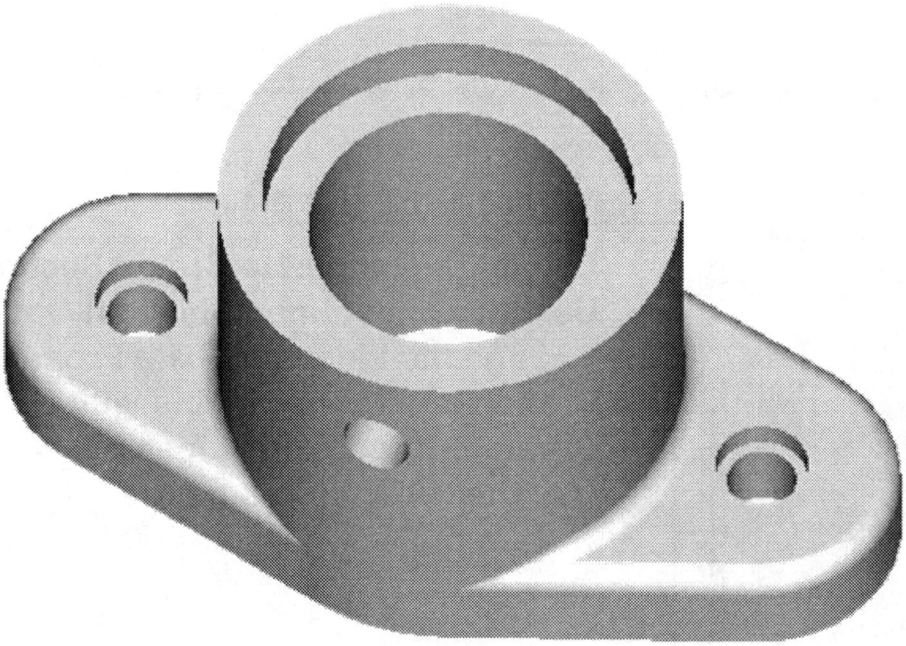

Starting Up *AutoCAD LT 2005*

1. Select the **AutoCAD LT 2005** option on the *Program* menu or select the **AutoCAD LT 2005** icon on the *Desktop*.

2. In the *Startup* dialog box, select the ***Use a Template*** option with a single click of the left-mouse-button.

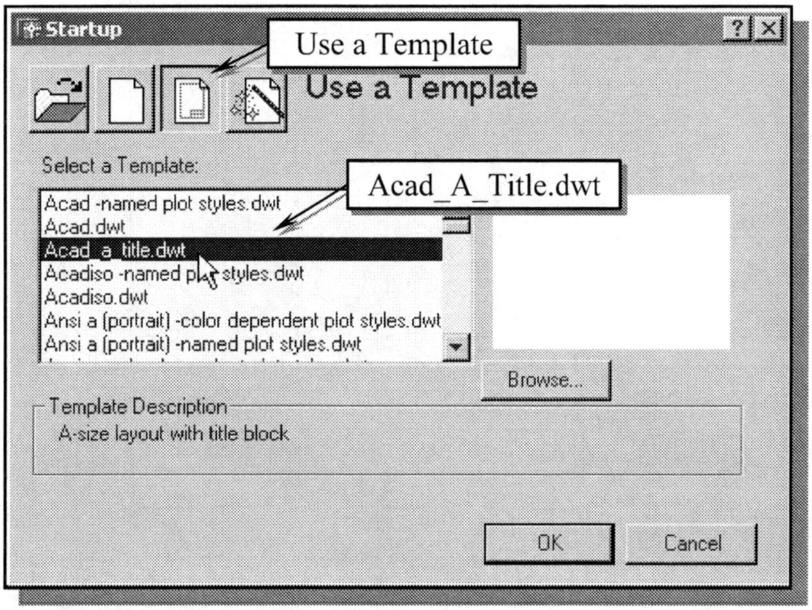

3. Select the ***Acad_A_Title*** template file from the list of template files. If the file is saved in a separate folder, click on the **Browse** button to locate the file.

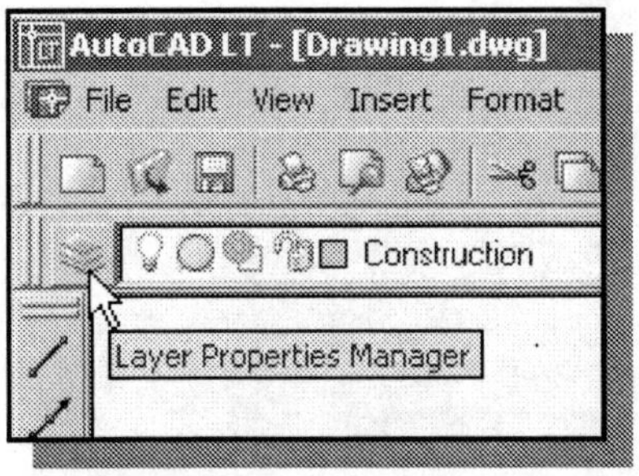

4. Pick **Layer Properties Manager** in the *Object Properties* toolbar.

5. Examine the layer property settings in the *Layer Properties Manager* dialog box.

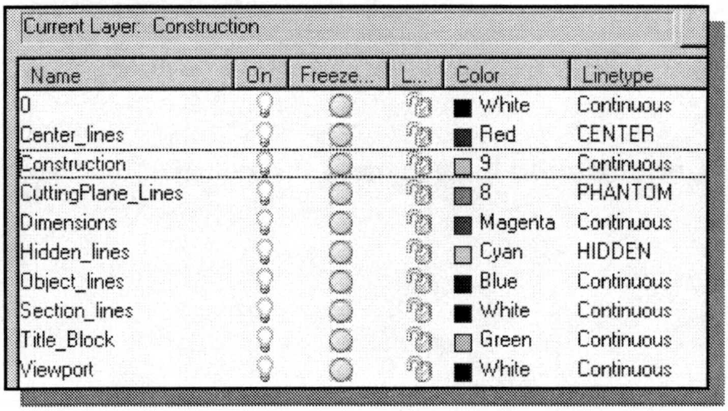

6. On your own, confirm that the layer ***Construction*** is set as the *Current Layer*.

7. Click on the **OK** button to exit the *Layer Properties Manager* dialog box.

The *Bearing* Example

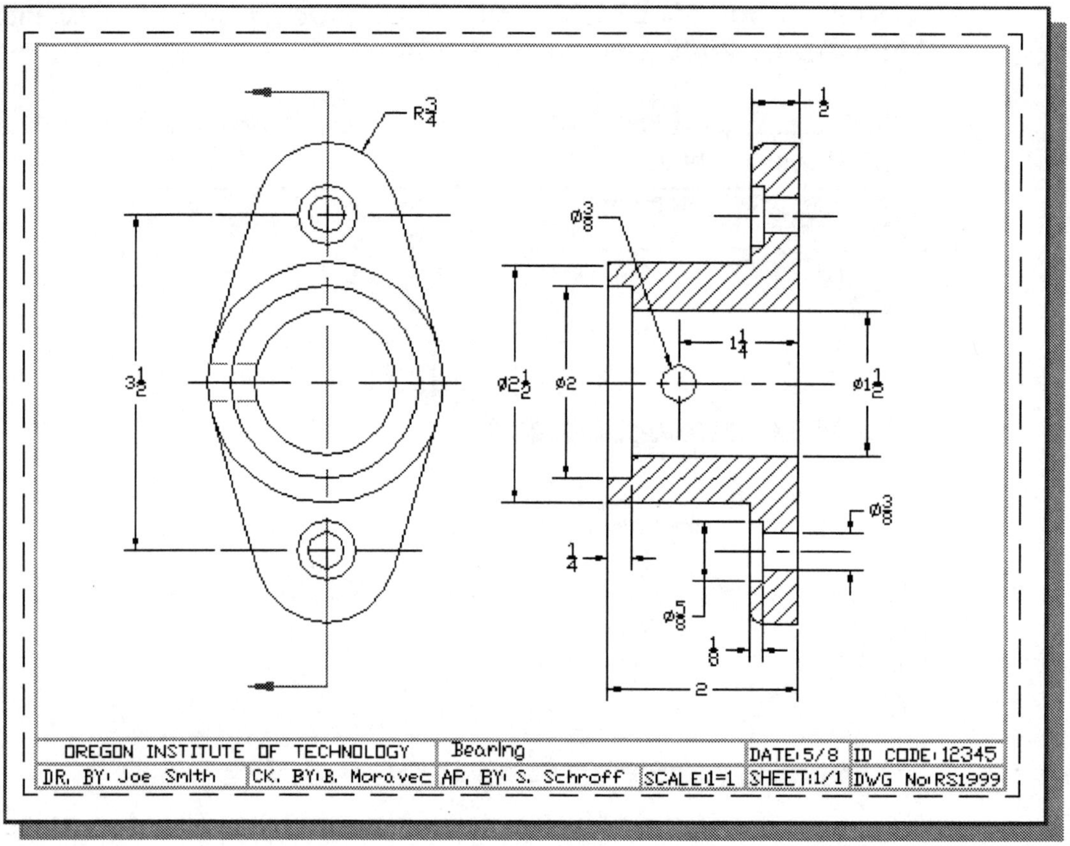

Setting Up the Principal Views

1. In the *Status Bar* area, reset the options and turn ***ON*** the *OSNAP, POLAR, LWT* and *MODEL* options.

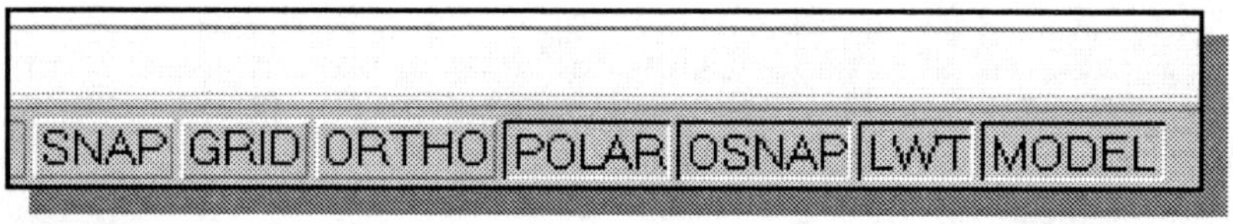

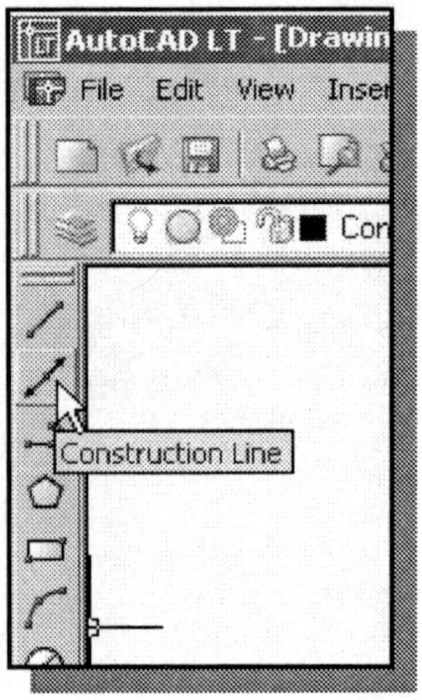

➢ We will first create construction lines for the front view.

2. Select **Construction Line** in the *Draw* toolbar.

3. In the command prompt area, the message *"_xline Specify a point or [Hor/Ver/Ang/Bisect/Offset]:"* is displayed. On your own, create a vertical line and a horizontal line as shown in the figure below. These lines will be used as the references for the circular features of the design.

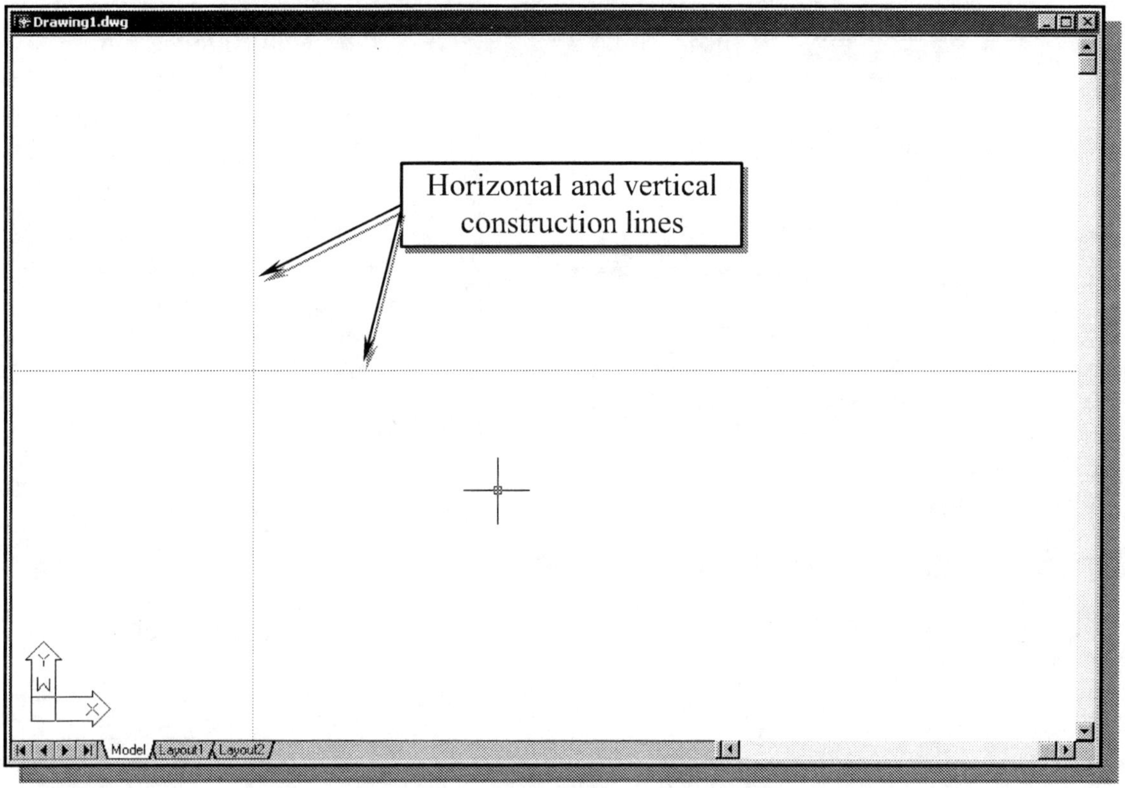

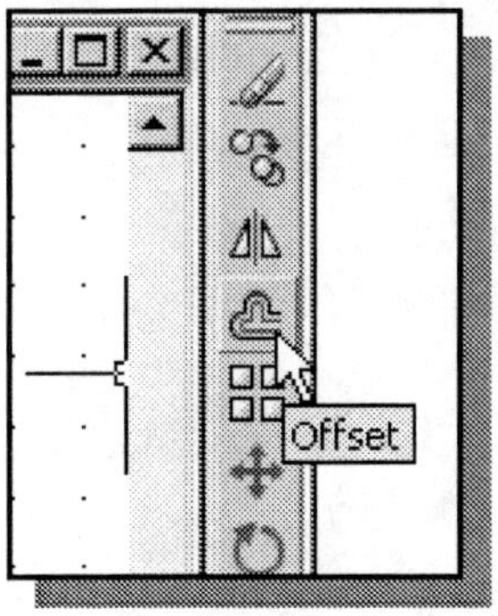

4. Click on the **Offset** icon in the *Modify* toolbar. In the command prompt area, the message *"Specify offset distance or [Through]:"* is displayed.

5. In the command prompt area, enter **1.75** [**ENTER**]

6. In the command prompt area, the message *"Select object to offset or <exit>:"* is displayed. Pick the **horizontal line** on the screen.

7. AutoCAD LT next expects us to identify the direction of the offset. Pick a location that is above the selected line.

8. We will also create a line that is below the original horizontal line at 1.75. Pick the original **horizontal line** on the screen.

9. Pick a location that is below the selected line.

10. Inside the graphics window, **right-mouse-click** to end the Offset command.

Creating Object Lines in the Front View

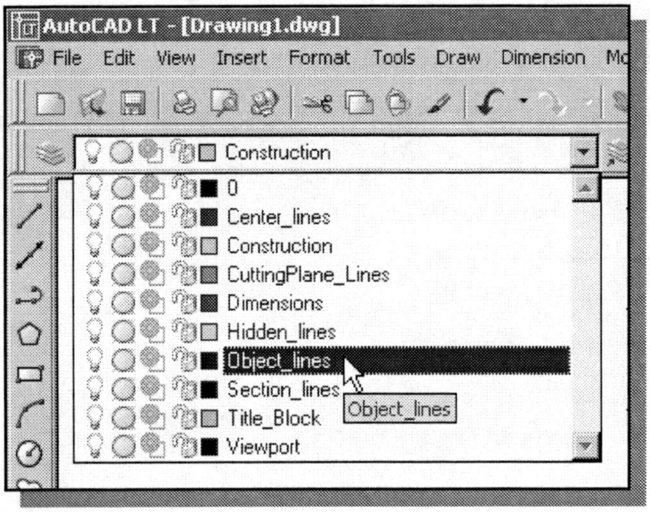

1. On the *Object Properties* toolbar, choose the ***Layer Control*** box with the left-mouse-button.

2. Move the cursor over the name of layer ***Object_Lines***; the tool tip *"Object_Lines"* appears.

3. **Left-mouse-click once** and layer *Object_Lines* is set as the *Current Layer*.

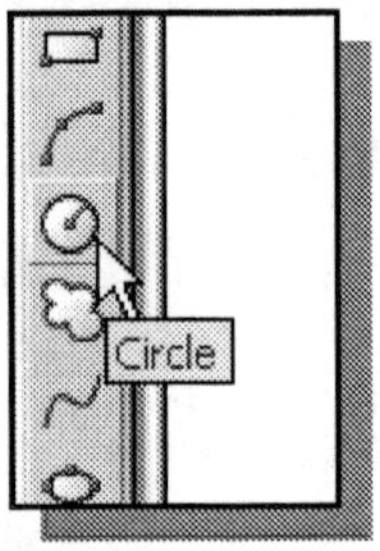

4. Click on the **Circle** icon in the *Draw* toolbar. In the command prompt area, the message *"Specify center point for circle or [3P/2P/Ttr (tan tan radius)]:"* is displayed.

5. Pick the center intersection point as the center of the circle.

6. In the command prompt area, the message *"Specify radius of circle or [Diameter]:"* is displayed. Enter **1.25** [**ENTER**]

7. Repeat the **Circle** command and create the two **1.5 diameter** circles as shown.

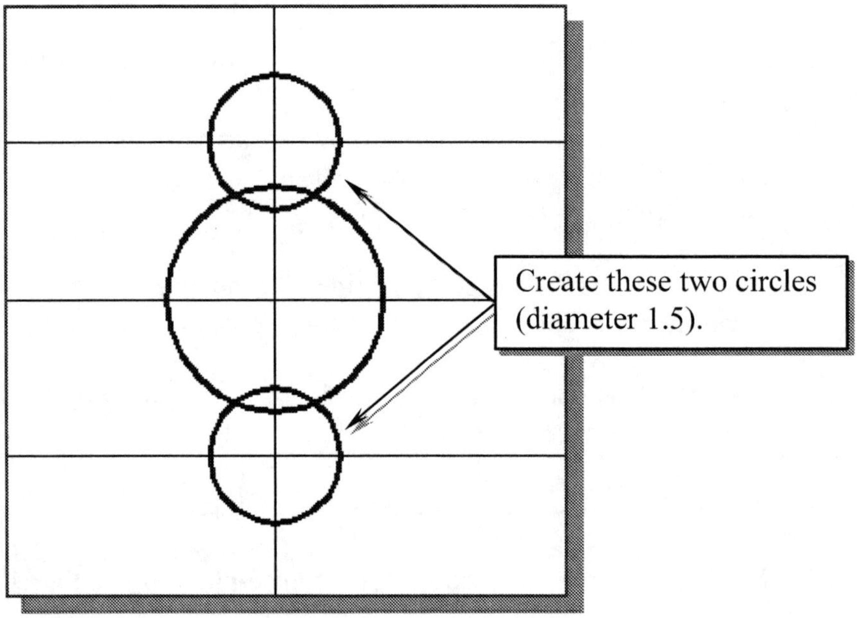

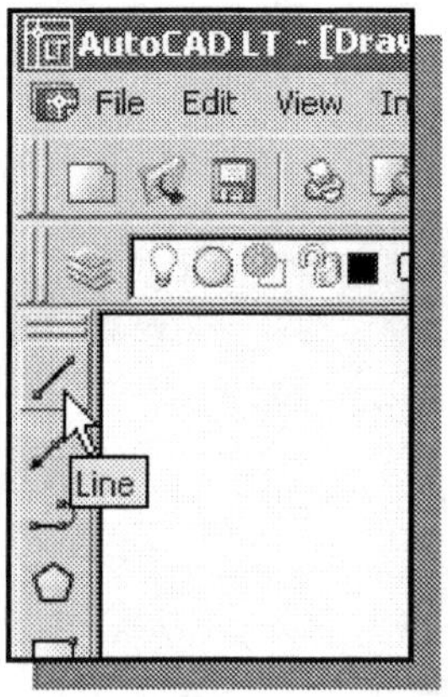

8. Select the **Line** command icon in the *Draw* toolbar. In the command prompt area, the message *"_line Specify first point:"* is displayed.

9. Inside the graphics window, hold down the **[SHIFT]** key and **right-mouse-click** once to bring up the *Object Snap* shortcut menu.

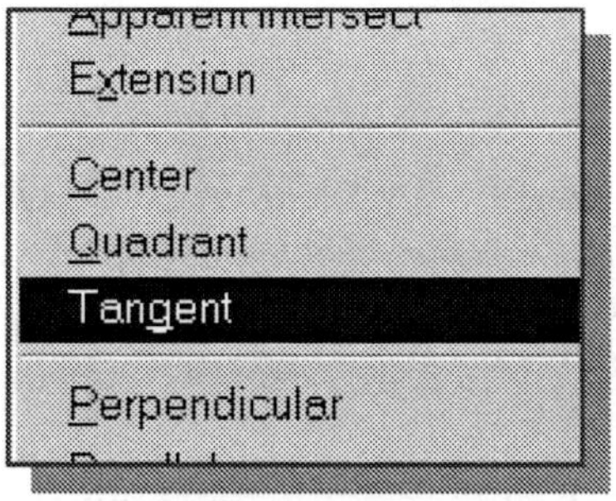

10. Select the **Tangent** option in the popup window. Move the cursor near the circles and notice the *Tangent* marker appears at different locations.

- The Tangent option enables us to create tangent lines; **select objects by clicking near the expected tangency locations.**

11. Pick the top circle by clicking on the upper right section of the circle.

12. In the command prompt area, the message *"Specify the next point or [Undo]:"* is displayed. Inside the graphics window, hold down the **[SHIFT]** key and **right-mouse-click once** to bring up the *Object Snap* shortcut menu.

13. Select the **Tangent** option in the popup menu.

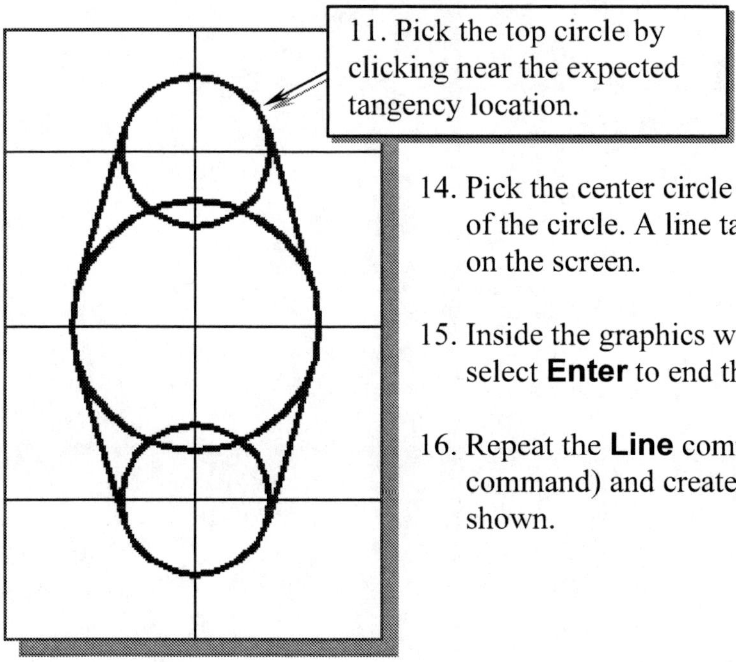

14. Pick the center circle by clicking on the right side of the circle. A line tangent to the two circles appears on the screen.

15. Inside the graphics window, right-mouse-click and select **Enter** to end the Line command.

16. Repeat the **Line** command (or use the **Mirror** command) and create the four tangent lines as shown.

Editing the Circles

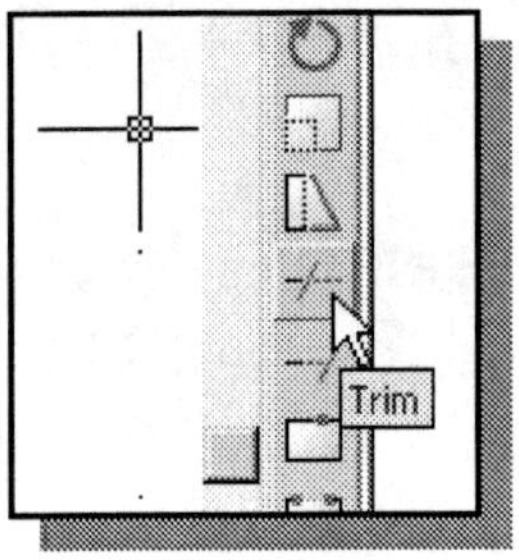

1. Select the **Trim** icon in the *Modify* toolbar. In the command prompt area, the message *"Select boundary edges... Select objects:"* is displayed.

2. Pick the four lines we just created as the *boundary edges*.

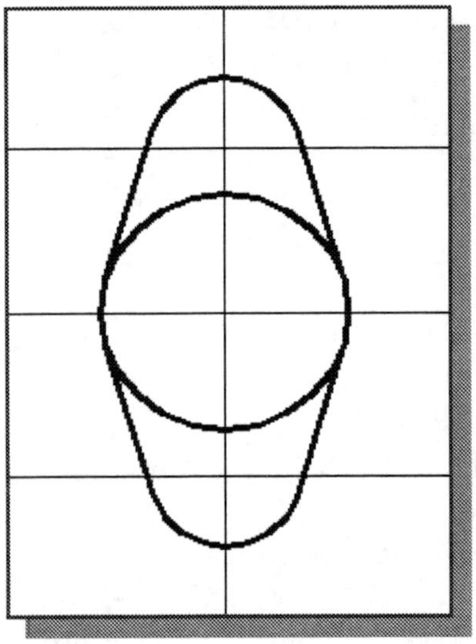

3. Inside the graphics window, **right-mouse-click** to proceed with the Trim command. The message *"Select object to trim or [Project/Edge/Undo]:"* is displayed in the command prompt area.

4. Trim the unwanted portions of the top and bottom circles and complete the outline of the front view as shown.

5. Inside the graphics window, right-mouse-click to activate the option menu and select **Enter** with the left-mouse-button to end the Trim command.

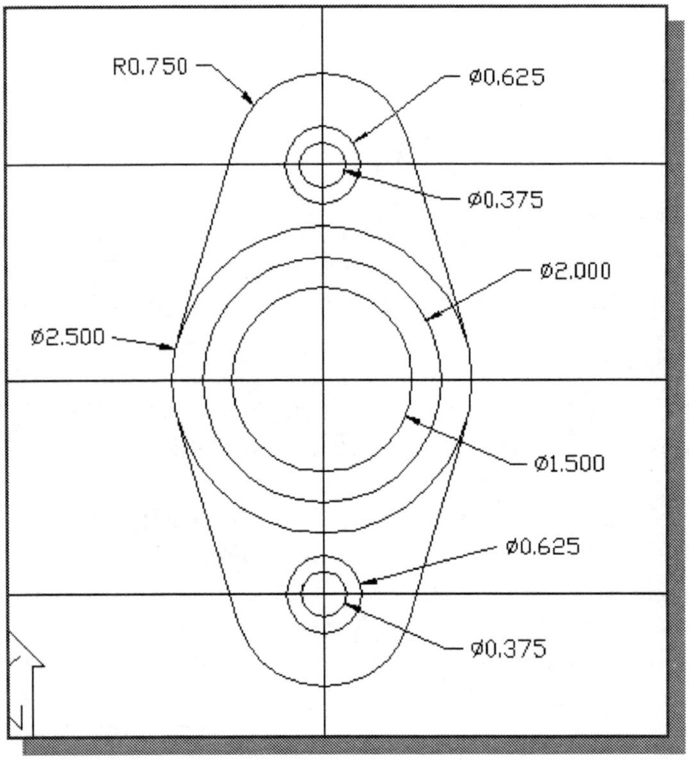

➢ On your own, create the additional circles as shown in the figure.

Setting Up the Side View

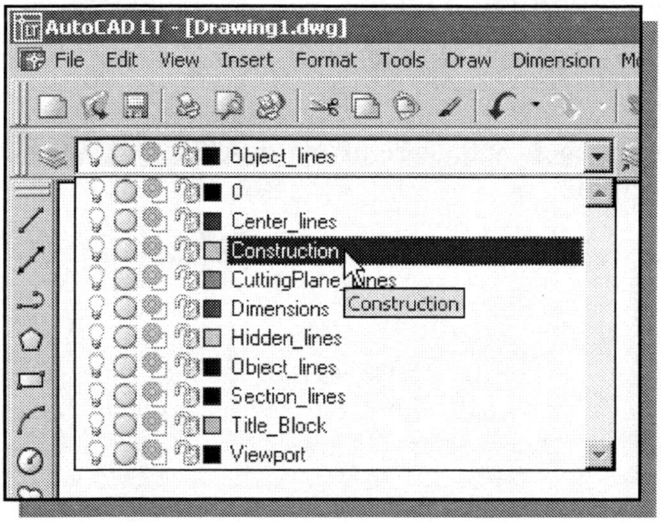

1. In the ***Layer Control*** box, set layer *Construction* as the *Current Layer*.

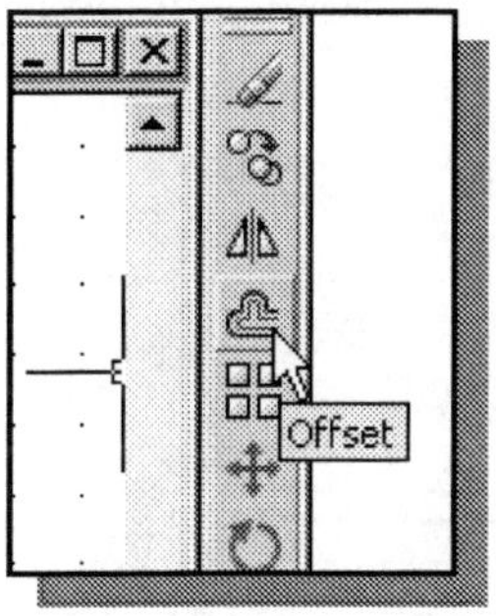

2. Select the **Offset** icon in the *Modify* toolbar. In the command prompt area, the message *"Specify offset distance or [Through]:"* is displayed.

3. In the command prompt area, enter **5.0** **[ENTER]**

4. In the command prompt area, the message *"Select object to offset or <exit>:"* is displayed. Pick the **vertical line** on the screen.

5. AutoCAD LT next expects us to identify the direction of the offset. Pick a location that is toward the right side of the selected line.

6. Inside the graphics window, **right-mouse-click** to end the Offset command.

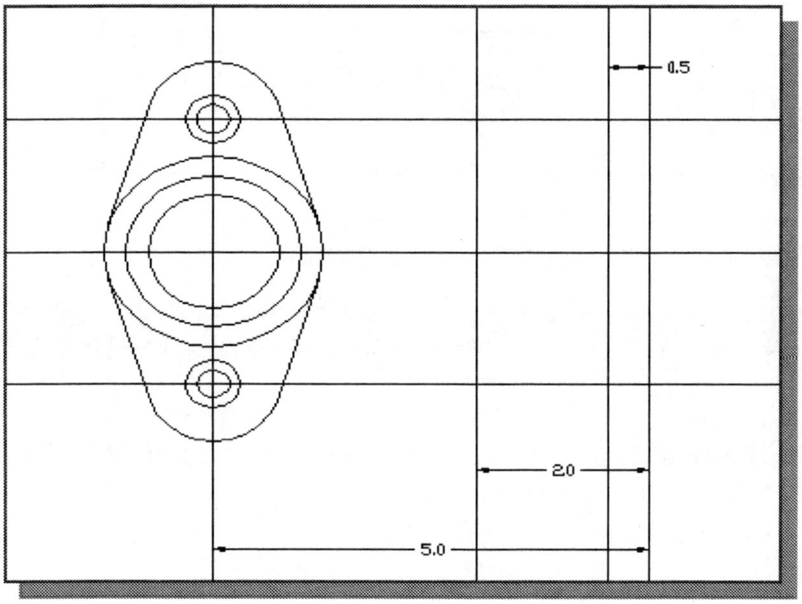

➢ On your own, repeat the Offset command and create two additional lines parallel to the line we just created as shown (distances of **0.5** and **2.0**).

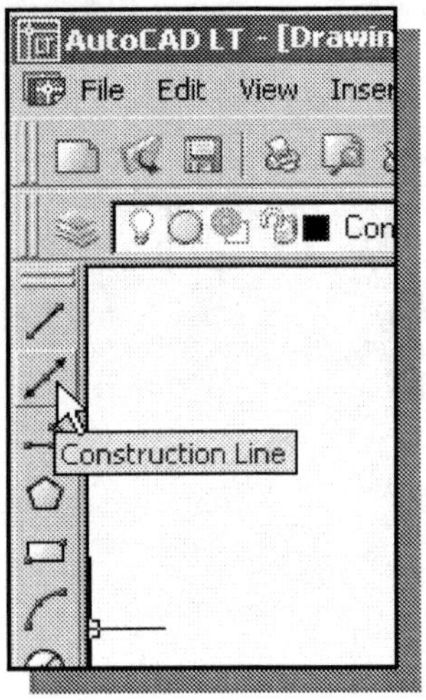

7. Select the **Construction Line** icon in the *Draw* toolbar. In the command prompt area, the message *"_xline Specify a point or [Hor/Ver/Ang/Bisect/Offset]:"* is displayed.

8. Inside the graphics window, **right-mouse-click** to bring up the popup menu.

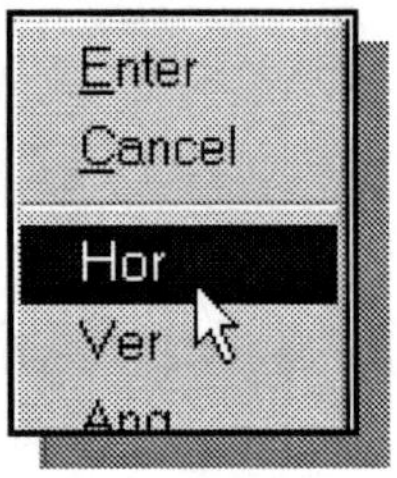

9. Select the **Hor** (horizontal) option in the popup menu.

➢ The **Horizontal** option enables us to create a horizontal line by specifying one point in the graphics window.

10. Create **projection lines** by clicking at the intersections between the vertical line and the circles (and arcs) in the front view.

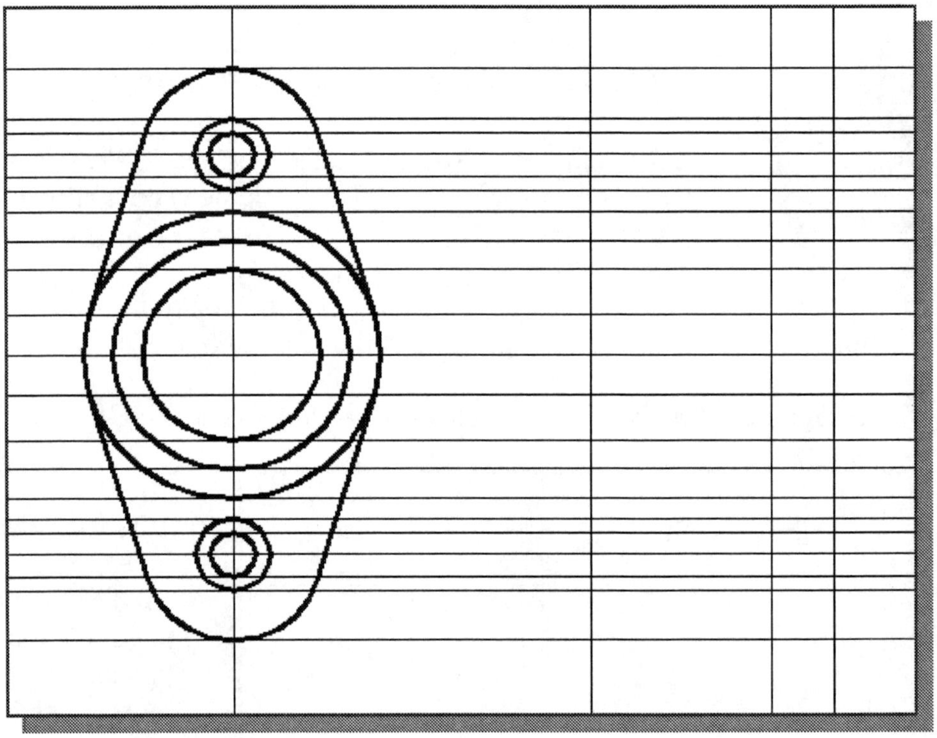

11. Also create two horizontal projection lines that pass through the two tangency points on the ∅2.5 circle.

12. Inside the graphics window, right-mouse-click to end the Construction Line command.

➢ On your own, create object lines to show the outline of the side view.

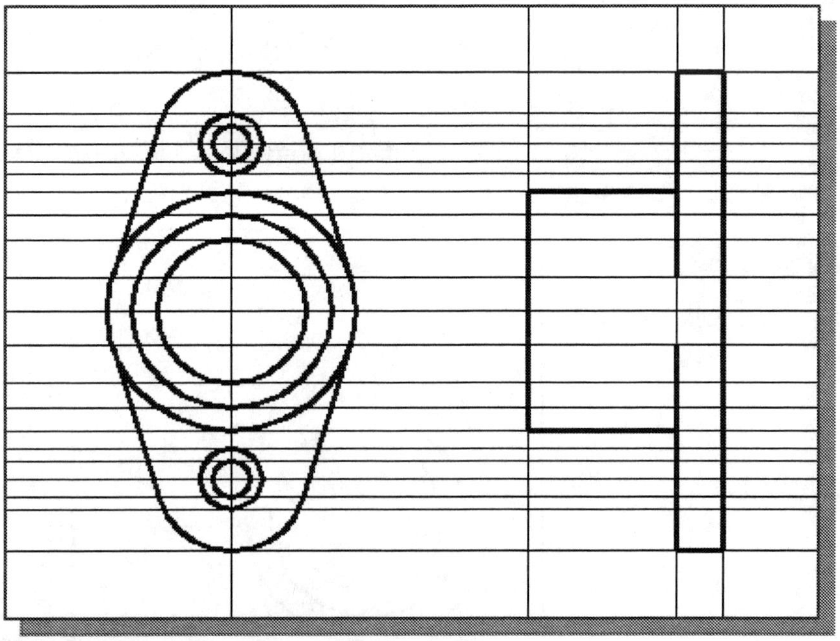

Adding Hidden Lines in the Side-View

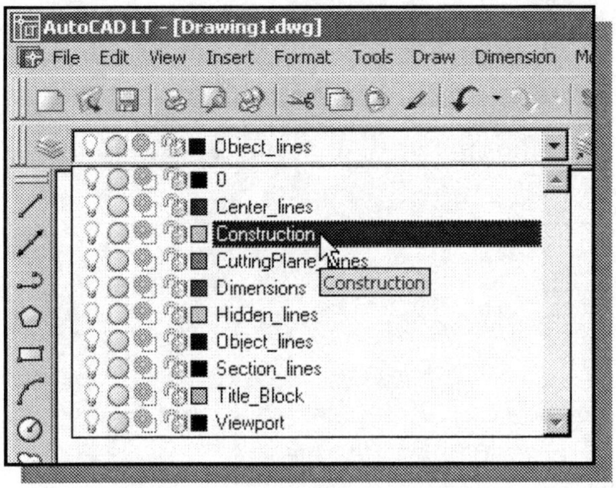

1. In the ***Layer Control*** box, set layer *Construction* as the *Current Layer*.

2. Use the **Offset** command and create the two additional vertical lines, for the counter-bore features, as shown.

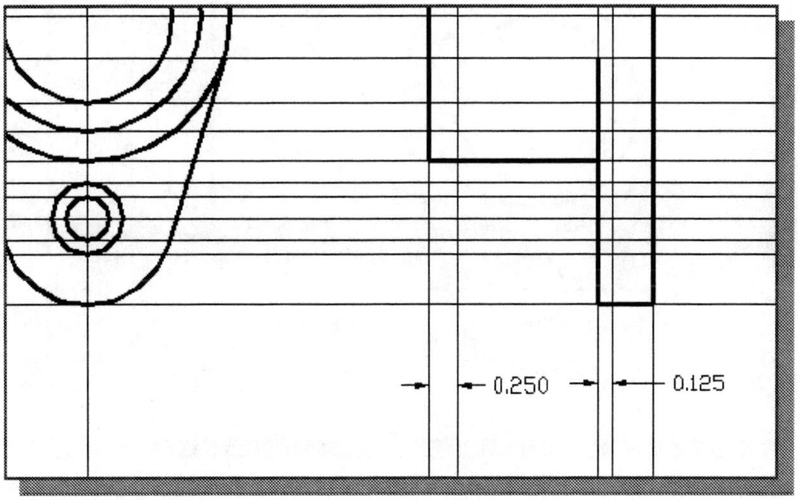

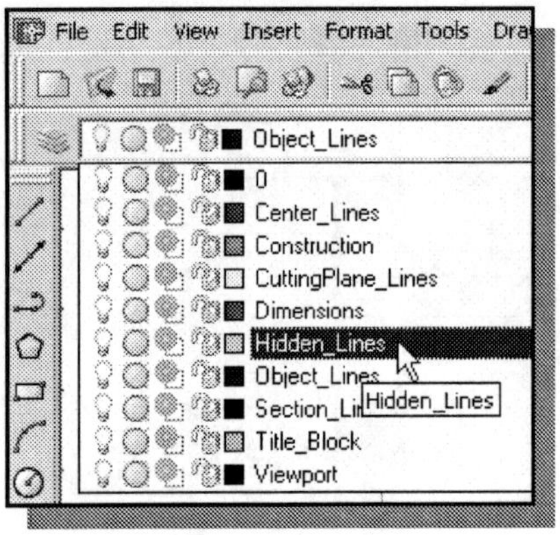

3. Set layer ***Hidden_Lines*** as the *Current Layer* in the ***Layer Control*** box.

4. Use the **Line** command and create the hidden lines as shown.

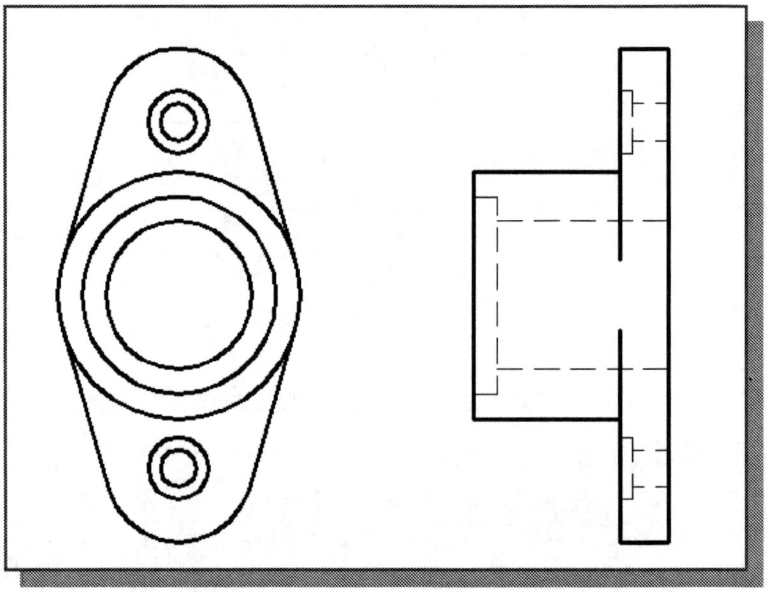

➤ On your own, complete the views by adding the side drill, the centerlines, and the rounded corners as shown.

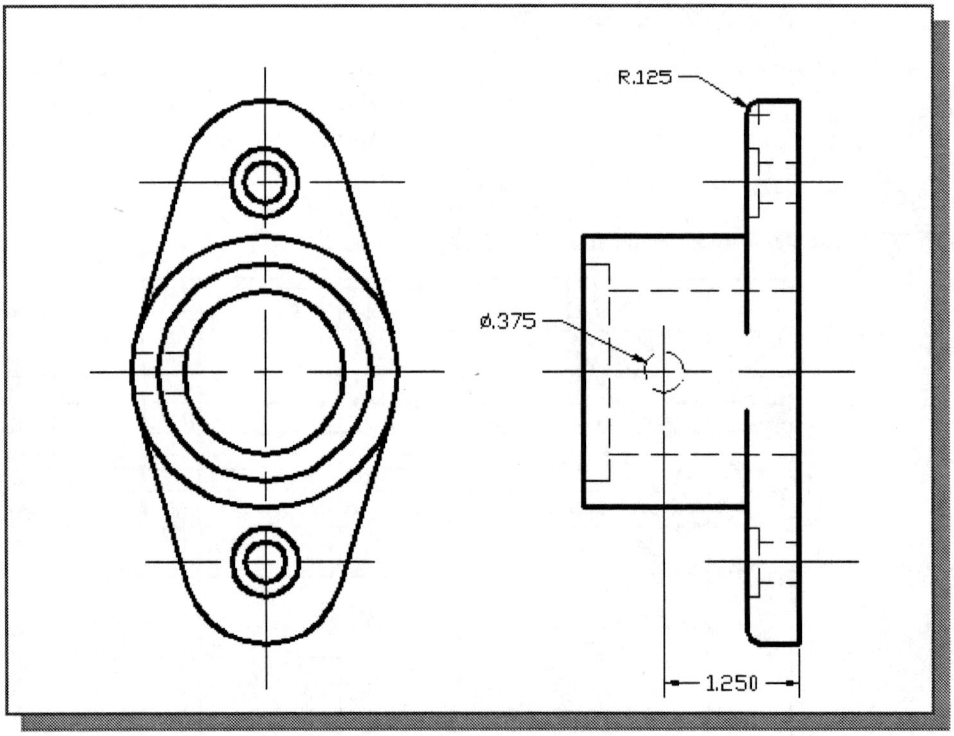

Changing the *Linetype Scale* Property

Looking at the side drill feature and the centerlines we just created; not all of the lengths of the dash-dot linetypes appeared properly on the screen. The appearance of the dash-dot linetypes can be adjusted by modifying the ***Linetype Scale*** setting, which can be found under the *Object Property* option.

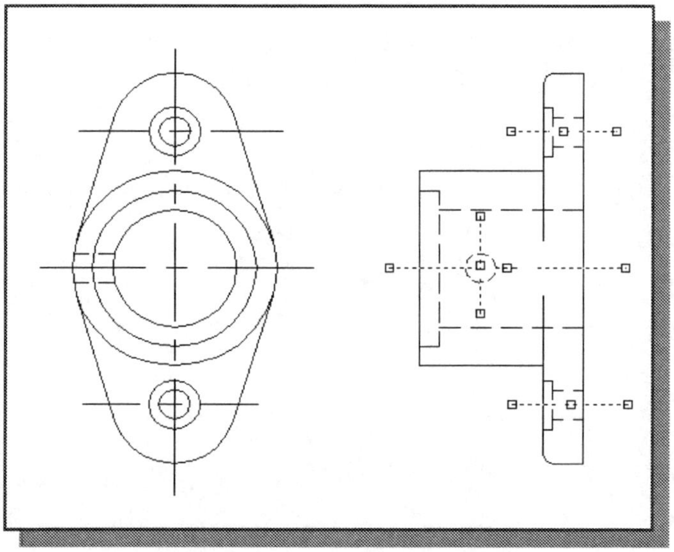

1. **Pre-select** the objects in the side view as shown (four lines and one circle).

2. In the *Standard* toolbar, select the **Properties** icon.

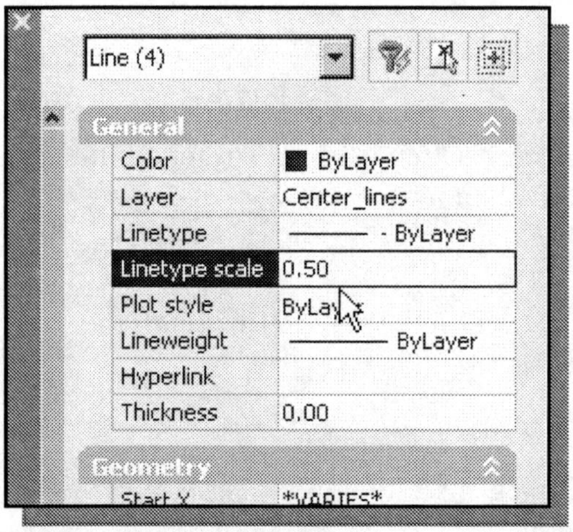

3. In the *Properties* dialog box, notice the default *Linetype scale* is **1.00**.

4. Left-click on ***Linetype scale*** in the list and enter a new value, **0.5** [**ENTER**]

5. Click on the [**X**] button to exit the *Properties* dialog box.

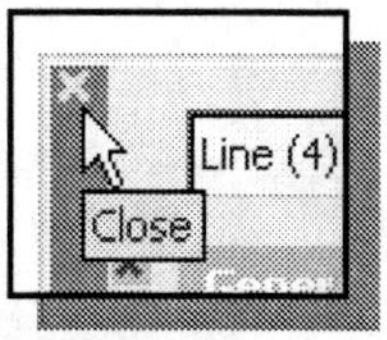

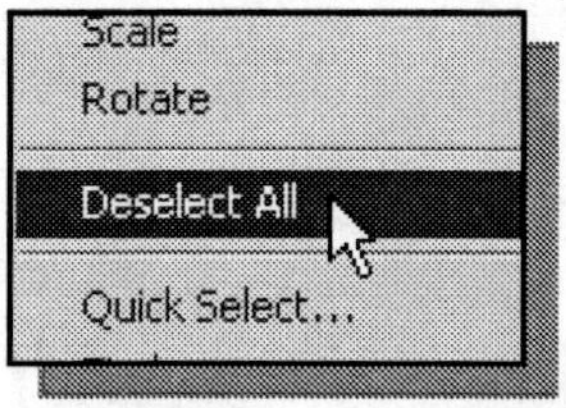

6. Inside the Graphics window, **right-mouse-click** and select **Deselect All**.

➢ The appearances of the dash-dot linetypes of the selected objects are adjusted to half-size of the other objects. Keep in mind that the dash-dot linetypes may appear differently on paper, depending on the type of printer/plotter being used. You may want to do more adjustments after examining a printed/plotted copy of the drawing. It is also more common to adjust the *Linetype scale* for all objects of the same linetype to maintain a consistent presentation of the drawing.

Stretching and Moving Objects with *GRIPS*

We can usually *stretch* an object by moving selected grips to new locations. Some grips will not stretch the object but will move the object. This is true of grips on text objects, blocks, midpoints of lines, centers of circles, centers of ellipses, and point objects.

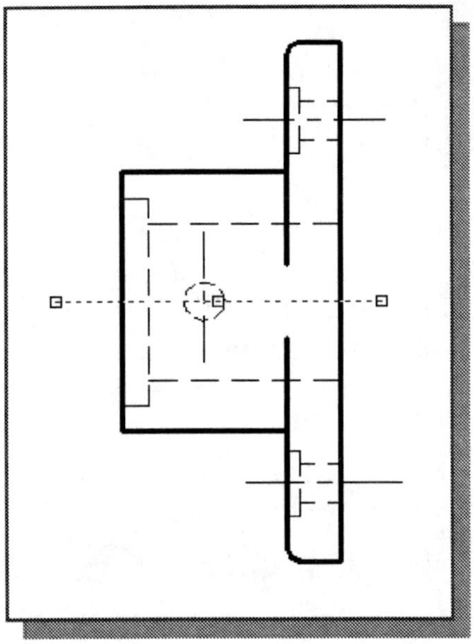

1. **Pre-select** the horizontal centerline that goes through the center of the part as shown.

2. Select the **right grip** by left-clicking once on the grip. Notice the grip is highlighted.

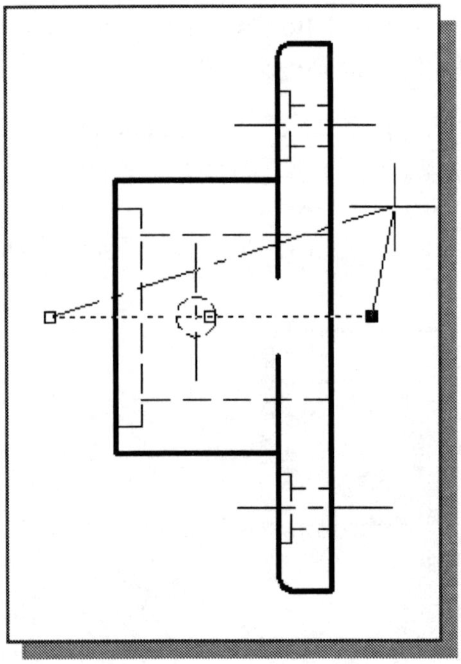

3. Move the cursor inside the graphics window and notice the center line is being stretched; the base point is attached to the cursor.

4. Pick a location on the screen to stretch the centerline.

5. Click on the **Undo** icon in the *Standard* toolbar area to undo the stretch we just did.

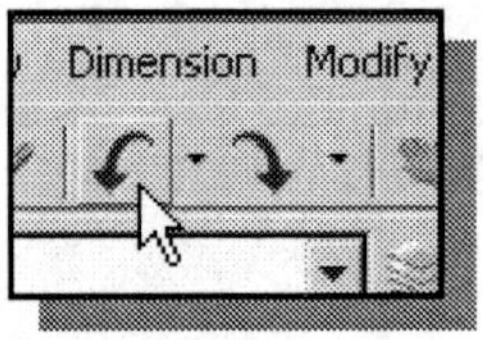

➢ On your own, experiment with moving the center grip of the centerline.

Drawing a Cutting Plane Line

Most section views require a cutting plane line to indicate the location on which the object is cut.

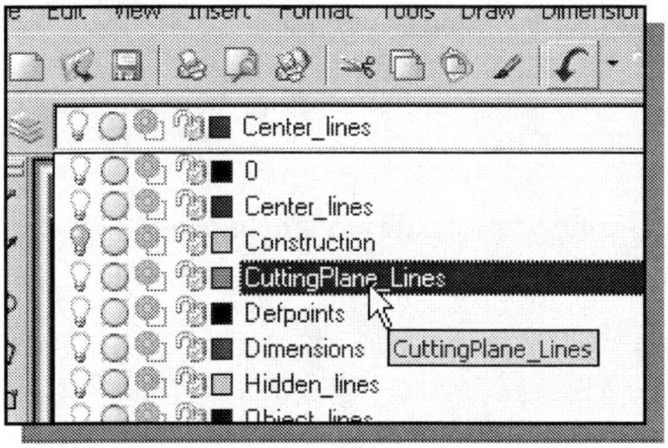

1. In the ***Layer Control*** box, turn ***OFF*** the ***Hidden_Lines*** layer and set layer ***CuttingPlane_Lines*** as the *Current Layer*.

2. Use the **Line** command and create the vertical cutting plane line aligned to the vertical centerline of the front view.

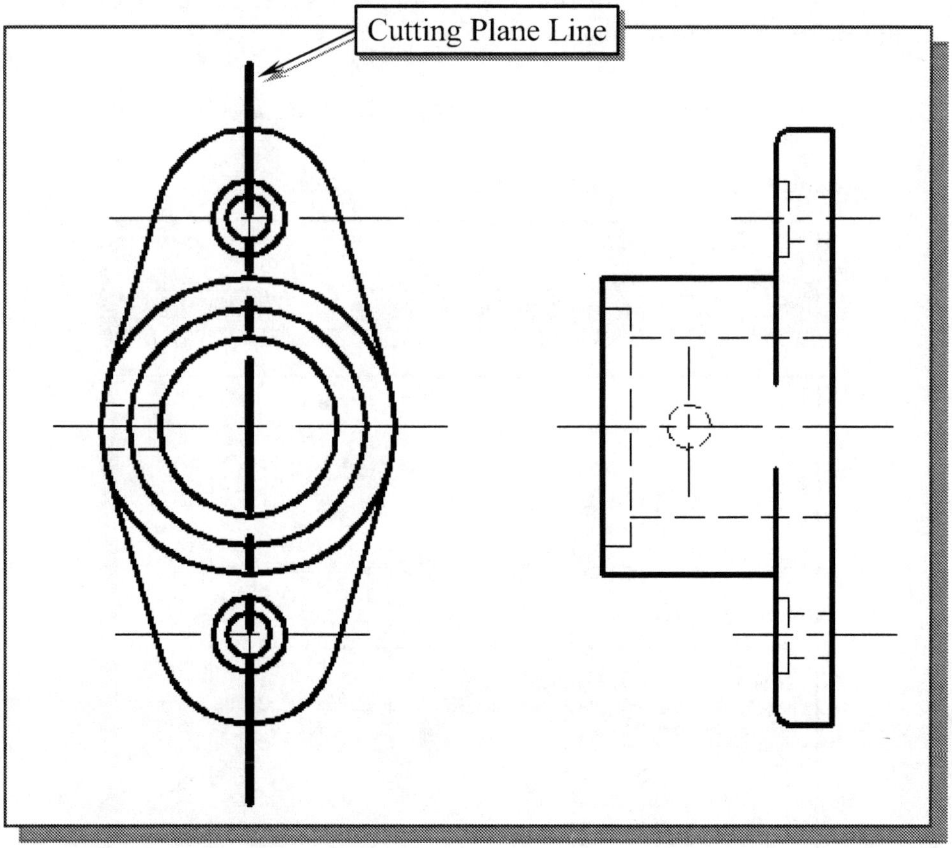

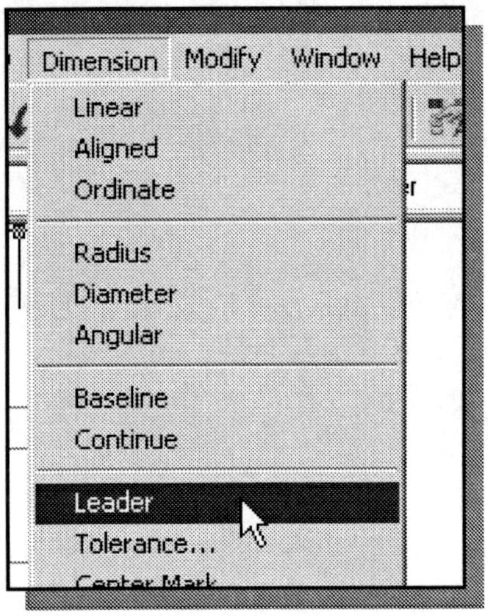

3. In the pull-down menus, select **[Dimension] → [Leader]**

4. Select a point that is toward the left of the top endpoint of the cutting plane line.

5. Pick the top endpoint of the cutting plane line to create a horizontal arrow.

6. Inside the graphics window, **right-mouse-click** to proceed with the Leader command.

7. In the command prompt area, the message *"Specify Text height <0.000>:"* is displayed. **Right-mouse-click** to accept the default **0.00** value.

8. In the command prompt area, the message *"Enter first line of annotation text <Mtext>:"* is displayed. **Right-mouse-click** to continue.

9. The *Multiline Text Editor* dialog box appears on the screen. Click on the **OK** button to close the dialog box.

10. Repeat the **Leader** command and create the other arrow as shown.

11. In the *Status Bar* area, turn ***OFF*** the *LWT* option.

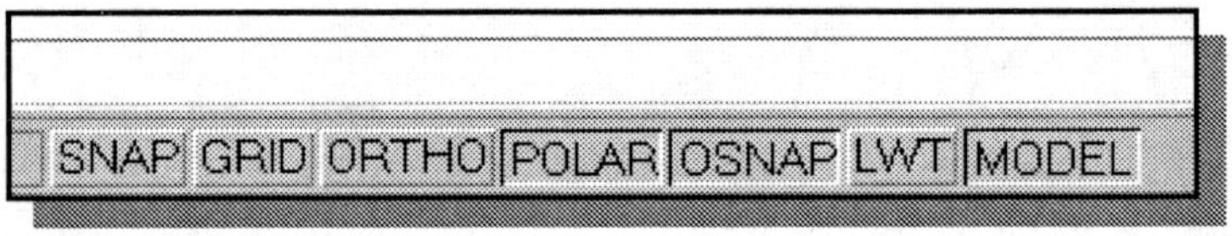

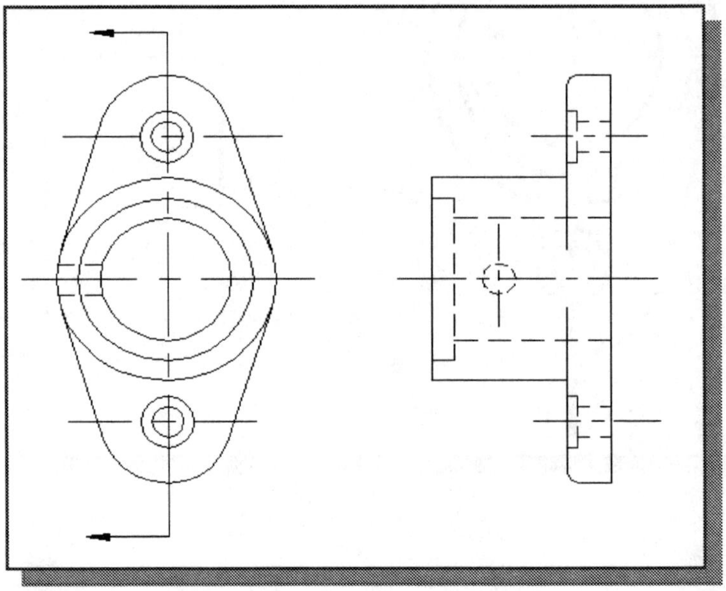

Converting the Side View into a Section View

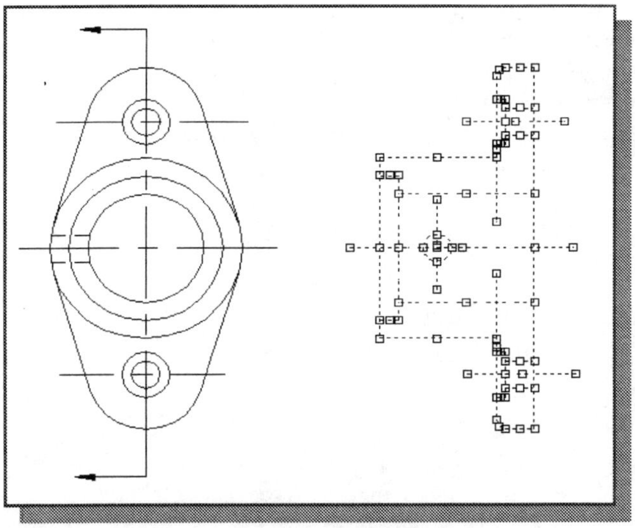

1. **Pre-select** all the objects in the side-view by using a selection window.

2. Inside the graphics window, **right-mouse-click** to bring up the popup option menu and select the **Quick Select** option.

The **Quick Select** option enables us to quickly select multiple objects by using various ***filter*** options.

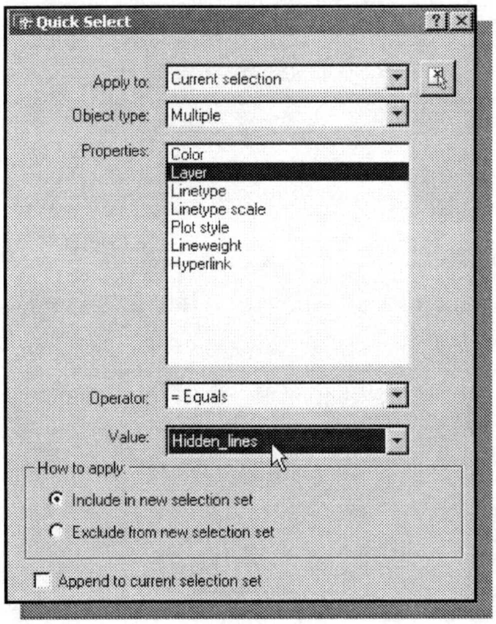

3. In the *Quick Select* dialog box, select ***Layer*** from the *Properties* list.

4. Set the *Value* box to ***Hidden_Lines***.

5. In the *How to apply section*, confirm the ***Include in new selection set*** option is selected.

6. Click on the **OK** button to accept the settings.

AutoCAD LT will now **filter out** objects that are not on layer *Hidden_Lines*.

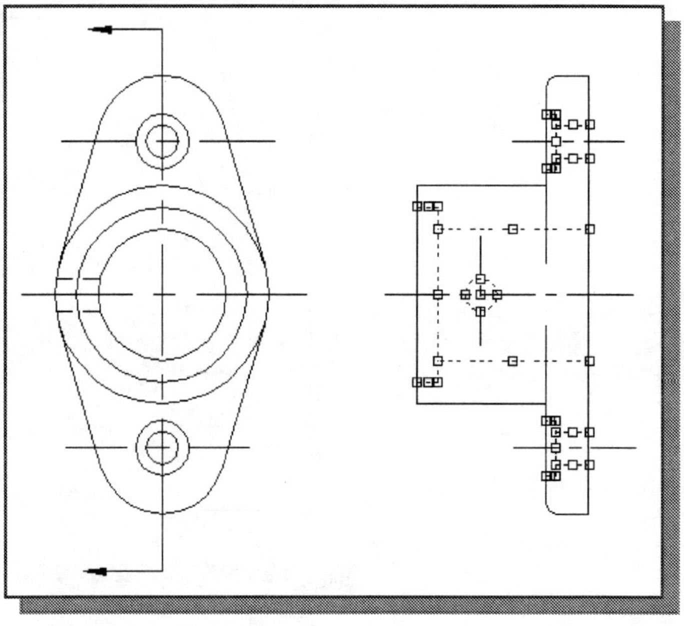

7. On the *Object Properties* toolbar, choose the ***Layer Control*** box with the left-mouse-button.

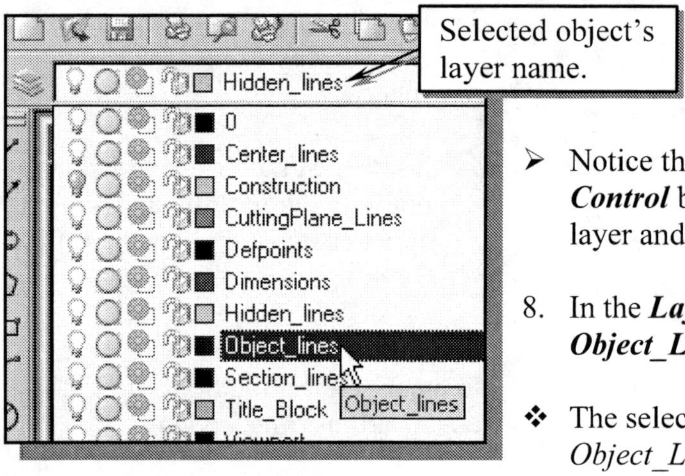

➢ Notice the layer name displayed in the ***Layer Control*** box is the selected object's assigned layer and layer properties.

8. In the ***Layer Control*** box, click on the ***Object_Lines*** layer name.

❖ The selected objects are moved to the *Object_Lines* layer.

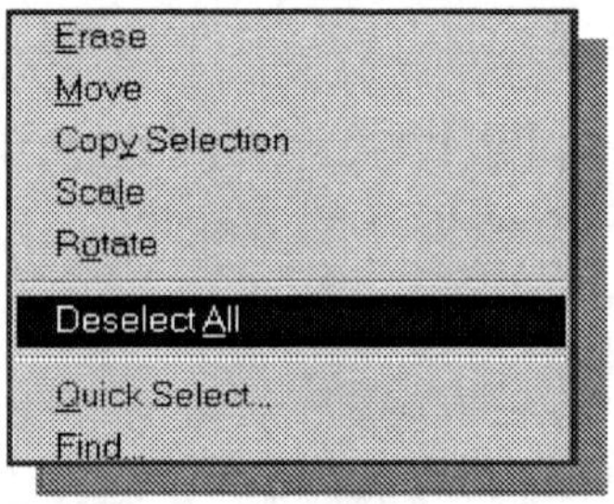

9. Inside the graphics window, **right-mouse-click** and select **Deselect All**.

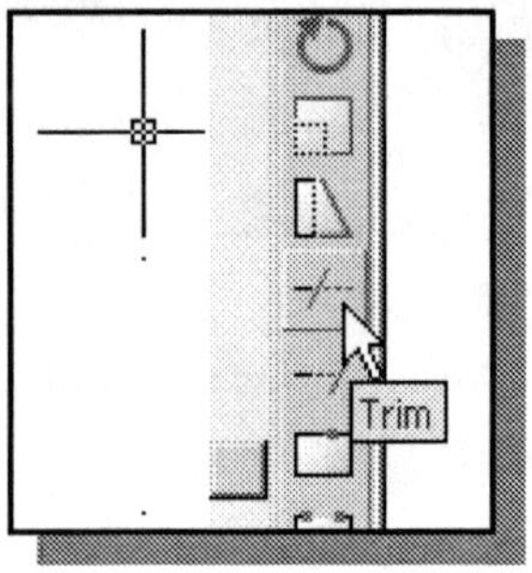

10. Use the **Trim** command and modify the side view as shown.

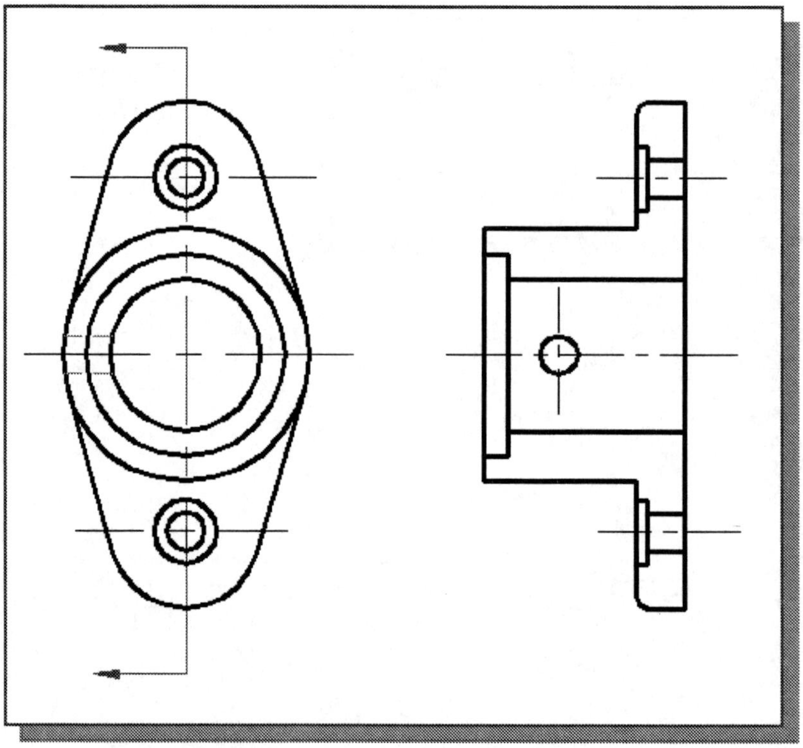

Adding Section Lines

1. In the ***Layer Control*** box, set layer ***Section_Lines*** as the *Current Layer*.

2. Select the **Hatch** icon in the *Draw* toolbar. The *Boundary Hatch* dialog box appears on the screen.

➢ We will use the *ANSI31* standard hatch pattern and create an associative hatch, which means the hatch is updated automatically if the boundaries are modified.

➢ We can define a boundary by **selecting objects** or **picking points**. The **Pick Points** option is usually the easier and faster way to define boundaries. We specify locations inside the region to be crosshatched and AutoCAD LT will automatically derive the boundary definition from the location of the specified point.

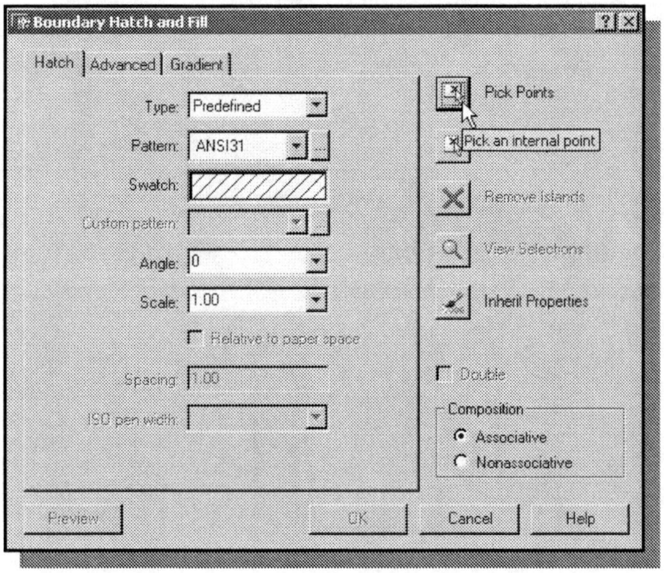

3. Click on the **Pick Points** button.

4. In the command prompt area, the message *"Select internal point:"* is displayed.

5. **Left-click** inside the four regions as shown.

6. Inside the graphics window, right-mouse-click to bring up the popup menu and select **Enter** to continue with the Hatch command.

7. Click on the **OK** button to close the *Boundary Hatch* dialog box.

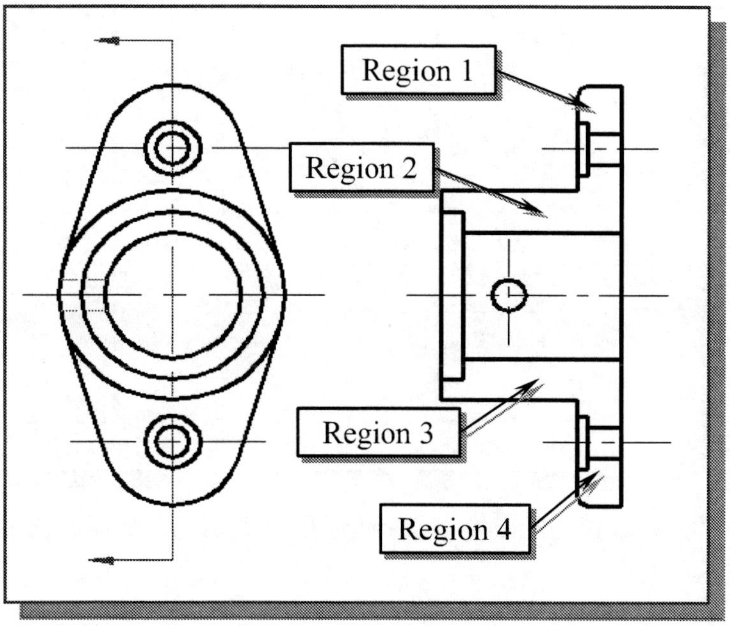

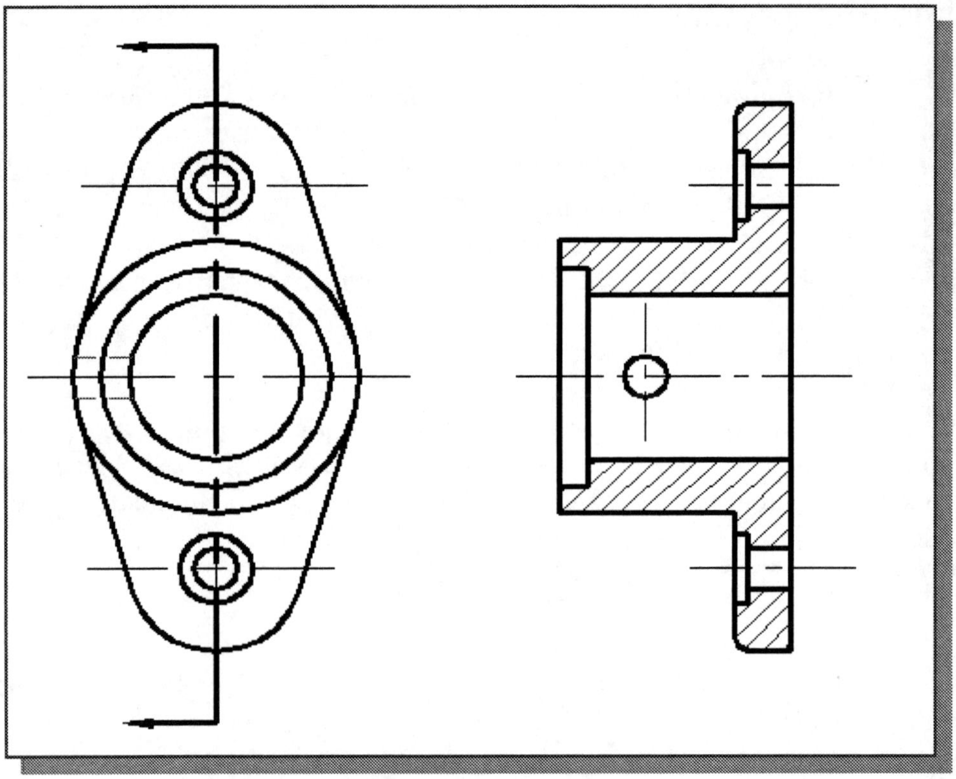

➤ Complete the drawing by adding the proper dimensions.

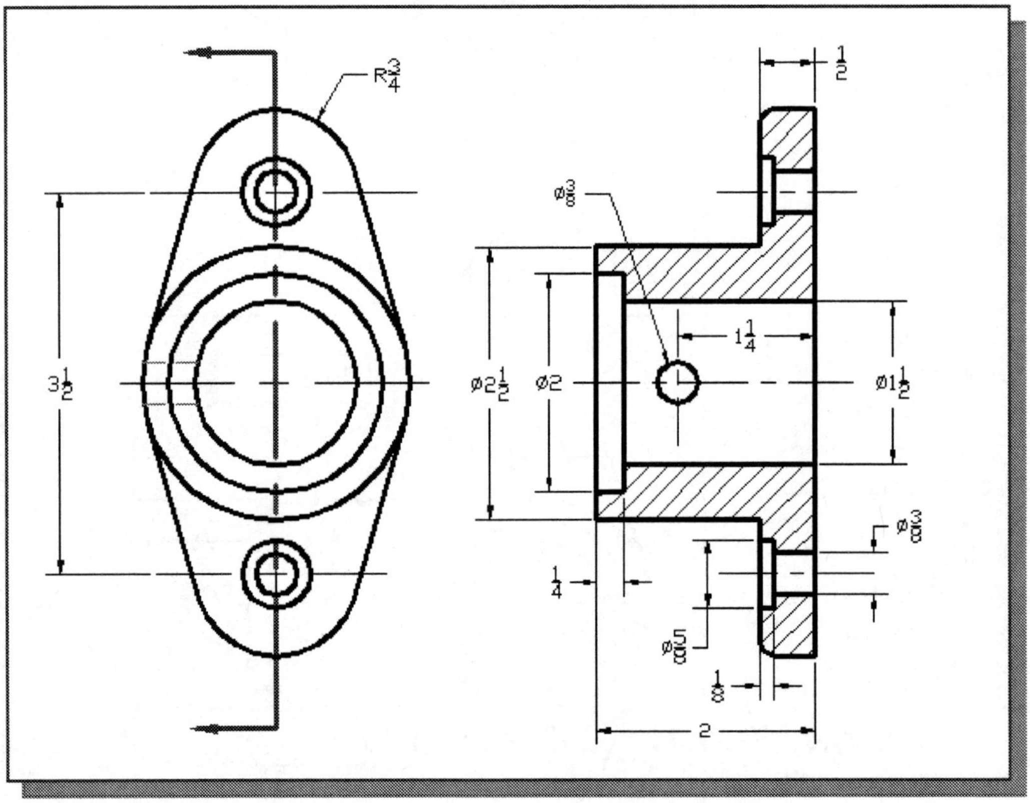

➤ On your own, create a drawing layout and print out the drawing.

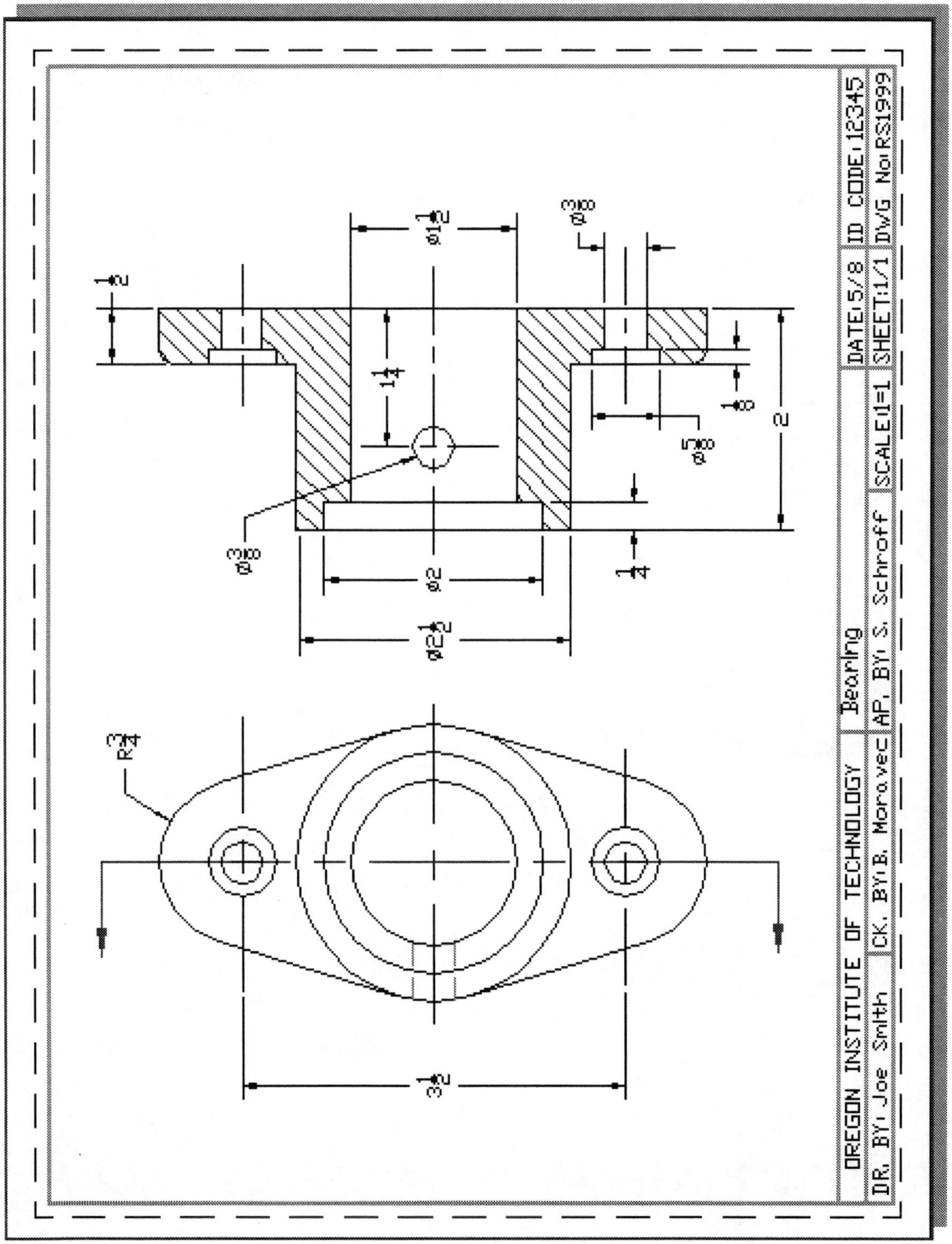
OREGON INSTITUTE OF TECHNOLOGY
Bearing
DATE: 5/8
ID CODE: 12345
DR. BY: Joe Smith
CK. BY: B. Moravec
AP. BY: S. Schroff
SCALE: 1=1
SHEET: 1/1
DWG No: RS1999

Questions:

1. When and why is a *section view* necessary?

2. Describe the general procedure to create a *section view* in **AutoCAD® LT 2005**.

3. In **AutoCAD® LT 2005**, can the angle and spacing of hatch patterns be altered?

4. Explain the concept of using a cutting plane line in a section view?

5. Identify the following commands:

(a)

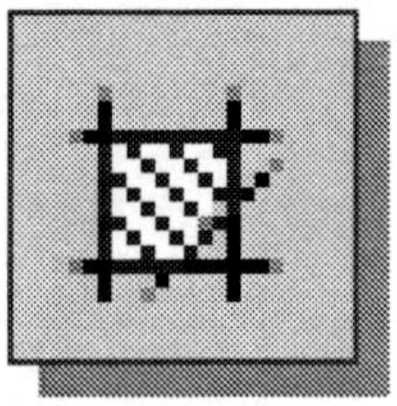

(b)

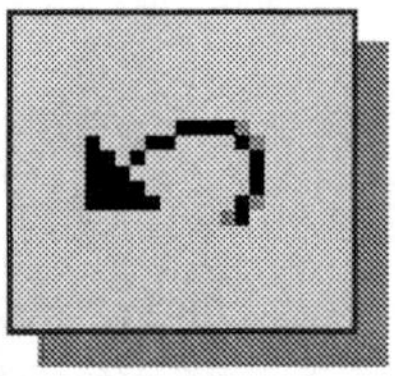

(c)

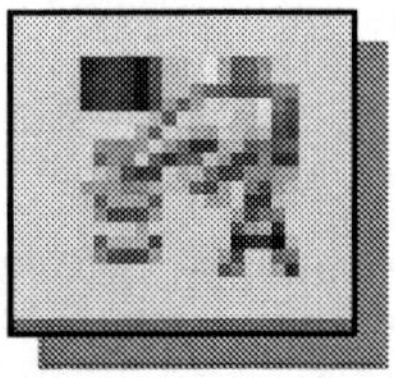

(d)

Exercises: (Unless otherwise specified, all dimensions are in inches.)

1.

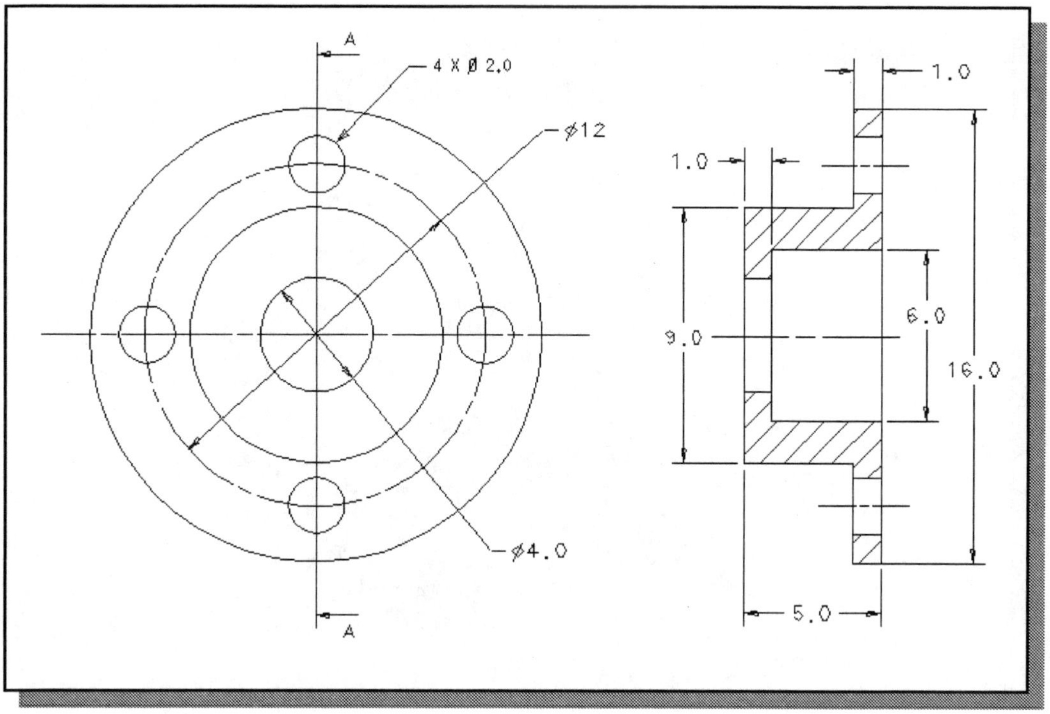

2.

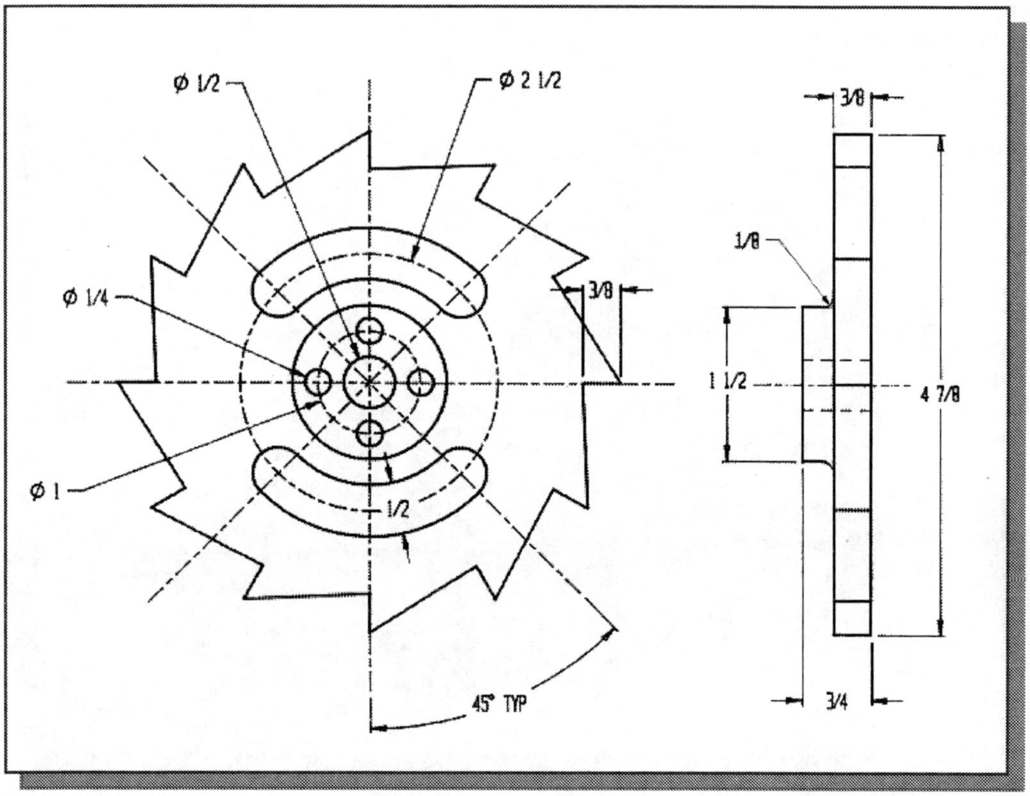

3.

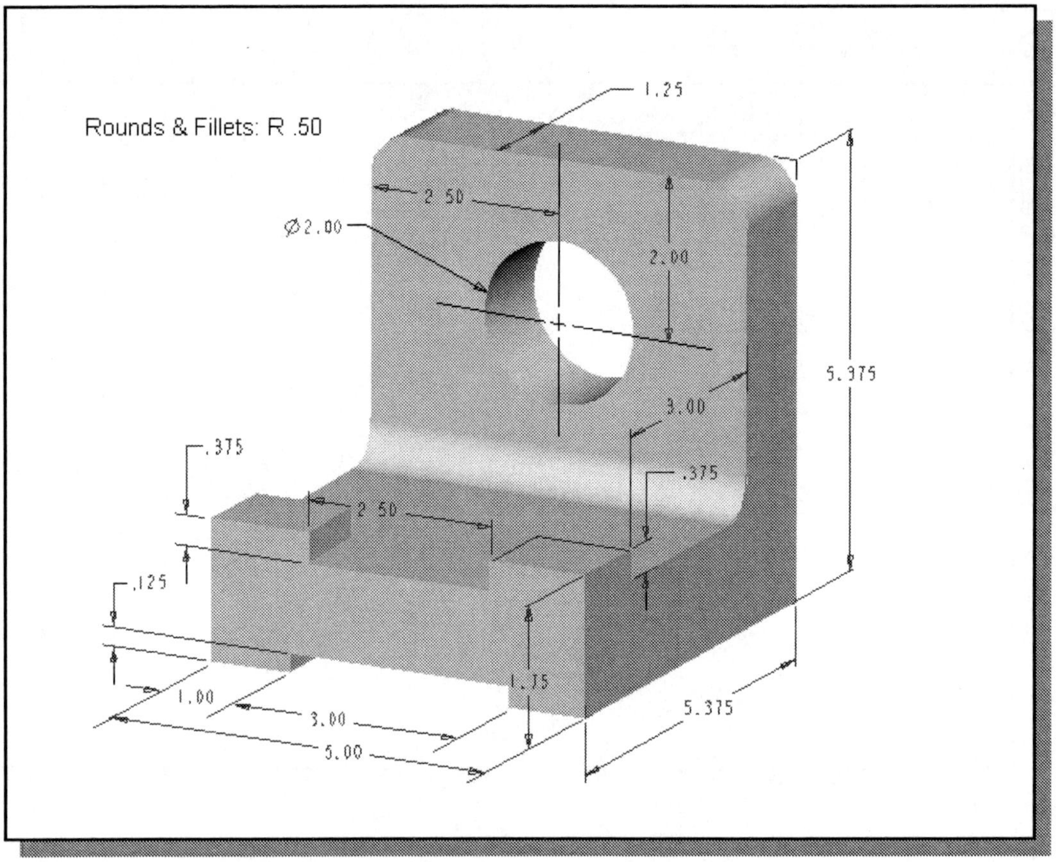
Rounds & Fillets: R .50
1.25
2.50
Ø2.00
2.00
5.375
3.00
.375
.375
2.50
.125
1.00
3.00
5.00
1.75
5.375

4.

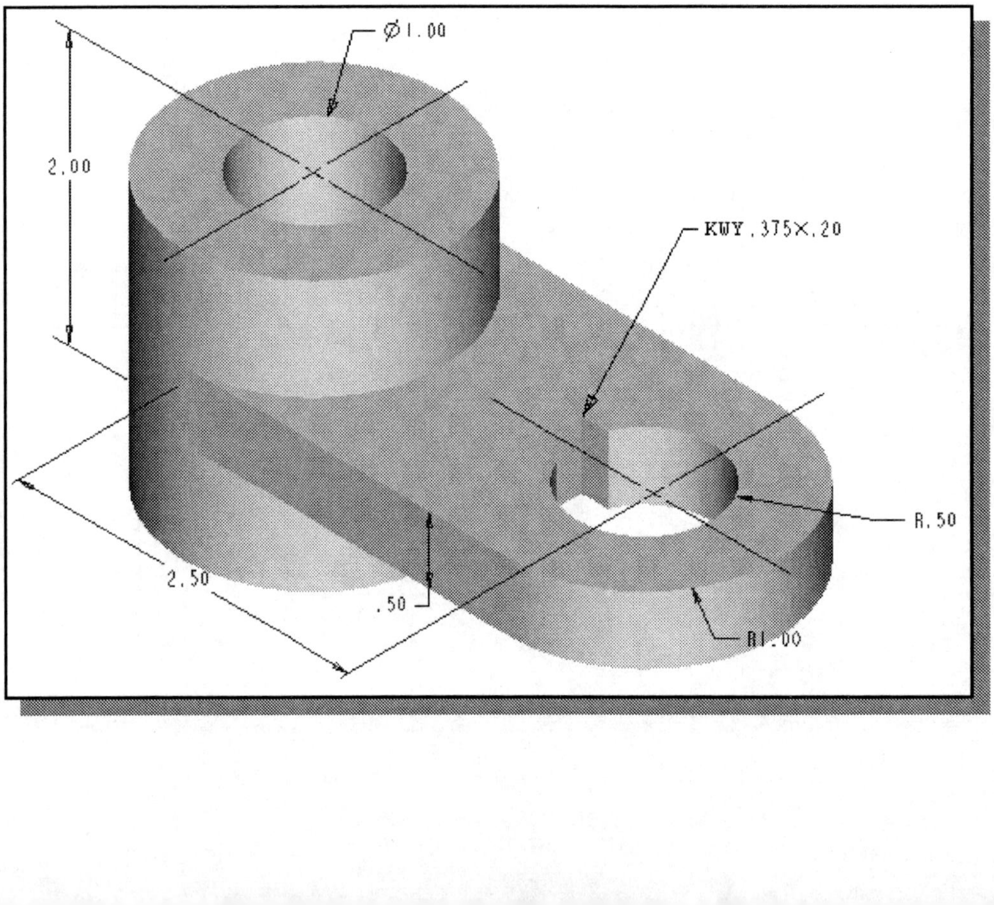
Ø1.00
2.00
KWY.375×.20
R.50
2.50
.50
R1.00

5.

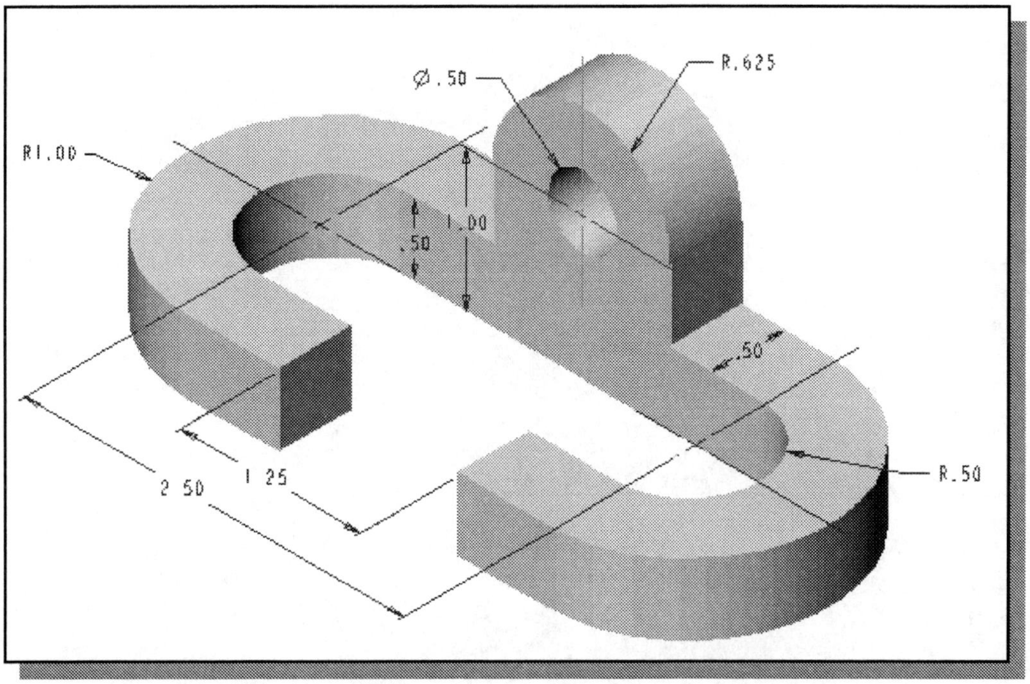
Ø.50
R.625
R1.00
1.00
.50
.50
R.50
2.50
1.25

6.

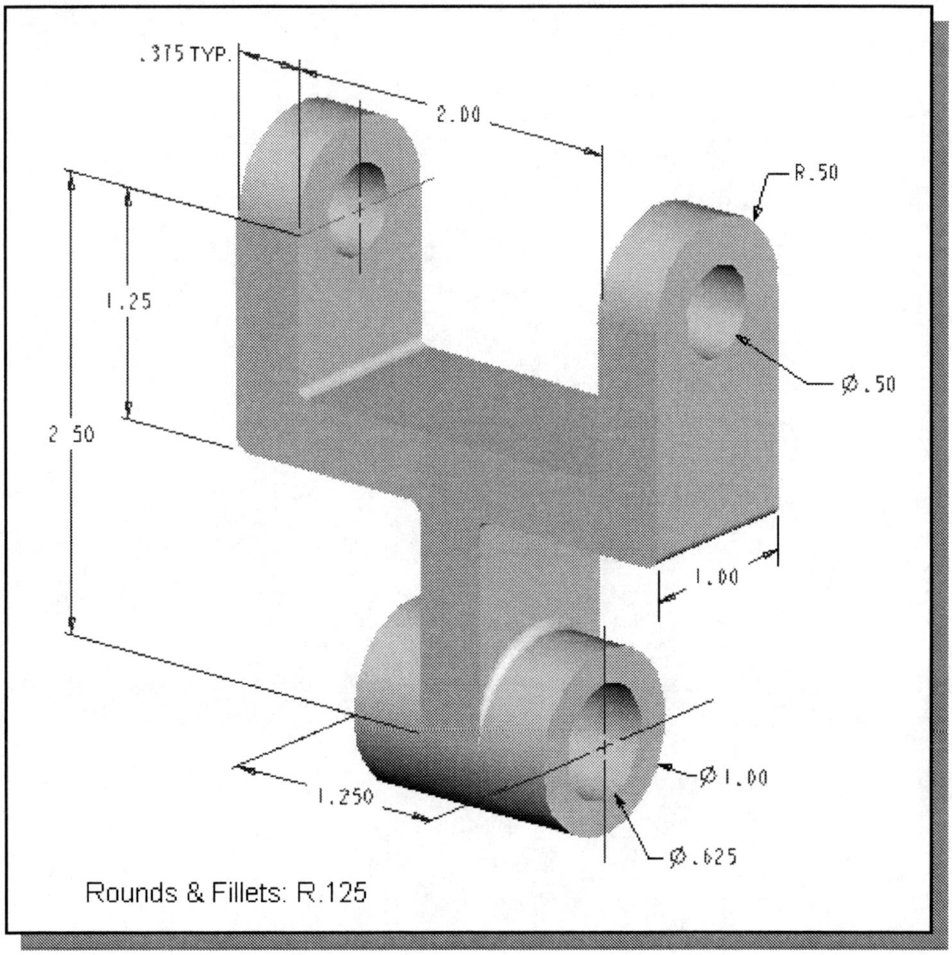
.375 TYP.
2.00
R.50
1.25
2.50
Ø.50
1.00
Ø1.00
1.250
Ø.625
Rounds & Fillets: R.125

Notes:

Lesson 9
Assembly Drawings and AutoCAD Blocks

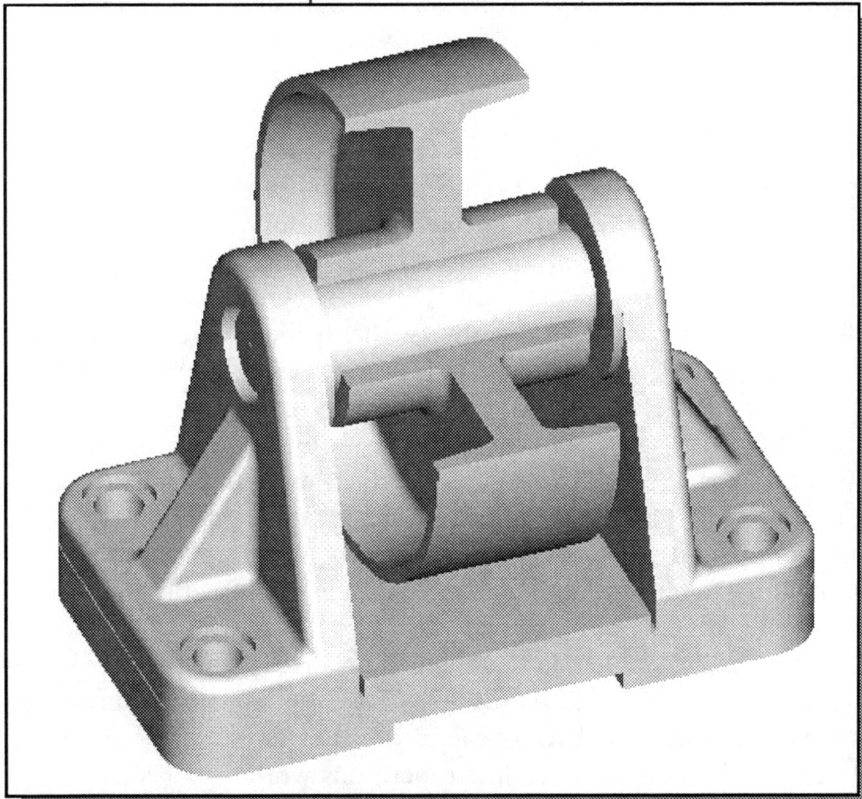

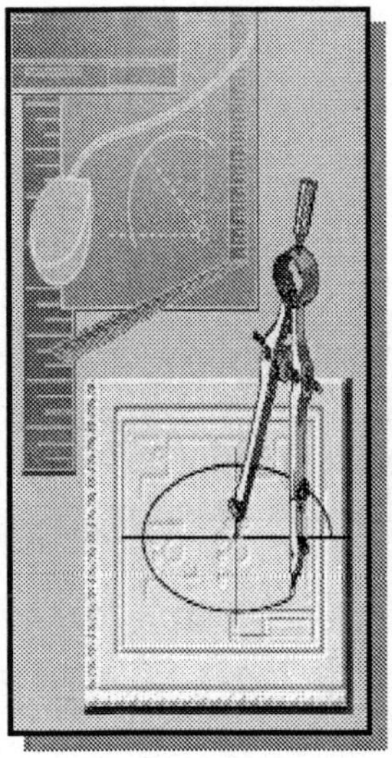

Learning Objectives

- Create an Assembly Drawing from Part Files
- Using AutoCAD LT with the Internet
- Load Multiple Drawings into a Single AutoCAD Session
- Define a Block
- Create Multiple Copies Using BLOCKS
- Copy and Paste with the Windows Clipboard
- Use the MOVE and ROTATE Commands

Introduction

The term **assembly drawing** refers to the type of drawing in which the various parts of a design are shown in their relative positions in the finished product. Assembly drawings are used to represent the function of each part and the proper working relationships of the mating parts. Sectioning is used more extensively on assembly drawings than on detail drawings to show the relationship of various parts. Assembly drawings should not be overly detailed since precise information is provided on the detail drawings. In most cases dimensions are omitted on assembly drawings except for assembly dimensions such as important center distances, overall dimensions, and dimensions showing relationships between the parts. For the purpose of clarity, *subassembly drawings* are often made to give the information needed for the smaller units of a larger assembly. Several options are available in **AutoCAD® LT 2005** to assist us in creating assembly drawings.

In **AutoCAD® LT 2005**, a **block** is a collection of objects that is identified by a unique name and essentially behaves as if it is a single object. Using blocks can help us organize our design by associating the related objects into smaller units. We can insert, scale, and rotate multiple objects that belong to the same block with a single selection. We can insert the same block numerous times instead of recreating the individual geometric objects each time. We can also import a block from a CAD file outside the current drawing. We can use blocks to build a standard library of frequently used symbols, components, or standard parts; the blocks can then be inserted into other drawings. Using blocks also helps us save disk space by storing all references to the same block as one block definition in the database. We can *explode* a block to separate its component objects, modify them, and redefine the block. **AutoCAD® LT 2005** updates all instances of that block based on the *block definition*. Blocks can also be nested, so that one block is a part of another block. Using blocks greatly reduces repetitious work.

In **AutoCAD® LT 2005**, we can now load multiple drawings into a single AutoCAD LT session. This new feature enables us to work with multiple drawings at the same time, and we can easily copy objects from one drawing to another by using the *Windows Clipboard*. Copying to and pasting from the *Clipboard* allow us to quickly assemble objects in different files and thus increase our productivity.

AutoCAD® LT 2005 also allows us to create a collaborative design environment, where files and resources can be shared through the Internet. We can open and save AutoCAD LT drawings to an Internet location, insert blocks by dragging drawings from a web site, and insert hyperlinks in drawings so that others can access related documents. To use the **AutoCAD® LT 2005** Internet features, *Microsoft Internet Explorer 6.0* (or a later version) and Internet or intranet connections are required.

In this lesson, we will demonstrate using the **AutoCAD® LT 2005** Internet features to access drawings through the Internet, as well as using blocks and the *Windows Clipboard* to create a subassembly drawing. We will use the ***Bearing*** part that was created in the previous lesson.

The *Shaft Support* Subassembly

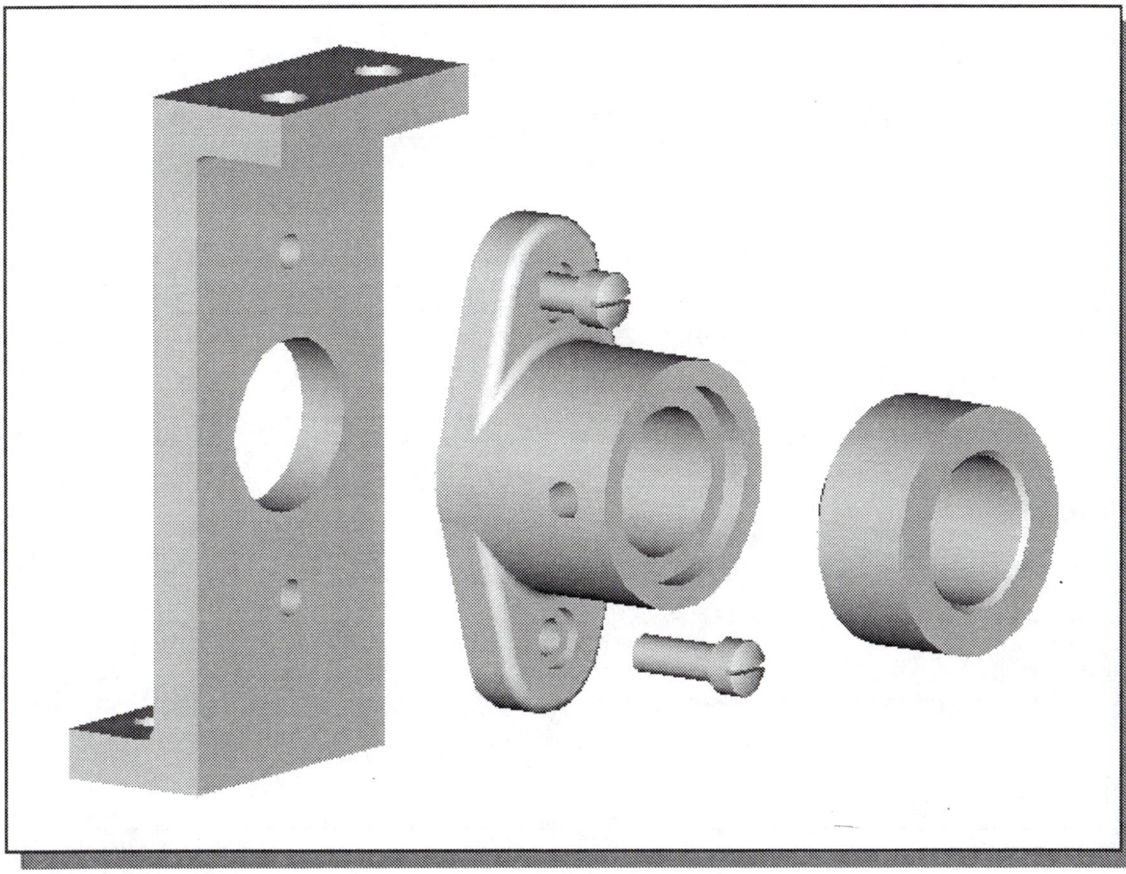

Additional Parts

Besides the ***Bearing***, we will need three additional parts: (1) ***Cap-Screw***, (2) ***Collar*** and (3) ***Base-Plate***. Create the three drawings as shown below, then save the drawings as separate part files (*Cap-Screw*, *Collar*, *Base-Plate*). (Exit **AutoCAD® LT 2005** after you have created the files.)

(1) ***Cap-Screw***
(Create this part only if you do not have Internet access. We will retrieve this drawing through the Internet.)

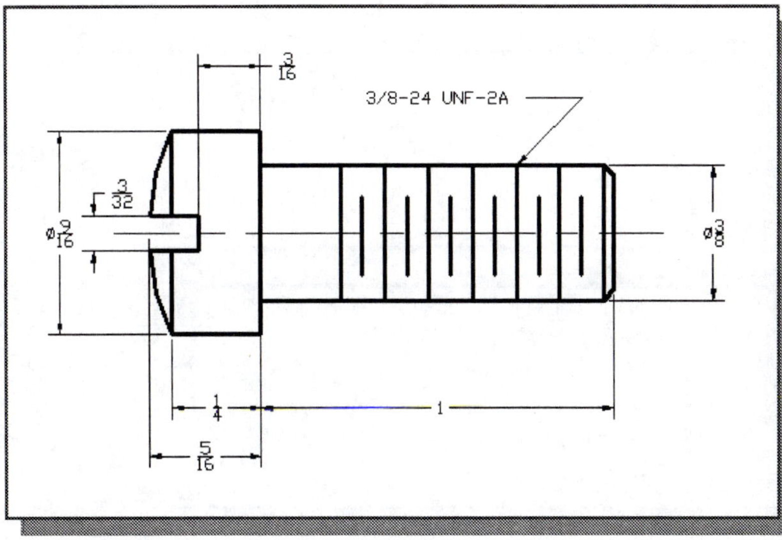

(2) ***Collar***

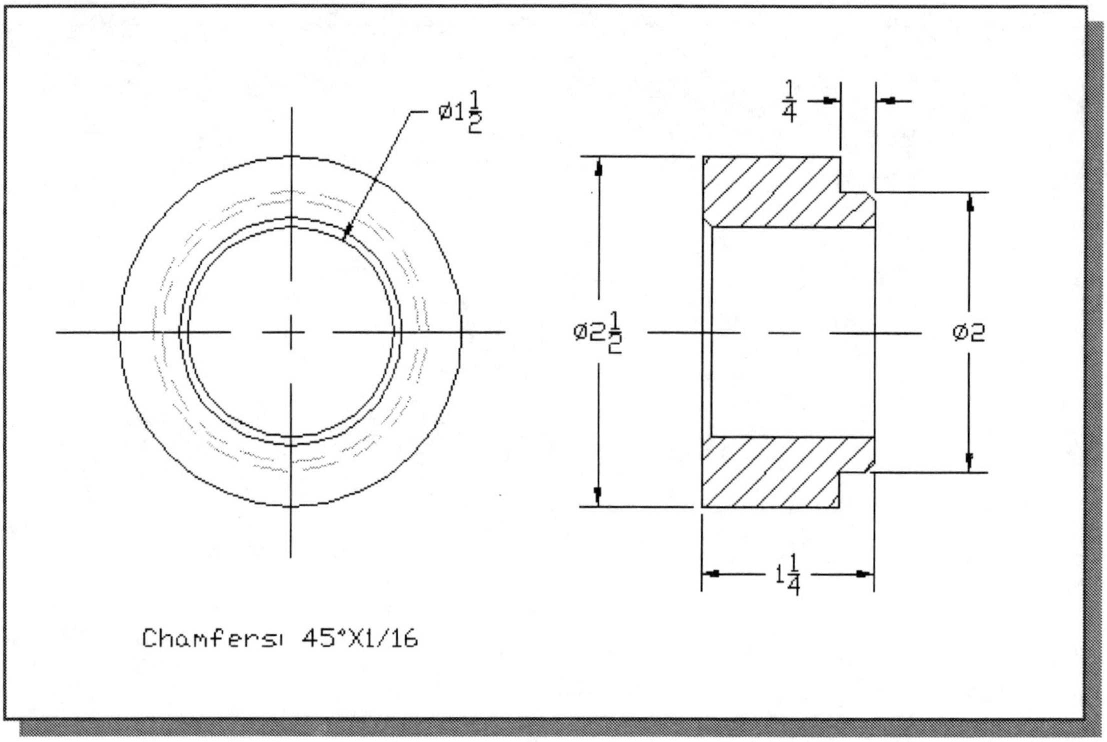

(3) ***Base-Plate***

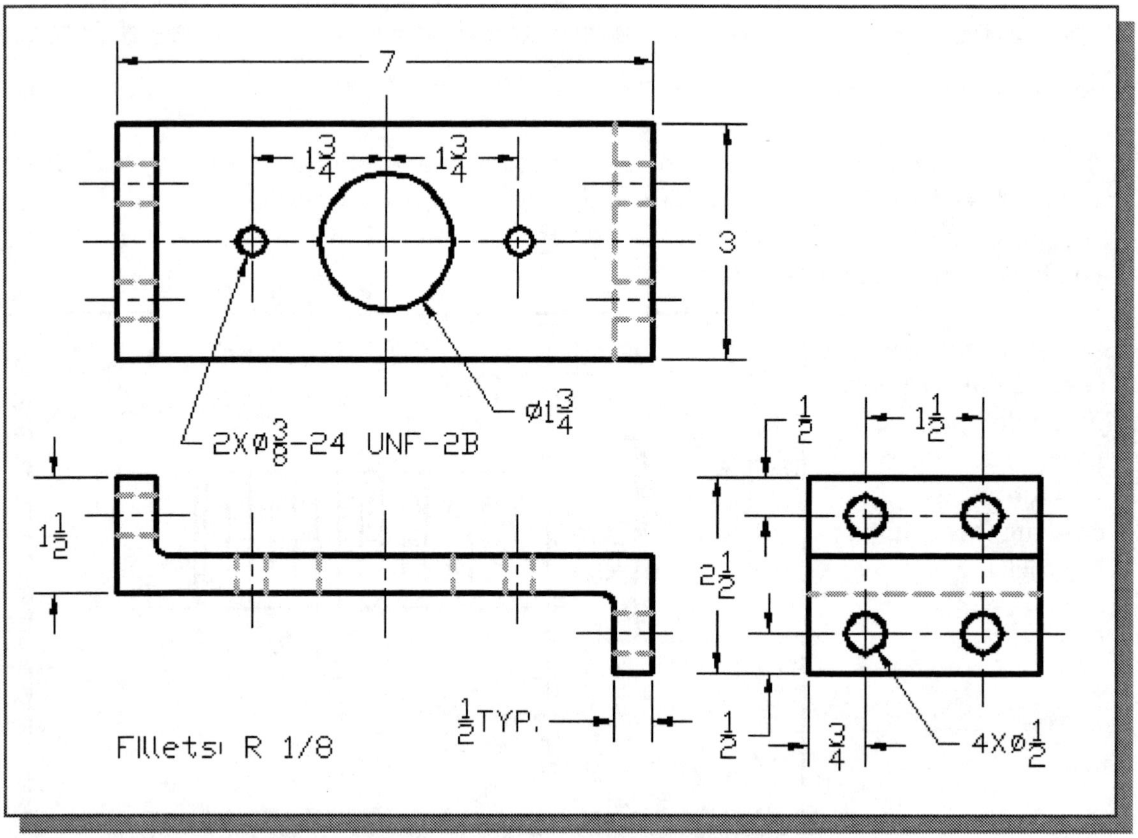

Starting Up *AutoCAD LT 2005*

1. Select the **AutoCAD 2005** option on the *Program* menu or select the **AutoCAD 2005** icon on the *Desktop*.

2. In the *Startup* dialog box, select the **Open Drawings** icon with a single click of the left-mouse-button.

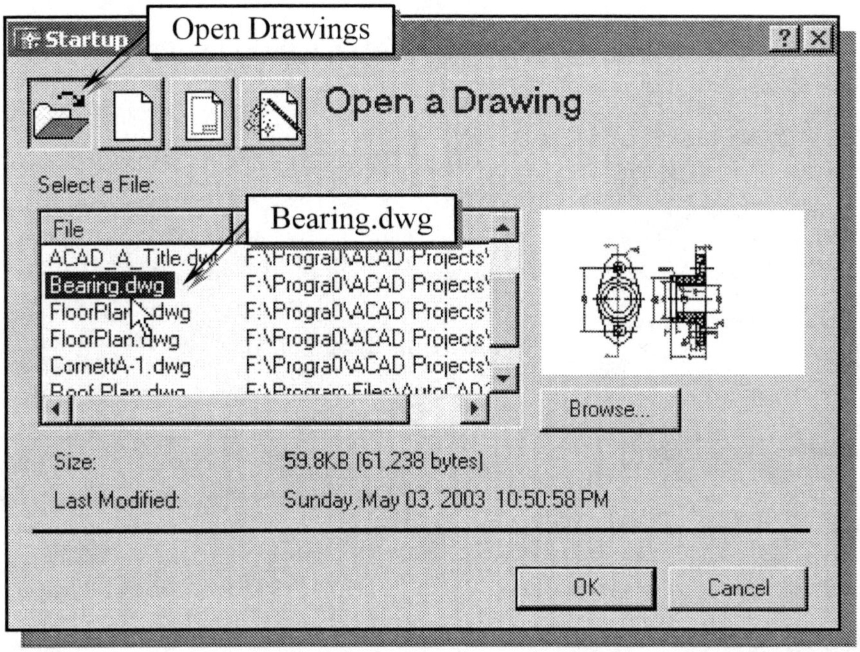

3. In the *File* list section, pick **Bearing.dwg** as the first drawing to be loaded. (If the file is not listed in the *File* list, use the **Browse** button to locate the file.)

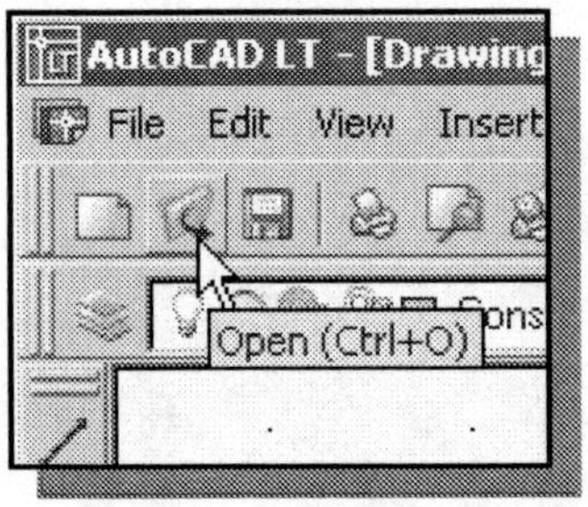

4. Select the **Open** icon in the *Standard* toolbar.

5. In the *Select File* dialog box, pick **Base-Plate.dwg** as the second drawing to be loaded.

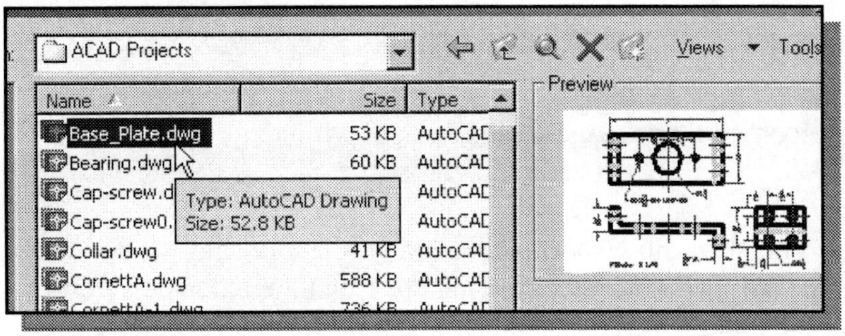

6. On your own, repeat the above steps and open the **Collar.dwg** file.

Using AutoCAD LT with the Internet

AutoCAD® LT 2005 allows us to share files and resources through the Internet. Drawings can be placed and opened to an Internet location, blocks inserted by dragging drawings from a web site, and hyperlinks inserted in drawings so that others can access related documents. Note that to use the *AutoCAD LT 2005* Internet features, *Microsoft Internet Explorer 6.0* (or a later version) and Internet or Intranet connections are required.

We will illustrate the procedure to open an AutoCAD LT file from the Internet by *Uniform Resource Locator* (URL).

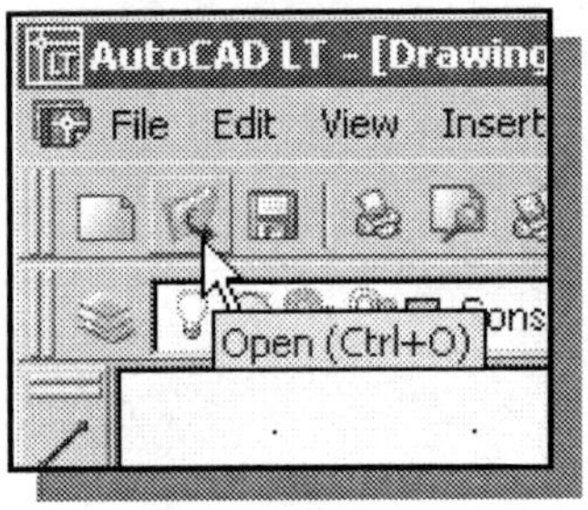

1. Click the **Open** icon in the *Standard* toolbar area as shown.

2. In the *Select File* dialog box, enter http://www.sdcACAD.com/acad2005/Cap-screw.dwg as shown in the figure below.

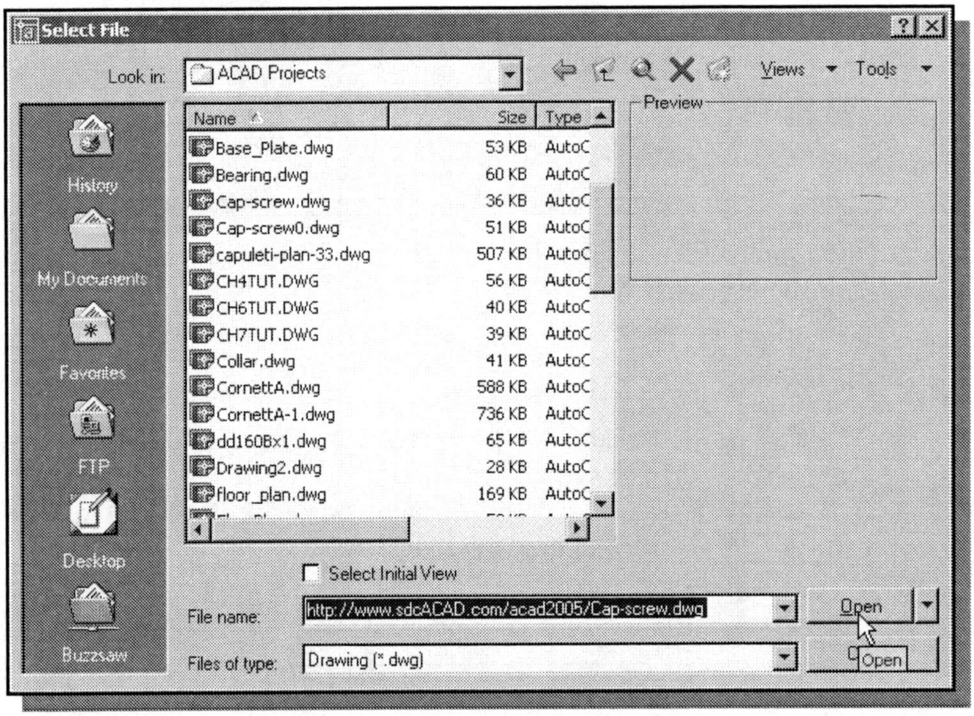

3. Click the **Open** icon and the *Cap-screw* file is downloaded from the www.sdcACAD.com web site to the local computer.

➢ The URL entered must be the *Hypertext Transfer Protocol* (http://) and the complete filename must be entered including the filename extension (.dwg or .dwt). Also, note that the directory and file names are **case sensitive**.

Rearrange the Displayed Windows

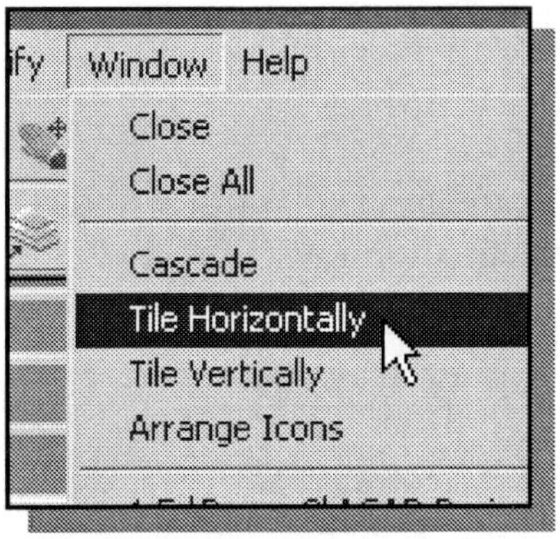

1. In the pull-down menus, select **[Window] → [Tile Horizontally]**

➤ Note that the highlighted window and the graphics cursor indicate the **active window** in the current AutoCAD LT session. We can switch to any window by clicking inside the desired window.

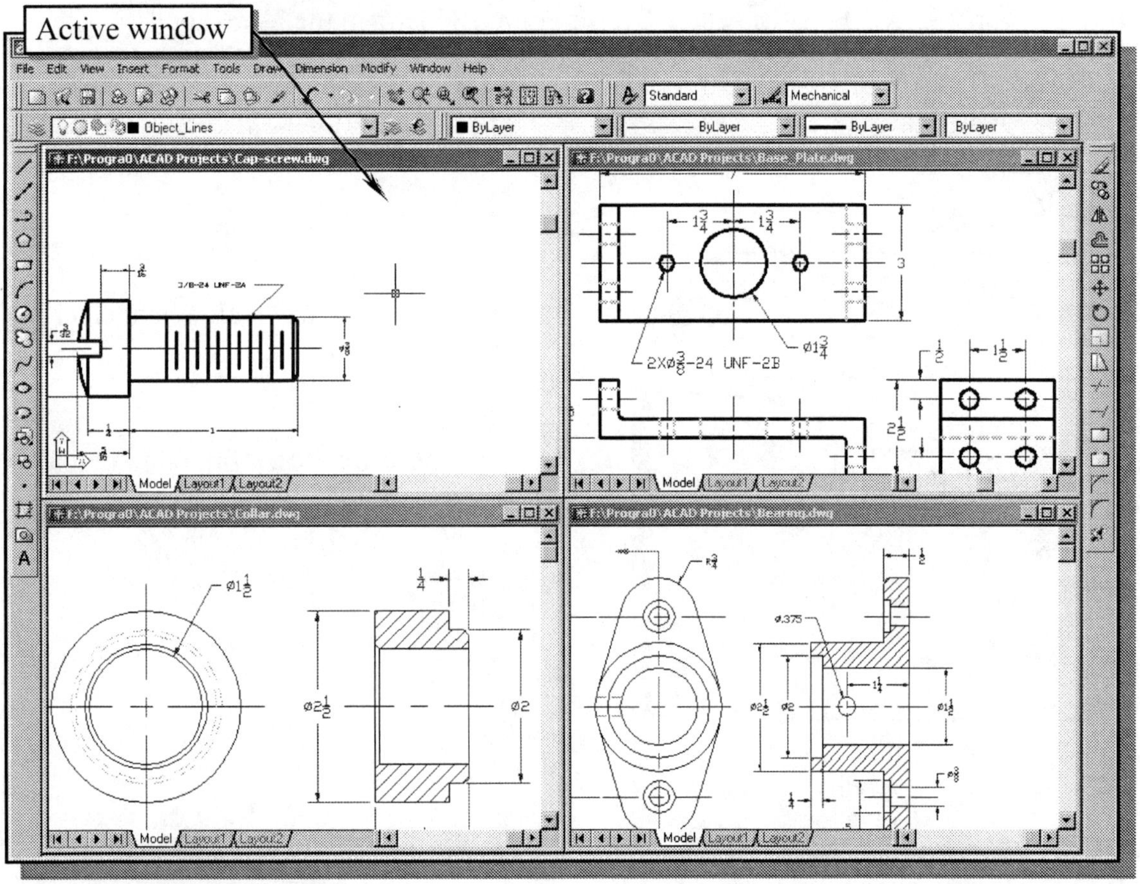

➤ On your own, adjust the display of each window by left-clicking inside each window and using the **Zoom Realtime** command.

Defining a *Block*

1. Set the ***Cap-Screw*** window as the *active window* by left-mouse-clicking inside the window.

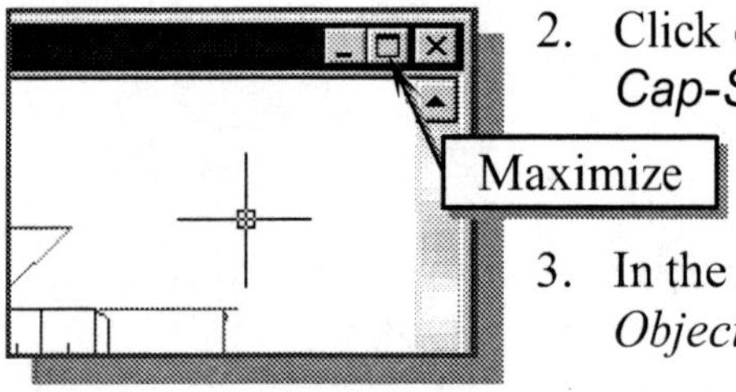

2. Click on the **Maximize** icon at the top right corner of the *Cap-Screw* window to enlarge the window.

3. In the *Layer Control* box, switch off all layers except the *Object_lines* and *Center_Lines* layers.

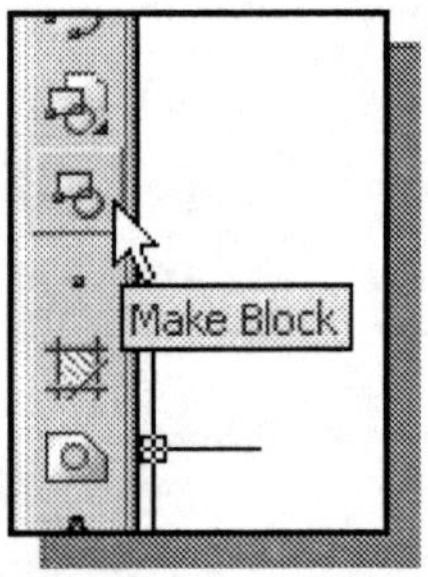

4. Pick the **Make Block** command icon in the *Draw* toolbar. The *Block Definition* dialog box appears on the screen.

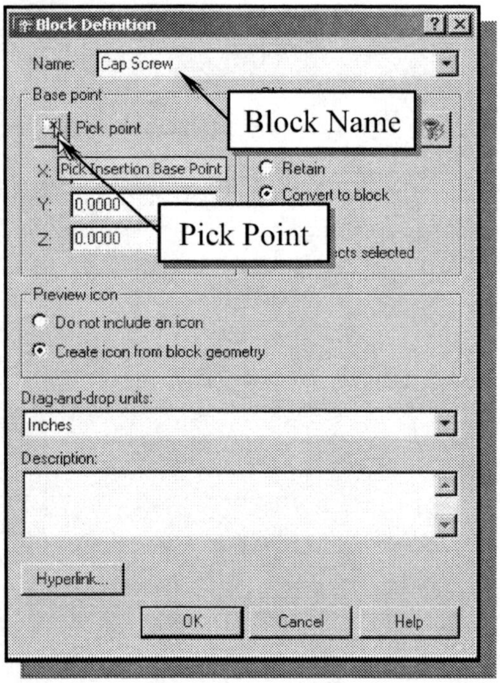

5. In the *Block Definition* dialog box, enter ***Cap Screw*** as the block *Name*.

6. Click on the **Pick Point** button to define a reference point of the block.

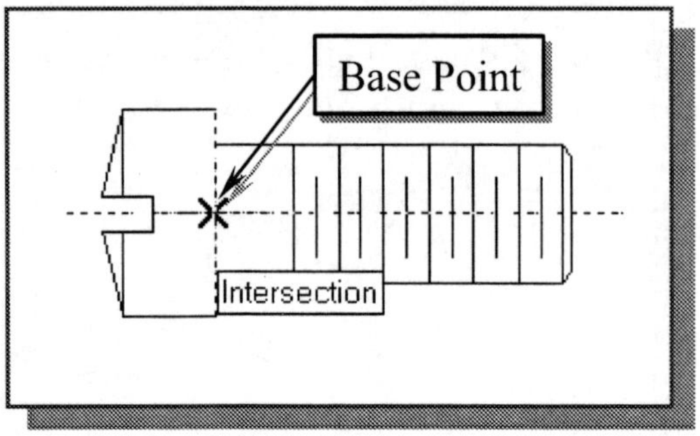

7. Pick the intersection of the centerline and the base of the *Cap-Screw* head as the base point.

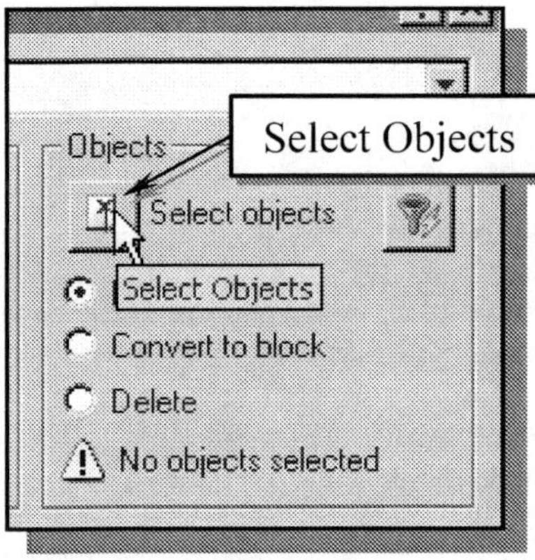

8. Click on the **Select Objects** icon to select the objects to be placed in the block.

9. Select all *object lines* and *centerlines* by using a selection window on the screen.

10. Inside the graphics window, **right-mouse-click** once to accept the selected objects.

❖ The selected objects will be included in the new block, and several options are available regarding the selected objects after the block is created. We can retain or delete the selected objects or convert them to a block instance.

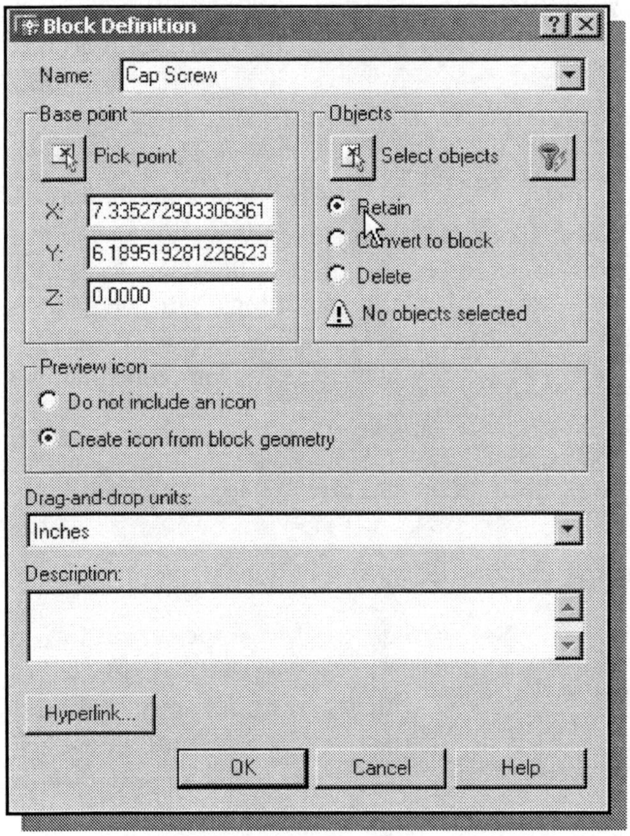

➢ ***Retain***: Keep the selected objects as regular objects in the drawing after creating the block.

➢ ***Convert to Block***: Convert the selected objects to a block instance in the drawing after creating the block.

➢ ***Delete***: Remove the selected objects from the drawing after creating the block.

11. Pick the ***Retain*** option to keep the objects as regular lines and arcs.

➢ Notice in the *Preview icon* section, the *Create icon from block geometry* option displays a small icon of the selected objects.

12. Click on the **OK** button to accept the settings and proceed to create the new block.

Inserting a *Block*

1. Pick the **Insert Block** command icon in the *Draw* toolbar. The *Insert* dialog box appears on the screen.

2. In the *Insert* dialog box, notice the block name ***Cap screw*** appears in the block *Name* box. (Note: In this example, we created only one block; AutoCAD LT allows us to define multiple blocks in the same drawing.)

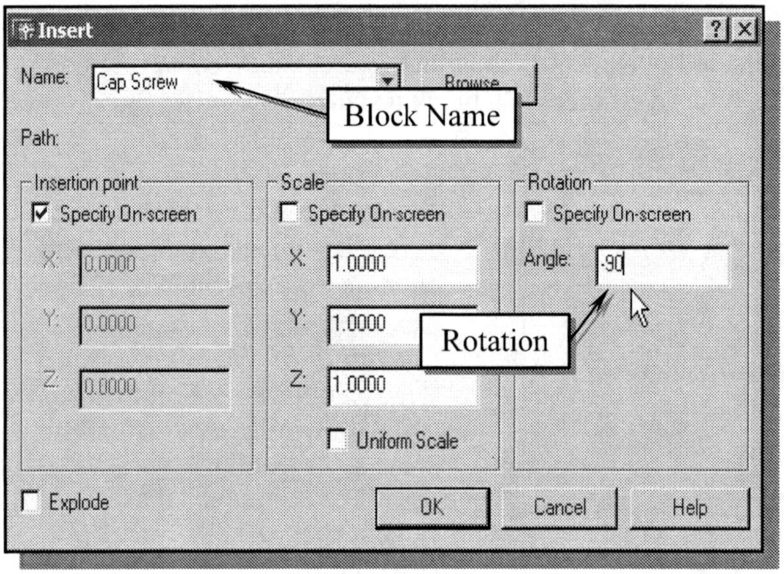

3. In the *Rotation* section, we will enter a **-90** angle to orient the *Cap screw* block in a vertical direction. Notice that other options are also available. The *Scale* option allows us to adjust the size of the block, and we can also position the block by entering coordinates.

4. Click on the **OK** button to accept the settings and proceed to insert the block into the drawing.

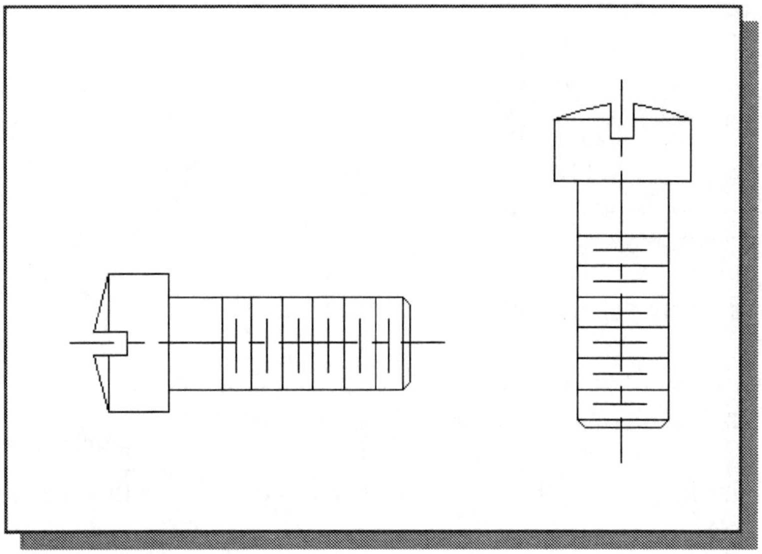

5. Move the cursor toward the right side of the original copy of the *Cap Screw*. Left-click to place a copy of the block.

➢ On your own, place additional copies of the block on the screen by experimenting with the block *Scale* and *Rotation* options.

Starting the Assembly Drawing

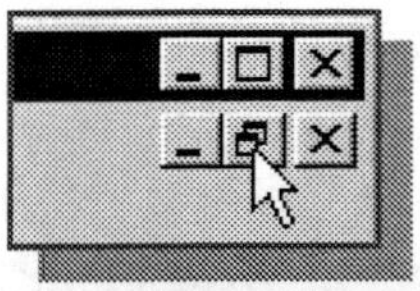

1. Switch back to the four tiled windows display by left-clicking on the **Minimize** icon near the upper right corner of the graphics window.

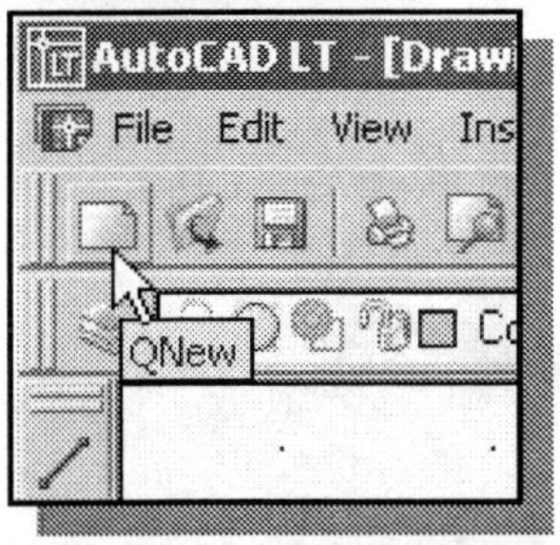

2. Select the **New** icon in the *Standard* toolbar area.

3. In the *AutoCAD LT* startup dialog box, select the ***Template*** option as shown in the figure.

4. Select the ***Acad_A_Title*** template file from the list of template files. If the file is saved in a separate folder, click on the **Browse** button to locate the file.

5. Click the **OK** button to open the selected template file.

6. On your own, resize the window as shown.

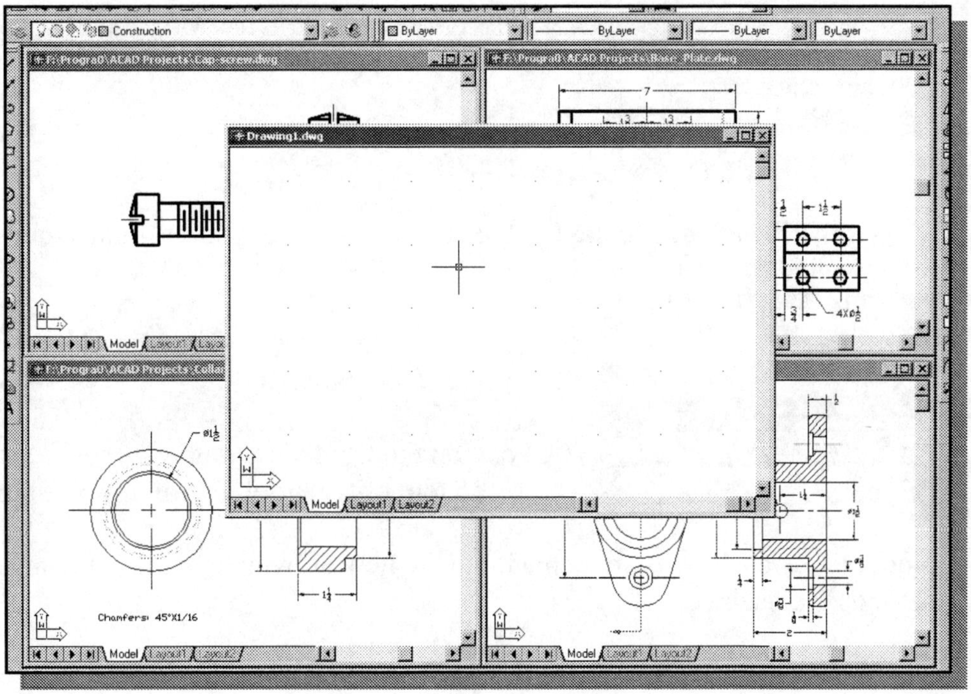

Copying and Pasting with the *Windows Clipboard*

1. Set the ***Base-Plate*** window as the *current window* by left-mouse-clicking inside the window.

2. In the ***Layer Control*** box, switch off all layers except the *Object_lines, Hidden_lines* and *Center_Lines* layers.

3. Select the **front view** of the *Base-Plate* by enclosing the front view using a selection window.

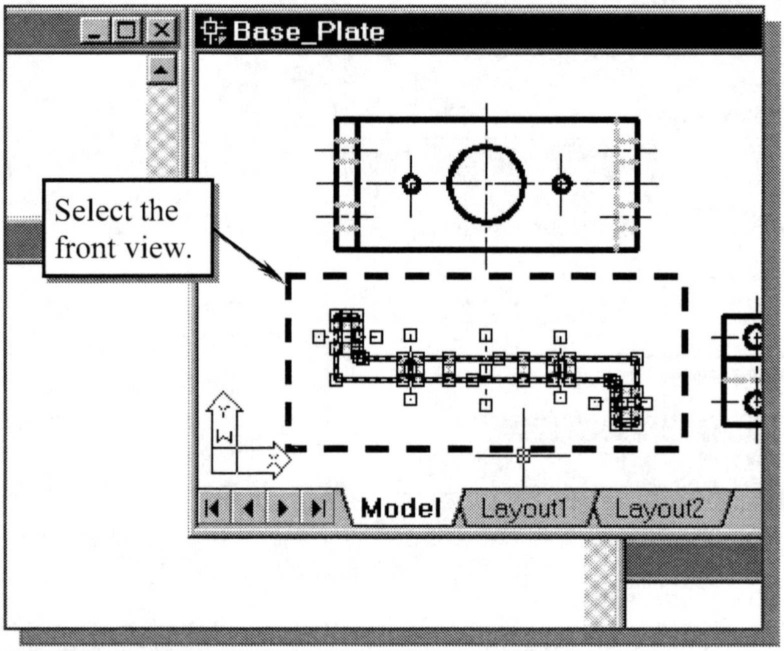

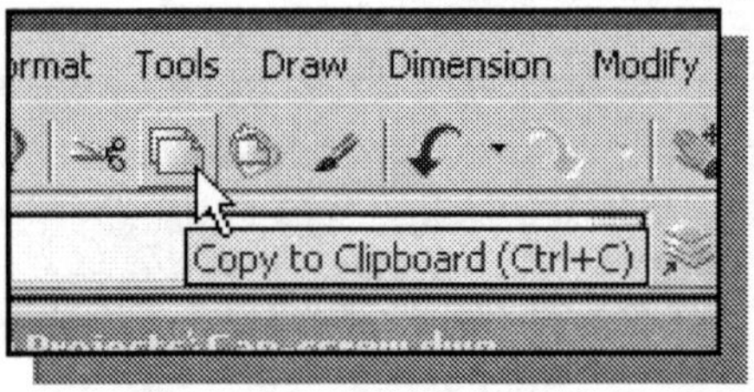

4. Select the **Copy to Clipboard** icon in the *Standard* toolbar area.

5. Set the ***Drawing1*** window as the *current window* by a left-mouse-click inside the window.

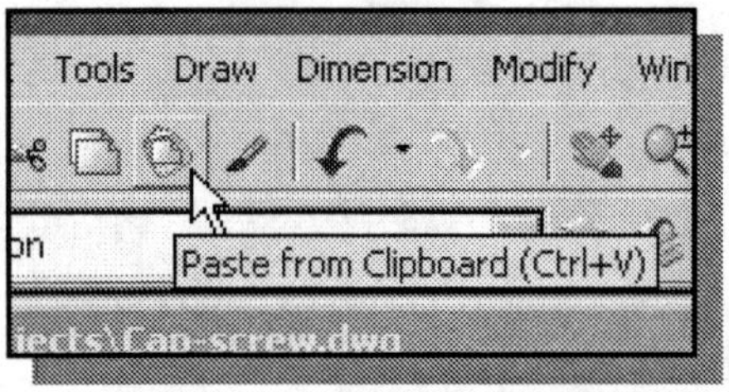

6. Select the **Paste from Clipboard** icon in the *Standard* toolbar area.

7. Position the front view of the *Base-Plate* near the bottom of the graphics window as shown.

➢ Note the selected items are copied into the new drawing and all of the layer settings are retained.

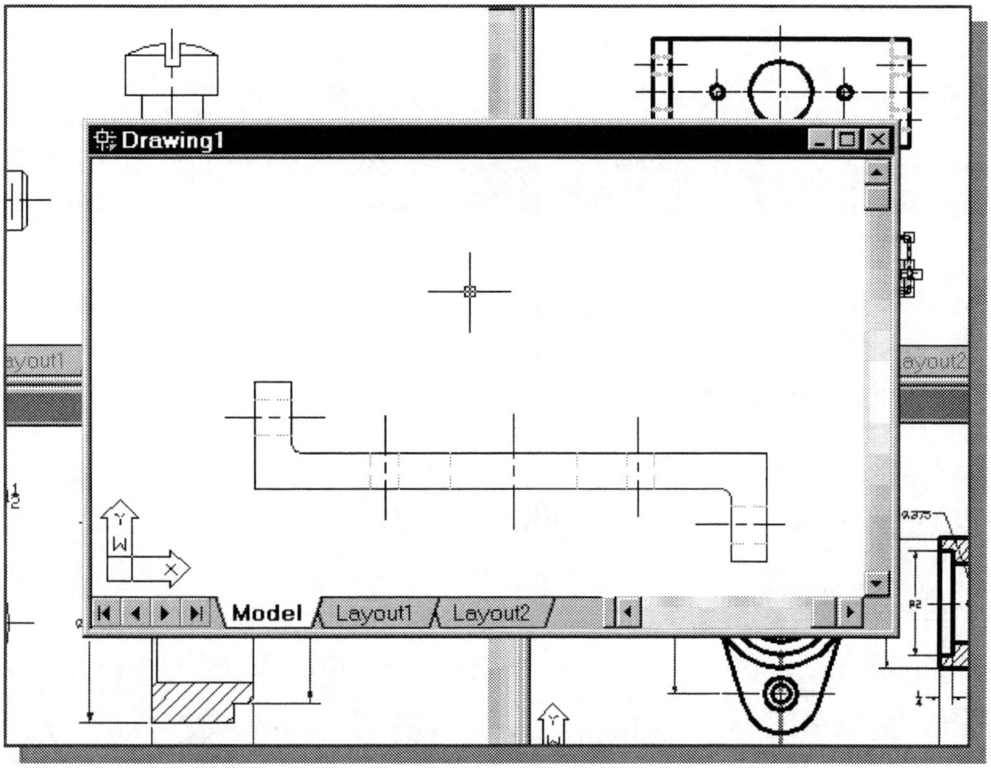

Converting the View into a Section View

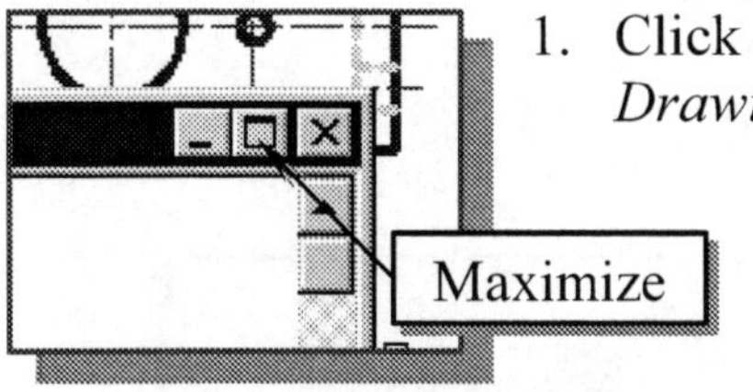

1. Click on the **Maximize** icon at the top right corner of the *Drawing1* window to enlarge the window.

2. **Pre-select** all the objects in the side view by using a selection window.

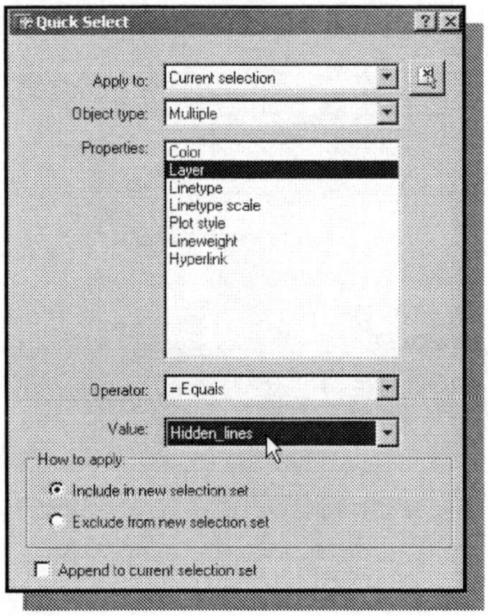

3. Inside the graphics window, **right-mouse-click** to bring up the popup option menu and select the **Quick Select** option.

4. In the *Quick Select* dialog box, select ***Layer*** from the *Properties* list.

5. Set the ***Value*** box to *Hidden_Lines.*

6. In the *How to apply* section, confirm the ***Include in new selection set*** option is selected.

7. Click on the **OK** button to accept the settings.

8. AutoCAD LT will now **filter out** objects that are not on layer *Hidden_lines*.

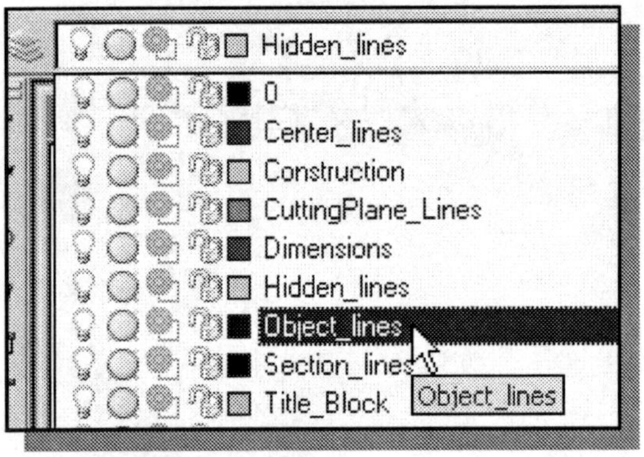

9. In the ***Layer Control*** box, click on the ***Object_Lines*** layer name to move the selected objects to the *Object_Lines* layer.

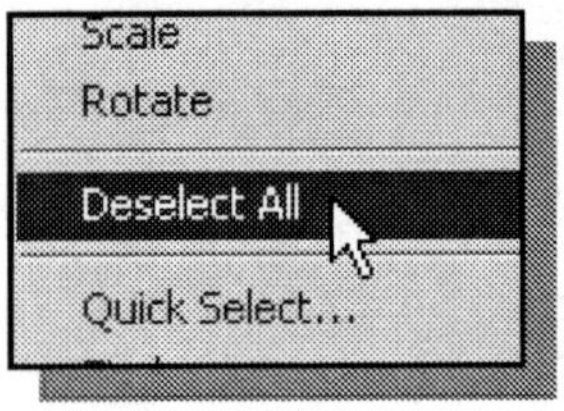

10. Inside the graphics window, **right-mouse-click** and select **Deselect All**.

11. In the ***Layer Control*** box, set layer *Section_Lines* as the *Current Layer*.

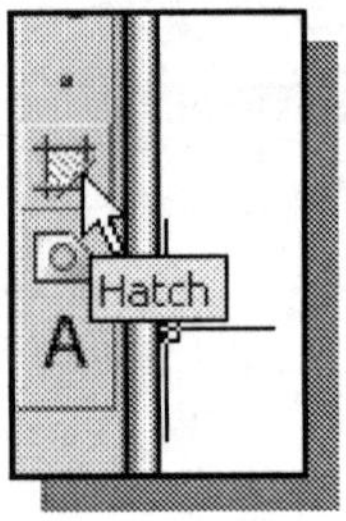

12. Select the **Hatch** icon in the *Draw* toolbar. The *Boundary Hatch* dialog box appears on the screen.

13. On your own, create the hatch pattern as shown.

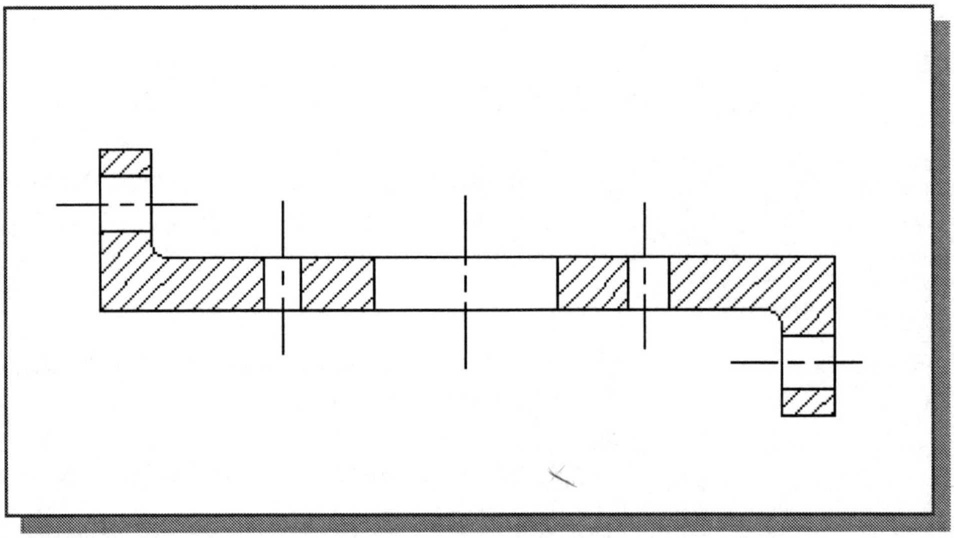

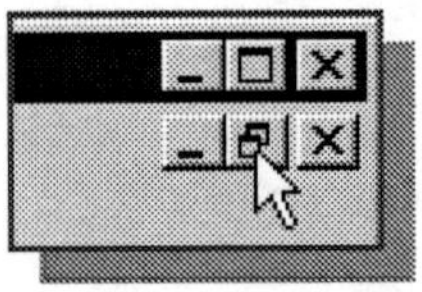

14. Switch back to the tiled windows display by left-clicking on the Restore Down icon near the upper right corner of the graphics window.

Adding the *Bearing* to the Assembly Drawing

1. Set the ***Bearing*** window as the current window by a left-mouse-click inside the window.

2. In the ***Layer Control*** box, switch off all layers except the *Object_lines, Hidden_Lines, Center_Lines* and *Section_Lines* layers.

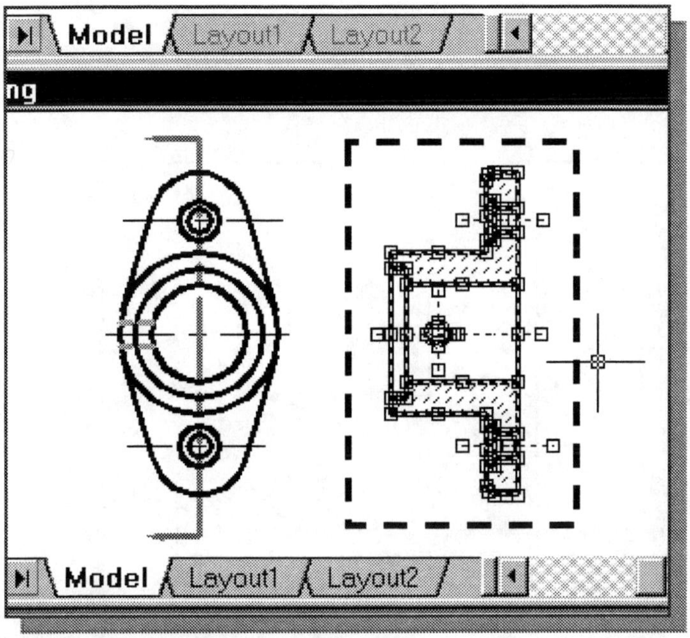

3. Select the **side view** of the *Bearing* by enclosing the side view using a selection window.

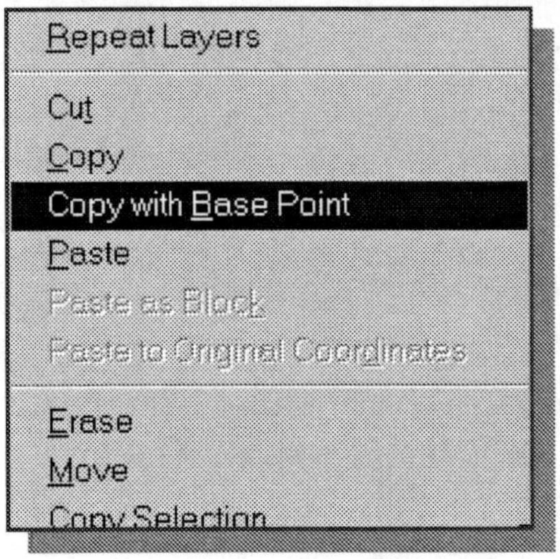

4. Inside the graphics window, **right-mouse-click** and select the **Copy with Base Point** option.

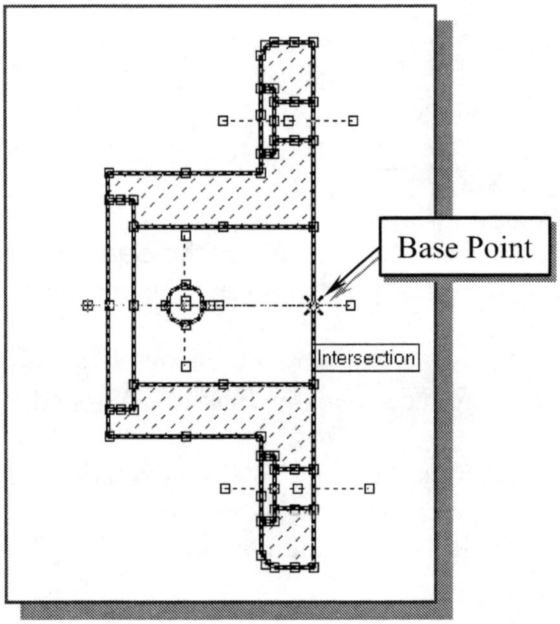

5. Pick the **center intersection** on the right vertical line of the side view as the base point.

6. Set the ***Drawing1*** window as the *current window* by left-mouse-clicking inside the window.

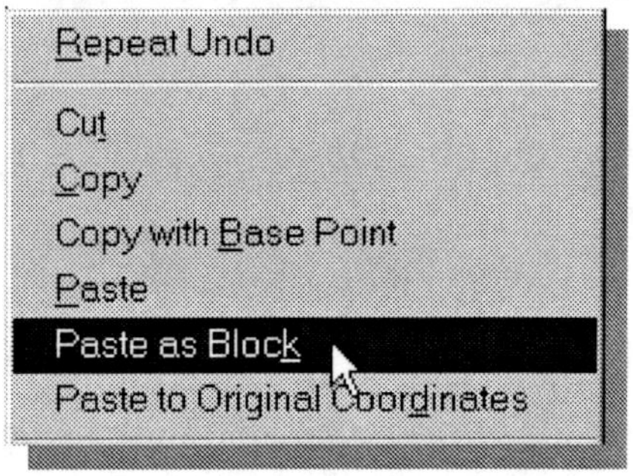

7. Inside the graphics window, **right-mouse-click** and select the **Paste as Block** option.

8. Align the side view of the *Bearing* to the top center intersection of the *Base-Plate* as shown.

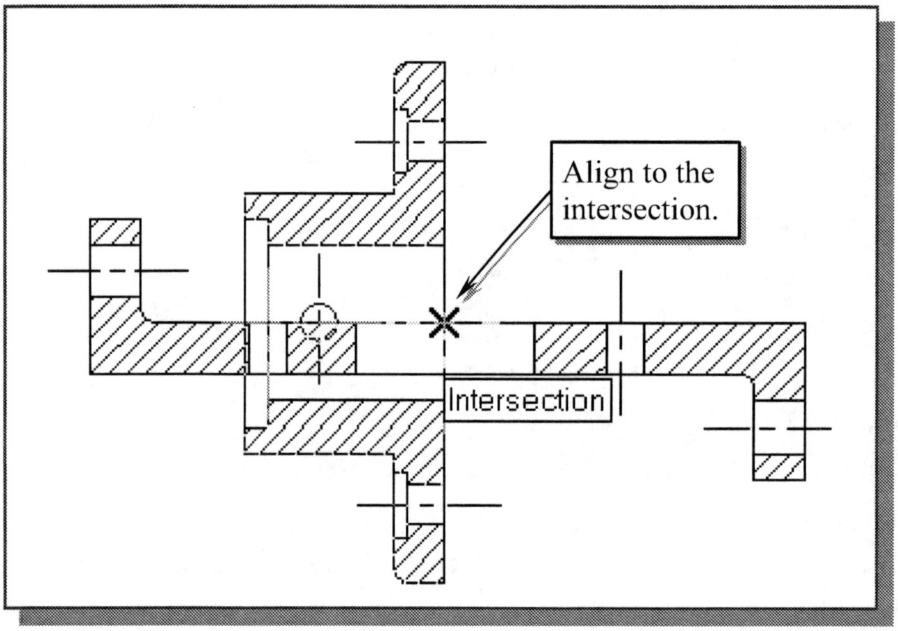

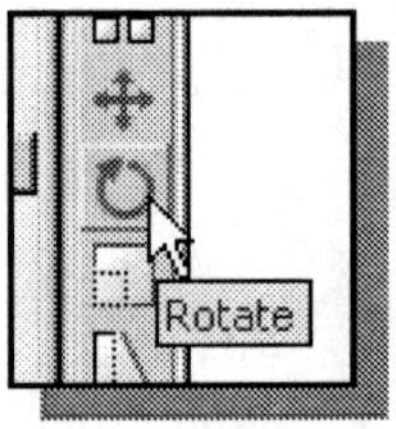

9. Click on the **Rotate** icon in the *Modify* toolbar.

10. Pick the side view of the *Bearing* we just placed into the assembly drawing. Notice the entire view is treated as a block object.

11. Inside the graphics window, **right-mouse-click** to accept the selection and proceed with the Rotate command.

12. Pick the base point as the rotation reference point.

13. Rotate and align the side view of the *Bearing* to the top of the *Base-Plate*.

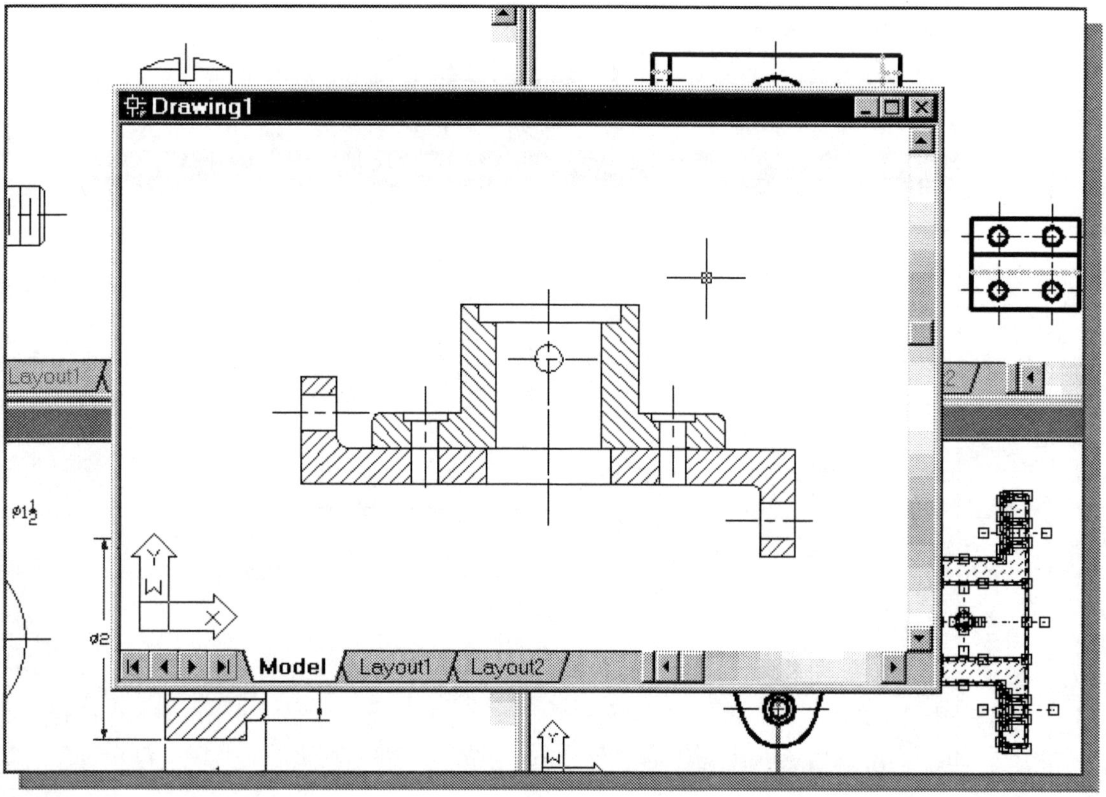

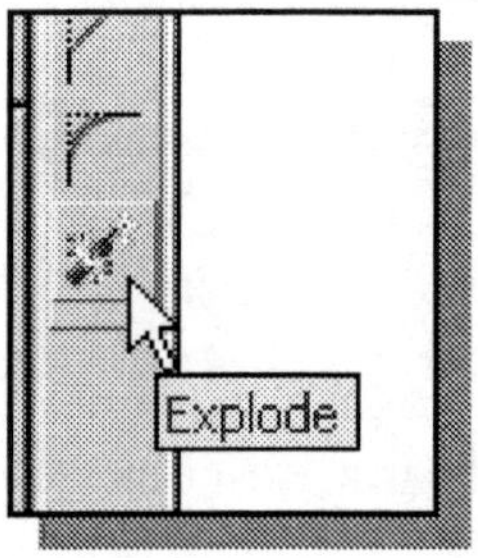

14. Select the **Explode** icon in the *Modify* toolbar.

15. Pick the *Bearing* to break the block into its component objects.

➢ On your own, copy and paste the *Collar* to the top of the bearing.

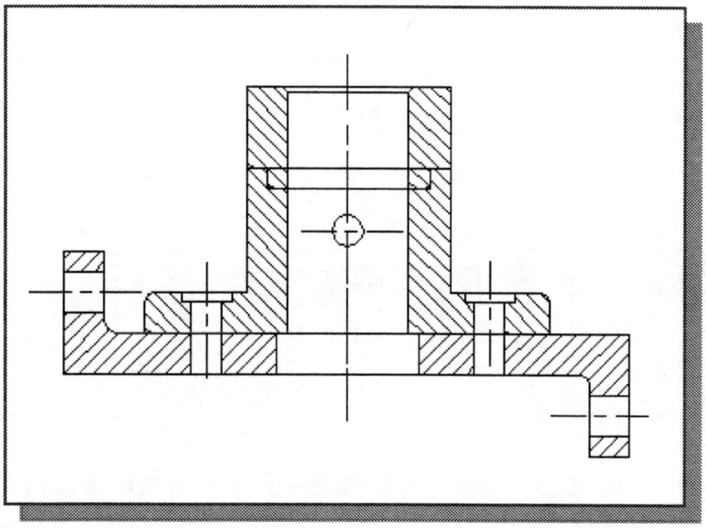

16. Use the **Explode, Trim** and **Erase** commands and modify the assembly as shown.

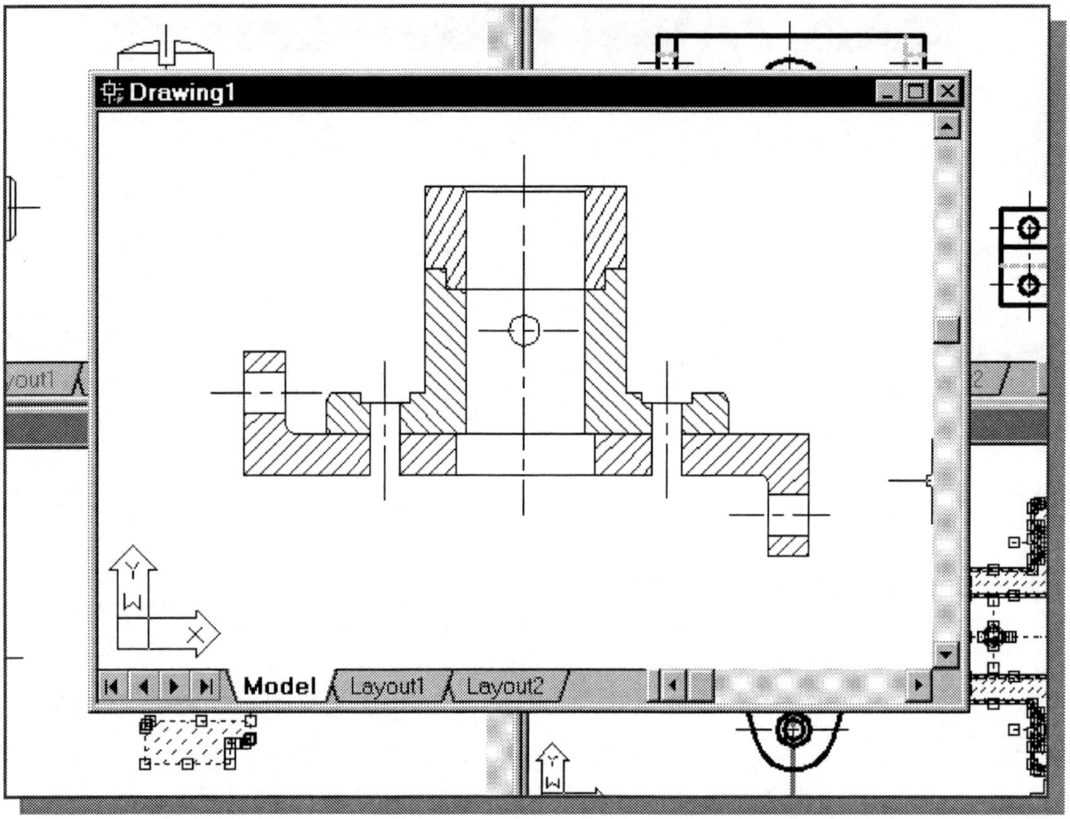

Adding the *Cap-Screws* to the Assembly Drawing

1. Set the ***Cap-Screw*** window as the *current window* by a left-mouse-click inside the window.

2. Pre-select the vertical *Cap-Screw*. Since all objects belong to a block we can quickly select the block.

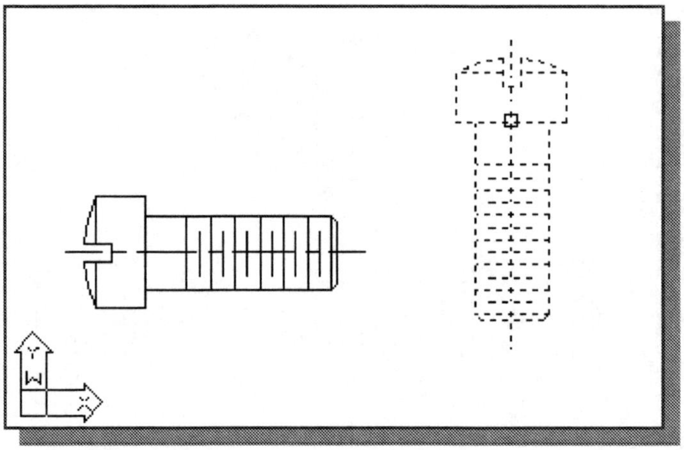

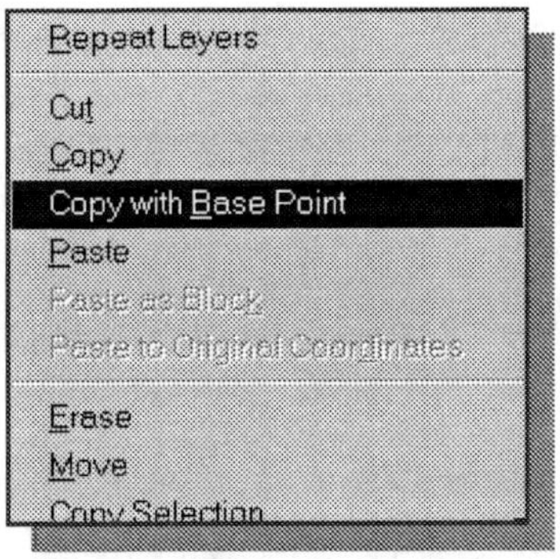

3. Inside the graphics window, **right-mouse-click** and select the **Copy with Base Point** option.

4. Pick the ***grip point*** as the copy base point.

5. Set the ***Drawing1*** window as the *current window* by left-mouse-clicking inside the window.

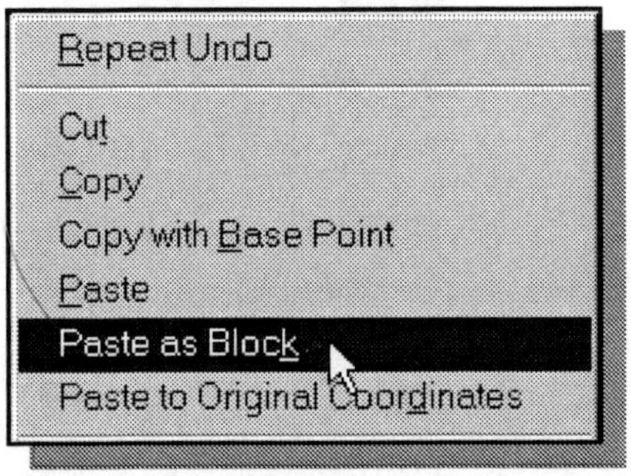

6. Inside the graphics window, **right-mouse-click** and select the **Paste** option.

7. Align the *Cap-Screw* as shown.

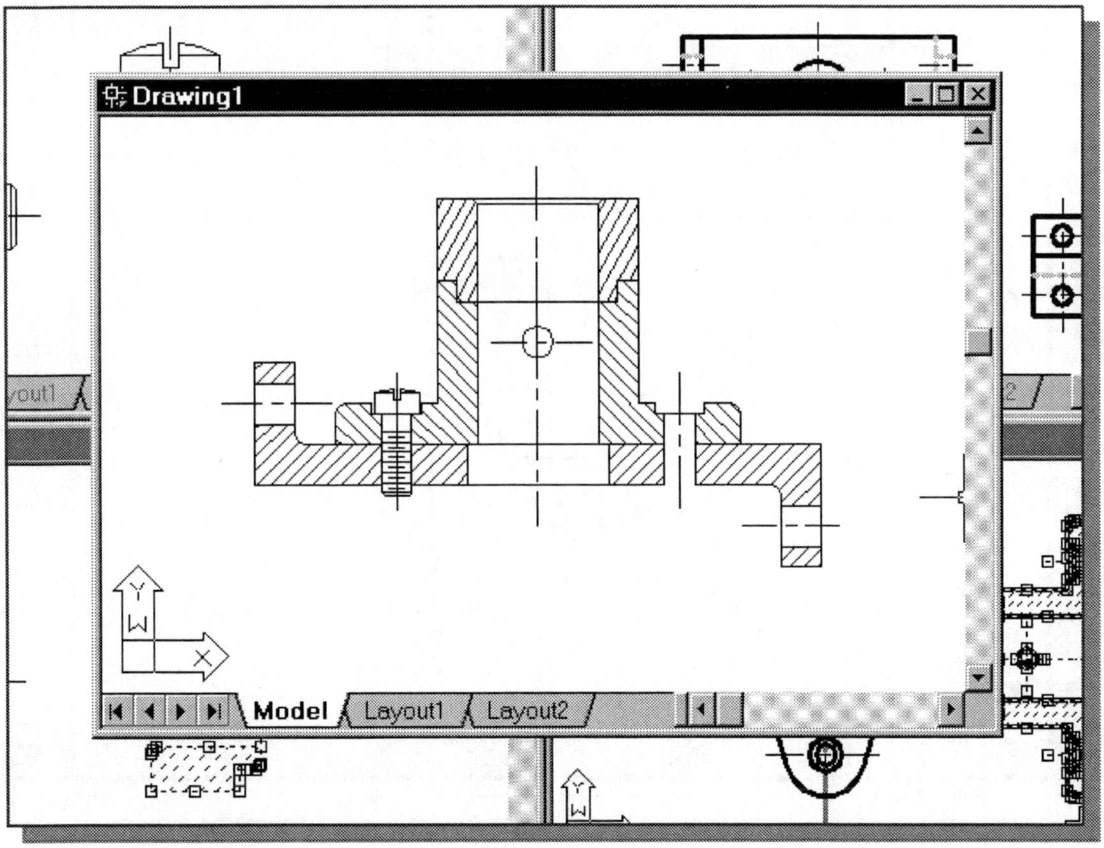

➢ On your own, repeat the steps and place another copy of the *Cap-Screw* in place.

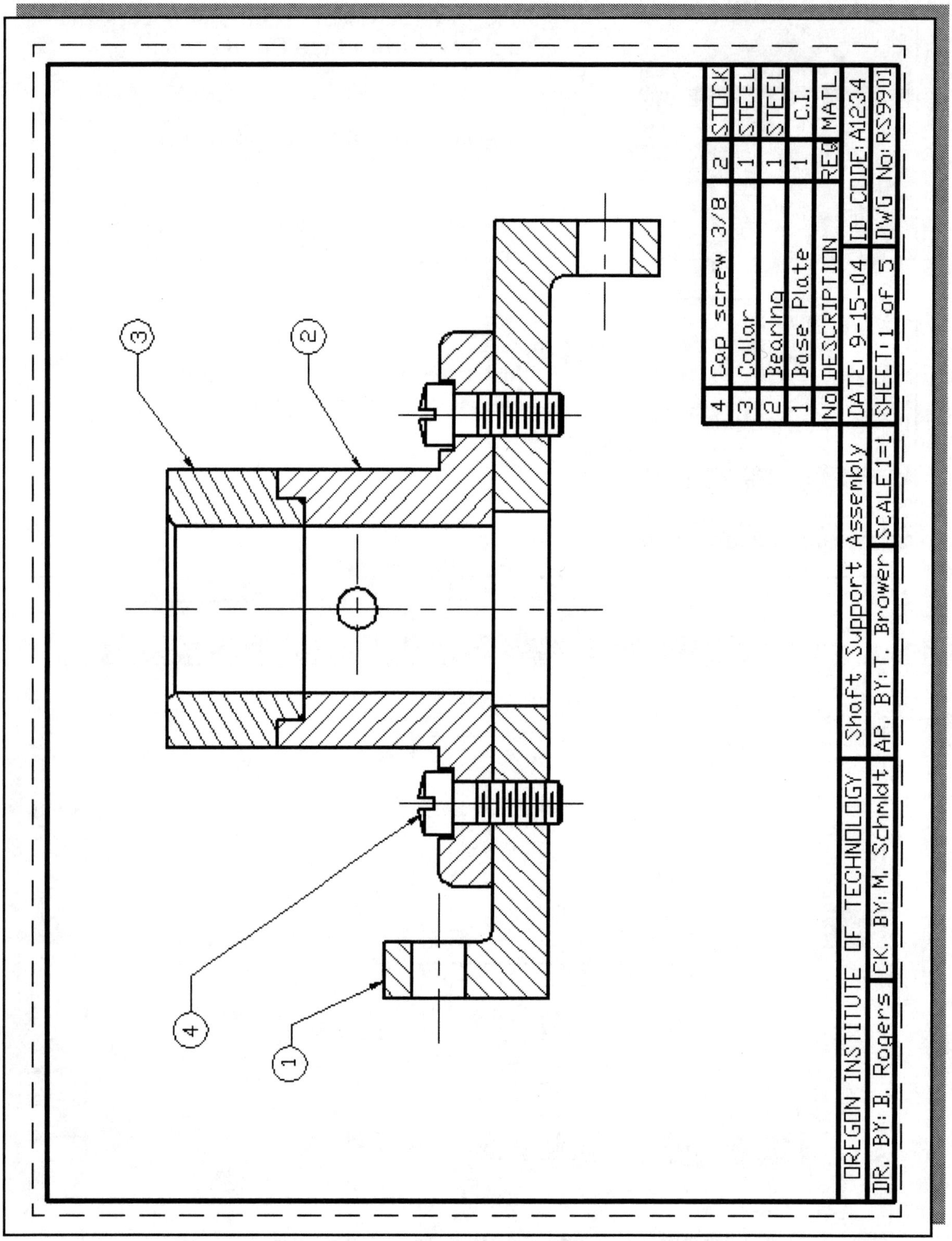

1
2
3
4
4 Cap screw 3/8 2 STOCK
3 Collar 1 STEEL
2 Bearing 1 STEEL
1 Base Plate 1 C.I.
No DESCRIPTION REQ MATL
OREGON INSTITUTE OF TECHNOLOGY
Shaft Support Assembly
DATE: 9-15-04
ID CODE: A1234
DR. BY: B. Rogers
CK. BY: M. Schmidt
AP. BY: T. Brower
SCALE 1=1
SHEET 1 of 5
DWG No: RS9901

Questions:

1. What is an *assembly drawing*? What are the basic differences between an assembly drawing and a detail drawing?

2. What is a *block*? List some the advantages of using blocks in AutoCAD LT.

3. What are the differences between "*Copying and pasting with the Windows Clipboard*" and "*Copying with GRIPS*"?

4. Which command allows us to separate a block into its component objects?

5. Describe the differences between Paste and Paste as Block.

6. Identify the following commands:

(a)

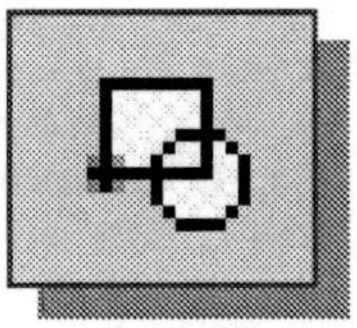

(b)

(c)

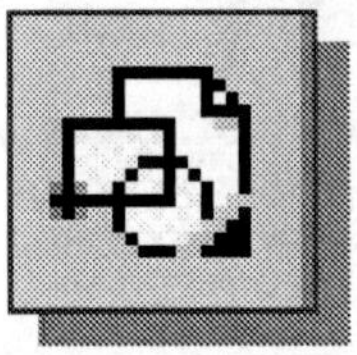

(d)

Exercises:

1. **Wheel Assembly**
   Create a set of detail and assembly drawings. (Dimensions are in mm.)

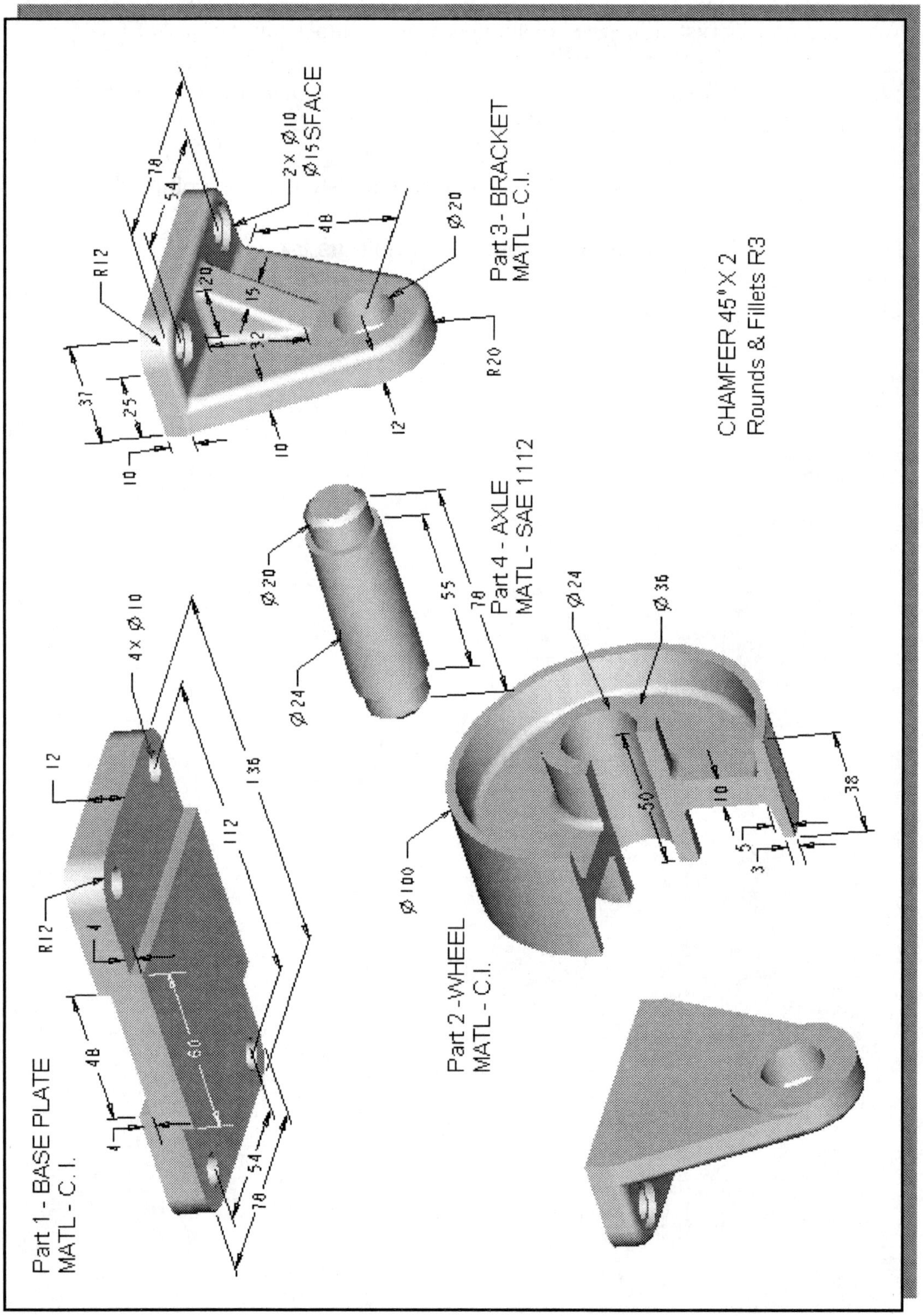

2. **Leveling Assembly**
   Create a set of detail and assembly drawings. (Dimensions are in mm.)

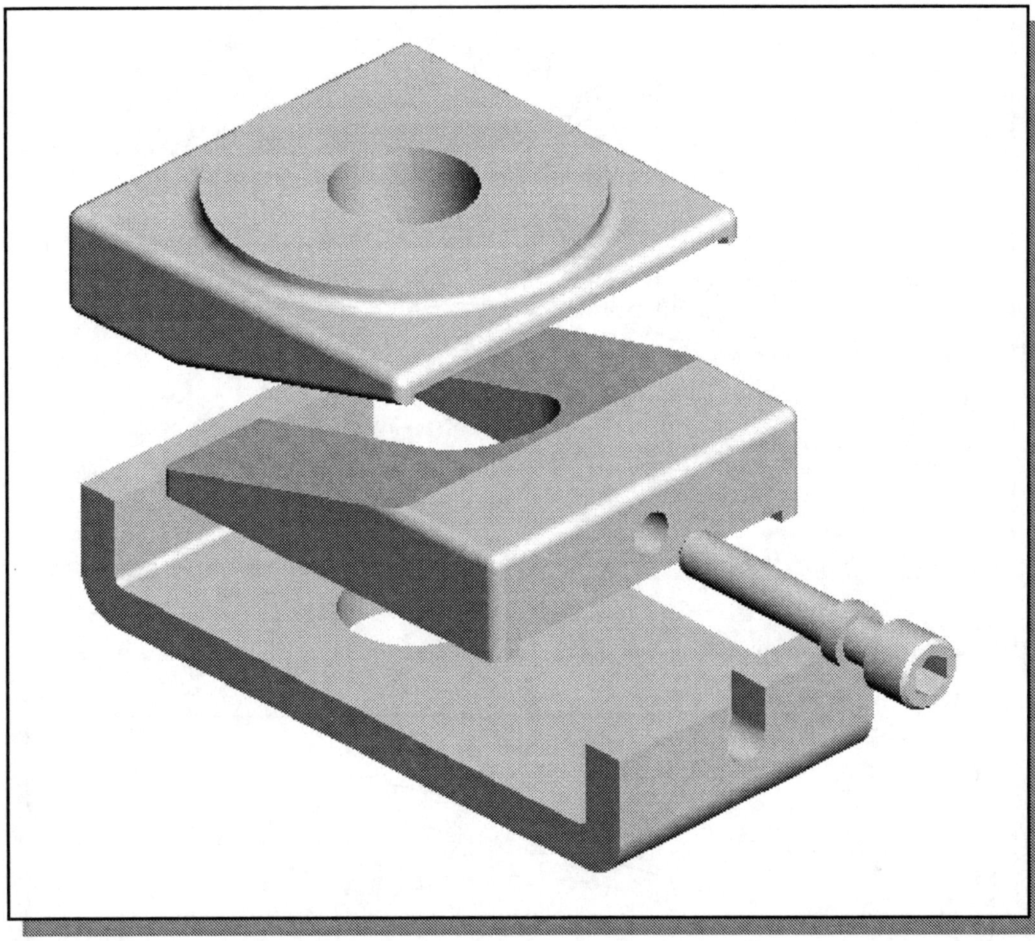

(a) **Base Plate**

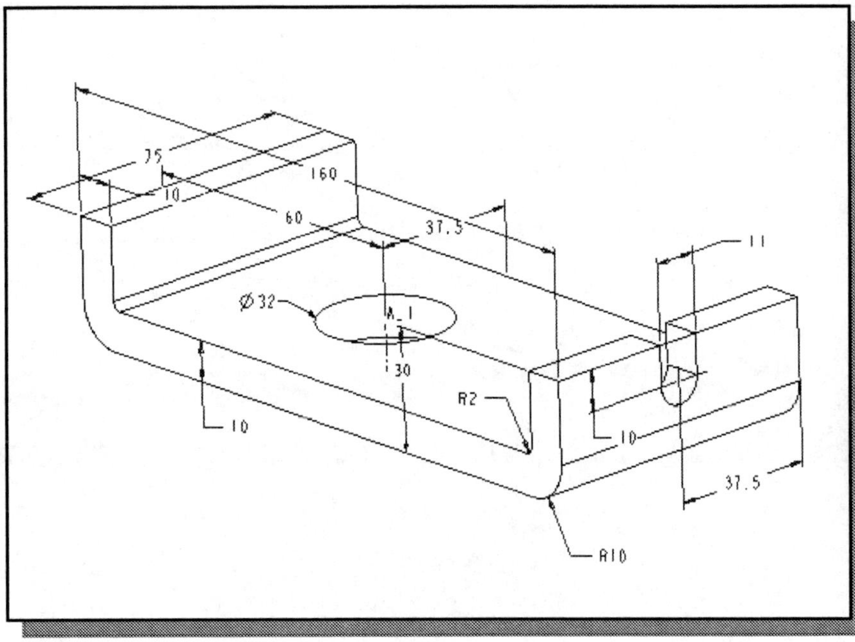

(b) **Sliding Block** (Rounds & Fillets: R3)

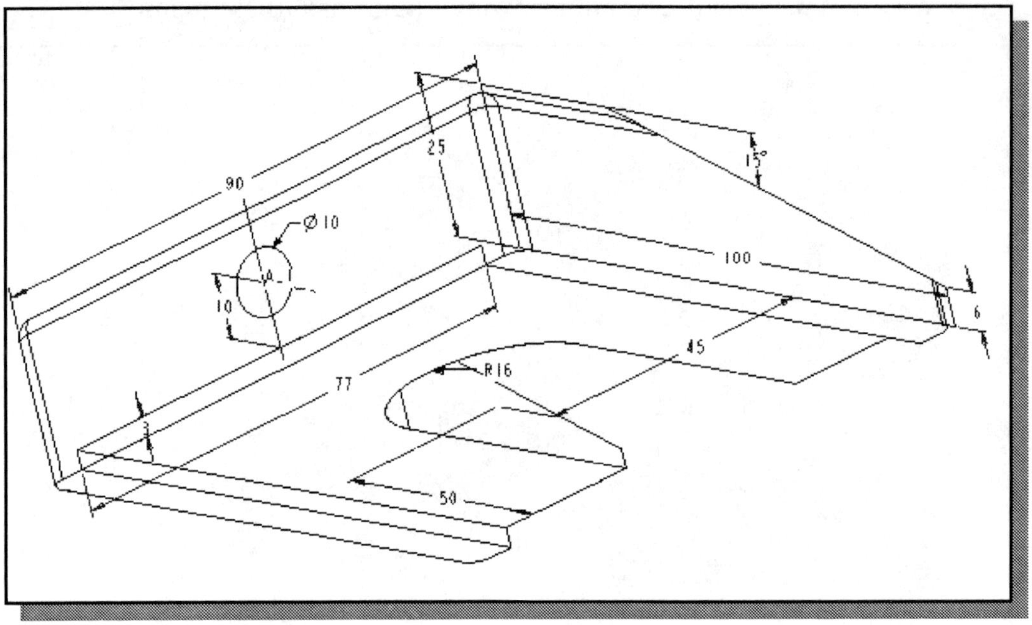

(c) **Lifting Block** (Rounds & Fillets: R3)

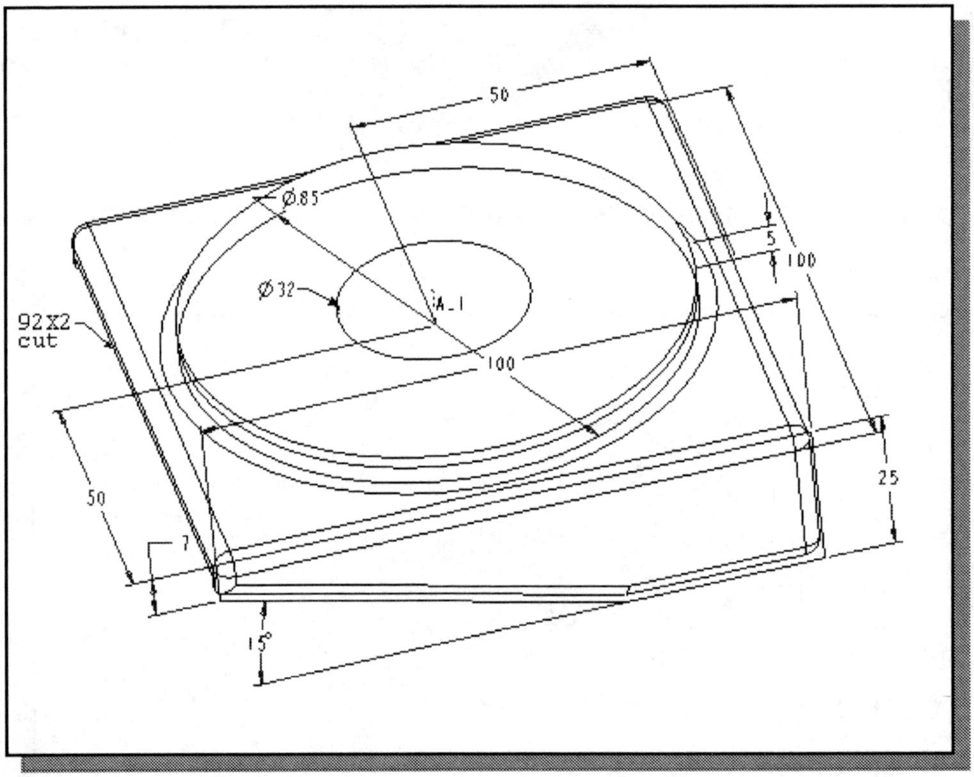

(d) **Adjusting Screw** (M10 × 1.5)

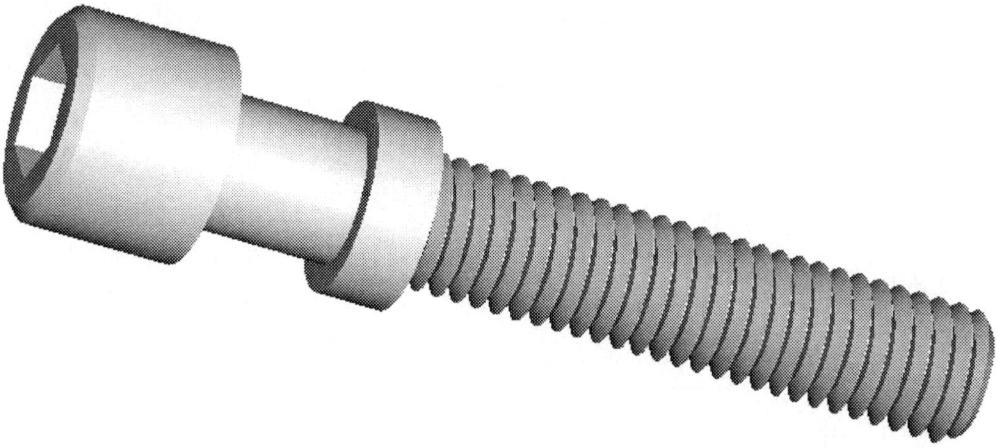

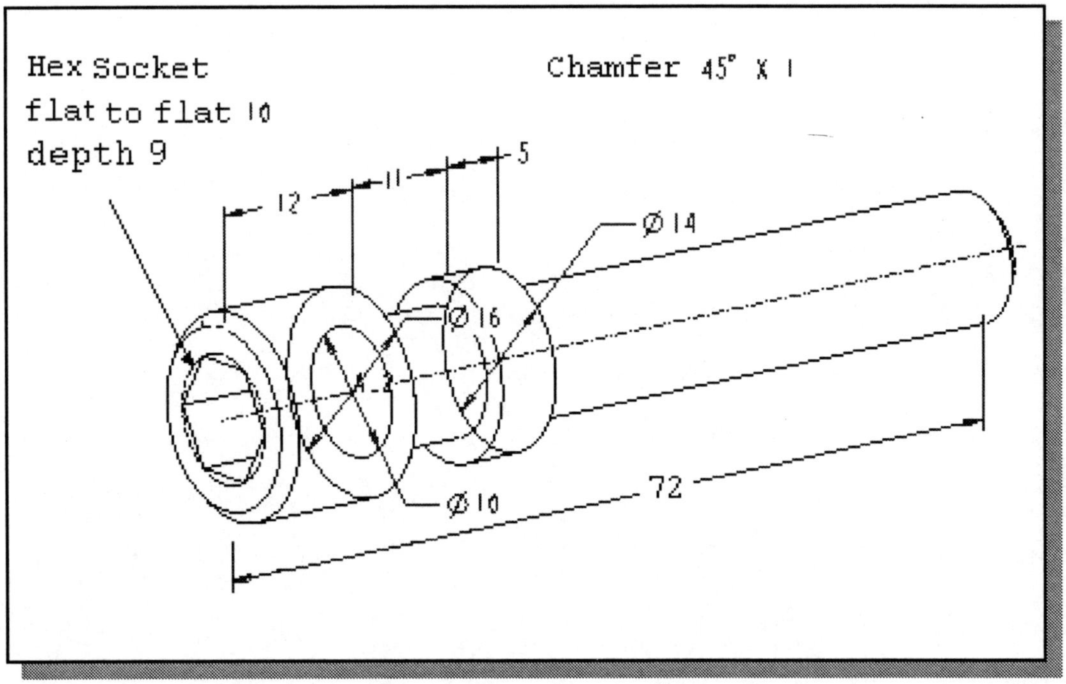

Notes:

Lesson 10
3D Wireframe Modeling

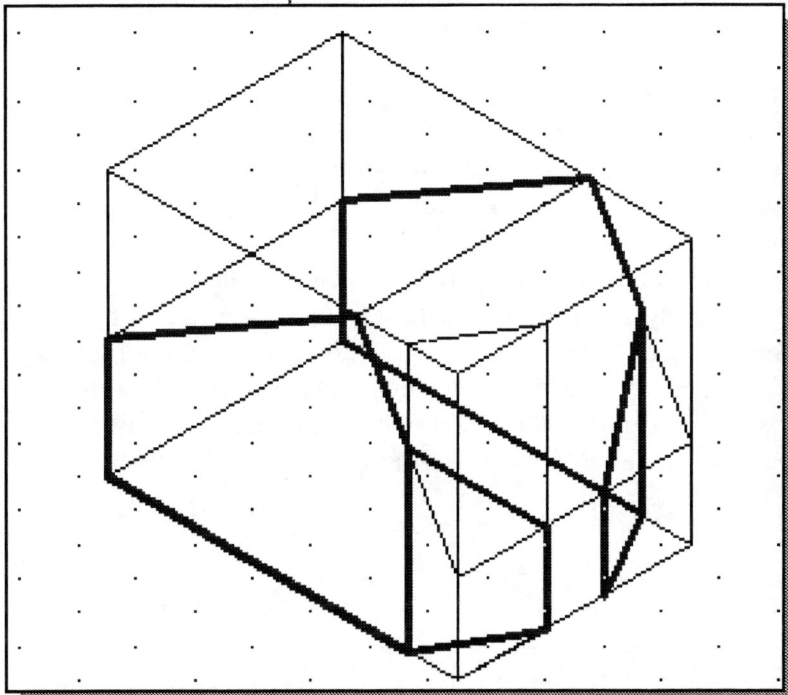

Learning Objectives

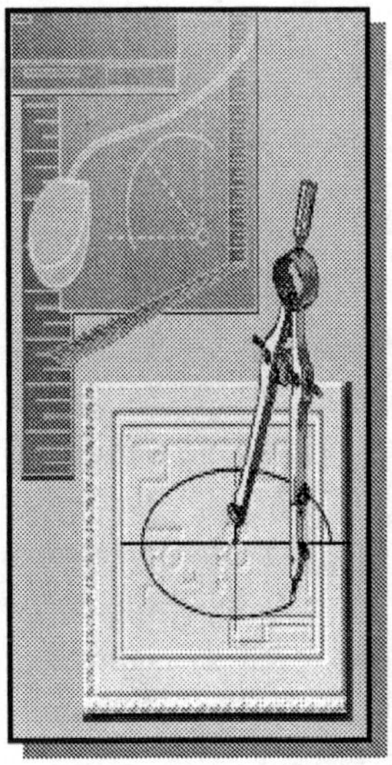

- ♦ Create 3D Wireframe Models
- ♦ Display and Orient 3D Views
- ♦ Understand and Apply the Basic Wireframe Construction Techniques
- ♦ Understand the Use of UCS
- ♦ Use the Named Views Option

Introduction

Design includes all activities involved from the original concept to the finished product. Design is the process by which products are created and modified. For many years designers sought ways to describe and analyze three-dimensional designs without building physical models. Although orthographic projections can be used to provide much of the information, they still require the designers to translate between the three-dimensional object and flat two-dimensional views. With the advancements in computer technology, the creation of three-dimensional models on computers offers a wide range of benefits. Computer models are easier to interpret and can be altered easily. Computer models can be analyzed using finite element analysis software, and simulation of real-life loads can be applied to the computer models and the results graphically displayed.

There are three basic types of three-dimensional computer geometric modeling methods: wireframe modeling, surface modeling, and solid modeling. The 3D wireframe models contain information about the locations of all the points and edges in space coordinates. The 3D models can be viewed from any direction as needed and are reasonably good representations of 3D objects. But because surface definition is not part of a wireframe model, all wireframe images have the inherent problem of ambiguity.

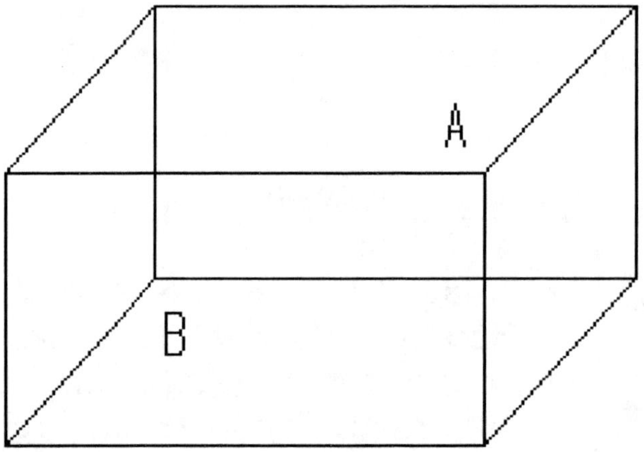

Wireframe Ambiguity: Which corner is in front, A or B?

Surface modeling describes part surfaces but not interiors. Designers are still required to interactively examine surface models to insure that the various surfaces on a model are contiguous throughout. Many of the concepts used in 3D wireframe and surface modelers are incorporated in the solid modeling scheme, but it is solid modeling that offers the most advantages as a design tool.

In the solid modeling presentation scheme, the solid definitions include nodes, edges, and surfaces, and it is a complete and unambiguous mathematical representation of a precisely enclosed and filled volume. Two predominant methods for representing solid models are the **constructive solid geometry** (CSG) representation and **the boundary representation** (B-rep). CSG defines a model in terms of combining basic solid shapes and B-rep defines a model in terms of its edges and surfaces.

In this lesson, we will discuss the fundamental concepts of 3D wireframe modeling. AutoCAD LT can be used to create 3D wireframe models, models that contain information about the locations of all the points and edges in space coordinates. Wireframe models often are used to represent the skeleton of designs. Many of the concepts and construction techniques used in wireframe modeling are also applicable to surface and solid modeling. As a comparison, the construction of a 3D wireframe model of the *V-Block* design from Lesson 7 will be illustrated.

The *V-Block* Design

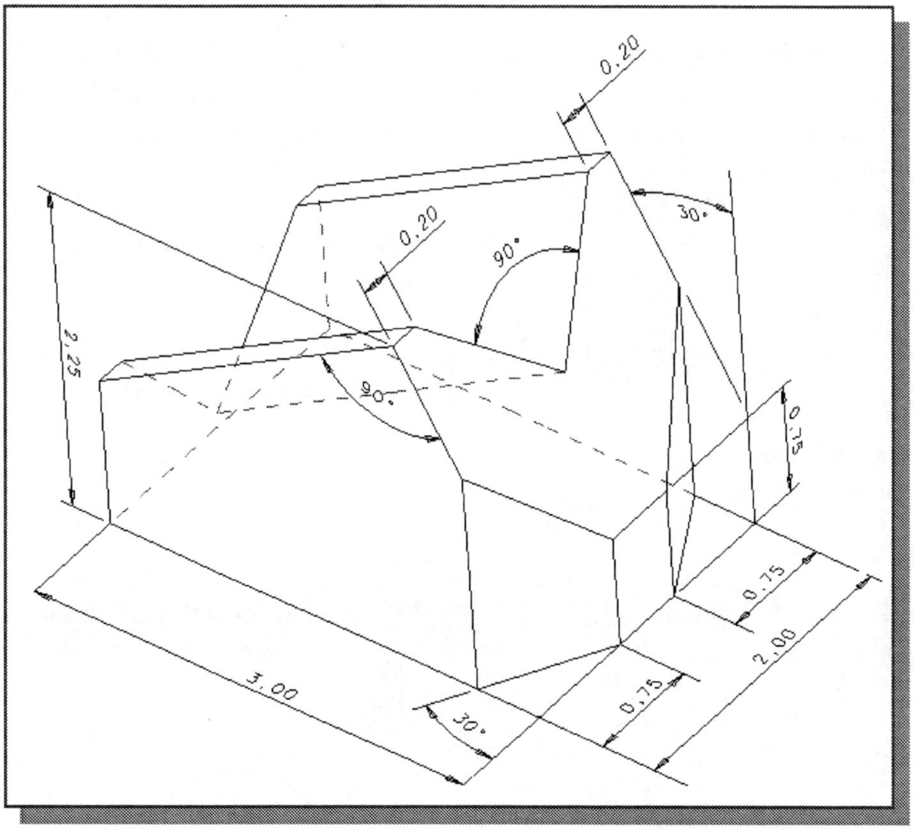

Starting Up *AutoCAD LT 2005*

1. Select the **AutoCAD LT 2005** option on the *Program* menu or select the **AutoCAD LT 2005** icon on the *Desktop*.

2. In the *Startup* dialog box, select the ***Use a Template*** option with a single click of the left-mouse-button.

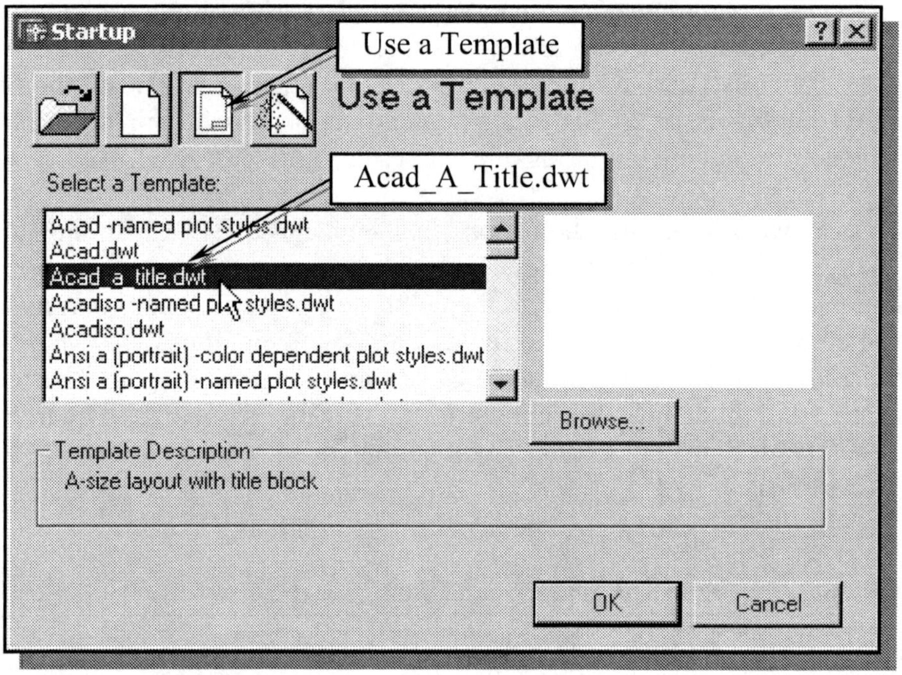

3. Select the ***Acad_A_Title*** template file from the list of template files. If the file is saved in a separate folder, click on the **Browse** button to locate the file.

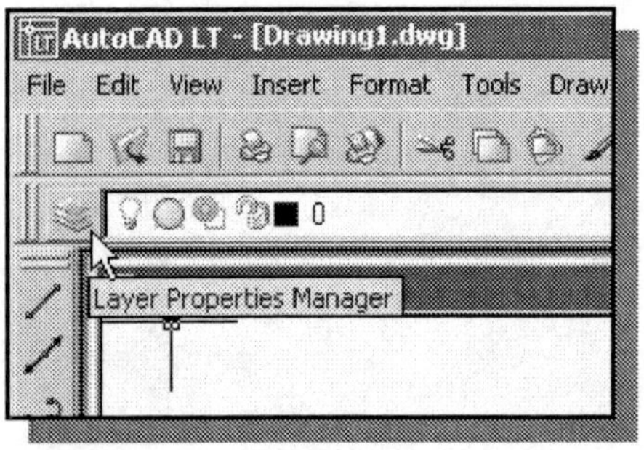

4. Pick **Layer Properties Manager** in the *Object Properties* toolbar.

5. Examine the layer property settings in the *Layer Properties Manager* dialog box.

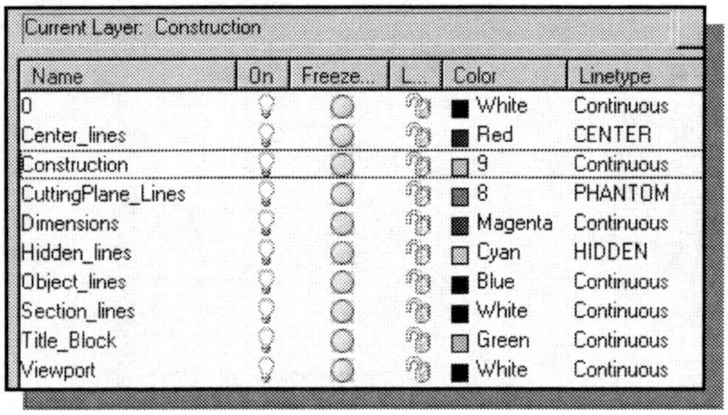

6. Click on the **OK** button to exit the *Layer Properties Manager* dialog box.

The 2D Sketch of the Base

We will first use construction geometry to define the outer edges of the design.

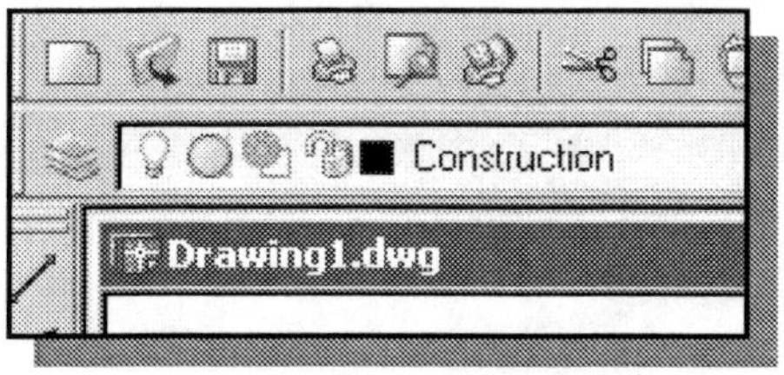

1. In the ***Layer Control*** box, confirm that layer *Construction* is set as the *Current Layer*.

2. In the *Status Bar* area, reset the options and turn ***ON*** the *GRID, POLAR, OSNAP, LWT* and *MODEL* options.

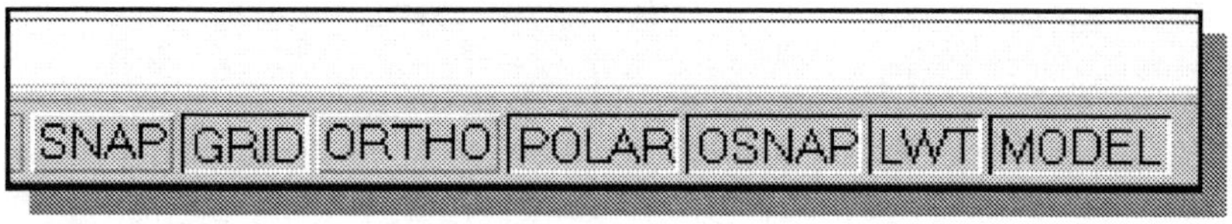

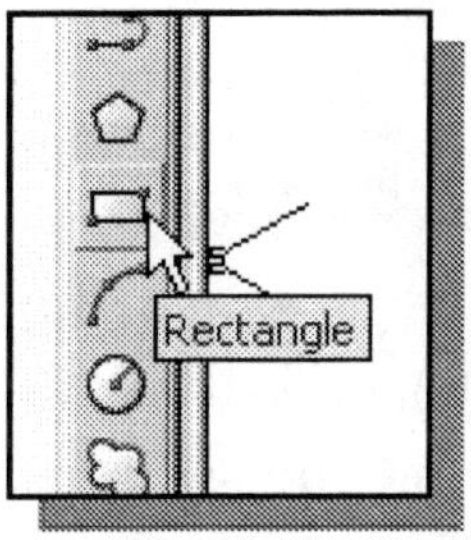

3. Select the **Rectangle** icon in the *Draw* toolbar. In the command prompt area, the message *"Specify first corner point or [Chamfer/Elevation/Fillet/Thickness/Width]:"* is displayed.

4. Place the first corner point of the rectangle near the lower left corner of the screen. Do not be overly concerned about the actual coordinates of the location; the drawing space is as big as you can imagine.

5. Next, create a 3″ x 2″ rectangle by entering **@3,2 [ENTER]**

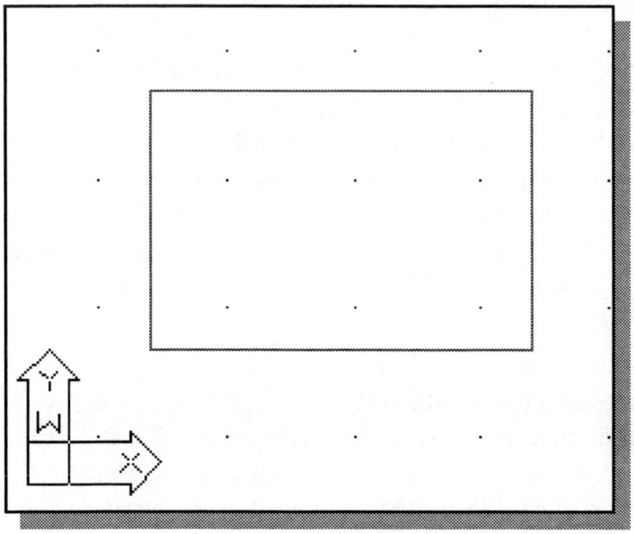

➢ The **Rectangle** command creates rectangles as *polyline* features, which means all segments of a rectangle are created as a single object.

UCS – It is an XY CRT, but an XYZ World

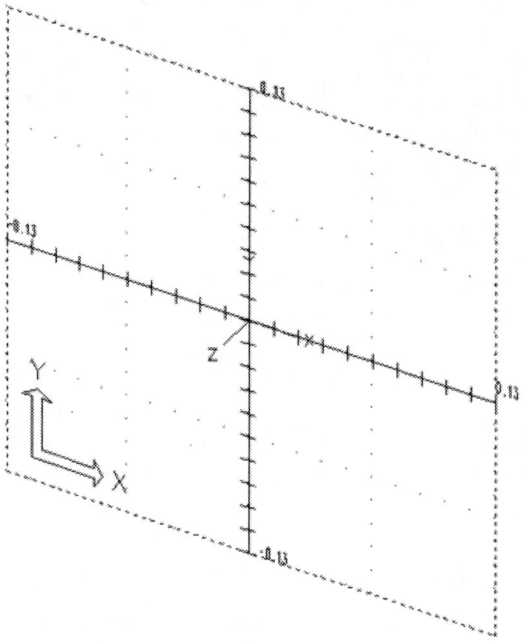

Design modeling software is becoming more powerful and user friendly, yet the system still does only what the user tells it to do. When using a geometric modeler, we therefore need to have a good understanding of what its inherent limitations are. We should also have a good understanding of what we want to do and what to expect as the results are based on what is available.

In most 3D geometric modelers, 3D objects are located and defined in what is usually called **world space** or **global space**. Although a number of different coordinate systems can be used to create and manipulate objects in a 3D modeling system, the objects are typically defined and stored using the world space. The world space is usually a **3D Cartesian coordinate system** that the user cannot change or manipulate.
In most engineering designs, models can be very complex, and it would be tedious and confusing if only the world coordinate system were available. Practical 3D modeling systems allow the user to define **Local Coordinate Systems (LCS)** or **User Coordinate Systems (UCS)** relative to the world coordinate system. Once a local coordinate system is defined, we can then create geometry in terms of this more convenient system.

Although objects are created and stored in 3D space coordinates, most of the geometry entities can be referenced using 2D Cartesian coordinate systems. Typical input devices such as a mouse or digitizer are two-dimensional by nature; the movement of the input device is interpreted by the system in a planar sense. The same limitation is true of common output devices, such as CRT displays and plotters. The modeling software performs a series of three-dimensional to two-dimensional transformations to correctly project 3D objects onto a 2D picture plane.

AutoCAD LT's **User Coordinate System (*UCS)*** is a special construction tool that enables the planar nature of the 2D input devices to be directly mapped into the 3D coordinate system. The **UCS** is a local coordinate system that can be aligned to the world coordinate system, an existing face of a part, or a pre-defined plane. By default, the UCS is aligned to the XY plane of the world coordinate system.

Think of UCS as the surface on which we can sketch the 2D profiles of the parts. It is similar to a piece of paper, a white board, or a chalkboard that can be attached to any planar surfaces. In the previous lessons, we used the default settings where the UCS is aligned to the XY plane of the world coordinate system.

Viewing the 2D Sketch in 3D Space

1. In the pull-down menus, select
   [View] → [3D Views] → [SE Isometric]

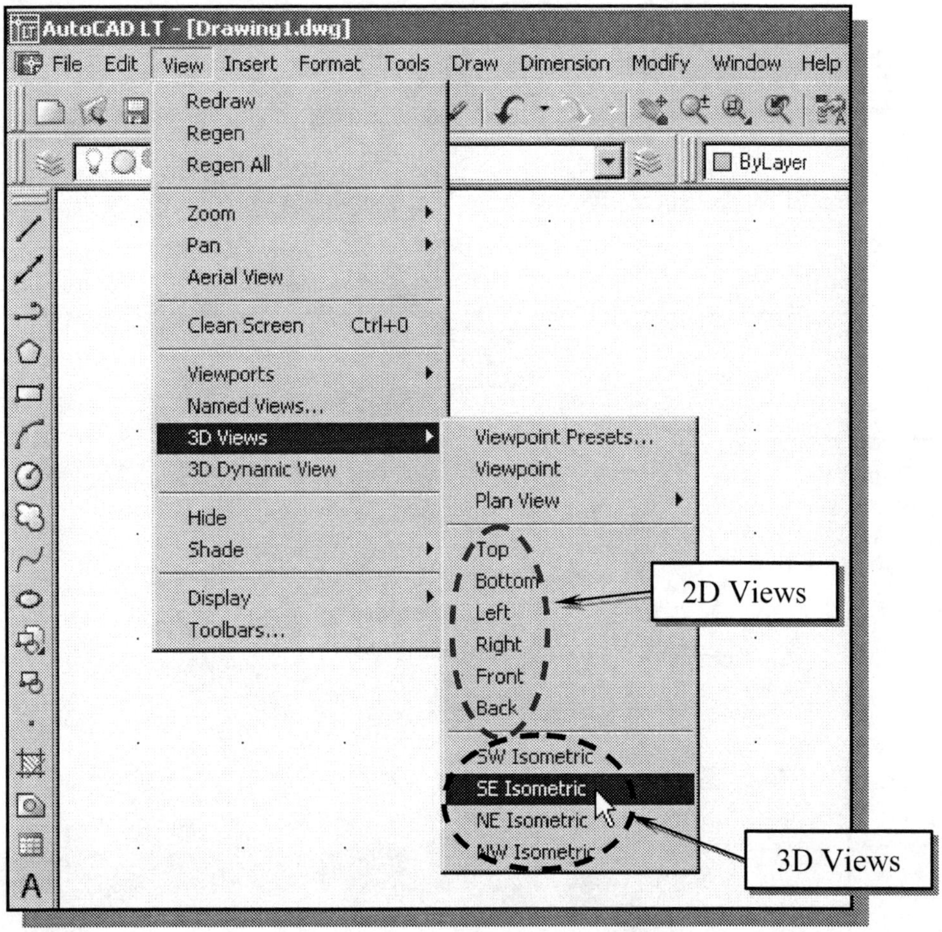

❖ AutoCAD LT provides a set of pre-defined views, which contains most of the standard 2D and 3D views as shown in the figure.

➢ The pre-defined **SE Isometric** view is oriented as shown in the below figure.

➢ The orientations of the preset views are based on the world coordinate system as shown below.

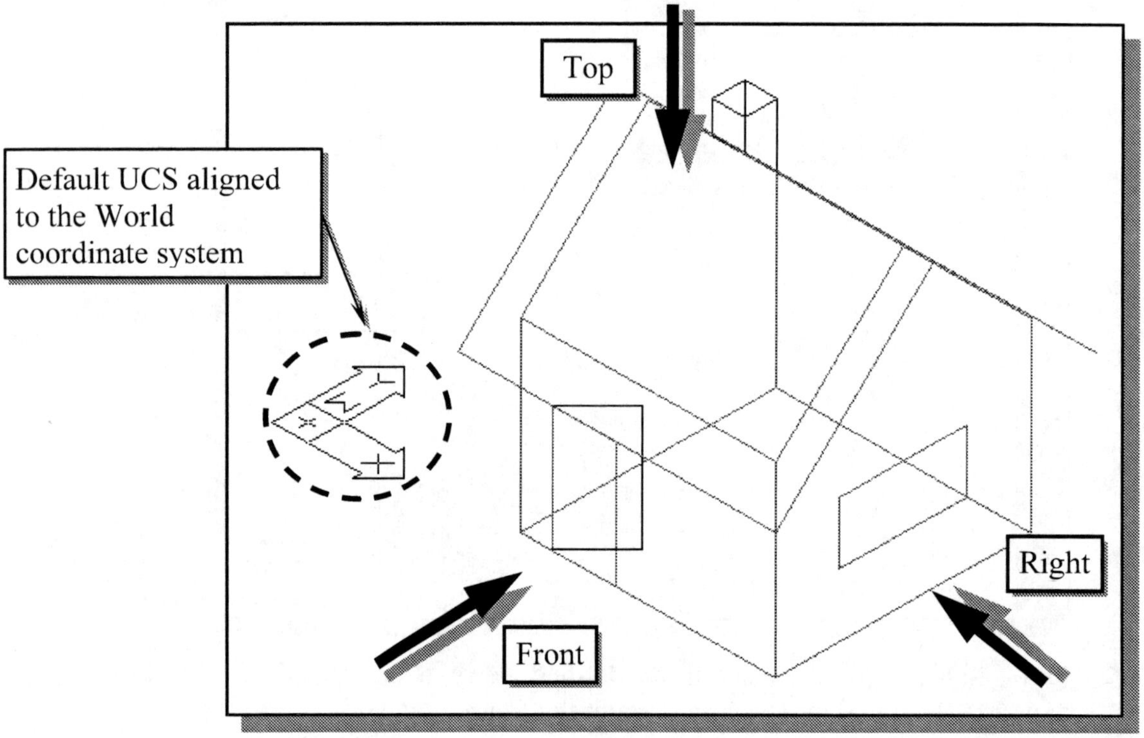

Creating a Wireframe Box

Next, we will use the **Copy Object** command to define the 3D boundary of the design.

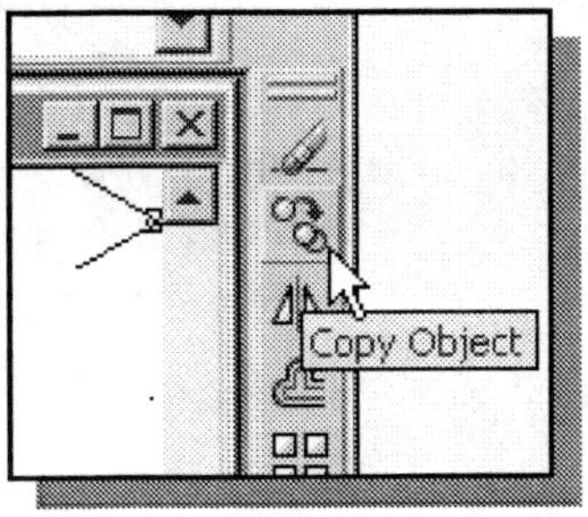

1. Click on the **Copy Object** icon in the *Modify* toolbar.

2. In the command prompt area, the message *"Select objects:"* is displayed. Pick any edge of the sketched rectangle.

3. In the command prompt area, the message *"Specify base point or displacement, or [Multiple]:"* is displayed. Pick any corner of the sketched rectangle as a base point to create the copy.

4. In the command prompt area, the message *"Specify second point of displacement or <use first point as displacement>:"* is displayed.

   Enter **@0,0,2.25** [**ENTER**]

➢ Note that the three values represent the distance measured in the X, Y and Z directions relative to the current UCS.

5. Use the **Zoom All** command to adjust the display.

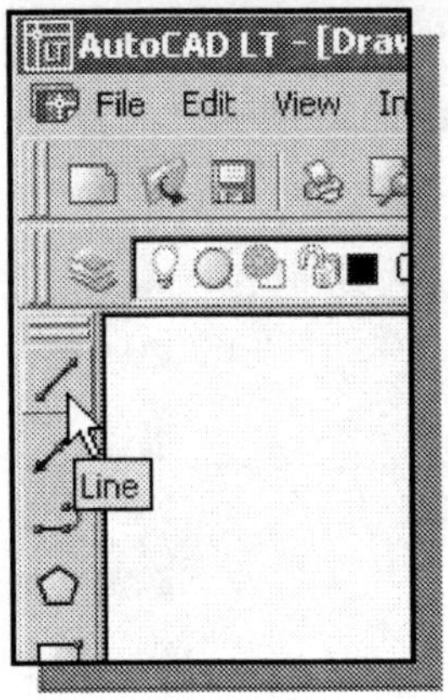

6. On your own, create four lines connecting the four corners of the two rectangles as shown below.

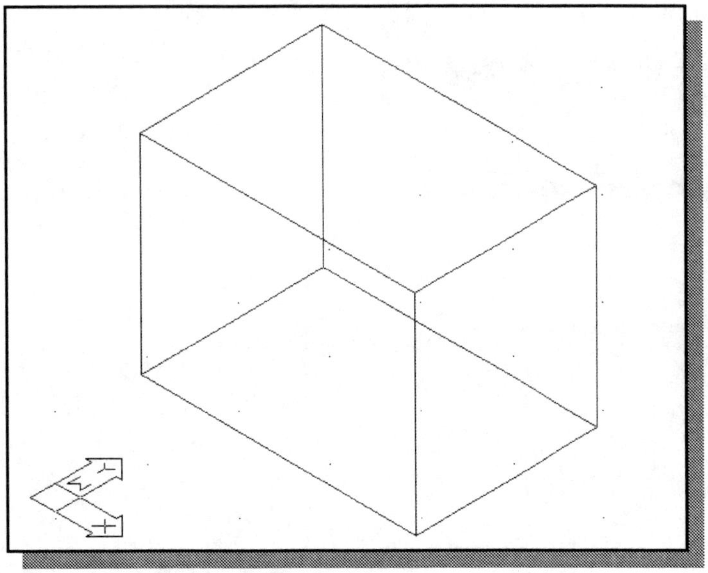

Using the *View* and *UCS* Toolbars

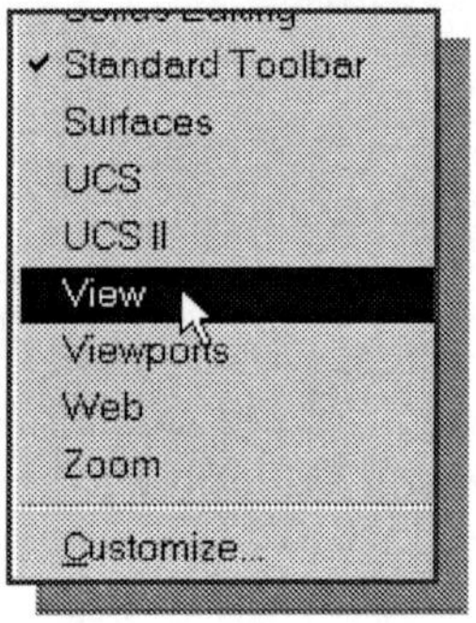

1. Move the cursor to the *Standard* toolbar area and **right-click** on any icon of the *Standard* toolbar to display a list of toolbar menu groups.

2. Select **View**, with the left-mouse-button, to display the *View* toolbar on the screen.

➢ The *View* toolbar contains two sections of icons that allow us to quickly switch to standard 2D and 3D views.

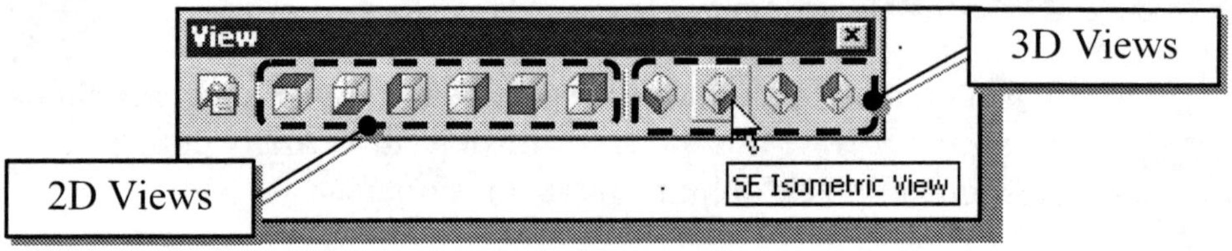

3. On your own, examine the wireframe model by using the different icons in the *View* toolbar. Reset the display to **SE Isometric View** before continuing.

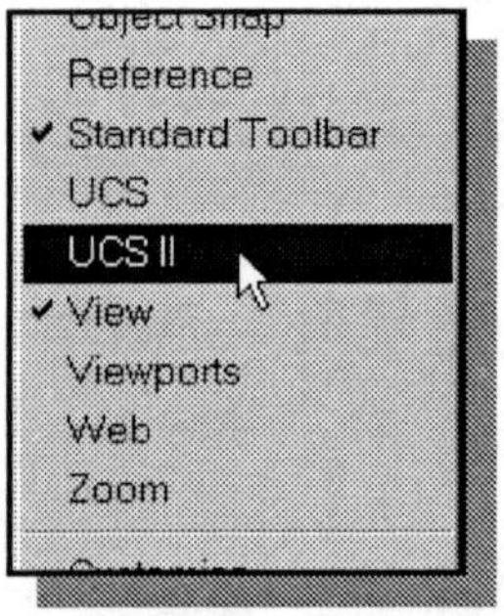

4. Move the cursor to the *Standard* toolbar area and right-click on any icon of the *Standard* toolbar to display a list of toolbar menu groups.

5. Select **UCS II**, with the left-mouse-button, to display the *UCSII* toolbar on the screen.

❖ The options available in *UCS II* toolbar allow us quickly align the UCS to the standard 2D views.

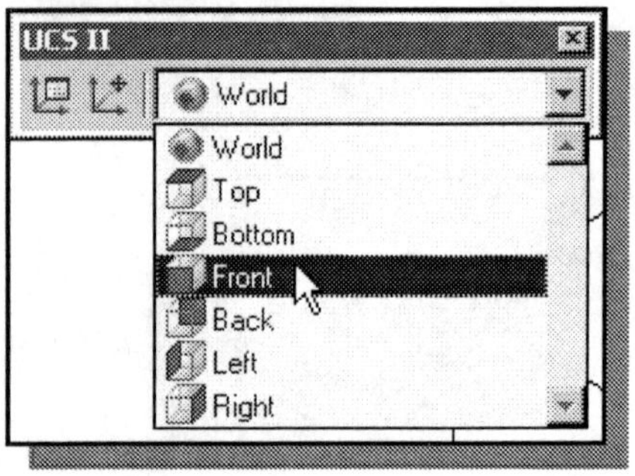

6. Note that the current UCS is aligned to the *World Coordinate System*. Select **Front** in the *UCS II* toolbar as shown.

➢ Note that the **UCS** icon is rotated and it is now aligned to the front view of the wireframe box as shown below.

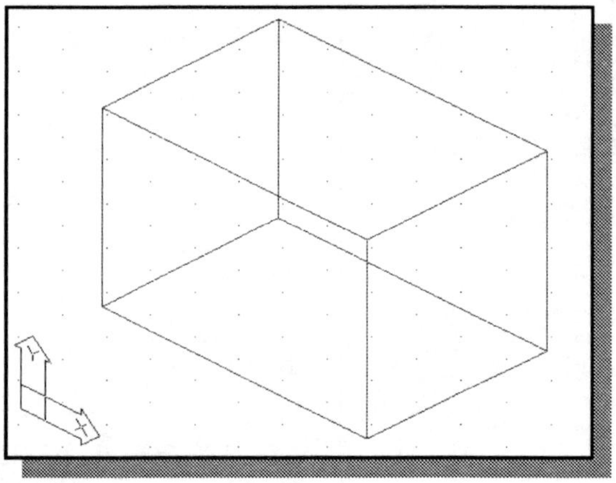

Creating Construction Lines in the Front View

1. Select the **Line** command icon in the *Draw* toolbar. In the command prompt area, the message *"_line Specify first point:"* is displayed.

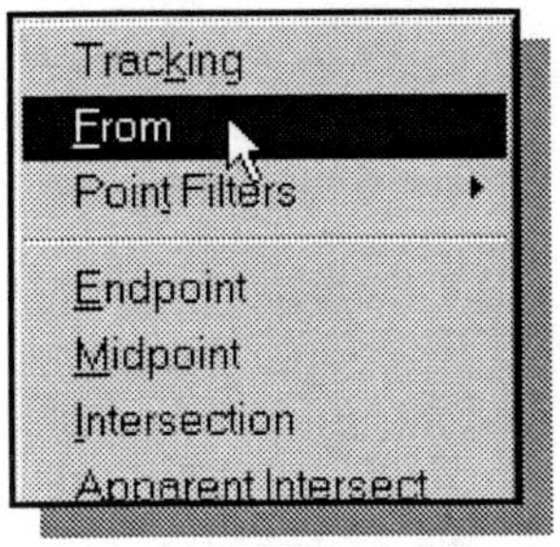

2. Inside the graphics window, hold down the **[SHIFT]** key and **right-mouse-click** once to bring up the *Object Snap* shortcut menu.

3. Select the **From** option in popup window.

4. Pick the lower right corner of the bottom horizontal line in the front view as the base point. Enter **@0,0.75 [ENTER]**

5. In the command prompt area, the message *"Specify next point or [Undo]:"* is displayed. Using the *Polar Tracking* option (30 degrees increment), create a line as shown in the figure below.

6. On your own, create a second line that is perpendicular to the last line we created. (Hint: Use the relative angle input option.)

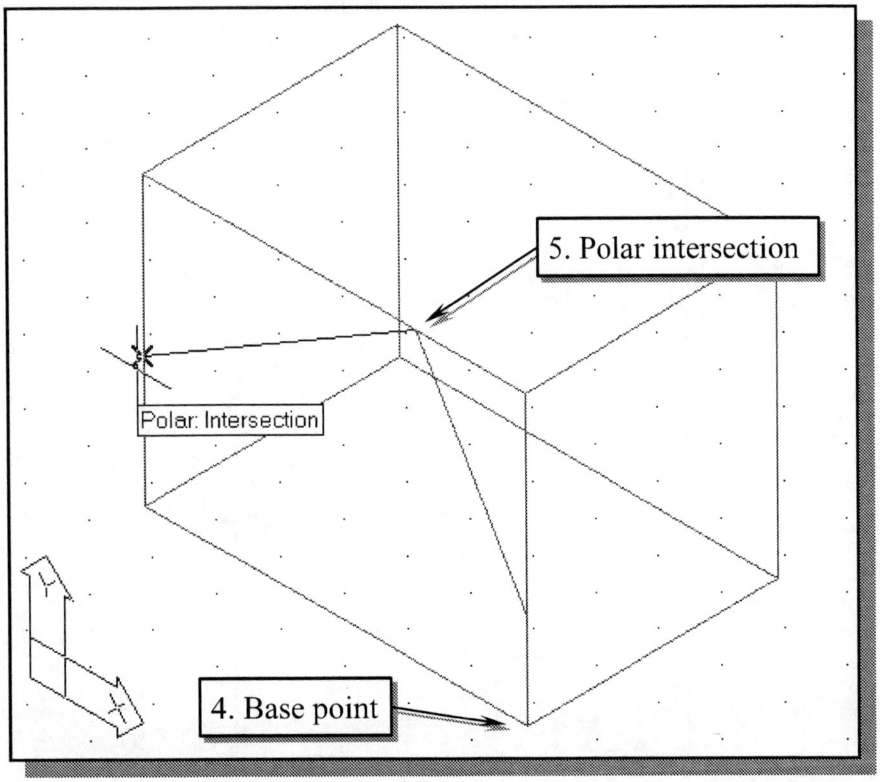

7. Inside the graphics window, right-mouse-click to activate the option menu and select **Enter** with the left-mouse-button to end the Line command.

Copying in the Negative Z Direction

1. Click on the **Copy Object** icon in the *Modify* toolbar.

2. In the command prompt area, the message *"Select objects:"* is displayed. Pick the two lines we just created.

3. In the command prompt area, the message *"Specify base point or displacement, or [Multiple]:"* is displayed. Pick any corner of the sketched rectangle as a base point to create the copy.

4. In the command prompt area, the message *"Specify second point of displacement or <use first point as displacement>:"* is displayed.

   Enter **@0,0,-2.0** **[ENTER]**

➤ Note that the negative value represents the distance measured in the negative Z direction relative to the current UCS.

5. On your own, create three lines to connect the corners of the two sets of lines we just created, as shown below.

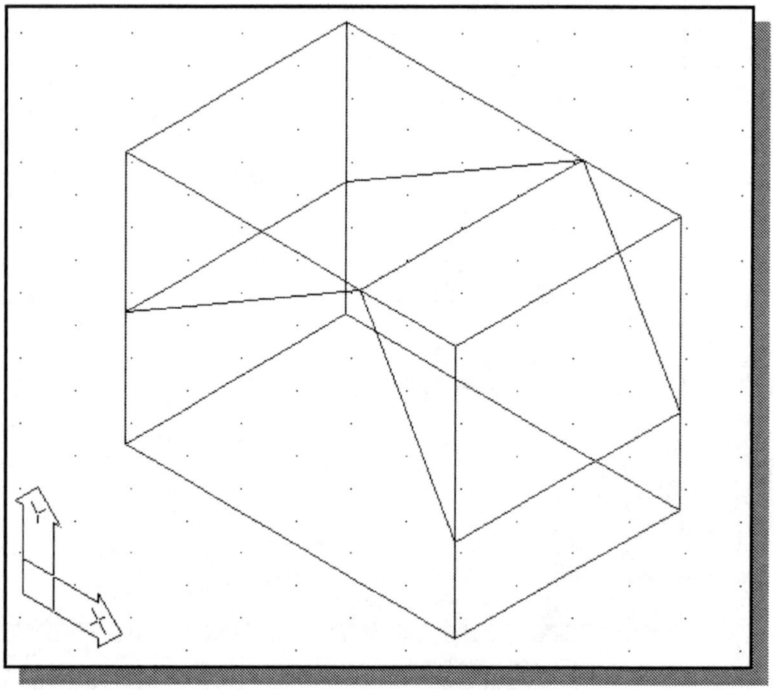

➤ In 3D wireframe modeling, the main emphasis is to establish the edges and corners of the design. The **Copy** option allows us to quickly establish planar edges and corners in the design.

Creating an Inclined Line at the Base of the Model

1. Select **Top** in the *UCS II* toolbar as shown.

2. Select the **Line** command icon in the *Draw* toolbar. In the command prompt area, the message *"_line Specify first point:"* is displayed.

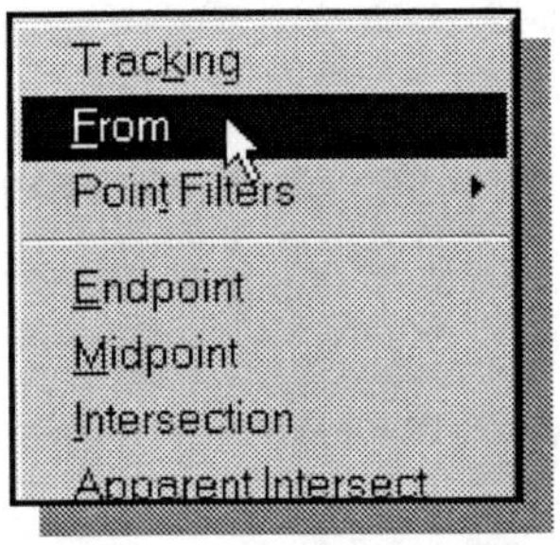

3. Inside the graphics window, hold down the **[SHIFT]** key and right-mouse-click once to bring up the *Object Snap* shortcut menu.

4. Select the **From** option in popup window.

5. Pick the lower right corner of the bottom horizontal line in the front view as the base point. Enter **@0,0.75 [ENTER]**

6. In the command prompt area, the message *"Specify next point or [Undo]:"* is displayed. Using the *Polar Tracking* option (30 degrees increment), create a line as shown in the below figure.

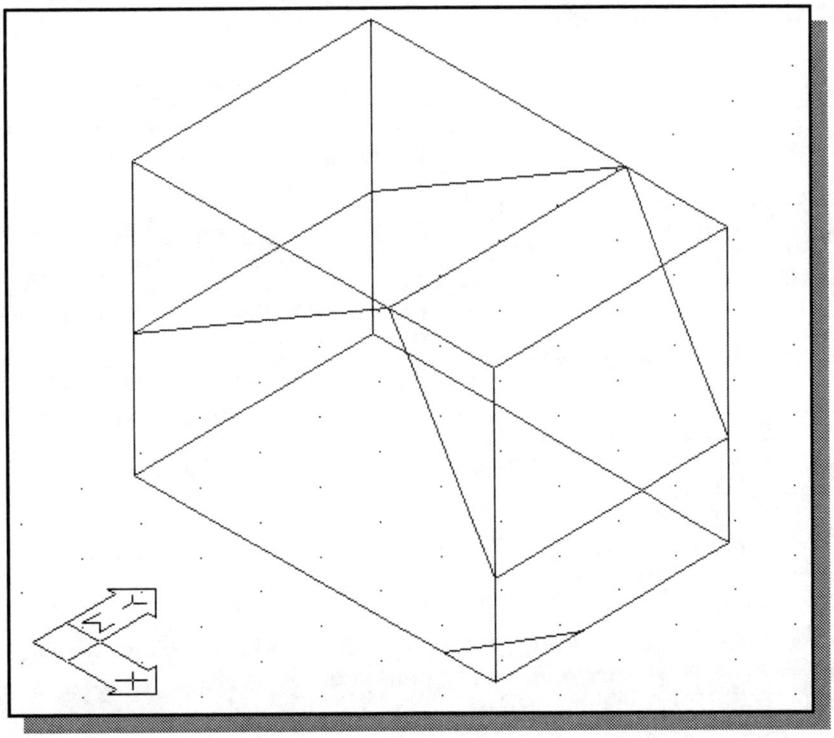

7. Inside the graphics window, right-mouse-click to activate the option menu and select **Enter** with the left-mouse-button to end the Line command.

➢ On your own, use the **Copy** and **Line** commands to create additional lines that the wireframe model appeared as shown below.

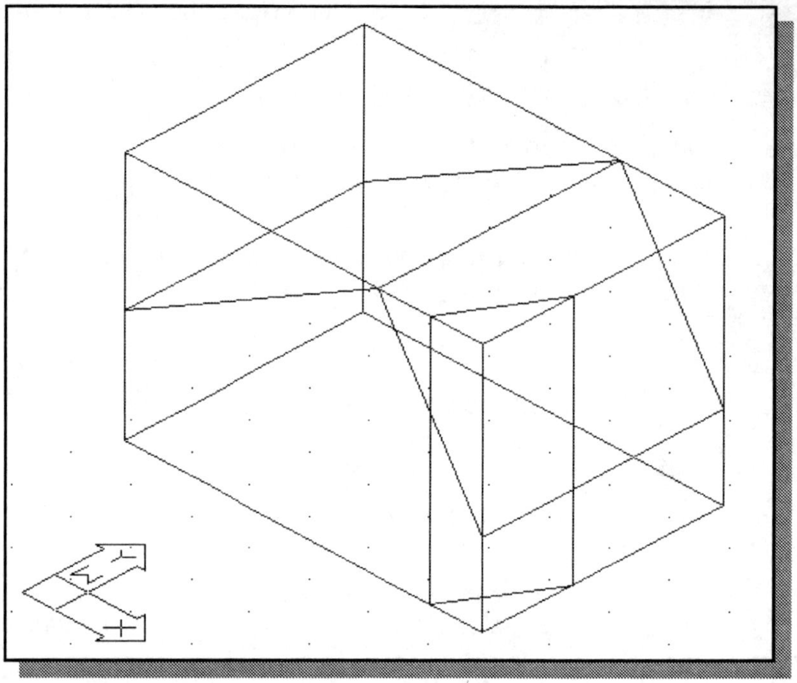

Creating Object Lines

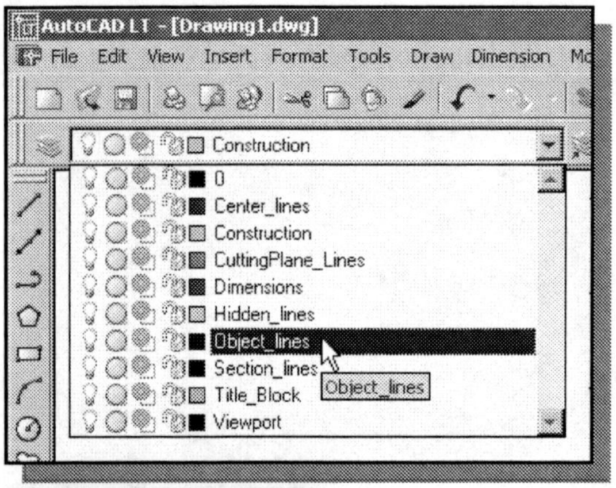

1. On the *Object Properties* toolbar, choose the ***Layer Control*** box with the left-mouse-button.

2. Move the cursor over the name of layer *Object_Lines*; the tool tip *"Object_Lines"* appears.

3. **Left-mouse-click once** and layer *Object_Lines* is set as the *Current Layer*.

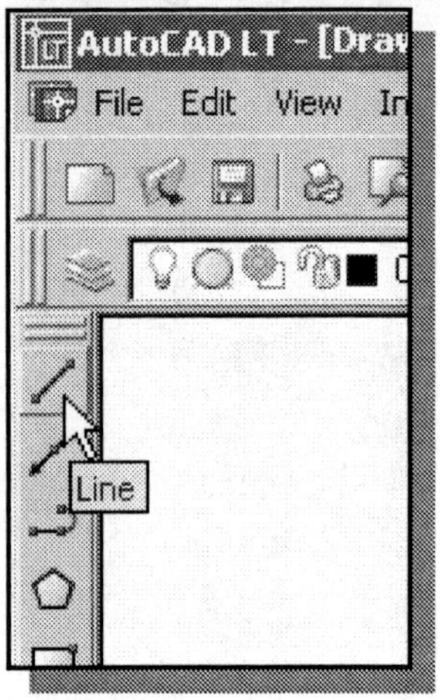

4. Select the **Line** command icon in the *Draw* toolbar. In the command prompt area, the message *"_line Specify first point:"* is displayed.

5. Pick the lower left corner of the bottom of the wireframe model as the starting point and create of the five line segments as shown.

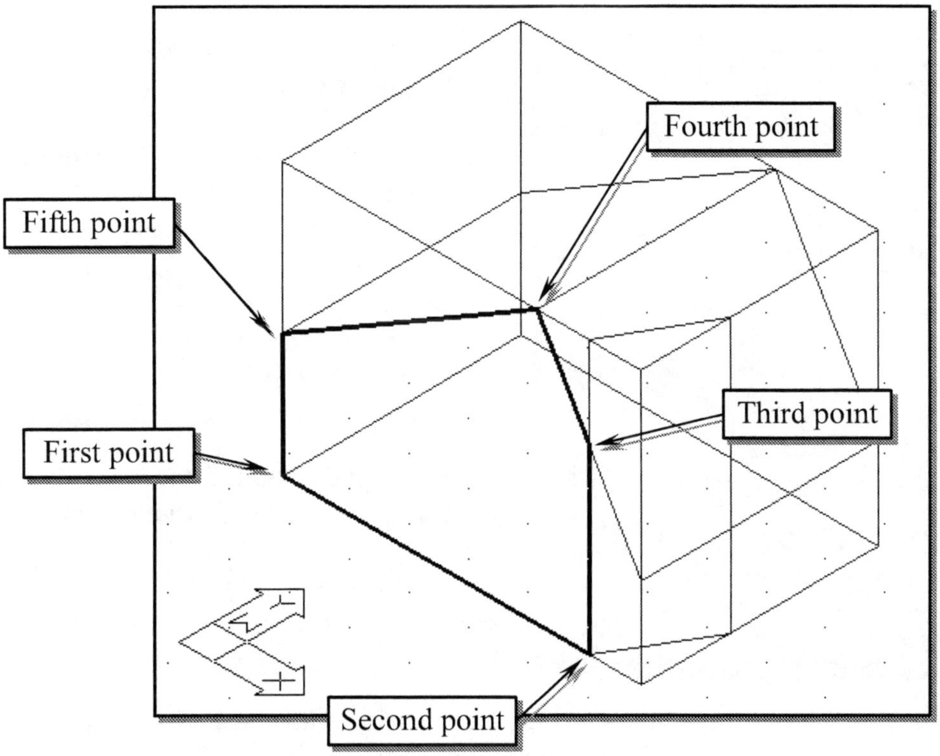

➢ Note that even though the UCS is aligned to the base plane of the model, the *OSNAP* option enables us to select points on the front plane of the model.

➢ On you own, create three additional lines representing the edges of the inclined face of the design as shown.

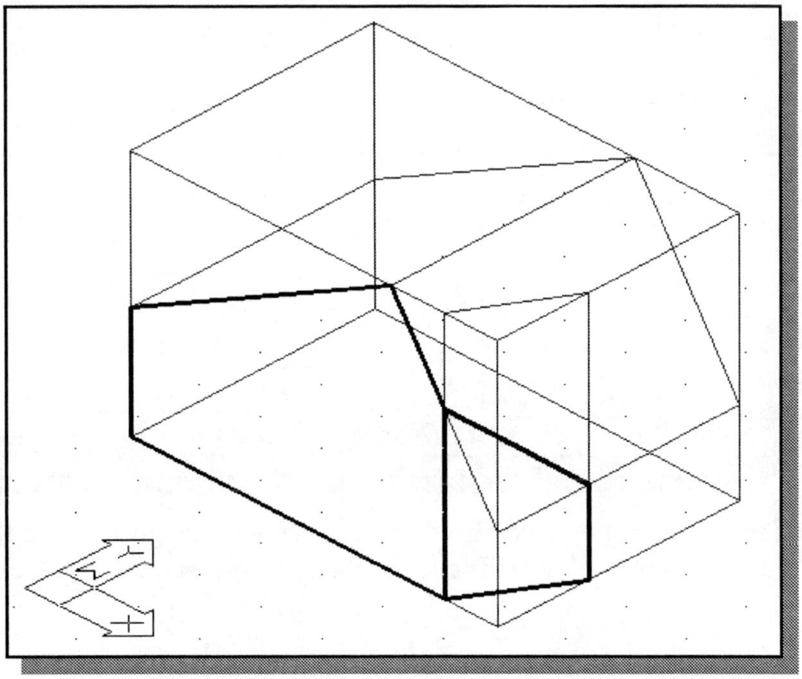

Multiple Viewports

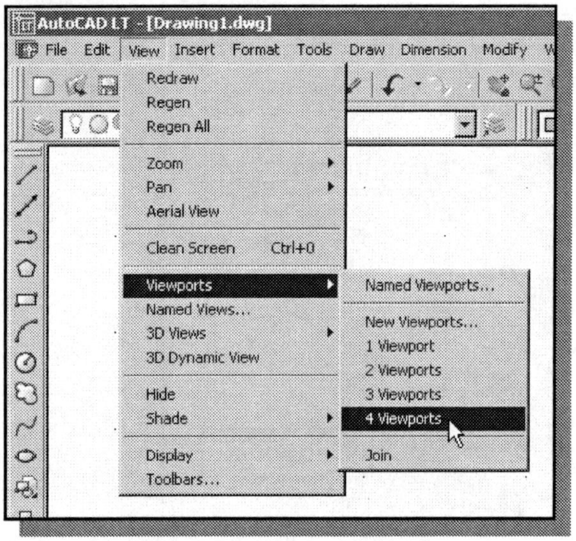

1. In the pull-down menus, select **[View] → [Viewports] → [4 viewports]**

➢ AutoCAD LT allows us to display different *views* of the model simultaneously. Only one *viewport* is activated at one time. The viewport with the darker border is the active viewport. Move the cursor inside each viewport and notice the different cursor display inside the active viewport.

2. Activate the top left viewport by left-clicking once inside the viewport.

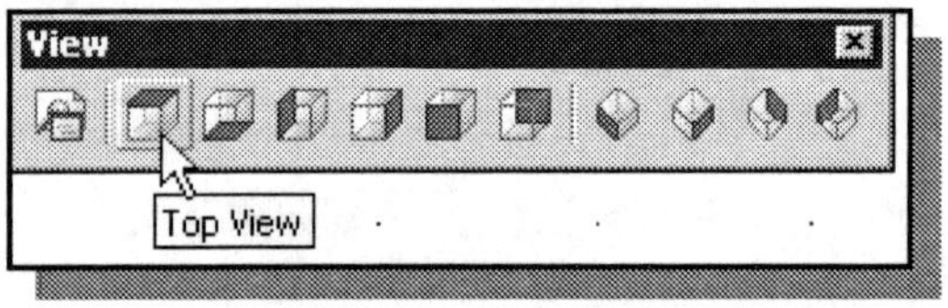

3. Select ***Top View*** in the *View* toolbar to change the display of the viewport.

4. On your own, repeat the above steps and use the Realtime Zoom command to adjust the displays of the viewports as shown below.

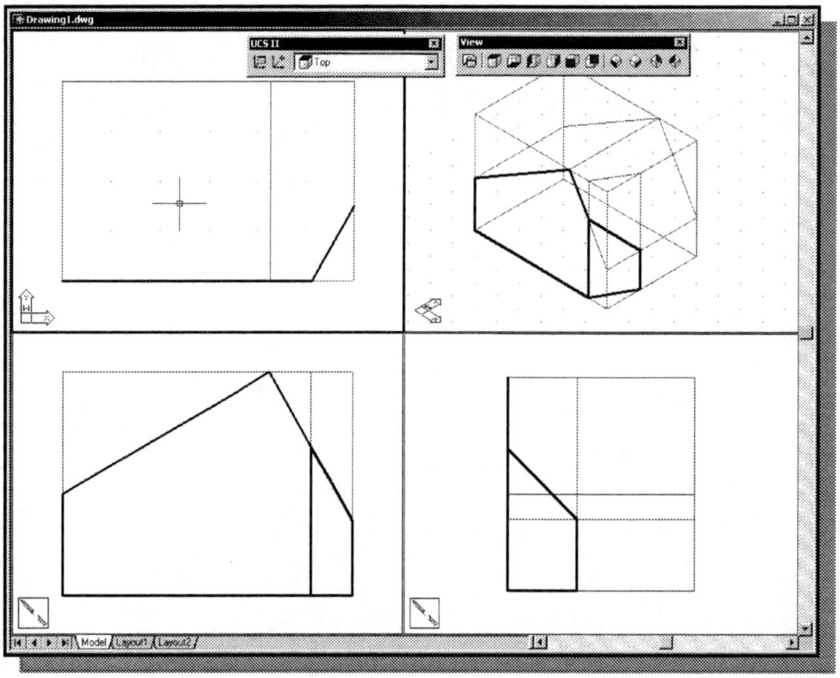

➢ Note that the *broken pencil* icon in the bottom viewport signifies that the UCS is not visible in the displayed views. (The UCS plane is perpendicular to the displayed view.)

Using the *Mirror* Command

1. Activate the top left viewport by left-clicking once inside the viewport.

2. **Pre-select** all the objects in the active viewport by using a selection window.

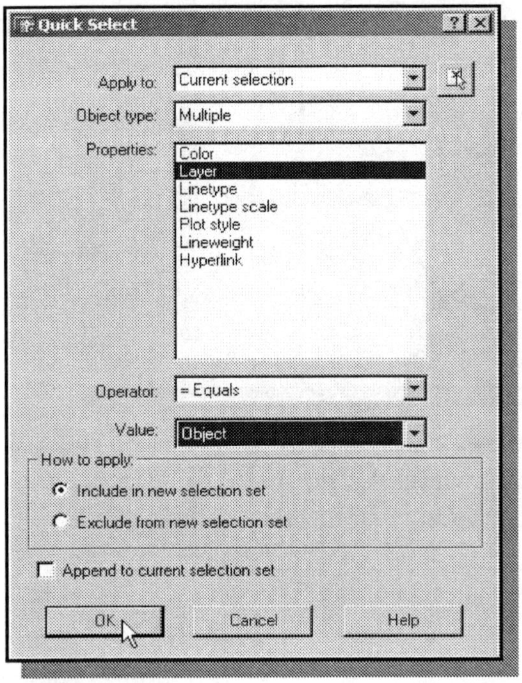

3. Inside the *active viewport*, right-mouse-click to bring up the popup option menu and select the **Quick Select** option.

4. In the *Quick Select* dialog box, select ***Layer*** from the *Properties* list.

5. Set the **Value** box to ***Object_Lines***.

6. In the *How to apply* section, confirm the ***Include in new selection set*** option is selected.

7. Click on the **OK** button to accept the settings.

8. AutoCAD LT will now **filter out** objects that are not on layer *Object_lines*.

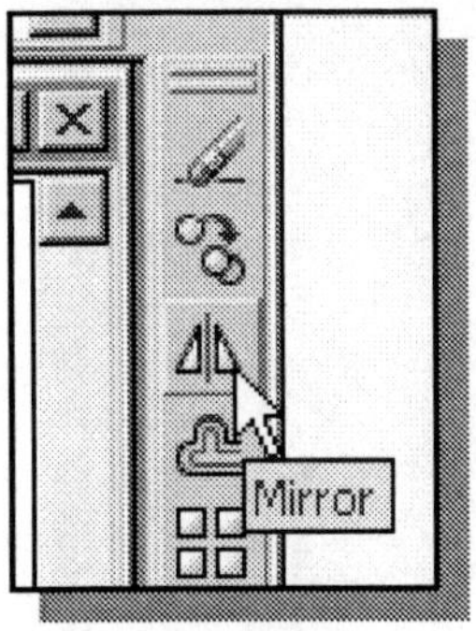

9. Click on the **Mirror** icon in the *Modify* toolbar.

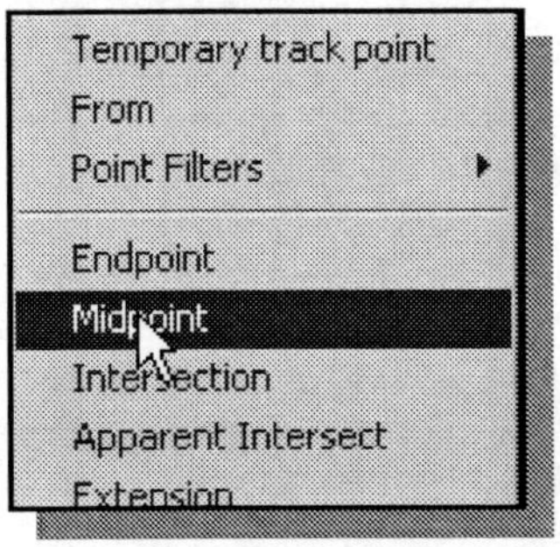

10. Inside the graphics window, hold down the **[SHIFT]** key and **right-mouse-click** once to bring up the *Object Snap* shortcut menu.

11. Select the **Midpoint** option in popup window.

12. Inside the active viewport, click on the left vertical line of the wireframe model.

13. Move the cursor toward the right vertical line in the active viewport; left-click once when the *Polar:Intersection* tooltip is displayed as shown below.

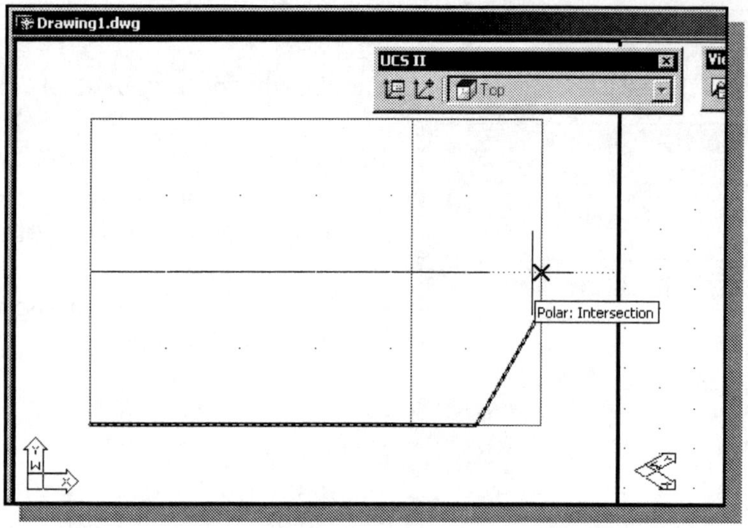

14. In the command prompt area, the message *"Delete Source Objects? [Yes/No] <N>:"* is displayed. Inside the graphics window, right-mouse-click once to bring up the option menu and select **No** to keep both sets of objects.

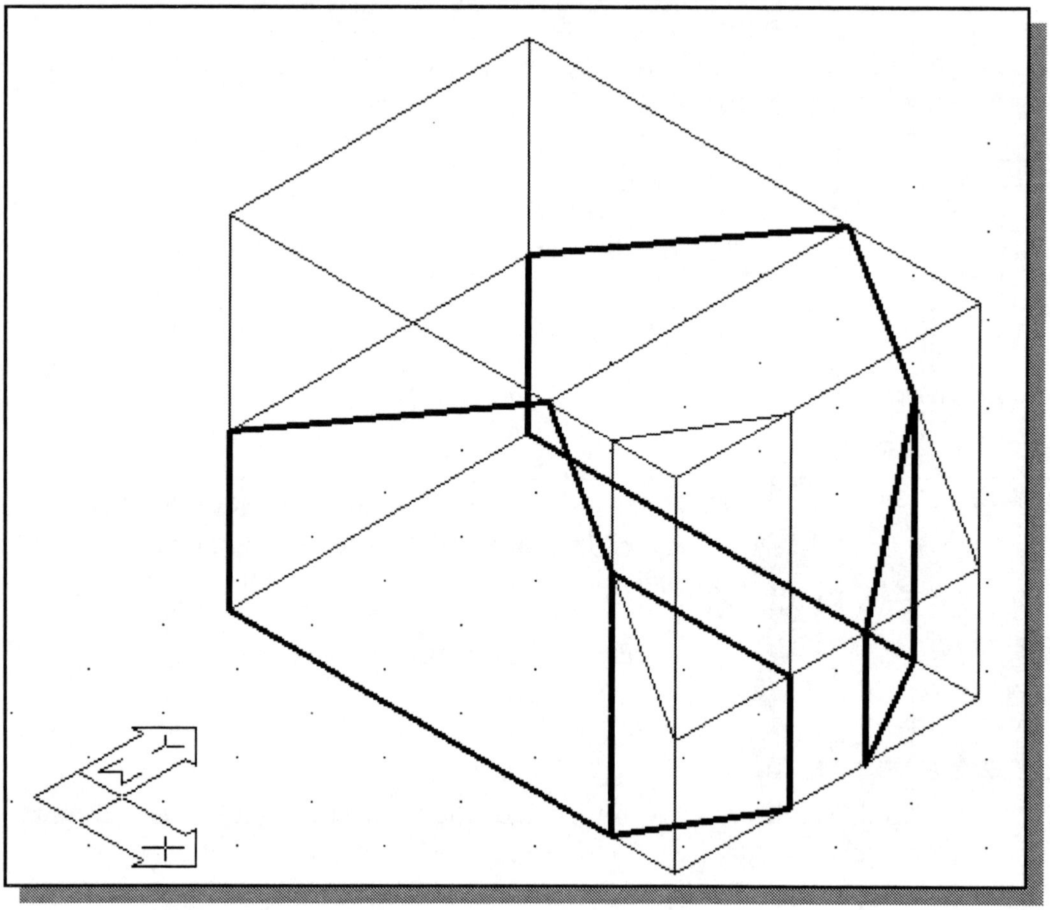

Turn *OFF* the Construction Lines

1. On the *Object Properties* toolbar, choose the ***Layer Control*** box with the left-mouse-button.

2. Move the cursor over the *light-bulb* icon for layer *Construction*, **left-mouse-click once** and notice the icon color is changed to a gray tone color, representing the layer (layer *Construction*) is *turned off*.

3. On your own, create the additional object lines connecting the two sets of objects as shown below.

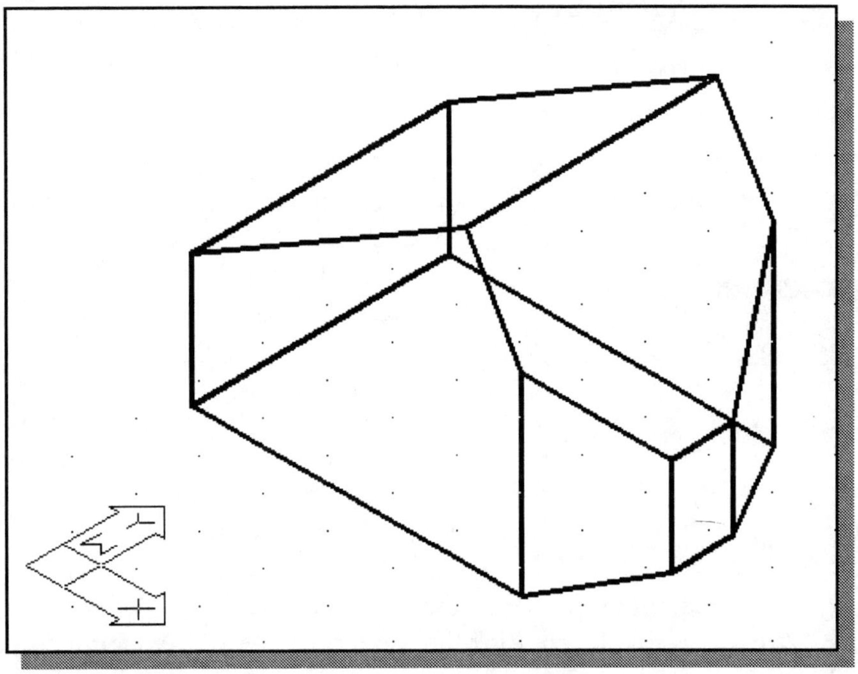

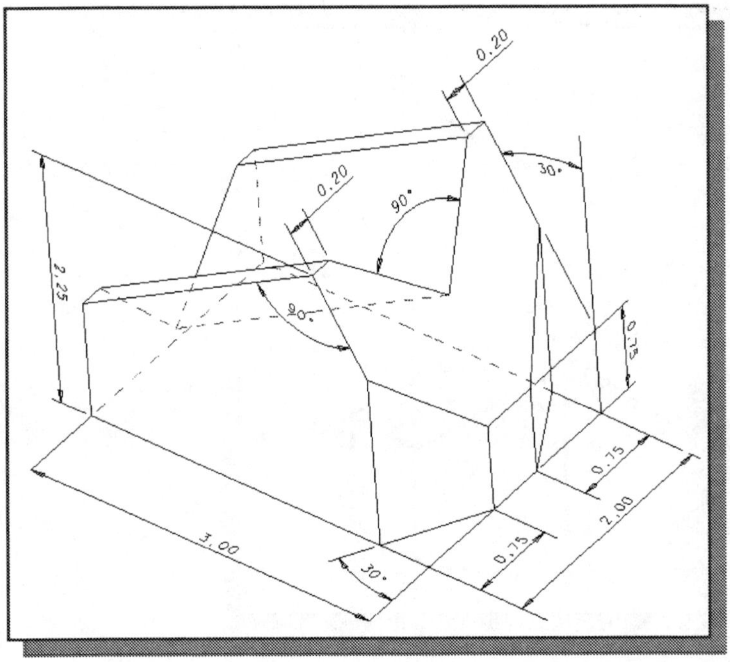

➢ The V-cut is the last feature we need to complete the 3D wireframe model of the *V-Block* design. Based on your knowledge of AutoCAD LT, how would you create this feature? What are the more difficult aspects of creating this feature as a 3D wireframe model?

Creating a NEW UCS

Besides using the preset UCS planes, AutoCAD LT also allows us to change our viewpoint and create new UCS planes. We will create an UCS plane aligning to the inclined plane of the design.

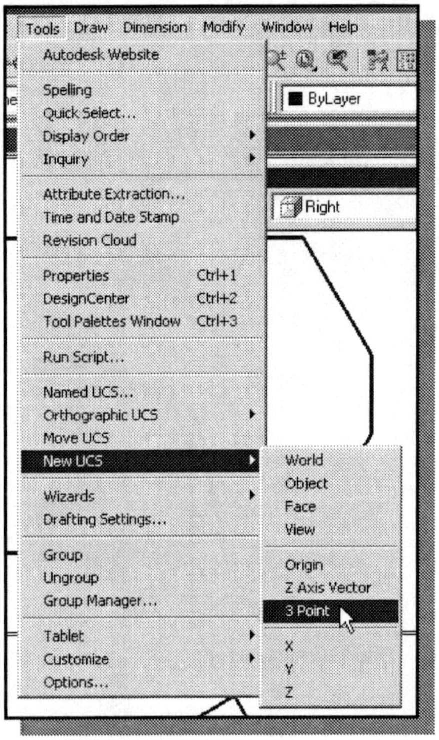

1. In the pull-down menus, select **[Tools] → [New UCS] → [3 points]**

➢ Note that other options are also available to aide the creation of new UCS planes.

2. In the command prompt area, the message *"Specify New Origin point <0,0,0>:"* is displayed. Pick the lower left corner of the inclined plane as shown below.

3. In the command prompt area, the message *"Specify point on positive portion of X-axis:"* is displayed. Pick the lower right corner of the inclined plane as shown below.

4. In the command prompt area, the message *"Specify point on positive portion of Y-axis:"* is displayed. Pick the top left corner of the inclined plane as shown below.

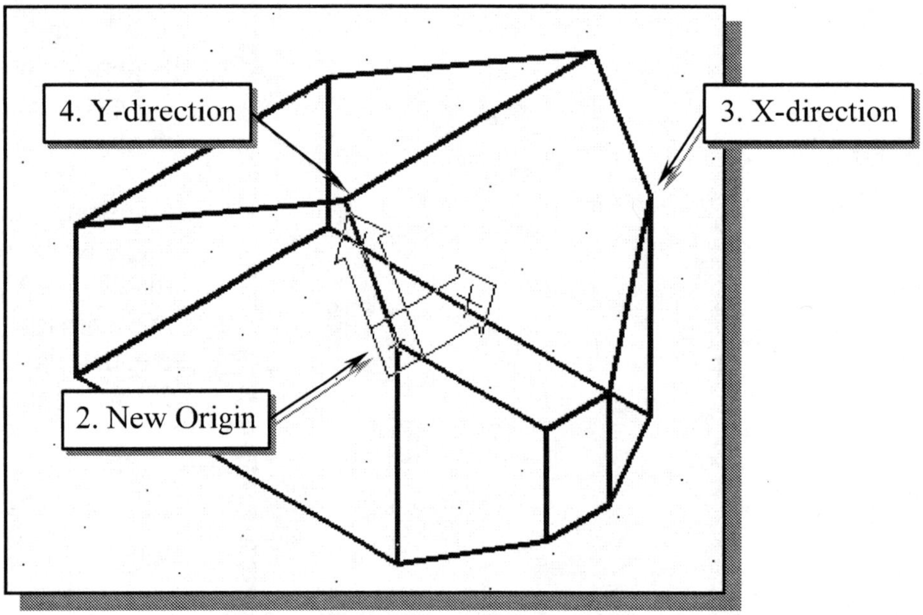

Changing the Displayed View and Creating a Named View

Besides using the preset views, AutoCAD LT also allows us to change our viewpoint and create new views, which can be saved and restored by name for convenient access. We will create a new view aligned to the new UCS plane we just created.

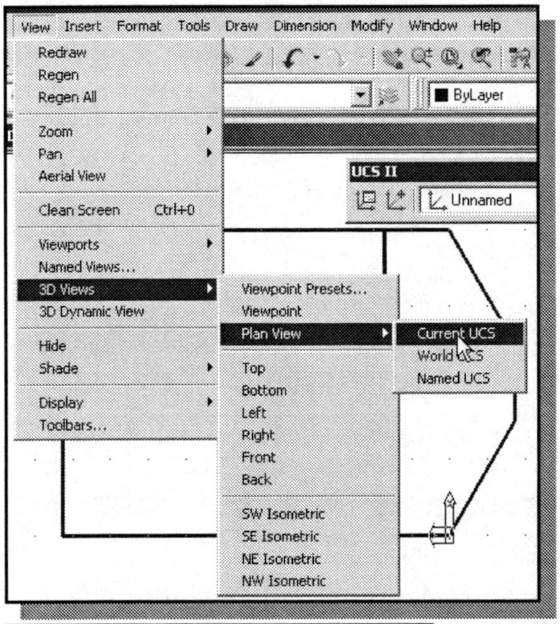

1. In the pull-down menus, select **[View] → [3D Views] → [Plan View] → [Current UCS]**

➢ The current viewport is now adjusted to display the current UCS plane.

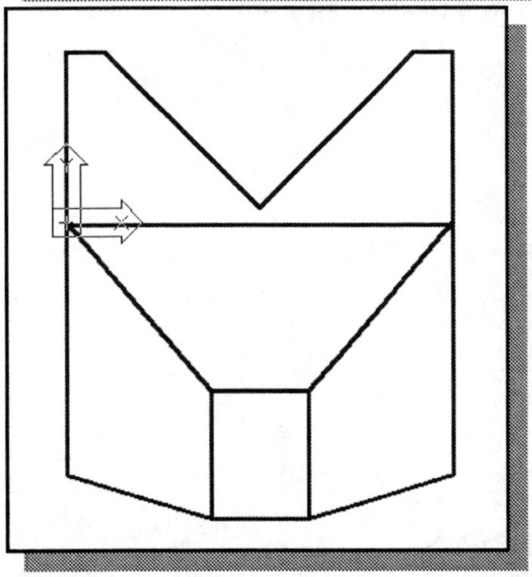

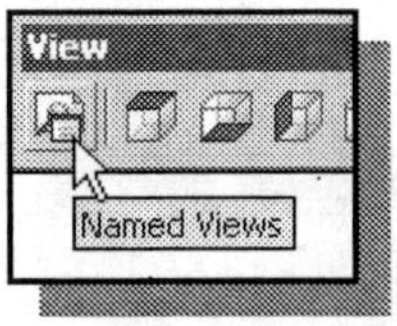

2. Click on the **Named Views** icon in the *View* toolbar.

3. In the *View* dialog box, click on the **New** button to create a new named view.

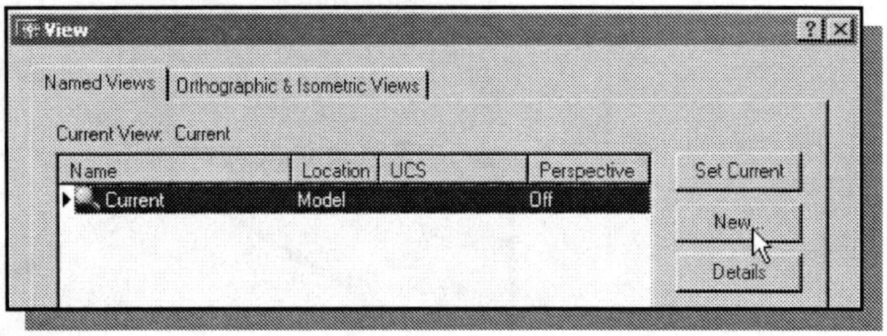

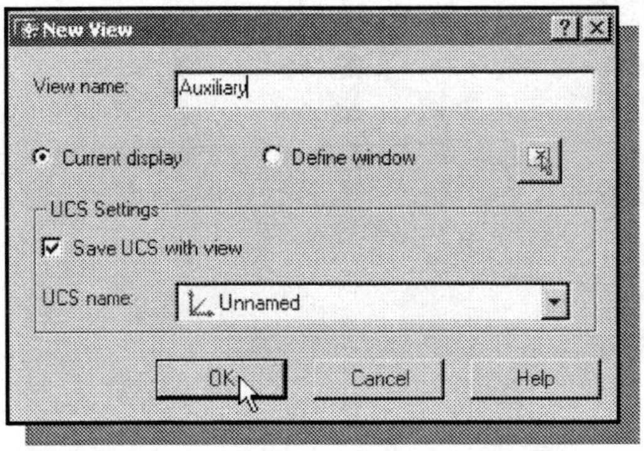

4. In the *New View* dialog box, enter ***Auxiliary*** as the new *View name* and confirm the ***Current display*** option and the ***Save UCS with view*** option are switched ***on*** as shown below.

5. Click on the **OK** button to accept the settings and create the named view.

6. In the *View* dialog box, the new named view (*Auxiliary*) is added to the *Named Views* list. We can also switch to this view by using the **Set Current** option.

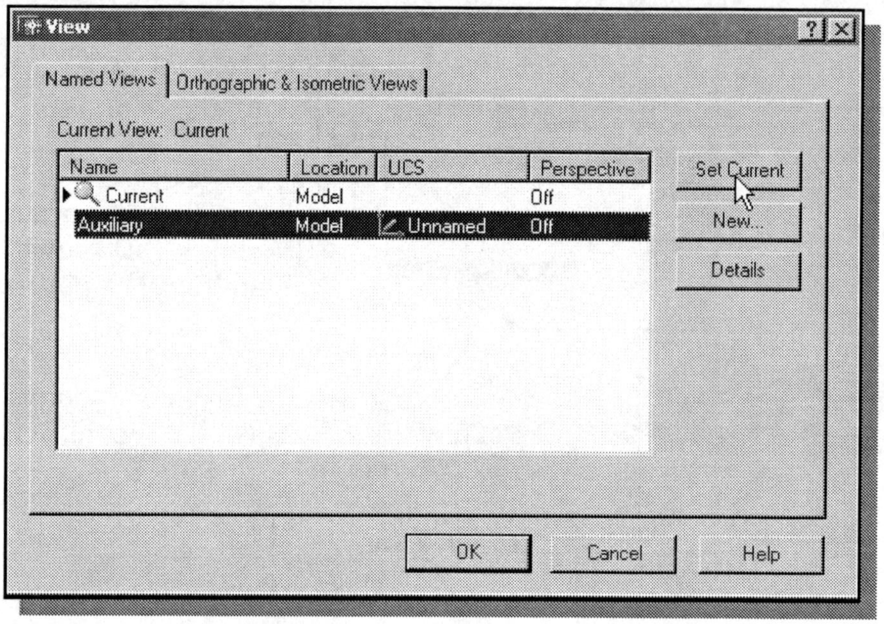

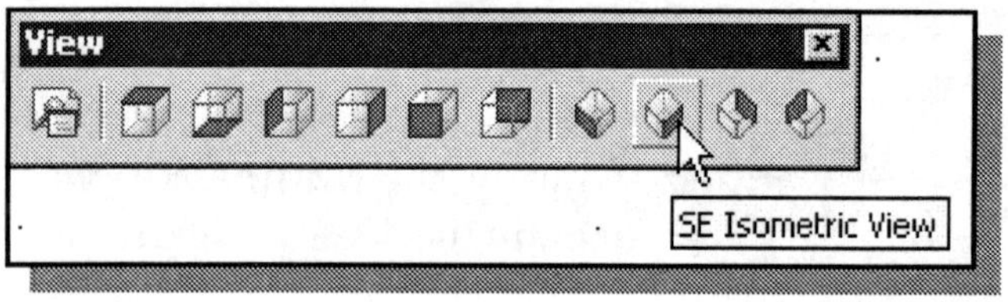

➤ On your own, reset the graphics window to one viewport and set the display to the SE Isometric view.

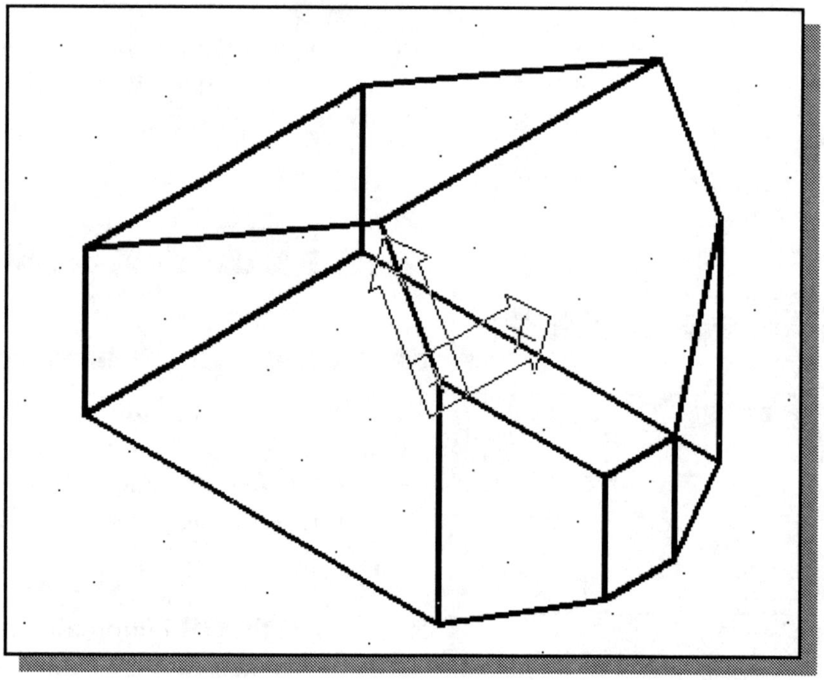

Creating the V-Cut Feature on the Inclined Plane

1. On your own, create two lines that are **0.2″** away from the top corners of the model, which are also rotated **45 degrees** relative to the top edge of the model.

2. Click on the **Copy Object** icon in the *Modify* toolbar.
3. In the command prompt area, the message *"Select objects:"* is displayed. Pick the two inclined lines we just created.
4. Inside the graphics window, **right-mouse-click** once to accept the selections.

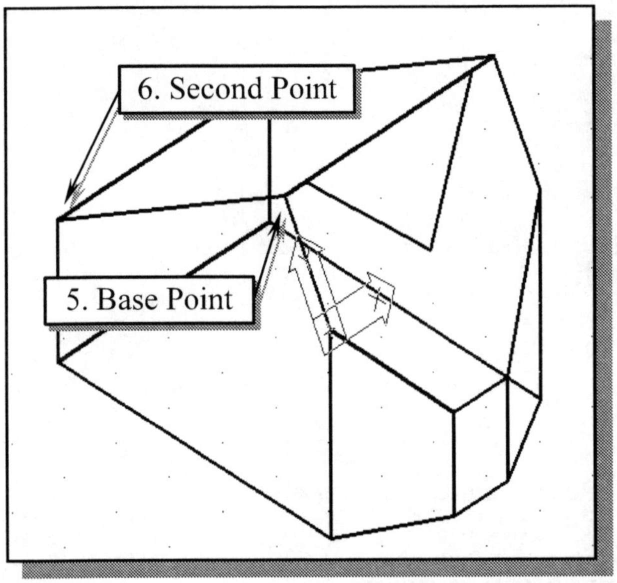

5. In the command prompt area, the message *"Specify base point or displacement, or [Multiple]:"* is displayed. Pick the top left corner as the base point to create the copy.
6. In the command prompt area, the message *"Specify second point of displacement or <use first point as displacement>:"* is displayed. Pick the corresponding corner on the back side of the model as shown in the figure below.

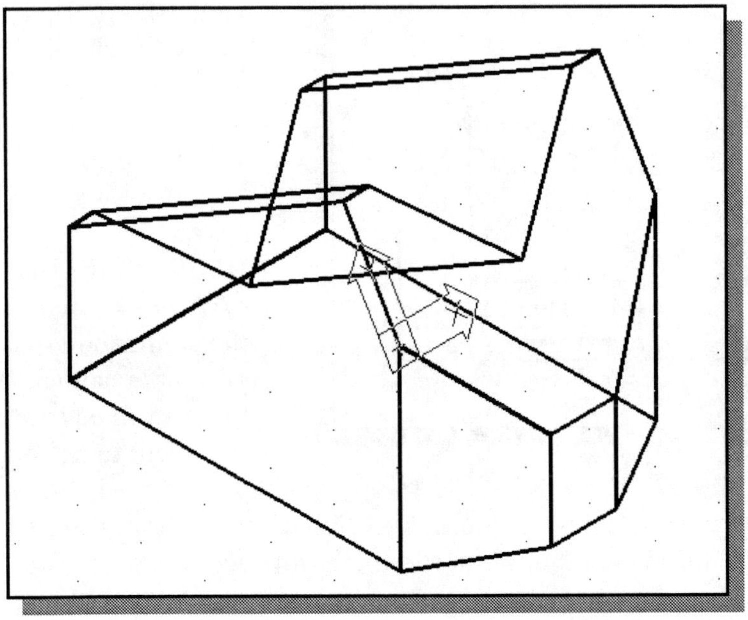

7. On your own, create addition lines to define the edges of the V-cut and use the Trim command to complete the model as shown below.

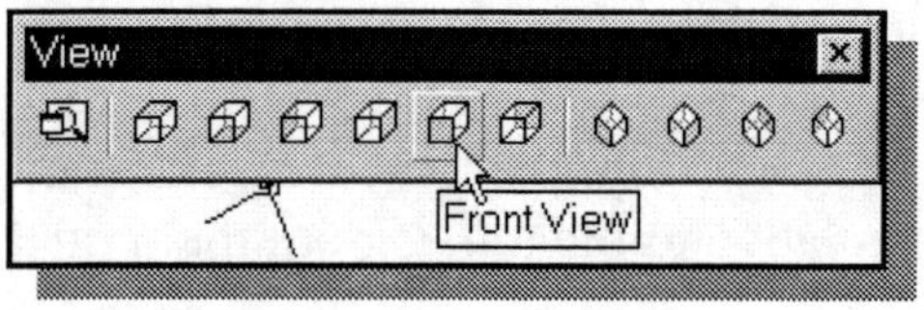

8. Click on the **Front View** icon in the *View* toolbar.

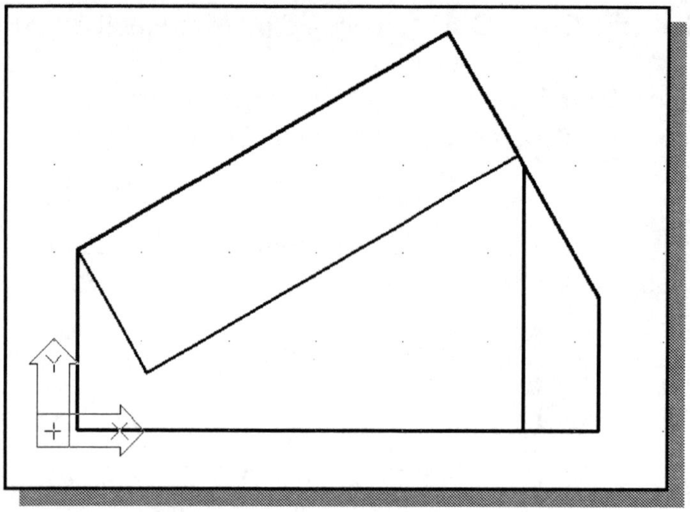

➤ Note that the V-cut we created, using the **Copy** command, does not represent a cut that passes through the entire block.

Extend the Cut and GRIP Editing

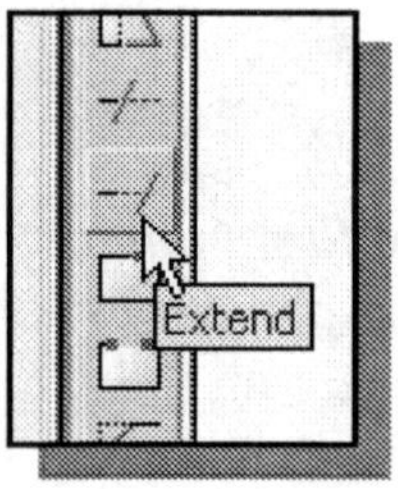

1. Select the **Extend** command icon in the *Modify* toolbar. In the command prompt area, the message *"Select boundary edges... Select objects:"* is displayed.

2. Pick the left vertical line as the *boundary edge.*

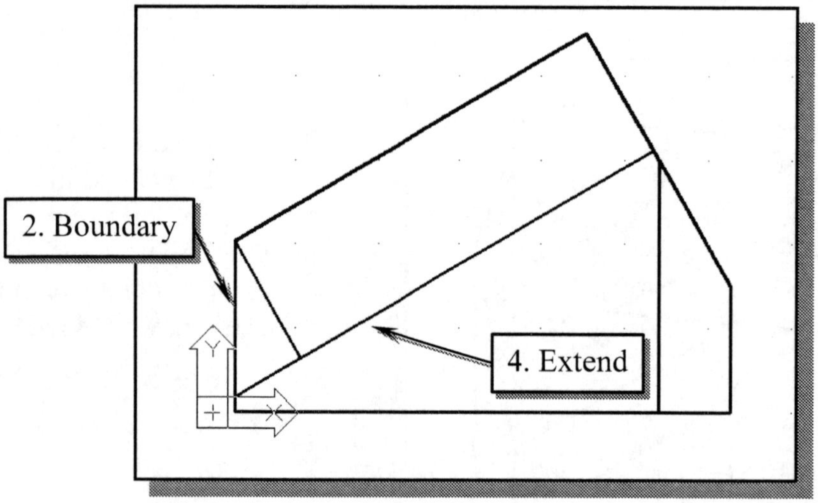

3. Inside the graphics window, **right-mouse-click** to accept the selection.

4. The message *"Select object to Extend or [Project/Edge/Undo]:"* is displayed in the command prompt area. Pick the bottom edge of the V-cut to extend.

5. Inside the graphics window, right-mouse-click to activate the option menu and select **Enter** with the left-mouse-button to end the **Extend** command.

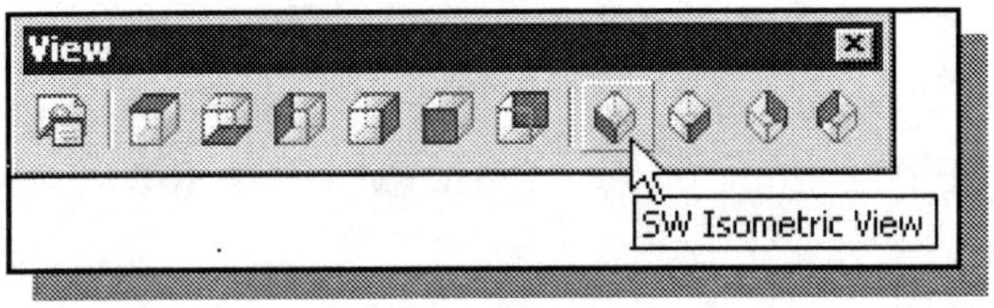

6. Click on the **SW Isometric View** icon to reset the display to the preset isometric view.

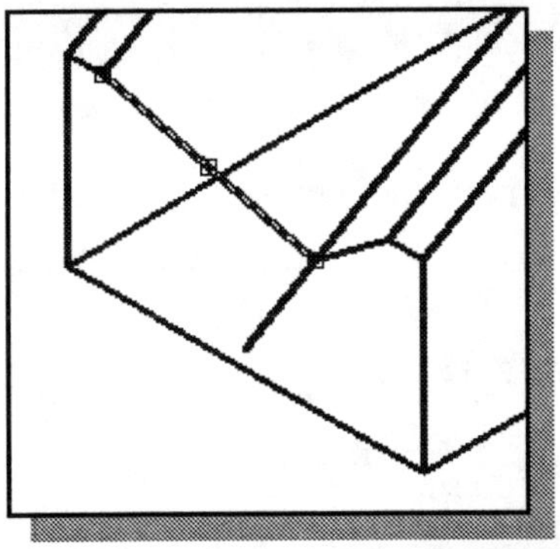

7. ***Pre-select*** the top edge of the *V-block* as shown.

8. Left-click once on the lower right grip point on the selected line.

❖ Selecting the grip points located at the end of the line or arc allows us to STRETCH the selected line.

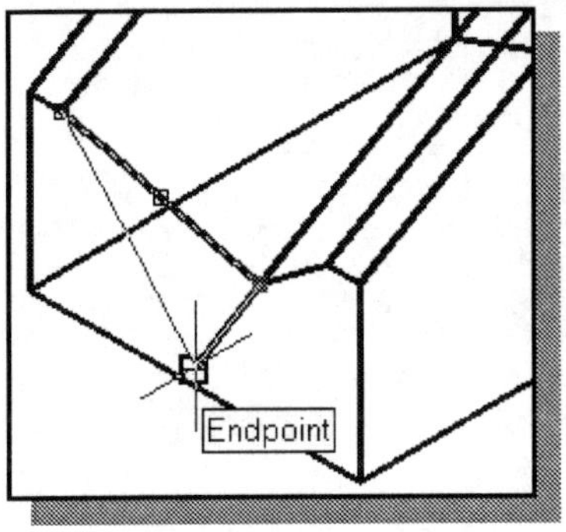

9. Move the cursor toward and select the lower corner of the V-cut as shown.

➢ On your own, repeat the above steps and use the grip editing options and complete the wireframe model as shown below.

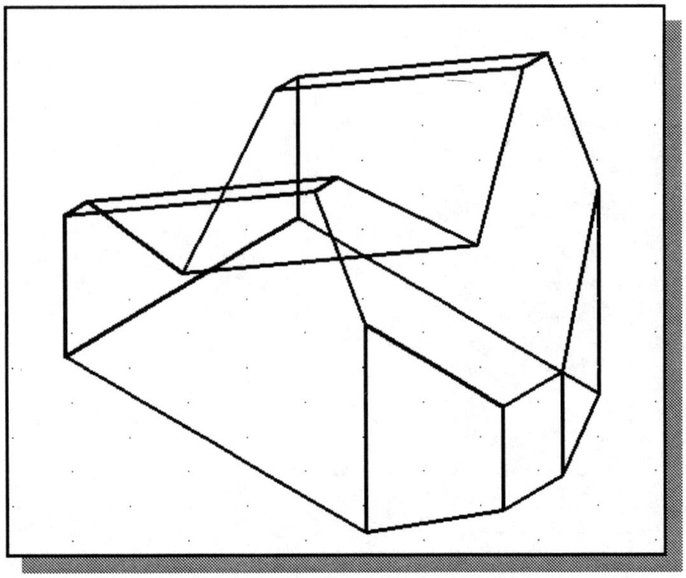

Conclusion

Throughout this text, various CAD techniques have been presented. Mastering these techniques will enable you to be effective and productive in creating CAD designs. In many instances, only a single approach to the construction tasks was presented; you are encouraged to repeat any of the lessons and develop different ways of thinking in accomplishing the same tasks. We have only covered the fundamentals of AutoCAD LT's functionality. The more time you spend using the system, the easier it will be to perform **computer aided design** with **AutoCAD® LT 2005**.

Questions:

1. List and describe three different types of 3D computer geometric modeling software available today?

2. What is a *named view*?

3. What does *UCS* stand for?

4. List and describe the methods available in AutoCAD LT to create a new UCS plane.

5. What is the difference between **Copy** and **Mirror** in AutoCAD LT?

6. Identify and describe the following commands:

a)

b)

c)

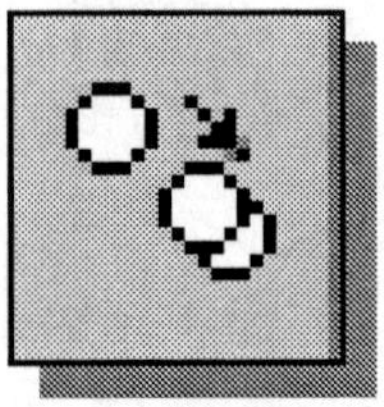

d)

Exercises:

1.

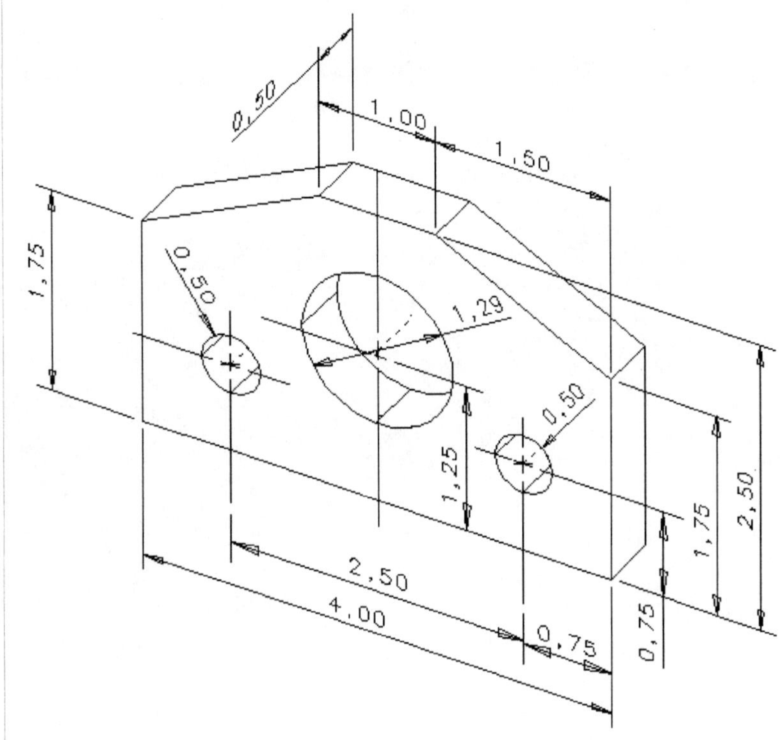

2.

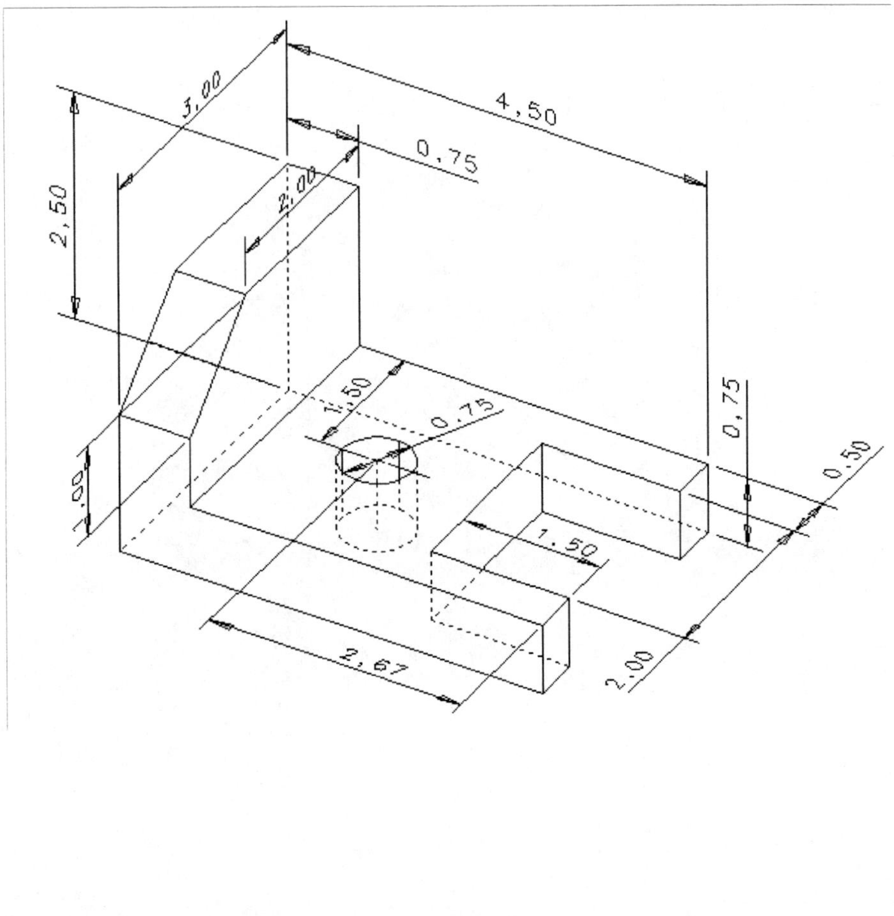

3.

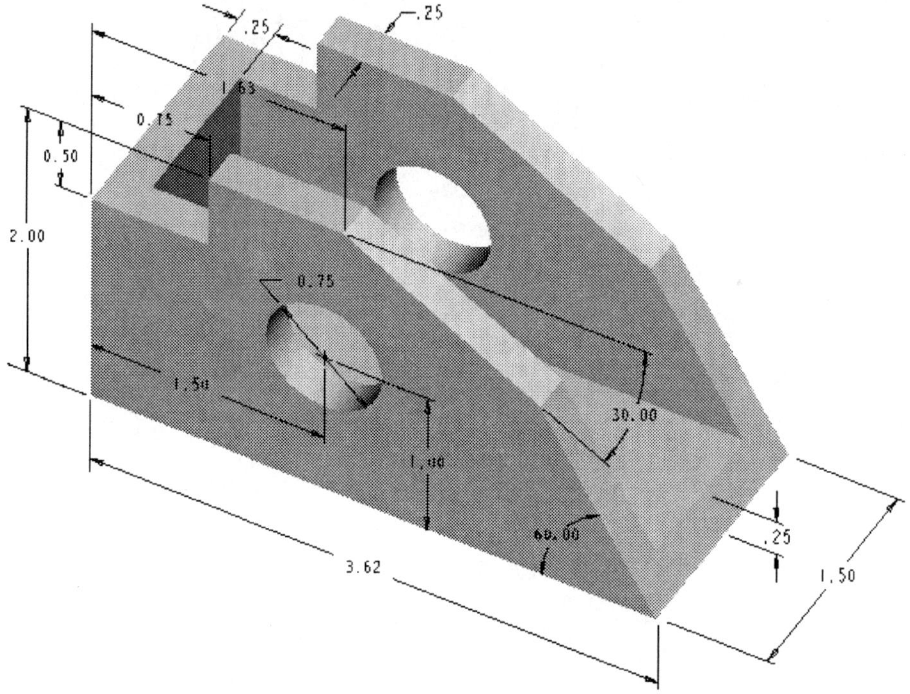
.25
.25
1.63
0.75
0.50
2.00
0.75
1.50
1.00
30.00
60.00
3.62
.25
1.50

4.

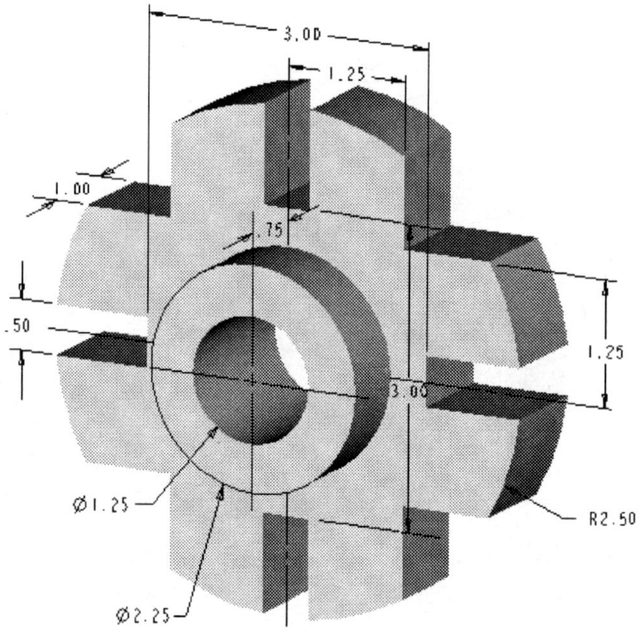
3.00
1.25
1.00
.75
.50
1.25
3.00
Ø1.25
R2.50
Ø2.25

INDEX

E

F

G

H

I

L

M

N

O

P